MW00580487

ADVANCE PRAISE FOR *CODE CRAFT*

"The mastery of a craft takes more than just tricks and tools; it also takes attitude and skill. For programmers that care, this is what they will get from *Code Craft*. With the able assistance of a large number of monkeys, this book invites readers to reflect and reason about what they are doing."

–KEVLIN HENNEY, INDEPENDENT CONSULTANT

"Readable, engaging, and even funny . . . this book is the distilled wisdom gained from years of actually working, suffering and triumphing in the world of software development . . . It's the book I wish I'd had when I started work as a programmer."

–STEVE LOVE, SENIOR DEVELOPER

"*Code Craft* is a goldmine of information that every professional software developer should be aware of."

–TIM PENHEY, C VU EDITOR

"Good judgment comes from experience. And experience—well, you get that from exercising bad judgment! Here is a chance to learn from someone else's hard-earned experience, more gain for less pain."

–LOIS GOLDTHWAITE, CONVENER OF C++ AND POSIX BSI STANDARDS PANELS

"This is exactly the kind of book you should give raw recruits. It tells it like it is, it's easy to read, and it covers the broad range of topics a newbie programmer needs to be aware of."

–JON JAGGER, SOFTWARE TRAINER-DESIGNER-CONSULTANT-MENTOR-PROGRAMMER

"A unique and practical guide to being a professional programmer in the modern workplace."

–ANDREW BURROWS, SOFTWARE DEVELOPER

"Pete has a rare ability. Not only can he identify techniques that the best professional software developers employ (often without realising it), but he can also describe these in a clear and concise manner."

–GREG LAW, CEO, UNDO LTD.

"I really wish that this book had been available at the start of my career, when I was being mentored. At least now I can use it with the programmers I'm mentoring."

–DR. ANDREW BENNETT, SENIOR ENGINEER, B.ENG., PH.D., MIET, MIEEE

"Those of you who have been fortunate enough to have seen Pete Goodliffe lecturing on a subject will immediately recognise the way he can bring a subject over with humour and clarity. In a teaching environment, this translates into directed, structured instruction that allows both the newbie and the experienced practitioner to learn and progress."

–ROBERT D. SCHOFIELD, M.SC., MIET FOUNDER, SCIENTIFIC SOFTWARE SERVICES LTD.

"Pete has a desire that code is not just written, but written well, with programmers using the right tools and techniques for the job. *Code Craft* explores a wide range of aspects of programming, and provides guidelines and principles that any developer who cares about their work should be familiar with."

–CHRIS REED, SOFTWARE DEVELOPER

"Pete Goodliffe's dedication to promote professionalism in software development is well known within the industry. Drawing on his authoritative knowledge, and blessed with an entertaining and informative writing style, Pete is an excellent mentor to novice and experienced developers alike."

–ROB VOISEY, DIRECTOR OF ENGINEERING, AKAI DIGITAL LTD.

"I like the monkeys best of all."

–ALICE GOODLIFFE, AGE 4 ½

CODE CRAFT

THE PRACTICE OF WRITING
EXCELLENT CODE

by Pete Goodliffe

**NO STARCH
PRESS**

San Francisco

CODE CRAFT. Copyright © 2007 by Pete Goodliffe.

All rights reserved. No part of this work may be reproduced or transmitted in any form or by any means, electronic or mechanical, including photocopying, recording, or by any information storage or retrieval system, without the prior written permission of the copyright owner and the publisher.

 Printed on recycled paper in the United States of America

10 09 08 07 06   1 2 3 4 5 6 7 8 9

ISBN-10: 1-59327-119-0
ISBN-13: 978-1-59327-119-0

Publisher: William Pollock
Production Editor: Elizabeth Campbell
Cover Design: Octopod Studios
Text Illustrations: David Brookes
Technical Reviewer: Jon Jagger
Copyeditor: Megan Dunchak
Compositors: Megan Dunchak, Riley Hoffman, and Christina Samuell
Proofreader: Stephanie Provines

For information on book distributors or translations, please contact No Starch Press, Inc. directly:

No Starch Press, Inc.
555 De Haro Street, Suite 250, San Francisco, CA 94107
phone: 415.863.9900; fax: 415.863.9950; info@nostarch.com; www.nostarch.com

Library of Congress Cataloging-in-Publication Data

Goodliffe, Pete.
  Code craft: the practice of writing excellent code / Pete Goodliffe.
      p. cm.
  Includes bibliographical references and index.
  ISBN-13: 978-1-59327-119-0
  ISBN-10: 1-59327-119-0
 1. Computer programming. 2. Programming languages (Electronic computers) 3. Computer software--
Development. I. Title.
QA76.6.G656 2006
005.1--dc22
                                                    2006015575

No Starch Press and the No Starch Press logo are registered trademarks of No Starch Press, Inc. Other product and company names mentioned herein may be the trademarks of their respective owners. Rather than use a trademark symbol with every occurrence of a trademarked name, we are using the names only in an editorial fashion and to the benefit of the trademark owner, with no intention of infringement of the trademark.

The information in this book is distributed on an "As Is" basis, without warranty. While every precaution has been taken in the preparation of this work, neither the author nor No Starch Press, Inc. shall have any liability to any person or entity with respect to any loss or damage caused or alleged to be caused directly or indirectly by the information contained in it.

All text illustrations copyright © 2006 by David Brookes.

To Bryony, my wonderful wife.
To Alice, who drew balloons on this book.
To Millie, who tasted this book.
And to Jessica, who never got a chance to.

Psalm 150

BRIEF CONTENTS

PART III
THE SHAPE OF CODE
239

PART IV
A HERD OF PROGRAMMERS?
293

PART V
PART OF THE PROCESS
365

CONTENTS IN DETAIL

PART I
AT THE CODEFACE

1
ON THE DEFENSIVE
Defensive Programming Techniques for Robust Code   3

2
THE BEST LAID PLANS
The Layout and Presentation of Source Code

23

3
WHAT'S IN A NAME?
Giving Meaningful Things Meaningful Names

39

4
THE WRITE STUFF
Techniques for Writing "Self-Documenting" Code   57

5
A PASSING COMMENT
How to Write Code Comments   73

6
TO ERR IS HUMAN
Dealing with the Inevitable—Error Conditions in Code   89

PART II
THE SECRET LIFE OF CODE

7
THE PROGRAMMER'S TOOLBOX
Using Tools to Construct Software

8
TESTING TIMES
The Black Art of Testing Code

9
FINDING FAULT
Debugging: What to Do When Things Go Wrong   **153**

10
THE CODE THAT JACK BUILT
Mechanisms to Turn Source Code into Executable Code   **175**

11
THE NEED FOR SPEED
Optimizing Programs and Writing Efficient Code

199

12
AN INSECURITY COMPLEX
Writing Secure Programs

223

PART III
THE SHAPE OF CODE

13
GRAND DESIGNS
How to Produce Good Software Designs   241

PART IV
A HERD OF PROGRAMMERS?

16
CODE MONKEYS
Fostering the Correct Attitude and Approach to Programming   295

17
TOGETHER WE STAND
Teamwork and the Individual Programmer   315

18
PRACTICING SAFE SOURCE
Source Control and Self-Control

349

PART V
PART OF THE PROCESS

19
BEING SPECIFIC
Writing Software Specifications

367

20
A REVIEW TO A KILL
Performing Code Reviews

385

21
HOW LONG IS A PIECE OF STRING?
The Black Art of Software Timescale Estimation 401

PART VI
VIEW FROM THE TOP

22
RECIPE FOR A PROGRAM
Code Development Methodologies and Processes 419

23
THE OUTER LIMITS
The Different Programming Disciplines — 441

24
WHERE NEXT?
All's Well That Ends Well — 459

ANSWERS AND DISCUSSION — 463

PREFACE

There are many things of which a wise
man might wish to be ignorant.
—Ralph Waldo Emerson

This book comes from the trenches. Well, it actually comes from deep within the software factory, but sometimes there isn't too much difference. This book is for programmers who *care* about what they're doing. If you don't, then shut the book now and put it neatly back on the bookshelf.

What's In It for Me?

Programming is your passion. It's sad, but it's true. As a hardcore techie, you practically program in your sleep. Now you're in the heart of the Real World, deep in the industry, doing what you could never imagine: being paid to play with computers. The truth is, *you'd* have paid someone for the privilege.

But this is an odd place, not what you were expecting at all. Surprised by the incursion of unrealistic deadlines and bad management (if management is what they call it), of shifting requirements and a legacy of awful code, you're left wondering if this is really *it*. The world is conspiring to prevent you from writing the code you always dreamed of. Welcome to life in the software factory. You're on the front line of a tough battle to create pieces of artistic mastery and scientific genius. Good luck.

That's where *Code Craft* comes in. This book is about what no one has taught you yet: how to program, properly, *in the Real World*. *Code Craft* picks up where the textbooks left off. Sure, it's about the technicalities and intricacies of good code. But it's also about something more than that: How to write the *right* code, in the *right* way.

What does that mean? Writing good programs in the Real World means many things:

- Crafting technically elegant code
- Creating maintainable code that others can interpret
- Understanding and adapting other people's messy code
- Working well alongside other programmers

You need all of these skills (and more) to be a crack coder. You must understand the secret life of code: What happens to it after you type it. You must have a sense of aesthetics: distinguishing beautiful code from ugly code. And you must have a head for the practicalities: to work out when shortcuts are justified, when to labor on the code design, and when to give up and move on (the pragmatic *quit when you're ahead* principle). This book will help you to achieve these goals. You'll learn how to survive the software factory, how to survey the battlefield and understand your enemy, how to work out tactics to avoid enemy traps, and how to produce truly *excellent* programs, despite it all.

Software development is an interesting profession. It's fast moving, full of fleeting vogues and transient fashions, get-rich schemes and peddlers of new ideologies. It's not mature. I'm not claiming to have any magic answers here, but I do have some practical, useful advice to impart. There's no ivory tower theory—just Real World experience and good practice.

By the time you've digested this stuff, you won't just be a better programmer. You will be a better inhabitant of the software factory. A real code warrior. You'll have learned code craft. If that doesn't sound exciting, then perhaps you should consider a career in the military.

Getting Better

So what sets *good* programmers apart from *bad* ones? More importantly, what sets *exceptional* programmers apart from merely *adequate* ones? The secret doesn't lie solely in technical competence—I've seen intellectual programmers who can write intense and impressive C++, who know their language standard by heart, but who write the most awful code. I've seen more humble programmers who stick to very simple code, but write the most elegant and well-thought-out programs.

What's the real difference? Good programming stems from your *attitude*. It lies in knowing the professional approach and always wanting to write the best software you can, despite the pressures of the software factory. Attitudes are the lenses through which we view things. They color our work and our actions. Good code needs to be carefully crafted by master artisans, not thoughtlessly hacked by sloppy programmers. *The code to hell is paved with good intentions.* To become exceptional programmers, we must learn to rise above intentions, foster positive perspectives, and develop these healthy attitudes.

In this book, we'll see how to do this. I cover a lot of ground, from the lowest hands-on code-writing issues to larger organizational concerns. Through all of these themes, I highlight what our correct attitude and approach should be.

ATTITUDES—AN ANGLE OF APPROACH

The more I've investigated and cataloged the world of software development, the more I've become convinced that it is specific *attitudes* that distinguish exceptional programmers. The dictionary definition of the word *attitude* looks something like this:

attitude (at.ti.tude)
1. A state of mind or a feeling; a disposition.
2. The position of an aircraft relative to a frame of reference.

That first definition isn't exactly surprising, but what's the second one about? It's actually more revealing than the first.

There are three imaginary lines of axis running through an aircraft; one from wing to wing, one from nose to tail, and one running vertically where the other two cross. A pilot positions his aircraft around these axes; they define the aircraft's angle of approach. This is known as the *attitude* of the aircraft. If you apply a little power to the aircraft while it has the wrong attitude, it will end up missing the target massively. A pilot has to constantly monitor his vehicle's attitude, especially at critical times like takeoff and landing.

At the risk of sounding like a cheesy motivational video, this closely parallels our software development work. The plane's attitude defines its angle of approach, and *our* attitude defines our angle of approach to the coding task. It doesn't matter how technically competent a programmer is, if his or her abilities aren't tempered by healthy attitudes, the work will suffer.

A wrong attitude can make or break a software project, so it's vital that we maintain the right angle of approach to programming. Your attitude will either hinder or promote your personal growth. To become better programmers, we need to ensure we have the right attitudes.

Who Should Read This Book?

Obviously, the people who should read this book are those who want to improve the quality of their code. We should all aspire to be better programmers; if you don't have that aspiration, then this book isn't for you. You might be a professional programmer, perhaps a few years into your employment. You might be an advanced student, familiar with programming concepts but unsure about how best to apply them. This book is also a useful aid if you are being mentored or are mentoring a trainee.

You must have programming experience. This book won't teach you how to program; it will teach you how to program *better*. While I've tried to avoid language bias and dogma, I need to show code examples. Most of these are written in C, C++, or Java, since they are in the family of popular contemporary languages. None of them require great language expertise to read, so don't panic if you're not a world-class C++ programmer.

The assumption here is that you are—or will be—writing code in the heat of the software factory. This often means employment in a commercial development organization, but it could be working on a chaotic open source development project, or becoming a hired gun (a contractor) providing software for a third party.

What's Covered?

This book addresses programmer attitudes, but it's not some kind of psychology textbook. We'll investigate many topics, including:

- Source code presentation
- Defensive coding techniques
- How to debug programs effectively
- Good teamworking skills
- Managing your source code

Take a quick glance through the table of contents to see exactly what's covered. What is the rationale behind my selection of topics? I've been mentoring trainee programmers for many years, and these are the topics that have come up time and time again. I've also worked in the software factory for long enough to have seen the recurring problems—I address these too.

If you can conquer all of these programming demons, you'll progress from an apprentice coder to a real code craftsman.

How This Book is Organized

I've tried to make this book as easy to read as possible. Conventional wisdom says you should start at the beginning and work to the end. Forget that. You can pick up this book, open it to a chapter that interests you, and start there. Each chapter stands on its own, with helpful cross referencing so you can see how they all fit together. Of course, if you enjoy being conventional, the beginning is as good a place to start as any.

Each chapter is similarly structured; you won't find any nasty surprises. They are split into these sections:

In This Chapter
At the very beginning, I list the highlights of the chapter. You'll get a few lines of content overview. Go on, skim through them all now to see what ground we'll cover.

The chapter
All the riveting stuff that you paid good money to read.

Dotted throughout the chapter are *key concepts*. These emphasize the important tips, issues, and attitudes, so watch out for them. They look like this:

KEY CONCEPT   *This is important. Pay attention!*

In a Nutshell

At the end of each chapter, this little section wraps up the discussion. It provides a bird's eye view of the material. If you're really pushed for time, you could just read the key concepts and these concluding sections. Just don't tell anyone I said that.

Afterwards, I contrast a good programmer's approach with that of a bad programmer to summarize the important attitudes you should aim to develop. If you're feeling brave, you can rate yourself against these examples; hopefully the truth won't hurt too much!

See Also

This list points you at the related chapters and explains how they tie in to the topic at hand.

Get Thinking

Finally, there are some questions to consider. These haven't just been included to fluff out the book—they are an integral part of each chapter. They don't ask for a banal rehashing of the material you just read, but are intended to *make you think*, and to think beyond the contents of the chapter. The questions are split into two groups:

- **Mull it Over** These questions investigate the chapter's topic in depth and raise some important issues.
- **Getting Personal** These questions probe the working practices and coding maturity of you and your software development team.

Don't skip these questions! Even if you're too lazy to sit down and seriously think about each answer (believe me, you'll gain a lot from doing so), at least read the questions and consider them in passing.

The final part of this book contains *answers and discussion* for each of these questions. It's not a straight answer set—few of the questions have a definite *yes* or *no* response. Once you've thought about them, compare your answers with mine. Many of my "answers" contain extra information that isn't covered in the main chapter.

The Chapters—a Closer Look

Each chapter covers a single topic, a specific problem area in modern software development. These are the common reasons people write bad code or write code badly. Each chapter describes the correct approaches and attitudes, which will make life on the front line more bearable.

The chapters are split into six parts; the contents page for each lists the chapters in the part with a short description of the material contained in each. These parts work from the inside, outwards. We'll start off looking at *what* code we write and end up looking at *how* we write it.

Our investigations begin at the codeface, focusing on the *micro* level of writing source code. I've deliberately put this first; cutting code is what programmers *really* care about:

Part I: At the Codeface

In this part we look at the nuts and bolts of developing source code. We'll investigate defensive programming techniques and how to format and lay out code. Then we'll move on to look at naming and documenting our code. Comment-writing conventions and error-handling techniques are also covered.

Part II: The Secret Life of Code

Next we'll take a look at the *process* of writing code; how we create it and work with it. We'll look at construction tools, testing methods, debugging techniques, the correct processes for building executables, and optimization. Finally, we'll consider how to write secure programs.

Part III: The Shape of Code

Then we'll look at the wider issues of source code construction. We'll discuss the development of a code design, software architecture, and how source code grows (or decays) over time.

We then move to the *macro* level, when we lift up our heads and see what's going on around us—life in the software factory. We can't write large-scale software without being part of a development team, and the next three parts contain tricks and techniques for getting the best out of these teams:

Part IV: A Herd of Programmers?

Few programmers exist in a vacuum. (It requires special breathing equipment.) In this part we'll move into the wider world with a look at good development practices and how they fit into a professional programmer's daily routine. Good personal and team programming skills and the use of revision control systems are covered here.

Part V: Part of the Process

Here we'll look at some of the rites and rituals of the software development process: writing specifications, performing code reviews, and the black art of timescale estimation.

Part VI: View from the Top

The final part provides a higher level look at the development process, investigating software development methodologies, and the different programming disciplines.

How to Use This Book

Work from the front cover to the back, or pick it up in the places that interest you—it doesn't matter.

What does matter is that you read *Code Craft* with an open mind, and think about how to apply what you read to what you do. *A wise man learns from his mistakes; a wiser man learns from the mistakes of others.* It's always good to learn from others' experiences, so look at this material, and then ask the opinion of a programmer you respect. Look over the questions and discuss them together.

As you learn code craft, I hope you enjoy yourself. When you have finished, look back and see how much more of the craft you appreciate, how your skills have grown, and how your attitudes have improved. If nothing has changed, then this book has failed. I'm sure it won't.

A Note to Mentors

This book is a great tool for mentoring less experienced programmers. It has been specifically designed with this in mind, and has proven to increase programmer maturity and insight.

The best approach to this material is not to methodically work through each section together. Instead, read a chapter separately, and then get together with your trainee to discuss the contents. The questions really work as a springboard for discussion, so it's a good idea to start there.

ACKNOWLEDGMENTS

There is always something for which to be thankful.
—Charles Dickens

This book was written over a period of several years.
They say *good things come to those who wait*. In that time
countless people have helped along the way . . .

No one deserves more thanks, and indeed sympathy, than my wife
Bryony who has put up with me and this project over its long gestation
period. *Phillipians 1v3*.

My good friend, excellent programmer, and illustrator extraordinaire,
David Brookes, took my awful monkey cartoons with lame jokes and turned
them into things of beauty. Thanks Dave! The lame jokes are still my fault.

Many people have read early drafts of this material in one form or
another. Specific thanks are due to ACCU (www.accu.org) which has been
a fertile proving ground for my writing skills. Thanks to the cthree.org geeks
Andy Burrows, Andrew Bennet, and Chris Reed who gave valuable feedback,
to Steve Love, and to the #ant.org geeks. Jon Jagger provided well balanced
technical review and lent his own war stories and battle scars, which have
improved the book considerably.

Most of this book is born from my experience and frustration with the
poor state of software development in the Real World, and a desire to help
people improve. "Thanks" are therefore also due to the various dysfunctional

companies I've worked in, and the awful programmers I've encountered there, who have provided me with almost a lifetime's worth of things to moan about! I never *really* realized how lucky I was.

Finally, thanks to all the guys at No Starch Press who have taken my painful XML formatted manuscript and turned it into a really great book. Thanks for your faith in the project, and for going the extra mile.

ABOUT THE AUTHOR

Pete Goodliffe is an expert software developer who never stays at the same place in the software food chain; he's worked in numerous languages on diverse projects. He also has extensive experience in teaching and mentoring programmers, and writes the regular "Professionalism in Programming" column for ACCU's *C Vu* magazine (www.accu.org). Pete enjoys writing excellent, bug-free code so he can spend more time having fun with his kids.

PART I

AT THE CODEFACE

Programmers write programs. It doesn't take a genius to figure that one out. But there is a more subtle distinction: Only good programmers habitually write good code. Bad programmers . . . *don't.* They create messes that take more effort to fix than they did to write.

Which would you rather be?

Code craft starts at the codeface; it's where we love to be. We programmers are never happier than when immersed in an editor, bashing out line after line of perfectly formed and well-executed source code. We'd be quite happy if the world around us disappeared in a puff of boolean logic. Sadly, the Real World isn't going anywhere—and it doesn't seem willing to keep itself to itself.

Around your carefully crafted code, the world is in a chaotic state of change. Almost every software project is characterized by flux: changing requirements, changing budgets, changing deadlines, changing priorities, and changing teams. These all conspire to make writing good code a very difficult job. Welcome to the Real World.

Good programmers naturally write neat code when left to their own devices. But they also have an array of battle tactics to help write robust code *on the front line*. They know how to defend themselves against the harsh realities of the software factory and write code that can survive the whirlwinds of change.

That's what we're looking at here. This first section delves into the painfully practical, gory details of code construction, the nuts and bolts of writing source code statements. You'll learn strategies to keep yourself afloat on the turbulent software development ocean and will be challenged to improve your code-writing skills.

These chapters focus on the following issues:

Chapter 1: On the Defensive
Defensive programming: How to write robust code when the world is conspiring against you.

Chapter 2: The Best Laid Plans
Good presentation: why it's important and how to present code well.

Chapter 3: What's in a Name?
Choosing clear names for the parts of your program.

Chapter 4: The Write Stuff
Self-documenting code. Practical strategies to explain code when you can't write a whole novel.

Chapter 5: A Passing Comment
Effective techniques for writing the most appropriate code comments.

Chapter 6: To Err Is Human
Handling errors: How to manage operations that *might* go wrong, and what to do when they do.

These form the path to sound code in an unsound world; they are solid code-writing techniques that should become second nature. If you don't write clear, understandable, defensive, easily testable, easily maintainable software, then you'll be distracted by tedious code-related problems when you should be preparing for what the software factory will throw at you next.

ON THE DEFENSIVE

Defensive Programming Techniques for Robust Code

We have to distrust each other. It's our only defense against betrayal.

—*Tennessee Williams*

When my daughter was 10 months old, she liked playing with wooden bricks. Well, she liked playing with wooden bricks and *me*. I'd build a tower as high as I could, and then with a gentle nudge of the bottom brick, she'd topple the whole thing and let out a little whoop of delight. I didn't build these towers for their strength—it would have been pointless if I did. If I had really wanted a sturdy tower, then I'd have built it in a very different way. I'd have shorn up a foundation and started with a wide base, rather than just quickly stacking blocks upon each other and building as high as possible.

Too many programmers write their code like flimsy towers of bricks; a gentle unexpected prod to the base, and the whole thing falls over. Code builds up in layers, and we need to use techniques that ensure that each layer is sound so that we can build upon it.

Toward Good Code

There is a huge difference between code that *seems* to work, *correct* code, and *good* code. M.A. Jackson wrote, "The beginning of wisdom for a software engineer is to recognize the difference between getting a program to work, and getting it *right*." (Jackson 75) There *is* a difference:

- It is easy to write code that *works* most of the time. You feed it the usual set of inputs; it gives the usual set of outputs. But give it something surprising, and it might just fall over.

- *Correct* code won't fall over. For all possible sets of input, the output will be correct. But usually the set of all possible inputs is ridiculously large and hard to test.

- However, not all correct code is *good* code—the logic may be hard to follow, the code may be contrived, and it may be practically impossible to maintain.

By these definitions, good code is what we should aim for. It is robust, efficient enough and, of course, correct. Industrial strength code will not crash or produce incorrect results when given unusual inputs. It will also satisfy all other requirements, including thread safety, timing constraints, and re-entrancy.

It's one thing to write this good code in the comfort of your own home, a carefully controlled environment. It's an entirely different prospect to do so in the heat of the software factory, where the world is changing around you, the codebase is rapidly evolving, and you're constantly being faced with grotesque *legacy code*—archaic programs written by code monkeys that are now long gone. Try writing good code when the world is conspiring to stop you!

In this torturous environment, how do you ensure that your code is industrial strength? *Defensive programming* helps.

While there are many ways to construct code (object-oriented approaches, component based models, structured design, Extreme Programming, etc.), defensive programming is an approach that can be applied universally. It's not so much a formal methodology as an informal set of basic guidelines. Defensive programming is not a magical cure-all, but a practical way to prevent a pile of potential coding problems.

Assume the Worst

When you write code, it's all too easy to make a set of assumptions about how it should run, how it will be called, what the valid inputs are, and so on. You won't even realize that you've assumed anything, because it all seems obvious to you. You'll spend months happily crafting code, as these assumptions fade and distort in your mind.

Or you might pick up some old code to make a vital last-minute fix when the product's going out the door in 10 minutes. With only enough time for a brief glance at its structure, you'll make assumptions about how the code works. There's no time to perform full literary criticism, and until you get a chance to prove the code is *actually* doing what you think it's doing, assumptions are all you have.

Assumptions cause us to write flawed software. It's easy to assume:

- The function won't *ever* be called like that. I will always be passed valid parameters only.
- This piece of code will *always* work; it will never generate an error.
- *No one* will ever try to access this variable if I document it *For internal use only.*

When we program defensively, we shouldn't make *any* assumptions. We should never assume that *it can't happen*. We should never assume that the world works as we'd expect it to work.

Experience tells us that the only thing you *can* be certain about is this: Your code will somehow, someday, go wrong. Someone *will* do a dumb thing. Murphy's Law puts it this way: "If it can be used incorrectly, it will." Listen to that man—he spoke from experience.[1] Defensive programming prevents these accidents by foreseeing them, or at least fore-guessing them—figuring out what might go wrong at each stage in the code, and guarding against it.

Is this paranoid? Perhaps. But it doesn't hurt to be a *little* paranoid. In fact, it makes a lot of sense. As your code evolves, you will forget the original set of assumptions you made (and real code does evolve—see Chapter 15). Other programmers won't have any knowledge of the assumptions in your head, or else they will just make their own invalid assumptions about what your code can do. Software evolution exposes weaknesses, and code growth hides original simple assumptions. A little paranoia at the outset can make code a lot more robust in the long run.

KEY CONCEPT   *Assume nothing. Unwritten assumptions continually cause faults, particularly as code grows.*

Add to this the fact that things neither you nor your users have any control over can go wrong: Disks fill up, networks fail, and computers crash. Bad things happen. Remember, it's never actually your program that fails—the software always does what you told it to. The actual algorithms, or perhaps the client code, are what introduce faults into the system.

As you write more code, and as you work through it faster and faster, the likelihood of making mistakes grows and grows. Without adequate time to verify each assumption, you can't write robust code. Unfortunately, on the programming front line, there's rarely any opportunity to slow down, take stock, and linger over a piece of code. The world is just moving too fast, and programmers need to keep up. Therefore, we should grasp every opportunity to reduce errors, and defensive practices are one of our main weapons.

---

[1] Edward Murphy Jr. was a US Air Force engineer. He coined this infamous law after discovering a technician had systematically connected a whole row of devices upside down. Symmetric connectors permitted this avoidable mistake; afterward, he chose a different connector design.

What Is Defensive Programming?

As the name suggests, defensive programming is careful, guarded programming. To construct reliable software, we design every component in the system so that it *protects* itself as much as possible. We smash unwritten assumptions by explicitly checking for them in the code. This is an attempt to prevent, or at least observe, when our code is called in a way that will exhibit incorrect behavior.

Defensive programming enables us to detect minor problems early on, rather than get bitten by them later when they've escalated into major disasters. All too often, you'll see "professional" developers rush out code without thinking. The story goes something like this:

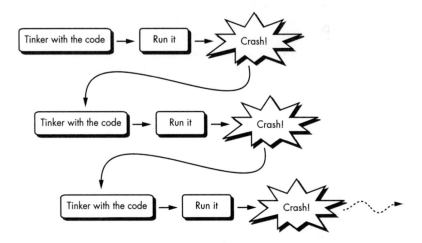

They are continually tripped up by the incorrect assumptions that they never took the time to validate. Hardly a promotion for modern day software engineering, but it's happening all the time. Defensive programming helps us to write correct software from the start and move away from the *code-it, try-it, code-it, try-it* . . . cycle. With defensive programming, the story looks more like this:

Okay, defensive programming won't remove program failures altogether. But problems will become less of a hassle and easier to fix. Defensive programmers catch falling snowflakes rather than get buried under an avalanche of errors.

Defensive programming is a method of prevention, rather than a form of cure. Compare this to debugging—the act of removing bugs *after* they've bitten. Debugging is all about finding a cure.

WHAT DEFENSIVE PROGRAMMING ISN'T

There are a few common misconceptions about defensive programming. Defensive programming is not:

Error checking

If there are error conditions that might arise in your code, you should be checking for them anyway. This is *not* defensive code. It's just plain good practice—a part of writing *correct* code.

Testing

Testing your code is not defensive. It's another normal part of our development work. Test harnesses aren't defensive; they can prove the code is correct now, but won't prove that it will stand up to future modification. Even with the best test suite in the world, anyone can make a change and slip it past untested.

Debugging

You might add some defensive code during a spell of debugging, but debugging is something you do after your program has failed. Defensive programming is something you do to *prevent* your program from failing in the first place (or to detect failures early before they manifest in incomprehensible ways, demanding all-night debugging sessions).

Is defensive programming really worth the hassle? There are arguments for and against:

The case *against*

Defensive programming consumes resources, both yours and the computer's.

- It eats into the efficiency of your code; even a little extra code requires a little extra execution. For a single function or class, this might not matter, but when you have a system made up of 100,000 functions, you may have more of a problem.

- Each defensive practice requires some extra work. Why should you follow any of them? You have enough to do already, right? Just make sure people use your code correctly. If they don't, then any problems are their own fault.

The case *for*

The counterargument is compelling.

- Defensive programming saves you literally hours of debugging and lets you do more fun stuff instead. Remember Murphy: If your code *can* be used incorrectly, it will be.

- Working code that runs properly, but ever-so-slightly slower, is *far* superior to code that works most of the time but occasionally collapses in a shower of brightly colored sparks.

- We can design some defensive code to be physically removed in release builds, circumventing the performance issue. The majority of the items we'll consider here don't have any significant overhead, anyway.

- Defensive programming avoids a large number of security problems—a serious issue in modern software development. More on this follows.

As the market demands software that's built faster and cheaper, we need to focus on techniques that deliver results. Don't skip the bit of extra work up front that will prevent a whole world of pain and delay later.

The Big, Bad World

Someone once said, "Never ascribe to malice that which is adequately explained by stupidity."[2] Most of the time we are defending against stupidity, against invalid and unchecked assumptions. However there *are* malicious users, and they will try to bend and break your code to suit their vicious purposes.

Defensive programming helps with program security, guarding against this kind of willful misuse. Crackers and virus writers routinely exploit sloppy code to gain control of an application and then weave whatever wicked schemes they desire. This is a serious threat in the modern world of software development; it has huge implications in terms of the loss of productivity, money, and privacy.

Software abusers range from the opportunistic user exploiting a small program quirk to the hard-core cracker who spends his time deliberately trying to gain illicit access to your systems. Too many unwitting programmers leave gaping holes for these people to walk through. With the rise of the networked computer, the consequences of sloppiness become more and more significant.

Many large development corporations are finally waking up to this threat and are beginning to take the problem seriously, investing time and resources into serious defensive code work. In reality, it's hard to graft in defenses *after* an attack. We look at software security in more detail in Chapter 12.

Techniques for Defensive Programming

Enough of the background. What does all this mean to programmers working in the software factory?

There are a number of common sense rules under the defensive programming umbrella. People usually think of *assertions* when they think of defensive programming, and rightly so. We'll talk about those later. But there's also a pile of simple programming habits that will immeasurably improve the safety of your code.

---

[2] Some historians attribute this quote to Napoleon Bonaparte. Now there's a guy who knew something about defense.

Despite seeming common sense, these rules are often ignored—hence the low standard of most software at large in the world. Tighter security and reliable development can be achieved surprisingly easily, as long as programmers are alert and well informed.

The next few pages list the rules of defensive programming. We'll start off by painting with broad strokes, looking at high-level defensive techniques, processes, and procedures. As we progress, we'll fill in finer detail, looking more deeply at individual code statements. Some of these defensive techniques are language specific. This is natural—you have to put on bulletproof shoes if your language lets you shoot yourself in the foot.

As you read this list, evaluate yourself. How many of these rules do you currently follow? Which ones will you now adopt?

Employ a Good Coding Style and Sound Design

We can prevent most coding mistakes by adopting a good coding style. This naturally dovetails with the other chapters in this section. Simple things like choosing meaningful variable names and using parentheses judiciously can increase clarity and reduce the likelihood of faults slipping past unnoticed.

Similarly, considering the larger-scale design before ploughing into the code is key. "The best documentation of a computer program is a clean structure." (Kernighan Plaugher 78) Starting off with a set of clear APIs to implement, a logical system structure, and well-defined component roles and responsibilities will avoid headaches further down the line.

Don't Code in a Hurry

It's all too common to see hit-and-run programming. Programmers quickly hack out a function, shove it through the compiler to check syntax, run it once to see if it works, and then move on to the next task. This approach is fraught with peril.

Instead, think about each line as you write it. What errors could arise? Have you considered every logical twist that might occur? Slow, methodical programming seems mundane—but it really does cut down on the number of faults introduced.

KEY CONCEPT   *More haste, less speed. Always think carefully about what you're typing* as *you type it.*

A particular C-family gotcha that snares speedy programmers is mistyping == as just =. The former is a test for equality; the latter a variable assignment. With an unhelpful compiler (or with warnings switched off) there will be no indication that the program behavior is not what was intended.

Always do *all* of the tasks involved in completing a code section before rushing on. For example, if you decide to write the main flow first and the error checking/handling second, you must be sure you have the discipline to do both. Be very wary of deferring the error checking and moving straight on to the main flow of three more code sections. Your intention to return later may be sincere, but later can easily become much later, by which time you will have forgotten much of the context, making it take longer and be more of a chore. (And of course, by then there will be some artificially urgent deadline.)

Discipline is a habit that needs to be learned and reinforced. Every time you don't do the right thing now, you become more likely to continue not doing the right thing in the future. Do it now; don't leave it for a rainy day in the Sahara. Doing it later actually requires *more* discipline than doing it now!

Trust No One

Your mother told you never to talk to strangers. Unfortunately, good software development requires even more cynicism and less faith in human nature. Even well-intentioned code users could cause problems in your program; being defensive means you can't trust anybody.

You might suffer problems because of:

- **Genuine users** accidentally giving bogus input or operating the program incorrectly.
- **Malicious users** trying to consciously provoke bad program behavior.
- **Client code** calling your function with the wrong parameters or supplying inconsistent input.
- **The operating environment** failing to provide adequate service to the program.
- **External libraries** behaving badly and failing to honor interface contracts that you rely on.

You might even make a silly coding mistake in one function or forget how some three-year-old code is supposed to work and then use it badly. Don't assume that all will go well or that all code will operate correctly. Put safety checks in place throughout your work. Constantly watch for weak spots, and guard against them with extra-defensive code.

KEY CONCEPT   *Trust no one. Absolutely anyone—including yourself—can introduce flaws into your program logic. Treat all inputs and all results with suspicion until you can prove that they are valid.*

Write Code for Clarity, Not Brevity

Whenever you can choose between concise (but potentially confusing) code and clear (but potentially tedious) code, use code that *reads* as intended, even if it's less elegant. For example, split complex arithmetic operations into a series of separate statements to make the logic clearer.

Think about who might read your code. It might require maintenance work by a junior coder, and if he can't understand the logic, then he's bound to make mistakes. Complicated constructs or unusual language tricks might prove your encyclopedic knowledge of operator precedence, but it really butchers code maintainability. *Keep it simple.*

If it can't be maintained, your code is not safe. In really extreme cases, overly complex expressions can cause the compiler to generate incorrect code—many compiler optimization errors come to light this way.

KEY CONCEPT   *Simplicity is a virtue. Never make code more complex than necessary.*

Don't Let Anyone Tinker with Stuff They Shouldn't

Things that are internal should stay on the inside. Things that are private should be kept under lock and key. Don't display your code's dirty laundry in public. No matter how politely you ask, people *will* fiddle with your data when you're not looking if given half a chance, and they *will* try to call "implementation-only" routines for their own reasons. Don't let them.

- In object-oriented languages, prevent access to internal class data by making it private. In C++, consider the Cheshire cat/pimpl idiom. (Meyers 97)

- In procedural languages, you can still employ object-oriented (OO) packaging concepts, by wrapping private data behind opaque types and providing well-defined public operations on them.

- Keep all variables in the tightest scope necessary; don't declare variables globally when you don't have to. Don't put them at file scope when they can be function-local. Don't place them at function scope when they can be loop-local.

SAY "WHEN"

When do you program defensively? Do you start when things go wrong? Or when you pick up some code you don't understand?

No, these defensive programming techniques should be used *all the time*. They should be second nature. Mature programmers have learned from experience—they've been bitten enough times that they know to put sensible safeguards in place.

Defensive strategies are much easier to apply as you start writing code, rather than retrofitting them into existent code. You can't be thorough and accurate if you try to shoehorn in this stuff late in the day. If you start adding defensive code once something has gone wrong, you are essentially debugging—being reactive, not preventative and proactive.

However, during the course of debugging, or even when adding new functionality you'll discover conditions that you'd like to verify. It's always a good time to add defensive code.

Compile with All Warnings Switched On

Most languages' compilers draw on a vast selection of error messages when you hurt their feelings. They will also spit out various *warnings* when they encounter potentially flawed code, like the use of a C or C++ variable before its assignment.[3] These warnings can usually be selectively enabled and disabled.

---

[3] Many languages (like Java and C#) classify this as an error.

If your code is full of dangerous constructs, you'll get pages and pages of warnings. Sadly, the common response is to disable compiler warnings or just ignore the messages. Don't do either.

Always enable your compiler's warnings. And if your code generates any warnings, fix the code immediately to silence the compiler's screams. Never be satisfied with code that doesn't compile quietly when warnings are enabled. The warnings are there for a reason. Even if there's a particular warning you think doesn't matter, don't leave it in, or one day it will obscure one that *does* matter.

KEY CONCEPT *Compiler warnings catch many silly coding errors. Always enable them. Make sure your code compiles silently.*

Use Static Analysis Tools

Compiler warnings are the result of a limited *static analysis* of your code, a code inspection performed *before* the program is run.

There are many separate static analysis tools available, like lint (and its more modern derivatives) for C and FxCop for .NET assemblies. Your daily programming routine should include use of these tools to check your code. They will pick up many more errors than your compiler alone.

Use Safe Data Structures

Or failing that, use dangerous data structures safely.

Perhaps the most common security vulnerability results from *buffer overrun*. This is triggered by the careless use of fixed-size data structures. If your code writes into a buffer without checking its size first, then there is always potential for writing past the end of the buffer.

It's frighteningly easy to do, as this small snippet of C code demonstrates:

```
char *unsafe_copy(const char *source)
{
    char *buffer = new char[10];
    strcpy(buffer, source);
    return buffer;
}
```

If the length of the data in source is greater than 10 characters, its copy will extend beyond the end of buffer's reserved memory. Then anything could happen. In the best case, the result would be data corruption—some other data structure's contents will be overwritten. In the worst case, a malicious user could exploit this simple error to put executable code on the program stack and use it to run his own arbitrary program, effectively hijacking the computer. These kinds of flaw are regularly exploited by system crackers—serious stuff.

It's easy to avoid being bitten by these vulnerabilities: Don't write such bad code! Use safer data structures that don't allow you to corrupt the program—use a managed buffer like C++'s string class. Or systematically use safe operations on unsafe data types. The C code above can be secured by swapping strcpy for strncpy, a size-limited string copy operation:

```
char *safer_copy(const char *source)
{
    char *buffer = new char[10];
    strncpy(buffer, source, 10);
    return buffer;
}
```

Check Every Return Value

If a function returns a value, it does so for a reason. Check that return value. If it is an error code, you *must* inspect it and handle any failure. Don't let errors silently invade your program; swallowing an error can lead to unpredictable behavior.

This applies to user-defined functions as well as standard library ones. Most of the insidious bugs you'll find arise when a programmer fails to check a return value. Don't forget that some functions may return errors through a different mechanism (i.e., the standard C library's errno). Always catch and handle appropriate exceptions at the appropriate level.

Handle Memory (and Other Precious Resources) Carefully

Be thorough and release any resource that you acquire during execution. Memory is the example of this cited most often, but it is not the only one. Files and thread locks are other precious resources that we must use carefully. Be a good steward.

Don't neglect to close files or release memory because you think that the OS will clean up your program when it exits. You really don't know how long your code will be left running, eating up all file handles or consuming all the memory. You can't even be sure that the OS will cleanly release your resources—some OSes don't.

There is a school of thought that says, "Don't worry about freeing memory until you know your program works in the first place; only then add all the relevant releases." Just say no. This is a ludicrously dangerous practice. It will lead to many, many errors in your memory usage; you *will* inevitably forget to free memory in some places.

KEY CONCEPT   *Treat all scarce resources with respect. Manage their acquisition and release carefully.*

Java and .NET employ a garbage collector to do all this tedious tidying up for you, so you can just "forget" about freeing resources. Let them drop to the floor, since the run time sweeps up every now and then. It's a nice luxury, but don't be lulled into a false sense of security. You still have to think. You have to explicitly drop references to objects you no longer care about, or they won't be cleaned up; don't accidentally hold on to an object reference. Less advanced garbage collectors are also easily fooled by circular references (e.g., *A* refers to *B*, and *B* refers to *A*, but no one else cares about them). This could cause objects to never be swept up; a subtle form of memory leak.

Initialize All Variables at Their Points of Declaration

This is a clarity issue. The intent of each variable is explicit if you initialize it. It's not safe to rely on rules of thumb like *If I don't initialize it, I don't care about the initial value.* The code will evolve. The uninitialized value may turn into a problem further down the line.

C and C++ compound this issue. If you accidentally use a variable without having initialized it, you'll get different results each time your program runs, depending on what garbage was in memory at the time. Declaring a variable in one place, assigning it later on, and then using it even later opens up a window for errors. If the assignment is ever skipped, you'll spend ages hunting down random behavior. Close the window by initializing every variable as you declare it; even if the value's wrong, the behavior will at least be predictably wrong.

Safer languages (like Java and C#) sidestep this pitfall by defining an initial value for all variables. It's still good practice to initialize a variable as you declare it, which improves code clarity.

Declare Variables as Late as Possible

By doing this, you place the variable as close as possible to its use, preventing it from confusing other parts of the code. It also clarifies the code using the variable. You don't have to hunt around to find the variable's type and initialization; a nearby declaration makes it obvious.

Don't reuse the same temporary variable in a number of places, even if each use is in a logically separate area. It makes later reworking of the code awfully complicated. Create a new variable each time—the compiler will sort out any efficiency concerns.

Use Standard Language Facilities

C and C++ are nightmares in this respect. They suffer from many different revisions of their specifications, with more obscure cases left as implementation-specific *undefined behavior.* Today there are many compilers, each with subtly different behavior. They are mostly compatible, but there is still plenty of rope to hang yourself with.

Clearly define which language version you are using. Unless mandated by your project (and there had better be a good reason), *don't* rely on compiler weirdness or any nonstandard extensions to the language. If there is an area of the language that is undefined, don't rely on the behavior of your particular compiler (e.g., don't rely on your C compiler treating char as a signed value—others won't). Doing so leads to very brittle code. What happens when you update the compiler? What happens when a new programmer joins the team who doesn't understand the extensions? Relying on a particular compiler's odd behavior leads to *really* subtle bugs later in life.

Use a Good Diagnostic Logging Facility

When you write some new code, you'll often include a lot of diagnostics to check what's going on. Should these really be removed after the event? Leaving them in will make life easier when you have to revisit the code, especially if they can be selectively disabled in the meantime.

There are a number of diagnostic logging systems available to facilitate this. Many can be used in such a way that diagnostics have no overhead if not needed; they can be conditionally compiled out.

Cast Carefully

Most languages allow you to *cast* (or convert) data from one type to another. This operation is some times more successful than others. If you try to convert a 64-bit integer into a smaller 8-bit data type, what will happen to the other 56 bits? Your execution environment might suddenly throw an exception or silently degrade your data's integrity. Many programmers don't think about this kind of thing, and so their programs behave in unnatural ways.

If you really want to use a cast, think carefully about it. What you're saying to the compiler is, "Forget your type checking: *I* know what this variable is, you don't." You're ripping a big hole into the type system and walking straight through it. It's unstable ground; if you make any kind of mistake, the compiler will just sit there quietly and mutter, "I told you so," under its breath. If you're lucky (e.g., using Java or C#) the run time might throw an exception to let you know, but this depends on exactly what you're trying to convert.

C and C++ are particularly vague about the precision of data types, so don't make assumptions about data type interchangeability. Don't presume that int and long are the same size and can be assigned to one another, even if you can get away with it on *your* platform. Code migrates platforms, but bad code migrates badly.

The Fine Print

There are many low-level defensive construction techniques, all part of a sensible coding routine and a healthy distrust of the Real World. Consider:

Providing default behavior
Most languages provide a switch statement; they document what happens in the default case. If the default case is erroneous, make that explicit in the code. If nothing happens, make *that* explicit in the code—that way the maintenance programmer will understand.

Similarly, if you write an if statement without an else clause, stop for a moment and consider whether you should handle the logical default case.

Following language idioms
This simple piece of advice will ensure that your readers understand all of the code you have written. They'll make fewer bad assumptions.

Checking numeric limits

Even the most basic calculations may cause numeric variables to overflow or underflow. Be on the lookout for this. Language specifications or core libraries provide mechanisms for determining the capacity of standard types—use them. Make sure you know all the available numeric types, and what each is most suitable for.

Check that each calculation is sound. For example, make sure you can't use values that would cause a *divide by zero* error.

Being const-correct

C/C++ programmers should be really vigilant about this—it will make life much easier. Make everything as const as you possibly can. It does two things: const qualifications act as code documentation, and const allows the compiler to spot silly mistakes that you make. It prevents you from modifying data that's off-limits.

Constraints

We've thought about the set of assumptions we make as we program. But how can we physically incorporate these assumptions into our software so they're not illusive problems waiting to emerge? Simply write a little extra code to check for each condition. This code acts as the documentation of each assumption, making it explicit rather than implicit.[4] In doing so, we're codifying the *constraints* on program functionality and behavior.

What do we want the program to do if a constraint is broken? Since this kind of constraint will be more than a simple detectable and correctable runtime error (we should already be checking for and handling those), it must be a flaw in the program logic. There are few possibilities for the program's reaction:

- Turn a blind eye to the problem, and hope that nothing will go wrong as a consequence.

- Give it an on-the-spot fine and allow the program to continue (e.g., print a diagnostic warning or log the error).

- Go directly to jail; do not pass go (e.g., abort the program immediately, in a controlled or uncontrolled manner).

For example, it is invalid to call C's strlen function with a string pointer set to zero, because the pointer will be immediately dereferenced, so the latter two options are the most plausible candidates. It's probably most appropriate to abort the program immediately, since derefencing a null pointer can lead to all sorts of catastrophes on unprotected operating systems.

There are a number of different scenarios in which constraints are used:

Preconditions

These are conditions that must hold true *before* a section of code is entered. If a precondition fails, it's due to a fault in the client code.

---

[4] This doesn't replace writing good documentation, though.

Postconditions
> These must hold true *after* a code block is left. If a postcondition fails, it's due to a fault in the supplier code.

Invariants
> These are conditions that hold true every time the program's execution reaches a particular point: between loop passes, across method calls, and so on. Failure of an invariant implies a fault in the program logic.

Assertions
> Any other statement about a program's state at a given point in time.

The first two listed here are frustrating to implement without language support—if a function has multiple exit points,[5] then inserting a postcondition gets messy. Eiffel supports pre- and postconditions in the core language and can also ensure that constraint checks don't have any side effects.

However tedious, good constraints expressed in code make your program clearer and more maintainable. This technique is also known as *design by contract*, since constraints form an immutable contract between sections of code.

What to Constrain

There are a number of different problems you can guard against with constraints. For example, you can:

- Check all array accesses are within bounds.
- Assert that pointers are not zero before dereferencing them.
- Ensure that function parameters are valid.
- Sanity check function results before returning them.
- Prove that an object's state is consistent before operating on it.
- Guard any place in the code where you'd write the comment *We should never get here.*

The first two of these examples are particularly C/C++ focused. Java and C# have their own ways of avoiding some of these pitfalls in the core language, as do other languages.

Just how much constraint checking should you do? Placing a check on every other line is a bit extreme. As with many things, the correct balance becomes clear as the programmer gets more mature. Is it better to have too much or too little? It is possible for too many constraint checks to obscure the code's logic. "Readability is the best single criterion of program quality: If a program is easy to read, it is probably a good program; if it is hard to read, it probably isn't good." (Kernighan Plaugher 76)

Realistically, putting pre- and postconditions in major functions plus invariants in the key loops is sufficient.

---

[5] There is a theological debate about whether functions *should* have multiple exit points.

Removing Constraints

This kind of constraint checking is usually only required during the development and debugging stages of program construction. Once we have used the constraints to convince ourselves (rightly or wrongly) that the program logic is correct, we would ideally remove them so as not to incur an unnecessary run-time overhead.

Thanks to the wonders of modern technology, all of this is perfectly possible. The C and C++ standard libraries provide a common mechanism to implement constraints—assert. assert acts as a procedural firewall, testing the logic of its argument. It is provided as an alarm for the developer to show incorrect program behavior and should not be allowed to trigger in customer-facing code. If the assertion's constraint is satisfied execution continues. Otherwise, the program aborts, producing an error message looking something like this:

```
bugged.cpp:10: int main(): Assertion "1 == 0" failed.
```

assert is implemented as a preprocessor macro, which means it sits more naturally in C than in C++. There are a number of more C++-sympathetic assertion libraries available.

To use assert you must #include <assert.h>. You can then write something like assert(ptr != 0); in your function. Preprocessor magic allows us to strip out assertions in a production build by specifying the NDEBUG flag to the compiler. All asserts will be removed, and their arguments will not be evaluated. This means that in production builds asserts have no overhead at all.

Whether or not assertions *should* be completely removed, as opposed to just being made nonfatal, is a debatable issue. There is a school of thought that says after you remove them, you are testing a *completely different* piece of code.[6] Others say that the overhead of assertions is not acceptable in a release build, so they must be eliminated. (But how often do people profile execution to prove this?)

Either way, our assertions must not have any side effects. What would happen, for example, if you mistakenly wrote:

```
int i = pullNumberFromThinAir();
assert(i = 6); // hmm - should type more carefully!
printf("i is %d\n", i);
```

The assertion will clearly never trigger in a debug build; its value is 6 (near enough *true* for C). However, in a release build, the assert line will be removed completely and the printf will produce different output. This can be the cause of subtle problems late in product development. It's quite hard to guard against bugs in the bug-checking code!

---

[6] In practice, more may change between development and release builds of software—compiler optimization levels and the inclusion of debugging symbols, for example. Both of these can make subtle differences to execution and may obscure the manifestation of other faults. During even the earliest stages of development, testing should be performed equally with development and release builds.

It's not difficult to envision situations where assertions might have even more subtle side effects. For example, if you assert(invariants());, yet the invariants() function has a side effect, it's not easy to spot.

Since assertions can be removed in production code, it is vital that only constraint testing is done with assert. Real error-condition testing, like memory allocation failure or filesystem problems, should be dealt with in ordinary code. You wouldn't want to compile that out of your program! Justifiable run-time errors (no matter how undesirable) should be detected with defensive code that can never be removed.

Java has a similar assert mechanism.[7] It can be enabled and disabled by controls on the JVM, and throws an exception (java.lang.AssertionError) instead of causing an instant program abort. .NET provides an assertion mechanism in the framework's Debug class.

OFFENSIVE PROGRAMMING?

The best defense is a good offense.
—Proverb

While writing this chapter, I wondered, *What's the opposite of defensive programming?* It's *offensive programming*, of course!

There are a number of people I know who you could call offensive programmers. But I think there's more to this than swearing at your computer and never taking baths.

It stands to reason that an offensive programming approach would be actively trying to *break* things in the code, rather than defending against problems. That is, actively attacking the code rather than securing it. I'd call that *testing*. As we'll see later in "Who, What, When, and Why?" on page 132, testing, when done properly, has an incredibly positive effect on your software construction. It improves code quality greatly and brings stability to the development process.

We should be all offensive programmers.

When you discover and fix a fault, it is good practice to slip in an assertion where the fault was fixed. Then you can ensure that you won't be bitten twice. If nothing else, this would act as a warning sign to people maintaining the code in the future.

A common C++/Java technique for writing class constraints is to add a single member function called bool invariant() to each class. (Naturally this function should have no side effects.) Now an assert can be put at the beginning and end of each member function calling this invariant. (There should be no assertion at the beginning of a constructor or at the end of the destructor, for obvious reasons.) For example, a circle class's invariant may check that radius != 0; that would be invalid object state and could cause later calculations to fail (perhaps with a divide by zero error).

---

[7] It was added in JDK 1.4 and is not available in earlier versions.

In a Nutshell

> *Draw water for the siege, strengthen your*
> *defenses! Work the clay, tread the mortar,*
> *repair the brickwork!*
> *—Nahum 3:14*

It is important to craft code that is not just correct but is also good. It needs to document all the assumptions made. This will make it easier to maintain, and it will harbor fewer bugs. Defensive programming is a method of expecting the worst and being prepared for it. It's a technique that prevents simple faults from becoming elusive bugs.

The use of codified constraints alongside defensive code will make your software far more robust. Like many other good coding practices (*unit testing*, for example—see "The Types of Test" on page 138), defensive programming is about spending a little extra time wisely (and early) in order to save much more time, effort, and cost later. Believe me, this *can* save an entire project from ruin.

Good programmers . . .

- Care that their code is robust
- Make sure every assumption is explicitly captured in defensive code
- Want well-defined behavior for garbage input
- Think carefully about the code they write, as they write it
- Write code that protects itself from other people's (or their own) stupidity

Bad programmers . . .

- Would rather not think about what could go wrong in their code
- Release code for integration that may fail and hope that someone else will sort it out
- Leave important information about how their code should be used locked in their heads, ready to be lost
- Apply little thought to the code they are writing, resulting in unpredictable and unreliable software

See Also

Chapter 8: Testing Times
Offensive programming—say no more.

Chapter 9: Finding Fault
When faults breach your careful defenses, you'll need a strategy to round them up.

Chapter 12: An Insecurity Complex
Defensive programming is a key technique for writing secure software systems.

You must document pre- and postconditions; how else will anyone know they exist? If you have any constraints specified, then you can add defensive code to assert them.

Get Thinking

A detailed discussion of these questions can be found in the "Answers and Discussion" section on page 463.

Mull It Over

1. Can you have *too much* defensive programming?
2. Should you add an assertion to your code for every bug you find and fix?
3. Should assertions conditionally compile away to nothing in production builds? If not, which assertions should remain in release builds?

4. Are exceptions a better form of defensive barrier than C-style assertions?

5. Should the defensive checking of pre- and postconditions be put *inside* each function, or around each important function *call*?

6. Are constraints a perfect defensive tool? What are their drawbacks?

7. Can you *avoid* defensive programming?

   a. If you designed a *better* language, would defensive programming still be necessary? How could you do this?

   b. Does this show that C and C++ are flawed because they have so many areas for problems to manifest?

8. What sort of code do you not need to worry about writing defensively?

Getting Personal

1. How carefully do you consider each statement that you type? Do you relentlessly check every function return code, even if you're *sure* a function will not return an error?

2. When you document a function, do you state the pre- and postconditions?

   a. Are they always implicit in the description of what the function does?

   b. If there are no pre- or postconditions, do you explicitly document this?

3. Many companies pay lip service to defensive programming. Does your team recommend it? Take a look at the codebase—do they really? How widely are constraints codified in assertions? How thorough is the error checking in each function?

4. Are you naturally paranoid enough? Do you look both ways before crossing the road? Do you eat your greens? Do you check for every potential error in your code, no matter how unlikely?

   a. How easy is it to do this thoroughly? Do you forget to think about errors?

   b. Are there any ways to help yourself write more thorough defensive code?

2

THE BEST LAID PLANS

The Layout and Presentation of Source Code

Stop judging by mere appearances, and make a right judgment.

—John 7:24

Coding style has been, is, and will continue to be the subject of holy wars among programmers—professional, amateur, and student—where, unfortunately, intense disagreements degrade into mere name-calling. *I'll show you where to stick your stupid brackets.*

The first company I ever worked for kick-started a process to define its internal coding standard. The guidelines were supposed to encompass several languages, defining common conventions and best practices. Months later, the group compiling the guidelines was still arguing about where to put brackets in C. I'm not sure if anyone ever followed the standard that was eventually produced.

Why *do* people get so worked up about this? As we'll see, presentation dramatically affects the readability of code—no one wants to work with code that isn't easy to read. Presentation is also a very subjective and personal thing—*you* may not like the style that turns *me* on. Familiarity breeds comfort, and an alien style puts you on edge.

Programmers are passionate about code, so presentation stirs deep emotions.

What's the Big Deal?

The layout and presentation of code is an issue in most modern programming languages. The freedom of formatting that permits individual artistic expression came *en vogue* in the early 1960s with the language Algol; the previously available Fortran versions had been more restricted in format. Since then, very few languages have deviated from that free-form approach.

A code presentation style governs a surprisingly large number of things; brace positioning is the most obvious[1] and perhaps the most contentious issue. The wider aspects of code style, like conventions for function and variable naming, tie in with other coding concerns such as program structure (e.g., *Don't use gotos*, or *Only write Single Entry, Single Exit functions*) to dictate the style in which you write a program. Altogether, this constitutes your *coding standard*.

Although there are many individual choices to make when you define a code presentation format, all are aesthetic. By definition, presentation has no syntactic or semantic meaning at all; the compiler ignores it.

However, presentation makes a real impact on the quality of code. Programmers read meaning into code based on its layout. It can illuminate and support your code's structure, helping the reader understand what's going on. Or it can confuse, mislead, and hide the code's intent. It doesn't matter how well designed your program is; if it looks like a thrown-together mess, it will be unpleasant to work with. But bad formatting not only makes code harder to follow; it may actually *hide* bugs from you. As a simple example of this, consider the following C code:

```c
int error = doSomeMagicOperation();
if (error)
    fprintf(stderr, "Error: exiting...\n");
    exit(error);
```

The layout shows what the author meant to happen, but he'll be surprised when the code actually runs.

Since we're conscientious craftsmen committed to high-quality code, we strive for clear presentation. There are already plenty of stumbling blocks in software development; we shouldn't let basic code presentation become one of them.

---

[1] *Brace* is a common name for the curly bracket (that is, { and }) so common in C-style programming languages.

Know Your Audience

To write effective source code, it's important to know *who* you're presenting it to. If you're going to confuse someone, you'd better know who deserves the apology. There are, in fact, three audiences for our source code:

Ourselves

My handwriting is so bad that sometimes even *I* can't read it. It's practically useless unless I concentrate on writing clearly. It's the same with code. You have to be able to read what you've written immediately after you write it, but also perhaps years later when you come back to it. Who would have expected to come back to archaic (relatively speaking) COBOL code to fix a Y2K bug?

The compiler

The compiler doesn't care what your code looks like, as long as it doesn't have any syntactic errors. The *intent* of the code is completely ignored. You can write detailed comments explaining what you *want* a function to do, but the compiler won't tell you if the instructions don't actually do what your comments say. As long as it's valid code, your development environment will be happy.

Others

This is the most important audience and often the least considered.

So you're working in a team, but you're the only person who will ever see your bit of code, right? Wrong. It never works that way.

You're at home writing some code for fun; no one will ever see it. You don't need to worry about making it neat, do you? No, you don't; but how would that benefit you? You aren't developing skills that will make you a professional. This is the perfect opportunity to practice really good discipline on a project with no external pressures. A chance to get into good habits. If you blow it here, is it any wonder you have no discipline on "real" projects?

Your source code is a document, describing the program you are creating. It needs to read clearly to whoever might come back to it. This will include those auditing (code reviewing) the work you have done and anyone who maintains it later. Be kind to people who have to look after your code—just imagine yourself in their shoes.

We tailor the elements of presentation style with our audiences in mind. How does the audience affect how we lay out code? Surprisingly, we care least of all about the compiler. Its job is to ignore all that unnecessary whitespace and get down to the serious business of interpreting our syntax. Presentation is not about syntactic meaning, and the compiler can cope with whatever freakish layout we throw at it.

Rather, we use layout to emphasize the *logical structure* of the code to human readers. It's about communication, and the clearer the better.

KEY CONCEPT *Understand the real audience for your source code: other programmers. Write for their benefit.*

What Is Good Presentation?

As you can see, good presentation means more than just being neat. Tidy code certainly gives an impression of high quality, but code can be both tidy *and* misleading. We strive for *clear* layout; the code structure must be *enhanced* by an indentation strategy, not hidden by it. If a particular flow of control is necessarily complex, the layout should be helping you to read the code. (If you've written a flow of control that is unnecessarily complex, you should change it immediately.)

Our code layout must convey meaning, rather than disguise it. I suggest the following as good metrics for the quality of a presentation style.

Consistent

The indentation strategy must be consistent across the project. Don't change styles halfway through a source file. Not only does this look unprofessional, it can confuse and give the impression that your source files are not really related.

The individual presentation rules should be internally consistent. The positioning of braces, brackets, and so on in different situations should all follow a single convention. The number of spaces of indent should always be the same.

Kernighan and Ritchie—the fathers of C—say, after stressing the importance of having good indentation: "The position of braces is less important, although people hold passionate beliefs. We have chosen one of several popular styles. Pick a style that suits you, then use it consistently." (Kernighan Ritchie 88)

Conventional

It's sensible to adopt one of the major styles currently in use in the industry rather than invent your own indentation rules. You can be sure of it being accessible to others who are reading your code. And you're less likely to make people vomit.

Concise

Can you concisely describe your indentation strategy? Think about it. If you do *this* unless *such-and-such*, in which case you do *this* if *X* holds; otherwise you do something else which depends on . . .

Someone may eventually need to extend the code you've written and should do so in the same style. If it's not easy to pick up, then is it really a useful presentation style?

Brace Yourself

To illustrate the impact presentation has on source code and the trade-offs involved in choosing a particular style, this case study investigates an important C-related layout issue. By looking at the variation in this one simple area, we'll see how important presentation is and what a profound impact it has on your code.

Brace positioning is a big concern for the curly bracket languages, although it's really only a fraction of the total code layout problem. As the most immediately visible artifact, it generates about 80 percent of the fuss. Other languages have their own similar layout concerns.

There are a number of conventional brace positioning styles. Which you pick comes down to your sense of aesthetics, the culture you code in, and what you're used to. Different styles are appropriate in different contexts—consider a magazine article versus a source editor (see "Well Presented" on page 28). You may prefer the exdented style, but in a magazine you're forced to use K&R to maximize use of the printed page.

K&R Brace Style

K&R style is the oldest flavor, established by the fathers of C Kernighan and Ritchie in their book *The C Programming Language*. (Kernighan Ritchie 88) For this reason, it is often considered the *original and best*. It was driven by the need to display the most information possible on a small screen. It's probably the dominant style for Java code.

```
int k_and_r() {
    int a = 0, b = 0;
    while (a != 10) {
        b++;
        a++;
    }
    return b;
}
```

Pros

- Takes up little room, so you can get more code on screen at once
- The closing brace lines up with the statement it matches, so you can scan up to find the construct being terminated

Cons

- The braces don't line up, so it's hard to visually match them
- You might not notice if an opening brace goes off the right of the page
- Code statements appear very densely packed

Exdented Brace Style

A more spacious approach is the so-called *exdented* (or sometimes *Allman*) style. This is my personal favorite.

```
int exdented()
{
    int a = 0, b = 0;
    while (a != 10)
    {
        b++;
        a++;
    }
    return b;
}
```

Pros

- A clear and uncluttered format
- Easier to scan code for opening braces since they're distinct; this makes each code block more obvious

Cons

- Takes up more vertical space
- Looks wasteful when you have lots of blocks containing only one statement
- Too much like Pascal for some hackers

WELL PRESENTED

How you present code depends on the context in which it will be read. There are more contexts than you might think. When you're reading some code, it's important to appreciate the forces that drove its presentation. The common code habitats are:

Source editor

This is most code's natural habitat. It raises all the presentation concerns programmers automatically think about. The code is read on a computer screen, usually in some dedicated editor or IDE. You scroll or navigate through a file to places of particular interest. It's an interactive world—more often than not, you're reading code *to make modifications*. This means that the code has to be malleable.

The editor may have horizontal scrollbars for long lines or may limit the page width and wrap them. Usually there's syntax coloring to aid comprehension. As you type, the editor performs some formatting work for you. For example, it intelligently positions the cursor on new lines.

Published code

Unless you live in a lonely, isolated little world, you'll regularly read published code. There are plenty of forums: listings in books and magazines, snippets from library documentation, or even lines in postings to newsgroups. These are formatted for clarity, but also favor a more compact representation since space is not cheap. Lines are compressed vertically to get the most code into a short space, and they are compressed horizontally to fit into narrow print margins.

This sort of code tends to omit error handling and anything not pertinent to the main idea of the example. It only serves to convey a point, not to be thorough.

You may never have to write code for this medium, but you'll certainly see plenty of it (you're reading code snippets in *this* book, at least). You need to understand the trade-offs and differences from normal code, so you don't unwittingly pick up any bad habits.

Printouts

When you print out project code you run into new issues. Column widths become a problem. Should you reformat before you print, scale pages down and cope with small fonts, or have haphazard line wrapping? There's no syntax coloring to enhance presentation (unless you're rich enough for a color printer and all that ink), so messy commenting or code disabled by large comment blocks suddenly becomes less obvious.

Although you may never print out a page of source, these are valid concerns that you should consider.

Indented Brace Style

Less common but still used is the *indented* style. Here the braces are indented with the code. It's also known as the *Whitesmith* style, since example code for the early Whitesmith's C compiler used it.

```
int indented()
    {
    int a = 0, b = 0;
    while (a != 10)
        {
        b++;
        a++;
        }
    return b;
    }
```

Pro

• Links code blocks to the braces that contain them

Con

• Many people don't like their blocks linked to their braces

Other Brace Styles

There are others. For example, the *GNU* style is sandwiched between exdented and indented; braces are placed halfway between each level of indent. There are also hybrids; the Linux kernel coding style is half K&R, half exdented. Most C# programmers also combine layout styles. If you're really perverse, you'll like this:

```
  int my_worst_nightmare()
  {
int a = 0, b = 0;
while (a != 10) {
        b++;
        a++;
        }
return b;
  }
```

I've seen plenty of surreal code like it, and I'm sure you could concoct something of equally nightmarish proportions if you tried.

KEY CONCEPT *Recognize the common code layout styles for your chosen language, and become familiar working with each of them. Appreciate their advantages and disadvantages.*

One Style to Rule Them All

Having seen seen what constitutes a good coding style, what it governs, and why it's necessary, you must now actually choose one. This is where the fights begin. Disciples of one presentation religion clash with the evangelists of the next, leading to programmer civil war. But the craftsman steps back from these petty squabbles and takes a more balanced view.

As long as you write in a style that's good, it doesn't matter what style that is. And there's no point in arguing about it. There is more than one good style; the quality and applicability of each will depend on context and culture.

KEY CONCEPT   *Pick a single good coding style, and stick to it.*

It could be argued that if your language standard defined the One True Presentation Style, the world would be a better place. After all, all code would look the same. The arguments would cease, and we'd all move on to something more useful instead. You could pick up anyone's code and get to grips with it immediately. Sounds pretty good, doesn't it?

The counterargument is *competition is a Good Thing*. If we had a single monopoly coding style, who would be able to say that it was the best one? By having more than one coding style, we are encouraged to think and improve the way we apply a style. It encourages style guidelines to improve. The upshot: It makes us write better code.

That argument is *not* a license to code in your own particular style, though. Remember that good presentation is *conventional*—a layout that readers expect.

COMMON CODING STANDARDS

A number of well-known coding standards are generally used.

Indian Hill
  The full title of this famous document is *Indian Hill Recommended C Style and Coding Standards*. It has nothing to do with Native Americans standing on mounds of earth; instead, it came from the renowned Indian Hill AT&T Bell lab.

GNU
  The *GNU's Coding Standards* are important since they influence most of the commonly used open source or free software out there.
  You can find them on the GNU Project's website (www.gnu.org).

MISRA
  The UK's *Motor Industry Software Reliability Association (MISRA)* has defined a well-known set of standards for writing safety critical embedded software in C. It consists of 127 guidelines, and a number of tools exist to validate your code against them. These guidelines are focused more on language use than code layout.

Project *foo*
  Most every project under the sun defines its own pet coding style. Just go on a hunt, and you'll find literally thousands. The Linux kernel, for example, has its own guidelines, as does the Mozilla project.

House Styles (and Where to Stick Them)

Many software companies have an internal (*house*) coding style that defines, among other things, its code presentation rules. But why bother—code that's been written in any good style is easy to read and maintain. If no one will have a hard time following it, do we really need this extra level of bureaucracy?

House styles *are* important and useful for a number of reasons. If everyone sings from the same hymn book (perhaps that should be *writes* on the same hymn book), then all source code will be consistent and homogenized. What value does this bring? It increases the code quality and makes software development safer. Here's how:

- Any code released outside the organization will be neatly presented and coherent, appearing to be well thought out. Having many conflicting styles in one project looks careless and unprofessional.

- The company can be assured that programs are written up to a certain standard, thanks to common idioms and methodologies. This doesn't guarantee good code, but it does help to protect against bad code.

- It makes up for poor tools; IDEs set in different ways will fight against each other, pulling code apart and generally molesting the layout. A standard provides level ground (and a common enemy for all the programmers).

- The appeal of being able to instantly recognize the shape of your peers' code and to quickly make appropriate maintenance alterations is clear. It saves reading time and therefore the company's money.

- Since the programmers won't be continually reformatting the code to suit their particular aesthetic fetishes, your version control history is very useful. If Fred reformats Bert's code to "his" style, what happens when, a bit later on, you look at a diff? Many diff tools are pretty crude and will now display a plethora of trivial whitespace and brace differences.

These house coding standards are a Good Thing. Even if you don't actually agree with the rules they mandate—if, for example, your indentation strategy is much prettier and easier to understand (in your opinion)—it shouldn't matter one iota. The benefits of everyone sharing the same style outweigh the burden on you to have to conform. If you don't agree with the standard, you should still work to it.

KEY CONCEPT   *If your team already has a coding standard, then* use it. *Don't use your own pet style.*

You may be surprised to find how much of your coding style is bred from familiarity and practice. If you use a house style for a while, it soon becomes second nature and seems perfectly normal.

What happens if you're working on code that originated from outside the company and doesn't conform to your house style? In this case, it makes more sense to write code conforming to the *existing* style of that source file. (This is why writing to a style that's easy to pick up is important.) The only other real alternative is to convert the file (and any others) into your house style. For most Real World projects, this latter course of action isn't feasible, especially if you are continually being fed with external source code updates.

Conform to the style of a given file or project, conform to your house style where this doesn't conflict, and sacrifice your own preferences. Don't surrender your style blindly, though; understand the benefits weighed against the costs. And what if your company doesn't have a house style? Push for one. . . .

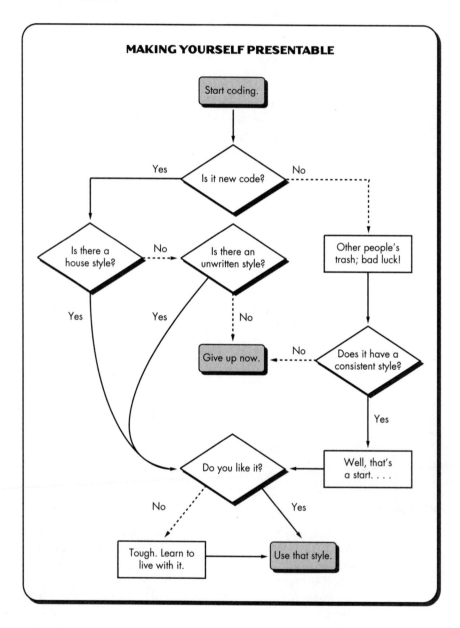

Setting the Standard

You've been tasked to draw up a code presentation style where there currently is none. Good luck! You can be sure that everyone will have an opinion on what the style should contain and that no one will be completely satisfied with the end result. Techies are helpful like that.

Creating a coding standard is a delicate task, and it should be approached tactfully but firmly. Why? Dumping edicts upon a group of programmers will neither make you nor your standard popular. But if you don't emphasize how important it is, programmers will not embrace it and will continue coding in their own peculiar ways.

The difficulty of this task depends on the people in the team:

- How many programmers there are
- How they code as individuals
- How similar their coding styles are already
- Whether they actually *want* a standard or not
- Whether they are prepared to change their styles at all

If their coding styles are all reasonably similar, then the job's a breeze. If they vary wildly, you're in for a bumpy ride. While people seldom agree on the best style, they will generally agree that some styles are better than others. You must aim to provide a sufficiently detailed set of layout directives while trying to satisfy as many programmers as possible—*and* produce something that will help them to work better as a team. Here's a collection of pragmatic advice for this herculean task:

What's it for?

Start off with a clear idea of the scope of the work—is the coding standard just for your immediate team, the department, or the whole company? This makes a big difference in how you'll develop and implement it.

Remember: What makes a good personal style is not necessarily the best for a whole team of programmers. You are creating something that shouldn't just serve *your* aesthetic fetishes; it should be a standard that will unite team code and avoid common problems. Keep this goal in mind as your develop the standard.

Determine the level of detail you intend to go into. Is this just a code layout document, or will it also touch on language usage concerns? It's best to keep it simple: Write one document for presentation and a different document for language use.

Get buy-in

Involve everyone on the team, so *they* own it. If the programmers feel like they contributed, they'll be more likely to follow the standard.

- Get everyone to agree that a standard is needed *before* you start working on it. Make sure the team understands the benefits of code consistency and the perils of ad-hoc code presentation.

- If you have more than a few programmers, *don't* try to design the standard by committee. Well, not unless you hide all the sharp objects in the office first. Select a small crack team to get the work done.

When the standard nears completion, review it with a panel of adopters. Make sure that you have a chairman who can make a final decision though, or everything will stall while 15 programmers sidetrack themselves in religious disputes.

Produce something

The end product should be an accessible document, not just a fuzzy set of agreed conventions. You should be able to refer to the document later, and point newcomers at it. The document contains a list of the rules, perhaps with justification for the more contentious decisions.

Standardize best practice

Make sure the standard embodies the team's current best practices—let them know that they're doing things right. If there's nothing that comes out of the blue, they will be more likely to adopt it. However, if you include random conventions from outside the team's experience, they'll revolt.

Focus on what matters

Concentrate your efforts on the things that really matter and will make the biggest improvements to your team's code. Don't try to create a presentation standard for C, C++, *and* Java if you only ever use C.

Avoid hotspots

Leave rare-but-tedious cases to individual taste if they won't actually make much difference. If people get really worked up over the layout of split lines in an `if` statement, give up and let them do what they want.

Don't be too restrictive; allow the rules to be broken if a violation can genuinely be justified.

Do it in pieces

A sensible approach is to develop your house style *a bit at a time*. Start by agreeing on brace layout and indent size. Just that. It will be difficult enough! Once you have that in place, progress will be *much* easier; any change is just more of the same. At some point, it won't be worth adding new rules, since the code will be sufficiently regular.

Plan for adoption

Have a clear idea how this coding standard will be adopted. Be realistic. People have to be happier *with* it, or they won't use it. Adoption will have to be based on some form of majority rule; if Fred still thinks that `switch` statements look better his way when everyone else managed to compromise, *too bad, Fred*. Don't be tempted to make it a democratic process, though. That just won't work.

Don't threaten people with the standard or induce punishments for not using it. That's not going to go down well. Instead, offer incentives—even if it's just public kudos in a code review.

Ultimately, the take-up of a standard depends on the authority with which it is introduced. Either the programmers themselves authorize it or the process gets management to back it. Or it's a big waste of time.

Does this sound like trying to persuade a load of school children to get along and play nicely? Funny, isn't it. . . . Still, you'll wade your way through a religious quagmire, emerging on the other side with a house style that will genuinely improve your team's code. Once the wounds heal, it will have been worth it.

Righteous Wars?

The quickest way of ending a war is to lose it.
—*George Orwell*

Engaging in holy wars over code layout is unproductive and a waste of time; there are far more important things to focus our attention on. But beware—code layout is not the only hot potato in the programming community. You could extend this to cover editors, compilers, methodologies, the One True Language,[2] and beyond.

These little commotions have been going on for years. They'll continue to go on. And no one will *ever* win. No one will ever manage to establish the *right* answer, because there is no right answer. These arguments are just an opportunity for one person to try to enforce his or her particular (carefully formed) opinion on others, and vice versa. After all, my opinion *must* be right, because it's *mine*. It's like trying to knit spaghetti—amusing for a while, but messy and totally pointless. It's usually only ever immature programmers that get involved. (The old-timers are already argued out.)

The key point to learn is: Holy wars are a waste of effort. As a professional, you should step back from such petty arguments. Of course, have an educated personal opinion, but don't arrogantly presume that it's correct.

KEY CONCEPT   *Holy wars:* Just say no. *Don't get involved. Walk away.*

In a Nutshell

Nothing succeeds like the appearance of success.
—*Christopher Lasch*

Presentation is one of the key features differentiating good code from bad code. Programmers glean a lot from code's appearance, so it *is* right to worry about layout. It's an important skill to be able to sensitively lay out code for maximum clarity, within the guidelines of any company coding standard that may exist.

---

[2] This brings to mind a C/C++ programming conference I attended some years ago. A speaker presented his discovery that you get fewer bugs (which are easier to fix) using Pascal rather than C, while the most difficult to fix and numerous bugs occur in C++. The reaction was wonderful—everyone's feathers were ruffled!

LOOKING FOR A FIGHT

Code layout is not the only excuse for a programmer flame war. There are many religious subjects that you'd best tactfully dodge for the sake of your blood pressure. Watch out for:

My OS is better than yours

. . . because it scales from a wristwatch to an alien mothership, only requires rebooting once every epoch, and performs most operations with a single two-letter command.

But *mine's* better than yours because you'll never see a single piece of text using it, it's tastefully color coordinated, and it can be operated by a blind squirrel. Anything you can't do with it is illegal in most civilized countries, anyway.

My editor is better than yours

. . . because it recognizes more than a million different syntax schemes, can edit files written in hieroglyphics, and each of its 400 operations are accessible with fewer than 10 simultaneous keystrokes. You can use it on the desktop, from a command line, over a modem, through a rising main, and over 128-bit encrypted smoke signals.

But *mine's* better than yours because it integrates with my underwear and knows what I want to type before I've even thought of it myself.

My language is better than yours

. . . because it implements the artificial intelligence of most major governments and is clever enough to interpret random gesticulations as meaningful sequences of instructions.

But *mine's* better than yours because it allows you to write in haiku and encodes information in combinations of whitespace characters.

It's reasonable to assume that code that has been carefully laid out will have been carefully designed. It's even more reasonable to assume that sloppily presented code hasn't been designed with much care. But there's more to this story than formatting source code.

Besides presentation skills, there are certain *attitudes* that separate good programmers from bad programmers. The moral is simple: *Avoid creating hot air.* Computers will do that for you (we don't need in-office heating because ours belch out so much heat). Know what you like and be *prepared* to defend it, to put your view across—but don't presume that you have to win or that you have to be right, and don't arrogantly do your own thing anyway.

Good programmers . . .

- Avoid pointless arguments and are sensitive to others' opinions

- Are humble enough to know that they're not right all the time

- Know how code layout impacts readability and strive for the clearest code possible

Bad programmers . . .

- Are close-minded and opinionated—*My view is the right one*

- Argue with anyone over the most trivial things; it's a chance to prove their superiority

Good programmers . . .	Bad programmers . . .
• Will adopt a house style even if it contradicts their personal preferences	• Have no consistent personal coding style • Trample over others' code in their own style

See Also

Chapter 3: What's in a Name?
A coding standard may mandate how you create names.

Chapter 4: The Write Stuff
Good presentation is key to writing code that's self-documenting.

Chapter 5: A Passing Comment
Describes how we write comments; some comment use relates to source code layout.

Get Thinking

A detailed discussion of these questions can be found in the "Answers and Discussion" section on page 466.

Mull It Over

1. Should you alter the layout of legacy code to conform to your latest code style? Is this a valuable use of code reformatting tools?

2. A common layout convention is to split source lines at a set number of columns. What are the pros and cons of this? Is it useful?

3. How detailed should a *reasonable* coding standard be?

   a. How serious are deviations from the style? How many limbs should be amputated for not following it?

   b. Can a standard become too detailed and restrictive? What would happen if it did?

4. When defining a new presentation style, how many items or cases need layout rules? What other presentation rules must be provided? List them.

5. Which is more important—good code *presentation* or good code *design*? Why?

Getting Personal

1. Do you write in a consistent style?

   a. When you work with other people's code, which layout style do you adopt—theirs or your own?

   b. How much of your coding style is dictated by your editor's auto-formatting? Is this an adequate reason for adopting a particular style?

2. Tabs: Are they a work of the devil, or the best thing since sliced bread? Explain why.

   a. Do you know if your editor inserts tabs automatically? Do you know what your editor's tab stop is?

   b. Some *hugely* popular editors indent with a mixture of tabs and spaces. Does this make the code any less maintainable?

   c. How many spaces should a tab correspond to?

3. Do you have a preferred layout style?

   a. Describe it in a series of simple statements. Be complete. Include, for example, how you format switch statements and split up long lines.

   b. How many statements did it take? Is that what you expected?

   c. Does your company have a coding standard?

   d. Do you know where it is? Is it advertised? Have you read it?

      i. If yes: Is it any good? Perform an honest critique, and feed your comments back to the document owners.

      ii. If no: Should it? (Justify your answer.) Is there a common unwritten code style that everyone adopts? Can you drive the adoption of a standard?

   e. Is there *more* than one standard used, perhaps one per project? If so, how is code shared among projects?

4. How many different layout styles have you followed?

   a. Which did you feel most comfortable with?

   b. Which was the most rigorously defined?

   c. Is there a link?

3

WHAT'S IN A NAME?

Giving Meaningful Things
Meaningful Names

When I use a word, Humpty Dumpty said, in a rather scornful tone, it means just what I choose it to mean—neither more nor less.

—Lewis Carroll

Ancient civilizations knew that to name something was to have power over it. This was more than a simple claim to possession. Some believed so strongly in the power of names that they would never give their own names to strangers, for fear the strangers might use it to inflict harm against them.

Names mean an awful lot. You may not live in fear of them, but don't underestimate the power of a name. A name describes:

Identity

Names are fundamental to our concept of identity. There are examples throughout history—even before 2000 BC, there are Biblical examples of meaningful place names and children named to reflect circumstances. In most cultures it's still convention for a woman to change her last name when she gets married, although the fact that some women choose not to shows how they attribute significant meaning to their names.

Behavior

A name not only promotes identity, but also implies behavior. Obviously, a name doesn't dictate what an object does, but it will influence how you interact with it and how the outside world interprets it. We're never fixed to one name per object. I'm known by different monikers in different contexts: the name my wife calls me,[1] the name my daughters know me by, the nickname I use in chat rooms, and so on. These names indicate different relationships and interactions with me and the roles I fulfil.

Recognition

A name marks something as a distinct entity. It elevates it from ethereal concept to well-defined reality. Before someone put a name to electricity, no one would have understood what it was, although they might have some vague idea of its effects by watching lightning or Benjamin Franklin's demonstrations. Once named, it became identifiable as a distinct force and, consequently, easier to reason about. The Basque culture believes that naming something proves its existence: *Izena duen guzia omen da*—That which has a name exists. (Kurlansky 99)

Today the act of naming has become a multimillion-dollar business, used (with varying degrees of success) by small firms, the largest multinational corporations, and everything in between. To launch, rebrand, and publicize products, these organizations need newer, ever more catchy names. These names help to build awareness of products and services.

Clearly, names are of immense importance.

As programmers, we wield this enormous power over our constructs when we name them. A badly named entity can be more than just inconvenient; it can be misleading and even downright dangerous. As a very simplistic example, consider the following C++ code:

```
void checkForContinue(bool weShouldContinue)
{
    if (weShouldContinue) abort();
}
```

---

[1] Which depends on whether she's in a good or bad mood at the time!

The parameter name is clearly a lie, or at least its sense is the opposite of what you'd expect. The function will not perform as anticipated and, as a consequence, your program will abort—a reasonably dire result from a single misnamed variable.

Sticks and stones may break my bones, but names will never hurt me. Not true.

Why Should We Name Well?

We need to carefully consider the names we give things. Remember that writing source code is all about clear communication. A name creates a channel of understanding, control, and mastery. Appropriate naming means that *to know the name is to know the object.*

Good names really matter. The human brain can only hold about seven pieces of information concurrently[2] (although I'm sure I have a couple of defective slots, reducing this capacity). It's already hard enough to cram all the information about a program into your head; we should not add complex naming schemes or require obscure references to make this task even harder.

Clear naming is one of the hallmarks of well-crafted code. The ability to name things well is an important skill of the code craftsman—he'll work hard to write easy-to-read code.

KEY CONCEPT   *Learn to name things* transparently—*an object's name should describe it clearly.*

What Do We Name?

In this chapter we'll spend some time thinking, as programmers, about what we name and how we name it. First: *What?* The things we name most often while writing code are:

- Variables
- Functions
- Types (classes, enums, structs, typedefs)
- C++ namespaces and Java packages
- Macros
- Source files

This list is by no means exhaustive—there are other, higher-level entities we'll give meaningful names to: states of a state machine, parts of messaging protocols, database elements, application executables, and so on. But these six are enough to start with.

---

[2] This is known as the *Miller number*, after George A. Miller's psychological research. (Miller 56)

Name Games

How do you name? The naming technique for each of these items will depend on any coding standard you're working to. However, while a standard might mandate certain naming conventions, it won't be specific enough to guide the *appropriate* naming of each and every part of a program.

In order to name well, it's essential to know exactly what you're naming before you think up a name for it. If you don't know what you're naming, how it will be used, and why it actually exists, how can you give it a meaningful name? Bad names are often a sign of poor understanding.

KEY CONCEPT *The key to good naming is to understand* exactly *what you're naming. Only then can you give a meaningful name. If you can't invent a good name for something, do you really know what it is, or even if it should exist at all?*

Before we look in detail at the specific categories of names we create, it's important to understand the forces that drive our choice of names and exactly what constitutes a good name. The next few sections explain the qualities of a good name.

Descriptive

Obviously a name must be descriptive. That's what you use it for—to describe something. Yet it's common to see puzzling identifiers that bear little resemblance to the data they describe.

Even an accurate name can be limiting. People often stick to their initial perceptions of a concept, despite the proverb about judging books by their covers. Therefore, it's important to convey the right first impression through careful naming. Choose names from the perspective of an inexperienced reader, not from your internal, knowledgeable perspective.

Sometimes finding a good description is difficult. If you can't come up with a good name, then you might need to change your design. It's an indication that something might be wrong.

Technically Correct

Modern programming languages impose some rules on how we name things. Most allow case-sensitive names, don't allow *whitespace* (spaces, tabs, newlines), and allow just alphanumeric characters plus certain symbols (like the underscore). These days, there are no appreciable limits on identifier length.[3] Although many languages permit use of Unicode identifiers, it's still common to select from the ISO8859-1 (ASCII) character set for simplicity.

There may be other technical restrictions. The C/C++ standards reserve specific ranges of names: You should not use any global identifier beginning with str followed by a lowercase letter, or beginning with an underscore, and

---

[3] Be aware that older versions of C limited external unique linkage to the first six characters, and case was not *necessarily* significant. You need to understand exactly what the target of your code is when you write it.

anything in a namespace called std. It's important to be aware of these kinds of restrictions so we can write robust, correct code.

Idiomatic

Just because a language permits certain combinations of characters doesn't meant they're automatically good names. Clear names follow conventions that the reader expects: the language's *idioms*. Just as fluency in a natural language depends on understanding its idioms, fluency in a programming language requires idiomatic usage.

Some languages have a single, common naming convention—the vast Java library establishes a prior art that is hard to ignore—while C and C++ have a lesser degree of convergence. There are several cultures, each with their own foibles; the standard libraries use one convention, Windows Win32 APIs another.

KEY CONCEPT *Know your language's naming rules. But more importantly, know the language's* idioms. *What are the common naming conventions? Use them.*

Appropriate

An *appropriate* name strikes a good balance in several areas:

Length
To create clear, descriptive names, we must use natural language words. Programmers have a built-in urge to abbreviate and shorten these words, but this leads to confused, messy names. It doesn't matter that a name is long if its meaning is unambiguous. a is not a realistic replacement for apple_count.

KEY CONCEPT *When naming, favor clarity over brevity.*

However, there is a case for short (even one letter) variable names: as loop counters. They actually make sense in *small* loops where variable names like loop_counter are not just overly verbose but can quickly become tedious.

KEY CONCEPT *Understand the trade-offs between short and long names—how they depend on the scope of the variable's use.*

Tone
The tone of a name *is* important. Just as a rude joke isn't appropriate at a funeral, an ill-judged name ruins the professionalism of your code. Is this serious? Yes—silly names make the reader doubt the ability of the original author.

Avoid jokey names like *blah* or *wibble*, or the bigger geek snares *foo* and *bar*. They can easily creep in, and while amusing at first, they just create confusion later on. (Objects given these names are usually quick temporary hacks that outlast their expected lifetime.) And, obviously, being professional means that you don't use expletives when naming.

FOOD FOR THOUGHT

So what's with all this *foo* and *bar* business? These words are a bit of geek humor, utterly meaningless and yet full of purpose. They are usually used as placeholders to represent arbitrary things. You might write: *for some variable foo, increment it by ++foo;*.

The words generally come in a series. There are several variant series, but you'll see *foo, bar,* and *baz* quite universally. What comes next may be up to the fickle finger of fate or to whatever geek folklore you prefer.

The etymology of these terms is debatable. Some trace them back to the World War II army slang FUBAR (Mucked Up Beyond All Repair). Needless to say, you should *never* use these names in production code.

KEY CONCEPT   *Name things well the first time, all the time.*

The Nuts and Bolts

The following sections investigate how to name each category of item we listed earlier. Even if you've been programming for years, this is a useful review of the broad spectrum of naming conventions.

Naming Variables

If a variable wasn't just an electronic entity, it would be the sort of thing you could hold in your hand, the software equivalent of a physical object. A name that reflects this will usually be a noun. For example, variable names in a GUI application might be ok_button and main_window. Even variables that don't correspond to Real World objects can be given noun names; consider elapsed_time or exchange_rate.

If not a noun, a variable will usually be a "noun-ized" verb, for example, count. A numeric variable's name describes the interpretation of the value, as in widget_length. A boolean variable name is often the name of a conditional statement, which is natural, considering the value will either be true or false.

There are a number of object-oriented language conventions for adorning member variables to show they are members, not ordinary local variables or (evil) global variables. This is a mild form of *Hungarian Notation*, which some programmers find useful.[4] For example, C++ members are commonly prefixed with an underscore, suffixed with an underscore, or prefixed with m_. The first method is frowned upon because it is somewhat risky and distasteful.[5] Besides, a leading or trailing underscore makes the variable pretty unnatural to read.

Some programmers adorn pointer types with a suffix like _ptr and reference types with one like_ref. This is another subtle infiltration of Hungarian

---

[4] Of course, this kind of naming convention won't have any impact on a class's public API because all of your member variables are private, aren't they?

[5] You can't have global identifiers beginning with an underscore followed by a capital letter. The archaic C naming rules make many such odd demands.

Notation, and it is redundant. The fact the variable is a pointer is implicit in its type. If your function is so large that you think this adornment is useful, then it's probably too large!

Another common variable-naming practice is using acronyms as concise, "meaningful" names. For example, you might declare a variable like this: `SomeTypeWithMeaningfulNaming stwmn(10);`. If the scope of use is small, this kind of name may be clearer than a long-winded variant.

Conventions that distinguish type names from variable names are generally best. Type names often have an uppercase initial letter, while variables have a lowercase one. This way, it's not unusual to see variables declared like this: `Window window;`.

KEY CONCEPT *Employ a helpful naming convention that differentiates variable names from type names.*

HUNGARIAN NOTATION

Hungarian Notation is a controversial naming convention that encodes information about a variable or function's type in its name with the belief that it will make the code more readable and maintainable. It originated at Microsoft in the 1980s and is widely used in the company's public Win32 APIs and the MFC library, which is the main reason for its popularity.

It is called Hungarian Notation because it was pioneered by Charles Simonyi, a Hungarian programmer. It's also called that because variable names look like they may as well have been written in Hungarian: Non-Windows programmers get confused by surreal names like `lpszFile`, `rdParam`, and `hwndItem`.

There are many subtly different and not-quite-compatible dialects of Hungarian Notation, which don't help matters.

Naming Functions

If a variable is like something you could hold in your hand, the *function* is what you do with it—you don't want to hold it forever. Since a function is an action, its name will most logically be (or will at least include) a verb. A function with a noun for a name wouldn't be clear; for example, what does the function `apples()` do? Does it return a number of apples, does it convert something into apples, or does it make apples out of thin air?

Meaningful function names avoid the words *be, do,* and *perform.* These are classic traps for beginners trying to consciously include verbs (*this function does XXX . . .*). They are just noise and don't add any value to the name.

A function should always be named from the viewpoint of the user, hiding all the internal implementation stuff neatly away. (That's the point of a function—it's a level of compression and abstraction.) Who cares if, behind the scenes, it stores an element in a list, makes calls over a network, or builds a new computer and installs a word processor on it? If the user only sees the function count apples, the function should be called `countApples()`.

KEY CONCEPT *Name functions from an external viewpoint, with a* doing *phrase. Describe the logical operation, not the implementation.*

The only time you might choose to break this rule is for simple query functions that request information. For these accessors, you can sensibly name the function after the data being requested. For an example of this, see the answer to question 9 in this chapter's "Mull It Over" section on page 478.

When you write a function, it should be well documented (either in a specification or using some literate programming method). However, the name should still be a clear statement of what the function does; it is part of the function's contract. What does void a() do? It could be anything.

CAPITALIZATION CONVENTIONS

Most languages prohibit us from using whitespace and punctuation in our identifiers, so we adopt a convention for joining up multiple words. These capitalization conventions cause as many programmer fist fights as the eternal Holy Editor Wars. There are a number of common methods that you'll see in modern code:

camelCase

camelCase is used extensively by the Java language libraries and also in many C++ codebases. It is so called because the capitalization resembles a camel's humps and was probably first used in Smalltalk in the early 1970s.

ProperCase

This is a close relative of camelCase, its only difference being that the first letter is also capitalized. It is sometimes known as *PascalCase*. Often the two conventions are used together. For example, Java class names are written in ProperCase and members in camelCase. The Windows API and .NET methods use ProperCase.

using_underscores

Proponents of this style are the implementers of the C++ standard library (look at all the names in the std namespace) and the GNU foundation.

There are also many other forms. How many can you think of? You can start by mixing ProperCase with underscores, or by dropping uppercase characters entirely.

Naming Types

Which types you can create depends on the language you're using. C provides typedefs, which are synonyms for other type names. You use them to provide easier, more convenient names. It stands to reason, then, that a typedef should be clearly named. Even if it's only a local typedef in a function body, it should still have a descriptive name.

Java, C++, and other OO languages are profoundly based on the creation of new types (*classes*). C also allows you to define compound types called structs. Just as good variable and function names are vital to the readability of the code, good type names are paramount. There aren't too many rigid heuristics for naming classes, though, because different classes serve different purposes.

- A class may describe some stateful data object. In that case, its name will probably be a noun.

It may be a function object (a *functor*) or a class implementing some virtual callback interface. Here the name will probably be a verb, perhaps including the name of a recognized design pattern. (Gamma et al. 94)

- If the class is a combination of both, then it's probably hard to name and possibly designed badly.

Interface classes (e.g., abstract C++ classes with pure virtual functions or `interface`s in Java and .NET) tend to be named according to the interface facility. Names like `Printable` and `Serializable` are common. .NET adds a Hungarian wart, prefixing all interface names with `I`, resulting in names like `IPrintable`.

Earlier, we discussed words to avoid in function names; there is similar quicksand here. For example, `DataObject` is a bad name: The class may very well contain data, and it's obviously going to be used to create an object—this doesn't need to be restated.

KEY CONCEPT   *Avoid redundant words in names. Specifically, avoid these words in type names:* class, data, object, *and* type.

Ensure that you describe the *class of data* and not an *actual object*. That's a subtle, but important distinction.

A CLASS OF BAD NAMES

A bad class name can serve to really confuse programmers. I once worked on an application that contained a state machine implementation. For some historical reason, the base class of each state was called `Window`, rather than something sensible like `State`. It was very confusing and threw off several programmers when they first saw it. To add insult to injury, the base class of a command pattern was called `Strategy`, when it wasn't actually implementing a strategy design pattern. It was never easy to figure out what was going on. Better naming would have provided a clear route into the code's logic.

Naming Namespaces

What name do you give something specifically designed to collate names? C++ and C# namespaces and Java `package`s are like bags, acting primarily as grouping mechanisms.

They are also used to prevent *name collisions*. When two programmers create different things with the same name and their code gets glued together, what will happen is anyone's guess. At best, the code will fail to link; at worst, all sorts of run-time carnage will ensue. Putting items into different namespaces avoids the danger of polluting the global namespace. This makes them valuable naming tools.

But namespaces on their own do not prevent collisions; your `utils` namespace could still clash with someone else's `utils`. To remedy this, we employ a *naming scheme*. Java defines a hierarchy of package names, nested like Internet domain names—you'll place code in your own uniquely named package. This neatly avoids the problem of collisions. Without such a convention, namespaces reduce, but do not eliminate, the likelihood of problems.

When picking a name for your namespace, choose something that describes the relationship of the contents. If they are all part of a library's interface, make it the library name. If the contents are a single section of a larger system, choose a name that describes this section; UI, filesystem, or controls are good names. Don't choose a name that redundantly implies a collection of items—controls_group is a bad name.

KEY CONCEPT *Give namespaces and packages names that reflect the logical relationships of their contents.*

Naming Macros

Macros are the walnut-cracking sledgehammers of the C/C++ world. They are search-and-replace tools for basic text that don't respect scope or visibility. They're tactless. However, there are some walnuts that just won't crack without them.

Macros have very drastic effects, so there is a well-established tradition for naming macros in a maximally obvious way: using CAPITAL LETTERS. Follow this without fail, and don't make any other name entirely capitalized. This makes macros stand out like sore thumbs, which is basically what they are.

Since they are simple text replacement tools, give macros names that are unique enough to not appear elsewhere in the code. Otherwise, carnage and confusion will ensue.

A unique file or project name prefix will help here. The macro name PROJECTFOO_MY_MACRO is much safer than MY_MACRO.

KEY CONCEPT *Macros in C/C++ are always capitalized to make them stand out and carefully named to avoid collisions. Don't capitalize anything else. Ever.*

Naming Files

The names of your source files can have a real impact on the ease of coding. Some languages have strict filename requirements—Java source filenames must correspond to the contained public class name. On the other hand, C and C++ are lax, with no restrictions at all.[6]

To make choosing filenames easy and obvious, each file should contain a single conceptual unit. Putting more stuff into one file is asking for trouble in the long run. Split your code into the maximum number of files you can; not only will it make them easier to name, but it will reduce coupling and make the project's structure clearer.

A C/C++ file that defines the interface for a *widget* should be called widget.h, not widget_interface.h, widget_decls.h, or any other variation. You should conventionally balance each widget.h with a matching widget.cpp or

---

[6] Except those imposed by your operating system or filesystem.

widget.c (see "All That Ends Well" on page 50) that implements whatever the widget.h declares. The shared base name ties them together logically. This is both obvious and conventional.

There are many other subtle, but important issues when naming files:

- Be aware of capitalization. Some filesystems can't get this right and ignore case when looking up filenames. But when porting to platforms where case *is* important, your code won't compile unless you've observed capitalization carefully. Perhaps the easiest way to avoid being tripped up is to mandate that all filenames be lowercase; as they say, *If you can't be good, be careful.* (Of course, that won't work for Java, which uses the PascalCase naming style for its classes and interfaces.)

- For the same reason, if your filesystem considers the filenames foo.h and Foo.h to be different, *don't* exploit it. Make sure that filenames in the same directory differ by more than just case.

- If you mix languages in a single project, don't create foo.c, foo.cpp, and foo.java in the same directory. It's messy—which file is used to create the object file foo.o, and which creates the executable called foo?

- Try to ensure that all the files you create have a distinct names, even if they're all spread across different directories. This makes it easier to reason about which file is which. It's obvious which header file you mean when you #include "foo.h". If there were two files with the same name, then a newcomer to the codebase would be confused. This becomes more of an issue as a system grows.

  One valid approach is to add some path information to the logical filename. Arrange your files so that you can include library_one/version.h and library_two/version.h without confusion.

File naming seriously impacts ease of coding. I once worked on a C++ project where the majority of the filenames matched the class names exactly; the class Daffodil was defined in Daffodil.h (names have been changed to protect the guilty). However, a handful of files were named in a *slightly* different manner, usually abbreviated, so HerbaciousBorder was held in HerbBdr.h. That made finding the right filename to #include complex and time consuming. On top of this, not all of the Daffodil class implementation was necessarily in Daffodil.cpp—some of it might have been in a shared FlowerStuff.cpp and perhaps also in Yogurt.cpp, for no adequately explained reason. As you can imagine, this made finding particular bits of code a nightmare. Source code browsers help in situations like this, but they are no substitute for plain old, well-named code.

A Rose by Any Other Name

There is more to the name game than you'd first think, and there are clearly a lot of considerations for naming bits of code. What are the main principles to pull out?

To invent a good name, do the following:

- Be consistent
- Exploit content
- Use names to your advantage

ALL THAT ENDS WELL

Choosing a suffix is integral to file naming. Java's build system insists that source filenames end in `.java`. C and C++ compilers are suffix agnostic, but calling header files `something.h` is such a universal convention that it would be like sticking pins in your eyes not to do it. We do feel some pain from the lack of rigid definition; there are several conventions for C++ implementation filenames, like the common suffixes `.C`, `.cc`, `.cpp`, `.cxx`, and `.c++`. Less common, but still seen, are C++ headers files suffixed with `.hpp`. Your choice may depend on the compiler, personal preference, and/or a coding standard. Consistency is the key; pick a file suffix scheme and use it consistently.

I have even worked on a platform that didn't support filename suffixes. Determining the filetype was a complex and messy business.

Be Consistent

This is perhaps the most important naming principle. Be *consistent*—not just within your own work, but with respect to company-wide practices. I have no confidence in the quality of a class interface if it looks like this:

```
class badly_named : public MyBaseClass
{
public:
    void doTheFirstThing();
    void DoThe2ndThing();
    void do_the_third_thing();
};
```

When a lot of people work together, it's very easy to end up with code like this—about as internally consistent as a random number generator. It's often a symptom of a more serious problem—perhaps that the programmers aren't respecting the fundamental design of the code they're simultaneously working on. This is where mandated coding standards and central design documents can be a big help.

Naming consistency goes beyond capitalization and formatting to the way you *create* names. A name establishes an implicit metaphor. Across a program or project, these metaphors should be consistent. Your naming approach should be holistic.

KEY CONCEPT *Choose a consistent naming convention—and use it consistently.*

With consistent naming, we get code that is intuitive and therefore easier to work with, easier to extend, and easier to maintain. In the long run, it's much cheaper to manage.

Exploit Context

Every name should make perfect sense when read in context. A name will only ever be read in its context, so you can delete all the superfluous bits that duplicate contextual information. We strive for succinct, descriptive names, without unnecessary baggage.

This contextual information may come from:

Scope

Things either live in a top-level, global scope or exist within some namespace, class, or function. Choose a name that makes sense in the context of that scope. The smaller and more specific a scope is, the easier it is to create a name within it and the easier it is for the reader to understand what that name really means. If a function counts the number of apples in a tree and is defined in a class `Tree`, then it needn't be called `countApplesInTree()`. Its fully qualified name would be an unambiguous description: `Tree::countApples()`. Put things in the smallest (and therefore most descriptive) scope you can.

The French language, like most other Romance languages, has two forms of the word *you*: *tu* and *vous*. Which one you use depends on how familiar you are with the person you're addressing. Similarly, the name you call a variable may depend on the context in which you're using it. You may see a variable named differently in a function's public declaration than in the function implementation.

Type

Everything has a type, and you'll know what that type is. A name doesn't need to restate this type information. (Restating this *is* the purpose of Hungarian Notation and is why it's an often derided convention.)

An inexperienced programmer will name his address `string` variable `address_string`. What good does the _string suffix do? Nothing, so get rid of it.

KEY CONCEPT   *The detail required in a name depends on its context. Use contextual information to your advantage when naming.*

Use Names to Your Advantage

There is power in a name—power that allows you to be more expressive than a language's syntax alone might allow. Think about how you can use similar names to group things together, using a common prefix. Or consider how you can imply which of a function's parameters are input or output by including this information in their names.

In a Nutshell

> *In your name I will hope, for your name is good.*
> —Psalms 52:9

Our ancient ancestors knew it, and good programmers know it: It's crucial to name things well. Good names serve more than just an aesthetic purpose; they convey information about the structure of code. They are an essential tool to aid comprehensibility and maintainability.

The main reason we write code in high-level languages is to communicate, and that communication is to an audience of code readers—other programmers—rather than to the compiler. Bad names have the potential to mislead. There *is* power in a name, and experienced programmers understand the balance of concerns involved when naming any part of their code.

GENERAL DOS AND DON'TS

We can condense a lot of the advice in this chapter into some general dos and don'ts. *Don't* create names that are:

Cryptic
You can create inexplicable names in a number of ways. Acronyms and abbreviations can appear quite random, and single letter names are far too magical.

Verbose
Avoid terse names, but don't create a variable called the_number_of_apples_ before_I_started_eating, either. It's neither remotely useful nor funny.

Inaccurate or misleading
As obvious as it seems, make your names accurate. Don't call something a widget_list if it has nothing to do with lists. Don't call something widget if it's a container of widgets.

Misspelling opens a minefield of confusion: *I thought the variable was called ignoramus, but I can't find it anywhere. Oops, it was misspelled ignoramous.* Sigh.

Ambiguous or vague
Don't use a name that could be interpreted in several ways. Don't use a hopelessly vague name like data or value unless it's perfectly clear what it represents. Avoid the vague temp or tmp unless you *really* need it.

Don't differentiate names by capitalization or by changes of a single character. Be wary of names that sound similar.

Don't gratuitously create local variables with the same name as something in an outer scope.

Too cute
Sexy little abbreviations, clever shortenings that are hard to remember, and interpretive use of numerals should be avoided. *i18n*, a common abbreviation for *internationalization*, reads like nonsense to the uninitiated.

On the other hand, *do* create appropriate names that are clear, specific, concise, accurate, and unambiguous. *Do* use common terms and frames of reference. Use words from the problem domain, and draw on descriptive design pattern names. (Gamma et al. 94)

Good programmers . . .	Bad programmers . . .
• Realize the importance of names and treat them with respect	• Care little for the clarity of their code
• Think about naming and choose appropriate names for everything they create	• Produce *write-once* code that is quick to write and poorly thought out
• Hold many forces in balance: name length, clarity, context, and so on	• Ignore the language's natural idioms
• Keep a view of the bigger picture, so their names hold together across a project (or projects)	• Are inconsistent in naming
	• Don't think holistically, failing to consider how their piece of code fits into the whole

See Also

Chapter 2: The Best Laid Plans

Discusses coding standards, which may guide you in naming things. Also talks about *holy wars*, which Hungarian Notation is definitely a cause of.

Chapter 4: The Write Stuff

Good names don't replace well-documented code—but they are an integral part of code documentation.

Get Thinking

A detailed discussion of the following questions can be found in the "Answers and Discussion" section on page 474.

Mull It Over

1. Are these good variable names? Answer with either *yes* (explain why, and in what context), *no* (explain why), or *can't tell* (explain why).

    a. `int apple_count`

    b. `char foo`

    c. `bool apple_count`

    d. `char *string`

    e. `int loop_counter`

2. When would these be appropriate function names? Which return types or parameters might you expect? Which return types would make them nonsensical?

    a. `doIt(...)`

    b. `value(...)`

    c. `sponge(...)`

    d. `isApple(...)`

3. Should a naming scheme favor the easy reading or easy writing of code? How would you make either easy?

    a. How many times do you write a single piece of code? (Think about it.) How many times do you read it? Your answers should give some indication as to the relative importances.

    b. What do you do when naming conventions collide? Say you're working on camelCase C++ code and need to do STL (using_underscore) library work. What's the best way to handle this situation?

4. How long should a loop be before you need to give a meaningful loop counter name?

5. In C, if assert is a macro, why is its name lowercase? Why should we name macros so they stand out?

6. What are the pros and cons of following your language's standard library naming conventions?

7. Can you wear out a name? Is it okay to repeat a local variable name in many different functions? Is it okay to use local names that override (and hide) global names? Why?

8. Describe the mechanics of Hungarian Notation. What are the pros and cons of this naming convention? Does it have a place in modern code design?

9. We see many classes containing member functions acting as *getters* and *setters*; reading and writing the value of certain properties. What are the common naming conventions for these functions, and which is the best?

Getting Personal

1. How good are you at naming? How many of these heuristics do you follow already? Do you consciously think about your naming and these sorts of rules, or do you just *do it* all naturally? In which areas can you improve?

2. Does your coding standard mention naming at all?

   a. Does it cover all the cases we've looked at here? Is it *sufficient*? Is it useful, or just superficial?

   b. How much naming detail *is* appropriate in a coding standard?

3. What's the worst name you've come across recently? How have names ever misled you? How would you have changed them to avoid future confusion?

4. Do you have to port code between platforms? How has this affected filenames, other names, and the overall code structure?

THE WRITE STUFF

*Techniques for Writing
"Self-Documenting" Code*

In this chapter:

- How to document your code
- Literate programming
- Documentation tools

Real seriousness in regard to writing is one of two absolute necessities. The other, unfortunately, is talent.
—Ernest Hemingway

Modern self-assembly (*flat-pack*) furniture is remarkable, leaving even the seasoned carpenter in a state of awe and confusion. Generally, it's cleverly designed and will *eventually* build into what you expect it to.

When assembling it, you have to rely on the supplied instructions—you'll build something more like modern art than furniture without them. The quality of the instructions drastically affects how easy construction is. Bad instructions make you sweat, swear, and continually take apart pieces of wood that should never have been attached in the first place.

It's a shame they don't make things like they used to.

Source code suffers from similar problems. It's true, they don't make it like they used to, but no one was ever *that* fond of punched cards or COBOL anyway. More importantly, without good instructions that explain how the code fits together, working with some programs can make you sweat, swear, and continually take apart pieces of code that should never have been attached in the first place.

Creating good code means creating *well-documented* code. The reason we write code is to communicate clear sets of instructions—not just to the computer, but also to the poor fools who have to fix or extend those instructions later on. Code in the Real World is never written and then forgotten about. It will be modified, extended, and maintained over the life of the software product. To do this we need instructions, a user guide—documentation.

Common wisdom for documenting code is that you should either write tons of documents *about* the code or write tons of comments *in* the code.

Both ideas are nonsense. Most programmers have an aversion to word processors and get bored with writing too many comments. Writing code *is* hard work. Documenting it shouldn't be more hard work. In the heat of the software factory, anything that requires extra work tends not to be done. Or if it is, it is done badly.

I've seen software systems propped up by design specifications, implementation notes, maintenance guides, and style guides. Unsurprisingly, this is the kind of code that's really tedious to work with. The problem with all of this supporting documentation is:

- We don't need extra work to do. Writing documentation takes a lot of time; so does reading it. Programmers would rather spend that time programming.

- All these separate documents must be kept up to date with any code changes. In a large project, that's an awful lot of work. The common alternative (never updating any documentation) leads to dangerously inaccurate and misleading information.

- A forest of documentation is hard to manage. It's not easy to find the right document or to locate a particular piece of information that could be in one of several places within a document. Like code, documentation has to be held under revision control, and you must make sure you're reading the corresponding document version for the version of source code you're working on.

- Important information in separate documents can easily be missed. If it's not beside the code, and there are no helpful pointers, things are overlooked.

KEY CONCEPT *Don't write code that needs to be propped up by external documentation. It's flimsy. Ensure that your code reads clearly on its own.*

The common alternative—documenting your code with detailed code comments—can be just as bad, if not worse. Reams of slavishly detailed comments obstruct good code. You'll end up writing poorly formatted documentation rather than a good program.

How do we avoid this nightmare? We write *self-documenting* code.

Self-Documenting Code

It sounds like a good idea, doesn't it? But what *is* self-documenting code? This program is self-documenting:

```
10 PRINT "I am very small and very pointless"
20 GOTO 10
```

It's not anything to be proud of, though. A more complicated, more useful self-documenting program requires a great deal of skill. Computer programs tend to be much harder to read than they are to write. Anyone who has used Perl will understand this; it has been described as the ultimate write-once language. Indeed, old Perl code can be truly unfathomable, but you can write opaque code in any language, and it doesn't take much effort.

The only document that describes your code completely and correctly is the code itself. That doesn't automatically mean it's the best description possible, but more often than not, it's the *only* documentation you'll have available.

You should, therefore, do everything you can to make it good documentation, the kind of documentation that anyone can read. By necessity, code is something that more people than just the author must be able to understand. Programming languages are our communication medium. Clear communication is vital. With clarity, your code gains quality because you're less likely to make mistakes (since errors are more obvious), and it is cheaper to maintain the code—it takes less time to learn.

Self-documenting code is easily readable code. It is comprehensible on its own, without relying on external documentation. We can improve the clarity of our code in many ways. Some techniques are very basic and have been drilled into us since we were taught to program. Others are more subtle and come with experience.

KEY CONCEPT *Write your code to be read. By humans. Easily. The compiler will be able to cope.*

Here's an example of a simple function that's about as far from self-documenting as you can get. What do you think it does?

```
int fval(int i)
{
    int ret=2;
    for (int n1=1, n2=1, i2=i-3; i2>=0; --i2)
    {
        n1=n2; n2=ret; ret=n2+n1;
    }
    return (i<2) ? 1 : ret;
}
```

DON'T JUDGE A BOOK . . .

A file of self-documenting code reads a lot like a good reference book. Such a book is carefully structured, sectioned, and laid out. It reads naturally from front to back and top to bottom, but you can just as easily dive into it as a reference. That's how our code should work. Let's compare the parts:

Introduction
> A book's introduction explains what's inside, sets the tone, and explains how it into the bigger picture. A source file should begin with a code comment header. It explains what's in the file and specifies to which project the source file belongs.

Table of contents
> Although some argue that the file header should include a list of all the contained functions, I strongly advise against this. It will rapidly become out of date. You can, however, list the contents of the file (all types and classes, functions, variables) with most modern editors or IDEs, providing useful directions to specific pieces of code.

Sections
> This book is divided into several parts. Source files may also split into major sections; perhaps a single file contains several classes or logical groups of functions. This is where *breakwater* comments help. Extravagant ASCII art is generally a Bad Thing, but these kinds of comments help to logically break up the file for easy navigation.
>
> Beware, though. Putting too many things in a single source file is *not* a good idea. A simple one-to-one file/class correspondence is best. Large, multipurpose files are confusing to understand and very hard to navigate. (If this advice leaves you with too many source files, then you need to improve the higher-level code structure.)

Chapters
> Each chapter of a book is a self-contained and well-named chunk. Source files typically contain a number of well-named functions.

Paragraphs
> Within each function, you'll group code into blocks of statements. The initial variable declarations will be in one logical block, separated from the following code by a blank line (well, at least they will be in older C code). This isn't a syntactic thing, just layout that helps you read the code.

Sentences
> Sentences naturally correspond to each single code statement.

Cross-references and index
> Again, this isn't a part of your source file markup, but a good editor or IDE will provide cross-referencing capabilities. Learn how to use them.

This is an interesting analogy, but what difference does it make for writing code? Many good book-writing techniques translate into good code-writing techniques. Learn them to make your code more readable. Split code into sections, chapters, and paragraphs. Use layout to emphasize the code's logical structure. Use simple, short code statements—just like short sentences, they're more readable.

That's a realistic example; countless millions of lines in production software look like that, and programmers on the front line suffer because of it. In contrast, the following code *is* self-documenting. You can probably work out what it does by just reading the first line.

```
int fibonacci(int position)
{
    if (position < 2)
    {
        return 1;
    }
    int previousButOne = 1;
    int previous       = 1;
    int answer         = 2;

    for (int n = 2; n < position; ++n)
    {
        previousButOne = previous;
        previous       = answer;
        answer         = previous + previousButOne;
    }
    return answer;
}
```

There's one thing you should notice about that function—the lack of comments. It's obvious what's going on without any. Comments would just add more stuff to be read. They'd be unnecessary noise and would make the function harder to maintain in the future. That's important—because even the smallest, most beautiful functions *will* need later maintenance.[1]

Techniques for Self-Documenting Code

Writing self-documenting code is traditionally thought to involve adding a copious amount of comments. Good commenting certainly is an important technique, but there's much more to it than that. In fact, we should actively *avoid* comments by writing clear code that doesn't need them.

The following sections list important self-documenting code techniques. You'll notice that they cover similar ground to the other chapters in this first part of the book. That's not entirely surprising—there are many overlapping characteristics of good code; the benefits of one technique will be seen in several areas of code quality.

Write Simple Code with Good Presentation

Presentation has an enormous impact on the clarity of code. Thoughtful layout conveys the structure of the code; it makes functions, loops, and conditional statements clearer.

- Make the "normal" path through your code obvious. Error cases should not confuse the normal flow of execution. Your *if-then-else* constructs should be ordered consistently (i.e., always place the "normal" case before the "error" case, or vice versa).

---

[1] Did you work out what that first example did? Both functions compute a value in the Fibonacci sequence. Which would you prefer to read?

- Avoid too many nested statements. They lead to complex code that needs lengthy explanation. Common wisdom claims that each function should have one and *only* one exit point; this is known as *Single Entry, Single Exit (SESE)* code. But this is actually too restrictive for readable code and leads to deep levels of nesting. I prefer the fibonacci example we saw previously to this SESE variant:

```
int fibonacci(int position)
{
    int answer = 1;
    if (position >= 2)
    {
        int previousButOne = 1;
        int previous = 1;

        for (int n = 2; n < position; ++n)
        {
            previousButOne = previous;
            previous       = answer;
            answer         = previous + previousButOne;
        }
    }
    return answer;
}
```

For the sake of an extra return statement, I'd rather avoid that gratuitous nesting—it has made the function much harder to read. returns deep in the middle of a function's logic *are* questionable, but simple short circuits at the top aid function readability immensely.

- Be wary of optimizing code so that it's no longer a clear expression of a basic algorithm. *Never* optimize code unless you've proved that it *is* a bottleneck to acceptable program function. Optimize only then, and clearly comment about what's going on.

Choose Meaningful Names

All variable, type, file, and function names should be meaningful, not misleading. A name should faithfully describe what it represents. If you can't name something meaningfully, then do you really understand what it's doing? Your naming scheme should be consistent so that there are no nasty surprises. Make sure that a variable is only ever used for what its name implies.

Good names are probably our best way of avoiding gratuitous comments. They are the nearest thing we have in code to the expressiveness of natural language.

Decompose into Atomic Functions

The way that you split the code into functions and the names you give those functions can either add meaning to code or totally strip it of sense.

- *One function, one action.* Make that your mantra. Don't write complex functions that make coffee, clean shoes, *and* guess the number you first thought of. In one function, do one action. Choose a name that unambiguously explains that action. A good name means that no extra documentation is needed.

- Minimize any surprising *side effects*, no matter how benign they appear. They require extra documentation.

- Keep it short. Short functions are easy to understand. You can get your head around a complex algorithm if it's broken into small pieces with descriptive names, but you can't if it's a sprawling mess of code on the page.

Choose Descriptive Types

As much as possible, describe constraints or behavior with the available language features. For example:

- If you are defining a value that will never change, enforce it as a constant type (use `const` in C).

- If a variable should not contain a negative value, use an unsigned type (if your language provides one).

- Use enumerations to describe a related set of values.

- Select appropriate types. In C/C++, put sizes in `size_t` variables and pointer arithmetic results in `ptrdiff_t` variables.

Name Constants

Stumbling over some code that reads `if (counter == 76)` will leave you scratching your head. What is the magic significance of the number 76? What is the intent of that test?

These so-called *magic numbers* are evil. They hide meaning. Writing

```
const size_t bananas_per_cake = 76;
...
if (count == bananas_per_cake)
{
    // make banana cake
}
```

is much clearer. If you use the constant 76 (sorry, `bananas_per_cake`) a lot in your code, you gain an additional benefit: When you need to change the banana-to-cake ratio, you only need to make one code change, rather than perform an error-prone search-and-replace for every 76 in the project.

KEY CONCEPT *Avoid magic numbers. Use well-named constants instead.*

This holds true for constant strings as well as numbers. Question the use of *any* literal in your code, especially when you use it several times over—can you use a more maintainable named constant instead?

Emphasize Important Code

Make important stuff stand out from mundane stuff. Draw the reader's attention to the right places. There are many coding opportunities to do this. For example:

- Order the declarations in a class helpfully. Public information should come first, since this is what the class user needs to see. Put the private implementation details at the end, since they are less important to most readers.
- Wherever possible, hide all nonessential information. Don't clutter the global namespace with unnecessary cruft. In C++ you can use the pimpl idiom to hide class implementation details (Meyers 97).
- Don't hide important code. Write only one statement per line, and keep each statement simple. You *can* write very clever for loops, putting all the logic on one line with an assortment of commas, but it's not easy to read. Don't do it.
- Limit the number of nested conditional statements. If you don't, the handling of important conditions will become hidden by a nest of ifs and braces.

KEY CONCEPT *Make sure all important code stands out and is easy to read. Hide anything that the client audience doesn't care about.*

Group-Related Information

Present all related information in one place. Otherwise, you'll not only make the reader jump through hoops, you'll require him to know via ESP where the hoops are. The API for a single component should be presented in a single file. If there is so much related information that it becomes messy to present it all together, question the code's design.

Whenever possible, group items by a language construct. In C++ and C# we can group items within a namespace. Java provides packages as grouping mechanisms. Related constant values can be defined in an enum.

KEY CONCEPT *Group information together intentionally. Use language features to make this grouping explicit.*

Provide a File Header

Place a comment block at the top of a file to describe its contents and the project to which it belongs. This takes only a little effort, but it can make a big difference. When someone comes to maintain that file, they'll have a good idea what to expect.

This header can be important: Most companies mandate that every source file contains a visible copyright notice for legal reasons. File headers commonly look something like the following.

```
/********************************************************
 * File: Foo.java
 * Purpose: Foo class implementation
 * Notice: (c) 1066 Foo industries. All rights reserved.
 ********************************************************/
```

Handle Errors Appropriately

Handle any error in the most appropriate context. If there is a disk I/O problem, you should handle it in code that accesses the disk. Perhaps handling this error would mean raising a different error (like a "couldn't load file" exception) to a higher level. This means that at each level in the program, an error is an accurate description of what the problem is *in that context*. Don't handle hard disk corruption in the user interface code—it doesn't make sense.

Self-documenting code helps the reader to understand where an error came from, what it means, and its implications for the program at that point.

KEY CONCEPT   *Don't return nonsensical errors. Present the appropriate information in each context.*

Write Meaningful Comments

As you can see, we've tried to avoid writing comments by using other implicit code documentation techniques. However, once you've written the clearest code you can, you need to comment what remains. Clear code contains an *appropriate* amount of commenting. What is this appropriate amount?

KEY CONCEPT   *Only add comments if you can't improve the clarity of the code in any other way.*

Think about all these other techniques first. Would a name change or a new subordinate function make the code clearer and avoid a comment?

SELF-IMPROVEMENT

How do you get better at writing self-documenting code? Let's head back into book-writing territory for some clues.

There's a simple principle for improving your writing skills: *If you read a lot, you become a better writer.* Critically reading the works of recognized authors teaches you what works and what doesn't. You pick up new techniques and idioms to add to your arsenal.

Similarly, if you read a lot of code, you'll become a better programmer. If you immerse yourself in *good* code, you'll soon be able to smell bad code a mile away. Customs officials see so many passports each day that a forged one stands out like a sore thumb. Even clever imitations become obvious. Bad code becomes so much more striking when you're sensitive to the warning signs.

With this experience you'll naturally find yourself using good techniques in your own code. You'll begin to spot when you write bad code; it will feel uncomfortable.

Practical Self-Documentation Methodologies

We'll conclude this chapter by comparing two specific code documentation methods. Remember that these methods come *after* the techniques we've just seen. Kernighan and Plaugher said, "Don't document bad code—rewrite it." (Kernighan Plaugher 78)

Literate Programming

Literate programming is an extreme self-documenting code technique, conceived by the renowned computer scientist Donald Knuth. He wrote a book by this name that described it. (Knuth 92) It is a radical alternative to the traditional programming model, although some people think the literate programming episode of Knuth's career was a large and unfortunate sidetrack. Even if it's not the One True Way to code, there are still things we can learn from it.

The idea behind literate programming is simple: You don't write a program, you write a document. The documentation language is bound up tightly with the programming language. Your document is primarily a description of *what* is being programmed, but also happens to compile *into* that program. The source code is the documentation, and vice versa.

A literate program is written almost as a story; it is easy for the human reader to follow, perhaps even enjoyable to read. It is not ordered or constrained for a language parser. This is more than just a language with inverted comments; it's an inverted method for programming. Literate programming is a whole different way of thinking.

Knuth originally mixed TeX (a markup language for document typesetting) and C in a system called *WEB*. A literate programming tool parses the program file and generates either formatted documentation or source code that can be fed into a traditional compiler.

Of course, this is just another programming technique, like structured programming or object-oriented programming. It doesn't *guarantee* quality documentation. That is, as ever, up to the programmer. However, literate programming shifts the emphasis toward writing a description of the program rather than just writing code that implements it.

Literate programming really comes into its own during a product's maintenance phase. With good quality (and quantity of) documentation directly on hand, it becomes much easier to maintain the source.

There are many useful qualities of literate programming:

- Literate programming places emphasis back on writing documentation.
- It makes you think about your code in a different way since you write explanations and justifications as you go along.
- You are more likely to update the documentation when you make changes to the code, since it's situated conveniently nearby.
- You are guaranteed to only have one document for the whole codebase. You'll always be able to view the correct version for the code you're working on—it *is* the code you're working on.

- Literate programming encourages the inclusion of items not normally found in source comments. For example: a description of the algorithms used, proofs of correctness, and the justification of design decisions.

However, literate programming isn't a magical cure-all. It has some serious drawbacks:

- Literate programs are harder to write, because most programmers don't find it natural. We tend not to think of code as a printed document that needs formatting. Rather, we mentally model control flows and interacting objects.

- Extra compilation steps are required, which make literate programs slower to work with. There is still no *really* good tool support.

  It's quite difficult to process a literate program, since the compiler needs to extract all the program fragments and reassemble them, in the correct order. While it's nice to write the document in any order, C can be quite specific about how it wants to see code; #includes must come first, for example. This leads to some practical compromises.

- You might end up documenting some code that doesn't really need it. And the alternative, not documenting swathes of simple code, often happens too. This is no longer a good literate program; you may as well not have bothered.

  When *everything* is being written about, you can miss the few important bits of documentation in all the noise.

- Knuth talked about *the programmer as essayist*. Many a programmer couldn't write an essay to save his life, but he can write the most exquisite code. Maybe these guys are exceptions to the rule, but not every good programmer is a capable literate programmer.

- Tying documentation intimately to code can be problematic. You may have frozen your code for a major release—no changes are allowed—but you still need to work on the documentation. Altering the documentation means altering the source code. Now you have an executable-release version and a documentation-release version of the same codebase that you have to tie together: a management nightmare.

A later chapter discusses software specifications; how does literate programming relate to specifications? A literate program will never replace a functional specification describing what work needs to be done. However, it should be possible to develop a literate program from such a specification. The literate program really is more of a combination of traditional code with a design and implementation specification.

Documentation Tools

There is a breed of programming tool that sits halfway between the literate programming approach and writing external specifications. These tools generate documentation from your source code by pulling out blocks of specially formatted comments. This technique has become particularly fashionable since Sun introduced Javadoc as a core component of the Java platform. All of the Java API documentation is generated by Javadoc.

To understand exactly how this works, we'll look at an example. The exact comment formats may differ, but to document a `Widget` class, you'd write something like:

```
/**
 * This is the documentation for the Widget class.
 * The tool knows this because the comment started
 * with the special '/**' sequence.
 *
 * @author Author name here
 * @version Version number here
 */
class Widget
{
public:
    /**
     * This is the documentation for a method.
     */
    void method();
};
```

The documentation tool will parse each of your project's files, extract the documentation, build a cross-referenced database of all the information it finds on the way, and spit out a pretty document containing this information.

You can document pretty much any code you write: classes, types, functions, parameters, flags, variables, namespaces, packages, and so on. There are facilities to capture a lot of information, including the ability to:

- Specify copyright information
- Document the date of creation
- Cross-reference information
- Mark old code as deprecated
- Provide a short synopsis for quick reference
- Present a description of each function parameter

There are many documentation tools available, both open source and commercial. We've already mentioned Javadoc; other popular tools are C#'s NDoc and the excellent Doxygen (www.doxygen.org).

This is an excellent approach to documentation, allowing you to document code at a sensible level of detail without writing a separate specification. You can easily read your documentation in the source files too, which can be very helpful.

Documentation tools offer many benefits:

- Like literate programming, this approach encourages you to write documentation and keep it up to date.
- No separate step is required to get compilable code.

- It's more natural, not requiring massive adjustments or a steep learning curve. While the code can be used to generate a document, you don't have to artificially make your code look like a book or worry about tedious text layout concerns.
- The documentation tools support rich searching, cross-referencing, and code-outlining features.

However, it is important to understand the consequences of comment-based code documentation:

- Unlike literate programming, it's really only useful for API documentation, not internal code documentation. You must use regular comments at the statement level.
- It's hard to glance at a source file and get an overview of the contents, since they are spaced out by reams of documentation comments. You'd have to use the overview output of the tool instead. This may be beautifully formatted, but it's inconvenient to view when you're immersed in the world of the code editor.

KEY CONCEPT *Use literate documentation tools to automatically generate documentation from your code.*

Although this is a powerful way to write documentation, you *can* still write bad documentation using it. These are some helpful heuristics for getting it right:

- For each publicly visible item, write a one- or two-sentence description; don't go overboard with reams of text. A slew of prose is slow to read and hard to update. Don't waffle.
- Document variables or parameters if it's not clear what they're used for, but don't document them if their names make it obvious. You don't need to document every last detail if it doesn't add any value. The tool's output will still include the item, just with no textual explanation.
- If some of a function's parameters are used for input and some for output, make this clear in their descriptions. Few languages provide a syntactic mechanism to express this, so you must document it explicitly.
- Document any function pre- or postconditions, what exceptions might be thrown, and any of a function's side effects.

In a Nutshell

> *The skill of writing is to create a context*
> *in which other people can think.*
> *—Edwin Schlossberg*

We write code primarily to communicate. Code without documentation is a perilous thing, hardly communicative. It is a high-maintenance problem. *Bad* documentation is no better, either misleading the reader or resulting in a flimsy program that relies on external explanation.

Often the only documentation we have for a piece of code *is* that code itself. Making the code self-documenting and clear to read goes some way to remedy this situation. Self-documenting code doesn't happen magically, you have to carefully think about it. The result is code that looks like it *was* easy to write.

Literate programming is one (quite extreme) method of writing self-documenting code. Another less extreme method employs documentation tools. These tools can generate API documentation very easily, but they don't necessarily replace all written specifications.

Good programmers . . .	Bad programmers . . .
• Seek to write clear, self-documenting code	• Are proud that they write unfathomable spaghetti
• Try to write the least amount of documentation necessary	• Try to avoid writing any documentation
• Think about the needs of programmers who will maintain their code	• Don't care about updating documentation
	• Think, "If it was hard for me to write, it should be hard for anyone else to understand."

See Also

Chapter 3: What's in a Name?
Good names are powerful tools when writing self-documenting code.

Chapter 5: A Passing Comment
When you do resort to writing comments, this is how to do it correctly.

Chapter 19: Being Specific

Code should document itself, but we still need separate specifications for many reasons.

Get Thinking

A detailed discussion of these questions can be found in the "Answers and Discussion" section on page 480.

Mull It Over

1. Grouping related code will make its relationships clear. How can we perform this grouping? Which methods document the relationships most strongly?

2. We should avoid using *magic numbers* in our code. Is zero a magic number? What should you call a constant value representing zero?

3. Self-documenting code makes good use of context to convey information. Show how you do this, and give an example of how a particular name would lead to a different interpretation in different functions?

4. Is it realistic to expect a newcomer to pick up some self-documenting code and understand it totally?

5. If code is truly self-documenting, how much other documentation is required?

6. Why must more people than the original author understand any piece of code?

7. This simple C *bubblesort* function could use some improvement. What specific things are wrong with it? Write an improved, self-documenting version.

```
void bsrt(int a[], int n)
{
    for (int i = 0; i < n-1; i++)
        for (int j = n-1; j > i; j--)
            if (a[j-1] > a[j])
            {
                int tmp = a[j-1];
                a[j-1]  = a[j];
                a[j]    = tmp;
            }
}
```

8. Working with code documentation tools brings up some interesting issues. What's your opinion on these?

    a. When you review the documentation, should you perform a *code review*, looking at the comments in the source files, or a *specification review*, looking at the generated documents?

b. Where do you put documentation of protocols and other non-API issues?

c. Do you document private/internal functions? In C/C++, where do you place this documentation—in the header file or implementation file?

d. In a large system, should you create a single, large API document or several smaller documents, one per area? What are the advantages of each approach?

9. If you're working on a codebase that isn't literately documented, and you need to alter or add new methods or functions, is it a good idea to give them literate documentation comments, or should you leave them undocumented?

10. Is it possible to write self-documenting assembly code?

Getting Personal

1. What do you consider to be the best documented code you've come across? What made it so?

a. Did this code have a large number of external specifications? How many of them did you read? How can you be sure you knew enough about the code without reading them all?

b. How much of this do you think was due to the author's programming style, and how much was because of any house style or guidelines he or she worked to?

2. If you write in more than one language, how does your documentation strategy differ in each?

3. In the last code you wrote, how did you make the important stuff stand out? Did you hide private information away appropriately?

4. If you're working on a team, how often do others come to you to ask you how something works? Could you avoid this with better-documented code?

A PASSING COMMENT

How to Write Code Comments

Comments are free but facts are sacred.
　　　　　　　—Charles Prestwich Scott

Comments are a lot like opinions. You're free to make them, but just because you do doesn't mean they're right. In this chapter, we'll spend a little time thinking about the details of writing these things. There's a lot more to writing comments than you'd think.

Probably one of the first things you learned when you were taught to program was how to write comments. You were told that comments aid the readability of code, and you were probably encouraged to write lots of them. But in this game, we need to be thinking more about *quality* than *quantity*. Comments are our lifelines, memory jogs, and guides through code. We should treat them with the respect they deserve.

I set my syntax-highlighting code editor to display comments in green. This way, I get an immediate feeling for the quality of a piece of codeand how easy it's going to be to work with as soon as I load up a source file. A nice proportion of green spread through in the right pattern makes me feel good about the world. The opposite makes me stroll to the kitchen for a strong coffee before going any further.

Comments can make the difference between bad code and good code, between a grossly complex and unfathomable morass of logic and a nice set of clear algorithms. But let's not overstate the case—there are things far more important to get right than comments. When you've written truly good code, your comments are the *icing on the cake*, delicately placed to add aesthetics and value, rather than liberally slapped on to cover up all the cracks and blemishes.

Good commenting is a strategy to avoid intimidating code. Comments aren't a magic additive to turn sour code sweet.

What Is a Code Comment?

Don't skip this section! Admittedly, this is an excruciating place to start. We all know what a code comment is, right? But it is more philosophical than you might think.

Syntactically, a comment is a block of source that the compiler will ignore. Put what you like in it, the names of your grandchildren or the color of your favorite shirt; the compiler won't bat an eye as it merrily parses its way through the file.[1]

Semantically, a comment is the difference between a dingy dirt track and a well-lit highway. The comment is an annotation of the code it's situated by. You can use it as a highlighter to make a particular problem area stand out or as a documentation medium in your header file. You might use comments to describe the shape of an algorithm, to aid the maintenance programmer (which could be you later on), or to mark the space between each function to help you navigate through a source file more quickly.

Comments are aimed at the human reader, not the computer. In this sense, comments are the most human-focused brick in the programming wall. They are ornately molded bricks, as opposed to structural breeze blocks. If we want to improve the quality of our comments, we need to look at and address what the human really needs as he reads code.

Code comments are not the only documentation that you should put in your code. Comments are not specifications. They are not design documents. They are not API references.[2] However, they are an invaluable form of documentation that will always be physically attached to the code (unless someone maliciously hits DELETE). Their close proximity means they're more likely to be updated and more likely to be read in context. It's an internal documentation mechanism.

As responsible programmers, we have a duty to comment well.

---

[1] Of course, the thing that chews up and spits out the comments differs with the kind of language you're using. In C/C++, the monstrous *preprocessor* beast devours comments before the compile stage begins. In other languages, the compiler itself throws away comments as it tokenizes the source. In interpreted languages, your intense commenting may slow down execution, since the interpreter has to jump over the names of all your grandchildren.

[2] Well, unless you use a literate programming tool, discussed in "Literate Programming" on page 66.

What Do Comments Look Like?

Well, they're green aren't they? At least they are for me.

C comments come in blocks between /* and */ and can span any number of lines. C++, C99, C#, and Java add the single line comment that follows //. Other languages provide similar *block* and *line* comment facilities, but with different syntaxes.

Again, this is elementary subject matter. But the different comment markers are often used in subtly different ways. We'll see examples as we go along. However, any commenting scheme that makes cute use of subtle syntax differentiations should be viewed warily.

How Many Comments?

Vigorous writing is concise.
—*William Strunk Jr.*

We need to focus on comment quality, not quantity, so more important than the amount of comments we write are the contents of those comments. The next section discusses this.

Student programmers are taught to write comments, and lots of them. But there is such a thing as *too much* commenting—you can obscure important sections of code in a dense forest of words. Code quality suffers when you have to spend more time wading through complex paragraphs of comments than the actual code that you need to read.

I liken this skill to being a good musician. Playing in a band is not about how much noise you can make at every conceivable opportunity. The more you play your instrument, the more complex the overall sound, and the worse the music. Likewise, too many comments muddle the code. A good musician doesn't have to think, *When should I stop playing and let someone else have a chance?* A good musician only plays when it will really add something. It's about playing the *minimum* you can to create the best sound possible. The beauty is in the space. We should only be writing comments when they really add something.

KEY CONCEPT *Learn to write* enough *comments, and no more. Favor quality, not quantity.*

The people who will read your comments can also read the code, so try to document as much as possible *in the code itself*, rather than in comments. It's what they'll believe, anyway—comments have a nasty tendency to lie. Consider your code statements the first level of comment, and make them self-documenting.

Well-written code doesn't actually need comments, because everything should be self-explanatory. Function names like f() and g() scream out for comments to describe them, but someGoodExample() doesn't ask for a comment at all. You can see it's a good example function name.

KEY CONCEPT *Spend your time writing code that doesn't need to be propped up by tons of comments.*

The fewer comments you write, the less chance you have of writing bad comments.

What Goes Inside Our Comments?

> *Of writing well the source and*
> *fountainhead is wise thinking.*
> *—Horace*

Bad comments are worse than no comments at all—they will misinform and mislead the reader. So what sort of thing should you write in comments? Here are a few basic steps to improve the quality of your comment content:

Explain Why, *Not* How

This is a key point, so read this paragraph twice. Then eat the page. Your comments should not describe *how* the program works. You can see that by reading the code. After all, the code is the definitive description of how the code works. And it has been written clearly and comprehensibly, hasn't it? You should instead focus on describing *why* something is written the way it is or what the next block of statements ultimately achieves.

Constantly check whether you're writing `/* update WidgetList structure from GlbWLRegistry */` or `/* cache widget information for later */`. They might equate to the same thing, but the latter conveys the intent of the code, while the former just tells you what it's doing.

As you maintain a section of code, the reason *why* it exists will change less often than *how* it achieves that purpose, making this sort of comment's maintenance much easier.

KEY CONCEPT   *Good comments explain* why *not* how.

You might also use a comment to explain why you have made a particular implementation choice. If you have two possible implementation strategies and you decide on one over the other, then consider whether it is worth adding a comment explaining this rationale.

Don't Describe the Code

Worthless descriptive comments can be obvious: `++i; // increment i`. They can also be more subtle: a lengthy comment description of a complex algorithm, followed by the implementation of the algorithm. There is no need to restate code laboriously in English unless you're documenting a really complex algorithm that's impenetrable without it. And then you should probably worry more about rewriting the algorithm than the comment.

KEY CONCEPT   *Honor the golden rule:* One fact—one source. *Don't duplicate code in a comment.*

Don't Replace Code

If you see a comment stating something that could be enforced by the language itself (e.g., `// this variable should only be accessed by class foo`), then look to express it in concrete syntax.

If you find yourself writing reams of comments to explain how a complex algorithm works, stop. First pat yourself on the back for trying to document what's going on. But then consider whether you could change the code or the algorithm to make it clearer.

- Perhaps you could split the code into several well-named functions to reflect the program logic.
- Don't write comments to describe the use of a variable; rename the variable. The comment you were going to write will often tell you what the name of the variable should be!
- If you are documenting a condition that should always hold, perhaps you should be writing an assertion.
- Remember that you don't need to prematurely optimize (and thus obfuscate) your code.

KEY CONCEPT   *When you find yourself writing dense comments to explain your code,* step back. *Is there a bigger problem to solve?*

Keep It Useful

A good comment usually takes several iterations to move up the quality ladder, just like code. Make sure your comments:

Document the unexpected
> If any bits of code are unusual, unexpected, or surprising, document them with a comment. You'll thank yourself when you come back later, having forgotten all about the problem. If there are specific work-arounds, say for an operating system issue, then mention this in a comment.
>
> The flip side of this is that you don't need to document the obvious. Remember: *Don't repeat the code!*

Tell the truth
> When is a comment not a comment? When it's a lie. Okay, you'll never deliberately write lies, but it's easy to accidentally introduce mistruths, especially when modifying code that has already been commented. Later code changes can easily render a comment inaccurate; "Working with Comments" on page 84 describes tactics to cope with this.

Are worthwhile
> Little witty cryptic comments may be witty, and they might be little, but *don't* put them in. They get in the way and cause confusion. Avoid expletives, inside jokes that only you understand, and comments that are unnecessarily critical—you never know where your code will end up in a month or year's time, so don't write comments that could cause you embarrassment later.

Are clear
> Your comment serves to annotate and explain the code. Don't be ambiguous. Be as specific as you can (without writing a thesis about each line).

If someone reads your comment and is left wondering what it means, then you have made the code *worse* and slowed down their comprehension.

Are comprehensible

You don't need to write complete, grammatically correct English sentences inside every comment you write. However, the comment *must* be readable. Cute abbreviations of words usually only serve to confuse the reader—especially if English is not his or her first language.

KEY CONCEPT   *Think about what you're writing in a comment; don't type without using your brain. Read it back again in the context of the code. Does it contain the right information?*

A WAR STORY

I once did some consulting work for a company that had a mixture of programmers: some were native English speakers, some native Greek speakers. The Greeks could all speak excellent English, but not one of the English speakers could speak Greek (no surprise there).

One of the Greek programmers wrote comments in Greek and, when politely asked, refused to change this practice. The English programmers couldn't read these comments because they were, quite literally, *all Greek to me!*

Avoid Distractions

Comments serve to illuminate the surrounding code, so we must avoid anything that distracts from it. Comments should only *add value*. Avoid comments that include:

The past

We don't need to keep a record of how we *used* to do something. The revision control system does that. We don't need to see old code reproduced in comments, nor a description of an old algorithm.

Code you don't want

Don't knock out code by enclosing it in comments. It's confusing. Even when debugging *commando style* (no pants, no debugger, and no printfs), *don't* hide code you need to remove in a comment block. Use C's #ifdef 0 ... #endif or some equivalent. These constructs nest and have clearer intent (especially important if you forget to come back later and tidy up).

ASCII art

Avoid ASCII art pictures or anything else that tries to highlight code in clever ways. This, for example, is a bad idea:

```
aBadExample(n, foo(wibble));
//              ^^^
//              My favorite
//              function
```

It won't make sense in editors with variable width display fonts. Comments are not supposed to double maintenance effort!

End of blocks

Some programmers comment the end of every control block, for example putting `// end if (a < 1)` after the closing brace of an `if` statement. This is a redundant form of comment; it needs to be filtered out before real comprehension can occur. The bottom of a block should be visible on the same page as the top, and the code layout should make its start and end clear. All extra verbiage should be avoided.

In Practice

The following example illustrates these commenting principles. Consider the following snippet of C++ code. Idiomatic criticisms aside, it is not at all clear what's going on.

```
for (int i = 0; i < wlst.sz(); ++i)
k(wlst[i]);
```

Yuck. There's some room for improvement here, so let's improve. The code can be made less cryptic by applying sensible layout rules and adding a few comments:

```
// Iterate over all widgets in the widget list
for (int i = 0; i < wlst.sz(); ++i)
{
    // Print out this widget
    k(wlst[i]);
}
```

Much better! Now it's entirely clear what the code snippet is supposed to be doing. I'm still not entirely happy, though. With appropriate function and variable names, we no longer need any comments at all, since the code describes itself:

```
for (int i = 0; i < widgets.size(); ++i)
{
    printWidget(widgets[i]);
}
```

Note that I didn't rename `i` to something more long-winded. It's a loop variable with a very small scope. Calling it `loopCounter` would have been overkill and would arguably have made the code *harder* to read.

It shouldn't be surprising that we ended up with no comments at all. Remember Kernighan and Plaugher's advice: "Don't document bad code—rewrite it." (Kernighan Plaugher 78)

A Comment on Aesthetics

You've no doubt heard people religiously touting about how you should format your comments. I'm not going to prescribe the One True Way to format (there is no such thing), but there are a few important aspects to consider. Interpret these as guidelines, according to your personal taste, rather than as rigid dictates.

Consistency

All commenting should be clear and consistent. Choose a specific way to lay out your comments, and use it throughout. Every programmer has a different sense of aesthetics, so choose what works for you. *Do* use a house style if one exists, or examine (good) existing code and follow the styles you see there.

Small formatting issues in comment writing may seem trivial—for example, should each comment start with a capital letter or not? However, if all your comments are randomly capitalized, it conveys a lack of cohesion in the code, as if the programmer didn't really think all that carefully when he crafted it.

Clear Block Comments

Syntax highlighting editors are great because they help comments to stand out. But don't rely on them too much. Your code might be read from a monochrome printout or viewed in an editor without syntax coloring. The comment work should still be easily readable.

A few strategies can help here, especially regarding block comments. Placing the start and end markers (e.g., /* and */ in C and C++) on their own lines makes them stand out. Placing a margin character down the left side of a block comment also helps to make it appear as a single item:

```
/*
 * This is much more readable
 * as a block comment in the midst
 * of a whole pile of code
 */
```

This is much better than the alternative:

```
 /*
a comment that might
    span a few lines but without
any margin character.
*/
```

At the very least, line up the comment text so it's not a jagged mess.

Indenting Comments

A comment shouldn't cut across the code and break up the logical flow. Keep it at the same level of indentation as the code around it. That way, the comment appears to apply to the correct level of the code. I always have to stare hard at code like this:

```
void strangeCommentStyle()
{
    for (int n = 0; n < JUST_ENOUGH_TIMES; ++n)
    {
// This is a meaningful comment about the next line.
        doSomethingMeaningful(n);
// But frankly, it's confusing the pants off of me.
        anotherUsefulOperation(n);
    }
}
```

In a loop without braces (which isn't a good idea anyway), *don't* put a comment before the single loop body statement—this can lead to all sorts of distaster. If you want a comment in there, wrap up the whole thing in braces. It's a far safer strategy.

End-of-Line Comments

Most comments are written on lines of their own, but sometimes a short single line comment can *follow* a code statement. In this case, it's good practice to space out the comment to mark it as clearly apart from the code. For example:

```
class HandyExample
{
public:
    ... some nice public stuff ...
private:
    int appleCount;         // End-of-line comments:
    bool isFatherADustman;  // Make them stand out
    int favoriteNumber;     // from the code
};
```

This is a good example of using comment layout to improve the appearance of your code. If each end-of-line comment came directly after the variable declaration, they'd look jagged, messy, and require more squinting to read.

Helping You to Read the Code

Comments are usually written *above* the code that they describe, not below it. This way, the source code reads downward, almost like a book. The comment serves to prepare the reader for what is to come.

Used with whitespace, commenting helps to break the code up into "paragraphs." A comment introduces a few lines, explaining what they intend to achieve; the code immediately follows, then a blank line, then the next block. This is such a convention that a comment with a blank line before it feels like a paragraph start, whereas a comment sandwiched in the middle of two code lines feels more like a statement in brackets or a footnote.

KEY CONCEPT   *Comments are part of the code narrative. Use them in a way that reads naturally.*

Choose a Low-Maintenance Style

It's sensible to choose a low-maintenance comment style, or you'll waste time fiddling with comments when you should be writing code.

Some C coders create comment blocks with a column of asterisks in the left margin *and* a column of asterisks as a right margin. Arguably this looks very pretty, but the amount of work required to adjust a paragraph of text within such margins is immense. When you could have moved on to the next task at hand, you have to manually realign all the asterisks on the right. If the programmer used tabs, then things get even nastier: If someone with a different-sized tab stop opens the file, he or she will wonder what the original programmer was up to—all the asterisks will look incredibly ugly and badly lined up.

The end-of-line comments we saw above are an example of alignment that requires some effort. How much work you're prepared to spend is up to you. There is always a balance between good-looking source code and maintenance effort. I suppose I prefer a little bit of effort to ugly code.

Breakwaters

Comments are often used as *breakwaters* between sections of code. This is where people's artistic sensibilities take over; programmers use different schemes to differentiate major comments (*this is a new section of code*) from minor comments (*this describes a few of lines of a function*). A source file implementing several classes may have something like this between each major section:

```
/**************************************************************************
 * class foo implementation
 **************************************************************************/
```

Some programmers insert large blocks of comment art between each function. Some use a long, single-line comment as a rule-off. I just place a couple of blank lines between functions. If your functions are so large that you need visual clues to see where they start and end, then you need to revise your code.

Avoid using these large rules to emphasize every comment in sight. Otherwise, nothing gets emphasized. Good indentation and structure, not impressive ASCII art, should group code together.

All that being said, well-chosen breakwater comments can help you to quickly navigate around a file.

Flags

Comments can also be used as inline *flags* in the code. There are a number of common conventions. You'll see //XXX, //FIXME, or //TODO littered though files that are still works in progress. Good syntax-highlighting editors display these comments prominently by default. XXX is used to mark troublesome code or something that needs to be reworked. TODO often marks missing pieces of functionality for a later return.[3] FIXME indicates something that's known to be broken.

File Header Comments

Every source file should begin with a comment block that describes its contents. This is just a quick overview, a preface, providing some essential information that you always want displayed as soon as a file is opened. If such a header exists, then any programmer who opens the file will have confidence in the contents; it shows the file was thoughtfully created rather than just hacked up as a dumping ground for some new code.

KEY CONCEPT *Give every source file a comment prologue.*

Some people advocate that this header should provide a list of every function, class, global variable, and so on that is defined in the file. This is a maintenance disaster; such a comment would rapidly become out of date. The kind of information this file header *should* contain is the purpose of the file (e.g., *implementation of foo interface*) and a copyright statement describing ownership and copying rights.

If a source file is automatically generated during the build process, then you must arrange for this file to receive a comment header that states very clearly (in BIG SCARY CAPITAL LETTERS) where it originated. This will prevent someone from mistakenly editing it, only to have the contents regenerated at the next build.

The header should *not* contain information that could easily become out of date, like the author(s), modifiers, or the date the file was last modified. This probably wouldn't be updated often, and would become misleading. Version control tells you this anyway. It also needn't contain a source file history describing every modification ever made. That information exists in your source control system and doesn't need to be duplicated here. Moreover, if you have to scroll through 10 pages of modification history to get to the first line of code, then the file becomes tedious to work with. For this reason, some programmers put it at the end of the file instead, but this will still make the file unreasonably large, slow to load, and bothersome to work with.

---

[3] Be careful with TODO comments. You might be better off throwing a TODO exception instead, which cannot be missed. That way, if you forget to implement the missing code, your program will fail in a well-defined way.

A WELL-PLACED COMMENT

We're focusing on *code* comments in this chapter, what we actually type into source code. But different breeds of comment graze in neighboring pastures:

Check in/out comments

Your revision control system maintains a history of how each file was modified over the life of the project. It associates *metadata* with each revision—at the very least, programmer-supplied *check-in comments*. It may also record *checkout comments* if it keeps tabs on which files are currently in use. You use these comments to describe what you are changing, as a record for posterity.

Such comments are invaluable, and should be created carefully. They should be:

- Short (so you can quickly browse a log of all modifications)
- Accurate (don't get information wrong, or the history is worthless)
- Complete (so you can see all that has happened in a file without manually *diff*ing revisions)

Document *what* has changed and *why*, not *how* it has changed. You can use the file revision differences to work out how you modified the code.

This is where comments about the past belong. It's also the right place for bug-tracking references. Don't be tempted to put information that belongs here into source code comments. Remember: *One fact—one source.*

README files

These are plaintext files that live in the directories alongside source code files. They are useful documentation, falling somewhere between formal specifications and code comments. They often contain practical information, perhaps on what each file does or on the structure of the file hierarchy; they are basically short notes.

READMEs tend to be either haphazard and poorly thought out or badly maintained and out of date—which is a shame. When you come across a README file, you naturally load it up to see what helpful information it contains. The presence of a README shows someone was thinking when they collected the source files together; there was something worth documenting and something worthwhile to say about it.

Working with Comments

Comments are convenient tools to use while you are writing code. But be careful not to abuse them.

Helping You to Write Routines

A common routine-writing approach is to fashion its structure in comments first and then fill in the code underneath each comment line. If you work this way, you should ask yourself, once finished, whether the remaining comments are still useful. Evaluate them against the criteria just discussed, and revise or remove them if necessary. Don't just leave them and move on.

The alternative is to write the new routine freehand, and then add any necessary comments afterward. The danger is that you'll forget to finish the job, or that you might not write the best comments—now knowing almost too well how the code works. The experienced programmer comments *as he goes along*. Practice shows you the right amount of commenting to use.

Don't be afraid of using the flags we saw earlier, like TODO, as markers to yourself. It will avoid the embarrassment of forgetting to tie up pesky little loose ends. You can easily search your entire codebase for these comments to find out what still needs to be completed.

Bug-Fix Notices

A common, but questionable, comment practice is placing notices where faults have been fixed. You may stumble over a comment like this in the middle of a function:

```
// <bug reference> - changed to use blah.foo2()
// method because blah.foo() didn't handle <some
// condition> properly
blah.foo2();
```

Although written with the best intentions (to help you see what's happened in the course of development), these comments often do more harm than good. To understand the real problem, you'd have to look up the fault in your fault-tracking system and pull out the previous revision of the file to investigate what changed. Few bug fixes require that kind of reading, so the newcomer can probably live in blissful ignorance. These comments proliferate in the later stages of development and during maintenance and litter the source code with sidelines, stale information, and distractions from the main thread of execution.

There *is* an argument for inserting a comment when you make a non-obvious fix—to prevent someone who is revising the code later from reintroducing the bug. However, in these well-chosen cases, you are actually *documenting the unexpected* rather than placing a bug-fix notice.

KEY CONCEPT *Comments should live in the* present, *not the past. Don't describe things that have changed, or tell what something used to do.*

Comment Rot

Comments rot. Well, all carelessly maintained code tends to rot, acquiring unsightly blemishes and losing the original neat design. However, comments seem to rot much more quickly than any other piece of code. They become out of date with the code they describe. This can be profoundly annoying.

A WAR STORY

I once worked on a section of code containing the comment *Features A and B not yet implemented.* I needed both these facilities, so I wrote them. Only after having done so did I discover that feature B *had* already been implemented—I had just wasted effort—and feature A was redundant, since the implementation of B handled it as well. If the programmer who did this had removed the incorrect comment, I would have been spared a *lot* of work.

The simple solution is this: When you fix, add, or modify any code, fix, add, or modify any comments around it. Don't just fiddle with a couple of lines and move on. Make sure that any code changes don't turn comments into lies. The corollary is: We must make comments easy to keep up to date, or they won't be updated. Comments must be clearly related to their section of code, not placed in obscure locations.

KEY CONCEPT *When you alter code, maintain any comments around it.*

Another bad habit is leaving blocks of code commented out. This will confuse you when you come back in a year's time, or when any other programmer stumbles across them. If you encounter some code in a comment block, you'll wonder why it's there. Was it a fix that was never completed? Is it still a work in progress? Did that code never work? Is the rest of the code functionally complete?

Either leave a note explaining why you have commented the code out or remove it completely—you can always get it back from the source control system. Even if you think you're only knocking something out temporarily, leave yourself a note; you may forget to finish it off.

Maintenance and the Inane Comment

As you wade though an old codebase, it's best not to remove any inane comments you find unless they are downright dangerous. Leave them as a warning for future maintenance programmers—they give a useful insight into the (lack of) quality of the surrounding code. Of course, if you're actually trying to improve that piece of code, then do rework the comments as you go! If you find a comment that *is* factually wrong or misleading, then you should rewrite it as a part of your maintenance of the code.

Learn the interesting area flags like XXX, and treat them with respect and caution. Also watch for output statements that have been commented out. These are a sure sign that there has been a problem area here in the past—treat the code with care!

Be aware of comment rot. Just because a comment says *this is defined in foo.c* doesn't mean that it is anymore. Always have faith in code and doubt comments.

In a Nutshell

> *Major writing is to say what has been seen,*
> *so that it need never be said again.*
> *—Delmore Schwartz*

We write a lot of comments. That's because we write a lot of code. Learning to write the right sort of comment is important, or our code may keel over under the weight of inappropriate and outdated commenting.

Comments are no more important than the code they annotate—you can't make bad code good using comments. Your aim should be self-documenting code that requires no comments at all.

Good programmers . . .	Bad programmers . . .
• Try to write a *few* really good comments	• Can't tell the difference between good and bad comments
• Write comments explaining *why*	• Write comments explaining *how*
• Concentrate on writing good code rather than a plethora of comments	• Don't mind if comments only make sense to themselves
• Write helpful comments that make sense	• Bolster bad code with many comments
	• Fill their source files with redundant information (revision history, etc.)

See Also

Chapter 2: The Best Laid Plans
Code layout and presentation schemes will affect how you lay out your comments.

Chapter 3: What's in a Name?
Another aspect of self-commenting code: choosing good names.

Chapter 4: The Write Stuff
Discusses *self-documenting code*, a tactic that makes heavy commenting redundant. Also describes *literate programming* techniques.

Chapter 18: Practicing Safe Source
Revision control systems hold file history so you don't need to explain it in comments.

Get Thinking

A detailed discussion of the following questions can be found in the "Answers and Discussion" section on page 485.

Mull It Over

1. How might the *need for* and the *content of* comments differ in the following types of code:
   a. Low-level assembly language (machine code)
   b. Shell scripts
   c. A single-file test harness
   d. A large C/C++ project
2. You can run tools to calculate what percentage of your source code lines are comments. How useful are these tools? How accurate a measure is this of comment quality?
3. If you come across some incomprehensible code, which is the better way to factor in some intelligibility: adding comments to document what you think is going on, or renaming variables/functions/types with more descriptive names? Which approach will most likely be easier? Which approach will be safer?
4. When you document a C/C++ API with a code comment block, should it go in the public header file that declares the function or the source file containing the implementation? What are the pros and cons of each location?

Getting Personal

1. Look carefully at the source files you've recently worked on. Inspect your commenting. Is it honestly any good? (I bet as you read through the code you'll find yourself making a few changes!)
2. How do you ensure that your comments are genuinely valuable and not just personal ramblings that only you can understand?
3. Do the people you work with all comment to the same standard, in about the same way?
   a. Who's the best at writing comments? Why do you think that? Who's the worst? How much of a correlation does this bear to these individuals' general quality of coding?
   b. Do you think any imposed coding standards could raise the quality of the comments written by your team?
4. Do you include history logging information in each source file? If yes:
   a. Do you do maintain it manually? Why, if your revision control system will insert this for you automatically? Is the history kept particularly accurate?
   b. Is this *really* a sensible practice? How often is this information needed? Why is it better if placed in the source file than in another, separate mechanism?
5. Do you add your initials to or otherwise mark the comments you make in other people's code? Do you ever date comments? When and why do you do this—is it a useful practice? Has it ever been useful to find someone else's initials and timestamping?

TO ERR IS HUMAN

*Dealing with the Inevitable—
Error Conditions in Code*

We know that the only way to avoid error is to detect it, that the only way to detect it is to be free to enquire.
—*J. Robert Oppenheimer*

At some point in life, everyone has this epiphany: *The world doesn't work as you expect it to.* My one-year-old friend Tom learned this when climbing a chair four times his size. He expected to get to the top. The actual result surprised him: He ended up under a pile of furniture.

Is the world broken? Is it wrong? No. The world has plodded happily along its way for the last few million years and looks set to continue for the foreseeable future. It's *our expectations* that are wrong and need to be adjusted. As they say: *Bad things happen, so deal with it.* We must write code that deals with the Real World and its unexpected ways.

This is particularly difficult because the world *mostly* works as we'd expect it to, constantly lulling us into a false sense of security. The human brain is wired to cope, with built-in fail-safes. If someone bricks up your front door, your brain will process the problem, and you'll stop before walking into an unexpected wall. But programs are not so clever; we have to tell them where the brick walls are and what to do when they hit one.

Don't presume that everything in your program will always run smoothly. The world doesn't always work as you'd expect it to: You *must* handle all possible error conditions in your code. It sounds simple enough, but that statement leads to a world of pain.

From Whence It Came

> *To expect the unexpected shows*
> *a thoroughly modern intellect.*
> *—Oscar Wilde*

Errors can and will occur. Undersirable results can arise from almost any operation. They are distinct from bugs in a faulty program because you *know* beforehand that an error can occur. For example, the database file you want to open might have been deleted, a disk could fill up at any time and your next save operation might fail, or the web service you're accessing might not currently be available.

If you don't write code to handle these error conditions, you will almost certainly end up with a *bug*; your program will not always work as you intend it to. But if the error happens only rarely, it will probably be a very subtle bug! We'll look at bugs in Chapter 9.

An error may occur for one of a thousand reasons, but it will fall into one of these three categories:

User error
> The stupid user manhandled your lovely program. Perhaps he provided the wrong input or attempted an operation that's absolutely absurd. A good program will point out the mistake and help the user rectify it. It won't insult him or whine in an incomprehensible manner.

Programmer error
> The user pushed all the right buttons, but the code is broken. This is the consequence of a bug elsewhere, a fault the programmer introduced that the user can do nothing about (except to try and avoid it in the future). This kind of error should (ideally) never occur.
>
> There's a cycle here: Unhandled errors can cause bugs. And those bugs might result in further error conditions occurring elsewhere in your code. This is why we consider defensive programming an important practice.

Exceptional circumstances
> The user pushed all the right buttons, and the programmer didn't mess up. Fate's fickle finger intervened, and we ran into something that couldn't be avoided. Perhaps a network connection failed, we ran out of printer ink, or there's no hard disk space left.

We need a well-defined strategy to manage each kind of error in our code. An error may be detected and reported to the user in a pop-up message box, or it may be detected by a middle-tier code layer and signaled to the client code programmatically. The same principles apply in both cases: whether a human chooses how to handle the problem or your code makes a decision—*someone* is responsible for acknowledging and acting on errors.

KEY CONCEPT *Take error handling seriously. The stability of your code rests on it.*

Errors are raised by subordinate components and communicated upward, to be dealt with by the caller. They are reported in a number of ways; we'll look at these in the next section. To take control of program execution, we must be able to:

- Raise an error when something goes wrong
- Detect all possible error reports
- Handle them appropriately
- Propagate errors we can't handle

Errors are hard to deal with. The error you encounter is often not related to what you were doing at the time (most fall under the "exceptional circumstances" category). They are also tedious to deal with—we want to focus on what our program *should* be doing, not on how it may go wrong. However, without good error management, your program will be brittle—built upon sand, not rock. At the first sign of wind or rain, it will collapse.

Error-Reporting Mechanisms

There are several common strategies for propagating error information to client code. You'll run into code that uses each of them, so you must know how to speak every dialect. Observe how these error-reporting techniques compare, and notice which situations call for each mechanism.

Each mechanism has different implications for the *locality of error*. An error is local in *time* if it is discovered very soon after it is created. An error is local in *space* if it is identified very close to (or even *at*) the site where it actually manifests. Some approaches specifically aim to reduce the locality of error to make it easier to see what's going on (e.g., error codes). Others aim to extend the locality of error so that normal code doesn't get entwined with error-handling logic (e.g., exceptions).

The favored reporting mechanism is often an architectural decision. The architect might consider it important to define a homogeneous hierarchy of exception classes or a central list of shared reason codes to unify error-handling code.

No Reporting

The simplest error-reporting mechanism is *don't bother*. This works wonderfully in cases where you want your program to behave in bizarre and unpredictable ways and to crash randomly.

If you encounter an error and don't know what to do about it, blindly ignoring it is *not* a viable option. You probably can't continue the function's work, but returning without fulfilling your function's contract will leave the world in an undefined and inconsistent state.

KEY CONCEPT   *Never ignore an error condition. If you don't know how to handle the problem, signal a failure back up to the calling code. Don't sweep an error under the rug and hope for the best.*

An alternative to ignoring errors is to instantly abort the program upon encountering a problem. It's easier than handling errors throughout the code, but hardly a well-engineered solution!

Return Values

The next most simple mechanism is to return a success/failure value from your function. A boolean return value provides a simple yes or no answer. A more advanced approach enumerates all the possible exit statuses and returns a corresponding *reason code*. One value means *success*; the rest represent the many and varied abortive cases. This enumeration may be shared across the whole codebase, in which case your function returns a subset of the available values. You should therefore document what the caller can expect.

While this works well for procedures that don't return data, passing error codes back *with* returned data gets messy. If int count() walks down a linked list and returns the number of elements, how can it signify a list structure corruption? There are three approaches:

- Return a compound data type (or *tuple*) containing both the return value and an error code. This is rather clumsy in the popular C-like languages and is seldom seen in them.

- Pass the error code back through a function parameter. In C++ or .NET, this parameter would be passed by reference. In C you'd direct the variable access through pointers. This approach is ugly and nonintuitive; there is no syntactic way to distinguish a return value from a parameter.

- Alternatively, reserve a range of return values to signify failure. The count example can nominate all negative numbers as error reason codes; they'd be meaningless answers anyway. Negative numbers are a common choice for this. Pointer return values may be given a specific invalid value, which by convention is zero (or NULL). In Java and C#, you can return a null object reference.

    This technique doesn't always work well. Sometimes it's hard to reserve an error range—all return values are equally meaningful and equally likely. It also has the side effect of reducing the available range of success values; the use of negative values reduces the possible positive values by an order of magnitude.[1]

---

[1] If you used an unsigned int then the number of values available would increase by a power of two, reusing the signed int's sign bit.

Error Status Variables

This method attempts to manage the contention between a function's return value and its error status report. Rather than return a reason code, the function sets a shared global error variable. After calling the function, you must then inspect this status variable to find out whether or not it completed successfully.

The shared variable reduces confusion and clutter in the function's signature, and it doesn't restrict the return value's data range at all. However, errors signaled through a separate channel are much easier to miss or willfully ignore. A shared global variable also has nasty thread safety implications.

The C standard library employs this technique with its errno variable. It has very subtle semantics: Before using any standard library facility, you must manually clear errno. Nothing ever sets a succeeded value; only failures touch errno. This is a common source of bugs, and it makes calling each library function tedious. To add insult to injury, not all C standard library functions use errno, so it is less than consistent.

This technique is functionally equivalent to using return values, but it has enough disadvantages to make you avoid it. Don't write your own error reports this way, and use existing implementations with the utmost care.

Exceptions

Exceptions are a language facility for managing errors; not all languages support exceptions. Exceptions help to distinguish the normal flow of execution from *exceptional* cases—when a function has failed and cannot honor its contract. When your code encounters a problem that it can't handle, it stops dead and throws up an *exception*—an object representing the error. The language run time then automatically steps back up the call stack until it finds some exception-handling code. The error lands there, for the program to deal with.

There are two operational models, distinguished by what happens after an exception is handled:

The termination model
> Execution continues after the handler that caught the exception. This behavior is provided by C++, .NET, and Java.

The resumption model
> Execution resumes where the exception was raised.

The former model is easier to reason about, but it doesn't give ultimate control. It only allows *error handling* (you can execute code when you notice an error), not *fault rectification* (a chance to fix the problem and try again).

An exception cannot be ignored. If it isn't caught and handled, it will propagate to the very top of the call stack and will usually stop the program dead in its tracks. The language run time automatically cleans up as it unwinds

WHISTLE-STOP TOUR OF EXCEPTION SAFETY

Resilient code must be *exception safe*. It must work correctly (for some definition of *correctly*, which we'll investigate below), no matter what exceptions come its way. This is true regardless of whether or not the code catches any exceptions itself.

Exception-neutral code propagates all exceptions up to the caller; it won't consume or change anything. This is an important concept for generic programs like C++ template code—the template types may generate all sorts of exceptions that template implementors don't understand.

There are several different levels of exception safety. They are described in terms of guarantees to the calling code. These guarantees are:

Basic guarantee

If exceptions occur in a function (resulting from an operation you perform or the call of another function), it will not leak resources. The code state will be *consistent* (i.e., it can still be used correctly), but it will not necessarily leave in a known state. For example: A member function should add 10 items to a container, but an exception propagates through it. The container is still usable; maybe no objects were inserted, maybe all 10 were, or perhaps every other object was added.

Strong guarantee

This is far more strict than the basic guarantee. If an exception propagates through your code, the program state remains completely unchanged. No object is altered, no global variables changed, nothing. In the example above, nothing was inserted into the container.

Nothrow guarantee

The final guarantee is the most restrictive: that an operation can *never* throw an exception. If we are exception neutral, then this implies the function cannot do anything else that might throw an exception.

Which guarantee you provide is entirely your choice. The more restrictive the guarantee, the more widely (re)usable the code is. In order to implement the strong guarantee, you will generally need a number of functions providing the nothrow guarantee.

Most notably, every destructor you write *must* honor the nothrow guarantee.* Otherwise, all exception handling bets are off. In the presence of an exception, object destructors are called automatically as the stack is unwound. Raising an exception while handling an exception is not permissible.

---

*That's the case in C++ and Java, at least. C# stupidly called ~X() a *destructor*, even though it was a finalizer in disguise. Throwing an exception in a C# destructor has different implications.

---

the call stack. This makes exceptions a tidier and safer alternative to hand-crafted error-handling code. However, throwing exceptions through sloppy code can lead to memory leaks and problems with resource cleanup.[2] You must take care to write *exception-safe* code. The sidebar explains what this means in more detail.

The code that handles an exception is distinct from the code that raises it, and it may be arbitrarily far away. Exceptions are usually provided by OO languages, where errors are defined by a hierarchy of exception classes.

---

[2] For example, you could allocate a block of memory and then exit early as an exception propagates through. The allocated memory would leak. This kind of problem makes writing code in the face of exceptions a complex business.

A handler can elect to catch a quite specific class of error (by accepting a leaf class) or a more general category of error (by accepting a base class). Exceptions are particularly useful for signaling errors in a constructor.

Exceptions don't come for free; the language support incurs a performance penalty. In practice, this isn't significant and only manifests around exception-handling statements—exception handlers reduce the compiler's optimization opportunities. This doesn't mean that exceptions are flawed; their expense is justified compared to the cost of not doing any error handling!

Signals

Signals are a more extreme reporting mechanism, largely used for errors sent by the execution environment to the running program. The operating system traps a number of exceptional events, like a *floating point exception* triggered by the maths coprocessor. These well-defined error events are delivered to the application in signals that interrupt the program's normal flow of execution, jumping into a nominated *signal handler* function. Your program could receive a signal at any time, and the code must be able to cope with this. When the signal handler completes, program execution continues at the point it was interrupted.

Signals are the software equivalent of a hardware interrupt. They are a Unix concept, now provided on most platforms (a basic version is part of the ISO C standard [ISO99]). The operating system provides sensible default handlers for each signal, some of which do nothing, others of which abort the program with a neat error message. You can override these with your own handler.

The defined C signal events include program termination, execution suspend/continue requests, and math errors. Some environments extend the basic list with many more events.

Detecting Errors

How you detect an error obviously depends on the mechanism reporting it. In practical terms, this means:

Return values
You determine whether a function failed by looking at its return code. This failure test is bound tightly to the act of calling the function; by making the call, you are implicitly checking its success. Whether or not you do anything with that information is up to you.

Error status variables
After calling a function, you must inspect the error status variable. If it follows C's errno model of operation, you don't actually need to test for errors after every single function call. First reset errno, and then call any number of standard library functions back-to-back. Afterward, inspect errno. If it contains an error value, then one of those functions failed. Of course, you don't know what fell over, but if you don't care, then this is a streamlined error-detection approach.

Exceptions

If an exception propagates out of a subordinate function, you can choose to catch and handle it or to ignore it and let the exception flow up a level. You can only make an informed choice when you know what kinds of exceptions might be thrown. You'll only know this if it has been documented (and if you trust the documentation).

Java's exception implementation places this documentation in the code itself. The programmer has to write an *exception specification* for every method, describing what it can throw; it is a part of the function's signature. Java is the only mainstream language to enforce this approach. You cannot leak an exception that isn't in the list, because the compiler performs static checking to prevent it.[3]

Signals

There's only one way to detect a signal: Install a hander for it. There's no obligation. You can also choose not to install any signal handlers at all and accept the default behavior.

As various pieces of code converge in a large system, you will probably need to detect errors in more than one way, even within a single function. Whichever detection mechanism you use, the key point is this:

KEY CONCEPT   *Never ignore any errors that might be reported to you. If an error report channel exists, it's there for a reason.*

It is good practice to always write error-detection scaffolding—even if an error has no implication for the rest of your code. This makes it clear to a maintenance programmer that you know a function may fail and have consciously chosen to ignore any failures.

When you let an exception propagate through your code, you are not ignoring it—you *can't* ignore an exception. You are allowing it to be handled by a higher level. The philosophy of exception handling is quite different in this respect. It's less clear what the most appropriate way to document this is—should you write a try/catch block that simply rethrows the exception, should you write a comment claiming that the code *is* exception safe, or should you do nothing? I'd favor documenting the exception behavior.

Handling Errors

> *Love truth, and pardon error.*
> *—Voltaire*

Errors happen. We've seen how to discover them and when to do so. The question now is: What do you do about them? This is the hard part. The answer largely depends on circumstance and the gravity of an error—whether it's possible to rectify the problem and retry the operation or to carry on regardless. Often there is no such luxury; the error may even

---

[3] C++ also supports exception specifications, but leaves their use optional. It's idiomatic to avoid them—for performance reasons, among others. Unlike Java, they are enforced at run time.

herald the beginning of the end. The best you can do is clean up and exit sharply, before anything else goes wrong.

To make this kind of decision, you must be informed. You need to know a few key pieces of information about the error:

Where it came from
> This is quite distinct from where it's going to be handled. Is the source a core system component or a peripheral module? This information may be encoded in the error report; if not, you can figure it out manually.

What you were trying to do
> What provoked the error? This may give a clue toward any remedial action. Error reporting seldom contains this kind of information, but you can figure out which function was called from the context.

Why it went wrong
> What is the nature of the problem? You need to know exactly what happened, not just a general *class* of error. How much of the erroneous operation completed? *All* or *none* are nice answers, but generally, the program will be in some indeterminate state between the two.

When it happened
> This is the locality of the error in time. Has the system only just failed, or is a problem two hours old finally being felt?

The severity of the error
> Some problems are more serious than others, but when detected, one error is equivalent to another—you can't continue without understanding and managing the problem. Error severity is usually determined by the caller, based on how easy it will be to recover or work around the error.

How to fix it
> This may be obvious (e.g., insert a floppy disk and retry) or not (e.g., you need to modify the function parameters so they are consistent). More often than not, you have to infer this knowledge from the other information you have.

Given this depth of information, you can formulate a strategy to handle each error. Forgetting to insert a handler for any potential error will lead to a bug, and it might turn out to be a bug that is hard to exercise and hard to track down—so think about every error condition carefully.

When to Deal with Errors

When should you handle each error? This can be separate from when it's detected. There are two schools of thought.

As soon as possible
> Handle each error *as* you detect it. Since the error is handled near to its cause, you retain important contextual information, making the error-handling code clearer. This is a well-known self-documenting code

technique. Managing each error near its source means that control passes through less code in an invalid state.

This is usually the best option for functions that return error codes.

As late as possible

Alternatively, you could defer error handling for as long as possible. This recognizes that code detecting an error rarely knows what to do about it. It often depends on the context in which it is used: A missing file error may be reported to the user when loading a document but silently swallowed when hunting for a preferences file.

Exceptions are ideal for this; you can pass an exception through each level until you know how to deal with the error. This separation of detection and handling may be clearer, but it can make code more complex. It's not obvious that you are deliberately deferring error handling, and it's not clear where an error came from when you do finally handle it.

In theory, it's nice to separate "business logic" from error handling. But often you can't, as cleanup is necessarily entwined with that business logic, and it can be more tortuous to write the two separately. However, centralized error-handling code has advantages: You know where to look for it, and you can put the abort/continue policy in one place rather than scatter it through many functions.

Thomas Jefferson once declared, "Delay is preferable to error." There is truth there; the actual *existence* of error handling is far more important than *when* an error is handled. Nevertheless, choose a compromise that's close enough to prevent obscure and out-of-context error handling, while being far enough away to not cloud normal code with roundabout paths and error handling dead ends.

KEY CONCEPT *Handle each error in the most appropriate context, as soon as you know enough about it to deal with it correctly.*

Possible Reactions

You've caught an error. You're poised to handle it. What are you going to do now? Hopefully, whatever is required for correct program operation. While we can't list every recovery technique under the sun, here are the common reactions to consider.

Logging

Any reasonably large project should already be employing a logging facility. It allows you to collect important trace information, and is an entry point for the investigation of nasty problems.

The log exists to record interesting events in the life of the program, to allow you to delve into its inner workings and reconstruct paths of execution. For this reason, all errors you encounter should be detailed in the program log; they are some of the most interesting and telling events of all. Aim to capture all pertinent information—as much of the previous list as you can.

For really obscure errors that predict catastrophic disaster, it may be a good idea to get the program to "phone home"—to transmit either a snapshot of itself or a copy of the error log to the developers for further investigation.

What you do *after* logging is another matter.

Reporting

A program should only report an error to the user when there's nothing left to do. The user does not need to be bombarded by a thousand small nuggets of useless information or badgered by a raft of pointless questions. Save the interaction for when it's really vital. Don't report when you encounter a recoverable situation. By all means, log the event, but keep quiet about it. Provide a mechanism that enables users to read the event log if you think one day they might care.

There *are* some problems that only the user can fix. For these, it is good practice to report the problem immediately, in order to allow the user the best chance to resolve the situation or else decide how to continue.

Of course, this kind of reporting depends on whether or not the program is interactive. Deeply embedded systems are expected to cope on their own; it's hard to pop up a dialog box on a washing machine.

Recovery

Sometimes your only course of action is to stop immediately. But not all errors spell doom. If your program saves a file, one day the disk will fill up, and the save operation will fail. The user expects your program to continue happily, so be prepared.

If your code encounters an error and doesn't know what to do about it, pass the error upward. It's more than likely your caller will have the ability to recover.

Ignore

I only include this for completeness. Hopefully by now you've learned to scorn the very suggestion of ignoring an error. If you choose to forget all about handling it and to just continue with your fingers crossed, *good luck*. This is where most of the bugs in any software package will come from. Ignoring an error whose occurrence may cause the system to misbehave inevitably leads to hours of debugging.

You can, however, write code that allows you to *do nothing* when an error crops up. Is that a blatant contradiction? No. It is possible to write code that copes with an inconsistent world, that can carry on correctly in the face of an error—but it often gets quite convoluted. If you adopt this approach, you must make it obvious in the code. Don't risk having it misinterpreted as ignorant and incorrect.

KEY CONCEPT *Ignoring errors does not save time. You'll spend far longer working out the cause of bad program behavior than you ever would have spent writing the error handler.*

Propagate

When a subordinate function call fails, you probably can't carry on, but you might not know what else to do. The only option is to clean up and propagate the error report upward. You have options. There are two ways to propagate an error:

- Export the same error information you were fed (return the same reason code or propagate exceptions).

- Reinterpret the information, sending a more meaningful message to the next level up (return a different reason code or catch and wrap up exceptions).

Ask yourself this question: Does the error relate to a concept exposed through the module interface? If so, it's okay to propagate that same error. Otherwise, recast it in the appropriate light, choosing an error report that makes sense in the context of your module's interface. This is a good self-documenting code technique.

Code Implications

Show me the code! Let's spend some time investigating the implications of error handling in our code. As we'll see, it is not easy to write good error handling that doesn't twist and warp the underlying program logic.

The first piece of code we'll look at is a common error handling structure. Yet it isn't a particularly intelligent approach for writing error-tolerant code. The aim is to call three functions sequentially—each of which may fail—and perform some intermediate calculations along the way. Spot the problems with this:

```
void nastyErrorHandling()
{
    if (operationOne())
    {
        ... do something ...
        if (operationTwo())
        {
            ... do something else ...
            if (operationThree())
            {
                ... do more ...
            }
        }
    }
}
```

Syntactically it's fine; the code will work. Practically, it's an unpleasant style to maintain. The more operations you need to perform, the more deeply nested the code gets and the harder it is to read. This kind of error handling quickly leads to a rat's nest of conditional statements. It doesn't reflect the actions of the code very well; each intermediate calculation could be considered the same level of importance, yet they are nested at different levels.

CRAFTING ERROR MESSAGES

Inevitably, your code will encounter errors that the user must sort out. Human intervention may be the only option; your code can't insert a floppy disk or switch on the printer by itself. (If it can, you'll make a fortune!)

If you're going to whine at the user, there are a few general points to bear in mind:

- Users don't think like programmers, so present information the way *they'd* expect. When displaying the free space on a disk, you might report Disk space: 10K. But if there's no space left, a zero could be misread as OK—and the user will not be able to fathom why he can't save a file when the program says everything's fine.

- Make sure your messages aren't too cryptic. *You* might understand them, but can your computer-illiterate granny? (It doesn't matter if your granny won't use this program—someone with a lower intellect almost certainly will.)

- Don't present meaningless error codes. No user knows what to do when faced with an Error code 707E. It is, however, valuable to provide such codes as "additional info"—they can be quoted to tech support or looked up more easily on a web search.

- Distinguish dire errors from mere warnings. Incorporate this information in the message text (perhaps with an Error: prefix), and emphasize it in message boxes with an accompanying icon.

- Only ask a question (even a simple one like *Continue: Yes/No?*) if the user fully understands the ramifications of each choice. Explain it if necessary, and make it clear what the consequence of each answer is.

What you present to the user will be determined by interface constraints and application or OS style guides. If your company has user interface engineers, then it's their job to make these decisions. Work with them.

Can we avoid these problems? Yes—there are a few alternatives. The first variant flattens the nesting. It is semantically equivalent, but it introduces *some* new complexity, since flow control is now dependent on the value of a new status variable, ok:

```
void flattenedErrorHandling()
{
    bool ok = operationOne();
    if (ok)
    {
        ... do something ...
        ok = operationTwo();
    }
    if (ok)
    {
        ... do something else ...
        ok = operationThree();
    }
    if (ok)
    {
        ... do more ...
    }
```

```
    if (!ok)
    {
        ... clean up after errors ...
    }
}
```

We've also added an opportunity to clean up after any errors. Is that sufficient to mop up all failures? Probably not; the necessary cleanup may depend on how far we got through the function before lightening struck. There are two cleanup approaches:

- Perform a little cleanup after each operation that may fail, then return early. This inevitably leads to duplication of cleanup code. The more work you've done, the more you have to clean up, so each exit point will need to do gradually more unpicking.

  If each operation in our example allocates some memory, each early-exit point will have to release all allocations made to date. The further in, the more releases. That will lead to some quite dense and repetitive error-handling code, which makes the function far larger and far harder to understand.

- Write the cleanup code once, at the end of the function, but write it in such a way as to only clean up what's dirty. This is neater, but if you inadvertently insert an early return in the middle of the function, the cleanup code will be bypassed.

If you're not overly concerned about writing *Single Entry, Single Exit (SESE)* functions, this next example removes the reliance on a separate control flow variable.[4] We do lose the cleanup code again, though. Simplicity renders this a better description of the actual intent:

```
void shortCircuitErrorHandling()
{
    if (!operationOne()) return;
    ... do something ...
    if (!operationTwo()) return;
    ... do something else ...
    if (!operationThree()) return;
    ... do more ...
}
```

A combination of this short-circuit exit with the requirement for cleanup leads to the following approach, especially seen in low-level systems code. Some people advocate it as the *only* valid use for the maligned goto. I'm still not convinced.

---

[4] Although this clearly isn't SESE, I contend that the previous example isn't, either. There *is* only one exit point, at the end, but the contrived control flow is simulating early exit—it *might as well* have multiple exits. This is a good example of how being bound by a rule like SESE can lead to bad code, unless you think carefully about what you're doing.

```
void gotoHell()
{
    if (!operationOne()) goto error;
    ... do something ...
    if (!operationTwo()) goto error;
    ... do something else ...
    if (!operationThree()) goto error;
    ... do more ...
    return;
error:
    ... clean up after errors ...
}
```

You can avoid such monstrous code in C++ using *Resource Acquisition Is Initialization (RAII)* techniques like smart pointers. (Stroustrup 97) This has the bonus of providing exception safety—when an exception terminates your function prematurely, resources are automatically deallocated. These techniques avoid a lot of the problems we've seen above, moving complexity to a separate flow of control.

The same example using exceptions would look like this (in C++, Java, and C#), presuming that all subordinate functions do not return error codes but instead throw exceptions:

```
void exceptionalHandling()
{
    try
    {
        operationOne();
        ... do something ...
        operationTwo();
        ... do something else ...
        operationThree();
        ... do more ...
    }
    catch (...)
    {
        ... clean up after errors ...
    }
}
```

This is only a basic exception example, but it shows just how neat exceptions can be. A sound code design might not need the try/catch block at all if it ensures that no resource is leaked and leaves error handling to a higher level. But alas, writing good code in the face of exceptions requires an understanding of principles beyond the scope of this chapter.

Raising Hell

We've put up with other people's errors for long enough. It's time to turn the tables and play the bad guy: Let's raise some errors. When writing a function, erroneous things will happen that you'll need to signal to your caller. Make sure you do—don't silently swallow any failure. Even if you're sure that the caller won't know what to do in the face of the problem, it *must* remain informed. Don't write code that lies and pretends to be doing something it's not.

Which reporting mechanism should you use? It's largely an architectural choice; obey the project conventions and the common language idioms. In languages with the facility, it is common to favor exceptions, but only use them if the rest of the project does. Java and C# really leave you with no choice; exceptions are buried deep in their execution run times. A C++ architecture may choose to forego this facility to achieve portability with platforms that have no exception support or to interface with older C code.

We've already seen strategies for propagating errors from subordinate function calls. Our main concern here is reporting fresh problems encountered during execution. How you determine these errors is your own business, but when reporting them, consider the following:

- Have you cleaned up appropriately first? Reliable code doesn't leak resources or leave the world in an inconsistent state, even when an error occurs, unless it's *really* unavoidable. If you do either of these things, it must be documented carefully. Consider what will happen the next time your code is called if this error has manifested. Ensure it will still work.

- Don't leak inappropriate information to the outside world in your error reports. Only return useful information that the caller understands and can act on.

- Use exceptions correctly. Don't throw an exception for unusual return values—the rare but not erroneous cases. Only use exceptions to signal circumstances where a function is not able to meet its contract. Don't use them non-idiomatically (i.e., for flow control).

- Consider using assertions (see "Constraints" on page 16) if you're trapping an error that should never happen in the normal course of program execution, a genuine programming error. Exceptions are a valid choice for this too—some assertion mechanisms can be configured to throw exceptions when they trigger.

- If you can pull forward any tests to compile time, then do so. The sooner you detect and rectify an error, the less hassle it can cause.

- Make it hard for people to ignore your errors. Given half a chance, someone *will* use your code badly. Exceptions are good for this—you have to act deliberately to hide an exception.

What kind of errors should you be looking out for? This obviously depends on what the function is doing. Here's a checklist of the general kinds of error checks you should make in each function:

- Check all function parameters. Ensure you have been given correct and consistent input. Consider using assertions for this, depending on how strictly your contract was written. (Is it an offense to supply bad parameters?)

- Check that invariants are satisfied at interesting points in execution.

- Check all values from external sources for validity before you use them. File contents and interactive input must be sensible, with no missing pieces.

- Check the return status of all system and other subordinate function calls.

AN EXCEPTION TO THE RULE

Exceptions are a powerful error reporting mechanism. Used well, they can simplify your code greatly while helping you to write robust software. In the wrong hands, though, they are a deadly weapon.

I once worked on a project where it was routine for programmers to break a while loop or end recursion by throwing an exception, using it as a non-local goto. It's an intersting idea, and kind of cute when you first see it. But this behavior is nothing more than an abuse of exceptions: It isn't what exceptions are idiomatically used for. More than one critical bug was caused by a maintenance programmer not understanding the flow of control through a complex, magically terminated loop.

Follow the idioms of your language, and don't write cute code for the sake of it.

Managing Errors

The common principle uniting the raising and handling of errors is to have a consistent strategy for dealing with failure, wherever it manifests. These are general considerations for managing the occurrence, detection, and handling of program errors:

- Avoid things that *could* cause errors. Can you do something that is guaranteed to work, instead? For example, avoid allocation errors by reserving enough resource beforehand. With an assured pool of memory, your routine cannot suffer memory restrictions. Naturally, this will only work when you know how much resource you need up front, but you often do.

- Define the program or routine's expected behavior under abnormal circumstances. This determines how robust the code needs to be and therefore how thorough your error handling should be. Can a function silently generate bad output, subscribing to the historic *GIGO* principle?[5]

---

[5] That is, *Garbage In, Garbage Out*—feed it trash, and it will happily spit out trash.

- Clearly define which components are responsible for handling which errors. Make it explicit in the module's interface. Ensure that your client knows what will always work and what may one day fail.

- Check your programming practice: *When* do you write error-handling code? Don't put it off until later; you'll forget to handle something. Don't wait until your development testing highlights problems before writing handlers—that's not an engineering approach.

KEY CONCEPT *Write all error detection and handling* now, *as you write the code that may fail. Don't put it off until later. If you must be evil and defer handling, at least write the detection scaffolding now.*

- When trapping an error, have you found a symptom or a cause? Consider whether you've discovered the source of a problem that needs to be rectified here or if you've discovered a symptom of an earlier problem. If it's the latter, then don't write reams of handling code here, put that in a more appropriate (earlier) error handler.

In a Nutshell

> *To err is human; to repent, divine; to persist, devilish.*
> —*Benjamin Franklin*

To err *is* human (but computers seem quite good at it, too). To handle these errors is divine.

Every line of code you write must be balanced by appropriate and thorough error checking and handling. A program without rigorous error handling will not be stable. One day an obscure error may occur, and the program will fall over as a result.

Handling errors and failure cases is hard work. It bogs programming down in the mundane details of the Real World. However, it's absolutely essential. As much as 90 percent of the code you write handles exceptional circumstances. (Bentley 82) That's a surprising statistic, so write code *expecting* to put far more effort into the things that can go wrong than the things that will go right.

Good programmers . . .	Bad programmers . . .
• Combine their good intentions with good coding practices	• Take a haphazard approach to writing code, with neither thought to nor review of what they're doing
• Write the error-handling code *as* they write the main code	• Ignore the errors that arise as they write code
• Are *thorough* in the code they write, covering every error possibility	• End up conducting lengthy debugging sessions to track down program crashes, because they never considered error conditions in the first place

See Also

Chapter 1: On the Defensive
Handing errors in context is one of the many defensive programming techniques.

Chapter 4: The Write Stuff
Self-documenting code ensures that error handling is integral to the code narrative.

Chapter 9: Finding Fault
Unhandled error conditions will manifest as bugs in the code. Here's how to squash them. (It's best to avoid them in the first place, though.)

Get Thinking

A detailed discussion of these questions can be found in the "Answers and Discussion" section on page 487.

Mull It Over

1. Are *return values* and *exceptions* equivalent error reporting mechanisms? Prove it.

2. What different implementations of *tuple* return types can you think of? Don't limit yourself to a single programming language. What are the pros and cons of using tuples as a return value?

3. How do exception implementations differ between languages?

4. Signals are an old-school Unix mechanism. Are they still needed now that we have modern techniques like exceptions?

5. What is the best code structure for error handling?

6. How should you handle errors that occur in your error-handling code?

Getting Personal

1. How thorough is the error handling in your current codebase? How does this contribute to the stability of the program?

2. Do you naturally consider error handling as you write code, or do you find it a distraction, preferring to come back to it later?

3. Go to the last (reasonably sized) function you wrote or worked on, and perform a careful review of the code. Find every abnormal occurence and potential error situation. How many of these were actually handled in your code?

    Now get someone else to review it. Don't be shy! Did they find any more? Why? What does this tell you about the code you're working on?

4. Do you find it easier to manage and reason about error conditions using *return values* or *exceptions*? Are you sure you know what is involved in writing exception-safe code?

PART II

THE SECRET LIFE OF CODE

This section investigates the art and craft of developing code—the daily activities of programming life. Although these topics aren't closely guarded secrets, you rarely hear expert discussion or see much written about them. Even so, mastering each practice is crucial if you want to write good programs; the code craftsman has a thorough understanding of all of these subjects.

We'll look at:

Chapter 7: The Programmer's Toolbox
A survey of the tools of our trade and how you should use them.

Chapter 8: Testing Times
No code is complete until it has been proved fit for purpose; until it has been tested. Here we look at the techniques for doing so.

Chapter 9: Finding Fault
Dealing with the inevitable: How to find and remove bugs in your code.

Chapter 10: The Code That Jack Built
"Building" code: The process of converting source code into executable programs.

Chapter 11: The Need for Speed

A look at the gory details of code optimization. What, why, when, and how.

Chapter 12: An Insecurity Complex

The thorny topic of software security—how to protect your code from willful abuse and malicious attack.

These are fundamental aspects of code construction. With the pressures and time constraints of the software factory, they are more than essential skills—they're survival tactics. With experience, they become second nature, so you can spend your precious time focusing on more pressing concerns: the architecture of your next system, the customer's changing requirements, and who's going to fetch your next cup of espresso.

THE PROGRAMMER'S TOOLBOX

Using Tools to Construct Software

Perilous to us all are the devices of an art deeper than we possess ourselves.

—J.R.R. Tolkien

To be a productive craftsman, you need a good set of tools. The contents of a plumber's toolbox will support him in whatever task he encounters, or else you wouldn't call him the next time your taps explode.

Not only the *existence* but also the *quality* of these tools is vital; a good craftsman can be let down by poor tools. If the compression valves are bad, there will be water everywhere, no matter how good your plumber is.

Of course, it's your *use* of these tools that sets you apart as a master craftsman. The tools, by themselves, will achieve nothing. Before power tools, carpenters were perfectly able to craft exquisite furniture. The tools were more basic, but their skill with them produced things of beauty.

The same is true of programming. To do a good job, you need to be supported by an appropriate kit of tools; tools that you have confidence in, know how to use, and are fit for the jobs you'll encounter. It takes a skilled craftsman, good tools, *and* mastery of those tools to craft great code.

This is serious stuff. How you use your tools can set you apart as a truly productive programmer. In extreme cases, these tools could provide the shortcut that determines your project's success or failure. The relentless pace of the software factory means that you should cling tightly to anything that will help you produce better code and produce it more quickly and reliably.

Other chapters cover issues that relate to particular tools. Here we'll broach the subject of *software tools* as a whole. Programming is a discipline that simply can't do without tools. From day to day, we use tools without much of a thought, taking the compiler for granted in much the same way you'd take a can opener for granted—it's fine while it works, but as soon as it goes wrong (or you need to open an oddly shaped can) you're stuck, no matter how fancy the can opener is. A cheap, basic can opener that works is better than some pretentious contraption that doesn't.

What Is a Software Tool?

We use a wide range of tools to construct software; they are *programs that build programs*—if that isn't too philosophical. Everything we use to create software is a tool of some form. Some tools help you write code. Some help you write *good* code. Some help sort out the mess of code you just created.

They come in all shapes and sizes and work in different ways. Obviously, the platform and environment they inhabit is a factor, but they also differ in:

Complexity

Some tools are elaborate environments with many, many features and incredible configurability. Some are minuscule utilities for a single task. Each approach has its pros and cons:

- A feature-rich tool is cool, when you've *finally* learned how to get it to make coffee and bring you doughnuts at the same time. If the many magical features make it hard to use, then it's less helpful.

- Simple tools are easier to learn; it's obvious what they do. You just end up with a lot of them, one for each task. But if you string them together, there are a lot of interface points, so they don't always work together seamlessly.

Different tools have different scopes, performing everything from very specific tasks (searching files for text strings) to entire projects (a collaborative project management environment).

Frequency of use

Some tools are used constantly; we can't live without them. Others are only dusted off once in a blue moon, but they're invaluable when you need them.

Interface

Some tools have pretty *graphical user interfaces (GUIs)*. Some are more basic, driven by a *command-line interface (CLI)* and directing their output to a file. Which you prefer depends on how your brain is wired and what you're used to.

Windows utilities tend to be graphical with no command-line access. The standard Unix utilities are the opposite, which makes them easier to automate and integrate into larger tools using scripts. The interface alters the way you harness a tool's power.

Integration

Some tools fit into a larger toolchain, often subsumed in a graphical *integrated development environment (IDE)*. Stand-alone command-line utilities tend to generate plaintext output in a format suitable as input to other tools, acting primarily as data filters.

Monolithic GUI interfaces can be very comfortable to use, and the integration can make you incredibly productive. On the other hand, they take time to set up just as you'd like them, and they seldom offer the full power of more manual command-line tools. But although they are incredibly powerful, the discrete Unix tools all have different cryptic interfaces that make them hard to use.

Cost

There are many excellent free tools.[1] However, you often get what you pay for. Free tools tend to have have poorer documentation, less support, or a smaller feature set. This doesn't always hold true, though. Some free tools are far superior to their commercial counterparts.

You can pay as much as you want for any type of tool, but a higher price tag doesn't guarantee a better product. I've worked with some fantastically expensive tools that were spectacularly poor. Which leads on to . . .

Quality

Some tools are really good. Some tools are really bad. I have a couple of critical tools that I'd gladly never see again; they do the job, but only barely, and are permanently on the brink of a crash. But without them, I can't produce the code I get paid for. How often have I been tempted to rewrite them myself? I can keep on dreaming.

You'll pick tools based on these characteristics, making appropriate compromises. Although it's important to get accustomed to your usual tool set, to learn it and to be productive with it, avoid the temptation to become religious about it. Most Windows users despise Unix-style development, while Unix hackers look down on Windows coders because they can't handle the command line. Get over it.

I challenge you to try working in a different environment on a reasonably large project. It will help you fully understand what makes a good toolchain and help you gain a real "world view" of software tools.

---

[1] *Free* has two meanings in the software world: free as in *beer* (the tool won't cost you anything to obtain) and free as in *speech* (open source software whose code you can view and modify). Which *free* is more important depends on how much of an idealist you are. See "Licenses" on page 361.

Why Worry About Tools?

It's impossible to create programs without a core set of software tools; you'd be stuck without an editor or compiler. There are other tools that you *can* get by without, but that are still genuinely useful. In order to improve your productivity, code quality, and craftsmanship, it's good to pay a little attention to the tools you're currently using and find out what they can really do.

When you understand how your tools work and which tool to use for which job, you are better able to produce code that works properly—and produce it more quickly. Smarter tool use will make you a smarter programmer.

KEY CONCEPT   *Know your common tools inside out. A little time invested to become proficient with them will quickly pay off.*

Let's be clear about why we actually use tools: Tools don't do our work *for us*—they *enable* us to do our work. The quality of software is always determined by the competence of its programmer. Remind yourself of that the next time your compiler spits out pages of error messages. You wrote the code, dimwit!

Programmers have wildly varying attitudes with regard to selecting and using tools. There's probably some deep psychological reasoning behind it all—something to do with whether you're an Evil Genius or not. On encountering a new lengthy task:

- Some programmers laboriously complete it by hand.
- Others write a tool in a scripting language to do the job automatically.
- Others spend hours searching for a pre-written tool to do the job for them.

Given a tool that *might* solve the problem:

- Some programmers fiddle with it until they get something near enough to what they want.
- Others carefully read the documentation to find out exactly what can be done and *then* start to use it.

Which the right approach? Well, it depends. Part of becoming a mature programmer is understanding how different situations require different solutions and applying the right tools for the right job. Everyone is different and everyone works differently—your colleagues may be most productive using different tools than the ones that are your favorites. But if you saw someone converting his C code into assembly by hand on a day-to-day basis, you'd question his sanity.

Invest your time and money in tools practically. Think about how you're going to use a tool. Search for or write a new tool only when the time it will take to do so *will* pay off. Don't spend a week writing a tool that will only save you one hour every month. Do spend a week writing a tool that will save you one hour every day.

KEY CONCEPT   *Adopt a pragmatic approach to software tools—use them only when they'll make your life easier.*

Power Tools

Since programming and tools go hand in hand, in order to be a super-programmer, you need to be a super–tool user. What does that mean?

First, it's important to have a good understanding of which tools are around. In the next section, we will run down a list of the common tools that every programmer should have on hand. You don't need to know every tool on the market; it makes for incredibly dull dinner party conversation, anyway. Just knowing the general categories of tools that exist, rather than specific products, is the important step forward. That will help you choose between finding a tool for a particular task, writing the tool yourself, or doing the task by hand.

Take the time to get informed. Check out where you can obtain some of these tools—there are shops that specialize in selling software tools and plenty of download sites on the Internet. Maybe you already have some installed but never needed them, or you didn't appreciate how useful they were. Learn what you can expect tools to do for you; it will prepare you for good tool usage.

KEY CONCEPT   *Know the sorts of tools that are available. Make sure you know where to get them, even if you don't need them right now.*

Be prepared to try a new tool and to take time to learn it; this is a healthy attitude. You may be forced to find new tools if you start a new project, move to a new platform, encounter a new kind of problem, or find that your old tools have become deprecated. But don't wait to be pushed—make sure that right now, you're using the best tools you can get your hands on.

Devote a portion of your time to honing your tools skills—just as you'd spend time reading a techie book or magazine or taking a professional training course. This stuff is important, so invest in it accordingly.

Here are a few simple steps to become a tool power user. For each weapon in your software construction arsenal . . .

Understand What It Can Do

Find out the feature set—what it can *really* do, not what you think it *should be able* to do. Even if you don't know how to wring out every last drop of goodness (maybe you'd have to look up the more esoteric command-line parameters), knowing what it's capable of will be helpful.

Are there particular things the tool *can't* do? Perhaps it doesn't support some facilities provided by its counterparts. Understand these limitations, so you know when to shop around for something better.

Learn How to Drive it

Just because you've run the tool without generating an error doesn't mean it has done *exactly* what you wanted it to do. You must know how to use it properly and be confident that you can make it do your bidding.

How does the tool fit into the whole toolchain? This will affect how you use it. For example, Unix tools can be used as sequential filters by *piping* them together—splicing small individual tools into a larger utility.[2] Understanding how to harness the power of each tool and learning about how they interoperate lifts your tool usage a notch.

Figure out the best way to use each tool—it might not be by calling it directly or by clicking somewhere in the GUI interface. Can it be triggered automatically? A compiler is often invoked through a build system, rather than manually.

Know What Tasks It's Good For

Know how each tool fits in the context of the other available tools. For example, I can set up keystroke recording macros, which allow me to save time on repetitive actions, in my text editor. Some of these alterations could also be done using a magic sed invocation.[3] However, it's better to use the keystroke macros in this context—I'm already using the editor and so it's quicker to fire them off.

You might not know how to use yacc,[4] but if you ever need to write a parser, you'll save yourself loads of effort knowing it's there.

KEY CONCEPT   *Use the right tool for the right task. Don't crack a walnut with a sledgehammer.*

Check That It's Working

Everyone becomes the victim of bad tools at some point. Your code doesn't work, but no matter how long you search for the errant behavior, there's no explanation. In desperation, you'll test random things—checking that the wind is blowing in the right direction and the light fittings have been secured correctly. Several hours later, you'll find a flaky tool doing something peculiar.

Compilers can produce faulty code. Build systems can get dependencies wrong. Libraries harbor bugs. Learn how to check for obvious failures before you rip out too much of your own hair.

Having access to the source code for your tools can be instrumental in diagnosing any problems you encounter, allowing you to work out exactly what a tool is doing. This might be a deciding factor in your choice of tool set.

---

[2] If you don't know much about this, I urge you to read up on it. The Unix command man bash is a good place to start; search the man pages for *pipelines*.

[3] sed is a stream editor command-line utility, explained in the next section.

[4] A parser generator. Don't worry—it's explained later too.

Have a Clear Route to Find Out More

You don't have to know it all. The trick is to know someone who does!

Find out where the tool's documentation is. Who provides support? How do you get more information? Look for manuals, release notes, online resources, internal help files, and man pages. Know where they are and how to access them on demand. Do the online versions have useful search tools and good indexing?

Find Out When New Versions Appear

Tools seem to develop at an incredible rate—in this industry, technology changes fast. Some tools develop much faster than others. You've barely installed the latest widgetizer when the authors release a newer version with a longer red stripe down the side.

It's important to stay informed about the tools you use so that you don't get out of date and end up with a potentially buggy and unsupported tool kit. But this should be done cautiously; don't blindly chase the latest version. The bleeding edge can be painful!

New versions may have new bugs and new higher prices. Adopt upgrades if they provide significant fixes and have been proven stable. Test first— sanity check the new tool on your old code to make sure that it behaves itself.

KEY CONCEPT   *Keep up to date with the latest developments in your tools, but don't upgrade carelessly.*

Which Tools?

There's a staggering array of software development tools. Over the years they have been developed to scratch particular itches, the needs that often crop up. When a task has been done many times, you can bet that someone has written a tool for it.

Exactly what comprises your tool kit will depend on your line of work. The available tools for embedded platforms are rarely as rich as those for desktop applications. We'll consider the common components below. Some are really obvious; others are less so.

While we'll look individually at each class of tool, don't forget that modern IDEs collect these disparate programs into a single, streamlined interface. This is undoubtedly convenient, but it's important to understand how each tool stands on its own, for these reasons:

- You'll know how to get the best from each feature that's available.
- You'll know what useful features your IDE lacks.

Most IDEs are modular—you can substitute one component with a better alternative and plug in facilities that are not available right out of the box. Learn what tool varieties are around, and you'll improve your IDE experience.

Source Editing Tools

A potter's medium is clay; a sculptor's, stone; and a programmer's, code. This is the fundamental thing we work with, so it's important to pick excellent tools to help us write, edit, and investigate source code.

Source Code Editor

The editor is probably your most important tool, even more important than a compiler. The compiler faces the computer, whereas the editor faces *you*. And you're the one driving. This is where you'll spend most of your programming life, so pick a good editor and learn to use it *really* well. Being productive with your text editor will dramatically improve how you write code.

KEY CONCEPT *Your choice of code editor is vital: It has a huge impact on how you write code.*

The One True Source Editor is an age-old debate that doesn't need to be stirred here, but you should select an editor that you are comfortable with and does what you require. Just because an editor is embedded in your visual IDE does not mean that it is the best editor for you. On the other hand, you may find that having it integrated is an incredible boon. For source code editing, I require at least the following from my editor:

- Comprehensive syntax coloring (with support for *many* languages—since I use many languages)
- Simple syntax checking (e.g., highlighting mismatched brackets)
- Good *incremental search* facilities (an interactive form of find that searches as you type)
- Keyboard macro recording
- Highly configurable
- Works across every platform that I use

My requirements and choice of editor may not be the same as yours, but that seems like a fair list of the most important facilities. I don't mind spending a little time learning how to get the best out of all these features. It's worth it if it makes me productive.

Depending on the type of work you're doing, you may find other types of editors useful. There are binary file editors (usually displaying file contents in hexadecimal; they're commonly called *hex editors*) and editors devoted to specific file formats, for example XML file editors.

Vim and Emacs are the infamous Unix-land editors, available now on pretty much any platform (probably even your electric toaster). These contrast with the default editors bundled with IDEs.

Source Manipulation Tools

The Unix philosophy is characterized by a large collection of small command-line tools. GUI environments have their counterparts for each tool, but they are rarely as powerful or easy to string together. The GUI versions are far simpler to learn, though.

The following Unix commands provide powerful mechanisms to investigate and modify source code:

diff
> Compares two files and highlights the differences between them. Basic diff spits output to the console, but more sophisticated graphical versions exist. There are even editors that allow you to work on the diffed files, displaying them side by side and updating the differences as you type. Exotic diffs can compare three files at once.

sed
> Stands for *stream editor*. Sed reads files a line at a time, applying a specified conversion rule. Sed can be used to reorder items, as a global search and replace tool, or to insert patterns into lines.

awk
> Imagine sed on steroids. Awk is another pattern-matching program that can process text files. It implements a full programming language for this task, so you can write quite advanced awk scripts to perform involved manipulation.

grep
> Searches for patterns of characters in a file. These patterns are described by *regular expressions*, a form of mini-language allowing wildcard characters and flexible match criteria.

find/locate
> These tools help to find files in the filesystem. They can hunt them down by name, date, or a number of other criteria.

These are only the tip of the iceberg, and there are many other tools. wc, for example, performs word/character counting. For more gems, look into sort, paste, join, and cut.

Source Navigation Tools

Really large projects have codebases like cities. Not even the town planners intimately know each and every back street. A few taxi drivers know the best routes around. Normal citizens know their own neighborhoods fairly well. Tourists get lost as soon as they step off a bus.

There is a breed of tool to help you delve into and understand code, map it out, and perform easy searches, navigation, and cross-referencing. Some tools produce call-graph trees so you can see how control flows around the system. They may produce a graphical map or integrate with your editor to provide auto-completion, function call help, and more. This can be invaluable on large codebases or when entering a project that is well established.

Good examples of freely available tools are LXR, Doxygen, and the venerable ctags.

Revision Control

We won't dwell on source control tools here, since we cover them in "Source Control" on page 351. Suffice to say: you *must* use one, or else have a limb forcibly amputated.

Source Generation

A number of tools automatically generate source code. Some are good; some frighten me.

One example is yacc, an LALR(1)[5] parser generator. You define the input grammar rules, then use it to generate programs that can parse well-formed input matching those rules. It spits out a C code parser with hooks for you to add functionality when items are parsed. Bison is a similar tool.

There is a class of code-generating tools that helps you to design user interfaces, spitting out the workhorse back-end code. These are especially used for complex GUI tool kits like MFC. If a library requires a tool to do *this much* legwork, then it implies that the library is too complex (or fundamentally broken) in the first place. Tread with caution!

Wizards that write reams of scaffolding code that you must later revise and modify should also be treated with caution. You must honestly understand the generated code before you begin to attack it, or you'll be bitten by your own ignorance. If you rerun the wizard after modifying any generated code, all your hand-edits will be silently overwritten. Ouch.

You can even write your own scripts to spit out repetitive sections of code. Sometimes this is an indicator that your code could have been designed better. Sometimes it *is* the right technical approach. In the past, I have written Perl scripts to generate code for me automatically. Having written the generator, I trusted the code it generated. Another programmer might look at it distrustfully, like any other code wizard.

Source Beautifiers

These tools homogenize source code formatting, creating a uniform *lowest common denominator* layout. I honestly think they are more hassle than they're worth—they can destroy as much important and helpful formatting as they fix.

Code Construction Tools

We don't want to stare at pretty source code all day. The fun bit is making it do something. We do this so often that we take the following tools for granted, assuming they all work, without thinking about what's going on behind the curtain.

Compiler

Besides a source editor, this is the most used software tool. Compilers convert your source code into an executable so you can marvel at the ways

---

[5] A cryptic techie (and dull) way of saying *reasonably complex grammar*.

your program fails to work. Since this tool is used so often, it's important that you can drive it properly. Do you really know all the options and facilities that it has? Many companies have a specific *buildmaster* who ensures that the build tools are used correctly, but this isn't an excuse to be ignorant of your compiler.

- Do you understand what level of optimization to employ and how that might affect the generated code? It's important—among other things, it will determine how surprisingly the code runs in the debugger, and even which compiler bugs you enable!

- Do you compile with all warnings switched on? There really is no excuse not to (perhaps only if you're maintaining legacy code that is already riddled with warnings). The warnings highlight potential errors, and their absence gives you extra confidence in the code.

- Is the compiler standards-compliant by default? The C++ ISO standard is, (ISO 98) the 1999 C standard is, (ISO 99) the Java language is defined by, (Gosling et al. 00) and C# by the ISO standard. (ISO 05) Does the compiler have any nonstandard extensions; if so, do you know what they are and how to avoid them?

- Is it generating code for the correct CPU instruction set? You may be churning out 386-compatible code when you'll only ever run it on the latest Intel whiz-bang chip. Get your compiler to spit out the most appropriate code possible.

I NEED A TOOL . . .

You need to perform a task. It's a dull task. It's repetitive. It's the kind of thing that *must* be better for a computer to do; it would be less error prone, less tedious, and far quicker. That's what computers were invented for! How do you find out if there's something to do the job for you?

- If it's mentioned in this list, you'll know already that a tool is available.

- If it's not in the list, but you're sure that you're not the first person to have this kind of problem, there's probably a tool out there *somewhere* that will help. You'd be surprised at some of the random programs a quick web search brings up.

- If your problem seems unique, you might have to write your own program for it. See "Rolling Your Own" on page 126 for more on this.

When looking for a tool, get as much advice as you can:

- Ask others on your team if they have any experience.

- Search the web, and read appropriate newsgroups.

- Go to tools vendors.

    Given the selection of available tools, you'll need to make an informed choice based on the criteria we saw in the first section. To make this decision, you must establish your requirements. Is it important that the tool is free? Or is it more important that you can get it *now*? Should it be easy to use for everyone on the team? How often will you use it—will it justify the expense?

A *cross compiler* targets a different platform from the development machine. This is primarily used when writing embedded software (after all, it's hard to run Visual C++ on a dishwasher).

The compiler is a single part of a larger toolchain, including the linker, assembler, debugger, profiler, and other object-file manipulators.

Some popular compilers include gcc, Microsoft's Visual C++, and Borland's C++ builder.

Linker

The linker is closely allied with the compiler. It takes all the intermediate *object files* that a compiler spits out and glues them together into a single executable lump of code. The C and C++ linkers are so closely bound to the compiler that sometimes the same executable does both tasks. For Java and C# the linker is tied to the run-time environment.

When using your linker, make sure you know:

- Does it *strip* the binary? That is, does it remove debugging symbols like the names of variables and functions? These can be used by a debugger to show useful diagnostic information, but they can also significantly bloat executables and make them slow to load.

- Does it eliminate replicated code sections?

- Can you make it spit out library objects rather than executables? What control do you have over the library—can you make it *statically* or *dynamically* loaded?

Build Environment

The entire build environment is more than just a compiler and linker. The kind of build tools that we use are the Unix make program or the build portions of your IDE. They automate the compilation process. Many open source Unix projects use the autoconf and automake tools to simplify building.

Learn how to get the most out of your integrated build environment, but not at the expense of knowing how to use each individual construction tool. We'll investigate these topics in more detail in Chapter 10.

Testing Toolchain

Note that this is a code construction tool, *not* a debugging tool! Appropriate testing is vital to the production of reliable, high-quality software. It is often neglected—perhaps because it's seen as too much work, distracting attention away from the important task of writing code. This is one of the biggest threats to good software. You cannot construct a reliable piece code unless you can prove that it works correctly, and the only way to do this is to construct tests for it as you write.

There are tools that help automate unit testing, offering a skeleton into which you can place your test code. These tools can be easily integrated into your build system, so testing becomes a central part of the code construction process.

As well as automated unit testing, there are tools that generate test data and formulate test cases. There are also tools that simulate a target platform, perhaps with the ability to model particular error conditions (low memory, high load, etc.).

Debugging and Investigative Tools

These tools characterize running code and help to track down problems—both things we have seen going wrong and potential disasters waiting to pounce. We'll look at them in greater detail in "Wasp Spray, Slug Repellent, Fly Paper . . ." on page 169.

Debugger

Having a quality debugger and understanding how to use it can save you hours of development time chasing surprising behavior. It allows you to investigate paths of execution in your program, break into it, investigate variable values, set breakpoints, and generally dissect your running code. It's an order of magnitude more sophisticated than peppering programs with `printf` logging statements!

gdb is GNU's open source debugger; it has been ported to almost every conceivable platform. ddd is an accomplished graphical interface for it. Every IDE and toolchain has its own debugger.

Profiler

This tool is used when your code runs unacceptably slowly. The profiler times sections of running code and identifies the bottlenecks. It is used to find targets for *sensible* optimization; armed with its results, you won't waste effort speeding up code that is rarely executed.

Code Validators

Code validators come in two varieties: *static* and *dynamic*. The former digest code in a similar way to a compiler, inspecting your source files to identify possible problem areas and flawed language use. lint is a well-known example; it performs static checks for a series of common coding errors in C. Much of its functionality is built into modern compilers, but there are still separate tools available for extra checking.

Dynamic validators modify and instrument the code as it is compiled and then perform checking at run time. Memory allocation/bounds checkers are a good example—they ensure that all dynamically allocated memory is freed appropriately and that array accesses do not occur out of bounds.[6] These tools can save hours of legwork looking for obscure bugs. They are *much* more useful than a debugger in most situations, since they act like prevention mechanisms rather than cures: They'll find faults before they have a chance to break your program.

---

[6] More socially responsible languages, like Java, avoid this kind of problem in the language design.

Metrics Tools

These tools perform code inspection and are usually a form of static analyzer (although dynamic metric tools do exist). They produce statistical assessments of the quality of your code. While statistics can easily mislead, these tools can powerfully highlight the most brittle areas. This information can help you pick specific targets for code reviews.

Metrics are usually gathered on a per-function basis. The most basic metric is *number of lines of code*, followed by the ratio of *comments to code*. Neither really tell you anything particularly useful, but there are plenty of more interesting metrics. *Cyclomatic complexity* is a measure of the complexity of code, considering the number of decision points and potential flows of control. A high cyclomatic complexity implies unintelligible code, which is more likely to be brittle and harbor faults.

Disassembler

This peers into executables, allowing you to inspect the machine code. Debuggers do contain this kind of support, but advanced disassemblers can attempt to reconstruct code where no symbols exist, generating a high-level language reinterpretation of the binary program file.

Fault Tracking

A good fault-tracking system provides a shared database that keeps track of the bugs found in your system. It allows colleagues to report faults, query, assign, or comment on them, and eventually mark faults as fixed. It's an essential tool to ensure the quality of a product—you need to manage faults systematically, or they'll slip through your fingers, and you'll release a flawed product. Capturing and storing this information is also useful when looking back over the project history.

Language Support Tools

To write in a high-level language, you need a lot of support. The language implementation provides everything you need to make coding possible, making it easier than wallowing in a swamp of machine code.

The Language

The language itself *is* a tool. Some languages provide facilities absent in others. These gaps may be filled by separate tools you can run over the program source. For example, C's much maligned preprocessor can be remarkably useful, and text-processing packages exist for other languages. Generic code facilities (like C++'s templates), and pre- and postcondition checking are other similarly useful language tools.

It's valuable to have a selection of languages under your belt. Understand how they differ, what tasks they lend themselves to, and what their weak points are. Then you can select the best language for any given task.

Learn several languages; each will teach you different ways to approach problems. Consider them tools, and select the most appropriate *language for each task.*

Run Time and Interpreter

Most languages can't be used without the requisite run-time support. Interpreted languages rely on their interpreter (or *virtual machine*), but directly compiled languages still lean on their support libraries. These libraries are often intimately entwined with the language itself, so the two can't be separated.

Just as you can pick a different compiler, you may be able to select a different language run time, with different characteristics.

Java's JVM (*The Java Virtual Machine*) is a common language interpreter. The C++ standard library supports the language, providing the default handlers for some core language features. Similarly, the C# language rests upon the run-time support of the .NET environment.

Components and Libraries

Yes, these are tools too! Reusing software components and finding libraries that do what you need avoids reinventing the wheel. A good library can increase productivity as much as any other software tool.

The scopes of these libraries vary—some are vast abstraction layers for an entire OS, while some do a very simple job, providing a humble *date* class. They look after their details and hide the complexity away so that you don't have to worry about it. You don't have to spend time writing, testing, and debugging your own versions.

All languages these days come with some level of library support. The C++ STL is a wonderful example of a powerful extensible library. The Java language and .NET environment ship with more standard libraries than you can shake a stick at. Many, many third-party libraries exist, both commercial and free.

Miscellaneous Tools

The story doesn't end here. You will come across plenty more tools. "See Also" on page 127 points out other places where we'll discuss software tools.

The following are some other interesting tool varieties.

Documentation Tools

Good documentation is invaluable; it's a key part of well-engineered code. Various tools help you to write it, both in the source code itself and separately (I describe some in "Practical Self-Documentation Methodologies" on page 66). Never underestimate how important a good word processor is.

Documentation needs to be read as well as written. Good online help systems (backed up by a quality bookshelf) are critical.

ROLLING YOUR OWN

What happens when you can't find a tool for a job and it'll take forever to do by hand? There's nothing wrong with "rolling your own" tools. Indeed, if this task is going to crop up repeatedly, a short tool development may save you hours in the long run.

Some tasks are naturally more tool-able than others. Make sure you're attempting something realistic, and check that the effort will be a cost-effective investment. These are the common ways to create a tool:

- Combine existing tools in a new ways, commonly using the Unix piping mechanism, perhaps writing a little connecting glue. You can put complex command-line incantations into a *shell script* (or *batch file* in Windows-land) so you don't have to type them in every time.

- Use a *scripting language*. Most small homegrown tools are written in some form of scripting language, often Perl. They're quick and easy to work with, yet powerful enough to provide the kind of support you need to write tools.

- Create a full-blown program from scratch. You only really want to do this if it's a serious tool that you'll be using over and over again. Otherwise, the effort probably isn't justified.

When writing the tool, consider:

- The audience—how polished does the tool have to be? Are a few rough edges acceptable? If it's only you and one other techie using it, you can cope. If other, more delicate souls may one day need it, perhaps you should upholster it tastefully.

- Can you extend an existing tool (wrap its command up, or perhaps create a plug-in for it)?

Project Management

Management and work collaboration tools allow you to report and track work against a schedule, manage faults, and monitor team performance. Depending on the scope of the management tool, humble programmers may not need to go near it. But more exotic systems may become the central hub of project activity, drawing in all users.

In a Nutshell

> *Give us the tools and we will finish the job.*
> —*Sir Winston Churchill*

Tools make software development possible. Good tools make it much easier.

Make a point of evaluating the set of tools you use. Do you really know how to use them all properly? Are there any missing tools you should have? Are you getting the most from the ones you do have?

A tool is only ever as good as its user. The proverb *A bad workman blames his tools* contains a lot of truth. Poor programmers create poor code, no matter how many tools they use. In fact, tools can help produce spectacularly worse code. Fostering a professional, responsible attitude toward your toolbox will make you a better programmer.

Good programmers . . .

- Would rather learn *once* how to use an appropriate tool, rather than repeat a tedious job *over and over and over* again
- Understand different toolchain models and are comfortable with each
- Use tools to make their lives easier but don't become slaves to them
- See everything they use as a tool, a replaceable utility
- Are productive, because the use of their tools is second nature

Bad programmers . . .

- Know how to use a few tools and look at every problem in terms of them
- Are afraid of taking the time to learn new tools
- Started using one development environment and now use it religiously, never trying out or even investigating alternatives
- Don't add to their toolboxes when they come across a valuable new tool

See Also

Chapter 10: The Code That Jack Built
The software build process is driven by tools. Just imagine compiling code by hand!

Chapter 13: Grand Designs
Contains a section discussing specific *design tools*.

Chapter 18: Practicing Safe Source
A chapter devoted to the use of *revision control tools*.

Get Thinking

A detailed discussion of these questions can be found in the "Answers and Discussion" section on page 491.

Mull It Over

1. Is it more important for everyone in a development team to use the same IDE, or for each person to pick the one that suits him or her best? What are the implications of different people using different tools?

2. What is the minimum set of tools that any programmer should have at his or her disposal?

3. Which are more powerful: command-line or GUI-based tools?

4. Are there construction tools that aren't programs?

5. What's most important for a tool?
   a. Interoperability
   b. Flexibility
   c. Customization
   d. Power
   e. Ease of use and learning

Getting Personal

1. What are the common tools in your toolbox? Which do you use every day? Which do you use a few times a week? Which do you only call on occasionally?
   a. How well do you know how to use them?
   b. Are you getting the most from every tool?
   c. How did you learn to use them? Did you ever spend any time improving your skill with them?
   d. Are these the *best* tools you could be using?

2. How up to date are your tools? Does it matter if they're not the latest cutting-edge versions?

3. Do you favor an integrated tool set (like a visual development environment) or a discrete toolchain? What are the advantages of the *other* approach? How much experience do you have with *both* ways of working?

4. Are you a *Default Dan* or a *Tweaker Tom*? Do you accept the default settings in your editor, or do you customize them to within an inch of their lives? Which is the "better" approach?

5. How do you determine your budget for software tools? How do you know whether a tool is worth its cost?

TESTING TIMES

The Black Art of Testing Code

Test everything. Keep what is good.
—1 Thessalonians 5:21

Write as much code as you like—there's one thing you can be sure of: It won't work perfectly the first time. It doesn't matter how long you took to carefully design it; software faults have a creepy ability to work their way into any program. The more code you write, the more faults you'll introduce. The faster you write, the more you'll introduce. I've yet to meet a really prolific programmer who created anything near bug-free code.

What do we do about this? We *test* our code. We do this to find any problems that exist, and once we've fixed them, we use the tests to maintain confidence in the quality of the code as we continue to modify it. It's suicide to release untested software, no matter how good a programmer you think you are. Untested software is *bound* to fail; testing is an essential part of our craft. Too many software factories underestimate the importance of thorough testing or try to squeeze it into a last-minute dash before the software ships. It shows.

Testing is not something relegated to the end of the development process, used to prove that your final program is okay. If that's all you ever try to do, you'll produce very poor code, indeed. Testing is a central construction technique. It's only by testing that you can prove that each bit of code works, which then tells you when you've finished it. How could you tell, otherwise? How do so many software factories think they can get away without decent testing?

TERMS AND CONDITIONS

The term *bug* is remarkably evocative and incredibly imprecise. It's easy to throw words around without really understanding what they mean. Using more specific terminology helps us to define what we're doing. These definitions are inspired by IEEE literature (IEEE 84):

Error

An *error* is something that *you* do wrong. It is a specific human action that results in software containing a *fault*. For example: Forgetting to check a condition in your code (like the size of a C array before indexing into it) is an error.

Fault

A *fault* is the consequence of an error, embodied in the software. I made an error, and this resulted in a fault in the code. At first, this is a *latent* problem. If the code I've just written is never executed, then this fault will never have a chance to cause problems. If execution often passes through the faulty code, but never in the particular way that triggers the fault, we'll never notice that there is a fault at all.

This subtle point is what makes debugging notoriously difficult. A faulty line of code may seem fine for years, and then one day it causes the most bizarre system tantrum you've ever seen; you won't suspect the aged code since it's been reliable for so long.

You might discover a fault in a code review, but you can't identify a fault from a running program.

Failure

When encountered, a fault may cause a *failure*. It may not. The failure, the manifestation of the fault, is what we really care about. It's probably the only thing we'll take notice of. A failure is the departure of your program's operation from its requirements, from its expected behavior. This is where we verge on philosophy. If a tree falls over in a forest, does it make a sound? If the running program doesn't exercise a bug, is the mistake still a fault? These definitions help to answer this.

Bug

The term *bug* is a colloquialism, often used as a synonym for fault. According to folklore, the first computer bug was an *actual* bug. It was discovered by Admiral Grace Hopper in 1947 at Harvard. A moth trapped between two electrical relays of the Mark II Aiken Relay Calculator caused the whole machine to shut down.

Reality Check

The two simple questions *What is testing?* and *Why do you test?* seem painfully obvious. Yet all too often, adequate software testing is not performed—or it is not performed at the appropriate stage of production. Good testing is a skill. Actually *doing* some testing is more than many programmers achieve; the mere mention of testing is enough to make most of them break out in a cold sweat. "The single most important rule of testing is to do it." (Kernighan Pike 99)

Testing is a distinct and separate activity from debugging, although their boundaries blur, and the two often get mixed up together. *Testing* is a methodical process of proving the existence, or lack thereof, of faults in your software. *Debugging* is the act of tracking down the cause of this faulty behavior. Testing leads to debugging, which leads to repair, which leads to more testing (we test again to prove that the fix worked).

KEY CONCEPT *Testing is not debugging. Don't get the two confused. They require different skills. Make sure you know when you're testing and when you're debugging.*

If you're programming well, you'll do a *lot* more testing than debugging. That's why this chapter comes before the debugging chapter.

Throughout the software development process, various things are tested:

- A large number of *documents* will go through a testing stage (more commonly known as a *review* process). Doing this ensures, for example, that the requirements specification correctly models the customer's needs, the functional specification implements the requirements specification, the various subsystem specifications are complete enough to fulfill the functional specification, and so on.

- Naturally, then, the implementation *code* is tested on the developer's machine. It is tested at several levels, ranging from line-by-line testing of each function as it's written, to the testing of individual modules, to integration tests when sections of code are glued together.

- Finally, the end *product* is tested. While this level of testing will (or *should*) indirectly test all the code components that have been developed, that is not the focus of these tests. Here we worry about whether or not the program, as a whole, is working as specified.[1]

  Product tests may be concerned with a number of things. Most importantly, they check that the system functions as intended. They also check that it installs correctly (if it's shrink-wrapped PC software) and that it's usable.

  This is the kind of testing performed by the QA department. It is this department's job to understand how the product should work and to ensure that it does, while also meeting any quality criteria that have been established for it.

In this chapter, we'll focus on the middle point—how we test our code as software developers. The other testing activities are large and separate topics, which are outside the scope of this book.

---

[1] Because, obviously, the correct behavior has been carefully specified beforehand, hasn't it?

QUALITY ASSURANCE

QA: *quality assurance*. Sounds painful, doesn't it? But just *who* or *what* is it? This name is given both to a tribe of software factory inhabitants and a development practice. To understand QA properly, it's important to separate colloquialisms and misconceptions from the real definiton.

People mistakenly bundle QA with *testing*, but the two differ significantly. Testing aims to detect erroneous behavior, where software diverges from its specification; it is effectively *detection*. Real QA is *prevention*. It ensures that our processes and development practices will result in high-quality software. Testing is a small part of QA—software quality includes more than just a low bug count. It means software that is delivered on time, to budget, and meeting all requirements and expectations (these two are not necessarily the same). Sadly, there still isn't a lot of high-quality software coming out of today's software factories.

Who's responsible for software quality? An organization's test department (often known as the QA department) is the group of people dedicated to *product* testing. They have the final say as to whether your program is good enough to release. This is an important piece of the quality jigsaw, but not the whole picture. Everyone in the development process is involved in producing quality software—it's not something you can tack on once the code is complete.

The responsibility for monitoring software quality often rests with the same group of people performing product testing. Otherwise, overall QA is the responsibility of project managers, while the testers are left to test.

Who, What, When, and Why?

For our software testing to be effective, we need to understand *why* we test, *who* does it, *what* it entails, and *when* it is done.

Why We Test

As software developers, our testing procedure exists for a few reasons: to help us to find faults and fix them, and to ensure the same faults don't reappear in later versions.

Note that testing can never reveal the absence of faults, only their existence. If your tests don't find any bugs, it doesn't necessarily mean they aren't there; it just means you haven't found them yet.

KEY CONCEPT *Testing can only discover the* presence *of faults. It can't prove the* absence *of faults. Don't be led into a false sense of security by code that passes a suite of inadequate tests.*

Software testing at the end of a development cycle may have another motivation. As well as *verifying* that a software component is correct and contains no faults, you may need to *validate* it—ensure that it fulfills the requirements originally established—to prove that it is good enough for release. Validation is one form of an acceptance test.

Who Tests

It is a *programmer's* responsibility to test the source code he or she writes. Tattoo that sentence backward across your forehead and stare in the mirror for 10 minutes every morning.

Too many developers, disillusioned by the trials of the software factory, crank out code and release it thoughtlessly to QA without having tested it themselves. This is irresponsible and unprofessional. In the long run, it'll cost you *more* time and effort than testing properly. It's plain stupid to release untested code in a product and almost as bad to supply untested code to the QA department. Its job *is* testing, but testing the product, not your new lines of code. It is likely to find the silly coding errors that you left behind, probably manifesting themselves in obscure and seemingly unrelated ways; but its job is to look for more fundamental errors that couldn't have been caught any earlier, not mop up after sloppy programmers.

KEY CONCEPT   *You must test every piece of code you write. Don't expect anyone else to do it for you.*

What Testing Involves

When writing software, we create individual functions, data structures, and classes and glue them together into a working system. Our main testing strategy is to exercise all this code and validate its behavior by writing more code—*test code.* This forms a harness around the test subject that prods, pokes, and drives it, provoking it to respond and checking that its response is correct.

We write test code for each level of the system, testing each important class and function, through to the superstructures composed of these smaller parts. For each test, you must be clear about the following:

- Exactly which piece of code you're testing. Clear modules with well-defined boundaries help here; the interfaces are your test points. Vague or complex interfaces make testing vague and complex.
- The method you're using to test (see "The Types of Test" on page 138).
- When you will be finished. This is one of the hardest and most important questions to answer—you could go on forever. When can you say that you've run enough test cases?

Another common testing strategy is to *inspect* the code in order to prove its correctness. Inasmuch as this is a human activity, it is prone to failure, and it also relies upon the requirements being well defined. *Code reviews* are a common inspection technique (see Chapter 20). Code inspection tools help, but they cannot magically perform all the tests for you. Too often, inspection is ad hoc and haphazard; it's so very easy to overlook faults. Prefer to use programmatic tests; they bring many benefits, which we'll see throughout this chapter. A combination of the two is most effective.

When We Test

Test your code *as it's written*, catching coding errors at the earliest possible opportunity. It's at this time when errors are easiest to fix, affect fewest people, and cause the least havoc. Testing early and thoroughly is the most effective way to ensure software quality.

The cost of a bug escalates as it works through the development process,[2] so it's essential to start testing code as soon as possible—during (or perhaps before) serious software development. The *test-driven development* approach, popularized by agile programmers, advocates testing as a central construction technique; you write test code *before* the code being tested!

KEY CONCEPT *Effective code testing starts early, so you catch bugs when they're least harmful. You can write tests before writing code!*

This is an essential point, and it is vitally important to absorb into your programming routine. For each piece of code you write, *immediately* write a test. Or write the test first. Prove that your code works, so you know that it's safe to move on. If you don't write a test at this point, you'll leave unproven, potentially buggy code behind. This destroys the stability of your codebase: When you hit a bug, you won't know which bit of code (in the mass you've accumulated since you last wrote a test) is causing the problem. So you end up in the debugger, which is a massive waste of time.

Writing the test later means you will test from a distance—either too late, when you've forgotten what the code is supposed to do, or as a consequence of testing a separate code module. This will not be an effective test. You're also far more likely to forget to write the test at all.

This testing strategy has profound implications: When you start to think about writing some code, you must simultaneously think about testing it. This will shape the way you design that code, for the better; we'll see why in "Design for Test" on page 144.

Every time you find a fault that managed to slip past your existing tests, you must add a new test to your test suite (after scolding yourself for missing it in the first place). The new test will help to prove that your bug fix is correct. It will also catch any later reappearance of the same bug; bugs can rise unexpectedly from the dead—this often happens when your code is modified later.

KEY CONCEPT *Write a test for every fault you find.*

So we write tests as early as possible, but how often do we run them? As often as humanly possible, if not more often (using computer support). The more often we run the tests, the more likely we are to detect problems. This is embodied in a *continuous integration* strategy (see "Automated Builds" on page 190), and begins to show why programatic tests (which are easy to run repeatedly) are so powerful.

KEY CONCEPT *Run your tests as often as you can.*

---

[2] See "The Economics of Failure" on page 157 for more on the cost of bugs.

Testing Isn't Hard . . .

Unless you do it badly, and then it's *really* hard. It does take thoughtful effort, though. To test whether a particular piece of code works, you need a test harness that demonstrates that:

- The correct output is generated for all valid inputs.
- The appropriate failure behavior is generated for all invalid inputs.

That sounds innocuous enough, yet for all but the simplest of functions, it is just not practical to exhaustively perform this testing. The set of valid inputs is usually very large, and it's impossible to test each input individually. You'll have to pick a smaller set of representative input values. The set of invalid inputs is almost always *much* larger than the set of valid inputs, so you have to pick a number of representative bad values, as well.

To illustrate this, here are two examples. This first function is easy to test:

```
bool logical_not(bool b)
{
    if (b)
        return false;
    else
        return true;
}
```

The set of valid inputs is of size two, and there are no invalid inputs. This means that the function's test harness is simple. It might look like this:

```
void test_logical_not()
{
    assert(logical_not(true)  == false);
    assert(logical_not(false) == true);
}
```

The function doesn't do anything particularly exciting, though. Now consider the following function (let's not critique its elegance at the moment). How much harder is it to test?

```
int greatest_common_divisor(int a, int b)
{
    int low  = min(a, b);
    int high = max(a, b);

    int gcd = 0;
    for (int div = low; div > 0; --div)
    {
        if ((low % div == 0) && (high % div == 0))
            if (gcd < div)
                gcd = div;
    }
    return gcd;
}
```

It's still a small snippet of code, but testing it is far more difficult for these reasons:

- Although there are only two parameters, the set of valid input is extremely large. You can't conceivably test every possible combination of values; it would take a *very* long time.[3] Adding more parameters to a function extends this problem exponentially.

- It contains a loop. Any form of branch (including a for loop) adds complexity and more potential for failure.

- There are several conditional statements. You now have to arrange to exercise the code running through each combination of conditions to check that each side works.

And that's just for a single small function. There's *already* a fault in there, did you notice it? Can you find it? Ten points and a gold star if you can.[4]

KEY CONCEPT *It's very easy to trust the code you read and to believe that it's correct. When you've just written some code, you'll read what you* intended *to write, not what you actually wrote. Learn to look twice—read* all *code cynically.*

Those three problems aren't the only reasons software gets harder to test. There are plenty of other ways to increase test complexity.

Code size

The more code there is, the more room for potential faults, and the more individual paths of execution that must be traced through to check validity.

Dependencies

Testing one small piece of code should be easy. But if the test harness has to attach the rest of the codebase before it will do anything, then it becomes too painful (and too time consuming) to write any tests. In this case, either testing doesn't happen, or the tests aren't comprehensive enough, since it's too hard to orchestrate all of the attached code components. This is an example of *untestable design*. We'll look at remedies for this later (in "Design for Test" on page 144).

The next two sections are also examples of kinds of inter-code dependency.

External inputs

Any reliance on the state of an external part of the system is essentially another input. Unlike function parameters, it's not easy to arrange for these external inputs to take on certain test values. A shared global variable can't be set to an arbitrary value without compromising other parts of the running program.

---

[3] The higher your input values, the longer the for loop will take. Assuming an int is a 32-bit value (meaning there are 2^{64} input combinations) and you have a nice, fast machine (let's say that every function call will take one millisecond—*that's one hell of a processor cache*), a brute-force test would take almost 600 million years! And that's without printing out any test results. . . .

[4] Look at the answer to this chapter's first "Mull It Over" question (page 494) to find out what it is.

External stimuli

The code may react to stimuli other than function calls. It's particularly troublesome when they may occur asynchronously (at any time), and with any frequency.

- A class can act on callbacks from other parts of the system, which may crop up at any time.
- Hardware interface code reacts to changes in physical device state.
- Communication with other systems may take any length of time. Physical connections are prone to interference, so they may degrade, and network connections can be unreliable.
- User interface code is driven by the user's mouse gestures. It's hard to physically automate a GUI in test conditions.

These conditions are hard to simulate in an artificial test environment, and they may be particularly timing sensitive (for example, the speed of mouse double clicks or the frequency of hardware-generated interrupts).

Some outside influences are unplanned: memory may run low, disk space may become exhausted, and network connections may fail. You have to ensure that your code is robust in *all* prevailing environmental conditions.

Threads

Multiple threads of control make testing more complex, since the concurrent code may intertwine in any arbitrary sequence. The complex interplay of execution paths means that any given test run may never be repeatable. Thread faults leading to deadlock or starvation may be hard to trigger, but they cause serious problems when they do crop up.

The program's threaded behavior will be different on truly parallel multiprocessor systems to the behavior exhibited under simulated concurrency on single-processor time-slicing environments.

Evolution

Software evolves. This evolution tends to break tests. If the requirements are not pinned down, your early tests will probably be invalid by the time you come to deliver because the APIs will have changed, the functionality will be completely different, and a full set of tests will not have been created because development never stood still long enough.

We require stable interfaces both in our own code and any external code we rely on. In the Real World, this is an impractical ideal—the code will never stand still—so we must craft small, malleable tests that can be easily modified alongside the code.

Hardware faults

Faults exist in hardware as well as in software. Work in an embedded environment is generally more likely to run into hardware errors, because you're closer to the metal. Hardware faults can be an order of magnitude more difficult to diagnose and fix; they are seldom repeatable, and you'll naturally distrust your software first.

Nasty failure modes

Code can fall over in a multitude of exciting and bizarre ways. Program faults don't just lead to *incorrect output*—there's more to contend with: infinite loops, deadlock, starvation, program crashes, OS lock-ups, and other potential failures raise their ugly heads to make testing a varied and exciting thing. A pathological software failure may even lead to physical damage to hardware![5] Write a test harness to check for *that*.

Writing a test harness is no small feat. When components get glued together and start relying on each other, the complexity of software expands exponentially. All of these problems gang up to make your life very complicated. This is when it becomes not just difficult, but technically infeasible to write harnesses that test the software *exhaustively*. The time and resources do not exist to generate all the test data necessary, and to run the software over all sets of inputs and stimuli. The brute-force method rapidly becomes impractical, and it seems more convenient to ignore testing and just hope that there aren't any bugs.

No matter how hard you test, you still can't produce fault-free software—writing test code is as hard and requires as much skill as writing regular code. Some errors will invariably slip through even the most rigorous testing (studies show that the most carefully tested software still contains 0.5 to 3 errors per 1,000 lines of code). (Myers 86) Testing in the Real World rarely proves that software is bulletproof—merely that it is *adequate*.

With this in mind, we need to focus on the key tests that are likely to capture the majority of software defects for the most effective testing. We'll see how to choose these later.

The Types of Test

There are many different kinds of software tests, and no one is better than any other. Each method approaches the code from a different direction and will catch a different class of faults. All are needed.

Unit testing

The term *unit test* is commonly used to mean testing a *module* of code (say a library, device driver, or protocol stack layer), but it really describes the testing of atomic units: each class or function.

Unit testing is performed in strict isolation. Any untrusted external code with which the unit interfaces is replaced with a stub or simulator—this ensures that you only trap bugs in *this* unit, not bugs caused by outside influences.

Component testing

A step up from unit testing, this validates the combination of one or more units into a full component. Often this is what people mean by *unit test*.

---

[5] This is no joke. The 68000 processor had an undocumented *stop and catch fire* instruction—a bus test operation that rapidly cycled the address lines, causing the circuit board to overheat and catch on fire.

Integration testing

This tests the combination of components as they are brought together in the system, ensuring that they interconnect properly.

Regression testing

This is retesting after fixes or modifications are made to the software or to its environment. You run regression tests to ensure that the software works as it did before and that your modification hasn't broken anything along the way. When you work with brittle software, a change in one place can cause strange faults to appear elsewhere. Regression testing helps to guard against this.

It can be difficult to determine how much retesting is needed, especially near the end of the development cycle. Automated test tools are especially useful for this type of testing. I'll discuss this in detail in "Look! No Hands!" on page 144.

Load testing

You perform load tests to ensure that your code can handle the expected volume of data being thrown at it. It's simple to write code that generates a good answer, but doing so in a timely manner is another thing. This can unearth problems related to the efficiency of a system, perhaps due to incorrect buffer sizes, bad memory usage, or inadequate database design. Load testing checks that the program "scales up" as expected.

Stress testing

Stress testing throws a *huge* amount of data at the code within a short space of time to see what it does. It's similar to load testing, often used for high-availability systems. Stress tests check the characteristics of the system: how tolerant it is to overloading. Load testing is performed to prove that the code can meet its *expected* demands; stress testing makes sure that it won't just crumple in a heap if it receives a real battering. The code doesn't have to keep working perfectly; it just has to fail gracefully and recover well.

Stress testing helps determine the capacity of the software—how hard you can push before it falls over. It is especially pertinent in threaded or real-time systems.

Soak testing

Soak testing is similar to stress testing. The focus is on running at a high load for a prolonged period of time—several days, weeks, or even months—to identify any performance problems that appear after a large number of operations have been executed. Soak testing reveals faults that might otherwise go undetected: small memory leaks that eventually crash the program or performance degradation as internal data structures slowly become fragmented.

Usability testing

Ensures that your software can be used easily by a shortsighted gerbil. There are various forms of end-user tests, often performed in *usability labs* under very controlled and scripted conditions. We also test software in *field trials*, putting it in a Real World setting to see what users think.

ALPHA, BETA, GAMMA . . .

What about *alpha* and *beta* testing? They are common terms, but not quite in the same league as the other tests we've looked at here. They are more focused on final *product* testing than on the implementation of particular bits of *code*. Nevertheless, they deserve some explanation.

Happily, the terms have no formal definition. Each company will have its own idea of what software in an *alpha* or *beta* state is. For all you know, alpha software might be made of lemon jelly and explode on exposure to light. Alpha or beta software is often released externally, as an advance customer preview—an early chance to elicit feedback and garner confidence.

These are common interpretations of the terms:

Alpha software

The first "code complete" stage. It may still have many, many bugs, and be completely unreliable. Alpha software provides a good representation of what the final product will be like, if you can look past the obvious flaws.

Beta software

Well past the alpha stage, beta software is *mostly* bug free; there are very few remaining problems. It's not too far from a final product. Beta testing (that is, testing *beta* software) is used in the run up to final release candidates to nail the remaining issues. Beta testing usually involves Real World field trials.

Release candidate

This is the final stage before a formal software release. Candidate builds go through verification and *assurance testing* (validation) prior to the production release. Release candidates are internal builds, usually going to the test department only.

If alpha and beta releases venture to the outside world, they may have some form of crippling (time-limited operation, for example). The release candidates are "pure" builds, without any of these limitations.

When we write unit and component tests, there are two main approaches to devising the test cases: *black box* and *white box* testing.

Black box testing

This is also known as *functional testing*. Black box testing compares actual functionality against intended functionality. The internal workings of the code are not known by the tester; it is seen as a *black box*. The designer and tester can be independent of each other.[6]

Black box testing is not concerned that every line of code is tested, only that it meets the software's specification—that if you put the right things into one end of the box, the right things come out the other. Therefore, without clear specifications and documented APIs, it is very hard to devise black box tests.

Black box test cases can be designed as soon as the software specification is complete. They rely on the specification being correct in the first place and on it not being radically altered after the tests have been devised.

---

[6] However, this isn't necessarily a good idea—a programmer is usually the best person to write the unit test for the code he or she creates.

White box testing

This is also known as *structural testing*. It is a code-coverage–based approach. Each line of code is scrutinized systematically to ensure correctness. Where you couldn't see into the black box beforehand, you now can and do. For this reason, white box testing is sometimes called *glass box* testing. It is really only concerned with testing the lines of code produced, and it doesn't guarantee that they meet their specifications.

There are *static* and *dynamic* methods of white box testing. Static tests do not run the code; instead, it is inspected and walked through to ensure that it represents a valid solution. Dynamic tests run the code and are concerned with path and branch testing—trying to visit every line of code and execute every decision. This may require some modification of the code to force control down certain paths. Such modification can be easier than trying to engineer test cases for all behavioral combinations.[7]

White box testing is laborious and much more expensive than black box; consequently, it is done a lot less. The completed code is needed before white box tests can even be planned. Black box testing is typically done before white box testing starts. The consequence of a failure at this stage is much more expensive. You'd have to code a fix, black box test again, then devise and run new white box tests.

Tools exist to instrument your code and measure the test coverage. Without tool support, white box testing could make your head explode.

Black box testing is concerned with faults of *omission* (where the software misses out some of the specified behavior), while white box testing discovers faults of *commission* (where parts of the implementation are faulty). In order to fully test a software unit, both black and white box testing is required.

TEST TIME

Each of these test methods is employed at different points in the development process. The following table illustrates this, showing which tests are most important at each point.

Stage of Development	Is Black or White Box Appropriate?	Common Testing Approaches at This Stage of Development	Who Performs the Test?
Requirements gathering	Black	Black box tests devised	Developers, QA
Code design	Black	Black box tests devised	Developers, QA
Code construction	Black, white	Unit, component, regression	Developers
Code integration	Black, white	Component, integration, regression	Developers
Alpha status	Black, white	Regression, load, stress, soak, usability	Developers, QA
Beta status	Black, white	Regression, load, stress, soak, usability	QA
Release candidate	Black, white	Regression, load, stress, soak	QA
Release	Black, white	It's too late by now . . .	Users (good luck)

---

[7] If you do modify the source code, then you're not actually testing the final executable, which is concerning.

Choosing Unit Test Cases

If testing is essential but exhaustive testing is impossible, you must judiciously choose the set of most effective tests. To do this, you need a thoughtful and methodical plan. You could take a *scattergun* approach—just prop the code up on a wall and then fire everything that comes to hand at it. . . .

That way you *might* find some flaws. But without a sensible, staged testing approach, you'll never have the quality tests that will give you proper confidence in your code. Instead of the scattergun, you should pick up a rifle with an accurate sight and aim careful shots at the code, hitting well-judged marks, to see how well it stands up.

Where do you aim? How do you determine the volley of test data to launch? Since you can't try every possible value, you need to select a handful of pertinent inputs. You must pick the tests that are most likely to disclose the software's faults, rather than run tests that just show the same few problems repeatedly.

KEY CONCEPT   *Write a comprehensive suite of tests, each one exercising a different aspect of the code. Fifteen tests that demonstrate the same fault over and over are less useful than fifteen tests that show fifteen different faults.*

To do this, you must understand the requirements for your piece of code. You can't write an accurate test case unless you know what it's supposed to do. It might be doing the wrong thing very well.

When black box testing, some test cases will be:

Some good input

Select a number of well-chosen *good* inputs to ensure that the software works properly in the normal cases.

Cover the whole range of valid input values; include some middle of the road values, some values from around the lower bounds of acceptable input, and some from the upper bounds.

Some bad input

Just as important are a certain number of well-chosen *bad* inputs. This ensures that the software is robust and doesn't give misleading answers to invalid input.

You must consider all sorts of bad data, including:

- Values that are numerically far too large or far too small (handling negative values is often overlooked)

- Input that is too long or too short (string lengths are a classic example—try sending an empty string to see what happens, or try different-sized arrays and lists)

- Data values that are internally inconsistent (what this means will depend on the contract of the function; perhaps it expects values in a certain order)

Boundary values

Test *all* the boundary cases—they are a rich source of error. Identify the highest and lowest inputs that are valid, or wherever the natural input boundaries are (perhaps where behavior changes). For each of these positions, test the code's behavior at:

- The boundary value itself

- The values just above it

- The values just below it

This ensures that your software works correctly right into the corners, and that it then gives up exactly when expected.

Boundary tests catch the all-too-easy mistakes, like typing > instead of >=, or getting loop count bases wrong (did you start counting from zero or one?). All three boundary tests are needed to check for these kinds of mistakes.

Random data

Test randomly generated sets of input data to avoid guesswork. This is a surprisingly effective test strategy. If you can write an automated test harness that repeatedly generates and applies random data, you stand a good chance of picking up subtle errors that you would have never thought of otherwise.

Zero

If the input is numeric, always test for the zero case. For some reason, programmers fail to think properly about zero, a blind spot in their reasoning.

C/C++ pointers are often given a zero value to mean *unset* or *undefined*. Try throwing zero pointers at your code to see if it reacts correctly. In Java, you can send `null` object references for a similar effect.

Design for Test

The quality of unit test you can write is determined largely by the quality of the interface you have to test. Testing is easier when your code is written thoughtfully and specifically designed to accommodate inspection and verification. You achieve this by crafting clear APIs, reducing reliance on other bits of code, and breaking any hard-coded links to other components. This way, it's easy to place a component into its test environment and stimulate it. If, instead, it's grafted intimately into other sections of code, you have to drag all of that code into the test environment and arrange for it to interact with your unit appropriately. This is not always easy, and often impossible, limiting your scope for possible tests.

KEY CONCEPT *Design your code for easy testing.*

There's a helpful side effect of this rule: When you structure code for testability, you will be structuring it in a sensible, understandable, and maintainable way. You'll reduce component coupling and increase cohesion. You'll make it more flexible, easy to use, and easier to wire up in different configurations. Your code will be better.

And since you've tested it well, the code is more likely to be correct.

You must design for tests up front. You can't easily return to an old component and bolt a "testable" interface onto it. If a lot of other code relies on the existing interface, then such modifications are hard. Remember: You're most likely to design geniunely testable code if you write unit tests alongside the code.

A few simple design rules lead to highly testable code:

- Make each section of code self-contained, without undocumented and tenuous dependencies on the outside world. Don't hard-code links to other parts of the system; rely on abstract interfaces that could be implemented by system components or by test simulators.

- Don't rely on global variables (or *singleton* objects, which are thin veneers for globals). Gather such states in a shared structure passed as an argument.

- Limit the complexity of your code; break it into small, comprehensible, bite-sized chunks that can be individually tested.

- Make the code observable, so you can see what it's doing, query internal state, and ensure that it's operating as expected.

Look! No Hands!

You can't hang around all day turning the handle on your test machinery. Manually invoking test after test isn't my idea of a great day's programming. Repeated regression testing would rapidly get boring. It wouldn't just be boring, but also slow, inefficient, and prone to human error. The golden testing rule is simple: *Automate.*

KEY CONCEPT *Automate your code testing as much as possible. It's quicker and easier than running tests by hand, and it's far safer: The tests are more likely to be run regularly.*

If the tests run without any intervention, they can be triggered as a validation phase of your build procedure. Before you play with some freshly built software, you'll know the unit tests have automatically run and passed; you're assured that there are no silly programming errors and that any new work hasn't broken old code.

KEY CONCEPT *Run unit tests automatically as a part of your build process.*

You can gather your individual pieces of test code together in an automated scaffold that marshals the test execution and gathers the results of the testing in a single place. This harness monitors which tests have been done; the more complex test harnesses maintain a history of test results over time. There are many such popular tools, like JUnit, a common Java unit test framework.

A high level of automation comes into its own during regression testing. If you make a modification to the code and want to ensure that you haven't accidentally broken anything, you can run the whole set of tests automatically; out of the end pops a *yes* or *no* answer. Of course, the regression test result is only ever as good as the tests put into the harness.

Automation really is a fundamental concept for solid code development. If you don't currently have an automated suite of unit tests, acting as a continual regression test of your codebase, then get one. Your work will quickly improve in quality.

Sadly, not all tests *can* be automated. Unit testing library functions is relatively easy; automatically testing user interfaces is very hard. How do you emulate mouse clicks, check the Urdu translation of a text string, or ensure that the correct sound clip is playing?

The Face of Failure

Our greatest glory is not in never falling,
but in rising every time we fall.
—Confucius

What do you do when your testing finds a program failure? Before you rush in headlong to debug it, step back and characterize the problem. This is especially important when you don't intend (or have no time) to repair it right away. Follow these steps to pin down the nature of the fault so that you, or any other developer, can come back later and attempt to sort it out.

1. Note what you were trying to do at the time and which actions triggered the failure.
2. Try it again. Discover whether the problem is repeatable, how frequently it crops up, and whether it coincides with any other activities going on at the same time.

3. Describe the fault. Fully. Be very specific. Include the following:
   - The context of problem
   - The simplest steps that can replicate it
   - Information about repeatability and frequency of occurrence
   - The version of the software, exact build number, and hardware used
   - Anything else that might conceivably relate
4. Record it. Don't lose it! Put this information in your fault-tracking system, even if it's a simple coding error that you intend to fix yourself (see "Can You Manage It?" next).
5. Write the simplest test harness that will demonstrate the failure, and add it to the suite of automatic tests. This will ensure that the fault cannot be lost or ignored and, once it's eventually fixed, won't reoccur later in development.

Remember, testing is *not* debugging—and these steps are *not* debugging! You've not tried to unveil the cause of the failure, or peek into the code, just to establish enough information to describe the problem to another developer.

Our favorite kind of fault is a repeatable fault. Really—we like code that falls over repeatedly: It's easy to replicate the problem; therefore it's easy to track down the fault and easy to prove that you've fixed it. Nasty failures are irregular, even random, and consequently hard to characterize. Failures that take an eon to manifest and depend upon the wind speed are a nightmare.

Can You Manage It?

You must be methodical and systematic in order to *find* faults. You must also be methodical and systematic in your management and handling of them. Before releasing code (or checking it into source control), you are the only person who'd be bitten by its gremlins. But as soon as it leaves your care, code takes on a life of its own. It's no longer just *you* who is concerned with its faults. The rules change as more players join the game:

- A programmer will find problems at the codeface—in his own code and in other people's.
- The code integrator will find errors as components are glued together.
- The QA department will find faults in the product as it tests.

With so many people finding so many problems while others are simultaneously trying to make fixes, there had better be a good procedure for managing it all. Otherwise, the result will be a mess, and development will come crashing down around everyone's heads.

Fault-Tracking System

Our key weapon in managing faults is a *fault-tracking system*. This tool is a specialized database with interfaces visible to everyone who has a hand in the testing process.

As bugs are discovered and dealt with, this database is updated to reflect the status of the software. In doing so, the fault-tracking tool becomes an integral part of the project's *fault-management procedure*. The general actions performed are:

Report a failure

When you find a bug, make a new entry for it in the database by creating a *fault report*. It becomes a fully paid-up member of the fault club, with its own personal membership number. This reference number uniquely identifies it for future use. The bug now cannot be overlooked. It *must* be addressed before the software is shipped.

Creating a report also alerts others in the team that this fault has been found; they don't need to enter the same information when they run into it.

Assign responsibility

This marks a fault report for a particular person's attention. It defines who is responsible for fixing (or making sure that someone fixes) each problem. Without this idea of ownership, every programmer will think that someone else is going to fix the fault, while the bug works its way through the cracks.

Prioritize reports

The fault-tracking system allows you to mark which faults are the most important. A repeatable startup crash is clearly more serious than a button that's occasionally shifted one pixel to the right.

By differentiating the show-stopping faults from little annoyances, developers can plan their work and choose which faults need to be fixed first. There may be various levels of severity supported by the tool—from critical faults, though medium-to-low priority issues, to feature requests.

Mark as fixed

A developer will do this once a repair has been made. It doesn't close the fault report but places it on a pile ready for verification. The person who submits the report is responsible for testing that the fix is correct, although he can delegate this task. A fix certainly shouldn't be verified by the person who made it, for obvious reasons.

Close a report

Once verified, a report can be closed, becoming nothing more than a distant memory (and perhaps a project statistic).

There may be other scenarios leading to report closure—the issue may not have been a fault at all, perhaps just a characteristic of the system, or even perfectly valid behavior. Testers are fallible too.

Instead of closing a report you don't intend to deal with, you can *defer* it, marking the fault to be fixed in a later software revision.

Query the database

You can query the fault-tracking system for information:

- Naturally, you can produce a list of all the pending fault reports, ordering them by software version, assignee, priority, or whatever.
- You can discover which faults have been assigned to you.
- You can produce a report on which faults have been fixed in each software version. This is helpful for preparing *release notes.*
- You can also view project statistics—how many faults have been reported during development, how many have been fixed, and the rate of closure versus generation. Presented graphically, this can give a good impression of how well the software is progressing.

Modify an entry

You can open a report and alter the information it contains. This includes:

- Adding comments for any new information you've found
- Attaching log files, containing example output, to illustrate the problem
- Marking a report as a duplicate of another fault, to prevent later confusion

There are plenty of fault-tracking tools available, both commercial and freely available versions, like the popular Bugzilla system developed as a part of the Mozilla project.

Bug Reviews

Toward the end of product development, as release deadlines inch ever nearer, *bug review* meetings become a part of life, occurring about once a week. These reviews are scheduled once functionality is complete but before all the bugs are ironed out—the long home stretch of the development process. They provide an overview of the project's progress to all interested parties, help plan the remaining repair work, and shepherd the software toward release.

These meetings are attended by an eclectic bunch of people:

- The software developers responsible for the product. (They'll be doing the fixing, after all.)
- Representatives from the test team, who will explain the context of faults and ensure the bug review is steering in the correct direction. (More often than not, it's their responsibility to convene the meeting.)
- Product managers, who will gain an overview of the progress and will make *the buck stops here* decisions.
- Commercial and marketing team members, who are the people that will have to sell this bug-ridden product. (Their viewpoint on the importance of each fault helps to decide which ones to fix and which to sweep under the digital carpet.)

A list of outstanding fault reports is generated from the fault tracking tool, and each fault is discussed in turn during the meeting. Test or development team members may present additional information, if required, and then commercial decisions on the importance of the problem are made. Nasty lingering faults are discussed, with a progress report of the repair. If work is struggling, a decision to apply additional resources might be made.

With such a large range of people, the meeting can rapidly get off track, and it takes a strong-willed chairman to keep discussion focused and to the point. The topic is fault reports and how to deal with them, not specific code fixes. Programmers love to talk technical and try to solve every issue in the meeting. This is not the place for it.[8]

In a Nutshell

Testing is critical to producing good software. In general, the more testing, the better—although the *quality* of the tests will be reflected in the quality of the final product. Poor tests will catch few faults, and the result will be a defective software release.

We test at various levels of development, from individual functions, through component integration, to the final assembled program. At each stage, you must adopt a methodical approach to finding and managing software faults.

It is each programmer's responsibility to test his or her code. The QA department has enough problems to deal with apart from your buggy code. You can't perform testing and then add in software quality at end of development—it must be designed in from the start, with tests being developed and run alongside the code.

Good programmers . . .	Bad programmers . . .
• Write tests for all their code (possibly even *before* they write the code)	• Don't consider testing to be an important and integral part of software development—*it's someone else's job*
• Test at the *micro* level, so *macro*-level testing is not hindered by stupid coding mistakes	• Release untested code to the QA department and look surprised when testing uncovers faulty behavior
• Care about product quality and take responsibility for it, playing their parts in the total testing effort	• Make their lives more complicated by discovering problems too late—not testing early enough and then being hit by a slew of hard-to-locate faults

---

[8] Tactics for successful meetings are described in "Meeting Your Fate" on page 340.

See Also

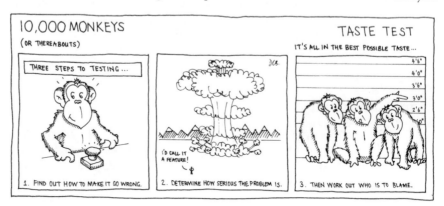

Get Thinking

A detailed discussion of these questions can be found in the "Answers and Discussion" section on page 494.

Mull It Over

1. Write a test harness for the greatest_common_divisor code example earlier in this chapter. Make it as exhaustive as you can. How many individual test cases have you included?

   a. How many of these passed?

   b. How many failed?

   c. Using these tests, identify any faults and repair the code.

2. How should the testing of a spreadsheet application and an automatic aircraft pilot differ?

3. Should you test all of the *test code* that you write?

4. How does a programmer's testing differ from a QA department member's testing?

5. Is it necessary to write a test harness for every single function?

6. *Test-driven development* encourages you to write tests first, before any code. What sort of tests should you write?

7. Should you write C/C++ tests to check for the handling of NULL (zero) pointer parameters? What's the value of such a test?

8. Your early code tests might not be on the final platform—you may not yet have access to it. Is it safest to defer testing until you *do* have a target test platform, or to steam ahead now?

    If the code is intended to run in a different environment (perhaps on a high-capacity server, or some embedded device), how can you be sure that your tests are representative and adequate?

9. How do you know when you've finished and can stop testing? How much is *enough*?

Getting Personal

1. For what percentage of your code do you write tests? Are you happy with this? Are your tests an automated part of the build process? What sort of testing do you give the remaining code? Is this adequate? What will you do about it?

2. How good is your relationship with the people in your QA department? What personal reputation do you think you have with them?

3. What's your usual response to finding an error in your code?

4. Do you file a fault report for every code problem you uncover?

5. How much testing are the project engineers expected to do?

FINDING FAULT

*Debugging: What to Do
When Things Go Wrong*

I have not failed. I've just found 10,000 ways that won't work.

—Thomas Edison

Nobody's perfect. Well, except for me. All day, I have to sit down and work through tedious problems in other people's code. The test department discovers that our software falls over when it does *such-and-such*. So I trawl through the system to find what Programmer Fred did wrong three years ago, patch it up, and send it back for them to break again.

Of course, you wouldn't find *me* making those sorts of elementary mistakes—not a chance. My code is watertight. Faultless. Low fat and cholesterol free. I never write a line without meticulous planning, I won't complete a code statement without considering all the special cases that might occur, and I type so carefully that I've never once misplaced = for == in an if statement.

Totally fault free, me. Really.

Well, perhaps not quite.

The Facts of Life

I don't think anyone sits trainee programmers down and explains the facts of life to them. *It's like this, son. There are the birds and the bees. Oh, and the bugs.* Bugs are the inevitable dark side of constructing software, a simple fact of life. Sad, but true. Whole departments, and even industries, exist to manage them.

We're all aware of the proliferation of faults in released software. How do bugs appear with such frightening regularity and in such great magnitude? It all comes down to human nature. Programs are written by humans. Humans make mistakes. They make mistakes for a number of reasons (or excuses). They make mistakes because they don't understand the system they're working on well enough or because they don't correctly understand what they are implementing, but more often than not, they make mistakes because they just don't pay enough attention to what they're doing. Most bugs are due to mindlessness. I once saw a wonderfully simple illustration of this; play along at home:

- The tree that grows from an acorn is called an . . .

- The noise a frog makes is a . . .

- The vapor that rises from fire is called . . .

- The white of an egg is called the . . .

The *yolk*, right? Think about it. If you didn't fall for that one, then you were probably only paying attention because I'd just warned you. (Give yourself a brownie point anyway.) But tell me, who warns you every time you're about to write a potentially flawed line of code? If that person existed, he'd deserve a lifetime supply of brownie points.

As programmers, we're all to blame for the bad state of software. We're all guilty. Do we learn to live with the guilt, or do we do something about it? There are two types of responses. The first is the *It's not a fault, it's a feature* school: Just make up an excuse and ignore it. A fault turns up, and we respond in the words of the great philosopher Bart Simpson: "I didn't do it. Nobody saw me do it. You can't prove anything!" (Simpsons 91) We blame compiler quirks, OS flaws, random climate changes, and computers with minds of their own. Or as I alluded to in the opening paragraphs, we blame other people. A Teflon raincoat is a handy programming tool.

However, we should really subscribe to the second school, the school that concedes that software errors are *not* entirely inevitable. Many mindless mistakes can be picked up or even prevented, and as responsible programmers, we should be taking steps to do so. Defensive programming and sensible testing are our main weapons. In this chapter, we'll look at good debugging techniques to employ when bugs do slip through the net.

Nature of the Beast

Contrary to popular belief, the term *bug* was in use before the advent of computers. In the 1870s, Thomas Edison talked about bugs in electrical circuits. The story of the Harvard University Mark II Aiken Relay Calculator tells of the first recorded computer bug. In 1945, the early days of computers when they took up whole rooms, a moth flew in and managed to lodge itself in some circuits, causing a system failure. They taped it into the logbook and wrote, *First actual case of bug being found.* For posterity's sake, it has been preserved in the Smithsonian Institute.

Bugs are bad news. But what are they, really? We outlined the correct nomenclature for these things in "Terms and Conditions" on page 130. It's worth identifying the varieties of bugs we encounter and understanding how they are born, how they survive, and how they can be exterminated.

The View from 1,000 Feet

Software bugs fall into a few broad categories, and understanding these will help us to reason about them. Some bugs are naturally harder to find than others, and this is related to their categories. Stepping back and squinting from a distance, these three classes of bugs emerge:

Failure to compile

It's really annoying when the code you've spent ages writing fails to compile. It means that you'll have to go back and fix a tedious little typo or a parameter type mismatch, and then wait for the compiler to run again before you can get to the real job of testing your handiwork. Surprisingly, this is the best type of error you can get. Why? Simply because it's the easiest to detect and fix. It's the most immediate and the most obvious.[1]

The longer it takes to detect faults, the more it will cost to fix them; this is demonstrated in "The Economics of Failure" on page 157. The sooner you catch and fix each fault, the sooner you can move on and the less fuss and cost they can incur. Compilation failures are very easy to notice (or rather, they are hard to ignore) and usually easy to fix. You can't run the program until you have taken care of them.

Most of the time, a compilation failure will be a silly syntactic mistake or a simple oversight, like calling a function with the wrong number or type of parameters. The failure might be due to a fault in a makefile, it might be a link stage error (perhaps a missing function implementation), or even a build server running out of disk space.

Run-time crash

After you fix the compilation errors, an executable pops out and you happily run it. Then it crashes. You'll probably swear and mutter something about random cosmic rays. After the 60th crash, you're threatening to throw your computer out the window. These kinds of errors are much harder to deal with than compilation errors, but they're still reasonably simple.

---

[1] Provided you have a sane build environment that stops when it encounters an error and provides some reasonable diagnostic messages.

That's because, like compilation errors, they are blindingly obvious. You can't argue with a dead program. You can't pretend a crash is a "feature." When it has kicked the bucket and shuffled off its mortal coil, you can step back and begin to figure out where your program went wrong. You'll have some clues (which input sequence preceded the crash and what it did before crashing), and you can employ tools to discover more information (more on this later).

Unexpected behavior

This is the really nasty one—when your program isn't pushing up the daisies, just pining for the fjords. Suddenly it does the wrong thing. You expected a blue square, and out popped a yellow triangle. The code continues to meander on its happy way with total disregard for your frustration. What caused the yellow triangle to appear? Has the program been overthrown by a militant army of guerrilla COM objects? It will almost certainly be a minute logic problem in the bowels of the code that executed over half and hour ago. Good luck finding it.

A failure may manifest itself because of defective single line of code, or it may only show up when several interconnecting modules whose assumptions don't quite match up are finally glued together.

The View from the Ground

If we move in a bit and take a closer look at run-time errors, more groupings of faults become clear. Here they are ranked in order of pain, from splinter to decapitation.

Syntactic errors

While these *are* mostly caught by the compiler at build time, sometimes language grammar errors slip through undetected. They generate weird and unexpected behavior. In C-like languages, the syntax error will often be one of these:

- Mistaking == for = or && for & in a conditional expression
- Forgetting a semicolon or adding one in the wrong place (the classic location is after a for statement)
- Forgetting to enclose a set of loop statements in braces
- Mismatching parentheses

The simplest way to avoid being tripped up by these sorts of errors is to keep all compiler warnings switched on; modern compilers moan about of lot of these problems.

KEY CONCEPT *Build your code with all compiler warnings switched on. It will highlight potential problems before they can bite.*

THE ECONOMICS OF FAILURE

The art of debugging is intimately bound to the topic of the previous chapter—*testing* your code. Testing will expose faults that need to be debugged. I've covered these topics in two separate chapters because they *are* different disciplines. However, the two in tandem are fundamental to reliable software development.

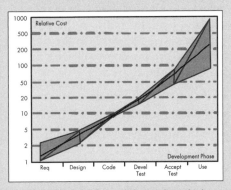

The frantic pace of the software factory demands code that's produced quickly and cheaply. This haste leads to software projects that are riddled with bugs and are consequently delivered incredibly late. Late software is a huge problem—it's not just embarrassing and inconvenient; it could spell disaster for any company.

In fact, the longer you ignore testing and allow bugs to remain, the worse it gets—this graph illustrates the escalating impact of bugs as they wriggle through the development process. It shows the average cost of finding and fixing an error relative to the phase of production in which it is discovered. (Boehm 81)

As you can see, the cost rises dramatically with time (note that the cost axis is a logarithmic scale). To make matters worse, the nearer we get to a project deadline, the less time we have to perform thorough testing. The added pressure of impending deadlines makes debugging that much harder—with the pressure on, you're even more likely to introduce fresh faults with each repair.

To save your skin and prevent a lot of debugging stress, test your code early and thoroughly. Eradicate any bugs you find as soon as possible, before they have a chance to cause major grief. There are established methodologies for this—look at test-driven development, one of the components of agile software development.

Build errors

While not a run-time fault *per se*, a build error may only manifest itself at run time. Be on the lookout and always distrust your build system, no matter how good you think it is. In these enlightened times, you're unlikely to come across a compiler bug. However, you may not always be running the code you thought you built.

I've been hit by this several times: The build system failed to rebuild a program or shared library (perhaps because the makefiles didn't contain adequate dependency information or the old executable had a bad time-stamp). Every time I tested my modifications, I was still unknowingly running the old buggy code. There are a number of ways to confuse a build system, but the worst is when you don't notice it failing—like a leprous limb.

It can take quite some time to figure this out. For this reason, when you feel at all wary of what's going on, it's sensible to do a total cleanout of your project and rebuild it from scratch. This should flush out any potential build system problems.[2]

Basic semantic bugs

The majority of run-time faults are due to very simple errors causing incorrect behavior. Using uninitialized variables is a classic example and can be quite hard to track; the program's behavior will depend on the garbage value previously in the memory location used by the variable. One time the program will work fine; another time it may fail. Other basic semantic faults are:

- Comparing floating-point variables for (in)equality[3]
- Writing calculations that don't handle numerical overflow
- Rounding errors from implicit type conversions (losing the sign of a char is common)
- Declaring an unsigned int foo, later writing if (foo < 0)—oops!

This type of semantic fault is often caught with static analysis tools.

Semantic bugs

These insidious errors that won't be caught by inspection tools are much harder to identify. A semantic bug might be a low-level error, like the wrong variable being used in the wrong place, not validating a function's input parameters, or getting a loop wrong. It may be a higher-level piece of wrong-headedness: calling an API incorrectly or not keeping an object's state internally consistent. Many memory-related errors fall into this category—they can be devilishly hard to find due to their ability to warp and corrupt your running code so that it behaves in totally unpredictable and unreasonable ways.

Programs often behave strangely. The only consolation is that they're doing exactly what we told them to.

The best kind of run-time failures are the repeatable ones. If they're reproducible, they are much easier to write tests for and track down the cause of. The failures that don't always occur tend to be memory corruptions.

The View from the Trenches

Now that we've arranged things into neat little boxes, let's zoom right in and take a look at some of the common types of semantic faults:

Segmentation faults

Also known as *protection faults*, segmentation faults come from accessing memory locations that have not been allocated for the program's use. They

---

[2] This presumes that you trust your build clean facility. To be really thorough, delete the entire project and check it back out again afresh. Alternatively, manually remove all intermediate object files, libraries, and executables. For large projects, both options are extremely tedious. *C'est la vie.*

[3] You can't do this meaningfully; floating point arithmetic is too approximate to offer an exact comparison that indicates anything.

result in the operating system aborting your application and producing some form of error message, usually with helpful diagnostic information.

This can be triggered far too easily by typing errors involving pointers or by poor pointer arithmetic. A common C typo causing a *segfault* is `scanf("%d", number);`. The missing & before `number` makes `scanf` try to write into the memory location referenced by the (garbage) contents of `number`, and *poof*—the program disappears in a wisp of smoke. If you're really unlucky, though, `number` happens to hold a value that equates to a valid memory address. Now your code will continue as if nothing is wrong, until the memory you just wrote over is used and your fate is in the lap of the gods.

Memory overruns

These are caused by writing past memory that has been allocated for your data structure, be it an array, a vector, or some other custom construct. When writing values into the wide blue yonder, you'll probably clobber the data in some other part your program. If you're running on an unprotected operating system (more common in embedded environments), you may even tamper with data from another process or the OS itself. Ouch.

Memory overrun is a common problem and difficult to detect; usually the symptom is random unexpected behavior manifesting at a much later point than the overrun, possibly many thousands of instructions later. If you're lucky, the memory overrun hits an invalid memory address and you get a segfault, which is hard to ignore. Use safe data structures wherever possible to insulate yourself from the possibility of such disaster.

Memory leaks

These are constant threats in languages that do not have garbage collection.[4] When you want some memory, you have to ask the run time for it nicely (using `malloc` in C or `new` in C++). Then you have to be polite and give it back when you're done (using `free` and `delete`, respectively). If you rudely forget to release memory, your program slowly consumes more and more of the computer's scarce resources. You may not notice it at first, but your computer's response will gradually degrade as memory pages thrash to and from the disk.

Two other classes of error relate to this: freeing a memory block *too many* times, causing unpredictable environmental failures, and not managing other scarce resources carefully, such as file handles or network connections. (Remember: Anything you manually acquire must be manually released.)

Running out of memory

This is always a possibility, as is running out of file handles or any other managed resource. It might be rare (modern computers have so much memory, how could this possibly happen?), but that's no excuse to

---

[4] It is also possible to leak memory in a language *with* garbage collection. Hand two object references to one another, and then let go of them both. Unless you have an advanced garbage collector, they will never be swept up.

ignore the potential for failure. Only sloppy code fails to make appropriate checks, and it will consequently perform in a very brittle manner when run in constrained situations. For this reason, you should always validate the return status of a memory allocation or filesystem call.

Some operating systems *never* return failure from a memory allocation call—every allocation returns a pointer to a reserved but unallocated memory page. When the program eventually tries to access this page, an OS mechanism traps the access and then really allocates memory to the page, resuming normal program operation. This all works nicely until the available memory is finally exhausted. Your program will then be sent error signals—a long time after the relevant allocation occurred.[5]

Math errors

These errors come in a number of guises: floating-point exceptions, incorrect mathematical constructions, overflow/underflow, or expressions that may fail (for example, divide by zero). Even trying to output a `float` but passing an `int` through `printf("%f")` can cause your program to bomb with a maths error.

Program hangs

These are usually caused by bad program logic; infinite loops with badly crafted terminal cases are the most common. We also see deadlock and race conditions in threaded code, and event-driven code waiting on events that will never occur. However, it is usually fairly easy to interrupt the running program, see where the code has stalled, and determine the cause of the hang.

Different OSes, languages, and environments report these errors in different ways, using different terminology. Some languages avoid whole classes of errors by not providing features you can shoot yourself in the foot with. Java, for example, has no pointers, and it automatically checks every memory access you make.

Pest Extermination

Weeding out bugs in your software is hard. You have to discover a bug, diagnose the problem, eradicate all traces of the unwanted behavior, make sure the bug hasn't bred elsewhere, and try not to break the code while you're doing all of it. The first step alone, finding a fault, is a major hassle: Humans make mistakes when writing, but they make just as many mistakes when reading. When looking over my prose or my code, I'll naturally read what I *meant* to write and not what I *really* wrote. Faulty code isn't obvious. The compiler isn't much help; in fact it's really quite pedantic. It can only produce *exactly* what you asked, not what you were hoping for.

---

[5] This is certainly the case for Linux, at least until you exhaust the virtual memory address space. At this point, `malloc` may return 0, but the system would probably have keeled over before you got a chance to notice.

Some programmers introduce far fewer faults than their peers (up to 60 percent less), can find and fix faults quicker (in as little as 35 percent of the time), and introduce fewer faults as they do so. (Gould 75) How do they do it? They are naturally able to pay more attention to the task and can focus on the microscopic level of the code they're writing, while still keeping the broader picture in mind.

This is the *art* of debugging; it's very much a skill to be learned. Experience teaches you how to become an effective debugger. And this is something that we *will* all get plenty of experience doing.

The single most important rule when debugging is this: *Use your brain.* Think. Consider what you're doing. Don't flail around, thoughtlessly hacking at bits of code until something appears to work.

KEY CONCEPT *Always follow the golden rule of debugging:* Use your brain.

There are two paths to pest extermination: the quicky-and-dirty *low road* and the theologically correct *high road.* We must be aware of them both; sometimes the low road looks like a good shortcut but will actually be slower, and sometimes the high road takes more effort to follow than is genuinely required.

The Low Road

The bug is really simple. The cause is obvious. You don't need to think too much about it, do you? Sometimes a quick tweak *will* achieve results; a few simple tests can pinpoint a problem quickly. So is it a justifiable thing to do? Perhaps, but don't fall into the trap of believing it will work every time. Too many programmers try to fix faults by tinkering, fiddling, poking, and prodding the code without any real thought about what they're doing. What happens is rarely anything useful—they just mask the original problem behind a myriad of other faults.

If you do make the conscious decision to do some quick-and-dirty stabbing around, set yourself a firm time limit to do it in. Don't spend an entire morning with the "just one more try" approach. After your time limit is up, follow the more methodical approach laid out here.

KEY CONCEPT *Set a reasonable time limit for "unstructured" debugging, and then resort to more methodical approaches if you don't find success.*

If your guesswork turns up trumps and you do find the fault, reengage your thinking gear. Look at "How to Fix Faults" on page 167, and make the change carefully and thoughtfully. Even if the fault was easy to find, the fix isn't necessarily as obvious.

The High Road

A better debugging technique is more methodical and considered. It recognizes that there are two distinct facets to removing a bug: *finding* the fault that caused it and *fixing* that fault.

Each presents its own challenges to overcome and problems to solve. It's very easy to forget the latter part and to presume that once you've found a fault, it will be easy and obvious to fix. Don't believe it. I'll cover both aspects in depth in later sections, and I'll outline a sensible approach to the task. But first, a few key principles govern the debugging game:

- How difficult a fault is to find depends on how well you know the code it's lurking in. It's hard to jump into some random source and make any kind of judgment about it without knowing the structure and how it's supposed to work. For this reason, if you have to debug some new code, take time to *learn* about it first.

KEY CONCEPT   *Learn the code you're debugging—you can't expect to find errors in code you don't understand.*

- Ease of debugging is also dependent on the control you have over the execution environment—how much you can play around with the running program and inspect its state. In an embedded world, debugging can be much harder because the tool support is more sparse. You're also probably running in an environment that is providing a lot less insulation from your own stupidity; little mistakes can have much bigger consequences.

- One of the most potent weapons in our debugging arsenal is a distrust of anyone's code mixed with a healthy dose of cynicism. The cause of your errant behavior could be absolutely anything, and in the act of diagnosis, you should start by eliminating even the most unlikely of candidates.

KEY CONCEPT   *When you look for a fault, suspect* everything. *Eliminate even the unlikeliest of causes first, rather than presume they have nothing to do with it.* Assume nothing.

Bug Hunting

How do you find bugs? If there was a simple three-step process, we'd all have learned it, and our programs would be perfect by now. As it is, there isn't, and they aren't. Let's try to distill the available bug-hunting wisdom.

Compile-Time Errors

We'll look at these first, since they are comparatively easy to deal with. When your compiler comes across something unpleasant, it will not normally just complain once, but will take the opportunity to sound off about life in general, spitting out a barrage of subsequent error messages. It's been told to do this; upon encountering any error, the compiler tries to pick itself back up and carry on parsing away. It rarely manages very well, but with code like yours, who could blame it?

The upshot is that the later compiler messages can be quite random and irrelevant. You only need to look at the very *first* error reported and sort out that problem. Have a glance farther down the list by all means; there may be some other useful errors there, but often there aren't.

CASE STUDY #1: PICTURE THIS

The program

A reasonably small utility with graphical interface.

The problem

The program was redesigned with an updated "look and feel"—new icons and a new layout. The old interface was intended to remain available as a configurable option. During redevelopment, everything worked fine until just before release, when someone tried to use the legacy interface. The program crashed just as a window was appearing but before you had a chance to see it fully.

The story

Thankfully, this was a nicely repeatable problem. The program was fired up in a debugger, and the point of failure was determined to be deep within the UI library in some image-rendering code.

On investigation, it seemed the failure was due to an invalid graphic being used. The program was trying to display an icon at memory location zero; a null pointer was causing the crash. We traced back up the call stack to see which graphic should have appeared. Armed with this information, a brief look at the legacy graphics directory showed that this particular icon was missing.

The icon load operation in the window's constructor had obviously failed, returning a zero pointer value to signify "No icon loaded." This return value was never checked—the author assumed that the graphic would always be present.

The fix would be twofold:

- Check the return values of all icon load routines so they deal with any other missing graphics more gracefully.
- Place the missing graphic in the correct directory.

Time to fix

A few hours to trace the problem, fix the fault, and verify the repair.

Lessons learned

- Check *all* function return codes, even the ones you don't think will fail.
- Test all program functionality as soon as possible, especially the rare conditions that won't be used very often.

KEY CONCEPT *When your build fails, look at the* first *compiler error. Trust this far more than the subsequent messages.*

Even this first compiler error may be cryptic or misleading, depending on the quality of the compiler (if you're really stumped by what an error means, try using another compiler). Hardcore C++ template code can provoke quite inspired errors from some compilers—listing reams and reams of mystical template incantations.

The syntax error usually *is* on the line that the compiler reports, but sometimes it may actually be on the *preceding* line—a syntax error there causes the following line to be nonsensical; this is what the compiler notices and moans about.[6]

---

[6] C++ has a great party trick here: The preceeding line might be in a different file! If you forget the ; at the end of your class declaration in a header file, the first line of the implementation file makes no sense. The compiler gives you a *very* crytpic error.

Linker errors, on the whole, are far less cryptic. The linker will tell you that it's missing a function or a library, so you'd better scurry off and find it (or write it). Sometimes the linker may complain about arcane v-table related C++ problems; this is usually a symptom of a missing destructor implementation or something similar.

Run-Time Errors

Run-time errors require more of a game plan. If your program contains a bug, then it's likely that a condition somewhere in the code that you believed to be true isn't. Finding the bug is a process of confirming what you think is correct until you find the place where that condition doesn't hold. You have to develop a model of how the code really works and compare this with how you'd intended it to work. Doing this methodically is the only sensible way.

KEY CONCEPT *Debugging is a* methodical *activity, slowly closing in on the location of a fault. Don't treat it like a simple guessing game.*

The *scientific method* is the process scientists use to develop an accurate representation of the world. That sounds akin to what we are trying to do, right? There are four steps to the scientific method:

1. Observe a phenomenon.
2. Form a hypothesis to explain it.
3. Use this hypothesis to predict the results of further observations.
4. Perform experiments to test these predications.

Although we're trying to *get rid of* the errant phenomenon rather than build a model of it, we need to understand a fault to truly fix it. The scientific method is a good debugging backbone, and you'll see it reflected in the steps below.

Identify a Failure

It all starts here, when you notice that the program doesn't do what it's supposed to do. It may crash or it may produce a yellow triangle instead of a blue square, but you know something's up, and you've got to fix it. The first thing to do is put a fault report into the fault database (see "Fault-Tracking System" on page 147). This is particularly valuable if you're in the middle of tracking some other bug or don't have time to handle the fault right away. Making a record ensures that the fault won't get lost. Don't just make a mental note to come back to a problem later—you'll forget.

Before you rush on and try to find a bug you've stumbled across, identify the nature of the errant behavior. Characterize the problem as completely as possible by answering questions like: Is it timing sensitive? and Does it depend on input, system load, or program state? If you don't understand the bug before you try to fix it, you'll just be changing code until the symptom disappears. You may only have masked a cause, so the same fault will crop up elsewhere.

Did the code work before? Skip back through your revision control system to find the last working version, and compare that working code with this faulty revision.

Reproduce It

This goes alongside characterizing the failure. Work out the set of steps you must take to reliably trigger the problem. If there is more than one way, then document them all.

KEY CONCEPT *The first step to locating a fault is finding out how to reproduce it reliably.*

You have a problem if the bug doesn't seem reproducible; the best you can do is set up mousetraps and see what information you can find out when it does occur. For these unreliable failures, keep careful notes of the information you collect; it may be a while until you see the problem crop up again.

Locate the Fault

This is the big one. You've got the scent; now you need to use what you've learned to track the beast and pinpoint its location. That is far more easily said than done. This is a process of eliminating all the things that don't contribute to the failure or can be shown to work correctly, Sherlock Holmes style. As you progress, you will find that you need to gather more and more information—the more answers you get, the more questions that arise. You may need to draft some new tests. You may need to poke around in the seedy underbelly of the code.

Analyze what you have learned about the failure. Without jumping to conclusions, draw up a list of code suspects. See if you can spot patterns of events that hint at causes. If possible, keep a record of the inputs and outputs that demonstrate the problem.

A good starting point for the investigation is where the error *manifests* itself—although this is rarely the actual habitat of the fault. Remember: Just because a failure exhibits itself in one module, it doesn't necessarily mean *that* module is to blame. Determining this location is easy if the program crashed; a debugger will tell you the line of code that failed, the value of all variables at that point, and who called this function. In the absence of a crash, start from a point you know exhibits incorrect behavior. Work backward from there, following the flow of control, checking that the code is doing what you expect it to at each point.

KEY CONCEPT *Start from what you know—the point of a program crash, for example. Then work back from there to the cause of the failure.*

There are a few common bug-hunting strategies:

- The worst thing to do is randomly change things to see if the failure goes away. This is an immature approach. (A professional will at least try to make it look scientific!)

- A far better strategy is to *divide and conquer*. Say you have the fault pinned down to a single function that consists of 20 steps. After the 10th step, print out the intermediate result, or set a breakpoint and investigate it in your debugger. If the value is good, then the fault lies in the instructions after this; otherwise, it's in the instructions before. Concentrate on those instructions and repeat until you've cornered the fault.

- Another technique is the *dry run* method. Rather than relying on intuition to locate the error, you play the role of the computer, tracing program execution through a trial run, calculating all intermediate values to get the final result. If your result and reality don't match, then you know a fault lies in the code—it's not doing what you expect it to. Although it is time consuming, this can be very effective because it highlights your bad assumptions.

Understand the Problem

Once you've found out where the fault is lurking, you've got to understand the *real* problem. If it's a simple syntactic error, such as using = instead of == (*d'oh!*), then the implications aren't too nasty. For more complex semantic problems, make sure you really know what the problem is and all the ways that it may manifest itself before you move on—you may have only found a part of the problem.

Often the fault is very subtle: The code will be doing exactly what it should do *and* what you thought it was supposed to do when you wrote it! The problem is a flawed assumption (remember how evil these are?). A function's writer and caller can easily presume that different behavior is acceptable in particular strange cases. Trace back and understand exactly what the cause of the problem is and whether or not any other bits of code may contain the same mistake.

KEY CONCEPT *Once you think you've found the cause of a bug, investigate it thoroughly to prove that you are right. Don't blindly accept your first hypothesis.*

This is a key principle in the fight against bugs. Otherwise, you'll join the ranks of the programmers who introduce *more* faults than they fix with every bit of repair work.

Create a Test

Write a test case to demonstrate the failure. You may have done this in the "Reproduce It" step if you were clever. If you didn't, then you really want to write one now. With your new understanding, make sure the test is rigorous.

Fix the Fault

And now the easy part: You've just got to fix the darned thing! This *should* actually be the easy part—you understand exactly why the faliure occurs, and you've got a reproducible way to excerise it. Given that depth of information, the fix is usually child's play. Most programmers find bug fixing hard because they skip the first two steps.

We'll look at fixing faults in more detail in the following section.

Prove You've Fixed It

Now you know why you wrote a test case. Run it again, and prove the world is a better place. The test case can be added to your regression test suite to ensure that the fault is never reintroduced at a later point.

KEY CONCEPT   *You haven't finished debugging until you've proved that the problem's been fixed and has gone away for good.*

That's it! Game over—mission accomplished. Well done. However . . .

If All Else Fails

Sometimes you try all of this but it just doesn't work; you're left wailing and gnashing your teeth, with a sore head from banging it against a brick wall for too long. When things get this bad, I always find it helps to explain the whole problem to someone else. Somewhere in the description, everything seems to slip into place and I see the one key piece of information I had been missing all along. Try it and see. This is one reason why *pair programming* is such a successful strategy.

How to Fix Faults

You'll notice that this section is much smaller than the preceding one. Funny. Usually the whole problem is *finding* the darned fault. Once you've worked out where it is, then the fix is obvious.

But don't let that lure you into a false sense of security. Don't stop thinking once you've diagnosed the source of your errant behavior. It's very important not to break anything else as you make the fix—it's surprisingly easy to trample over something in the flower bed as you stroll over to pluck out a weed.

KEY CONCEPT   *Fix bugs with the utmost care. Don't risk breaking anything else with your modification.*

As you modify code, always ask yourself, *What are the consequences of this change?* Be aware of whether the fix is isolated to a single statement or if it affects other surrounding bits of code. Might the effect of your change ripple out to any code that calls this function; does it subtly alter the behavior of the function?

CASE STUDY #2: HUNG, DRAWN, AND QUARTERED

The program

Embedded software controlling a consumer electronics device.

The problem

A random lockup, occurring after about a week's continuous operation. It resulted in the total death of the device; there was no UI response, no network connectivity, not even an interrupt being handled—the processor was completely stalled. This was *particularly* nasty, leaving no easy way to find out the cause.

The story

The lockup happened so rarely that it was remarkably hard to track. In an attempt to pinpoint the cause, we tried a number of tests, leaving each to run for the week-long gestation period. First we tried different usage patterns to see if we could make the fault happen sooner and thereby determine what was causing it. These tests made no difference whatsoever.

The nature of the lockup seemed to imply that it was a gnarly hardware problem. We tried running the software on different versions of the mainboard with different peripheral components and different CPU versions. Weeks of testing later, we were still no nearer to figuring out the problem, but we did have less hair (and what remained was graying). No matter what configuration we used, the software still ran for about a week and then locked up.

Next we tried removing different sections of code from the system. After a lot of iterative testing, we tracked the problem down to a single component: Its presence in the build heralded a lockup; its absence prevented it. Finally, progress!

Working out *why* this software component caused such problems wasn't straightforward. It was layered on top of a third-party library, which itself was built against a core OS library. We discovered that this core OS library had been upgraded to a more recent version, but the third-party library had not been rebuilt. We'd been continually linking against an inappropriate piece of code. While theoretically, this shouldn't have made a difference—the OS library change was supposedly *binary compatible*—a rebuild of the third-party library fixed the problem for good.

Time to fix

The total process took about four months, elapsed time. It involved many people on and off over that period, consumed lots of test resources, tied up many bits of hardware, and caused more review meetings than you'd believe were possible. As bugs go, this one had a nasty sting, and caused the company a lot of pain (not to mention expense).

Lesson learned

Rebuild the *whole* software platform whenever *any* component changes to prevent subtle version mismatches.

Convince yourself that you have really found the root *cause* of the problem, and you're not just hiding another *symptom*. Then you can feel confident that you've put a fix in the right place. Consider whether similar mistakes may have been made elsewhere in any related modules; go and fix them if necessary.[7]

---

[7] This is why *copy and paste programming*—duplicating code, perhaps with minor modifications—is bad. It's dangerous; you'll mindlessly duplicate bugs, and then you won't be able to fix them in a single place.

KEY CONCEPT   *When you fix a bug, check to see if the same mistake is lurking in related sections of code. Exterminate the bug once and for all: Fix all occurences of the fault now.*

Finally, try to learn from your mistake. We must learn, or else we will be doomed to repeat the same errors for all eternity. Is it a simple programming error you keep making or something more fundamental, like the incorrect application of an algorithm?

KEY CONCEPT   *With each fault you fix, learn the lessons. How could you have prevented it? How could you have discovered it more quickly?*

Prevention

Anyone will tell you that "an ounce of prevention is worth a pound of cure." The best way to manage the population of bugs is to not introduce them. Sadly I don't think that we'll ever completely reach this ideal. For as long as programming involves problem solving, it will always be difficult—not only do you have to solve the problem correctly, you have to understand the whole problem *fully* in the first place. Despite this, careful defensive programming can avoid many problems. Good programming is about discipline and attention to detail. Thorough testing will prevent faults from leaking out in your software releases.

This section could be enormous, but all prevention advice boils down to that one simple statement: *Use your brain.* Enough said.

Wasp Spray, Slug Repellent, Fly Paper . . .

Many useful debugging tools exist, and you'd be stupid not to take advantage of them. Some are *interactive*, allowing you to inspect the code while it is running. Others are *noninteractive*, often running as a code filter or parser spitting out information about the program following analysis. Learn how they work to immesurably reduce your debugging time.

Debugger

This is the best known debugging tool; the name belies its purpose. A debugger is an interactive tool that allows you to view the internals of your running program and poke around with it. You can follow the flow of control, inspect the contents of variables, set *breakpoints* in the code for later interruption, and even run arbitrary sections of code at will.

Debuggers come in many shapes and sizes; some are command-line tools, and others are graphical applications. There will be at least one available for your particular development platform (although the ubiquitous gdb seems to be ported to every conceivable platform these days).

A debugger relies on *symbols* being left in your executable (these are elements of the compiler's internal information that are normally stripped out at the final link stage)—it uses these to provide you with information about function and variable names and the location of the source files.

Although debuggers are rich and powerful tools, I believe that they are often misused or overused, and can actually *inhibit* good debugging. Programmers easily become wrapped up chasing what the program is doing, getting sidetracked by observing the wrong variable values, stepping into the wrong functions, and they forget to step back and *think* about the problem they are trying to solve. A little more thought about a failure may pinpoint the specific fault far more quickly than it would take to hunt it down in a debugger.

KEY CONCEPT *Use debuggers sparingly, when you encounter behavior you can't explain. Don't reach for them routinely to use as an alternative to* understanding *how your code works.*

Memory Access Validator

This interactive tool inspects your running program for memory leaks and overruns. It can be remarkably useful, revealing reams of memory release errors you never knew existed.

System Call Tracing

System call trace utilities, like Linux's strace, show all the system calls issued by an application. This is a good way to see how a program is interacting with its environment and is particularly useful when it appears to be stalled on some external activity that is not happening.

Core Dump

This is a Unix term for the OS-generated snapshot of a program that is produced when it exits abnormally. The term derives from archaic machines with *ferrite core* memory; the dump file is still called *core* today. It contains a copy of the program's memory when it died, the state of the CPU registers, and the function call stack. The core dump can be loaded into an analyzer (which is often the debugger) to reveal a great deal of useful information.

Logging

Logging facilities allow you to programmatically generate information about your application as it runs. Rich logging systems allow you to assign priorities to the output (e.g., debug, warning, fatal) and then filter out a particular message level at run time. The program's log gives a history of activity that can help pinpoint the circumstances that triggered a failure.

Even without a good logging facility (either as part of the operating environment or from a third-party library), you can achieve the same effect by peppering your code with basic print statements on an ad hoc basis. However, these printouts may interfere with normal program output, and they all must be carefully removed in the production code release.

Sometimes even lowly print instructions aren't available. Once, when bringing up a new piece of hardware, the only diagnostic output I had was a single eight-segment LED display and a scope attached to a spare system bus. It's impressive how much information you can shoehorn into a few lights when you try!

There are downsides to logging: It can slow down program execution, bloat the executable size, and even introduce bugs of its own. Some logging systems, in which the crash destroys the buffer containing log messages, are useless for trapping a program crash. Be sure you know how well your logging mechanism behaves, and always send diagnostic print statements to an unbuffered output stream.

Static Analyzer

This is a noninteractive tool that inspects your source code for potential problems. Many compilers perform basic static analysis when set to their maximum warning level, but good analysis tools go far beyond this. Products exist to detect problem code and any usage of undefined behavior or non portable constructs, to identify dangerous programming practices, to provide code metrics, to enforce coding standards, and to create automatic test harnesses.

Use of a static analysis tool can eradicate many errors before they have a chance to bite—a handy safety net. It's a pragmatic idea to use a static analyzer from a different company than your compiler manufacturer—two companies are less likely to have made the same set of assumptions or mistakes.

In a Nutshell

> *I can remember the exact instant when I realized that a*
> *large part of my life from then on was going to be spent in*
> *finding mistakes in my own programs.*
> *—Maurice Wilkes*

Like death and taxes, no matter how hard we try to avoid them, bugs happen. Sure, you might be able to mitigate the effects of the first two by using every sort of antiwrinkle cream available and manipulating your money in cunning ways, but if you don't know how to deal with faults when they stare you in the face, your code is doomed.

Debugging is a skill you develop. It doesn't rely on guesswork, but on methodical detection and thoughtful repair.

Good programmers . . .	Bad programmers . . .
• Don't cultivate bugs; they write code carefully to prevent introducing them in the first place	• Don't debug; they flail around, sinking in a sea of bad code
• Understand what their code does and write careful tests to ensure that it won't be broken easily	• Spend most of their life in a debugger, figuring out what their code is doing
• Hunt for bugs methodically and carefully, rather than rush in headfirst without a battle plan	• Encounter a failure and try to hide it—they actively avoid debugging
• Know their limitations and will ask others to help find a fault when they're stuck	• Have unrealistic expectations of the quality of their code and of their ability to fix faults
• Change code carefully, even when making a "simple" repair	• "Fix" bugs by masking symptoms rather than tracing the problem back to its real cause

See Also

Chapter 1: On the Defensive
How to prevent bugs from ever gaining a foothold in your code.

Chapter 8: Testing Times
You can't fix a fault until you know it exists. Thorough testing is a prevention mechanism that stops faults from leaking out into your software releases.

Chapter 20: A Review to a Kill
Code reviews help to pinpoint and eradicate bugs and can identify problem areas that would otherwise go undetected.

Get Thinking

A detailed discussion of these questions can be found in the "Answers and Discussion" section on page 500.

Mull It Over

1. Is it best for faults to be fixed by the original programmer who wrote the code? Or is the programmer who discovered the problem better placed to make a fix?

2. How can you tell when to use a debugger and when to use your brain?

3. You should learn unfamiliar code before you start trying to find and fix faults in it. But the time pressures of the software factory often dictate that you can't spend any serious time studying and understanding the program you're repairing. What's the best way forward?

4. Describe good techniques to avoid memory-leak bugs.

5. When is it justifiable to have a quick stab at finding and fixing a fault, rather than adopting a more methodical approach?

Getting Personal

1. How many debugging techniques/tools do you routinely use? What others have you seen that you might find useful?

2. What are the common problems and pitfalls in your language(s) of choice? How do you guard against these kinds of bugs in your own code?

3. Are most of the bugs that occur in your code sloppy programming errors, or are they more subtle issues?

4. Do you know how to use a debugger on your platform? How routinely do you use it? Describe how to do the following:

   a. Produce a backtrace

   b. Inspect variable values

   c. Inspect value of fields within a structure

   d. Run an arbitrary function

   e. Swap thread contexts

THE CODE THAT
JACK BUILT

*Mechanisms to Turn Source Code
into Executable Code*

*What you spend years building may be destroyed
overnight. Build anyway.*

—Mother Teresa

The programmer (*Geekus maximus*) is usually found in its natural habitat, hunched in the ethereal glow of a monitor, entering profound combinations of punctuation characters into a text editor. Occasion-ally, this timid beast will leave the confines of its lair to forage for coffee or pizza. Quickly it returns to safety, continuing its ritual at the keyboard.

If typing language constructs was all there was to programming, then our job would be a great deal easier, although we'd risk being replaced by the proverbial infinite number of monkeys with their infinite number of text editors. Instead, we must run our source code through a compiler (or interpreter) to obtain something that might just function as we intend it to. Invariably, it doesn't. Rinse and repeat.

The task of converting carefully honed, high-level language into an executable that can be distributed is commonly referred to as *building* code (although you'll find that this term is used pretty interchangeably with *making* and *compiling* in most contexts).

This act of building is a fundamental part of what we do—we can't develop code without performing a build. It's important, then, to understand what's involved and how your project's build system works in order to have any confidence in the code that's generated. There are a lot of subtle issues at play here, especially when a codebase reaches a reasonable size. Interestingly, almost all programming textbooks will gloss over this kind of topic; they present single-file example programs that don't show any real build complexity.

Many developers rely on their IDE's build system, but this doesn't remove the burden of understanding how it works. It's very convenient to hit a button and have all your code generated, but if you don't know which options are being passed to the C compiler or which level of instrumentation is left in your object files, then you're not really in control. The same holds true if you type a single *build* instruction at a command prompt. You must understand what's going on under the hood to be able to repeatably perform reliable builds.

Language Barriers

There are several varieties of programming languages, each with its own mechanical process of constructing an executable program from source code. Some construction models are more complex than others, and each has its strong and weak points.

There are three main mechanisms: *interpreted* languages, *compiled* languages, and *byte-compiled* languages. These are shown in Figure 10-1.

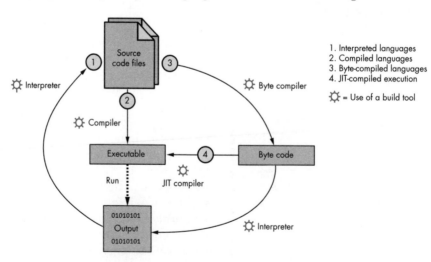

Figure 10-1: Programing language build and execution methods

DO WE REALLY *BUILD* SOFTWARE?

Building is often used as a metaphor for programming, equating what we do to the "traditional" building industry. There are many striking parallels, since both are construction processes. We have, in fact, seen some sort of overlap and collaboration between the two disciplines, as the software patterns movement (see "Design Patterns" on page 255) learned from Christopher Alexander's architectural work. (Alexander 79)

It's valuable to understand how far this metaphor stretches and how useful it really is. No metaphor is perfect, after all. Although philosophical and a bit of an aside, it *does* matter because the comparison will inevitably prejudice our approach to development. The metaphor is helpful in places; elsewhere it's less than perfect (even potentially harmful).

The good

Like the physical construction process of a house, we start from nothing and build by placing one layer of structure atop another. Before the construction begins, a process of gathering requirements and careful design and architecture should have been performed. While you can probably build a garden shed without much planning, you'd be crazy to hope an unplanned skyscraper had a chance of standing up; you need serious design and planning up front. This neatly parallels our software construction.

The bad

The metaphor stretches thin in other areas, though. We can modify the foundational layers of our software constructions more easily than the foundations of a house. It's far cheaper to tear down a software edifice than a physical one. This means that the software world offers the opportunity to prototype and explore more often than the physical world does.

Real World building mandates sound engineering principles; this is enshrined in statute and enforced by public liability. Many software firms wouldn't know an engineering principle if it slapped them in the face.

The ugly

Our entire development procedure *is* akin to a physical construction process, comprising system conception, design, implementation, and testing. But what we're actually thinking about in this chapter is subtly different—it revolves around *compilation* and the procedures involved in *this kind* of building task. The metaphor's a bit out of kilter here too. Each time you take a fresh copy of some source code, you "build" it, creating an executable program; *that* is what we're looking at here. Be clear about these two different uses of the term "build."

The software build process follows its own rules—if you modify a function, you must then perform a system rebuild. In contrast, you don't have to rebuild the walls in your house every time you paint the doors.

Interpreted Languages

Code written in interpreted languages does not need to go through a specific build phase. After writing some code, you need only tell the interpreter where it is; it parses and acts on the instructions in real time. Common interpreted languages are Perl, Python, and JavaScript. The majority of OO languages are interpreted, largely because they have been developed more recently as computers have become better able to run interpreters at reasonable speeds.

The main advantage of interpreted languages is their speed of development; with no intermediate *compile* stage; you can test each change very quickly. You also gain platform independence—popular language interpreters run on many different platforms. Your program will work wherever the interpreter has been ported.

But interpreted programs have some disadvantages: They execute more slowly than a compiled equivalent since the language run time has to read, parse, interpret, and act on each individual code statement. That's a lot of work. Modern machines are so fast that this is only a problem for the most computing-intensive applications. There are various interpreter technologies that improve code performance: Some languages precompile the source file before execution (slowing down startup time) or employ *Just-In-Time (JIT)* compilation, compiling each function as it's about to be run (slowing down each function's first call). For most programs, this isn't an appreciable overhead, and JIT-compiled performance is indistinguishable from native compiled code.

Scripting languages are often interpreted. These languages support a very fast development cycle by being very forgiving to questionable code (with lax language rules and weak typing) and by avoiding complex features. Scripting languages are often used as glue to invoke other utilities in more convenient ways. Unix shell scripts, Windows batch files, and Tcl are examples of scripting languages.

Compiled Languages

Compiled languages employ a build toolchain to convert your source code files into machine instructions that will execute natively on the target platform. The target execution platform is usually the same as the development platform, but embedded developers often build on a PC and target very different machines, using a *cross compiler.* Large projects are compiled in several stages; each individual source file is compiled into an intermediate *object file*, and then these objects are linked into a final executable. This build model is illustrated by the cake-baking metaphor, shown in Figure 10-2, where individual ingredients (source files) are mixed (compiled) and finally baked together (linked).

C and C++ are the most popular compiled languages, although most structured languages are compiled. By its very nature, a compiled application will run faster than its interpreted counterpart (at least, without JIT compilation), although in practice, you won't notice this—most applications are not computing-intensive; they spend most of their time stalled and waiting for user, disk, or network input.

The compiled language build procedure is more complex than an interpreter, so there are more possible points of failure. An application has to be recompiled for each target platform you want to run it on.[1]

---

[1] Target platforms are distinguished by their processor types and the host operating systems. Other factors, like the available peripheral hardware, may be important.

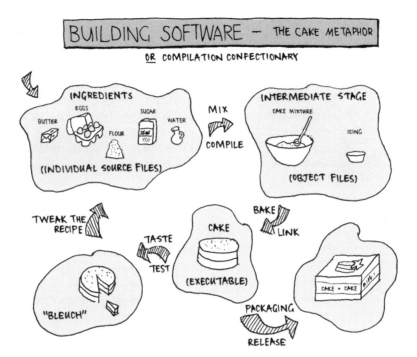

Figure 10-2: Compilation confectionary

Byte-Compiled Languages

Byte-compiled languages sit halfway between interpreted and compiled languages. They involve a compilation step but don't produce a native executable program. Instead, the product is a file of *byte code*; a pseudo machine language that can be executed by a *virtual machine*. Java and C# are common byte-compiled languages.

A common misconception is that executing byte code is *necessarily* slower than executing an equivalent compiled binary. This is not always so. A JIT optimizer can make intelligent decisions about the code that may make it particularly fast (for example, tailoring itself to the exact hardware the program is executing on).

As a compromise, byte compilers inherit some of the advantages and disadvantages of the previous approaches. Byte code can be executed on any platform the virtual machine has been ported to, so you gain portability (although some language run times are more widely ported than others).

Making Mountains out of Molehills

The compiled (and byte-compiled) build models are the hardest to reason about, so let's investigate what compiling software entails. It's shocking how few newly trained programmers really understand this, so we'll start from first principles. If you already know this stuff, feel free to skip ahead.

For a good understanding, it's best to think about each manual step rather than rely on your IDE to do all the rebuilding work for you. This five-part story of a simple program's development will explain:

1. You're starting a new project, coded in C. It will solve all the ills of the software development world and will usher in a new era of world peace. However all you have at first is a single file containing `main`. You've got to start somewhere.

   It's easy to build and run this single-file program—you just type `compiler main.c`,[2] and out pops an executable for you to run and test. Simple.

2. The program grows. To help organize the parts, you split it into multiple files, one per functional block. The build is still a simple process. Now you type `compiler main.c func1.c func2.c`. The same executable program pops out, leaving you to carry on testing as before. No sweat.

3. Soon, you recognize that some sections of the code are really individual components with isolated concerns, almost like stand-alone libraries. It would be easier to reason about these sections of code by placing them in their own directories—grouping the similar sections of code together. Now the project is beginning to spread out. The simple way to build this new file structure is to compile each individual source file by hand, using a compiler call that doesn't build an executable, just intermediate object files. Afterward, `main.c` is compiled and linked with all the intermediate object files. To do this, you may also have to point the compiler at some other directories' include files. Now things are getting a little more complex.

   Whenever you change some code in one of the new directories, you have to fire off the compile command in *that* directory and then issue the final "link everything" command once more. Quite manual. Additionally, if you change a header file that other directories use, all of *those* directories have to be rebuilt too. If you forget, the linker will probably generate a slew of cryptic complaints.

   To eliminate this huge command-line burden, you can write a *shell script* (or *batch file* in Windows) that walks around each directory and fires off the requisite build commands. Having hidden all that messy work and the tedious compiler parameters, you can get back to the serious business of code development with the peace of mind that you don't have to memorize unnecessary build fluff.

4. Later on, these subdirectories become real stand-alone libraries; they are also used in other projects. You tidy up the code so it's a little friendlier to use, add some good user-facing documentation, and then alter the build commands to generate *shared libraries* rather than object files. This requires some more changes to your build script, but it's a relatively hidden change and isn't too painful.

---

[2] Obviously, you would replace `compiler` with the command to prod your C compiler—this is a hypothetical example.

5. Development carries on like this for some time. Code is added rapidly. Many new subdirectories and sub-subdirectories are created. Although the file structure seems pretty neat, build times become a problem— each time you fire up the build script, it recompiles every source file, even those that haven't changed. The temptation here is to track all changes yourself and to issue subdirectory builds by hand again (perhaps by creating individual directory build scripts as a halfway house). The project is now so large that it would be very easy to miss some dependencies. This would lead to hard to resolve build errors, or even subtler problems (e.g., you may encounter flaws that don't stop the link from working, but that do make the program behave in incorrect ways).

    Now your development is on the brink. You can't trust the system being used to build the code. It's not safe. You can only really trust the executable if you've done a complete cleanout and rebuilt from scratch.

Enter the tool for just this occasion. The classic solution is a command-line program imaginatively called make. (Feldman 78) It deals with all of the intermediate object files and compilation rules for you and, most importantly, tracks which files depend on which other files. You tell it what to do by writing makefiles that provide the necessary build rules. It looks at the source file time-stamps to check what has changed since you last performed a make, and then it recompiles just those files, along with anything dependent on them. It's a more intelligent version of the scripts we wrote above, specifically tailored to the task of compiling and recompiling software.

Over the years, many variants of the humble make have appeared, these days many with pretty GUI façades. GNU Make is one of the most widely used tools (it's free and very flexible). If you haven't been initiated into the Cult of Make, "Make: A Tourist's Guide" on page 183 explains its basic operation.

There are many other build systems in common use. Look at SCons, Ant, Nant, and Jam for examples. They are each tailored to a specific kind of build environment (for example, Nant is used to build .NET projects) or for a particular quality (many aim to simplfy the syntax of make, which is quite baroque!).

Building Builds

In that sinking morass of software construction, we've seen some of the main issues of a build procedure. Essentially, any software build process takes one or more source files as input, and it spits some executable program out the other end. It may even produce an entire release distribution, including an executable, help files, an installer, and so on, all packaged neatly and ready to be burned onto CD.

TERMS AND CONDITIONS

These terms comprise the main software construction terminology:

Source code

Source code is physically contained in the files that you write, and it usually occurs in a high-level language. These language constructs can be converted into a functioning program with the appropriate tools.

Compilation

Source code is converted into an executable in one of two ways. One is to *compile* it into an executable program. The alternative is to *interpret* the source code in real time—a language run time parses and acts on the source code as the program is run.

Build

This is a vague term, often used as a synonym for *compile*. Compilation is a single construction step, whereas a build describes the entire construction process. The term *make* is used in a similarly vague fashion; even worse, it is also the name of a common software build tool.

Object code

Object code is held in an *object file*. It represents the compiled version of a file of source code. Object code is not directly executable; it relies on other files of code (most programs are made of more than one source file). An object file must be *linked* with other objects to create an *executable*.

Library

A code *library* is akin to an object file—it is a collection of compiled code and not itself a whole program. A library contains a cohesive collection of useful functionality that can be incorporated into any program. A library can be *static* or *dynamic*. The former is linked like an object file, whereas the latter is dynamically loaded by the application when it is run.

Machine code

Some compilation steps produce *machine code* rather than object files. This is a form of source code that represents the exact CPU instructions for a program. Machine code is converted into real CPU instructions by an *assembler*, which is why it's also known as *assembly code*.

Some low-level OS libraries and embedded programs are written in assembly language, but we generally work in high-level languages and leave assembly to the internal workings of the compiler.

Linking

The *linker* combines one or more *object files* (and perhaps libraries) into a final executable or into a partially linked code *library*.

Executable

The outcome of a compile or link step. This is a self-contained program that can be run directly on your computer.

Like the cumulative story from which I shamelessly pilfered this chapter's title, as our software develops and matures, the build process develops and matures with it. Maybe yours didn't start in as basic a state as the example above, but build scaffolding tends to start simple and grow alongside the code it builds. A large project often has a bewildering build process that requires (but doesn't necessarily always have) adequate documentation. We can see that the act of compiling a single source file is at the lowest level of the build food chain, and we will raise a tower of extra work upon this simple act.

A build process is not *just* about compiling source files. It may also involve preparing some text registration files from templates, creating internationalized strings for the UI, or converting graphics files from their source resolution to some destination format. Practically all such activities can hang off a build system and be run in the normal course of a build. This does presume that all the tools are scriptable—that they can be run by some other program (e.g., by make).

It's important to consider your build system a part of the entire source tree, not something separate. Makefiles are kept under revision control alongside other source files, are maintained alongside the source, and are as much a part of the program as any other source file. They're essential—you can't create the application without them.

KEY CONCEPT *Consider the build system a part of the source tree, and maintain the two together. They are intimately entwined.*

MAKE: A TOURIST'S GUIDE

Make is one of the most widely used build systems in the programming world. Here is a whirlwind tour of what it is and what it can do.

Make is driven by *makefiles*, which usually reside in directories beside the source code they build. These makefiles contain *rules* describing how to build the application. Each rule describes a *target* (that is, a program or intermediate library to build), details what it depends on, and how to create it. Comments in the file are prefixed by #. Here's a short example (using the hypothetical compiler program to build source):

```
# This first rule says ".o files can be built from
# .c files and here's the command to do it." $< and
# $@ are magic names for the source and destination
# file. Yes, make's syntax can be a little cryptic...
%.o: %.c
    compiler -object $@ $<

# This rule says "the program myapp is built from these
# three .o files, and here's how to link them together"
myapp: main.o func1.o func2.o
    linker -output $@ main.o func1.o func2.o
```

That's the general idea. If you save this with the magic filename Makefile and then issue the make myapp command, it will be loaded and parsed. Since myapp depends on some .o files, these will first be built from their respective .c files using the rule provided. Then the linker command will be run to create the application.

There are many ways to neaten this up so that it's more manageable. For example, makefiles can define variables; the myapp rule looks nicer like this:

```
OBJECT_FILES=main.o func1.o func2.o
myapp: $(OBJECT_FILES)
    linker -output $@ $(OBJECT_FILES)
```

A deeper description of the nuts and bolts of make usage is outside the scope of this book, but it's something every developer ought to know. There are many more useful features available. GUI build tools are essentially wrappers around this kind of functionality, hiding the detail of writing makefiles. They are generally easier to set up, but can be a hindrance when you want to do some advanced build configuration.

What Makes a Good Build System?

Following are a few important qualities of a good build system.

Simplicity

The build system must be accessible to *all* programmers, not just the build gurus. Every developer must be able to perform a build, or he can't get any work done. If a build system is too complicated, it's practically useless. It must be:

Simple to learn

That is, a new developer should be able to join the team and quickly understand how to build software. He won't be productive until he's mastered the build procedure. I've worked in companies where it was considered a *rite of passage* to figure out how the build works and to perform one. That is not just an unhelpful attitude, it is dangerous—what happens when everyone who really knows how to build the code leaves?

As software grows, it becomes larger and harder to understand. As the build system grows alongside it, it becomes larger and harder to understand. Builds tend to become more clever and more cryptic as new facilities are introduced. Resist complexity.

Simple to set up

Setting up a build means:

- Taking a clean PC (with just a fresh copy of the host OS)
- Installing all the necessary software (compilers, translators, source control, installers, plus patches/service packs)
- Installing all the necessary libraries (noting the correct versions)
- Creating the correct environment to perform a build in (this may involve setting up directory structures, assigning environment variables, getting the correct tool licenses, and so on)

Without clear instructions for setup, how can you be sure that your build is a repeatable procedure?

Unsurprising

It's best to use common, well-known build tools. They are what people expect and know how to use, so the learning curve is less steep. Complex build tools that do things no one really understands are worrying.[3]

Uniformity

It's essential that everyone uses the same build system. Otherwise they're not building the same software. Different build mechanisms may seem equivalent— *I use my IDE while he uses makefiles*—but you're increasing the maintenance

---

[3] I have an built-in distrust of anything more clever than GNU Make, but that probably says more about me than the other clever make tools. GNU Make is *quite* clever enough, thank you!

effort and the potential for error. Subtle differences can creep in—for example, compiler options may not be the same, resulting in a different executable.

This dovetails with the requirement to maintain the build system alongside the source tree. If the build system physically *is* a part of the code, then it can't be ignored or avoided.

KEY CONCEPT *Every programmer on a project must use the same build environment. Otherwise you're not all building the same software.*

This may seem blindingly obvious, but it's incredibly easy to get wrong. Even if you *are* all happily sharing makefiles, other differences can slip past unnoticed—mismatched versions of libraries, tools, or the build scripts can all lead to a different program being built.

Repeatable and Reliable

Builds must be deterministic and reliable. You should be able to determine the set of input files easily before performing the build. Performing two separate builds on the same set of files should give you exactly the same executable both times—the build should be *repeatable.*

KEY CONCEPT *A good build system allows you to repeatedly create physically identical binary files.*

You can then mark this set of source files in the revision control system as a particular version of the software (or archive the files to a backup store), and perform many identical builds at any time in the future.

This is crucial—an important customer may find a significant bug in an old revision of software, and if you can't get back to that version and generate the exact same program, you may never be able to reproduce the failure, let alone find the fault.

KEY CONCEPT *You must be able to pull out a source tree from three years ago and rebuild it correctly.*

A build process that spits out an unreproducible binary is worrying. If what comes out of a build depends on the lunar cycle, the world becomes a hard place to reason about. This means that gratuitous use of C's __DATE__ or other potentially changeable information should be kept to an absolute minimum in the source files.

The build must work perfectly all the time—it must be *reliable.* If it falls over every other day or occasionally produces a broken binary, then it is worse than useless—it's dangerous. How can you be sure that you're testing a good binary? How can you be sure that your company is releasing an acceptable product? Problems with the build system really hamper development.

The build should be almost invisible; the only thing you need to worry about is how to turn the handle, and you should be assured that the right things will come out at the end.

Atomic

The ideal build system takes undoctored *virgin source* and compiles it all at once, with no human intervention. There should be no special steps you have to go through to perform the build. You should not have to fire up another application halfway through and prod a file. You shouldn't even need to run more than one command to perform the build. This ensures that no information is locked away in your head, just waiting to be lost. All the build magic is documented in a reliable place—the build script itself. The build is always repeatable. It's safe.

KEY CONCEPT *A good build is presented as a single step. You need only push a button or issue one command.*

If you can't reach this ideal (and it's not *at all* unreasonable), then the less manual a build is, the better. All of the manual steps need full documentation. It is acceptable (in fact, it's advisable) to break the procedure up into these separate parts:

1. Obtain the virgin source.
2. Build it.
3. Create the release distribution from this.

See how the notion of *building* the code is separate from *obtaining* it—the same build instruction could potentially create any version of the software, depending on the version of source you start with. *Packaging* the program is also a separate step; for development work, you don't always want to waste time creating a full install package.

A WAR STORY

Repeatable builds are essential; you must be able to regenerate any released version of your software. You'll get into trouble otherwise. I once worked for a company that struggled with this exact problem.

They had made a live change to the code on a customer's site and did not replicate the change in their master copy under version control. The customer was no longer running an "official" software release. Later on, when the customer found a critical bug, the programmers couldn't reproduce it. But of course no one could figure out why, because the on-site tweak had been long forgotten.

Why did they do this? Because it was much, much easier to make a quick-and-dirty change than to do it properly (i.e., fix the bug in the main codebase, test it, make an official software release, ship it to the customer, and then get the appropriate approval and sign-off before installation). When your client's business depends on your software and its entire production line is waiting for you to fix a bug, the pressure for a dirty hack is enormous.

Coping with Errors

At the end of development, when the dust settles over finished code, there will be *no* build errors. But during development you'll be breaking things all over the place. The build system has to cope with this and should lend a hand to deal with it.

- Your build system should not continue after an error. It should stop and leave you with no doubt about what broke and where it can be fixed. If the build process continues, other problems will almost certainly result as a consequence of that first skipped error. These will be very hard to understand. For your own sanity, don't break this rule!

- The build system should remove any incomplete objects when a build step fails. Otherwise the next time you run a build, it will assume that file is actually intact and pick up after it. This will cause much pain later on; errors that magically hide themselves are great fun.

- Builds should not be *noisy*. This isn't determined so much by the build process as the source code that you've written.[4] If your code generates compiler warnings, then there is something in it that you should be looking into. Persuade the compiler to be quiet by writing better code. Copious silly warnings can cloak the more insidious messages that you *should* be reading.

  For maximum peace of mind, build with all compiler warnings enabled—switching them off does not fix the problem; it hides it.

  The only real way to follow this advice is from the very start: Think about the build process at the beginning of your project. Trying to add the flag that says *all warnings enabled* when you've already written a lot of code will result in an instant flood of warnings. The overwhelmingly likely response is to quickly turn the flag off again and pretend it never happened. Anything for an easy life. You really have to start as you mean to go on.

The Mechanics

Beyond those quality concerns are the practicalities of a build system. To discuss this in concrete terms, we'll talk about make, a specific build system, and makefiles a lot—don't worry too much; barring syntactic differences, other build systems follow similar conventions (even the pretty graphical ones).

Choice of Targets

Makefiles define *rules* that describe how to build *targets*. (Remember: Other build systems work in a very similar manner, even if the terminology is subtly different.) The system is clever enough to infer all intermediate targets and

---

[4] Actually, it could be—you can disable compiler warnings to remove the noise. This is the *wrong* way to solve the problem.

build those along the way. A single makefile can contain multiple targets. This allows you to use one build system to generate several different outputs, such as:

- Distinct programs (commonly seen when two programs have some common code components and so live in the build source tree)
- Different target platforms to build your application for (say a Windows/Apple/Linux version, or a desktop/PDA release)
- Product variants (the full *release build* or a *demo* version with save/print disabled)
- The development build (with debugging support enabled, logging switched on, and assertions made fatal)
- Differing *levels* of build (build just the internal libraries, build the application, build an entire distribution)

You might even require some combination of these targets, say a "demonstration PDA" build.[5] You can design your source tree so that each of these targets can be built from the same place. Rather than type just make, you might type make desktop or make pda, and an appropriate executable will come out the other end. (The name following make is the rule it should attempt to build.)

There is a huge benefit in doing this rather than having separate source trees for each target. Maintaining several source trees across which most of the code is identical would be an intense and error-prone task. You could easily forget to apply one of your modifications to all copies of the code.[6]

So how do these target rules differ? The actual differences can boil down to a number of things:

- Different files being built (e.g., save_release.c or save_demo.c)
- Different macro definitions being passed through to the compiler (e.g., the compiler predefines a DEMO_VERSION macro to select appropriate #ifdefed code in save.c)
- Different compiler options being used (e.g., to enable debugging support)
- Different tool sets or environments being selected for building (e.g., using the correct compiler for the target platform)

While you could have any number of targets for all sorts of minor differences, it opens the possibility of making your build system complex and unwieldy. Some selections can be moved to build configuration options. Some configuration can actually be done at code install time, or even at run time. This is preferable if it reduces the number of different builds that exist and require testing.

---

[5] In this case, the mechanism changes: You can only build one target at a time, so the "demo-ness" would become a build configuration rather than a target. A later section discusses configurations.

[6] Note how this dangerous approach is different from maintaining multiple *branches* of a project in a revision control system. Revision control systems provide a mechanism to *merge* changes across branches and to easily compare branches for differences.

LIFE AFTER MAKE

A lot of the issues we're investigating here are quite specific to the C-style development cycle, where a compiler generates object code and libraries from source files, and these are linked into a final executable. Some languages follow a different model. Java simplifies the build process greatly; the javac compiler takes over the role of make, performing dependency checks automatically. It locks you down more, enforcing a particular build tree structure, but makes your life easier by doing so.

Simple Java programs don't need an elaborate build system; one javac command can safely rebuild the world. However, a reasonably large Java project often *will* employ make. We've seen that there is more to a build than just compiling source. You need a mechanism to prepare supporting files, to run automated tests, and to create the final distribution. Make is a good framework for this to hang off of, so it isn't entirely redundant.

Housekeeping

For every target rule you define, there should be a corresponding *clean* rule that undoes all the build operations—removing the program executable, intermediate library, object files, and any other files created during the build. The source tree should revert to its original virgin state—it's relatively easy to verify that it does.[7]

This implies that a build system that physically alters the source files is nasty—how can you easily revert from these changes? You should instead use the original files as templates, and send modifications to a different output file.

Clean rules are a good housekeeping convention. They allow you to easily sweep everything away and rebuild from scratch when you think that a build gremlin is catching up to you.

KEY CONCEPT   *For every build rule, have a corresponding clean rule that undoes the action.*

Dependencies

How does a build system know which files depend on which others? Short of ESP, it's a difficult task, and so we will elicit help from the people who do know.

You provide dependency information in your makefile rules: a recipe in make's preferred format. Make can build and follow the tree of dependencies, inspect each file's timestamp, and work out which parts need to be rebuilt after any modification.

This is simple enough for an executable build rule—you just need to specify which object files and libraries comprise it. You don't, however, want to laboriously specify dependency information for every single source file; no doubt there are many #included files, which themselves #include many others. Quite a list. It would be really easy to type incorrectly at first and very likely to become out of date; you could easily add a new #include and forget to alter the makefile correspondingly.

---

[7] Just do a build, do a clean, and then check the tree for differences from the start state.

Who *does* know about all this dependency information? The compiler does—it's the one component in the build system that actually traces all source file dependencies. Helpfully, all good compilers have an option that causes them to spit out dependency information. The trick is to write a make rule that gathers this dependency information, places it in an appropriately formatted file, and then includes *that* in the dependency tree.

Automated Builds

If your build procedure is atomic, a simple matter of firing off one command, you can easily set up overnight builds of the entire source tree.[8] A regular overnight build takes the code that has been produced during the day and applies the full build procedure to it. This is a remarkably helpful practice with many benefits:

- Every morning there's a fresh copy of the state of the art. Developers often spend the day in their own little worlds, forgetting to synchronize their code with colleagues' check-ins. This technique provides a painless integration test, checking that everything knits together properly.

- It identifies build problems early on, with no extra work on your part. When you sit down at your desk in the morning, coffee in hand, you can see whether the source tree is in a buildable state. You'll know immediately where to start fixing, rather than wait for your own build to complete.

- You can add automated regression and stress tests to the overnight build. This is a good way to sanity-test code before anyone ever tries to use it. During the day, you may not have time to run the full test suite with every build—this ensures that it never gets overlooked. It's a potent validation mechanism.

- The overnight build can be used as a yardstick of project progress. Publish the overnight test results and, as more and more tests pass, the developers gain a sense of achievement.

- You can make actual product releases from the overnight build. You'll trust this build to have not suffered from command-typing mistakes, misconfiguration, or other human errors.

- It proves that you really know how to build the software and that the build procedure really *is* atomic. Without running automatic builds, how do you know that your build process doesn't rely on some other activity, like one of the developers cleaning away the old build tree first?

KEY CONCEPT *Establish an automatic build of your software. Use it to ensure that your codebase is in a consistent state.*

Automated builds are especially good for big systems (where a build of *everything* may take hours and hours) or for systems with many people working alongside one another (where each developer may not have a copy of the absolute latest system source at any given point).

---

[8] Time-delayed commands can be set up in Unix using the cron utility or in Windows using the Scheduled Tasks facility.

A good practice with nightly builds is to capture the *build log* (the output of the build procedure) and make it publicly accessible. Perhaps even email the results around when the build fails, to highlight the problem. It's important to know what happened each time a build ran, especially when something goes wrong.

The overnight build becomes a central heartbeat of project development. The code is developing healthfully and happily if the builds are successful. A great rule enforced on many projects is: *Don't break anything in the source tree*—checking in code that breaks during the nightly build is punishable by something extremely painful and unpleasant (preferably involving public humiliation). A second rule is this: *If the build breaks, it's everyone's problem.* If the overnight build fails, all developers must put down their down tools until it works again.

You can take this automatic build procedure to the extreme, and use tools that perform a build whenever the source repository is altered. This is known as *continuous integration* and is a powerful way to check that your code is consistent and buildable at any point in time.

Build Configuration

A good build system allows you to configure certain aspects on a per-build basis. This could be via options in your IDE, but makefiles usually achieve this by defining *variables*. Variables can be picked up from a number of places:

- Inherited from the calling environment
- Set on make's command line
- Defined explicitly within a makefile

Configuration variables are commonly used in the following ways:

- A PROJECT_ROOT variable is defined, pointing to the root of the build tree. This allows the build system to know where to look for other files—for example, to establish paths for header files. You really don't want to hard-code the location of the build tree on your development machine. If you did, you could never move it around, and you wouldn't be able to manage two build trees at the same time.
- Other variables may specify where to find each external library (so you can point the build at different versions for testing purposes).
- They may specify the kind of build to produce (*development* or *release*, for example).
- The command to invoke each build tool (compiler, linker, etc.) can be placed into a variable. This makes it easy to test a different set of command-line parameters, or to employ a different vendor's tool.

You can put default values into the makefile. This serves two purposes: it documents all the available options and means you don't *have* to provide values for every config option all the time.

Recursive Make

Source code naturally nests into directories. If all the files in a large project got dumped into one directory, things would rapidly become unmanageable. Since the source tree nests, the build system has to nest too. Far from making life more complex, accommodating this nesting can make the build system more flexible.

A makefile in one directory can invoke the makefiles in subordinate directories by firing off another make command, just as it would invoke a compiler. This is a common technique known as *recursive make*; the build system that recurses into each subdirectory builds the components in there and returns to build the components in this directory. In this way, you can type make from the project root directory to build the whole codebase, or within a subcomponent's directory for a partial build. Whatever you want to be built is built.

Recursive make helps to compartmentalize and manage build components, but introduces some problems of its own. It is slow (as it fires off many child processes to traverse into subdirectories), and since each child-make only sees its portion of the entire build tree, it can get dependency information incorrect. Be wary of recursive make if you see it—prefer to make non-recursive build systems. (For more on this, see the answer to this chapter's "Mull It Over" question 7 on page 506.)

Please Release Me

Some builds are particularly important and require more care in their preparation. These are *release builds*, builds that are made with a special purpose, rather than in the course of code development. A release could be one of a number of exciting events: a beta version, the first official product release, or a maintenance release. It may also be an internal development milestone or an interim release to the test department; these builds won't leave the company but are held in as high regard as external releases, almost a fire drill for an official release.

If the build system is carefully crafted, there shouldn't be any extra preparation needed for a release build. However, these important builds must be handled thoughtfully, so we need to make sure that no build issues compromise the final executable. The key concerns with release builds are:

- Release builds should always come from a virgin source tree, not from someone's half-built development tree. Start from scratch. We need to know the exact state of the source files being built. Do not trust the files on Joe's computer to be in a "good enough" state.

- Prior to the build itself, a specific step identifies which source code and which particular file versions to include in this release. It then marks them in some manner, usually by tagging or labeling them in the source control system. The release's file set is now retrievable at any later point.

THE (SOURCE) TREE OF KNOWLEDGE

All code lives in a *source tree*; a file structure housing directories and source files. The structure of this tree affects how easy the code is to work with. A messy glob of files is far harder to understand than a neatly arranged hierarchy. We can use the source file structure to our advantage, making development easier. This tree structure goes hand-in-hand with the build system, since the build system physically is a part of the source tree (hence the term *build tree* is used interchangeably with *source tree*). A modification to one requires meddling with the other.

We divide code into separate modules, libraries, and applications. A good source tree reflects that structure. The code composition should map neatly into files, using directories as a logical grouping mechanism. This helps to manage development with multiple programmers—each person will probably be working in his own self-contained directory, removed from other people's work by a reasonably safe distance.

Libraries

Place each library in its own self-contained directory. Use the tree structure to differentiate the library *interface* (the public header files) from private *implementation* details. It is a good idea to place the public API within a directory on the compiler's lookup path and keep any private headers out of the way.

Applications

Structuring is easier; there are no public files as such, just a collection of source files that link to libraries. Even so, wrap each application in its own directory to make its bounds clear. If the application is large enough to have distinct constituent parts, they should be separated into subdirectories, or even libraries, and built separately. Make the build tree reflect the program structure.

Third-party code

The source tree should clearly mark *your own* code from third-party work. Projects increasingly rely on others' code; common libraries are brought in from outside (from commercial vendors, free software projects, or even other parts of the company). These external files should be kept separate.

Other stuff

Program documentation can live in the source tree. Put it in directories beside the code it refers to. The same holds for graphics and any other supporting files.

- Each release build has a particular name you identify it by, sometimes a cool code name, sometimes just a build number. This should tally with the source control label the code was marked with. If you and I agree that we're talking about "build five" when investigating a fault, then we're working in harmony. If you are working with build five, but I found a fault in build six, how do we know we'll see the same issues?

KEY CONCEPT *Release builds are always made from virgin source. Ensure that these pristine sources can always be retrieved from source control or a backup archive in the future.*

- There may be some extra packaging stage after the code has been built, like preparing a CD, adding documentation, integrating licensing information, or whatever. This step should also be automated.

- Each release should be archived and stored for future reference. Obviously you store a copy of the final built executable in whatever form it ships to the user (the exact shipped Zip file, self-extracting EXE, or whatever). You should also capture the final state of the build tree if possible, but often this will be enormous and impractical.

- At the very least, the *build log*, the exact sequence of commands issued and the response generated, should be retained. These logs allow you to look back over old builds and see which compiler errors were overlooked or exactly what happened during the build. Sometimes this can give a clue into a fault reported in a years-old version of product that has long since been discontinued.

- Each release has a *release note* that describes what has changed. It may or may not be a customer-facing document, depending on exactly what you're building. These notes should also be archived. Usually the release note describes the changes since the last release and contains updates subsequent to the printing of the official documentation, any known issues, upgrade instructions, and so on. It is an important part of the release procedure and shouldn't be overlooked.

- When performing release builds, you must select the correct set of compiler switches—they might differ from those used in development builds. Debugging support gets switched off, for example. You also need to choose what level of code optimization is appropriate. Optimization may be disabled for development builds since the optimizer often takes a particularly long time to execute. This can become unbearable on very large build trees. However, ramping the optimizer up to warp speed nine may expose compiler bugs that break your code; you have to carefully choose (and test) a level.

  If you use different sets of compiler options for development and release builds, beware. You *must* test the release builds regularly, long before a deadline approaches. Aim to minimize the differences between release and development builds.

KEY CONCEPT   *Ensure that you test the release configuration of your application, not just the development builds. Subtle differences may adversely affect the code's behavior.*

Since creating a release build is a relatively involved task and is so important to get right, responsibility is usually delegated to a nominated team member (perhaps one of the coders, perhaps someone in QA). That person produces all the release builds for the project to make sure that each build is of the same high quality. Release builds are as much about procedure as they are about the build system.

Jack-of-All-Trades, Buildmaster Of?

Many organizations employ a specific person to fulfill a *build engineer* role, often known as the *buildmaster*. This person's job is to maintain the build system. The role may also involve planning and managing release schedules, or it may be purely technical. The buildmaster knows the build system intimately.

He or she probably sets it up, adds new targets as required, maintains the overnight build scripts, and so on. The buildmaster also owns the build system documentation, and probably administers the source control system.

The buildmaster performs the release builds, and for this reason is often heavily involved with tracking component stability. He or she is charged with ensuring the reliability and safety of the release process.

The buildmaster is not always a specific full-time position; sometimes a programmer will double in this task.

In a Nutshell

It is easier to pull down than to build up.
—Latin proverb

On the face of it, building software is easy if you have the right tools. But you have to know how to use the tools properly. The quality of your build system is paramount; without a safe, reliable build process, you can't realistically develop solid code. Producing trustworthy release builds for production is an even more involved matter—it requires a thorough approach and a well-defined procedure. It is important to have an understanding of what's going on when you fire off a build, even if you don't have to alter the build system every day.

Performing good builds is not a straightforward task; our jobs are safe from the proverbial infinite number of monkeys. They're too busy arguing about which of their infinite number of text editors is the better one, anyway.

Good programmers . . .

- Understand how their build system works, how to use it, and how to extend it
- Craft simple, atomic build systems, and maintain them alongside the source code
- Automate as many build activities as possible
- Use overnight builds to catch integration problems

Bad programmers . . .

- Ignore build system mechanics, then get caught by silly build problems
- Don't care how unsafe and unreliable their build system is
- Expect newcomers to pick up their baroque build procedure in an almost adversarial manner
- Create thrown-together release builds without following a defined release procedure

See Also

Chapter 9: Finding Fault
Describes how to deal with build errors.

Chapter 18: Practicing Safe Source
The build tree is held in a source control system, and the two are intimately linked.

Get Thinking

A detailed discussion of these questions can be found in the "Answers and Discussion" section on page 502.

Mull It Over

1. Why should people with nice integrated development environments worry about using a command-line make utility, when they can just hit a single button to build their project?

2. Why is it important to treat the extraction of source code as a separate step from building it?

3. Where should the intermediate files from construction steps (e.g., object files) be put?

4. If you add an automated test suite to the build system, should it run automatically after the software is built, or must you fire a separate command to invoke the tests?

5. Should the overnight build be a *debug* or *release* build?

6. Write a make rule to automatically generate dependency information from your compiler. Show how to use this information in the makefile.

7. Recursive make is a popular method of creating a modular build system spanning several directories. However, it is fundamentally flawed. Describe its problems and suggest alternatives.

Getting Personal

1. Do you know how to perform different types of compilation using your build system? How can you build a debug or release version of the application from the same sources, with the same makefiles?

2. How good is your current project's build process? Does it rate well against the characteristics in this chapter? How could you improve it? How easy is it to:

   a. Add a new file to a library?

   b. Add a new directory of code?

   c. Move or rename a file of code?

   d. Add a different build configuration (say, a demo build)?

   e. Build two configurations in one copy of the source tree without doing a clean in between?

3. Have you ever created a build system from scratch? What drove you to its particular design?

4. Everyone suffers from flaws in a build system from time to time. When programming a build script, you're as likely to introduce bugs as you are when programming real code.

   What kinds of build errors have you been bitten by, and how could you fix, or even prevent, them?

11

THE NEED FOR SPEED

Optimizing Programs and Writing Efficient Code

In this chapter:

- Why efficient code matters
- Designing efficient code
- Improving the performance of existing code

There is more to life than increasing its speed.
—*Mahatma Gandhi*

We live in a fast food culture. Not only must our dinner arrive yesterday; our car should be fast and our entertainment instant. Our code should also run like lightning. I want my result. And I want it *now*.

Ironically, writing fast programs takes a long time.

Optimization is a spectre hanging over software development, as renowned computer scientist W.A. Wulf observed: "More computing sins are committed in the name of efficiency (without necessarily achieving it) than for any other single reason—including blind stupidity." (Wulf 72)

Optimization is a well-worn subject, on which everyone has offered their two cents' worth, and the same advice has been served time and time again. But despite this, a lot of code is *still* not developed sensibly. Optimization seems like a good idea, but programmers get it wrong all too often: They get sidetracked by the lure of efficiency, they write bad code in the name of performance, they optimize when it's really not necessary, or they apply the wrong kind of optimizations.

In this chapter, we'll address this. We'll tread the familiar ground, but look out for some new views on the way. Don't worry—if the subject is optimization, it shouldn't take too long. . . .

What Is Optimization?

The word *optimization* purely means to make something better, to improve it. In our world, it's generally taken to mean "making code run faster," measuring a program's performance against the clock. But this is only a part of the picture. Different programs have different requirements; what's "better" for one may not be "better" for another. Software optimization may actually mean any of the following:

- Speeding up program execution
- Decreasing executable size
- Improving code quality
- Increasing output accuracy
- Minimizing startup time
- Increasing data throughput (*not necessarily* the same as execution speed)
- Decreasing storage overhead (i.e., database size)

Conventional optimization wisdom is summed up by M.A. Jackson's infamous laws of optimization:

1. Don't do it.
2. *(For experts only)* Don't do it yet.

That is, you should avoid optimization at all costs. Ignore it at first, and only consider it at the end of development when your code is not running fast enough. This is a simplistic viewpoint—accurate to a point, but potentially misleading and harmful. Performance is really a valid consideration right from the humble beginnings of development, before a single line of code has been written.

Code performance is determined by a number of factors, including:

- The execution platform
- The deployment or installation configuration
- Architectural software decisions
- Low-level module design

- Legacy artifacts (like the need to interoperate with older parts of the system)
- The quality of each line of source code

Some of these are fundamental to the software system as a whole, and an efficiency problem there won't be easy to rectify once the program has been written. Notice how little impact individual lines of code have; there is so much more that affects performance. We must manage performance issues at every step of the development process and deal with any problems as they arise. In a sense, optimization (while not a specific scheduled activity) is an ongoing concern through all stages of development.

KEY CONCEPT *Think about the performance of your program from the very start—do not ignore it, hoping to make quick fixes at the end of development.*

But don't use this as an excuse to write tortured code based on your notion of what is fast or not. Programmers' gut feelings for where bottlenecks lie are seldom right, no matter how experienced they are. In the following sections, we'll see practical solutions to this code-writing dilemma.

But first, the golden rule. Before you consider a stint of code optimization, you must bear this advice in mind:

KEY CONCEPT Correct *code is far more important than* fast *code. There's no point in arriving quickly at the wrong answer.*

You should spend more time and effort proving that your code is correct than making it fast. Any later optimization must not break this correctness.

A WAR STORY

I once discovered that a module I'd written was running unbelievably slowly. I profiled it and tracked the problem down to a single line of code. It was called frequently and appended a single element to a buffer.

Upon inspection, the buffer (which I was given and hadn't written) was expanding itself by a *single element* each time it got full! In other words: Every single append was allocating, copying, and deallocating the entire buffer. Ouch. Needless to say, I was not expecting this behavior.

This helps to show how we get suboptimal programs: by growth. Few people willfully attempt to write an ambling program. As we glue software components into a larger system, we can easily make assumptions about the performance characteristics of the code and end up with a nasty shock.

What Makes Code Suboptimal?

In order to improve our code, we have to know the things that will slow it down, bloat it, or degrade its performance. Later on, this will help us to determine some code optimization techniques. At this stage, it's helpful to appreciate what we're fighting against.

Complexity

Unnecessary complexity is a killer. The more work there is to do, the more slowly the code will run. Reducing the amount of work or breaking it up into a different set of simpler, faster tasks can greatly enhance performance.

Indirection

This is touted as the solution to all known programming problems, summarized by the infamous programmer maxim: *Every problem can be solved by an extra level of indirection.* But indirection is also blamed for a lot of slow code. This criticism is often leveled by old-school procedural programmers, aimed at modern OO designs.

Repetition

Repetition can often be avoided and will inevitably ruin code performance. Repetition can often be avoided and will inevitably ruin code performance. It comes in many guises—for example, failing to cache the results of expensive calculations or of remote procedure calls. Every time you recompute, you waste precious efficiency. Repeated code sections unnecessarily extend executable size.

Bad design

It's inevitable: Bad design will lead to bad code. For example, placing related units far away from each other (across module boundaries, for example) will make their interaction slow. Bad design can lead to the most fundamental, the most subtle, and the most difficult performance problems.

I/O

A program's communication with the outside world—its input and output—is a remarkably common bottleneck. A program whose execution is blocked waiting for input or output (to and from the user, the disk, or a network connection) is bound to perform badly.

This list is nowhere near exhaustive, but it gives us a good idea of what to think about as we investigate how to write optimal code.

Why Not Optimize?

Historically, optimization was a crucial skill, since early computers ran very, very slowly. Getting a program to complete in anything like reasonable time required a lot of skill and the hand-honing of individual machine instructions. That skill is not so important these days; the personal computer revolution has changed the face of software development. We often have a surplus of computational power, quite the reverse of the days of yore. It might seem that optimization doesn't really matter anymore.

Well, not quite. The software factory still throws us situations requiring high-performance code, and if you're not careful, you'll need a mad optimization dash at the last minute. But it is preferable to avoid optimizing code if at all possible. Optimization has a *lot* of downsides.

There's always a price to pay for more speed. Optimizing code is the act of trading one desirable quality for another. Some aspect of the code will suffer. Done well, the (correctly identified) more desirable quality is enhanced. These trade-offs are the top reasons to avoid optimizing code:

Loss of readability

It's rare for optimized code to read as clearly as its slower counterpart. By its very nature, the optimized version is not as direct an implementation of the logic or as straightforward. You sacrifice readability and neat code design for performance. Most "optimized" code is ugly and hard to follow.

Increase in complexity

A more clever implementation—perhaps exploiting special backdoors (thereby increasing module coupling) or taking advantage of platform-specific knowledge—will add complexity. Complexity is the enemy of good code.

Hard to maintain/extend

As a consequence of increased complexity and a lack of readability, the code will be harder to maintain. If an algorithm is not clearly presented, the code can hide bugs more easily. Optimization is a surefire way to add subtle new faults—these will be difficult to find because the code is more contrived and harder to follow. Optimization leads to dangerous code.

It also stunts the extensibility of your code. Optimizations often come from making more assumptions, limiting generality and future growth.

Introducing conflicts

Often an optimization will be quite platform specific. It might make certain operations faster on one system, at the expense of another platform. Picking optimal data types for one processor type may lead to slower execution on others.

More effort

Optimization is another job that needs to be done. We have quite enough to do already, thank you. If the code is working adequately, then we should focus our attentions on more pressing concerns.

Optimizing code takes a long time, and it's hard to target the real causes. If you optimized the wrong thing, you've wasted a lot of precious energy.

For these reasons, optimization should be quite a way down on your list of concerns. Balance the need to optimize your code against the requirement to fix faults, to add new features, or to ship a product. Often optimization is not worthwhile or is uneconomical. If you take care to write efficient code in the first place, you're less likely to need to optimize anyway.

Alternatives

Often code optimization is performed when it's not actually necessary. There are a number of alternative approaches that we can employ without altering our exisiting good-quality code. Consider these solutions *before* you get too focused on optimization:

- Can you put up with this level of performance—is it really *that* disastrous?

- Run the program on a faster machine. This seems laughably obvious, but if you have enough control over the execution platform, it might be more economical to specify a faster computer than spend time tinkering with code. Given the average project duration, you are guaranteed that by the time you reach completion, processors will be considerably faster. If they're not much faster, then they'll have double the number of CPU cores embedded in the same physical space.

  Not all problems can be fixed by a faster CPU, especially if the bottleneck is not execution speed—a slow storage system, for example. Sometimes a faster CPU can cause drastically *worse* performance; faster execution can exacerbate thread-locking problems.

- Look for hardware solutions: Add a dedicated floating-point unit to speed up calculations; add a bigger processor cache, more memory, a better network connection, or a wider-bandwidth disk controller.

- Reconfigure the target platform to reduce the CPU load on it. Disable background tasks or any unnecessary pieces of hardware. Avoid processes that consume huge amounts of memory.

- Run slow code asynchronously, in a background thread. Adding threads at the last minute is a road to disaster if you don't know what you're doing, but careful thread design can accommodate slow operations quite acceptably.

- Work on user interface elements that affect the user's perception of speed. Ensure that GUI buttons change immediately, even if their code takes over a second to execute. Implement a progress meter for slow tasks; a program that hangs during a long operation appears to have crashed. Visual feedback of an operation's progress conveys a better impression of the quality of performance.

- Design the system for unattended operation so that no one notices the speed of execution. Create a batch-processing program with a neat UI that allows you to queue work.

- Try a newer compiler with a more aggressive optimizer, or target your code for the most specific processor variant (with all extra instructions and extensions enabled) to take advantage of all performance features.

KEY CONCEPT *Look for alternatives to optimizing code—can you increase your program's performance in any other way?*

Why Optimize?

Having seen the dangers of code optimization, should you now give up any foolish notion of ever optimizing your code? Well, no: You should still avoid optimization wherever possible, but there are plenty of situations where optimization is important. And contrary to popular belief, some areas are *guaranteed* to require optimization.

- Games programming always needs well-honed code. Despite the huge advances in PC power, the market demands more realistic graphics and more impressive artificial intelligence algorithms. This can only be delivered by stretching the execution environment to its very limits. It's an incredibly challenging field of work; as each new piece of faster hardware is released, games programmers still have to wring every last drop of performance out.

- *Digital signal processing (DSP)* programming is all about high performance. Digital signal processors are dedicated devices specifically optimized to perform fast digital filtering on large amounts of data. If speed didn't matter, you wouldn't be using them. DSP programming generally relies less on an optimizing compiler, since you want to have a high degree of control over what the processor is doing at all times. DSP programmers are skilled at driving these devices at their maximum performance.

- Resource constrained environments, such as deeply embedded platforms, can struggle to achieve reasonable performance with the available hardware. You'll have to hone the code for acceptable quality of service or work hard to fit it into the device's tight memory.

- *Real-time* systems rely on timely execution, on being able to complete operations within well-specified quanta. Algorithms have to be carefully honed and proven to execute in fixed time limits.

- Numerical programming—in the financial sector, or for scientific research—demands high performance. These huge systems are run on very large computers with dedicated numerical support, providing vector operations and parallel calculations.

Perhaps optimization is not a serious consideration for general-purpose programming, but there are plenty of cases where optimization *is* a crucial skill. Performance is seldom specified in a requirements document, yet the customer will complain if your program runs unacceptably slowly. If there are no alternatives, and the code doesn't perform adequately, then you have to optimize it.

There is a shorter list of reasons to optimize than not to. Unless you have a specific need to optimize, you should avoid doing so. But if you do need to optimize, make sure you know how to do it well.

KEY CONCEPT *Understand when you* do *need to optimize code, but prefer to write efficient* high-quality *code in the first place.*

The Nuts and Bolts

So how do you optimize? Rather than learn a list of specific code optimizations, it's far more important to understand the correct *approach* to optimizing. Don't panic; we will see some programming techniques later, but they must be read in the context of this wider optimization process.

The six steps for speeding up a program are:

1. Determine that it's too slow, and prove you do need to optimize.
2. Identify the slowest code. Target this point.
3. Test the performance of the optimization target.
4. Optimize the code.
5. Test that the optimized code still works (very important).
6. Test the speed increase, and decide what to do next.

This sounds like a lot of work, but without it you'll actually waste time and effort and end up with crippled code that runs no faster. If you're not trying to improve execution speed, adjust this process accordingly; for example, tackle memory consumption problems by identifying which data structures are consuming all the memory and target those.

It's important to begin optimization with a clear goal in sight—the more optimization you perform, the less readable the code becomes. Know the level of performance you require, and stop when it's sufficiently fast. It's tempting to keep going, continually trying to squeeze out a little extra performance.

To stand any chance of optimizing correctly, you must take great care to prevent external factors from changing the way your code works. When the world is changing under your feet, you can't compare measurements realistically. There are two essential techniques that help here:

KEY CONCEPT *Optimize your code separately from any other work, so the outcome of one task doesn't cloud the other.*

> . . . and . . .

KEY CONCEPT *Optimize release builds of your program, not development builds.*

The development builds may run very differently from release builds, due to the inclusion of debugging trace information, object file symbols, and so on.

Now we'll look at each of these optimization steps in more detail.

Prove You Need to Optimize

The first thing to do is make sure you really *do* need to optimize. If the code's performance is acceptable, then there's no point in tinkering with it. Knuth said (himself quoting C.A.R. Hoare): "We should forget about small efficiencies, say about 97 percent of the time: Premature optimization is the root of all evil." There are so many compelling reasons *not* to optimize that the quickest and safest optimization technique is to prove that you don't need to do it.

You make this decision based on program requirements or usability studies. With this information you can determine whether optimization takes priority over adding new features and fixing bugs.

Identify the Slowest Code

This is the part that most programmers get wrong. If you're going to spend time optimizing, you need to target the places where it will make a difference. Investigations show that the average program spends more than 80 percent of its time in less than 20 percent of the code. (Boehm 87) This is known as the *80/20 rule*.[1] That's a relatively small target that is very easy to miss, which means you might waste effort optimizing code that's rarely run.

You might notice that a part of your program has some relatively easy optimizations, but if that part is seldom executed, then there's no point in optimizing—in this situation, clear code is better than faster code.

How do you figure out where to focus your attention? The most effective technique is to use a *profiler*. This tool times the flow of control around your program. It shows where that 80 percent of execution time is going, so you know where to concentrate your effort.

A profiler *doesn't* tell you which parts of the code are slowest; this is a common misconception. It actually tells you where the CPU spends most of its time. This is subtly different.[2] You have to interpret these results and use your brain. The program might spend most of its execution time in a few perfectly valid functions which cannot be improved at all. You can't always optimize; sometimes the laws of physics win.

There are plenty of benchmarking programs around—many excellent commercial programs and a number of freely available tools. It's worth spending money on a decent profiler: Optimization can easily eat into your time; this is also an expensive commodity. If you don't have a profiler available, there are a few other timing techniques you can try:

- Put manual timing tests throughout your code. Make sure you use an accurate clock source and that the time taken to read the clock will not affect program performance too much.

- Count how often each function is called (some debug libraries provide support for this kind of activity).

- Exploit compiler-supplied hooks to insert your own accounting code when each function is entered or exited. Many compilers provide a means to do this; some profilers are implemented using such a mechanism.

---

[1] Some go so far as to claim this should be the *90/10 rule*.

[2] All code runs at a fixed rate, based on the speed of the CPU clock, the number of other processes being juggled by the OS, and the thread's priority.

- Sample the program counter; interrupt your program periodically in a debugger to see where control is. This is harder in multithreaded programs and is a very slow, manual approach. If you have control over the execution environment, you can write scaffolding to automate this kind of test—effectively writing your own form of profiler.

- Test an individual function's impact on the total program execution time by making it slower. If you suspect that a particular function is causing a slowdown, try replacing its call with two calls in succession, and measure how it affects execution time.[3] If the program takes 10 percent longer to run, then the function consumes approximately 10 percent of execution time. Use this as a very basic timing test.

When profiling, make sure that you use realistic input data, simulating Real World events. The way your code executes may be drastically affected by the kind of input you feed it or by the way it is driven, so make sure that you provide true representative input sets. If possible, capture a set of real input data from a live system.

Try profiling several different data sets, to see what difference this makes. Select a very basic set, a heavy use set, and a number of general use sets. This will prevent you from optimizing for the particular quirks of one input data set.

KEY CONCEPT   *Select profiling test data carefully to represent Real World program use. Otherwise, you might optimize parts of the program that are not normally run.*

While a profiler (or equivalent) is a good starting point to choose optimization targets, you can easily miss quite fundamental problems. The profiler only shows how the code in the current design executes—and encourages you to perform code-level improvement only. Look at larger design issues too. The lack of performance may not be due to a single function, but rather a more pervasive design flaw. If it is, then you'll have to work harder to remedy the problem. This shows how important it is to get the initial code design right, with knowledge of established performance requirements.

KEY CONCEPT   *Don't rely solely on a profiler to find the causes of program inefficiency; you might miss important problems.*

Having completed this step, you've found the areas of your code where a performance improvement will have the most benefit. Now it's time to attack them.

Testing the Code

We recognized three testing phases in the optimization procedure. For each piece of code targeted, we test its performance before optimization, confirm

---

[3] This won't *necessarily* make the function run twice as slowly. Filesystem buffers or CPU memory caches can enhance the performance of repeated code sections. Treat this as a very rough guide—more qualitative than quantitative.

that the code still works correctly once optimized, and test its performance after optimization.

Programmers often forget the second check: that the optimized code still works correctly in *all* possible situations. It's easy to check the normal mode of operation, but it's not in our nature to test each and every rare case. This can be the cause of weird bugs late in the day, so be very rigorous about this.

You *must* measure the code's performance before and after modification to make sure that you have made a real difference—and to make sure that it is a change for the better; sometimes an "optimization" can be an unwitting *pessimization*. You can perform these timing tests with your profiler or by inserting timing instrumentation by hand.

KEY CONCEPT Never *try to optimize code without performing some kind of before and after measurement.*

These are some very important things to think about when running your timing tests:

- Run both the before and after tests with exactly the same set of input data so that you're testing exactly the same thing. Otherwise, your tests are meaningless; you're not comparing apples to apples. An automated test suite is best (see "Look! No Hands!" on page 144)—with the same kind of live representative data we used in the profiling step.
- Run all tests under identical prevailing conditions, so that factors like the CPU load or amount of free memory don't affect your measurements.
- Ensure that your tests don't rely on user input. Humans can cause timings to fluctuate wildly. Automate every possible aspect of the test procedure.

Optimizing the Code

We'll investigate some specific optimization techniques later. Speed-ups vary from the simple refactoring of small sections of code to more serious design-level alterations. The trick is to optimize without totally destroying the code.

Determine how many different ways exist to optimize the identified code, and pick the best. Only perform one change at a time; it's less risky, and you'll have a better idea of what improved performance the most. Sometimes it's the least expected things that have the most significant optimization effects.

After Optimization

Don't forget to benchmark the optimized code to prove that you've made a successful modification. If an optimization is unsuccessful, remove it. Back out your changes. This is where a source control system is useful, helping you to revert to the previous code version.

Also remove the *slightly* successful optimizations. Prefer clear code to modest optimizations (unless you're absolutely desperate for an improvement, and there are no other avenues to explore).

Optimization Techniques

We've avoided this for long enough; now it's time to look at the really gory details. Having followed the optimization procedure outlined above, you've proved that your program performs badly and have found the worst code culprit. Now you need to whip it into shape. What can you do?

There's a palette of optimizations to choose from. Which is the most appropriate will depend on the exact cause of the problem, what you're trying to achieve (e.g., increased execution speed or reduced code size), and how much of an improvement is required.

These optimizations fall into two broad categories: *design* changes and *code* changes. A change at the design level will usually have a more profound effect on performance than a code-level tweak. An inefficient design can strangle efficiency more than a few bad lines of source code, so a design fix—while more difficult—will have a bigger payoff.

Most often, our goal is to increase execution speed. The speed-based optimization strategies are to:

* Speed up slow things
* Do slow things less often
* Defer slow things until you really need them

The other common optimization goals are to reduce memory consumption (mainly by changing the data representation, by tweaking the pattern of memory consumption, or by reducing the amount of data accessed at once), or to reduce executable size (by removing functionality or by exploiting commonality). As we'll see, these goals often conflict: Most speed increases come at the expense of memory consumption, and vice versa.

Design Changes

These are the *macro* optimizations, the fixes on a large scale that improve the internal design of your software. Bad design is hard to fix. The nearer a project is to a release deadline, the less likely you are to perform design changes; the risk is too great.[4] We end up plastering over the cracks by employing small, code-level fixes instead.

When brave enough, the kinds of design optimization we can perform include:

* Adding layers of caching or buffering to enhance slow data access or prevent lengthy recalculations. Precompute values that you know will be needed, and store them for immediate access.

---

[4] Sadly, it's often only near project deadlines that anyone notices that performance isn't good enough.

- Creating a pool of resources to reduce the overhead of allocating objects. For example, preallocate memory, or hold a selection of files open rather than repeatedly opening and then closing them. This technique is often used to speed up memory allocation; older OS memory allocation routines were designed for simple non-threaded use. Their locks stall multithreaded applications, leading to horrible performance.

- Sacrificing accuracy for speed if you can get away with it. Dropping floating-point precision is the obvious example. Many devices have no *floating-point unit (FPU)* hardware and employ slower FPU emulation software instead. You can switch to fixed-point arithmetic libraries to bypass a slow emulator, at the expense of numeric resolution. This is particularly easy in C++ by taking advantage of its abstract data type facilities.

  Accuracy is not solely due to your choice of data types; this tactic can run far deeper to your use of algorithms or the quality of your output. Perhaps you can let users make this decision—allow them to select *slow but accurate* or *fast but approximate* operation modes.

- Changing the data storage format or its on-disk representation to something more suited to high-speed operation. For example, speed up text file parsing by using a binary format. Transmit or store compressed files to reduce network bandwidth.

- Exploiting parallelization and using threading to prevent one action from being serialized after another. As advances in processor speeds tail off, CPU manufacturers are increasingly introducing multi-core, multi-pipeline processors. To use these effectively, your code *must* be designed with a threaded model at its heart. The front line of the optimization battle is rapidly moving in this direction.

- Threading efficiently: Avoiding or removing excessive locking. It inhibits concurrency, generates overhead, and often leads to deadlock. Employ static checking to prove which locks are necessary and which aren't.

- Avoiding overuse of exceptions. They can inhibit compiler optimizations[5] and will hamper timely operation when used too frequently.

- Forgoing certain language facilities if it will save code space. Some C++ compilers allow you to disable RTTI and exceptions, consequently reducing executable size.

- Removing functionality: The quickest code is code that doesn't run at all. A function will be slow if it is doing too many things, some of which are unnecessary. Cut out the superfluous stuff. Move it elsewhere in the program. Defer all work until it's really necessary.

- Compromising design quality to gain speed. For example, reducing indirection and increasing coupling. You can do this by breaking encapsulation: leaking a class's private implementation through its public interface. Knocking down module barriers will cause irreparable damage to the design. If possible, try a less disruptive optimization mechanism first.

---

[5] Like functions, try/catch blocks act as barriers to an optimizer. It's not possible to look through the barrier to perform optimization, so some potential speed-ups will be lost.

COMPLEXITY NOTATION

Algorithmic complexity is a measure of how well an algorithm scales—how long it takes in proportion to the size of input. It's a *qualitative* mathematical model, allowing you to quickly compare the performance characteristics of different implementation approaches. It doesn't measure exact execution time (this is highly dependent on CPU speed, OS configuration, etc.).

Complexity is determined by the amount of work an algorithm must perform: the number of basic operations it executes. A basic operation is something like an arithmetic operation, an assignment, a test, or a data read/write. Algorithmic complexity doesn't count the *exact* number of operations performed, just how this value relates to the problem size. We are usually interested in the worst case performance of an algorithm, the most work that will ever need to be done. A good comparison looks at the best case and average time complexity as well.

Algorithmic complexity is expressed using *Big O* notation, invented by the German number theorist Edmund Landau. For a problem with input size n, it might have a complexity of:

$O(1)$: **Order 1**

This is a *constant time* algorithm. No matter how large the input set, it always takes the same amount of time to complete the task. This is the best performance characteristic possible.

$O(n)$: **Order n**

A *linear time* algorithm's complexity rises in line with the input size. Searching a linked list will involve visiting more nodes as the list size grows; the number of operations is directly related to the size of the list.

$O(n^2)$: **Order n squared**

This is where performance really begins to get bad: Complexity is increasing faster than the rate of input growth. A *quadratic time* algorithm may seem fine when you give it a small set of data, but large data sets take a seriously long time. The bubblesort algorithm is $O(n^2)$.

Of course, complexity may be of any order; the quicksort algorithm averages $O(n \log n)$. This is worse than $O(n)$, but far better than $O(n^2)$. A simple optimization route for a slow bubblesort algorithm is to replace it with a quicksort algorithm, especially since there are plenty of freely available quicksort implementations.

These Big O expressions don't include constants or low-order terms. You'll rarely see any talk about a complexity of $O(2n+6)$. When n gets large enough, these constants and low-order terms dwarf into insignificance.

The major design-level optimizations involve improvements in *algorithms* or *data structures*. Most speed degradation or memory consumption comes down to a bad choice of one or both, and a subsequent change will rectify this.

Algorithms

Algorithms have a profound impact on the speed of execution. A function that works acceptably in a small local test may not scale up when Real World data gets thrown at it. If profiling shows that your code spends most of its time running a certain routine, you must make it run faster.

One approach is at the code level, chipping small improvements from each instruction. A better approach is to replace the entire algorithm with a more efficient version.

Consider this realistic example: A particular algorithm runs a loop 1,000 times. Each iteration takes 5 milliseconds (ms) to execute. The operation therefore completes in around 5 seconds. By tweaking the code inside the loop, you can shave 1 ms from each iteration—that's a saving of 1 second. Not bad. But instead, you can plug in a different algorithm, where an iteration takes 7 ms, although it only iterates 100 times. That's a saving of almost 4 and a half seconds—significantly better.

For this reason, prefer to look at optimizations that change fundamental algorithms, not that tweak specific lines of code. There are many algorithms to chose from in the computer science world, and unless your code is particularly dire, you'll always gain the most significant performance improvements by selecting a better algorithm.

KEY CONCEPT *Prefer to replace a slow algorithm with a faster variant than to tinker with the algorithm's implementation.*

Data structures

Data structures are intimately related to your choice of algorithms; some algorithms require certain data structures, and vice versa. If your program is consuming far too much memory, changing the data storage format may improve matters, although often at the expense of execution speed. If you need to quickly search a list of 1,000 items, don't store them in a linear array with $O(n)$ search time; use a (larger) binary tree with $O(\log n)$ performance.

Selecting a different data structure seldom requires you to implement the new representation yourself. Most languages come with library support for all common data structures.

Code Changes

And so now we creep anxiously on to the really disgusting stuff: the *micro*-level, small-scale, shortsighted, code-tweaking optimizations. There are many ways to molest source code for the sake of performance. You must experiment to see what works best in each situation: Some changes will work well; others will have little, or even negative effect. Some may prevent the compiler's optimizer from performing its task, producing startlingly worse results.

The first task is easy: Turn on compiler optimization or increase the optimization level. It often gets disabled for development builds since the optimizer can take a very long time to run, increasing the build time of large projects by an order of magnitude.[6] Try configuring the optimizer, and test what affect this has. Many compilers allow you to bias optimization toward extra speed or reduced code size.

---

[6] It has to do complex inspection of the parsed code to determine the set of possible speed-ups and select the most appropriate ones.

There are a few very low-level optimizations that you should know about but should generally avoid. These are the kind of changes that a compiler is able to perform for you. If you've switched the optimizer on, it'll be looking in these areas already—enable optimization and make the most of its help. You will rarely need to apply these by hand, which is good: They butcher your code's readability, since they warp its fundamental logic out of shape. Only consider using one of these optimizations if you can *prove* that it's really required, that your optimizer hasn't already done it, and that there are no better alternatives.

Loop unrolling

For loops with very short bodies, the loop scaffolding may be more expensive than the looped operation itself. Remove this overhead by flattening it out—turn your 10-iteration loop into 10 consecutive individual statements.

Loop unrolling can be done partially; this makes more sense for large loops. You can insert four operations per iteration, and increment the loop counter by four each time. But this tactic gets nasty if the loop doesn't always iterate over a whole number of unrolls.

Code inlining

For small operations, the overhead of calling a function might be prohibitive. Splitting code into functions brings significant benefits: clearer code, consistency through reuse, and the ability to isolate areas of change. However, this can be removed to increase performance, by merging the caller(s) and the callee.

There are a number of ways to do this. With language support, you can request it in the source code (in C/C++ using the inline keyword); this method preserves a lot of the code's readability. Otherwise, you have to merge the code yourself, either by duplicating the function over and over again or using a preprocessor to do the work for you.

It's hard to inline recursive function calls—how would you know when to stop inlining? Try to find alternative algorithms to replace recursion.

Inlining often opens the way for further code-level optimizations (that were not previously possible across a function boundary) to be performed.

Constant folding

Calculations involving constant values can be computed at compile time to reduce the amount of work done at run time. The simple expression return 6+4; can be reduced to return 10;. Carefully ordering the terms of a large calculation might bring two constants together, enabling them to be reduced into a simpler subexpression.

It's unusual for a programmer to write something as obvious as return 6+4;. However, these sorts of expressions are common after macro expansion.

Move to compile time

There is more you can do at compile time than just constant folding. Many conditional tests can be proved statically and removed from the code. Some kinds of tests can be avoided altogether; for example, remove tests for negative numbers by using unsigned data types.

Strength reduction

This is the act of replacing one operation with an equivalent that executes faster. This is most important on CPUs with poor arithmetic support. For example, replace integer multiplication and division with constant shifts or adds; x/4 can be converted to x>>2 if it's faster on your processor.

Subexpressions

Common subexpression elimination avoids the recalculation of expressions whose values have not changed. In code like this:

```
int first  = (a * b) + 10;
int second = (a * b) / c;
```

the expression (a * b) is evaluated twice. Once is enough. You can factor out the common subexpression, and replace it with

```
int temp   = a * b;
int first  = temp + 10;
int second = temp / c;
```

Dead code elimination

Don't write needless code; prune anything that's not strictly necessary to the program. Static analysis will show you the functions that are never used or the sections of code that will never execute. Remove them.

While those are particularly distasteful code optimizations, the following ones are slightly more socially acceptable. They focus on increasing program execution speed.

- If you find that you're repeatedly calling a slow function, then don't call it so often. Cache its result and reuse this value. This might lead to less clear code, but the program will run faster.

- Reimplement the function in another language. For example, rewrite a critical Java function in C using the Java Native Interface (JNI) facility. Conventional compilers still beat JIT code interpreters for execution speed.

  Don't naïvely assume that one language is faster than another—many programmers have been surprised by how little difference using JNI makes. It has been commonly claimed that OO languages are far slower than their procedural counterparts. This is a lie. Bad OO code *can* be slow, but so can bad procedural code. If you write OO-style code in C, it is likely to be *slower* than good C++; the C++ compiler will generate better-tuned method dispatch code than your attempts.

- Reorder the code for improved performance.

     Defer work until it's absolutely necessary. Don't open a file until you're about to use it. Don't calculate a value if you might not need it; wait until it's wanted. Don't call a function yet if the code will work without it.

     Hoist checking further up the function to avoid needless work. If a test leading to an early return can be placed at the top of a function or halfway though it, prefer to place it at the top. Make the check sooner to avoid delays.

     Move invariant calculations out of a loop. The most subtle source of this problem is a loop condition. If you write for (int n = 0; n < tree.appleCount(); ++n), but appleCount() manually counts 1,000 items on every call, you'll have a very slow loop. Move the count operation before the loop:

```
int appleCount = tree.appleCount();
for (int n = 0; n < appleCount; ++n)
{
    ... do something ...
}
```

     However, don't forget to profile first to prove that the loop truly is a problem. This is a great example of how optimizations are local to a particular execution environment: In C#, the new version could well be *slower* because the unoptimized code is a pattern the JIT compiler understands and can optimize away itself.

- Use *lookup tables* for complex calculations, trading time for space. For example, rather than write a set of trigonometric functions that individually calculate their values, precalculate the return values and store them in an array. Map input values to the closest index into this array.

- Exploit *short-circuit evaluation.* Make sure that the tests likely to fail are placed first to save time. If you write a conditional expression if (condition_one && condition_two), make sure that condition_one is statistically more likely to fail than condition_two (unless, of course, condition_one acts as a guard for condition_two's validity).

- Don't reinvent the wheel—reuse standard routines that have already been performance tuned. Library writers will have already carefully honed their code. But be aware that a library may have been optimized for different goals than yours; perhaps an embedded product was profiled for memory consumption, not for speed.

Size-focused, code-level optimizations include:

- Producing compressed executables that unpack their code before running. This doesn't necessarily affect the size of the running program, but it reduces the storage space required.[7] This might be important if your program is stored in limited flash memory.

---

[7] This may have the pleasant side effect of decreasing program startup time: A compressed executable will load from disk much faster.

- Factoring common code into a shared function to avoid duplication.
- Moving seldom-used functions out of the way. Put them into a dynamically loaded library or into a separate program.

Of course, the ultimate hard-core optimization technique is to reimplement a section of code in assembly—the one environment where you have *full* control over the CPU and can do exactly what you want (including shooting yourself in the foot). This is always a last resort and is almost certainly unnecessary. These days, compilers produce perfectly acceptable code, and the lost time spent writing, debugging, and maintaining "optimized" sections of machine code far outweighs the advantages gained.

Writing Efficient Code

If the best approach is *not* to optimize, how can we avoid any need to improve code performance? The answer is to *design for performance*, planning to provide adequate quality of service from the outset, rather than trying to whittle it out at the last minute.

Some argue that this is a dangerous road to follow. Indeed, there are potential hazards for the unwary. If you try to optimize as you go along, then you'll write at a lower level than needed; you'll end up with nasty, hacky code full of low-level performance enhancements and back-door interfaces.

How do we reconcile these seemingly opposing views? It isn't hard, because they're not actually at odds. There are two complementary strategies:

- Write efficient code.
- Optimize code later.

If you make a point of writing clear, good, efficient code *now*, you will not need to perform heavy optimizations later. Some claim that you don't know whether any optimization is necessary at first, so you should write everything *as simply as possible*, and only optimize when profiling proves that there is a bottleneck.

This approach has obvious flaws. If you know that you need a data structure with good search performance (because your program must perform fast searches), pick a binary tree over an array.[8] If you're not aware of any such requirement, *then* go for the most appropriate thing that will work. This still might not be the simplest—a raw C array is a hard data structure to manage.

As you design each module, don't blindly chase performance—only spend the effort when necessary. Understand the mandated performance requirements and justify how your choices will meet these requirements at each stage. When you know what level of performance is required, it's easier

---

[8] But, as always, it's not necessarily that simple. Arrays often provide better cache coherence (since binary tree nodes can easily become scattered across memory). An array that is kept sorted (you amortize time when inserting) would be a worthy consideration. Measure, measure, measure.

to design for appropriate efficiency. It also helps you to write explicit tests that prove you do achieve these performance goals.

Some simple design choices that will increase efficiency and aid later optimization are:

- Minimizing your reliance on functions that might be implemented on remote machines or that will access the network or a slow data storage system

- Understanding the target deployment and how the program is expected to be run so you can design it to work well in these situations

- Writing *modular* code so it's easy to speed up one section without having to rewrite other sections too

PESSIMIZATIONS

Without careful measurement, you can easily end up writing optimizations that are not at all optimal. A perfectly good optimization for one situation might turn out to be a performance disaster in another. Here's a case study. Exhibit A: The copy-on-write string optimization.

This was a common optimization applied to C++ standard library implementations around 1990. Programs that performed intensive string manipulation experienced a massive overhead when copying long strings, both in terms of execution speed and memory consumption. Copying large strings means duplicating and shoveling around large quantities of data. Many string copies are automatically generated, temporary objects that are created and then thrown away shortly after—they are never actually modified. The expensive copy operation is an unnecessary cost.

The copy-on-write (COW) optimization turns the string data type into a form of *smart pointer*; the actual string data is held in a (hidden) shared representation. The string copy operation now only has to perform an inexpensive smart pointer copy (attaching a new smart pointer to the shared representation), rather than duplicate the entire string contents. Only when you make a modification to a shared string is the internal representation copied and the smart pointer remapped. This optimization avoids a large number of unnecessary copy operations.

COW worked well in single-threaded programs; it was shown to greatly speed up performance. However, a problem became apparent when multithreaded programs used COW strings. (Indeed, this problem also manifests in single-threaded programs if the COW string class is built with multithreading support). The implementation requires very conservative thread locking around the copy operations—these locks become a *major* bottleneck. Suddenly, a lightning-fast program slowed down to a crawl. The COW optimization proved to be a serious pessimization.

Far better multithreaded performance was achieved by reverting to classic string implementations and writing more careful code that reduced automatic string copying. Thankfully, C++ library vendors now provide more intelligent versions of the string class, which are both thread safe and fast.

In a Nutshell

Technological progress has merely provided us
with more efficient means for going backwards.
—Aldous Huxley

High-performance code is not as important as some people think. Although you sometimes *do* have to roll your sleeves up and tinker with code, optimization is a task you should actively avoid. To do this, make sure that you know the software's performance requirements before you start working on it. At each level of design, ensure that you provide this quality of service. Then optimization will be unnecessary.

When you do optimize, be very methodical and measured in your approach. Have a clear goal, and prove that each step is getting you closer to it. Be guided by solid data, not your hunches. As you write code, ensure that your designs are efficient, but don't compromise on quality. Worry about code-level performance only when it proves to be a problem.

Good programmers . . .	Bad programmers . . .
• Avoid optimizing unless it proves to be absolutely necessary	• Start optimizing before the code proves to be inadequate
• Attempt optimization methodically, taking a considered and measured approach	• Dive in feet first, attacking the pieces of code they *think* are bottlenecks without measuring or investigating
• Look for alternatives and investigate design improvements before ever resorting to code-level optimizations	• Never consider the wider picture: what the full implications of their optimization are in other code areas and usage patterns
• Prefer optimizations that won't destroy the code's quality	• Think speed is more important than code quality

See Also

Chapter 1: On the Defensive
Optimizations that remove "unnecessary" code often clash with any extra defensive code.

Chapter 4: The Write Stuff
The needs of optimized code are often at odds with self-documenting code.

Chapter 13: Grand Designs
Efficiency must be *designed* into the codebase from the start of a project.

Chapter 19: Being Specific

Performance requirements must be carefully specified before construction begins so you know how much optimization is necessary.

Get Thinking

A detailed discussion of these questions can be found in the "Answers and Discussion" section on page 510.

Mull It Over

1. Optimization is a process of making trade-offs—sacrificing one quality of code for another desirable quality. Describe the kinds of trade-offs that lead to a performance increase.

2. Look at each of the optimization alternatives listed in "Why Not Optimize?" on page 202. Describe what trade-offs are being made, if any.

3. Explain these terms and their exact relationship:
   - Performance
   - Efficiency
   - Optimized

4. What are the likely bottlenecks in a slow program?

5. How can you avoid the need to optimize? What methods will prevent you from writing inefficient code?

6. How does the presence of multiple threads affect optimization?

7. Why *don't* we write efficient code? What stops us from using high-performance algorithms in the first place?

8. A List data type is implemented using an array. What is the worst case algorithmic complexity of each of the following List methods?
   a. The constructor
   b. append—places a new item on the end of the list

c. insert—slides a new item in between two existing list items, at a given position

d. isEmpty—returns true if the list contains no items

e. contains—returns true if the list contains a specified item

f. get—returns the item with a given index

Getting Personal

1. How important (honestly) is code performance in your current project? What is the motivator for this performance requirement?

2. In your last optimization attempt:

    a. Did you use a profiler?

    b. If yes, how much improvement did you measure?

    c. If no, how did you know whether you made any kind of improvement?

    d. Did you test that the code still worked after optimizing?

    e. If yes, how thoroughly did you test?

    f. If no, why not? How could you be sure the code still worked properly for *all* cases?

3. If you've not yet attempted to optimize the code you're currently working on, take a guess at which parts are the slowest and which bits consume the most memory. Now run it through a profiler—how accurate were you?

4. How well specified are your program's performance requirements? Do you have a concrete plan to test that you meet these criteria?

AN INSECURITY COMPLEX

Writing Secure Programs

Security is mostly a superstition. It does not exist in nature. . . . Life is either a daring adventure or nothing.

— *Helen Keller*

Not so long ago, computer access was a scarce commodity. The world contained only a handful of machines, owned by a few organizations and accessed by small teams of highly trained personnel. In those days, computer security meant wearing the right lab coat and pass card to get past the guard on the door.

Fast-forward to today. We carry more computational power in our pockets than those operators ever dreamed of. Computers are plentiful and, more pertinently, highly connected.

The volume of data carried by computer systems is growing at a fantastic rate. We write programs to store, manipulate, interpret, and transfer this data. Our software must guard against information going astray: into the hands of malicious attackers, past the eyes of accidental observers, or even disappearing into the ether. This is critical; a leak of top-secret company information could spell financial ruin. You don't want sensitive personal information (your bank account or credit card details, for example) leaking out for anyone to use. Most software systems require some level of security.[1]

Whose responsibility is it to build secure software? Here's the bad news: It's *our* headache. If we don't consider the security of our handiwork carefully, we will inevitably write insecure, leaky programs and reap the rewards.

Software security is a really big deal, but generally we're very bad at it. Nearly every day you'll hear of a new security vulnerability in a popular product or see the results of viruses compromising system integrity.

This is an enormous topic, far larger than we have scope to go into here. It's a highly specialized field, requiring much training and experience. However, even the basics are not adequately addressed by modern software engineering teaching. The aim of this chapter is to highlight security issues, explore the problems, and learn some basic techniques to protect our code.

The Risks

Better be despised for too anxious apprehensions,
than ruined by too confident security.
—Edmund Burke

Why would anyone bother to attack your system? It's usually because you've got something that they want. This could be:

- Your processing power
- Your ability to send data (e.g., spam)
- Your privately stored information
- Your capabilities—perhaps the specific software you have installed
- Your connection to more interesting remote systems

People might even attack you for the sheer fun of it or because they dislike you and want to cause harm by disrupting your computer resources. While malicious people *are* lurking around looking for easy, insecure prey, a security vulnerability might also be caused by a program that accidentally releases information to the wrong audience. A lucky user might exploit the leak and cause you harm.

KEY CONCEPT *Know what important assets you possess. Do you have particularly sensitive information or specific capabilities that an attacker might want? Guard them.*

---

[1] As we'll see, this is true whether they handle sensitive data or not. If a noncritical component has a public interface, then it poses a security risk to the system as a whole.

To understand the kinds of attack you might suffer, it's important to differentiate protecting an entire computer *system* (comprising of several computers, a network, and a number of collaborating applications) from writing a single secure *program*. Both are important aspects of computer security; they blur together since both are necessary. The latter is a subset of the former. It takes just one insecure program to render an entire computer system (or network) insecure.

These are the common security risks and compromises of a live, running computer system:

- A thief who acquires a laptop or PDA can read any unsecured sensitive data. The stolen device might be configured to automatically dial into a private network, allowing a simple route straight through all your company's defences. This is a serious security threat and one that you can't easily guard against in code! What we can do is write systems that aren't immediately accessible to computer thieves.

- Flawed input routines can be exploited, leading to many types of compromise—even to the attacker gaining access to the whole machine (we'll see this in "Buffer Overrun" on page 229).

  Break-ins through an unsecured public network interface are particularly worrying. While vulnerbilities in a GUI interface can only be exploited by people actually *using* that UI, an insecure system running on a public network could lead to the whole world trying to break down your door.

- *Privilege escalation* occurs when a user with limited access rights tricks the system to gain a higher security level. The attacker could be an authentic user or someone who has just broken into the system. His or her ultimate aim is to achieve *root* or *administrator* privilege, where the attacker has total control of the machine.

- If communication is unencrypted and traverses an insecure medium (e.g., the Internet), then any computer en route can syphon off and read data, like a phone tap. A variant of this is known as a *man-in-the-middle attack*: An attacker's machine pretends to be the other communicant and sits between both senders, snooping on their data.

- Any system has a small set of trusted users. Malicious authorized users can wreak havoc by copying and sharing data they're not supposed to or entering bad data to compromise the quality of your computer system.

  It's hard to guard against this. You have to trust that each user is responsible enough to handle the level of system access he or she has been designated. If the user isn't trustworthy, you can't write a program to fix it. This shows that security is as much about administration and policy as it is about writing code.

- Careless users (or careless administrators) can leave a system unnecessarily open and vulnerable. For example:

  - People forget to log off; if there is no session timeout, anyone can pick up your program later and start using it.

- Many attackers use dictionary-based password-cracking tools that fire off many login attempts until one works. Users choose easy-to-memorize passwords that are also easy to guess. Any system that allows weak, easy-to-guess passwords is vulnerable. More secure systems suspend a user's account after a few unsuccessful logins.

- *Social engineering*—the art of acquiring important information from people, items in an office, or even the outgoing trash—is usually a lot easier (and often quicker) than worming a way into your computer system. People are easier to con than computers, and attackers know this.

- Out-of-date software installations permit many compromises. Many vendors issue security warnings (or *bulletins*) and software patches. An administrator can easily fall behind the cutting edge, leaving the system open to attack.

- Setting lax permissions will allow users access to sensitive parts of your system—for example, letting casual viewers read everyone's salary details. The cure could be as basic as setting correct access permissions on the database files.

- Virus attacks (self-replicating malicious programs, commonly spread by email attachment), Trojans (hidden malicious payloads in seemingly benign software), and spyware (a form of Trojan that spies on what you are doing, the web pages you visit, etc.) infect machines and can cause all sorts of mayhem. They can capture even the most complex password with keystroke loggers, for example.

- Storing data "in the clear" (unencrypted)—even in memory—is dangerous. Memory is not as safe as many programmers think; a virus or Trojan can scan computer memory and pull out a lot of interesting tidbits for an attacker to exploit.

The risks increase as the number of routes into a system grows, with more input methods (web-access, command-line, or GUI interfaces), more individual inputs (different windows, prompts, web forms, or XML feeds), and more users (there is a better chance of someone discovering a password). With more outputs, there are more chances for bugs to manifest in the display code, leaking out the wrong information.

KEY CONCEPT   *The more complicated a computer system is, the more likely it is to contain security vulnerabilities. Therefore, write the simplest software possible!*

The Opposition

It's probably difficult to believe that anyone would take the time and effort to hack your application. But these people exist. They're talented, motivated, and very, very patient. In the battle to write secure software, it's important to know who you're fighting against. Understand exactly what they're doing, how they do it, the tools they're using, and their objectives. Only then can you formulate a strategy to cope.

SECURE IN THE KNOWLEDGE

These important terms help us to reason about security problems:

Flaw
A security flaw is an unintended problem in an application. It is a program fault (see "Terms and Conditions" on page 130). Not all flaws are security problems.

Vulnerability
A vulnerability exists when a flaw opens the possibility for a program to be insecure.

Exploit
This is an automated tool (or a manual method) that employs a program vulnerability to force unintended—and insecure—behavior. Not all vulnerabilities are found and exploited (that's called *luck*).

Who

Your attacker might be a common crook, a talented cracker, a *script kiddie* (a derogatory name for crackers who run automated cracker scripts—they exploit well-known vulnerabilities with little skill themselves), a dishonest employee cheating the company, or a disgruntled ex-employee seeking revenge for unfair dismissal.

Crackers are well informed. There is a cracker subculture where knowledge is passed on and easy-to-use cracker tools are distributed. Not knowing about this doesn't make you innocent and pure, just naïve and open to the simplest attack.

Where

Thanks to pervasive networking, attackers could be anywhere, on any continent, using any type of computer. When working over the Internet, attackers are very hard to locate; many are skilled at covering their tracks. Often they crack easy machines to use as covers for more audacious attacks.

When

They could attack at any time, day or night. Across continents, one person's day is another's night. You need to run secure programs around the clock, not just during business hours.

Why

With such a large bunch of potential attackers, the motives for an attack are diverse. It might be malicious (a political activist wants to ruin your company or a thief wants to access your bank account), or it might be for fun (a college prankster wants to post a comical banner on your website). It might be inquisitive (a hacker just wants to see what your network infrastructure looks like or practice his cracking skills) or opportunist (a user stumbles over data he shouldn't see and works out how to use it to his advantage).

In a networked world, you usually won't know who your enemies actually are until after they have struck. You might not even find out who they are then; your forensic skills might not be able to work back from a smouldering pile of digital debris. But like any good boy scout: *Be prepared.* Don't ignore vulnerabilities and assume no one is interested in attacking your systems—someone out there *is* interested.

KEY CONCEPT   *Don't ignore vulnerabilities and pretend that you're invincible. Someone, somewhere wants to exploit your code, guaranteed.*

CRACKER VS. HACKER

These two terms often get confused and used inappropriately. Their correct definitions are:

Cracker
   Someone who purposefully exploits vulnerabilities in computer systems to gain unauthorized access.

Hacker
   Often used incorrectly to mean *cracker*, a *hacker* is really someone who hacks at—works on—code. This is a 1970s term used with pride by a particular breed of programming geek. A hacker is a computer expert or enthusiast.

   You might also see these two hacker terms in use:

White hat
   White hat hackers consider the consequences of their work, scorning the actions of crackers and unethical computer users. They believe that their work is for the good of society.

Black hat
   This is a programmer from the dark side who enjoys abusing computer systems. Black hats are crackers who actively seek to use systems dishonestly. They have no regard for other people's property or privacy.

Excuses, Excuses

How do attackers manage to break into code so often? They're armed with weapons we don't have or (due to lack of education) know nothing about. Tools, knowledge, skills: These all work in their favor. However, they have one key advantage that makes all the difference—time. In the heat of the software factory, programmers are pressed to deliver as much code as humanly possible (probably a little bit more) and to do so on time, or else. This code has to meet all requirements (for functionality, usability, reliability, etc.), leaving us precious little time to focus on other "peripheral" concerns, like security. Attackers don't share this burden; they have plenty of time to learn the intricacies of your system, and they have learned to attack from many different angles.

The game is stacked heavily in their favor. As software developers, we must defend all possible points of the system; an attacker can pick the weakest point and focus there. We can only defend against the known exploits; attackers can take their time to find any number of unknown vulnerabilities. We must be constantly on the lookout for attacks; attackers can strike at will. We have to write good, clean software that works nicely with the rest of the world; attackers can play as dirty as they like.

Software security presents a myriad of extra—but important—problems and challenges for the poor, overworked programmer. What does this tell us? Simply that we *must* do better. We must be better informed, better armed, more aware of our enemies, and more conscious of the way we write code. We must design in security from the outset and put it into our development processes and schedules.

Feeling Vulnerable

The programmer's role in this mess is to write secure code, so let's survey the weak points in our software to determine where we must focus our effort. These are specific types of code vulnerabilities, holes that can be compromised by an attacker.

Insecure Design and Architecture

This is the most fundamental flaw, and consequently the hardest to fix. Failure to consider security at the architectural level will lead to committing security sins everywhere: sending unencrypted data over public networks, storing it on easily accessible media, and running software services that have known security flaws.

Security should appear on the radar as soon as development starts. Every system component must be considered for security holes; a computer system is only as safe as its least secure part, which may not even be the code you're writing. For example, a Java program can be no more secure than the JVM executing it.

Buffer Overrun

Most applications are public facing, listening on an open network port or handling input from a web browser or GUI interface. These input routines are prime sites for security failure.

C code programs often use the standard library function sscanf to parse input. Although it's part of C's standard library and appears in C code regularly, sscanf unashamedly provides subtle ways to write insecure code.[2]

---

[2] This example is written in C and is common in C code, but remember that this exploit is far from a C-only problem.

You might see code like this:

```
void parse_user_input(const char *input)
{
    /* first parse the input string */
    int my_number;
    char my_string[100];
    sscanf(input, "%d %s", &my_number, my_string);
    ... now use it ...
}
```

Can you see the glaring problem? An ill-formed `input` string—anything over 100 characters—will overrun the `my_string` buffer and smear arbitrary data across invalid memory addresses.

The results depend on what memory is trashed. Sometimes the program will carry on unaffected; you've been very, very lucky.[3] Sometimes the program continues, but its behavior is subtly altered—this can be hard to spot and confusing to debug. Sometimes the program will crash as a consequence, perhaps taking other critical system components down with it. But the worst case is when the spilt data gets written somewhere in the CPU's execution path. This isn't actually hard to do and allows an attacker to execute arbitrary code on your machine, potentially gaining complete access to it.

Overrun is easiest to exploit when the buffer is located on the stack, as in the example above. Here it's possible to direct CPU behavior by overwriting the stack-stored return address of a function call. However, buffer overrun exploits can abuse heap-based buffers too.

Embedded Query Strings

This breed of attack can be used to crash programs, execute arbitrary code, or fish for unauthorized data. Like buffer overrun, it relies on a failure to parse input, but rather than burst buffer boundaries, these attacks exploit what the program subsequently does with the unfiltered input.

Format string attacks are a classic example of this problem in C programs. A common culprit is the `printf` function (and its variants), used as follows:

```
void parse_user_input(const char *input)
{
    printf(input);
}
```

A malicious user could provide an input string containing `printf` format tokens (like `%s` and `%x`) and coerce the program to print data from the stack or even from locations in memory, depending on the exact form of the `printf` call. An attacker can also write arbitrary data to memory locations using a similar ploy (exploiting the `%n` format token).

---

[3] Or, to look at it another way, you've been very *unlucky*. You didn't spot the flaw when testing; it will enter production code, just waiting for a cracker to exploit it.

Solutions to this problem aren't hard to find. Writing `printf("%s", input)` will avoid the problem by ensuring that `input` is not interpreted as a format string.

There are many other situations where an embedded query can maliciously exploit a program. SQL statements can be surreptitiously fed into database applications to force them to perform arbitrary database lookups for an attacker.

Another variant exhibited by lax web-based applications is known as a *cross-site scripting* exploit, due to the way the attack works across the system: from an attacker's input, through the web application, finally manifesting on a victim's browser. An attacker's bogus comment on a web-based messaging system will be rendered by all browsers viewing the page. If the message contains hidden JavaScript code, the browsers will execute it without their users realizing it.

Race Conditions

It is possible to exploit systems that rely on the subtle ordering of events, to provoke unintended behavior or crash the code. This is generally exhibited in systems with complex threading models or that are comprised of many collaborating processes.

A threaded program might share its memory pool between two worker threads. Without adequate guarding, one thread might read information in the buffer that the writer thread did not intend to release yet—part of a privileged transaction or a different user's information.

This problem isn't restricted to threaded applications, though. Consider the following fragment of Unix C code. It intends to dump some output to a file and then change file permissions on it.

```
fd = open("filename");            /* create a new file */
/* point A (see later) */
write(fd, some_data, data_size);  /* write some data */
close(fd);                        /* close the file */
chmod("filename", 0777);          /* give it special privileges */
```

There is a race here that an attacker can exploit. By removing the file at point A and replacing it with a link to his own file, the attacker gains a specially privileged file. This can be used to further exploit the system.

Integer Overflow

Careless use of mathematical constructs can cause a program to cede control in unusual ways. Integer overflow will occur when a variable type is too small to represent the result of an arithmetic operation. The unsigned 8-bit data type (uint8_t) renders this C calculation erroneous:

```
uint8_t a = 254 + 2;
```

The contents of a will be 0, not the 256 you'd expect; 8 bits can only count up to 255. An attacker can supply very large numeric input values to provoke overflow and generate unintended program results. It's not hard to see this causing significant problems; the following C code contains a heap overrun waiting to happen, thanks to integer overflow:

```
void parse_user_input(const char* input)
{
    uint8_t length = strlen(input) + 11; /* a uint8_t might overflow */
    char *copy = malloc(length);         /* so this might be too small */
    if (copy)
    {
        sprintf(copy, "Input is: %s", input);
        /* oh dear, we might have overrun the buffer */
    }
}
```

It's true that uint8_t is an unlikely candidate for the string length variable, but the exact same problem manifests itself with larger data types. It's less likely in normal operation, but just as exploitable.

This kind of problem also occurs with subtraction operations (where it's called integer *underflow*), mixed signed and unsigned assignments, bad type casting, and multiplication or division.

Protection Racket

> *The more you seek security, the less of it you have.*
> —*Brian Tracy*

We've seen how software construction is like building a house (see "Do We Really *Build* Software?" on page 177, and Chapter 14). We must learn to secure our programs just like we'd protect a house, locking all doors and windows, employing a sentry, and adding security mechanisms (like a burglar alarm, electronic pass cards, identity badges, etc.). But you must still be constantly vigilant: A door can be left ajar regardless of any fancy lock devices, and a burglar alarm can be left unset.

Our software security strategies apply at different levels:

The system *installation*
The exact OS configuration, network infrastructure, and version numbers of all running applications have important security implications.

The software system *design*
We need to address design issues like whether the user can remain logged in for indefinite periods, how each subsystem communicates, and which protocols are used.

The program *implementation*
It must be flaw-free. Buggy code leads to security vulnerabilities.

The system's usage *procedure*

If it is routinely used incorrectly, any software system can be compromised. We should prevent this as much as possible with sound design, but users must be taught not to cause problems. How many people write down their username and password on paper beside their terminals?

Creating a secure system is never easy. It will always require a security/functionality compromise. The more secure a system is, the less useful it becomes. The safest system has no inputs and no outputs; there's nowhere for anyone to attack. It won't do much, though. The easiest system has no authentication and allows everyone full access to everything; it's just terribly insecure. We need to pick a balance. This depends on the nature of the application, its sensitivity, and the perceived threat of attack. To write appropriately secure code, we must be very clear about such *security requirements*.

Just as you would take steps to secure a building, the following techniques will protect your software from malicious attackers.

System Installation Techniques

No matter how good your application is, if the target system is insecure, your program is vulnerable. Even the most secure application must run in its operating environment: under a particular OS, on a specific piece of hardware, on a network, and with a certain set of users. An attacker is just as likely to compromise one of these as your actual code.

- Don't run any untrusted, potentially insecure program on your computer system.

  This raises the question: What makes you trust a piece of software? You can audit open source software to prove that it's correct (if you have the inclination). You can opt for the same software that everyone else uses, thinking that there's safety in numbers. (However, if a vulnerability is found in that software, you, and many other people, must update.) Or you can pick a supplier based on their reputation, hoping that it's a worthwhile indicator.

KEY CONCEPT *Only run trusted software on your computer system. Have a clear policy to decide who you trust.*

- Employ security technologies like firewalls and spam and virus filters. Don't let crackers in through a back door.

- Prepare for malicious authorized users by logging every operation, recording who did what and when. Back up all data stores periodically so that bogus modifications don't lose all of your good work.

- Minimize the access routes into the system, give each user a minimal set of permissions, and reduce the pool of users if you can.

- Set up the system correctly. Certain OSes default to very lax security, practically inviting a cracker to walk straight in. If you're setting up such a system, then it's vital to learn how to protect it fully.

- Install a *honeypot*: a decoy machine that attackers will find more easily than your real systems. If it looks plausible enough, then they'll waste their energy breaking into it, while your critical machines continue unaffected. Hopefully you'll notice a compromise of the honeypot and repel the attacker long before he gets near your valuable data.

Software Design Techniques

This is the essential place to get your security story straight. You can try to shoehorn security into code at the end of a development cycle, and you'll fail. It must be a fundamental part of your system's architecture and design.

KEY CONCEPT *Security is an essential aspect of every software architecture. It's a mistake to gloss over it during early development work.*

The simplest software design has the fewest points of attack and is consequently the easiest to secure. More complex designs naturally lead to more interactions between constituent parts, and so provide more places for a cracker to attack. If you're one of the 99.9 percent of programmers who can't run your program in a sealed box in an underground bunker in an undisclosed location in the middle of a desert, then you need to consider how to make your design as simple as possible.

As you design the code, think about how to actively prevent anyone from abusing it. Here are the winning strategies:

- Limit the number of inputs in your design, and route all communication through one portion of the system. This way, an attacker can't get all over your code—only through a single (secured) bottleneck. His influence is limited to a secluded corner, and you can focus your security efforts there.[4]

- Run every program at the most restrictive privilege level possible. Don't run a program as the system superuser unless it's absolutely necessary, and then take *even more* care than usual. This is especially important for Unix programs that run setuid—these can be run by any user but are given special system privileges when they start.

- Avoid any features that you don't really need. It will not only save you development time, but also reduce the chance of bugs getting into the program—there's less software for them to inhabit. The less complicated your code, the less likely it is to be insecure.

- Don't rely on insecure libraries. An insecure library is anything you don't *know* to be secure. For example, most GUI libraries aren't designed for security, so don't use them in a program run as the superuser.

KEY CONCEPT *Only rely on known, secure third-party components in your program design.*

- Tailor your code to an execution environment that manages security issues. The .NET run time offers offers a *code access security* infrastructure that allows you to assert, for example, that the calling code has been

---

[4] Of course, it's never quite *that* simple. A buffer overrun could occur anywhere in your code, and you must be constantly vigilant. However, most security vulnerabilities exist at, or near, the sites of program input.

signed by a trusted third party. This doesn't remove all potential problems (the company's private key could always go astray), and you must learn how to use it correctly, but it does help to manage security problems.

- Avoid storing sensitive data. If you must, encrypt it so that prying eyes can't easily read it. When you handle secrets, be very wary of where you put them; lock memory pages containing sensitive information so that your OS's virtual memory manager can't swap it onto the hard disk, leaving it available for an attacker to read.
- Obtain secrets from the user carefully. Don't display passwords.

The least impressive security strategy is known as *security through obscurity*, yet this is really the most prevalent. It merely hides all software design and implementation behind a wall so that no one can see how the code works and figure out how to abuse it. Obscurity means that you don't advertise your critical computer systems in the hope that no attacker will find them.

It's a flawed plan. Your system *will* one day be found, and it *will* one day be attacked.

It's not always a conscious decision, and this technique works very conveniently when you forget to consider security in the system design at all—that is, it's convenient until someone *does* compromise your system. Then it's a different matter.

KEY CONCEPT   *Expect your software to be attacked, and design each part with this in mind.*

Code Implementation Techniques

With a bulletproof system design, your software is unbreakable, right? Sadly, it is not. We've already seen how security exploits can capitalize on flaws in code to wreak their particular brand of chaos.

Our code is the front line, the most common route an attacker will try to enter through and the place our battles are fought. Without a good system design, even the best code is vulnerable to attack; but upon the foundation of a well-thought-out architecture, we must build strong walls of defense with secure code. Correct code is not necessarily secure code.

- Defensive programming is the main technique to achieve sound code. Its central tenet—*assume nothing*—is exactly what secure programming is about. Paranoia is a virtue, and you can never assume that users will employ your program as you expect or intend them to.

  Simple defensive rules like "check *every* input" (including user input, startup commands, and environment variables), and "validate *every* calculation" will remove countless security vulnerabilities from your code.

- Perform *security audits*. These are careful reviews of the source code by security experts. Normal testing won't find many security flaws; they are generally caused by bizarre combinations of use that ordinary testers wouldn't think of (for example, very long input sequences that provoke buffer overrun).

- Spawn child processes very carefully. If an attacker can redirect the subtask, then he can gain control of arbitrary facilities. Don't use C's system function unless there's no other solution.

- Test and debug mercilessly. Squash bugs as rigorously as you can. Don't write code that can crash; its use could bring down a running system instantly.

- Wrap all operations in atomic transactions so attackers can't exploit race conditions to their advantage. You could fix the chmod example in "Race Conditions" on page 231 by using fchmod on the open file handle, rather than chmoding the file by name: It doesn't matter if the attacker replaces the file, you know exactly which file is being altered.

Procedural Techniques

This is largely a matter of training and education, although it helps to select users who aren't totally inept (if you have that luxury).

Users must be taught safe working practices: not to tell anyone their password, not to install random software on a critical PC, and to use their systems only as prescribed. However, even the most diligent people will make mistakes. We design to minimize the risk of these mistakes, and we hope that the consequences are never too severe.

In a Nutshell

> *Security is a kind of death.*
> *—Tennessee Williams*

Programming is war.

Security is a real issue in modern software development; you can't stick your head in the sand and hide from it. Ostriches write poor code. We can prevent most security breaches by better design, better system architecture, and greater awareness of the problems. The benefits of a secure system are compelling, since the risks are so serious.

Good programmers . . .	Bad programmers . . .
• Understand the security requirements for each project they work on	• Dismiss security as an unimportant concern
• Instinctively write code that avoids common security vulnerabilities	• Consider themselves security experts (very few people *are* security experts)
• Design security into each system; they don't patch it in at the end	• Only think about security flaws in their programs when vulnerabilities are discovered, or worse, when their code is compromised
• Have a security test strategy	• Focus on security when writing code and ignore it at the design and architectural levels

See Also

Chapter 1: On the Defensive
Defensive programing is an important technique for writing secure code.

Chapter 8: Testing Times
We must rigorously test our software for security issues.

Chapter 13: Grand Designs
Security is similarly essential to the design of each section of code.

Chapter 14: Software Architecture
Security is one of the fundamental architectural concerns of a computer system. It must be designed in from the outset.

Get Thinking

A detailed discussion of the following questions can be found in the "Answers and Discussion" section on page 515.

Mull It Over

1. What is a "secure" program?
2. What input must be validated in a secure program? What sort of validation is required?
3. How can you guard against attacks from the pool of trusted users?
4. Where can an exploitable buffer overrun occur? What functions are particularly prone to buffer overrun?
5. Can you avoid buffer overruns altogether?
6. How can you secure the memory in use by your application?
7. Are C and C++ inherently less secure than alternative languages?
8. Has the experience of C led to C++ being a better, more securely designed language?
9. How do you know when your program has been compromised?

Getting Personal

1. What are the security requirements for your current project? How were these requirements established? Who knows about them? Where are they documented?
2. What's the worst security bug in one of your shipped applications?
3. How many security bulletins have been posted against your application?
4. Have you ever run a *security audit*? What kinds of flaws did it reveal?
5. What kind of person is most likely to attack your current system? How is this influenced by
   - Your company
   - The type of user
   - The type of product
   - The popularity of the product
   - The competition
   - The platform you run on
   - The connectedness and public visibility of the system

PART III

THE SHAPE OF CODE

Unlike a fine wine, your code is not likely to get any better the longer you leave it. If it starts like a small pile of something that the dog produced, then it will no doubt end up like a large pile of something an elephant produced.

This is no secret, yet software factories continually churn out elephantine creations and then suffer the consequences. Their products are neither adaptable, extensible, or malleable enough to suit their future requirements, nor easy enough to develop: They fail to deliver on time and to budget. As programmers, this hurts our pride—but it hurts managers' wallets, hard.

The answer? One solution is to never attempt code development in the first place, but that's hardly practical. The other is to develop code with a view to the entire system's structure. Good code doesn't happen by accident; it is the product of careful crafting, with much emphasis placed on prior planning and design. But it also stems from a nimble development approach, from being agile enough to cope with the inevitable problems and changes that you'll encounter en route.

This section explores this process. We'll look at:

Chapter 13: Grand Designs
Code micro design: low-level construction tips for individual code modules.

Chapter 14: Software Architecture
Larger-scale system design—the first construction stage of any software development.

Chapter 15: Software Evolution or Software Revolution?
A look at how software grows and expands over time, with some practical suggestions for grafting new work into an old codebase.

These are not optional extras or nice-to-haves. They are essential stages of our craft and are therefore crucial to the production of quality software. Ignore this stuff at your peril.

13

GRAND DESIGNS

*How to Produce Good
Software Designs*

A camel is a horse designed by committee.
—Sir Alec Issigonis

Some code just makes you sigh.

I once had to write a device driver for an embedded product. The driver's interface to the OS was quite complex. The interface to the hardware I was using was also complex. To keep myself sane, I split the code into two sections. The first was an internal library that accessed the hardware, performed some data buffering, and provided a simple API to access that buffered data. Then I wrote a second, distinct layer that implemented the finicky OS driver interface in terms of this internal library. The structure of the device driver looked like Figure 13-1.

Later, the manufacturer of the hardware sent me a sample implementation of the same device driver. The author of this code had clearly not thought it out at all. The code was a sprawling mess, tightly intermingling the complex OS interface with the hardware logic in a completely incomprehensible manner. An approximation of its structure is shown in Figure 13-2.

OS interface   Hardware interface

Figure 13-1: Pete's sane software design   *Figure 13-2: How not to design software*

Now, I'm not trying to toot my own horn (any more than is necessary, anyway). The point of this illustration is clear. The first design is better. It is easier to understand because it's so straightforward, it is easier to implement, and consequently it is easier to maintain.

C.A.R. Hoare wrote, "There are two ways of constructing a software design: One way is to make it so simple that there are *obviously* no deficiencies, and the other way is to make it so complicated that there are no *obvious* deficiencies. The first method is far more difficult." (Hoare 81)

One of the signs of a mature programmer is the design quality of his or her code. In this chapter, we'll look at what constitutes a good design and investigate how to craft high-quality software designs.

Programming as Design

It's a popular belief that "design" is a stage you complete before moving on to writing code. Its product is some form of *design specification*, which is sufficient for a generic code monkey to implement.

The truth is very different. Programming—the act of writing code—is a *design activity*.

Even the most detailed specification has holes, or else it would *be* the code—you can't describe every minuscule detail in a design document. The act of programming verifies the initial design decisions and performs the remaining design work. It exposes holes, inconsistencies, and errors and allows you to find a route around them. "Some programmers don't think they're doing design when they program, but whenever you write code, you're always doing design, either explicitly or implicitly." (Page Jones 96)

KEY CONCEPT   *Programming is a design activity. It's a creative and artistic act, not mechanical code generation.*

A good development process recognizes this and doesn't shy away from writing code when it's appropriate. Practitioners of Extreme Programming advocate that design *is* the code. (Beck 99) There is no separate design activity;

there is no team of designers. It's the programmers who constantly refine and extend the design by refining and extending the code. This is enshrined in their *test-driven design* approach: Code tests are written before any code, as a design verification tool. This is a wise idea.

Does this mean that you don't need to think before starting to hack at code? Not at all! Deep inside a text editor is not the place to plan what you're writing. That's like trying to drive from Berlin to Rome without deciding a route first. You'll end up in Moscow before you've worked out which way is north. By definition, design is something you do *first*.

KEY CONCEPT *Think before you type; establish a coherent design. Otherwise you'll end up with chaotic code.*

What Do We Design?

Programmers design code structures, obviously. But this means different things at different stages of the development process. At each stage, design is a process of decomposing the task into its constituent parts and figuring out how each part works.

These levels of software design are:

The system architecture

Here we look at the system as a whole, identify the main subsystems, and work out how they communicate. The architectural design has the most influence on the performance and characteristics of the system *as a whole* and the least impact on specific lines of code. It is the most important design act and is covered in the next chapter. In this chapter, we're concerned with the internal design of code, which involves the subsequent design levels.

Modules/components

The architectural subsystems are usually too large to directly implement in code, so the next step is to break each one down into comprehensible modules. It's very easy to be vague about design at the module level. In some ways, a "module" does not really exist. *Module* may mean something different depending on the design approach; it might be a logical clump of code, perhaps some physical unit like a Java package, C++/C# namespace, or a reusable library. It might be a class hierarchy or maybe even a free-standing executable.

This design stage often produces published interfaces. These can't be easily changed later on, since they form strict contracts between code modules and between the teams of programmers writing them.

Classes and data types

Next, we break a module into bite-sized chunks. Interface design tends to be less formal and easier to change behind the module. The tendency is to do this micro design at the keyboard. This urge should be resisted, or else you'll write the first code that comes into your head, not the best code for the problem.

Functions

This may be the lowest design level in the food chain, but it's of no less importance. A program is built from routines: If the routines are poorly designed, then the entire system will suffer. After having established exactly which functions are required, we design how they work internally, how the flow of control is routed, and which algorithms are used.[1] This is usually a mental exercise rather than a documented procedure, but a diligent design is essential.

What's All the Fuss About?

You won't find anyone arguing *for* bad design, but nonetheless, there's a lot of badly designed code out there. After a few years on the front line, any developer has the scars to prove it. (Battle-hardened veterans are already nodding their heads and mentally rehearsing their war stories.) But why is this the case?

Sloppy design can be the product of inexperienced programmers, but more often it is caused by the commercial pressures of the software factory squeezing out any time that might have been spent on good design. No one listens to the poor, protesting coders. Programming in the Real World is necessarily bound by the drive to ship software—any software—on time. The irony is that in almost every case, a lack of a good design ultimately costs more than doing it properly would have. As they say, "There's never time to do it right, but there's always time to do it twice."

Getting design right is really *very* important. The design of your code is the foundation upon which it is built. If it's wrong, then the code will be unstable, unsafe, and not fit for purpose—dangerous. A bad design foundation leads to the software equivalent of the Leaning Tower of Pisa. While novel that it manages to stand up under the strain of real use, it will never be as good as it ought to be, and in time this inevitably shows.

A sound design makes code:

- Easier to write (there's a well-defined plan of attack, and it's clear how it's all going to fit together)

- Easier to understand

- Easier to fix (you can identify the location of problems)

- Less likely to harbor bugs (program errors are not hidden behind mystifying design problems)

- More resilient to change (the design will encourage extensions and accommodate modification)

---

[1] Key algorithms will often span multiple functions; they'll be determined at the module design stage.

Good Software Design

For any programming problem, there will be *many* potential code designs. Your job is to find one. The best one. Or at least a sufficiently good one. It's not an easy task. . . .

- How do you know that your design will work? After completing a bullet-proof plan of attack, you confidently begin implementing it. Later, an unexpected problem will show its ugly head. Back to the drawing board.

- How do you know when your design is finished? You can't know until you've actually implemented it and found that it works. Many issues can't be fore-guessed; you have to step out, implement the design, and see whether or not it's complete. It's only by attempting a solution that you even *begin* to understand the original problem. Armed with this new knowledge, you can then try to solve it again properly.

- How do you know it's the *best* design solution for the problem? You can't tell unless you try out every possibility. This isn't practical. Instead, how do you know it's good *enough*? If performance is a requirement, you won't really know until the system *is* performing.

The best design approaches address these problems. They are:

Iterative
Avoid too many nasty surprises by doing a small amount of design, implementing it, assessing the implications, and feeding this into to the next design round. This incremental construction approach is very powerful.

Cautious
Don't try to design too much at once. If something fails, it might be because of any number of design decisions. Limit the room for failure, and you'll find it easier to progress. Small, sure design steps are more likely to succeed than large, clumsy ones.

Realistic
A prescriptive design process will not work all of the time, every time. The outcome depends on the quality of the requirements established, the experience of the team, and the rigor with which the process is applied. A pragmatic approach takes the best of all methodologies and admits that it relies on the programmers' gut feeling—experience has a lot to do with shaping good design.

Informed
You must fully understand all requirements and motivating principles to be clear about the problem you're solving, and also about the important qualities of the right solution. If you don't, you'll solve the wrong problem. You need this information to get early design decisions right, and some are hard to reverse.

Your design approach is inevitably affected by the overall development methodology in use (see "Programming Styles" on page 420 for a description of these). A good design *process* is a step towards creating a good design, but no guarantee. It still comes down to the quality of the design *decisions* you make. Different trade-offs lead to different designs. A design for speed will differ from design for extensibility, for example. Ultimately, there is no *right* or *wrong* design. At best, there are *good* designs and *bad* designs.

Good designs have a number of attractive characteristics, whose opposites are sure indicators of bad design. We'll discuss these next.

Simplicity

This is the single most important characteristic of well-designed code. A simple design is easy to understand, has no unnecessary warts or blemishes, and is easy to implement. It is coherent and consistent.

Simple code is as small as possible but no smaller. This takes some doing, as the mathematician Blaise Pascal appreciated: "I am sorry for the length of my letter, but I had not the time to write a short one." Carefully work out how *little* code is needed, and then write just that. Remember, you can always add more code later for extra functionality, but you can rarely remove something that has become intimately entwined.

MAKING A TRADE

Software design is a process of making decisions—of decomposing the system into its constituent parts, but also balancing the contending forces that pull in different directions. There are trade-offs to be made that shape the final design.

These are common examples of such tightropes and games of tug-of-war:

Extensibility vs. simplicity
A design for extensibility provides plenty of interface points for future code to be plugged into and ensures the scaffolding is sufficiently general to support any later requirements. Simplicity avoids the complication of extra levels of indirection and needless generality.

Efficiency vs. safety
Gains in performance often come by sacrificing purity of design—putting in special back doors for certain important operations or adding lots of coupling to prevent too much indirect access. Highly optimized systems are generally less clear and more brittle in the face of change.

Not all efficient designs are bad, though; many good designs naturally perform well *because of* their simplicity.

Features vs. development effort
At project initiation, there are a thousand desired features and a reasonable idea of when they should be delivered by (tomorrow, if not sooner). Without an infinite number of monkeys and their infinite number of PCs, you'll never get it all done. More features take more time to implement.

Which of these characteristics is most important depends on the project requirements. That's why it's so important to be clear about them up front.

Laziness *can* pay off. Work your design so you can defer as much work as possible, and only concentrate on the immediate problems.

KEY CONCEPT   Less is more. *Strive for simple code that does a lot with a little.*

A simple design is not necessarily easy to create. It takes time. For all but the most basic programs, a great deal of information must be sifted through to reach a final solution. Well-designed code *looks* obvious, but it probably took an awful lot of thought (and a lot of refactoring) to make it that simple.

KEY CONCEPT   *It's a complicated job to make something simple. If a code structure looks obvious, don't assume that it was easy to design.*

There are many ways to make a design unnecessarily complex, including incorrect component decomposition, the thoughtless proliferation of threads, inappropriate choice of algorithms, complex naming schemes, and excessive or inappropriate module dependencies.

Elegance

Elegance embodies the aesthetic aspects of design and often goes hand in hand with simplicity. It means that your code isn't baroque, confusingly clever, or overly complex. Well-designed code has a beauty in its structure. These are desirable characteristics:

- Control flowing gracefully around the system. A single operation doesn't pass through every module, converting the format of its parameter between 16 different representations, before finally ignoring it.
- Each part complements the others, adding something distinct and valuable.
- The design is not riddled with special cases.
- It associates similar things.
- No nasty surprises lurk around the corner.
- There is a small locality of change: A single, simple change in one place doesn't lead to modifications of the code in many other places.

Good design has a lot to do with balance and aesthetics. I won't go so far as to say programming is art, although some could argue a convincing case for this. Elegance and simplicity underpin most of the remaining characteristics in this list.

Modularity

As we attack a design problem, we naturally divide it into parts called *modules* or *components*. We decompose into subsystems, libraries, packages, classes, and so on. Each part is less complex than the original problem, but put together, they form a complete solution. The quality of this decomposition is paramount.

Key qualities of modularity are *cohesion* and *coupling*. We aim for modules with:

Strong cohesion

Cohesion is a measure of how related functionality is gathered together and how well the parts *inside* a module work as a whole. Cohesion is the glue holding a module together.

Weakly cohesive modules are a sign of bad decomposition. Each module must have a clearly defined role and not be a grab bag of unrelated functionality (like the pitifully common utils namespace—why *do* people write these things?).

Low coupling

Coupling is a measure of the interdependency *between* modules—the amount of wiring to and from them. In the simplest designs, modules have little coupling and so are less reliant on one another. Obviously, modules can't be totally decoupled, or they wouldn't be working together at all!

Modules interconnect in many ways—some direct, some indirect. A module can call functions on other modules or be called by other modules. It may use another module's data types or share some data (perhaps variables or files). Good software design limits the lines of communication to only those absolutely necessary. These communication lines are part of what determines the code design.

Once identified, each module can be worked on in isolation and tested separately. This is an advantage of modularity; it allows you to split tasks between programmers. Take care, though; Conway's Law warns that software structure may follow team structure: "If you have four teams working together to build a compiler, it will become a four-pass compiler" (see "Organization and Code Structure" on page 320). Make sure the decomposition is sensible and based on the problem, not the team organization.

KEY CONCEPT   *Design modules that are internally cohesive with minimal coupling. The decomposition must represent a valid partition of the problem space.*

Good Interfaces

Modules help us separate concerns and partition the problem. Each module defines an *interface*, the public façade behind which it hides an internal implementation. This set of available operations is often called an *application programming interface (API)*. It is the sole route to a module's functionality, and its quality determines the quality of that module, at least as seen from the outside.

KEY CONCEPT   *Draw lines in the sand that people don't need to cross: Identify clear APIs and interfaces.*

To create a good interface, follow these steps.

1. Identify the client and what it *wants* to do.
2. Identify the supplier and what it's *able* to do.

You can only successfully separate the user and implementer with an interface if both parties have been correctly identified and their individual needs are understood. Once you're clear about this, you stand a chance of creating an interface that will satisfy its users and is actually implementable.

Bad design puts operations in the wrong place, making it a nightmare to follow the application logic and difficult to extend the design. It leads to increased module coupling and reduced cohesion.

3. Infer the type of interface required.

    Is it a function, a class, a network protocol, or something else? This is probably dictated by who supplies the functionality, but an interface may also be wrapped up to present it in different ways. For example, wrapping a CORBA object around a library publishes its functionality to a network of collaborating computers.

4. Determine the nature of operation.

    What functionality *really* needs to be provided—is it more general than this client's specific requirement? Inside every function, there is often a more useful operation waiting to get out.

There are a few key principles that help us to reason about the nature and quality of our interfaces. As illustrated in Figure 13-3, these are:

Partitioning

An interface forms a point of contact, but also a line of separation between client and implementer. They can only communicate in the defined manner, not in any other ad hoc way.

Well-designed code clearly defines *roles and responsibilities*. Knowing who the main actors are in a system and what they are all supposed to do ensures that interfaces are crisp and effective.

A good example is my house: Its main interface is the front door. The door partitions occupants from visitors and determines where they meet. There are a number of other interfaces for other operations: windows, telephones, the chimney, and so on.

Abstraction

An abstraction allows the viewer to concentrate on important decisions, selectively ignoring certain details. It neatly organizes reality behind a simpler representation, helping us to cope with complexity. It's a particularly important concept in OO design. When designing an interface, you create an abstraction by carefully choosing exactly what is important for the user and what can be usefully hidden from them.

Given a bowl of fruit, you can happily say, "*Eat* the item on top," and then "*Eat* the next one," without worrying exactly what that entails; a grapefruit needs to be peeled, while rhubarb needs to be boiled and smothered in sugar. These details are hidden behind the abstraction *eat*; you only care that the fruit *was* eaten, not how.[2]

---

[2] This ability to hide multiple physical behaviors behind a single logical abstraction is known as *polymorphism* and is described in "Polymorphism" on page 423 .

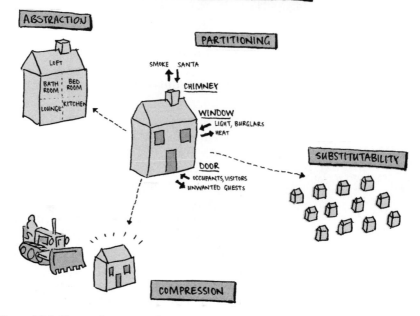

Figure 13-3: The interfaces provided by a house

Abstractions can form a hierarchy. You can view my house at different *levels of abstraction*, depending on whether you're a builder, a particle physicist, or a bank manager. It can be considered:

- A collection of rooms
- An arrangement of walls, floors, and ceilings
- A construction of bricks and timber
- A collection of molecules, or even atoms
- A mortgage that needs to be paid

Compression

This is the ability of an interface to represent a large operation with something simpler. Compression is often the result of making good abstractions, but bad abstractions can lead to more verbose code.

Substitutability

You can substitute one implementation of an interface with another, if it meets the same contract. If you define a sort interface in your program, then any algorithm can sit behind it: It could be a quicksort, a heapsort, or (heaven forbid) a bubblesort. You can change it at any point, as long as the visible behavior through the interface is the same.

In class inheritance hierarchies, any object can be substituted for its supertype.

If you want me to open my front door, you'll ring the doorbell. It used to be a wired switch that ran to the bell mechanism, but I've just invested in a new-fangled wireless doorbell. This doesn't affect you at all, in fact you won't even know I've changed it; you push a button, and I appear.

ABOUT FACE

Most of computer science is built around defining interfaces and organizing complexity around them. The infamous maxim is, "Any problem can be solved by adding an extra level of indirection"—that is, hiding new complexity behind another interface. There are many types of interfaces. They all present some *public* face to their clients and hide the gory implementation details behind this façade.

Common forms of interfaces that you'll create are:

- Libraries
- Classes
- Functions
- Data structures (particularly more exotic ones with additional behavior, like semaphores)
- OS interfaces
- Protocols (network communications, for example)

Extensibility

Well-designed code allows extra functionality to be slotted in at appropriate places, when necessary. The danger is that this may lead to over-engineered code, trying to cope with any potential future modification.

Extensibility can be accommodated through software scaffolding: dynamically loaded plug-ins, carefully chosen class hierarchies with abstract interfaces at the top, the provision of useful callback functions, and even a fundamentally logical and malleable code structure.

KEY CONCEPT   *Design for extensibility, but don't be hopelessly general—you'll end up writing an OS, not a program.*

A good designer thinks carefully about how his or her software will be extended. Randomly sprinkling code with hooks for extensibility may actually degrade quality. You should balance the functionality needed now, what will definitely need to be added later, and what might be needed to determine how extensible the design should be.

Avoid Duplication

Well-designed code contains no duplication; it never has to repeat itself. Duplication is the enemy of elegant and simple design. Unnecessary redundant code leads to a brittle program: Given two similar pieces of code that differ only in minor details, you may find and fix a bug in one and then forget to fix the same bug in the other. This clearly compromises code safety.

Most duplication comes through *cut-and-paste programming*—copying code in the editor. It can arise more subtly through the reinvention of wheels by programmers who don't understand the whole system.

- If you see strikingly similar things being done by separate sections of code, generalize it in a function with appropriate parameters. There's now a single place to fix any faults. This has the benefit of making the code's intent clearer with a descriptive function name.

- Classes that are strikingly similar indicate that some functionality could be pushed up to a superclass or that there's a missing interface to describe the common behavior.

KEY CONCEPT   *Do it once. Do it well. Avoid duplication.*

Portability

A good design is not *necessarily* portable; it depends on the code's requirements. A lot *can* be done to prevent platform dependence, but compromising code for unnecessary portability is bad design. A good design is *appropriately* portable and manages portability concerns when they are an issue.

The story is familiar: Your code was never intended to run in any other environment, so it wasn't designed to cope. Later development unexpectedly required a new runtime platform; it was simpler to adapt the old program than write a new one. The code didn't lend itself to portability, and there wasn't enough time to refactor or redesign for cross-platform support. The result? A tangled mess of code, whose design has been irreparably warped, riddled with `#ifdef NEW_PLATFORM` constructions. It has not been programmed by an engineer; it has been plumbed by a philosopher.

Make careful choices about the structure of your OS-dependent or hardware-dependent sections of code. It will pay dividends in the future, and need not affect performance or clarity (sometimes it may even improve clarity). It's important to think about this as early in the design as possible; it is expensive to rework old assumptions.

The common approach is to create a platform abstraction layer (which may be a simple veneer over a few OS interface functions). You can implement this layer differently on each platform.

KEY CONCEPT   *Manage the portability of your code in its design, rather than hacking it in as an afterthought.*

Idiomatic

A good design naturally employs best practices, fitting in with both the design methodology (see "Programming Styles" on page 420) and the implementation language's idioms. This allows other programmers to immediately understand the code's structure.

Given the implementation language (which may be fixed or may be part of the design domain) you must understand how to use it *well*. C++, for example, has idioms like *Resource Acquisition Is Initialization (RAII)* and operator overloading, which make a big difference to how you design code. Learn them. Understand them. Use them.

Well-Documented

Last, but by no means least, a good design should be documented. Don't leave readers to infer the structure by themselves. This is particularly important at the higher levels of design. The documentation should be small because the design is so simple.

At one end of the spectrum, architectural designs are documented in a specification. At the other end, functions employ self-documenting code. In the middle, you'll probably use literate programming for API documentation.

How to Design Code

Always design a thing by considering it in its next larger context—a chair in a room, a room in a house, a house in an environment, an environment in a city plan.
—*Eliel Saarinen*

How do you learn to design well? Are good designers born or made? Can design be taught or caught? Some programmers have a natural flair for good design; it fits the way their brains work. They naturally appreciate aesthetics and can comprehend enough of a problem to make balanced judgments. Nevertheless, you *can* learn to design more effectively.

When I was born, I wasn't very good at pottery. (I've never met anyone who was.) I'm still terrible now, but I took some lessons once. I understand the mechanics and can produce (almost recognizable) pots. I'd probably be much better if I practiced a little, but I'll never become a master artisan.

Similarly, no one is born able to design code: We learn. We are taught design methodologies and good engineering practice. These aim to make design a repeatable process, but they are no substitute for *craftsmanship*. The creative thought process and construction of innovative designs is much harder to convey; there will always be better designers who grasp this.

Good software design is aesthetic; to create this digital art requires skill, experience, and practice. This chapter cannot attempt a paint-by-numbers description of how to design software. A shame: If I could bottle good design, I'd be a millionaire. To be a good designer, you must understand what constitutes a good design and learn to avoid the characteristics of bad design. Then practice. For a long time.

Apart from personal ability, there are design methods and tools that promise much to the programmer. We'll conclude by investigating how they can (or can't) help us.

Design Methods and Processes

There are many software design methodologies. Some emphasize a notation, others the process. A systematic approach is better than *seat of your pants* design; which method you use is usually dictated by company practice and culture. I'm always wary of getting too bogged down in a *particular* process—satisfying its minuscule details tends to stifle creativity.

Modern design methods fall into two main families, the fundamental design philosophies upon which they are based:

Structured design

This is primarily about *functional decomposition*, breaking up the functionality of the system into a series of smaller operations. Routines are the main structuring devices; the design is composed of a hierarchy of routines. Structured design is characterized by the *divide-and-conquer* approach, splitting a problem into successively smaller procedures until each piece can be decomposed no more.

There are two main lines of attack: *top-down* and *bottom-up*.

- Not surprisingly, a top-down approach starts with the entire problem and breaks it down to smaller activities. These, in turn, are designed as self-contained units, until no more division is necessary.

- In contrast, bottom-up design starts with the smallest units of functionality, the simple things you know the system *must* do. It then stitches these functions together until it arrives at an entire solution.

In practice, these are used in tandem, and the design process ends where they meet, somewhere in the middle.

Object-oriented design

Whereas structured design focuses on representing the operations a system must perform, OO design focuses on the data within that system. It models the software as an interacting set of individual units, known as *objects*.

An OO design identifies the primary objects in the problem domain and determines what their characteristics are. The behavior of these objects is established, including the operations they provide and which other objects they each relate to. The objects are weaved into a design, incorporating any implementation domain objects needed. Design is complete when all object behavior and interaction is determined.

Object-oriented programming was hailed as the savior of the software design world, a new paradigm to usher in world peace, so much so that people are often embarrassed to not be performing OO design. But it has largely lived up to the hype, allowing software designs to manage the complexity of far bigger problems.

See "Programming Styles" on page 420 for a more detailed description of design methods and processes.

DESIGN PATTERNS

Patterns have become a buzzword in the OO programming community over the last few years. Popularized by the book *Design Patterns: Elements of Reusable Software* (Gamma et al. 94) by the authors affectionately known as the "Gang of Four" (hence it's often known as the *GoF* book), design patterns are the software version of Christopher Alexander's architectural work. (Alexander 99)

Patterns establish a vocabulary of proven design solutions, and each pattern describes a recognizable structure of collaborating objects. These aren't clever invented designs, but recurring patterns found in *real code* that have been shown to work. *Pattern languages* collate a catalog of design patterns, showing how they relate to and complement one another. Each pattern in a language follows a common form, describing the *context*, the *problem*, and the *solution*. This information allows you to apply the pattern appropriately in your designs.

Patterns crop up at several levels in a software system. Architectural patterns have a profound influence on the organization of a system. Design patterns are midlevel collaborations of software components. Language-level patterns are specific code techniques, known more commonly as language *idioms*.

The names of design patterns have entered common parlance, a testament to their usefulness. You'll hear programmers happily talking about *adaptors*, *observers*, *factories*, and *singletons*.

There is far more to design patterns than this quick description can do justice. They are a genuinely useful concept, and it's worth devoting some time to learn about them. Read the GoF book and material beyond it.

Design Tools

Our designs are ultimately expressed in code, but it can often be helpful to work at a more abstract level. Tools help us to reason about a design, help us produce more effective designs, and help us to communicate those designs to other programmers—documenting what we *intend* to produce and what we have *already* created.

In a sense, methodologies are tools, but there's a broad range of other design aids that complement them.

Notations

Pretty pictures are worth their weight in words. Many graphical notations exist to help us express our designs pictorially. Most became fleetingly fashionable and then quietly slunk out of the limelight to be replaced by an even sexier way of drawing boxes and lines. The *Unified Modeling Language (UML)* is currently the most popular and well-specified notation. It provides a standard way to model and document practically every artifact generated by the software development process. In fact, it has grown so comprehensive that you can use it to visualize far more than just software; it has been used to model hardware, business processes, and even organizational structures.

Notations provide a medium to help you express, think about, and discuss your software design. They serve two purposes:

- They allow you to scrawl quick "back of an envelope" designs and share thoughts around a whiteboard.
- They allow you to formally document designs.

To maintain your sanity in the latter case, diagram creation must be automated with a dedicated drawing tool. Otherwise, diagrams will be hard to update and will diverge from reality as you develop the code. Spend your time doing something useful, not drawing boxes and lines.

I prefer to not be bogged down by overly formal use of a notation, happily using it as a method of communicating the essential elements of a design. Knowing enough to be able to communicate is good enough for me; I don't want to get too concerned about what *every* diamond and dotted line means in *every* type of picture.

Design patterns
A powerful design tool providing a vocabulary of proven design techniques, and showing how to apply them in practice. "Design Patterns" on page 255 discusses design patterns in more depth.

Flowcharts
A particular kind of graphical notation, used to visualize algorithms. They're good for giving a high-level overview but are less precise than code and become another thing to be kept in sync with code changes. For this reason, it's best to use them sparingly.

Pseudocode
Pseudocode helps you draft function implementations. It's one of the most curious inventions in software design—halfway between a natural language and a programming language, a sort of pidgin English. Its advantage is the freedom from any particular language's syntax and semantics. You can concentrate on what needs to be done, not on language mechanics, and you can include arbitrary amounts of descriptive prose for clarity.

These aren't incredible benefits compared to the downsides. The pseudocode will require translation into an implementation language. You could have started to write in *that* language anyway and saved yourself some effort. If pseudocode is being used as design documentation, then you'll have to keep it in sync with code.

Program Design Language (PDL) is an even more absurd invention— a formalized pseudocode. I guess it made sense to somebody at the time. I'd love to have seen their pseudocode compiler.

Design in code
This is a useful informal approach to code design. During the initial design stages, you capture all APIs and the lower-level interfaces in code, but without implementing any of them—you just write stubs that return plausible values, putting comments inside each describing what should be done. When you have reached a sufficiently mature design, the system already has a lot of code written.

This can be a mixed blessing, as it can lead to less fluid designs. The more you change the design, the more stubbed code you have to alter.

CASE tools

Computer-aided software engineering (CASE) tools assist in all or part of the design process, automating tedious jobs and managing the workflow. Most are capable of generating code (of variable quality) from your pretty pictures. Some even update the pictures when you modify the code; this is known as *round-trip engineering* (or *round-tripping*). Many CASE tools support collaborative work, allowing teams of programmers to contribute to a single large-scale design.

A breed of CASE tool worthy of mention is *Rapid Application Development (RAD)* tools: environments for quickly building applications. They tend to work well in their specific domain (usually simple UI-focused applications) but aren't good general-purpose software design models.

KEY CONCEPT *Take a pragmatic approach to design tools and methodologies—use them when they are genuinely helpful—but don't become a slave to them.*

In a Nutshell

> *Out of intense complexities, intense simplicities emerge.*
> *—Winston Churchill*

Good code is well designed. It has a certain aesthetic appeal that makes it *feel good.* You must plan a design before beginning to write code, or you'll end up with an unpleasant mess. Consider things like clean structure, possible future extensions, correct interfaces, appropriate abstractions, and portability requirements. Aim for simplicity and elegance.

Design involves a strong element of craftsmanship. The best designs come from experienced and skilled hands. Ultimately, a good designer is what makes a good design. Mediocre programmers do not produce excellent designs.

Good programmers . . .

- Want to leave anything they touch in a good state
- Think of programming as a creative process and weave an element of artistry into their work
- Think about the structure of code before they start working on it
- Feel the need to tidy up and refactor messy code before they do any extra work on it
- Constantly learn about the design of other software, building up knowledge of successes and failures

Bad programmers . . .

- Keep knitting more and more code into a tight ball until they think they've done enough and then complain about the result
- Don't notice a bad design or feel any distaste when working with dense code
- Are happy to hack quickly and run away, leaving someone else to clean up the mess
- Don't appreciate or respect the internal design of code they're working on; they trample over it in an unsympathetic manner

See Also

Chapter 8: Testing Times
Describes how to *design code for testing*—making it easier to prove that your code works properly.

Chapter 14: Software Architecture
The highest level of software design is known as *software architecture*. It provides its own specific problems and is dealt with in this chapter.

Chapter 19: Being Specific
Software designs are often captured in a specification document.

Chapter 22: Recipe for a Program
Design fits into the overall software development process.

Chapter 23: The Outer Limits
The type of system you're building has an inevitable influence on the software's internal design.

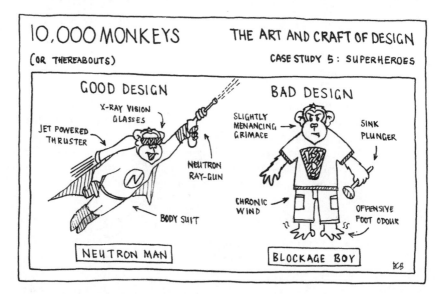

Get Thinking

A detailed discussion of these questions can be found in the "Answers and Discussion" section on page 519.

Mull It Over

1. How does project size affect your software design and the work involved in creating it?

2. Is a well-documented bad design better than an undocumented good one?

3. How can you measure the design quality of a piece of code? How can you quantify its simplicity, elegance, modularity, and so on?

4. Is design a team activity? How important are teamworking skills in creating a good design?

5. Are different methodologies more suitable to different projects?

6. In what ways can you determine whether a design is highly cohesive or weakly coupled?

7. If you've solved a similar design problem in the past, how good an indicator is it of how difficult *this* problem will be?

8. Is there a place for experimentation in design?

Getting Personal

1. Look back and think about how you learned to design code. How could you convey the knowledge you've gained to a total novice?

2. What experience do you have with using particular design methodologies? Were these good or bad experiences? What was the resulting code like? What might have worked better?

3. Do you find it important to stick rigidly to the methodology you're using?

4. What was the best designed code you've ever seen? What was the worst designed?

5. A programming language is essentially a tool to implement your design, not a religion to argue about. How important is it *really* to know language idioms?

6. Do you think programming is an *engineering discipline*, a *craft*, or an *art?*

14

SOFTWARE ARCHITECTURE

*Laying the Foundations
of Software Design*

Architecture is the art of how to waste space.
—Philip Johnson

Go into a city. Stand in the middle of it. Look around. Unless you've picked an unusual place, you will be surrounded by a large number of buildings of varying ages and styles of construction. Some fit into their surroundings sympathetically. Others look totally out of place. Some are aesthetically pleasing and seem well proportioned. Others are downright ugly. Some will still be there in 100 years' time. Many will not.

The architects who designed these buildings took a lot into consideration before they put pencil to paper. During the process of design, they worked carefully and methodically to ensure that the building was feasible to fabricate, and they balanced all the contending forces: user requirements, construction methods, maintainability, aesthetics, and so on.

Software is not made of bricks and mortar, but the same careful thought is required to ensure that a system meets similar sets of requirements. We have been erecting buildings far longer than we've been writing software, and it shows. We're still learning about what makes good software architecture.

In this little foray into the world of software architecture, we'll investigate some common architectural patterns and look at what software architecture really is, what it really isn't, and what it's used for.

UNDERGROUND MOVEMENT

I joined a project that had produced a large amount of undocumented software, erected without plan or purpose, with no architect to guide the construction process. Naturally, it had become an unsightly carbuncle. The time came when we needed to understand how it all *really* worked, and an architectural diagram of the system was drawn up. There were so many different components (many largely redundant), inappropriate interconnections, and different methods of communication that the diagram was an intense jumble of tightly woven lines in many interpretive colors—almost as if a spider had fallen into a few different cans of paint and then spun psychedelic webs across the office.

Then it struck me. We had all but drawn a map of the London Underground. Our system bore such a striking resemblance, it was uncanny—it was practically incomprehensible to an outsider, with many routes to achieve the same end, and the plan was still a gross simplification of reality. This was the kind of system that would vex a traveling salesman.

The lack of architectural vision had clearly made its mark on the software. It was hard to work with and hard to understand, with bits of functionality strewn across completely random modules. It had gotten to the point where the only useful thing you could do with it was throw it away.

In software construction, as in building construction, *the architecture really matters.*

What Is Software Architecture?

Is this just another term that stretches the *building* metaphor a little thinner (see "Do We Really *Build* Software?" on page 177)? Maybe so, but it is a genuinely useful concept. Software architecture is sometimes known as *high-level design*; regardless of the terms used, the meaning is the same. Architecture is a more evocative description of the concept.

Software Blueprints

As an architect prepares his blueprint for a building, the software architect prepares a blueprint for the software system. However, while a building's blueprint is a rigorously detailed plan with all the important features included, our software architecture is a top-level definition, an overview of the system that specifically avoids too much detail. It is macro, not micro.

In this high-level view, all implementation details are hidden; we just see the essential internal structure of the software and its fundamental behavioral characteristics. The architectural view does the following:

- Identifies the key software modules (or components, or libraries; at this point call them what you like—*blobs*)

- Identifies which components communicate with each other
- Helps to identify and determine the nature of all the important interfaces in the system, clarifying the correct *roles and responsibilities* of the various subsystems

This information allows us to reason about the system as a whole without having to understand how every individual part will work. The architecture provides a framework into which the later development fits. It shows how work can be split between teams and allows you to weigh different implementation strategies.

Not only does the architecture give a picture of how the system is composed, it also shows how it should be extended over time. In large teams, a program will develop more elegantly when there's a clear, unified vision of how the software should be adapted, of what should be put in each module, and of how modules connect.

KEY CONCEPT *The architecture is the single largest influence on the design and future growth of a software system. It is therefore essential to get it right in the early stages of development.*

As an up-front activity, the architecture is our first chance to map the *problem domain* (the Real World problem we are solving) to a *solution domain*. There isn't always a simple one-to-one mapping of objects and activities between the two, so the architecture shows how to think about one in terms of the other.

Exactly what needs to be addressed by the software architecture will differ from project to project. The target platform is not important at this stage; it may be possible to implement the architecture on a number of different machines using different languages and technologies. However:

- For certain projects, it may be important to specify particular hardware components, most likely for embedded designs.
- For a distributed system, the number of machines and processors and the split of work between them might be an architectural issue. Minimum and average system configurations should be considered.
- The architecture may also describe specific algorithms or data structures if they are fundamental to the overall design (although this is far less likely).

There is always a trade-off. The more information that is set in stone at the architectural level, the less room for maneuverability there is at a later design or implementation stage.

Points of View

In physical architecture, we use a number of different drawings or views of the same building: one for the physical structure, one for the wiring, one for the plumbing, and so on. Similarly, we develop different software views in the architectural process. Four views are commonly recognized:

The conceptual view
Sometimes called the *logical view*, this shows the major parts of the system and their interconnections.

The implementation view

This view is seen in terms of the real implementation modules, which may have to differ from the neat conceptual model.

The process view

Designed to show the dynamic structure in terms of tasks, processes, and communication, this view is best used when there's a high degree of concurrency involved.

The deployment view

Use this view to show the allocation of tasks to physical nodes, in a distributed system. For example, you may split functionality between a database server and a farm of web interface gateways.

You don't start with all of these. Particular views arise as development work progresses. The main result of the initial architectural phase is the *conceptual view*, and that's what we're concentrating on here.

FOR WHAT IT'S WORTH

Software architecture has wide-ranging implications—far beyond the initial structure of the code, right into the heart of the software factory. The architecture will be a lasting legacy, both in the technological and practical realms. Architecture affects how the code will grow and how teams of people will work together to extend it; software design affects workflow. With a three-tiered architecture, you'll end up with *three* teams of people working on the separate parts. There will probably be *three* sets of admin staff too, and *three* management reporting lines. Someone's early design decision will affect which desk you sit at.

Since the architecture determines how malleable the software is and how well the codebase can accommodate future requirements, it ultimately influences the commercial success of your company. A bad architecture is more than just inconvenient—it could cost you your livelihood. Serious stuff.

As programmers, it affects us most directly—it will affect how fun our work will be. No one wants to labor intensely to add a minuscule feature that would have taken two seconds with a correct initial design. At conception, check that the architecture supports what *you* think it should, not just what the architects believe.

Where and When Do You Do It?

The architecture is captured in a high-level document called something imaginative like the *architecture specification*. This specification explains the system's structure and shows how it fulfills the requirements, including important issues like the strategy to reach any performance requirements and how acceptable fault tolerance will be achieved.

KEY CONCEPT   *Capture system architecture in a known place; a document accessible to everyone involved—programmers, maintainers, installers, managers (perhaps even customers).*

The architecture is the initial system design. It is therefore the *first* developmental step after the requirements have been agreed upon. It's important to generate a specification up front because it provides a first chance to review and validate the design decisions that will have the most significant impact on the project. It will expose weaknesses and potential problems. Reversing a bad decision this early on will save a lot of time, effort, and money. It's expensive to change the foundation of a system once a lot of code has been built upon it.

Architectural work is a form of design, but it is separate from the module design phase, and distinct from low-level code design, although it certainly overlaps somewhat. Later work on detailed design may feed changes back up to the system architecture. This is natural and healthy.

WHOSE JOB?

We've seen that software architecture affects *everyone* on the project—not just the programmers. In contrast, the architecture is determined by a far smaller group of people. What a responsibility.

The architecture designer is called a *software architect*. This is a grandiose title and, like *engineer*, somewhat contentious. "Real" architects must study, qualify, and reach levels of professional excellence to even be called architects. There are no such requirements in the software world.

Software architects are among the project initiators, working right at the beginning of the development cycle. As development ramps up, programmers will join the effort to implement this established architecture.

However, on smaller projects requiring less specialized architectural experience, the programmers themselves will devise the architecture. No big guns are drafted in. Be ready to contribute to architectural design.

What Is It Used For?

Architecture is the initial system design. But its uses stretch even further. We use the system architecture to:

Validate

The architecture is our first chance to validate what is going to be built. With it, we can mentally check that the system will meet all requirements. We can check that it really is feasible to build. We can ensure that the design is internally consistent and hangs together well with no special cases or gratuitous hacks. Nasty blemishes in the high-level design will only lead to more dangerous hacks at lower levels.

The architecture helps to ensure that there is no duplication of work, wasted effort, or redundancy. We use it to check that there are no gaps in the strategy, that we have included all the necessary pieces. We ensure that there will be no mismatches as separate sections are brought together.

Communicate

We use the architecture specification to communicate the design to all interested parties. These may be system designers, implementers, maintainers, testers, customers, or managers. It's the primary route to understand the system and is an important piece of documentation that should *always* be kept up to date as changes are made.

KEY CONCEPT *An architecture specification is an essential device to communicate the shape of your system. Ensure that you keep it in sync with the software.*

The architecture conveys the vision of your system, mapping the problem domain to the solution domain. It should neatly identify how future extensions fit in, helping to maintain the system's *conceptual integrity*. (Brooks 95) It implicitly provides a set of conventions and contains an element of style. For example, it's clear that you shouldn't introduce a new component with custom socket-based communication if the rest of the design uses a CORBA infrastructure.

The architecture provides a natural route into the next level of design without being too prescriptive.

Discriminate

We use the architecture to help us make decisions. For example, it identifies build versus buy decisions, determines whether a database is required, and clarifies the error-handling strategy. It will flag problem areas, areas of particular risk on the project, and help us plan to minimize this risk. Just as an architect's primary goal is to ensure his building stays up when it's built—under all expected conditions (and some unusual conditions too)—so should we ensure the resilience of our software structure. A little wind or extra load shouldn't topple the thing over.

We need this systemwide perspective to make the appropriate trade-offs, ensuring that the design meets its required properties. These important issues are considered at the beginning rather than grafted in toward the end of development.

KEY CONCEPT *Make all software design decisions in the context of the architecture. Always check that you're working in line with the system vision and strategy. Don't create a little wart on the side that doesn't complement anything else.*

Of Components and Connections

Architecture mostly concerns itself with *components* and *connections*. It determines the number and type of each.

Components

Architecture captures information about each component, whatever *component* means in the architecture's context. It could be an object, a process, a library, a database, or a third party product. Each of the system's components is identified as a clear and logical unit. Each performs one task and does it well. No component includes a kitchen sink unless there's a specific kitchen-sink module.

While it won't dwell on component implementation issues, the architecture will describe all exposed facilities and perhaps the important externally visible interfaces. It defines the *visibility* of the component: what it can see and what it can't, and what can see it and what can't. Different architectural styles imply different visibility rules, as we'll see later.

ARCHITECTS VS. MARKETERS

An architecture is inadequate if it doesn't fulfill the product requirements for initial deployment or any future development; design quality is about more than just technical excellence. Technical issues must be addressed alongside product management and marketing considerations.

There is no point in developing a product that no one wants; it would obviously be a huge waste of time. But you can miss vital business opportunities by omitting marketing requirements from technical consideration. The marketing department identifies core business objectives including sales strategies (do you charge a one-off fee or employ a licensing/billing model?), the product's position in the marketplace (is it a high-end, feature-packed, high-cost product or a cheap, mass-produced item?), and the importance of a unique brand running through the system.

In some situations, visibly good architecture may be a *unique selling point* and may provide a strong competitive advantage. Other markets care less about the internal system structure, but an architecture that anticipates and handles future customer requirements is still essential to establish and maintain a strong market position.

Technical architects must work closely with the marketing decision makers to understand how new software will fit into the company's overall strategy and what the customer requires for a truly exceptional solution. The software architecture will address marketing issues such as usability, reliability, upgradeablity, and extensibility. Each of these has a real influence on the software design. Support for different charging methods alone may have a huge impact on the profitability of the project—the inclusion of rich logging support will pave the way for per-transaction billing, which may lead to increased product revenue. However, it may mandate the inclusion of additional security and fraud-prevention measures in the architectural planning.

Marketing requirements feed into the technical architecture. Technical considerations will also feed back to the marketing strategy. A truly great architecture is born when technical and strategic visions meet to create a product that stands out from its competitors.

Connections

The architecture identifies all the inter-component connections and describes the connection properties. A connection may be a simple function call or data flow through a pipe. It may be an event handler or a message passing through some OS or network mechanism. A connection can be *synchronous* (blocking the caller until the implementation has completed the request) or *asynchronous* (returning control to the caller immediately and arranging for a reply to be posted back at a later date). This is important, since it affects the flow of control around the system.

Some communication is indirect (and consequently quite subtle). For example, components can share certain resources and talk through them—rather like posting messages on a shared whiteboard. Examples of shared communication channels are: a subordinate component, a shared memory region, or something as basic as the contents of a file.

What Is Good Architecture?

The key to good architecture is *simplicity*. A few well-chosen modules and sensible communication paths are the aim. It also needs to be *comprehensible*, which often means visually represented. We all know that *a picture speaks a thousand words*.

KEY CONCEPT *Good system architecture is* simple. *It can be described in a single paragraph and summarized in one elegant diagram.*

In a well-designed system, there should be neither too few nor too many components. This criterion scales with the size of the problem. For a small program, the architecture may fit on (or even be done on) the back of an envelope, with just a few modules and some simple interconnections. A large system naturally requires more effort and more envelopes.

Too many fine-grained components lead to an architecture that is bewildering and hard to work with. It implies that the architect has gone into too much detail. *Too few* components means that each module is doing far too much work; this makes the structure unclear, hard to maintain, and hard to extend. The correct balance is somewhere between the two.

The architecture does not dictate the inner workings of each module—that's what module design is for. The goal is that each module should know very little about the other parts of the system. We aim for low coupling and high cohesion (see "Modularity" on page 247) at this level of design, as with all others.

KEY CONCEPT *Architecture* identifies *the key components of the system and how they interact. It* doesn't define *how* they work.

The architecture specification lists the design decisions made and makes it clear why this approach is being favored over any alternative strategies. It doesn't need to labor these other approaches, but should justify the chosen architecture and prove that some serious thought went into it. It must have correctly identified the primary goal of the system: For example, *extensibility* is a different game from *performance* and will lead to different architectural design decisions.

A good architecture leaves room for maneuverability; it allows you to change your mind. It may specify that we wrap third party components with abstract interfaces so we can swap one version out for another. It may suggest technologies that make it easy to select different implementations during deployment. As a project gains momentum, the correct implementation choices become clear—they aren't always obvious at first. A successful architecture is flexible, providing a mechanism for nimble design during these initial uncertainties. The architecture is the first pivot on which to balance contending forces; it will show how we trade one quality for another.

KEY CONCEPT *A good architecture leaves space for maneuverability, extension, and modification. But it isn't hopelessly general.*

The architecture must be clear and unambiguous. Preexisting, well-known architectural styles or well-known frameworks are best (see the next section for more on these). Architecture must be easy to understand and work with.

Like a good design, good architecture has a certain aesthetic appeal that makes it *feel* right.

Architectural Styles

Form ever follows function.
—Louis Henry Sullivan

Just as an immense gothic cathedral and a quaint Victorian chapel, or an imposing tower block and a 1970s public lavatory employ different architectural styles, there are a number of recognized software architectural styles that a system may be built upon. A style may be chosen for various reasons, good or bad—perhaps on sound technological grounds, or perhaps based on the architect's prior experience, perhaps even by what style is currently in fashion. Each architecture has different characteristics:

- Its resilience to changes in the data representation, algorithms, and required functionality
- Its method of module separation and connection
- Its comprehensibility
- Its accommodation of performance requirements
- Its consideration of component reusability

In practice, we might see a mixture of architectural styles in one system. Some data processing may progress through a pipe and filter process, while the rest of the system employs a component-based architecture.

KEY CONCEPT *Recognize the key architectural styles and appreciate their pros and cons. This will help you to sympathetically work with existing software and perform appropriate system design.*

The following sections describe some of the common architectural styles. And then compare them to pasta.

No Architecture

A system always has an architecture, but like my London Underground project, it may not have a *planned* architecture. Before long, this state of affairs becomes an albatross around the neck of your development team. The resulting software will be a mess.

Defining an architecture is essential if you want to build good software. Not planning an architecture is a surefire way to doom development before you've even started.

> Architecture as Pasta:
> *Spaghetti Ball*
>
> Messy, uncontrollable, unmanagable morass of interwoven gloop.

Layered Architecture

This is probably the most commonly used architectural style in conceptual views. It describes the system as a hierarchy of layers, with a building-block approach. It is a very simple model to comprehend; even a non-techie can quickly grasp what it's telling him.

Architecture as Pasta: *Lasagne*

Several distinct layers, arranged one on top of another.

Each component is represented by a single block in the stack. The positions in the stack indicate what lives where, how the components relate to each other, and which components can "see" which other components. Blocks may be placed alongside each other on the same level and can even become tall enough to span two layers.

A famous example of this is the OSI seven-layer reference model for network communication systems. (ISO 84) A more interesting example is the Goodliffe seven-layer trifle reference model shown in Figure 14-1.

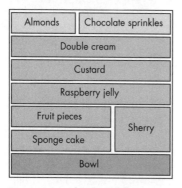

Figure 14-1: The Goodliffe seven-layer trifle reference model

At the lowest level of the stack, we find the hardware interface, if the system does indeed interact with physical devices. Otherwise, this level is reserved for the most basic service, perhaps the OS or a middleware technology like CORBA. The highest level will likely be occupied by the fancy interface that the user interacts with. As you rise further up the stack, you move further away from the hardware, happily insulated by the layers in between in the same way that the roof of a house doesn't have to worry about the magma at the earth's core.

At any point, you can brush out all the lower layers and slot in a new implementation of the layer below—the system will function as before. This is a key point: It means that you can run the same C++ code on any computing platform that supports your C++ environment. You can swap the hardware platform without touching your application code—relying on the OS layer (for example) to swallow the technical differences. Handy.

Higher levels use the public interfaces of the layer directly below. Whether they can use the public interfaces of the lower levels depends of your definition of layering. Sometimes the diagram is fiddled to represent this, like the sherry brick in the trifle stack. Whether or not components on the same layer can interconnect is also not rigidly defined. You certainly can't use anything from a higher level; if you break this edict, you no longer have a layered architecture, just a meaningless diagram drawn in stack form.

As you can see, most layer diagrams are informal. The relative size and position of boxes gives a clue as to importance of a component, and that is generally sufficient as an overview. Component connections are implicit, and the methods of communication irrelevant. (However, this can be a key architectural concern for the efficiency of the system—you won't send gigabytes of data down an RS232 serial port.)

Pipe and Filter Architecture

This architecture models the logical flow of data through the system. It is implemented as a string of sequential modules that each read some data, process it, and spit it out again. At the start of the chain is a data generator (maybe a user interface or perhaps some hardware harvesting logic). At the end is a data sink (perhaps the computer display or a log file). It's the old through-the-grapevine telephone game in digital form. The data flows down the pipe, encountering the various filters en route. The transformations are usually incremental; each filter does a single simple process and tends to have very little internal state.

Architecture as Pasta: *Cannelloni*

Good conduit for its contents, suits particular situations very well.

The pipe and filter architecture requires a well-defined data structure between each filter; it has the implicit overhead of repeatedly encoding the output data for transmission down the pipe and parsing it back again in each subsequent filter. For this reason, the data stream is usually very simple—just a plaintext format.

This architecture makes it easy to add functionality by just plugging a new filter into the pipeline. Its main downside is error handling. It is hard to determine where an error originated in the pipeline by the time a problem manifests itself at the sink. It's cumbersome to pass error codes down the chain toward the output stage; they need extra encoding and are hard to handle uniformly over several separate modules. The filters may use a separate error channel (e.g., stderr), but error messages can get mixed up all too easily.

Client/Server Architecture

A typically network-based architecture, the client/server model separates functionality into two key pieces: the *client* and the *server*. It differs from the older *mainframe* style of networked design in the division of work between each part; a mainframe "client" is a dumb terminal—little more than a means to capture and transmit keypresses, with some output display.

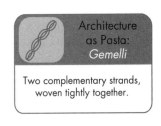

Architecture as Pasta: *Gemelli*

Two complementary strands, woven tightly together.

A SLAP IN THE INTERFACE

A key software construction principle is *modularity*, designing systems from replaceable components. This is almost a "LEGO brick" approach to construction. Done correctly, you should be able to take out a square, blue brick and replace it with a slightly fancier red one. If the bricks are the same size and shape and have the same kinds of connector, they will fit into the same hole and do the same job.

How do we implement this in software? We define *interfaces*; these are our connection points and component barriers. They define the size and shape of each component (as seen from the outside, at least) and determine what you have to do to provide a like-for-like replacement. Key types of interfaces are:

APIs

Application programming interfaces (APIs) are specified as collections of functions in a physically linked application. To replace a component that implements a particular API, you just reimplement all the functions and relink the code.

Class hierarchies

You can design an abstract "interface" class (in Java and C#, you'd actually define an `interface`). Then provide any number of concrete implementations that derive from it and implement that interface.

Component technologies

Technologies such as COM and CORBA allow your program to determine the correct implementation component at run time. Typically, interfaces are defined in an abstract *Interface Definition Language (IDL)*. The beauty of this approach is that components can be written in any language. It requires middleware or OS support.

Data formats

These formats can form a connection point in designs focused on the movement of data rather than the flow of control. You can replace any component in the data chain with an analog that interacts with the same data types.

As you can see, architecture—indeed, most of software design—is about crafting appropriate interfaces. Each of these interface techniques maps to a particular architectural style. Pick an interface mechanism that complements the architecture.

The clients of a client/server architecture are richer, more intelligent, and generally able to present data in an interactive, graphical manner. Here is a more detailed look at the role of the two elements:

Server

The server provides certain well-defined services to clients. It will generally be a powerful computer dedicated to providing specific functionality or to managing a resource (shared files, printers, a database, or pooled processing power).

The server waits for requests from clients and responds to them. It may be able to handle any number of simultaneous client connections or might be limited to certain usage patterns.

Client

The client consumes a server's services. It sends off requests and processes the results that are returned. Some clients are dedicated terminals which only fulfill one role; other clients serve many functions (for example, a "client" application may run on a standard desktop PC that can also browse the web and view email).

There can be many different types of clients using one server, all performing the same set of requests but in different ways. One client might be web based, one might have a GUI interface, while another might provide command line access.

This client/server approach is sometimes known as a *two-tier* architecture, for obvious reasons. It's very common and is seen throughout the software development world. The means of communication between client and server varies—it's simplest to use standard network protocols, but you may also see use of remote procedure calls (RPC), remote SQL database queries, or even proprietary application-specific protocols.

There are various ways of splitting work between the two components. The main application logic (also known as *business logic*) may run on either the client or server, depending on how intelligent and specialized the client is supposed to be. As more application logic is pushed down to the client, the design becomes less flexible—separate clients have to reimplement similar features, negating the benefit of the central server. Clients are generally concerned with providing sensible human interfaces to the published server functionality.

We sometimes see an extension of this two-tier design, which introduces another layer (the *middle tier*). This component is explicitly designed to contain the business logic, separating it from both the client application (which is now most definitely only an interface) and the back-end data storage. This is a *three-tier* architecture.

A client/server approach is different from a *peer-to-peer* architecture, where no network node has more capability or importance than any other. Peer-to-peer architectures are harder to deploy but more tolerant of faults. The client/server design is crippled when the server is unavailable (through some software fault or routine maintenance): No client will be able to operate until the server comes back to life. For this reason, client/server installations generally require a designated administrator to keep all systems running smoothly.

Component-Based Architecture

This architecture decentralizes control and splits it into a number of separate collaborating *components* rather than a single monolithic structure. It is an object-oriented approach, but doesn't necessarily require implementation in an OO language. Each component's public interface is typically defined in an *Interface*

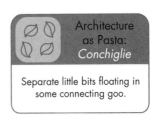

Architecture as Pasta: *Conchiglie*

Separate little bits floating in some connecting goo.

Definition Language (IDL) and is separate from any implementation, although some component technologies (like .NET's built-in component support) can determine this from the implementation code itself.

Component-based design arrived with the lure of assembling applications quickly out of prefabricated components, supposedly enabling plug-and-play solutions. It's still up for debate how much of a success this has been. Not all components are designed for reuse (it's hard work), and it's not always easy to find a component that does what you want it to do. It's easiest for UIs, where popular frameworks and established marketplaces exist.

The core of a component-based architecture is a communication infrastructure, or *middleware*, which allows components to be plugged in, to broadcast their existence, and to advertise the services they provide. Components are used by looking up this information through a middleware mechanism, rather than by hardwiring a direct connection between two components. Common middleware platforms include CORBA, JavaBeans, and COM; each have different strengths and weaknesses.

A component[1] is essentially an implementation unit. It honors one (maybe more) specific published IDL interfaces. This interface is how clients of the component interact with it. There are no back doors. The client is concerned with dealing with an instance of that interface, rather than in how the component is implemented.

Each component is an individual, independent piece of code. Behind its interface, it implements some logic (perhaps business logic or user interface activity) and contains some data, which may just be local or may be published (say a filestore or database component). Components don't need to know much about one another. If they *are* tightly coupled, then the architecture is just an obfuscated monolithic system.

Component-based architectures can be deployed in a networked environment with components on different machines, but they can just as easily exist as a single machine installation. This may depend on the type of middleware in use.

Frameworks

Instead of developing a new architecture for a specific project, it may be appropriate to use an existing *application framework* and add development into that skeleton. A framework is an extensible library of code (usually a set of co-operating classes) that forms a reusable design solution for a particular problem domain. Most

Architecture as Pasta: *Canned Ravioli*

Most of the work's already been done for you. Just heat and serve.

of the work in a framework has been done for you, with the remaining pieces following a fill-in-the-blanks approach. Different frameworks follow different architectural models; by using a framework, you commit to its particular style.

---

[1] We've already talked about components as modules, ephemeral implementation units. But this is a new definition for the word, quite specific to the world of component-based architecture. Sadly, the terms are overloaded with multiple meanings.

Frameworks differ from traditional libraries in the way they interact with your code. When using a library, you make explicit calls into the library components under your own thread of control. A framework turns this around; it is responsible for the structure and flow of control. It calls into your supplied code as and when necessary.

Sitting alongside off-the-shelf frameworks are architectural *design patterns*. While not an architectural style in their own right, patterns are small-scale architectural templates. They are micro-architectures for a few collaborating components, distilling a recurring structure of communication. Architectural patterns describe common component structures at the architectural design level, explaining how they fulfill the requirements of a given context. Patterns are a set of design best practices, described in the ubiquitous GoF book (Gamma et al. 94) and numerous subsequent publications (see "Design Patterns" on page 255).

In a Nutshell

The Roman architect Vitruvius made a timeless statement of what constitutes good architectural design: strength (*firmitas*), utility (*utilitas*), and beauty (*venustas*). (Vitruvius) This holds true for our software architectures. Without a well-defined, well-communicated architecture, a software project will lack a cohesive internal structure. It will become brittle, unstable, and ugly. Eventually, it will reach a breaking point.

All this talk of pasta has made me hungry. I'm off to build a seven-layer reference trifle. . . .

Good programmers . . .

- Understand their software architecture and write new code within it

- Can apply the appropriate architecture to each design scenario

- Create simple architectures that are beautiful and elegant—they appreciate the aesthetics of software design

- Capture the system architecture in a live document that is continuously updated

- Relay problems with the structure back to the system architects in an attempt to improve the design

Bad programmers . . .

- Write code regardless of any overall architectural vision—resulting in unsympathetic blemishes and unintegrated components

- Fail to perform any high-level design before ploughing into code, ignoring any architectural alternatives

- Leave architectural information locked inaccessibly in people's heads or in a dangerously out-of-date specification

- Put up with inadequate architectures, adding more badly designed code rather than fixing the underlying problems—they can't be bothered to open a larger can of worms

See Also

Chapter 12: An Insecurity Complex
Security concerns must be addressed by a system architecture.

Chapter 13: Grand Designs
Code *design* is the subsequent level of code construction.

Chapter 15: Software Evolution or Software Revolution?
Architecture is the start of your software's life, but it is by no means the only thing that steers its development.

Chapter 22: Recipe for a Program
Where architectural design fits into the software development process.

Get Thinking

A detailed discussion of these questions can be found in the "Answers and Discussion" section on page 522.

Mull It Over

1. Define where *architecture* ends and *software design* begins.
2. In what ways can a bad architecture affect a system? Are there parts that wouldn't be affected by architectural flaws?
3. How easy is it to repair architectural deficiencies once they become apparent?
4. To what extent does architecture affect the following things?
   a. System configuration
   b. Logging
   c. Error handling
   d. Security

5. What experience or qualifications are required to be called a *software architect*?

6. Should sales strategy influence architecture? If so, how? If not, why?

7. How would you architect for *extensibility*? How would you architect for *performance*? How do these design goals affect the system, and how do they complement one another?

Getting Personal

1. How diverse is the range of architectural styles to which you are accustomed? What do you have the most experience with—how does it affect the software you write?

2. What personal experience do you have of architectures that succeeded or failed? What made them winning solutions or a hindrances?

3. Get every developer on your current project to draw a picture of the system architecture—individually (without talking to anyone) and without any reference to system documentation or the code. Compare the pictures. See what strikes you about each developer's efforts—aside from the relative artistic merit!

4. Do you have an architectural description that's commonly available for your current project? How up to date is it? Which kinds of view are you using? If you needed to explain the system to a newcomer or a potential customer, what would you really need to have documented?

5. How does your system's architecture compare to the architecture of your competitors in the marketplace? How has your architecture been defined to determine your project's success?

SOFTWARE EVOLUTION OR SOFTWARE REVOLUTION?

How Does Code Grow?

In this chapter:

- How software grows over time
- Software rot—how decay sets in
- How to manage the risks of old code

I cannot say whether things will get better if we change; what I can say is they must change if they are to get better.
—G.C. Lichtenberg

If only software grew like a plant. You'd put the seed of an idea into some fertile programming soil, add a little water, and wait. You'd tend it carefully: Fertilize it, keep it in good light, and cover it to keep the birds off. In time, a code seedling would sprout, and when the program plant was big enough, you could release it to the world. For extra functionality you'd keep watering and add some more fertilizer, and it would continue to develop. The trunk would strengthen in order to support the new branches and the program would stay in perfect balance. If it grew in a direction you didn't like, a little pruning would soon set it straight.

Unfortunately, the Real World does not work like this. Not by a long shot.

Software *is* a live entity. It's not sentient or organic, but it has its own kind of life: It is conceived, develops steadily, and eventually reaches maturity. Then it's sent out into the Big Wide World to make a living and hopefully garner respect and admiration. It may continue to develop, perhaps to the point where it gains a middle age spread and loses its youthful looks. Over time, it grows tired and old and is eventually retired, put out to pasture in a digital farmyard where it can gracefully die.

This chapter looks at how we cultivate software, especially after the initial round of development. Programs require thoughtful tending and seldom receive the care and attention they really deserve. What can we do to prevent a slowly spreading code cancer that leads to early death?

To answer this, we'll work backward. We'll take a look at the symptoms of bad code growth, explore how we grow our code, and determine some strategies to develop healthier software.

MORE METAPHORS FOR SOFTWARE CONSTRUCTION

We've already examined the metaphor of *building* and discussed what it tells us about the software construction process (see "Do We Really *Build* Software?" on page 177). In this chapter, I'll introduce some more metaphors. They provide different insights into our programming methods:

Growing software

This relates to how we *extend* existing software, usually by adding new features. Bug fixing isn't growth: It is tending to diseased parts of the code.

Our code *does* grow as we add to it, but programming is not a perfect analog of plant growth—we have far more control and influence over code growth than over a seedling. Code grows more like an oyster making a pearl: slowly, by the progressive accretion of small extra parts.

Evolving software

Another common construction metaphor is the *evolution* of software. We start with a single-celled code organism and gradually see it develop into a larger, more complex beast. This is an incremental process; the software develops through a number of evolutionary stages. However, there are a few key differences to biological evolution:

- *We* are the ones deliberately making changes; the software doesn't develop by itself.
- We don't employ *natural selection* to choose the best design. We have neither the time nor the inclination to develop many different variants of the same program.

We do have the opportunity to iteratively improve the quality of our code, mimicking evolutionary development somewhat. We can use experience gained from previous releases to adapt the code to its natural habitat, ensuring its long-term survival.

Software Rot

When you're green, you're growing. When you're ripe, you rot.
—Ray Kroc

Bad things happen to good code. No matter how well you start, no matter how honorable your intentions, no matter how pure your design and how clean the first release's implementation, time will warp and twist your masterpiece. Never underestimate the ability of code to acquire warts and blemishes during its life.

There is a misconception that software only develops during its initial stages of life. The *maintenance* phase of software development[1] is always the longest. It's where most of the overall effort goes—even if this effort is not scrunched into a compact ball, like the initial design and development work. B.W. Boehm, a respected computer science professor, observed that 40 to 80 percent of total development time is spent in maintenance. (Boehm 76)

Software is never expected to stand still after a release. There will always be odd faults to fix, no matter how much testing went on. Customers demand new features. Requirements change under the development team's feet. Assumptions that were made during development prove to be incorrect in the Real World and require adjustments. The upshot: More code is written *after* the project is considered complete.

During the initial development stages, you can keep a firm grip on your code and play with it as much as you like within the available time constraints. After it has been released, you're more restricted. These restrictions may be practical:

- Changes have to be minimized to reduce their impact on the carefully tested codebase.
- Published APIs are already being used by clients, so they are harder to modify.
- The UI is familiar to users and can't be changed gratuitously.

The restrictions may also be psychological, based on the developers' (potentially erroneous) preconceptions:

- The code has always worked *this* way, so we can't change it like *that*.
- It's too hard to revise the architecture at this late stage.
- It's not worth the time or expense to make this modification properly now; the product won't be around for very much longer.

The restriction might even be a simple lack of understanding—a maintenance programmer may not understand original author's mental model of the code; this leads to inappropriate modifications.

There is a fine line between maintaining an existing product and developing the next version. Where it lies is a moot point. But whatever you're doing, the original codebase gets modified—sometimes by the original author,

---

[1] That is, work done after initial delivery that isn't considered a major new release.

often by someone else. This is where the rot sets in. It's a *damned if you do, damned if you don't* scenario; whatever you do, the code will rot.

If you never touch the code again, if you don't keep it up to date with fixes and modifications, the program will degrade. In the worse case, it will stop working as the OS changes or its assumptions become outdated. The Y2K bug is a glorious example of this.[2] Or the program will putrefy as competing solutions develop more features and gain more popularity. Untouched code slowly rots away.

If you do make extensions and fixes as the code grows, it might still rot. When fixing a fault, the programmer often introduces more faults as a side effect. Brooks found that as many as 40 percent of fixes introduced new faults. (Brooks 95) "The Programmer's Drinking Song" (sung to the tune of "99 Bottles of Beer on the Wall"), written by a minstrel unknown, sums this up neatly:

> 99 little bugs in the code, 99 bugs in the code,
> Fix one bug, compile it again, 101 little bugs in the code.
>   (Repeat until BUGS == 0)

Even bug-free modifications can cause code turmoil. Quick-and-dirty fixes pile atop one another, putting nail after nail into the original design's coffin, making future maintenance harder. The plant analogy is useful here: If more heavy branches grow at the top and nothing is reinforcing the trunk, the entire codebase becomes less stable. Eventually, and inevitably, it totters over. Healthy plants don't grow like that; why should we expect our code to?

KEY CONCEPT   *Be aware of how easily code degrades as it is modified. Don't be satisfied with changes that leave the system in a worse state.*

Does all this sound unduly pessimistic? Surely code won't rot if you're careful? Perhaps, but adequate care is not taken in today's software factories. It's a culture thing. Fixes must be quick and cheap. Programs have a habit of hanging around longer than they were ever intended to. Many quick hacks live on, well past their expected lifetimes.

The Warning Signs

Switch on your code radar, and constantly look out for rotten code. Beware of the telltale signs: Rot sets in with any change that leads to a lack of clarity or that makes the system more complex. Unnecessary complexity comes in many guises.
Here are some, the flashing red lights and Klaxon calls:

- The code is littered with many large classes and convoluted functions.
- Function names are cryptic or misleading. Functions have suprising side effects not implied by their names.

---

[2] Many old programs were never expected to be operational in the year 2000, so programmers considered it safe to encode years in two digits—76 rather than 1976. As the digits rolled over to 00, all their date calculations went awry.

- There is no structure: It's not clear where to look for a certain bit of functionality.

- There is duplication: Many separate bits of code crop up to do the same thing.

- There is high coupling: Complex module interconnections and dependencies mean that a small change in one place ripples out across the entire code, even into seemingly unrelated modules. (See "Modularity" on page 247).

- As data flows through the system it is repeatedly converted between different representations (e.g., display data is transferred between std::string, char*, Unicode, UTF-8, and back again).

- APIs become blurred; once neat interfaces are now far too broad in scope, with new features being thoughtlessly added.

- APIs change rapidly between code revisions.

- Bits of private implementation leak out of public APIs to enable other quick hacks.

- The code is littered with work-arounds: fixes for symptoms but not for causes. They hide the real problems. The edges of the system are cluttered with these, leaving faults lurking at the core.

- There are functions with enormous parameter lists. Many don't use these parameters, passing them through to subordinate function calls.

- You find code that's too scary to even think about improving. You have no idea if you'll improve it, break it subtly, or make it even worse.

- New features are added with no supporting documentation; the existing documents are out of date.

- The code compiles noisily, with many warnings generated.

- You find comments saying, *Don't touch this.* . . .

Many of these forms of rot are particularly visible in the code and can be seen with a quick inspection or using certain tools. However, there is a class of more subtle, invisible degradations that usually manifest at a higher level than syntactic gunk. Modifications that fudge the original code architecture or that subtly circumvent program conventions are much harder to spot until you're deeply immersed immersed in the system.

KEY CONCEPT *Learn to detect putrid code. Know the warning signs and handle rotten code with the utmost care.*

Why do we make such a big mess of code? The answer is simple: *complexity*. A program is a huge collection of information organized on many levels: the architecture, its component design, the interfaces, the implementation of each bit of code, and so on. That's a lot to understand before you start work on a project. With tight deadlines, there isn't enough time to work out how a few lines actually work, let alone how they fit into the overall picture. We haven't yet learned to manage this vast complexity.

How Does Code Grow?

No code development ever follows the classic model of lock down all requirements, design completely, code completely, integrate, test, release. Unexpected modifications happen to an existing codebase. New pieces are grafted in somehow. It's an incremental development cycle toward ever shifting goalposts.

Code growth happens by one of the following mechanisms, loosely ranked in order of disgust:

Luck

This is the most frightening way to make code, and far too common. Code that grows by luck never had any design. It was modified without thought. Its structure is down to happenstance, and it's a miracle it works at all.

Even if your code originally *was* designed carefully, maintenance modifications can follow this happy-go-lucky approach. Hit-and-hope fixes may just mask the immediate problem and make the real fix harder later on.

Accretion

We need to add a new feature. Doing it properly would involve ripping up the interfaces between a few key modules and revising a lot of code. There's no time to do all this and, even if we did, it would probably still be too complicated. We'll just graft on another clump of code. It'll hang off one of the existing modules—well, perhaps a few of them—and use its own special back door interface to talk to them. We'll have something working really quickly.

Okay, it's a monstrous kludge. Oh, and the performance will be awful. And the modules will no longer have clear roles and responsibilities. There won't be a neat design anymore, and maintaining it in the future will be a nightmare. But we'll get this version out quickly, and we don't have any time to do it the right way now, anyway.

Maybe we'll come back later and do it properly. . . .

Rewrite

When you recognize that the code you're working on is truly awful—unintelligible, fragile, and inextensible—it needs a rewrite. Based on prior experience, a rewrite is often quicker and safer than hacking at the original mess. However, rewrites are rarely done. It takes courage and vision.

Rewrites get riskier as you attack more code at once. Rewriting a whole product is a different prospect from rewriting a troublesome function or class. Good modularity and separation of concerns means that you needn't rewrite the whole system, just the module you're working on, keeping its original interface. If the interface is terrible, or you need to rewrite because the system isn't actually modular enough, then a lot more work is involved.

DOUBLING UP

The software had reached a major crossroad. There wasn't much future in the existing codebase—it really needed to be rewritten. Finally the management accepted this fact, and a plan was formed. The developers were split into two teams. Some continued to hack away at the existing codebase to try and limp it along for just a bit longer. The rest of the programmers got to start the entire application again from scratch.

One task was glamorous: devising a sleek new design with interesting implementation challenges and the chance to work on a fresh, cruft-free codebase. The other task was menial: patching up holes in a sinking ship until the new cruise liner was ready (at which time all the old work would be left for scrap). Which team would you rather have been on?

Not surprisingly, this led to a build up of resentment and frustration and a rivalry between the teams. Many programmers relegated to the old application asked to change projects or left the company to seek greener pastures. The work on the old codebase was second rate, as it was the second-rate project.

Refactor

A formalized cousin of rewrite. If your code is mostly okay, but bits of it need some work, you can *refactor* these unpleasant parts. Refactoring is a process of making small changes to a body of code in order to improve its internal structure without changing its external behavior. It improves the design so that you can work with it more easily in the future. It's not about performance improvement, just design enhancement. Not as drastic as a complete rewrite, refactoring is a series of gentle massages of what you already have.

This is a fancy name for particular kinds of code modification. Martin Fowler has formalized it, documenting a number of small, understandable code refinements. (Fowler 99)

Design for growth

You'll often have an idea how your code will expand in the future; perhaps some features have been deferred until the next release. You can carefully design the system so that it's easy to make these future additions. Most of the time, this won't make the design work much harder.

Even if you don't know the set of future additions, careful design affords room for growth. An extensible system provides hinge points for new functionality to be plugged in. Be careful that this isn't an exercise in chasing the wind, though,[3] trying to guess the future when you don't have a clue how the system will expand. Extensibility comes at the cost of complexity. If you correctly guess where this complexity is needed, you win; if you guess incorrectly, then you'll make an unnecessarily complicated system. This is the danger of *over-design*, and it's especially likely when design occurs by committee.

There is a school of thought, exemplified in Extreme Programming, that insists on the absolute simplest design that can possibly work in

---

[3] Ecclesiastes 2:11

any given situation. This could be at odds with the design for growth mentality (depending on how malleable the initial simple design is). Exactly how much design for growth you should employ can be a hard—but important—balance to strike.

CHAOS THEORY

Code is obviously shaped by design, but the organization that built it and its life history also play a large role. Years ago, I joined a project with particularly disgusting user interface code. It worked (usually), but was unfathomable, an intense lump of intertwining logic with no discernible architecture and labyrinthine paths of execution. And it was like that for a reason: history.

The code was initially created as a simple one-off television UI for a single customer, with minimal specifications. Successfully built, it served its purpose well. Sadly, the story didn't end there.

It was then sold to a second customer, who wanted it to look different. A second skin (visual appearance) was hacked on. Then it was sold to another customer in a different country. Internationalization was bolted on, with another skin. Then it was sold to a third customer, who wanted some new UI facilities—these were shoehorned in. This story continued. For a long time. Today the UI is unrecognizable from its former self, and it's now also unmaintainable: Each addition has been a quick hack since the whole thing was always a temporary system.

If the initial design had incorporated all these features, then the code would still be lean and logical. However, it would have been far too much work up front, and the company would never have started the project. Pity the poor programmers that work under these Real World conditions.

Believe the Impossible

Perhaps the reason we see so much bad code and so many dirty hacks is the mistaken belief that it takes longer to do the job properly. When you factor in the time spent debugging and the ease of making later modifications, this proves to be a false assumption. You may be able to close a single fault report quickly by hacking out a fix, but it's not a good solution. True craftsmen take responsibility for what they do to code.

In the corporate world, there is often a management expectation of quick fixes. It's reasonably easy to show a manager that a five-ton block of concrete stuck on top of a flimsily erected flagpole won't stay up for very long. It's harder to make him stand underneath the thing. And it's *much* harder to get the same message across when we're talking about software. Managers just don't get it. As far as they're concerned, programmers are magicians who practice dark mystical arts and have limitless powers. Tell them what to do, provide a deadline, and it will happen, however many all-night coding sessions are required.

Being gifted and dedicated, sometimes we meet these expectations. This actually makes matters worse, as management now expects that this tactic will always work. Worse, they assume that it's *our* fault when it doesn't. Sadly, there comes a time when hastily hacked software just cannot be made to expand any more, when it really just wants to keel over and find its final resting place in a quiet corner somewhere. Management will not be happy.[4]

Code growth is easier if the company's culture is to develop software in small incremental steps (see "Iterative" on page 245 and "Iterative and Incremental Development" on page 432). This way, evolution is built into the design strategy, and rewriting code to accommodate change is expected. The alternative, when you have to attack a monolithic code edifice with a small pickaxe in 20 seconds flat, is unreasonable—but not unusual.

What Can We Do About This?

> *God grant me the serenity to accept the things*
> *I cannot change, the courage to change the things*
> *I can, and the wisdom to know the difference.*
> —*Reinhold Niebuhr*

Now that we've identified some of the problems of an evolving codebase, how do we manage the mess? What strategies can we adopt to avoid this?

The first and most important step is to recognize the problem. Too many programmers hack away without thinking about the quality of their code. As long as they silence the users' screams in the shortest time possible, they don't care what state they leave the code in. Someone else can deal with it next time.

KEY CONCEPT   *Code conscientiously. Good programmers care more about how their code will look after a few years' work than how much effort it takes to write now.*

Writing New Code

Before we think about how to work with *legacy* (existing) code, here are a few tactics for creating brand-new code that will greatly aid later maintenance:

- Consider the interconnection of modules, and reduce coupling as much as possible. Avoid having one central module that every other module depends on; a change there will affect every other module in the system.

- Modularity and information hiding (see page "Modularity" on page 247) are the cornerstones of modern software engineering. Isolate any likely changes to a small part of the system, making your system more viscous and therefore stable under change.

- Extension and malleability need to be designed in—but, as we've seen, not at the expense of complexity. Modern component/object based paradigms promise greater reuse and extensibility. They give clear interface points between code modules. However, if the interfaces don't support later extension, then the code can't grow. Think very carefully about your system interfaces as you create them.

---

[4] Of course this is a gross generalization, but not too inaccurate. Many managers used to be programmers themselves and understand the tensions. A good manager listens to the programmers' objections. A good programmer will *make* his or her boss listen. Too often, neither happens, and the software suffers.

- Write neat, clear code that can easily be understood and worked with, accompanied by good documentation and well-defined, clearly named APIs. Consider literate programming tools to document interfaces.

- *KISS*. That is, *Keep It Simple, Stupid*. Don't over-complicate; don't over-engineer. Optimize an algorithm only when you *know* that there are performance issues, not just because you think you know a good way to make code run faster. Simplicity is nearly always more desirable than performance, and it certainly makes later maintenance easier.

KEY CONCEPT   *Write new code with a view to its modifiability. Make it readable, extensible, and simple.*

Maintenance of Existing Code

Maintaining *good* code requires a different battle plan than maintaining *bad* code. With the former, you must carefully preserve the integrity of the design and ensure that you don't introduce anything out of place. With the latter, you must try to not make the mess any worse and, if possible, improve things on your way through. If you can't rewrite the offending code, a little refactoring will go a long way.

Before you touch any code, these organizational issues should be considered:

- *Prioritize* any changes that are needed. Balance the importance of each task against its complexity, and decide which should be done first. What early changes will have an impact on later work?

- Only change what's necessary. *If it ain't broke, don't fix it.* Don't gratuitously "improve" bits of code because you think they need it—only make the changes that are really required. Refactor the bad code you need to work with. Give the rest a wide berth.

- Monitor how many modifications are being made at once. Making several parallel modifications *yourself* is either incredibly clever or foolish; most likely the latter. Do one thing at a time. Carefully.

  If several people are working on the code at once, be aware of what's changing around you. There is a danger of too many separate hacks causing odd conflicts. Methodical change by a single developer gives clearest visibility of where the code is being stretched and where the most care is needed. Several simultaneous modifications might stretch the code thin without anyone understanding or noticing.

KEY CONCEPT   *Manage changes carefully. Make sure you know who else is trying to modify code near where you're working.*

- Just as the initial code should be reviewed during its development, subsequent changes should also be reviewed. Organize formal reviews, and try to include the code's original author and reviewers. It's very easy to introduce subtle new bugs with small code extensions; reviews will catch many of these errors.

KEY CONCEPT   *Review sensitive changes, especially in the run-up to a release. Even the simplest change can break other code.*

Once at the codeface, how do we tackle existing source? Here are practical suggestions:

- To make good modifications, you must be informed about the code you're working on. Before you modify a file or code module, understand:
  - Where it sits within the whole system
  - What interdependencies it has (i.e., which components might be affected by your change)
  - What assumptions were made when the code was created (hopefully documented in the code's specifications)
  - The history of modifications that have already been made

  Inspect the code's quality. This is surprisingly easy to do, and rapidly gives you a sense of how easy the code is going to be to work with. You may find it helpful to use tools that visualize the code and generate quality metrics; this will highlight where hidden gotchas could be lurking. Collate all relevant documentation.

- Adopt the correct attitude—avoid the *just one more hack* mentality. Don't dismiss code, thinking that it will be thrown away or rewritten in the future. It won't be.

  Be constantly aware of the warning signs cataloged in "The Warning Signs" on page 282. If your modification moves the codebase nearer to one of those states, refactor the code to alleviate the problem. Take responsibility for these problems.

  Be prepared to do some redesign work. Don't be afraid to unpick the code and perform major surgery when necessary. Sometimes a modification will be costly right now (in terms of your time and effort), but the investment will pay off later: Future work with the code will be much, much easier. For legacy code, this may be considered uneconomical. Sadly, it's legacy code that makes cash and is unlikely to be phased out. If you know that you'll be working on a section of code a lot in the future, make sure that the code structure will support future extension.

KEY CONCEPT   *Don't mindlessly fiddle with code. Step back and look at what you're doing.*

- Try not to introduce extra dependencies with newly added code. An increase in coupling makes code more complicated and harder to change next time.

- When maintaining any code, retain the programming style of the source files you are working with, even if it's not your favorite style or the house style. A file with code in several formats is confusing and hard to work with. Apply presentation tidy-ups as you go if they're not too gratuitous, but be aware that source code diffs across versions will be harder if you do so. Maintain the comments around the code you're working on (see "Maintenance and the Inane Comment" on page 86).

- Use the code's test suite to check that you don't break anything. Exhaustive regression testing is the only real way to have confidence in the changes you've made.

  Ensure that you have an adequate test suite, and run it regularly.

KEY CONCEPT *Carefully test any modification you make, no matter how simple. It's really easy for silly faults to slip past unnoticed.*

- If you are fixing a fault, do you really understand the cause? Write a test harness to trigger it; this demonstrates your understanding and will prove that you have made the fix. Add it to the suite of regression tests.

  Once you have made a successful fix, look around the codebase for similar faults. This overlooked step can make a big difference: Many problems hang around in packs, and it's much easier to defeat them in one crushing blow than to slowly chip away as they each individually manifest.

- If you make a bad change, back it out quickly. Don't litter code with unnecessary dead wood.

As a code craftsman, you should always shy away from the pressure to do a quick bodge job. Strive to make careful, considered changes. Unfortunately, we don't work in ivory towers, and compromise is sometimes required on the battle front; it's not always commercially feasible to complete a task in the theologically correct way.

This explains why so much code is brittle, flaky, and dangerous. But it also explains why there's any code out there at all. If there wasn't the commercial drive to get software shipped, programmers would spend forever tweaking their software to get it just right, writing and rewriting. The company would have collapsed around them long before they'd finished.

However, don't introduce pragmatic (but distasteful) modifications without a plan to fix them at a later date. Place a tidy-up task on the development schedule.

In a Nutshell

> *Change in all things is sweet.*
> —*Aristotle*

I'm not sure that I agree with Aristotle. Change can be a real pain in the rear end. We should manage code changes carefully. Then a good program will evolve into something greater, rather than degrade into an unstable mess.

It's important to maintain software well and expand it correctly, preserving the code design and making sympathetic modifications. Don't expect maintenance to be easy. You may need to invest a lot of time to rewrite, redesign, or refactor.

See Also

Chapter 17: Together We Stand
We build and maintain software as a team. Team dynamics inevitably affect the final shape of your code.

Chapter 18: Practicing Safe Source
A history of your code's development is recorded in the *revision control system*.

Chapter 22: Recipe for a Program
The software development lifecycle: the procedures we follow to create and grow software.

Good programmers . . .

- Write maintainable software with clean structure and logical layout
- Recognize and are prepared to deal with bade code
- Try to understand as much of the code and the author's original mental model as possible, prior to working on it
- Care about the quality of code they're working on; they refuse to clumsily patch code

Bad programmers . . .

- Create complex code without thinking about the needs of maintenance programmers
- *Avoid* maintaining old code, preferring to ignore problems rather than fix them
- Favor an easy patch over thinking about a good solution
- Litter code with quick and dirty hacks; they employ every shortcut they can find
- Focus attention in the wrong places, tinkering with code that didn't actually need to be fixed

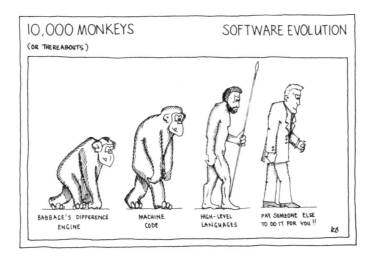

10,000 MONKEYS (OR THEREABOUTS) — SOFTWARE EVOLUTION

BABBAGE'S DIFFERENCE ENGINE — MACHINE CODE — HIGH-LEVEL LANGUAGES — PAY SOMEONE ELSE TO DO IT FOR YOU!!

Get Thinking

A detailed discussion of the following questions can be found in the "Answers and Discussion" section on page 527.

Mull It Over

1. What is the best metaphor for software growth?

2. Looking at a program's development through the colorful lifetime metaphor I talked about in the introduction, what Real World events correspond to a program's:

    - Conception
    - Birth
    - Growth
    - Coming of age
    - Sending out into the Big Wide World
    - Middle age
    - Growing tired
    - Retirement
    - Death

3. Is there a limit to software life—how long can you keep developing and working on a program before you have to start afresh?

4. Does the size of a codebase correspond to the maturity of the project?

5. How important is *backward compatibility* when maintaining code?

6. Is code likely to rot more quickly if you alter it or if you leave it alone?

Getting Personal

1. Is the majority of the code you write brand new or a modification of existing source?

    a. If it's brand-new code, do you create entirely new systems or new extensions to existing systems?

    b. Does this affect *how* you write? In what ways?

2. Do you have experience of working with preexisting codebases? If so:

    a. How has it shaped your current skill set? What lessons did you learn?

    b. Was it predominantly good or bad code? What did you have to judge it against?

3. Have you ever made changes that degraded the quality of code? Why?

4. How many revisions has your current project gone through?

    a. How much changed functionally between revisions? How did the code change?

    b. Has it grown by *luck*, by *design*, or something between the two? How is this evident now?

5. How does your team safeguard code so that it can't be changed by more than one programmer at once?

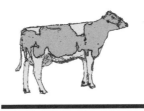

PART IV

A HERD OF PROGRAMMERS?

Cubicle after cubicle, arranged in long, dreary rows. A soul farm. The corporate drudgery of unrealistic schedules, bad management, and disastrous software. No natural light and awful coffee.

Welcome to the software factory.

Some programmers freelance, hopping from office to office. Some write open source code at home for kicks. But most are institutionalized in uninspiring software factories, serving time for a cause they still love passionately.

We're a funny bunch: antisocial by nature, preferring the company of a compiler and web browser. However, to create software masterpieces, we are forced to work together, against our natural instincts. As we'll see, the quality of your software is determined by the quality of your programmers and their collaboration. Without sound tactics to cope in the Real World, you're sunk.

This section investigates how culture and dynamics affect the shape of your code. We'll see:

Chapter 16: Code Monkeys
The essential skills and personal qualities of potent programmers.

Chapter 17: Together We Stand

How to work as an effective and productive software team.

Chapter 18: Practicing Safe Source

Managing source code that's shared between many programmers: how to avoid disaster and heartache.

So what *is* the collective noun for a group of programmers? It's certainly not a *swarm*: We're nowhere near as fast and rarely as organized. It's not a *pride*: We're neither as fierce as lions, nor likely produce something worthy of boast. The answer (at least for C-family coders) is clear: The collective noun is a *brace* of programmers.

16

CODE MONKEYS

Fostering the Correct Attitude and Approach to Programming

We are just an advanced breed of monkeys on a minor planet of a very average star. But we can understand the Universe. That makes us something very special.
—*Stephen Hawking*

Pop quiz: How many programmers does it take to change a light bulb? Is it:

1. None. The bulb's not broken; it's a power-saving feature.

2. Just the one, but it will take all night and an inordinate amount of pizza and coffee.

3. Twenty. One to fix the initial problem, and nineteen to debug the resultant mess.[1]

---

[1] That's no joke: I have a friend who's only ever changed two light bulbs in her life. The first time, glass showered all over the carpet. The second time, an electrician had to fit a new light socket afterward.

What's the correct answer? It could be any of those, depending on who does the work. Different programmers work in different ways and will have their own individual approaches to solving the same problem. There is always *more than one way to do it,*[2] and different programmers' attitudes will lead them to make very different decisions.

Throughout this book, we've been identifying the important attitudes of a good programmer. This chapter focuses specifically on this: We'll investigate programmer attitudes, good and bad, and identify the key ones for successful programming. This includes how we approach the task of coding and also how we relate to other programmers. We'll come to some surprising conclusions about what makes the best coders.

Monkey Business

The software factory is inhabited by a strange collection of freaks and social misfits, the *code monkeys.* Any serious software system is built by a bunch of these people, with their different skill levels and attitudes, all working toward a common goal.

The way we work together and the kind of code we write will inevitably be shaped by our attitudes toward the work as much as by technical competence. If everyone was a diligent, pragmatic, hardworking genius, our software would be a lot better—delivered on time, to budget, with no bugs. But we're not perfect, and unfortunately, it shows in the code we write.

To work out strategies to deal with this, I'll lead us on a guided tour through a gallery of programmer stereotypes. These are all directly based on the types of people I have met in the software factory. Of course it's a necessarily general list; you'll know programmers who fall into categories other than those listed here, or even fit several descriptions at once.

Even so, this shameless categorization highlights important facts and shows us how to improve. We'll see:

- What motivates the different types of code monkeys
- How to work with each of them
- How each code monkey can improve
- What we can learn from each of them

As you read each code monkey description, ask yourself:

- Are *you* this type of programmer? How closely does the description match your programming style? What lessons can you learn to improve your approach to coding?
- How many people do you know like this? Are they close colleagues? How could you work with them better?

---

[2] The Perl programmer's mantra.

The Eager Coder

We'll start with this guy, because he[3] probably embodies the traits of most programmers reading this book. The Eager Coder is fast and fleeting; he thinks in code. An impulsive, natural-born programmer, he writes code as soon as an idea forms in his head. He won't stand back and think first. So, although an Eager Coder does have very good technical skills, the code he writes never shows his true potential.

The Eager Coder often tries to use a new feature or idiom because it's fashionable. His desire to try out new tricks means that he applies technology even when it isn't appropriate.

Strengths

Eager Coders are productive, in terms of code quantity. They write a *lot* of code. They love learning new stuff and are really enthusiastic—even passionate—about programming. The Eager Coder loves his job, and genuinely *wants* to write good code.

Weaknesses

Because of his unfettered enthusiasm, the Eager Coder is hasty and doesn't think before rushing into the code editor. He does write a lot of code, but because he writes so fast, it's flawed—the Eager Coder spends *ages* debugging. A little forethought would prevent many silly errors and many hours ironing out careless faults.

Unfortunately, the Eager Coder is a really bad debugger. In the same way he rushes into coding, he dives straight into debugging. He's not methodical, so he spends ages chasing faults down blind alleys.

He's a poor estimator of time. He'll make a reasonable estimate for the case when it all goes well, but it never *does* go according to plan; he always takes longer than expected.

What to do if you are one

Don't lose that enthusiasm—it's one of the best characteristics of a programmer. Because your joy lies in seeing programs work and standing back and admiring the beauty of code, work out practical ways to do this. Writing units tests as an integral part of code development is a great idea. But it mostly boils down to this simple piece of advice: *Stop and think.* Don't be hasty. Work out personal disciplines that will help you, even something basic like writing *THINK* on a Post-It note and sticking it on your monitor!

How to work with them

When they work well, these are some of the best people to program alongside. The trick is to channel their energy into productive code rather than mindless flapping. They are great to work with in pair programming.

Ask an Eager Coder about what he's doing each day and what his plans are. Show an interest in his design—it will encourage him to really think about it! If you rely on an Eager Coder's work, ask for early pre-releases, and ask to see his unit tests too.

---

[3] I'll describe all code monkeys as male, for no other reason than clarity of prose.

An Eager Coder benefits from appropriate management, to help with his discipline. Make sure his time is carefully placed on a project plan (you don't have to plan his time yourself).

The Code Monkey

If you ever needed an infinite number of monkeys, these guys would be your first choice. (I wouldn't advise it though; you'll be picking monkeys for a *loooong* time!)

The Code Monkey writes solid but uninspired code. Given an assignment, he faithfully plods through it, ready to be handed the next one. Because of their menial work, these guys are also known—perhaps unfairly—as *grunt programmers.*

Code Monkeys have quiet personalities. Afraid to push for good jobs, they are sidelined on unglamorous projects. They carve out niches as maintenance programmers, keeping the aged codebase going while the pioneers are off writing exciting replacements.

A junior Code Monkey will learn and progress given time and mentoring, but he is given low risk assignments. An older Code Monkey has probably stagnated and will retire as a Code Monkey. He'll be quite happy to do so.

Strengths

Give them a job and they'll do it—reasonably well, reasonably on time. A Code Monkey is reliable and can usually be counted on to put in extra effort when it comes to crunch time.

Unlike Eager Coders, Code Monkeys are good estimators of time. They are methodical and thorough.

Weaknesses

Although Code Monkeys are careful and methodical, they don't *think outside of the box.* They lack design flair and intuition. A Code Monkey will follow the existing code design conventions unquestioningly, rather than address any potential problems. Since they are not accountable for the design, they don't accept responsibility for any problems that arise and often won't take the initiative to investigate and fix them.

It's hard to teach a Code Monkey new stuff; he's just not interested.

What to do if you are one

Do you want to explore new areas and broaden your responsibility? If so, start to strengthen your skills by practicing on personal projects. Grab some books and study new techniques.

Push for more responsibility, and offer to join in the design work. Take the initiative in your current work—identify possible failure points early, and work out plans to avoid them.

How to work with them

Don't look down on a Code Monkey, even if you have stronger technical skills or greater responsibility. Encourage him—compliment his code and teach him techniques to improve his work.

Write your code thoughtfully to make the maintenance programmer's (that is, the maintenance Code Monkey's) job as easy as possible.

The Guru

This is the fabled mystic genius: a program wizard. The Guru tends to be quiet and unassuming, perhaps even a little odd.[4] He writes excellent code, but he can't communicate well with mere mortals.

The Guru is left alone to work on the fundamental stuff: frameworks, architectures, kernels, and so on. He holds the deserved respect (and sometimes fear) of his colleagues.

Omniscient, the Guru knows all and sees all. He turns up sagely in any technical discussion to dispense his expert opinion.

Strengths

Gurus are the experienced magicians. They know all the modern techniques and understand which old tricks are better. (Gurus invented all the cool techniques in the first place.) They have a wealth of experience and write mature maintainable code.

A good Guru is a wonderful mentor—there's so much to learn from him.

Weaknesses

Few Gurus can communicate well. They're not always tongue tied, but their ideas fly so fast and at a level beyond mere mortals', so it's hard to follow them. A conversation with a Guru makes you feel stupid, confused, or both.

The poorer a Guru's communication skills, the worse mentor he will make. Gurus find it hard to understand why others don't know as much or don't think as fast as they do.

What to do if you are one

Try to step off of your cloud and live in the Real World. Don't expect everyone to be as quick as you are or to think in the same way as you do. It takes a lot of skill to explain something simply and clearly. Practice this.

How to work with them

If you cross paths with a Guru, learn from him. Absorb what you can—and not just technical stuff. Becoming established as a Guru takes a certain temperament and personality—knowledge but not arrogance. Observe this.

---

[4] Well, more odd than "normal" programmers, anyway. *Eccentric* is probably the polite way to put it.

The Demiguru

The Demiguru *thinks* he's a genius. He isn't. He talks knowledgeably, but it's a load of trash.

This is probably the most dangerous type of code monkey; a Demiguru is hard to spot until the damage is done. Managers believe he's a genius because he sounds so plausible and self-assured.

A Demiguru is generally louder than a Guru. He's more boastful and full of himself. He appoints himself to a position of authority. (Gurus, on the other hand, are *recognized* as experts by their peers.)

Strengths

It's easy to assume that a Demiguru has *no* strengths, but his great asset is his belief in himself. It's important to trust your own abilities, and to be secure that you write high-quality code. However . . .

Weaknesses

The Demiguru's great weakness is his *belief in himself.* He overestimates his abilities, and his decisions will jeopardize your project's success. He's a serious liability.

The Demiguru will haunt you, even after he's moved on to new pastures. You'll be left with the consequences of his bad design and overly clever code.

What to do if you are one

Right now, take an honest appraisal of your skills. Don't oversell yourself. Ambition is a good thing; pretending to be something you're not isn't.

You may not be doing this on purpose, so be objective about what you can and cannot do. Be more concerned about the quality of your software than how important or clever you look.

How to work with them

Be very, very careful.

Once you have recognized a Demiguru, you've won half the battle. Most of the damage he can cause will occur while you haven't got him figured out. Keep a careful watch on the Demiguru: You must filter the garbage he speaks, grapple with his flawed designs, and inspect his wretched code.

The Arrogant Genius

This guy is a subtle, but significant, variation on the Guru species. A killer programmer, he's fast, efficient, and writes high-quality code. Not quite a Guru, but he's hot. *But* because he's all too aware of his own skills, he is cocky, condescending, and demeaning.

The Genius is terminally argumentative because he's usually right and always has to promote his correct view over others' wrong opinions. He's become used to it. The most annoying thing is that most of the time, he *is* right, so you're bound to lose any argument with him. If you are correct, he'll keep talking until the argument moves on to something *he* is right about.

Strengths

The Genius has considerable technical skill. He can provide a strong technical lead and will catalyze a team when everyone agrees with him.

Weaknesses

The Genius doesn't like to be proved wrong and thinks that he must *always* be right. He feels compelled to act as an authority; The Genius knows everything about everything. He can never say *I don't know*, suffering from a full humility bypass.

What to do if you are one

Not everyone achieves Godlike status, but there are plenty of good programmers worthy of respect. Recognize this. Practice humility, and honor other people's opinions.

Look for people who might have a more experienced viewpoint, and learn from them. Never pretend or cover your inexperience—be honest about what you do and do not know.

How to work with them

Do show a Genius respect, and show respect *to other programmers* around him. Avoid nonconstructive quarrels with him. But stand your ground— assert your reasonable opinions and views. Don't be daunted by him. Discussing technical issues with a Genius can make you a better programmer; just learn to detach your emotions first. If you know that you're correct, gain allies to help argue with him.

Take heed and avoid being cocky or argumentative yourself.

> ## GETTING PERSONAL
>
> This classification of programmer attitudes isn't particularly scientific. Psychologists have devised more formal personality classifications; authoritative ways of calling you a freak. They don't focus exclusively on the software development world, but do give a valuable insight into programmer behavior.
>
> The *Myers Briggs Type Indicator* is perhaps the most popular tool. (Briggs 80) It decomposes your personality across four axes: extrovert (E) or introvert (I); sensing (S) or intuitive (N); thinking (T) or feeling (F); and judging (J) or perceiving (P). This classification results in a four letter descriptor; ISTJ would be common for a Code Monkey.
>
> Belbin's *Team Roles* is a taxonomy of attitudes, defined as *a tendency to behave, contribute, and interrelate with others in a particular way.* (Belbin 81) This is a means to characterize your natural social behavior and ability to form relationships, to determine how it helps or hinders the progress of a team. It shows how your personality type affects your teamworking skills. Belbin identifies nine specific behavioral roles: three action-oriented, three people-oriented, and three cerebral personalities. Understanding these enables us to build effective teams from people with complementary skills; if every programmer was a *coordinator*, then nothing would ever get done.
>
> Neither of these personality taxonomies have a one-to-one mapping with my programmer classifications. They also have a distinct lack of primates.

The Cowboy

The Cowboy is a bad programmer who actively avoids hard work. He'll take as many shortcuts as he can find. Some would incorrectly classify this guy a *Hacker*. He's not a hacker in the classic sense of the word. *Hacker* is a term used by geeks to proudly describe a heroic coder.[5]

The Cowboy dives straight into code and does the minimum amount of work to solve the immediate problem. He won't care if it's not a very good solution, if it compromises the code structure, or will not satisfy future requirements.

A Cowboy is anxious to complete each task and move on to the next. If he's read a little about processes, he'll call this Agile Programming. It's really just laziness.

Strengths

Cowboy code *works*, but isn't particularly elegant. Cowboys like to learn new things, but seldom get around to it (it's too much like hard work).

Weaknesses

You'll spend ages cleaning up after a Cowboy. His aftermath is not a pleasant place to be. Cowboy code always requires later repair, rework, and refactoring. They have a limited palette of techniques to use, and no real engineering skills.

What to do if you are one

Learn to *hack* code in the right sense of the word. Take pride in your work, and spend more time over it. Admit your failings, and try to improve.

How to work with them

Never go into a Cowboy's house; if his code is anything to go by, it'll be a DIY disaster! Understand that they're not a malicious breed, just a little lazy. Organize reviews of their code. Get him pair programming. (A Cowboy might work well with an Eager Coder; if you want to see fur fly, pair him with a Planner.)

The Planner

The Planner thinks about what he's doing so much that the project has been canned long before he's started writing any code.

It's true, you *must* plan up front and establish a cohesive design, but this guy forms an impenetrable cocoon around himself and refuses any contact with the outside world until he's finished. Meanwhile, everything's changing around him.

Terminally educated, the Planner studies and reads a lot. A common sub-species is the Process Weenie; he knows all about the "proper development process" but is weak on hitting deadlines or getting anything done. (Process Weenies eventually become middle managers, and then they get fired.)

---

[5] It has also been subverted by ignorant people and used mistakenly to mean *cracker*—someone who breaks into computer systems without permission. See "Cracker vs. Hacker" on page 228.

Strengths

They *do* design. They do think. They don't hack out thoughtless code.

Weaknesses

When a Planner sets to work, there is a very real danger of *over design*. He tends to create very complex systems. Planners are the key cause of *analysis paralysis*—where development becomes more focused on methods and modeling than on prototyping and creating a solution. The Planner likes to generate endless documents and call meetings every other hour.

He spends ages thinking and not enough time doing anything. He knows a lot, but it doesn't all make the leap from theory to practice.

What to do if you are one

It *is* important to create careful designs up front, but consider incremental development and prototyping as methods to verify your design. Sometimes you can't commit to a design until you've actually started to implement it. Only then will you appreciate all the problems.

Try to establish a better balance of planning and action. Console yourself that it's better to spend too long designing than to write awful code—the latter is far harder to fix.

How to work with them

Ahead of time, agree on all milestones and deadlines for a Planner's work. Throw in a *design complete* milestone; a Planner will be happy that it has been recognized as an important task and will be encouraged to complete his design work on time. This is usually enough to crystallize a Planner into action.

Avoid meetings with a Planner. You'll spend an hour arguing about how to decide the agenda.

The Old Timer

This old boy is a senior programmer from the old school. Sit back and listen to him reminisce about the Good Old Days, when he used punch cards and machines without enough memory to hold the result of an integer addition.

The Old Timer is either happy that he's still doing what he loves the most or bitter that he's missed promotion countless times. He's seen it all, knows all the answers, and won't learn new tricks (he'll tell you that there's nothing new to learn; we just repackage the same old ideas). He's reluctant to learn new languages: "I don't need C++. I can get by perfectly well in Assembler, thank you very much."

An Old Timer doesn't suffer fools gladly. He's a bit cranky and is easily irritated.

Strengths

He's been programming for years, and so he has considerable experience and wisdom. The Old Timer has a mature approach to coding. He has learned which qualities make good and bad programs and how to avoid the common pitfalls.

Weaknesses

The Old Timer won't willingly learn new techniques. Fed up with fashionable ideas that promise much and deliver little, he's a bit slow and can be resistent to change.

He has little patience, thanks to years of corporate ineptitude. He's been at the receiving end of countless tight deadlines and unreasonable managers.

What to do if you are one

Don't be too judgmental of younger, more enthusiastic programmers. You were once like them, and *your* code wasn't awful, was it?

How to work with them

You don't know how easy you have it, you young programmers. Don't mess with an Old Timer, or you'll find out how he survived this long in the software factory. Choose your battles with him wisely. Show him respect, but treat him as a peer, not a deity.

Understand the Old Timer's motivation. Find out if he's programming because he loves to, or because he's in a career dead end.

The Zealot

The Zealot is a brainwashed convert, a disciple who blindly thinks that everything *BigCo* produces is excellent. Teenage girls have rock stars to worship; programmers have their own idols. In his enthusiasm, the Zealot takes it upon himself to become an unpaid technology evangelist. He'll try to incorporate BigCo products into every assignment he is given.

The Zealot follows BigCo to the exclusion of all other approaches and rarely knows about alternatives. Anything that's not excellent in the current BigCo product line will surely be fixed in the next version, which we *must* upgrade to immediately.[6]

Strengths

He knows BigCo's products inside out and will produce genuinely good designs based on them. He is productive with that technology, but not necessarily maximally productive—other unfamiliar approaches might be more effective.

Weaknesses

Being a Zealot, he's neither objective nor pragmatic. There may be better non-BigCo designs that he will miss. Worse, though, are the Zealot's continual rants about BigCo.

What to do if you are one

No one expects you to turn away from your beloved BigCo. It is valuable to understand its technologies and know how to deploy them. But don't be a technology bigot. Embrace different approaches and new ways of thinking. Don't look at them with an air of superiority or prejudge them.

---

[6] Zealots don't only idolize software vendors. A Zealot might be an open source advocate or hanker after an obsolete software package.

How to work with them

Don't bother getting into philosophical arguments with a Zealot. Don't try to explain the virtues of your preferred technology—he won't listen. Watch out: One conversation with this guy can turn *you* into a Zealot. He's contagious.

Zealots are generally harmless (and amusing to watch from a distance), unless your project is at a critical design stage. At this point, provide a clear, unbiased perspective on the problem domain and insist on a thorough evaluation of all implementation approaches. Remember: He might be right.

If you encounter silly arguments, counter them with well-prepared, accurate, detailed information about the strengths of your approach and the weaknesses of his.

The Monocultured Programmer

This is the archetypal geek, the guy who lives and breathes technology. It's his whole life; he probably dreams about it.

The Monocultured Programmer has a remarkable one-track mind. Taking work home with him, he returns with the whole system designed and written, all the major bugs fixed, and a plan for how to implement the rest of the project. He's done it all before you've had breakfast.

Strengths

The Monocultured Programmer is focused and determined. He'll ensure that the project works, or he'll die trying. He's willing to put in a *lot* of extra effort, and he's really useful as deadlines draw near.

Weaknesses

He expects others to be as obsessive and focused as he is and might be disapproving of those who aren't. His biggest danger is overlooking things, since he permanently lives too close to the problem.

What to do if you are one

Take up stamp collecting—or anything—to help you switch off. *All work and no play makes Jack a dull boy.* But you probably don't care anyway.

How to work with them

These guys are great to work with. Their enthusiasm is contagious, and the project will move quickly when they're on board. But don't let them take over. Given half a chance, the Monocultured Programmer will do all your work too! Although that might sound good, you'll be left maintaining foreign code. It's not worth the hassle.

Don't worry about their lack of a personal life, and don't feel pressured to spend all the hours God sends on the project—sometimes the best design tool is a relaxing night off.

The Slacker

The Slacker is a work-shy sluggard. He's hard to detect, because he's learned to make it look like he's overloaded with jobs. His "design" is playing solitaire, his "research" is looking at fast cars on the Web, and his "implementation" is working on his own stuff. The Slacker actively avoids all assignments. (Oh, I'm *far* too busy to do *that*.)

A more subtle Slacker will only work on the things he wants to or the bits he thinks should be done, not on what he's supposed to. Despite working constantly, he'll never get his jobs done.

The Slacker knows how to have fun. He parties too much and can usually be found sleeping under his desk. His diet consists mostly of coffee, except for lunchtime, when you'll find him in the bar.

This guy can be a burnout; one too many failed projects has killed his desire to work.

Strengths

At least he knows how to have fun.

Weaknesses

A Slacker is an obvious liability. It's hard to prove he's slacking—some hard problems *do* take a while to sort out. A programmer might not be slacking; he just might not have enough skill to solve the problem quickly.

What to do if you are one

Work on your morals, and start to put some effort in. Or learn to live with the guilt.

How to work with them

It's best not to complain about a Slacker—you have your own flaws. He'll get his come-uppance in good time.

Take measures to prove that you are working effectively, and that delays are the Slacker's fault. It might help to keep a methodical diary of your work. A clear set of deadlines is generally enough to get a Slacker working. Don't start writing his stuff too, even in desperation. He'll only expect you to do this next time.

Avoid burnout yourself; try to have fun as you work. Perhaps you should hit the bar with him sometimes.

The Reluctant Team Leader

This is the organizational classic; a developer who's been promoted to team leader when there was no further technical route for him to advance.

You can plainly see that he is uncomfortable in this role. He doesn't have the correct skill set, and he struggles to keep up. He is a programmer, and he wants to program. This guy is not a natural organizer or manager of people, and he is a bad communicator.

Most programmers make spectacularly bad leaders. There are few genuinely excellent software team leaders; it requires a particular skill set that is both technical and organizational.

The Reluctant Team Leader is usually quite mild mannered and indecisive—how else did he get persuaded to take on this job? He becomes squashed between the development team and management, taking the blame for slippage and poor software. An increasingly harassed expression grows on his face until he finally burns out.

Strengths

The Reluctant Team Leader has a real sympathy for the programmer's plight—he's been there and now wishes he was back. Often, he is far too willing to take responsibility for late software delivery to prevent the programmers being picked on by management. Just as he's not good at delegating work, he's not good at apportioning blame.

Weaknesses

When a Team Leader tries to write code, it will be awful. He never has enough time to write, design, or test carefully enough. He naïvely plans himself a full day's coding alongside team leading duties. He can't fit it all in, and so the Reluctant Team Leader spends longer and longer in the office, trying to keep up. He can't organize well, can't explain things to managers, and can't manage his team members properly.

What to do if you are one

Get training. Quickly.

If you're not happy in this role, push for a career move. This is not admitting defeat; it's pointless to burn yourself out doing something you hate and aren't good at. Not everybody has the skills or passion for management. Move to an area you do have skill and passion for.

If you like herculean tasks, try to sort out the promotion path at your company. Get the company to recognize that a managerial position should *not* be the next step up from senior developer. Few programmers make decent managers; their brains aren't wired up the right way.

How to work with them

Be sympathetic, and do everything you can to help the Team Leader. Give him reports on time, and try to get your work done on schedule. If you might miss a deadline, let the Team Leader know early on, so he can plan around it.

You

In the interest of politeness, we'll say no more about this curious beast. Sadly, some people are beyond help. . . .

The Ideal Programmer

From this tangled mess, it's clear that we're a strange breed. Which of these code monkeys should we aspire to be? What code monkey cocktail will create the *Ideal Programmer*?

Unfortunately, in the Real World, there are no perfect programmers—the beast is an urban legend. Therefore, this is an academic question, but finding an answer will give us something to aim for.

The fabled Ideal Programmer is part:

Politician

He must be diplomatic, able to deal with the peccadilloes of these weird code monkeys and the many, many more creatures that inhabit the software factory—managers, testers, support, customers, users, and so on.

Relational

He works well with others. He isn't territorial about his code and isn't afraid to get his hands dirty if a task is for the common good. He communicates well—he can listen as well as talk.

Artistic

He can design elegant solutions and appreciate the aesthetic aspects of a high-quality implementation.

Technical genius

He writes solid, industrial-strength code. He has a broad palette of technical skills and understands how and when to apply them.

Reading that list again, it's quite clear what we should be. If you haven't realized yet, I'll spell it out: The ideal programmer is a

Well, that's something to aspire to.

So What?

> *Only the wisest and stupidest of men never change.*
> —*Confucius*

While it's entertaining to stare into the cages of these code monkeys and have a laugh at their expense, what should you do about this? If you do nothing, then it has been little more than mere entertainment; you'll walk away doing exactly the same stupid things you've always done.

To improve as a programmer, you must change. Change is hard—it runs contrary to our nature. The saying goes, a leopard doesn't change his spots. If he did, he wouldn't be a leopard anymore. Perhaps that's the key. More of us should be wildebeests or rhinoceroses.

Take a moment to think about the following questions. You might find it useful to use the *action sheet* at the end of this chapter to record your answers.

1. What kind of code monkey are you most like? If you're honest, there's probably a little of each of them in you. Identify the one or two that describe you best.

2. What are your particular strengths and weaknesses?

3. Look over your code monkey description again and see what practical things you could change. What specific techniques will help you to overcome bad attitudes? How can you capitalize on your good ones?

KEY CONCEPT *Know what kind of programmer you are. Determine how to exploit your strengths and compensate for your weaknesses.*

The Stupidest of Men

To help us think about the kinds of change required, what lessons can we learn from each of the code monkeys? We all have individual personality flaws, but this summary shows some good attitudes and a few common areas of improvement. To be a good programmer, you must learn to become

That is:

Team player
Learn to work with others effectively. Try to understand each of your colleagues' particular traits, and learn how to respond to them better.

Honest and humble
Be realistic about your capabilities: Know your strengths and weaknesses. Don't pretend that you are more able. Adopt an attitude that seeks to help others and to work with them effectively.

Improving constantly
No matter what you know, how much experience you have, and how good your code is, there is *always* more to learn, new skills to acquire, and bad attitudes to address. Confucius said, "Real knowledge is to know

the extent of one's ignorance." Acknowledge that you're not perfect. A good programmer is in a constant state of improvement.

Considerate

Train yourself to always think about what you're doing. Silly mistakes creep in when you're not paying attention. Always use your brain. Consider what you're doing *before* you write each piece of code. Then read back what you've written, even if it's a simple change.

Keen

Try to maintain the enthusiasm of the Eager Coder. If you love learning new skills, then keep reading and keep practicing. If you work best with regular breaks, then plan that vacation! If you relish facing new challenges, then position yourself where you'll be most stimulated.

If you become staid and bored, your attitude will worsen, and the quality of your code will suffer.

In a Nutshell

> *Darwinian Man, though well-behaved,*
> *At best is only a monkey shaved!*
> —Gilbert and Sullivan

Programmers are a social species (which is odd considering their lack of social skills). They are social by necessity; you can't create excellent large software systems without a closely working team of programmers who are knit into a larger social structure (be it a department, company, or an open source culture).

Each of these programmers has their own foibles and peculiarities. Their underlying attitudes affect how well they program, shaping their approach to the code and to their relationships with teammates.

If you want to be an exceptional programmer, you need to foster the correct positive attitudes. Remember: Aim to be a *thick prat*.

Good programmers . . .	Bad programmers . . .
• Are *PRAT*s: politicians, relational, artistic, and technical	• Are not interested in writing good code
• Are *THICK*: team players, honest and humble, improving constantly, considerate, and keen	• Do not work well on a team
	• Try to look better than they really are
	• Stagnate—they don't seek to improve themselves

See Also

Chapter 17: Together We Stand
Discusses team dynamics in more depth.

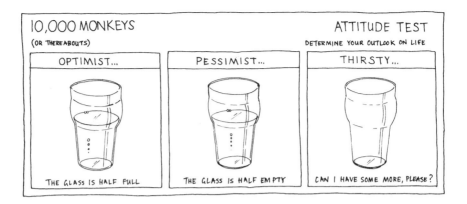

Action Sheet

Look at the following action sheet. Take some time to fill it in and figure out how to put what you've learned into practice.

Code Monkeys	ACTION SHEET
Take some time to fill out this form thoughtfully. Refer to the code monkey descriptions for more information.	
I am a . . . Check the code monkey that applies the most. You can check a second code monkey if you think that you fall into more than one category. If you want to check more than two, I can recommend a good psychiatrist.	☐ Eager Coder ☐ Planner ☐ Code Monkey ☐ Old Timer ☐ Guru ☐ Zealot ☐ Demiguru ☐ Monocultured ☐ Arrogant Genius ☐ Slacker ☐ Cowboy ☐ Reluctant Team Leader
My strengths are . . . List what you think are your best characteristics, skills, and abilities. Compare them to the description of your code monkey.	• • • •
My weaknesses are . . . List what you think are your worst characteristics, skills, and abilities. Compare them to the description of your code monkey.	• • • •
I can improve by . . . How can you capitalize on your strengths and compensate for or improve upon your weaknesses?	• • • •
I work with . . . Think about the programmers you work with most closely. What kind of code monkeys are they? Check all that apply. Consider how you can interact with these guys better. Does identifying their personality types help you to work with them more effectively?	☐ Eager Coder ☐ Planner ☐ Code Monkey ☐ Old Timer ☐ Guru ☐ Zealot ☐ Demiguru ☐ Monocultured ☐ Arrogant Genius ☐ Slacker ☐ Cowboy ☐ Reluctant Team Leader
Our team can improve by . . . How can you write software better together as a team? Are there specific steps you could take to help with this?	• • • •

Get Thinking

A detailed discussion of these questions can be found in the "Answers and Discussion" section on page 532.

Mull It Over

1. How many programmers *does* it take to change a light bulb?

2. Is it better to be enthusiastic and less skilled (not incompetent) or to be incredibly talented and unmotivated?

    a. Who will write the better code?

    b. Who is the better programmer? (Not the same thing.)

    Which does more to shape the code you write: your technical competence or your attitude?

3. There are various different types of programs we write, differentiated by code "heritage." How does writing the following types of code differ?

    a. A "toy" program

    b. A brand-new system

    c. Extensions to an existing system

    d. Maintenance work on an old codebase

4. If programming is an art, what is the correct balance of consideration and planning versus intuition and gut instinct? Do you program by gut or by plan?

Getting Personal

1. If you haven't done so already, fill out the action sheet on the previous page carefully. Make sure you figure out how to improve, and start acting it out!

2. Here's an interesting game you can set up for your development team to help each programmer work out his or her natural coding approach.

The teams

If there are a lot of you, split into smaller groups of three to five programmers.

The task

You are a team of programmers tasked with the development of the following new product. In the time available, design the system. Explain how you'll split it into components and arrange the work among your team members.

You don't have to write the code yet (although there might be bonus points if you manage to show a working prototype!). Don't get hung up on perfectionism (there's no time); just start to design something that will work.

The system

Due to massive NASA cutbacks, you are the entire team writing control software for the next Mars probe. It must be able to:

- Drive around
- Take pictures
- Measure atmospheric conditions
- Communicate with Earth control
- Be *very* reliable

The time limit

Here's the fun part. You've only got five minutes. Of course, this is totally unreasonable, but it's a good metaphor for our project timescales. (Just watch the slippage. . . .)

Afterward

Look at how well people worked together. Which teams were most successful? Which failed? Why was this? How did different people approach the task? The outcome of this task is nowhere near as important as how people attempted to perform it.

Answering these kinds of questions will show quite clearly which type of code monkey each team member is most like.

TOGETHER
WE STAND

*Teamwork and the
Individual Programmer*

The most important single ingredient in the formula of success is knowing how to get along with people.
—Theodore Roosevelt

It's Saturday night, and you're settling down with popcorn and drinks to watch a film. Perhaps you've persuaded some unsuspecting, non–computer nerds to watch it with you. You didn't tell them it was *The Matrix*, did you?

The production that you're watching is the result of enormous effort by dedicated teams of people, all working together to create the final movie. Although you can't necessarily see it, there have been many, many man-hours (man-days, and "mythical" man-months) put into the production.

When you see some films, though, you have to wonder if they really should have bothered.

Compare that vast coordination of effort to how we write software. If you tried to create a movie on your own, the result would be poor. No one person can make a film on his or her own—or at least, not a film that's any good. To get a complete, edited movie to your television takes more effort: marketing, manufacture, distribution, retailing, and more. Perhaps you could create an entire "professional" software package yourself, but it would take a phenomenally long time. In the commercial world, who would give you such a risky contract?

In most professions, good products are the result of good teamwork. Software development is no exception. In fact, teamwork is *vital* to the survival of a project. An ineffective team will quickly stifle any software development activity, leaving progress to the heroic efforts of a few dedicated individuals working against huge odds. Being a good software engineer means more than just being a good programmer. You might be able to compute PI to ridiculous accuracy in less than five lines of code. Well done. But there are many other skills required, and one of these is teamworking.

KEY CONCEPT   *Teamwork is an* essential *skill of a high-quality software developer.*

In this chapter, we'll examine teamwork as it applies to us, as programmers. We'll look at what constitutes good teamwork and how we can be more effective in our teams.

Our Teams—The Big Picture

Over the years, many types of teams have worked together to produce software products. They range from the highly formal teams (suits in offices), with rigid structures and defined processes, to the new frontier work of the open source movement, where anyone can contribute and changes are incorporated on merit.

Both methods of working have had great successes, and both have had great failures. The IBM OS/360 and the Linux kernel are notable successes for each camp, respectively. The Ariane 5 is a legendary flop—this European launcher exploded during its maiden take-off because two software teams misunderstood the formally defined interface. Mozilla is an interesting open source flop—when Netscape open sourced its code, they expected rapid development and improvement. Years of Mozilla development were disappointing compared to other open source projects.

A software developer typically participates in various levels of teams, each with different dynamics and requiring different levels of contribution. Consider this scenario:

- You're creating a distinct software component that is part of a larger project. You may develop it by yourself or as part of a team of programmers: Team One.

- The component will fit into a wider product. All the people involved with this product (including any hardware designers, software developers, testers, and other non-engineering roles such as management and marketing) form Team Two.

- You are also part of a company that may be working on many different products simultaneously—Team Three.

In reality, there are more levels of teamwork in any reasonably large software-development company. These are shown in Figure 17-1, along with an example of the different dynamics at play. Inter-team dynamics, when separate teams interact, introduces the most complex teamwork considerations: Politics and managerial mistakes plague intra-organizational collaboration. Although a company is effectively one large team, it's not unusual for it to be layered with a "them and us" mentality between departments and groups. This is not an ideal atmosphere for effective product development.

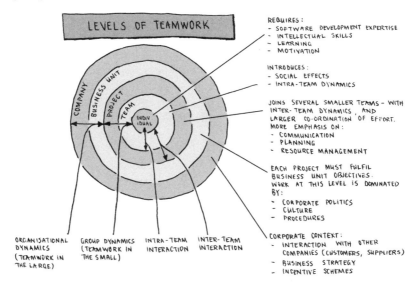

Figure 17-1: The levels of teamwork

As programmers, we are directly involved in the smaller level of team activity: in our day-to-day development teams. We have the most control and influence over this world. It is the level we are responsible for, where we have authority to make design and implementation decisions and to report on team progress. Programmers are less responsible for the effects of higher level teams, but we are affected by teamwork "in the large" as much as we are by teamwork "in the small," even if it's not as immediately obvious.

Development team size dictates the dynamic and nature of shared software construction work as much as the team's place in the organizational food chain. A lone engineer is given responsibility for all software architecture, design, and implementation work. In really small outfits, they may also have to work on gathering requirements and create and run a thorough test plan.

As soon as more developers are added to this mix, the nature of the programming task changes. It's no longer just about coding skill; it requires social interaction, coordination, and communication skills. This is where your teamworking skills will affect the software you build—for better or worse.

KEY CONCEPT   *Both the interactions within and outside your development team will affect the code you produce. Notice how they affect your work.*

Team Organization

The structure of a software development team is inevitably shaped by the management approach and the division of responsibility among its members. These two factors will naturally determine the amount of code and the size of the units that you work on. This shows us that the code we produce is shaped by the organization of our teams.

Management Approach

A project may be managed on a peer basis, with no coder considered more important than any other, or under the leadership of an über–programmer/ manager. The programming team could be considered part of a software production line: Fed designs from a team upstream, they produce code to specification.[1] Enlightened software engineers are given more autonomy and responsibility.

Tasks may be allotted months in advance on long-range plans (which can rapidly become out of date and inaccurate), or just-in-time by assigning each work package when a developer finishes his previous one. Programmers might work alone on their individual parts of the system, or work collaboratively via *pair programming* to spread responsibility and knowledge.

Division of Responsibility

The axis of responsibility determines how each line of development is split amongs programmers:

- With a *vertical team organization,* you employ a team of generalists who are skilled in a wide number of roles. They are each given a piece of work and implement it end-to-end—from the architecting and designing, right through implementation and integration, to development testing and documentation.

  The main advantage of this approach is that developers gain a wider range of skills and become more experienced in the whole software system. With one key developer per feature, there is cohesion in its design and implementation. However, generalists are expensive and hard to find. They don't have expertise in all areas and therefore take longer

---

[1] Here, management expects replaceable, commodity—grunt—programmers. See "The Code Monkey" on page 298.

to solve some problems. There is likely to be less cohesion between separate features, since they are implemented by different developers. The customer has to work with more people, since there's no specific liaison point—each developer needs to give input to scope the requirements and validate the design.

To make this kind of team work, you must define common standards and guidelines. You must have good communication to prevent people from reinventing the wheel. A common architecture must be agreed upon early on, or a chaotic and haphazard system will ensue.

- In contrast, a *horizontally organized team* is built from a team of specialists, and every development task is split between them, using their respective talents at the appropriate times. Because each aspect of work (requirements gathering, design, coding, etc.) is done by a specialist, it should be of a higher quality.

This has many opposite characteristics to the vertical arrangement: We build cohesion between separate work packages, but there's a danger that each set of work holds together less well because more people have

---

IT'S ALL GOING PAIR SHAPED

Pair programming is a collaborative software development approach, especially fashionable in agile development circles. It has claimed to make programmers more efficient: producing code faster, with fewer faults.

Two developers code together—at the same time, *at the same terminal*. While one (the driver) types, the other (the navigator) thinks about what's being done and acts as second pair of eyes, removing many mistakes before they have a chance to bite. The pair periodically swaps roles. The navigator sees consequences that the driver would miss, removing the common danger of being focused narrowly on the code as it's typed. Two people think of more than two ways to solve any problem, so you're far more likely to hit upon the best code design. Because of this unusually close collaboration, pair programming best suits talented programmers who have positive attitudes.

Studies claim that, once trained, two programmers are more than twice as productive on any given task. According to data published in *The Economist*, "Laurie Williams of the University of Utah in Salt Lake City has shown that paired programmers are only 15 percent slower than two independent individual programmers, but produce 15 percent fewer bugs. Since testing and debugging are often many times more costly than initial programming, this is an impressive result." (Economist 01)

Pair programming has many advantages. It promotes knowledge transfer and aids mentoring, increases your focus (you are less likely to daydream, take long phone calls, or tune out), increases discipline and reduces interruptions (you're less likely to interrupt two people working closely together than a single programmer staring vacantly into space). It works as an early real-time inspection mechanism—an instant code review—and brings the benefits of better code. It's a social process; with the right people, it improves morale (although it can be disastrous when two people grate against each other). The programmers get to know each other more closely and better understand how to work together. Pair programming promotes collective code ownership, spreads good coding culture and values, and emphasizes the development process.

worked on it. Interaction outside the team (with customers or other company factions) is made by a small number of specialists. This is easier to manage for the team itself and the external contacts.

You must take care to ensure that the specialists are well coordinated and that they see right through to the end of each work package, or their work will be narrow-sighted. With many people involved in each development procedure, the team is harder to manage; there is more workflow. This arrangement requires good communication, defined processes, and smooth handoffs between developers.

There is no "right" kind of organization. Which one is most appropriate depends on the team members, the size of the team, and the nature of the work produced. The pragmatic arrangement is probably somewhere in the middle.

Organization and Code Structure

A team's organization has an inevitable affect on the code it produces. This is enshrined in software folklore as *Conway's Law*. Simply stated, it says, "If you have four groups working on a compiler, you'll get a four-pass compiler." Your code inevitably takes on the structure and dynamics of your interacting teams. The major software components lie where teams gather, and their communications follow the team interactions. Where groups work closely, component communication is simple and well defined. When teams separate, the code interacts clumsily.

We naturally aim to create well-defined interfaces between each team's work to facilitate our interaction with that team. We do so even in cases where reaching into some internal part of another component might be a valid and better approach. In this way, teams can foster arbitrary divisions; despite our good intentions, design decisions are forced by team composition.

Of course, there's nothing wrong with encapsulation and abstraction; but they must be designed in for the right reasons. If anything, you should let the code you are building define the team membership and organization.

KEY CONCEPT   *Organize your team around the code you're building, not your code around the team.*

Teamwork Tools

There are foundational tools that help us to organize a functioning software team. They facilitate collaboration and help to elevate joint development from chaos to a well-oiled machine. On their own, they won't make you a team of commando programmers, but they're the arsenal every crack outfit relies on—the prerequisites for effective software developer interaction.

Source control

A development team revolves around the source code, and this is where it is held. Source control helps to marshal who is doing what and when, provides the definitive latest code snapshot, and allows you to manage changes, undo mistakes, and make sure that no one misses source code updates. You need it equally on a 100-strong team and on a one-man project.

Faults database

We've already looked at how this aids development (see "Fault-Tracking System" on page 147), but notice how it facilitates interaction between teams: A fault-tracking system acts as the pivot between test and development. It helps to organize test and repair work, prioritize faults, assign problems to individuals, and track pending fixes in the software. It identifies which faults are currently a developer's responsibility and which are a tester's.

Groupware

A team needs effective communications infrastructure, especially when geographically separated. A centralized calendar, address book, and meeting booking system provide a digital administrative backbone.

You also need a mechanism to share and collaborate on documents. Consider using wikis (web-based community documentation tools) and internal newgroups (email discussion boards with permanent storage) to facilitate group interaction.

A methodology

It's important to establish a defined and universally understood development methodology, or else work will be chaotic and performed on an ad hoc basis. One developer will release code, while another will refuse to let go until it has been thoroughly tested and debugged. One developer will halt all coding until an intricately detailed specification has been produced, while another will rush straight into prototyping the code. Holy Wars are made of smaller things than this.

A methodology defines the development process details, who is responsible for what work, and how work is passed along. With this, each developer knows what's expected and how to work as a part of the team. You must pick an appropriate methodology, based on the size of the team, the kind of code you are producing, and the talent, experience, and dynamics of people. This is described in Chapter 22.

Project plan

To produce any work in a predictable, timely manner you need some organization. This is provided by the project plan, detailing who is doing what over the course of development. To be of any use, the plan must be based on sound estimates and kept up to date with any changes required.

Programmers are notoriously poor at estimating, and managers are notoriously poor at planning. We must not be pressured to work to an unrealistic project plan. This is a geniunely hard problem that we dissect in Chapter 21.

Team Diseases

*Recovering from failure is often easier
than building from success.*
—Michael Eisner

Even with good programmers and wonderful organization, you can still have a dysfunctional team. Teams fail to produce results for many reasons, and just as we stereotyped different species of programmer, we can also identify categories of doomed development teams—to see what we can learn from them.

Here are some of the classic team disasters. In each case we'll see:

- The particular road to ruin
- The warning signs (so you can recognize when you're headed in this direction)
- How to turn around a team stuck in that particular rut
- How to be a successful programmer in that team situation (sometimes *despite* the team)[2]

Hopefully you won't recognize your current team in the following list.

Tower of Babel

Just like the Biblical builders, a Babel-esque team suffers a massive communication breakdown. Once programmers fail to communicate, development work is doomed—if anything works, then it's more likely by luck than by design.

With ineffective communication, people make incorrect assumptions. Bits of work fall between the cracks, potential error cases are ignored, faults are forgotten about, programmers duplicate effort, interfaces are misused, problems aren't addressed, and small slippages, unnoticed, grow into mammoth project delays because no one's monitoring progress.

The original Babel builders were fragmented by multiple spoken languages.[3] However, multinational projects rarely suffer from Babel

---

[2] I don't claim that these strategies will solve the team's general problem; they're deliberately shortsighted ways to get *your* work done now, with minimum risk of problems.

[3] Genesis 11:1–9

syndrome—with language barriers to cross, people make more of an effort to communicate well.

It's not only different spoken languages that can separate developers. Different backgrounds, methodologies, programming languages, and even different personalities cause team members to misunderstand one another. A small seed of confusion, unchecked, will eventually grow; resentment and frustration will build up. At worst, Babel teams end up not talking at all, with each programmer sitting in his own corner, doing his own thing.

This problem can brew within the immediate software team and also between interacting teams. Extra-team Babel syndrome occurs when developers fail to talk to testers or the management team is disconnected from development.

Warning Signs

You can tell that your team is headed toward Babel when one developer can't be bothered to ask another about something, feeling it's not worth the effort. It creeps in with a lack of detailed specifications and with ambiguous code contracts. You see too few or too many emails flying about. Too many emails means that everybody's shouting, and no one's listening: Nobody has time to keep up with the constant barrage of information.

On the road to Babel, there are no team meetings, and no one person knows exactly what's going on in the project. If you pick someone at random, they can't tell you whether development is on course or not.

Turnarounds

Talk to people. Go on—open the floodgates! Soon they'll all be doing it.

Babel attitudes are difficult to redress once the rot has set in, because morale has been dragged to an all time low, apathy is rampant, and no one believes that change is possible. The most effective strategy is to work at boosting team morale, to bring the developers closer together. Do something social to shake the team up: Consider a team-building exercise, even a simple trip out for a drink together. Buy pizza one day for lunch, and share with the team.

Then develop some strategies to force people to talk to one another. Create small focus groups to scope new features. Put two people in charge of a piece of design work. Introduce pair programming.

Success Strategies

To write good code in the face of such problems, you have to be very disciplined. Before you start a work package, ensure that it's rigorously defined. Write the specification yourself if you have to, and mail it to all the people involved to get their buy-in (provide a time limit for comments, stating that no feedback is assumed to be agreement). Then it's clear when you've succeeded because you have fulfilled the agreed spec.

Lock down all your external code interfaces fully, so there's no confusion about what you're relying on or what people can expect of your code.

Dictatorship

This is the original *one-man show*, a team led by a strong-willed, strong personality who is (usually) a highly skilled programmer. Other programmers are required to be yes men, even if they don't want to be, following the Dictator's mandates without question.

In some teams this works fine—with a well-chosen benevolent leader and a team who respects him. Problems loom when a Dictator's personality doesn't support his position, or when he is technically substandard (see "The Demiguru" on page 300). If his ego gets in the way, the team is in trouble: They will resent him and grind to a frustrated halt.

When fashioned on purpose, this kind of team is a hierarchy, with lines of defined authority. This structure was likened to a *surgical team* by Frederick Brooks. (Brooks 95) The surgical team places the most highly qualified technical individual, the lead surgeon,[4] at the top of the pile: acting as a code writer, *not* a manager. He performs the bulk of the development and has ultimate responsibility if bad things happen (if the patient dies). He is backed up by a deliberately chosen team. This includes a junior surgeon who performs smaller, lower-risk tasks, supports the lead surgeon, and learns the trade. The team also involves the software equivalent of anaesthetists, nurses, and perhaps more junior surgeons learning skills (e.g., sewing up the patient).

There are two dangers with this kind of team. The first comes when external pressures force the Dictator to become more of a manager; his technical specialism almost guarantees a lack of management skills. His focus will shift away from the software and the project will collapse. The second danger is a self-appointed Dictator, who isn't recognized by the team. Workflow will stall as the team is neither structured nor prepared to support his leadership.

Warning Signs

This team structure tends to develop slowly and subtly, as a would-be Dictator slowly modifies the focus of his work role and presumes his level of authority. You can see a Dictated team brewing when you often find yourself saying:

- *I can't do this without consulting . . .*
- *Oh, . . . will moan if we do it like* that.
- *But . . . says we must do . . . first.*

---

[4] Usually this guy is a technology specialist, as defined by Belbin's team roles.

Turnarounds

If you have a Dictator who is not a worthy team leader, then you must address the situation. Otherwise, the team will petrify under this authoritarian tyrant. Either work the issues through with him (in all honesty, this is unlikely to work—change is hard, especially for people with an inflated ego), or unseat him from the throne by confronting a manager on the issue.

After overthrowing the king, you either need a team restructure or a new king. Lead surgeons are hard to come by, so it's probably better to restructure the team.

Success Strategies

In a (functional or dysfunctional) Dictatorship, determine your level of authority and responsibility. Confer on this with the person whose opinion really counts—your manager or team leader.

However, once you've asserted your rightful development role, you (and the other programmers) must still listen to and work with the Dictator, even if you don't like his current position. Otherwise, you won't work well together and won't write complementary code. There must be consensus in the design, or the software will not work.

Don't be disrespectful or rude toward a Dictator; it'll just bring down the team morale and make you more angry.

Development Democracy

An old proverb says, *All men are created equal*, and here this is outworked. This is a team of peers— programmers with similar levels of skill and complementary personalities—who organize themselves in a nonhierarchical fashion. It's an unusual beast in the corporate world, which expects that someone must be boss. The idea of a self-organizing team seems heretical. However, it has been shown to be a team model that can work well. Some democratic teams run by periodically electing a leader from their ranks, based on whose skills are most in demand at this stage of the project. Often there is not a clear leader, and all decisions are taken by consensus. Open source development often follows this pattern.

We tend to forget the other half of that proverb: All men are created equal, but by practice grow apart. It takes a special set of individuals to make this team culture work. The danger with a team founded on this laudable principle is that as it grows, or when a certain member leaves (the one who crystallizes the group into making decisions), things begin to drift. The team can lose its focus, failing to agree on anything, and failing to produce results in a timely fashion. In the worst case, the team ends up arguing forever about a single issue, contemplating its navel, and never actually achieving anything.

With endless meetings and circular discussions, the team is in danger of *analysis paralysis*: of becoming focused on process, not on delivery of the project. Like a real democracy, the genuine team business can get lost in a sea of politicking.

You can accidentally end up with a Development Democracy if you have a ineffective team leader who is incapable of making decisions. This kind of bumbling leader will slowly phase himself out without realizing it. The frustrated team ends up jointly taking over his role—forcing decisions to be made and choosing the direction of development.

Democracy is a particularly difficult team structure in a crisis, even when established on purpose. If personality friction prevents the election of the right leader for a situation, then an outside leader must be brought in to steer the project.

Warning Signs

You can smell a sick Democracy a mile off: The rate of decision making drops like a stone. If there is a software team leader, then everyone bypasses him, rather than be stalled by his dithering. He is now a leader in name only; no one recognizes his authority or his ability to achieve anything.

Without leadership, no one is assigned responsibility for each task; it's never clear who should be ensuring a task's completion, and so nothing gets done. Weeks can go by without a specification being completed and with no visible progress.

In a rampant Development Democracy, the smallest decision forces the team into committee mode, and it takes days to conclude. Or a decision is made: Let's say *yes* until we decide to do something else. "Let your 'yes' be yes, and your 'no' be no,"[5] otherwise you'll spend ages ripping up old code and redoing it whenever someone changes his mind.

You might also notice that junior programmers feel alienated because they'll never be elected leader.

Turnarounds

Democracies aim to remove a specific bottleneck: where all decisions must be made by the boss, who is not always the most appropriate person to make them (especially when the boss isn't technical). In a dysfunctional Democracy, there is no decision-making process, and no decisions are made at any level. To return to a healthy Democracy, ensure that leadership can move around the team freely and that replacing the leader is easy. Don't attempt to run a Democracy unless you have enough potential leaders.

As with any other slipping project, make sure that problems are visible to everybody, both developers and managers. Make sure that it's clear who's responsibility this problem is—especially if it's not yours!

You can attempt to correct indecisive Democracies by showing some strong will; don't be content to let matters continually slide. You'll probably be named as a troublemaker, but eventually you'll also be named as someone who achieves results. Beware, though, of the danger of becoming a demi-Dictator as a backlash.

---

[5] Matthew 5:37, unless you're a Babel builder, in which case your "yes" might be *Oui* and your "no," *Nein*!

Success Strategies

For your own sanity, avoid ditherers—the people who cannot decide the simplest thing.

Ensure that you are allotted a well-defined part of the project and have clear and realistic deadlines. This is a major anchor against the ebb and flow of uncertain leadership.

Satellite Station

A Satellite team—split from the main development team—presents its own world of potential pain and pitfalls. It's hard to work as a cohesive unit when part of the team is physically separated, like a severed limb.

The Satellite might be an entire peripheral department, or a part of your immediate software team separated off in a different location. *Tele-commuting* (working from home) is a special case, with only one person in the Satellite.

It's not unusual for members of upper management to be in a head office elsewhere, but since they have little input on day-to-day programming activities, this isn't problematic. However, if part of the development team is many miles away, then you need to put measures in place to ensure that the project succeeds. You must be deliberate about this—split teams don't work together by accident.

Programming requires close team interaction because our individual pieces of code must interact closely. Anything that threatens our human interactions also threatens our code. Satellite teams present these threats:

- Physically disjointed development teams lose the informal, spontaneous conversations that spring up beside the coffee machine. The chance for easy dynamic cooperation disappears. With it goes a level of shared insight and the group understanding of the code.

- There is a lack of cohesion in development. Each site's local practices and development culture will differ (even if only slightly). Inconsistent methodologies make handing over work more complex.

- Since you don't know people in the Satellite very well, there is an inevitable lack of trust and familiarity. A *them and us* attitude emerges.

- An old proverb says, "Out of sight, out of mind." When you don't see Satellite programmers regularly, you'll forget them, you won't know their progress, and you won't think about whether or not your work impacts them (technically or procedurally).

- Satelites make the simplest conversation difficult. You need greater awareness of other programmers' schedules; when they're in meetings or on vacation.
- Cross-country projects introduce time zone problems. There is a smaller communication window between teams and a larger eclipse period.

Warning Signs

Geographically split teams are obvious, but also be wary of separated teams within the same office. Splitting developers into different rooms or even across corridors imposes an artificial divide that can impede collaboration.

Watch out for separation between departments too. It can be just as damaging. For example, test teams are often hived off separately from the developers, sometimes in a different office or section of the building. This is a real shame; it hinders essential interaction between the teams, with the result that the QA process is not very fluid.

Turnarounds

A Satellite Station team is not necessarily doomed; it just requires careful monitoring and management. The problems are not insurmountable, but definitely inconvenient—avoid them if you can.

An essential survival strategy is to get all team members meeting face-to-face early in the project. This helps to build a rapport, trust, and understanding. Regular meetings are even better. Provide food and drink when the team assembles; this sets people at ease and creates a more social atmosphere.

Arrange the Satellite so that its work requires the least collaboration and coordination with the mothership. This will minimize the impact of any communication problems.

Avoid code interaction problems by defining interfaces between the separate sites' work early on. But beware of designing your code around the team; you might not be creating the most appropriate design. Programming is a process of making pragmatic choices, so choose well.

Groupware becomes an essential tool in a Satellite to make communication effective. Also consider using instant message communication between sites. And remember: Don't be scared of the telephone!

Success Strategies

If you have to work with off-site people, make sure that you know them well—personally and professionally. It makes a big difference. You'll know how they react and when they are being sincere or sarcastic. Make an effort to be friendly to Satellite programmers—it's easy to be mistaken for a grumpy idiot when they only ever phone you at inconvenient times.

Make sure that you know exactly who is off site. Learn everyone's names, and find out what they do and how to contact them. Work at improving your communications skills. Don't be afraid to contact someone when you need to: Think about whether or not you'd talk to them if they were sitting beside you.

The Grand Canyon

This team is comprised of members whose skill levels and experience lie at oppostite ends of the spectrum. There is a clear skills gap; the chasm between the senior developers and the junior developers has not been bridged, and so two distinct factions have grown. In almost every Grand Canyon team, this is both a social and technical phenomenon: The junior programmers socialize among themselves, and the senior 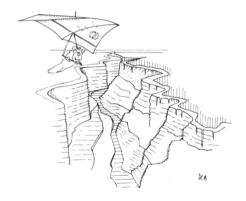 programmers socialize among themselves. This isn't helped when the senior developers sit in one enclave, and the junior developers in a separate ghetto.

The reason for Grand Canyon culture is often historical: A project starts with a small number of crack developers who must quickly establish an architecture and get proof-of-concept code out the door. They are naturally seated together and learn to work as a swift, cohesive unit. As the project progresses, more programmers are required, and junior members are brought in. Because of the existing office layout, they are seated on the periphery and then given smaller programming tasks in order to learn the structure of the system.

Without careful checking, the senior developers adopt a superior attitude and look down on the junior developers. They hand over small, tedious chunks of work and continue with the interesting grand design work. The senior developers reason that it would take a prohibitively long time to teach a junior about the bigger picture, and there *is* an element of truth there. In this way, the junior developers never get a chance to gain responsibility and do more fun programming. They become frustrated and disillusioned.

Junior programmers want to learn the trade, have a youthful enthusiasm, and have a passion for programming. Senior programmers may have a very different (more jaded?) worldview, with aspirations for management or more senior development roles. These different personal motivations pull the factions in different directions.

Warning Signs

Watch your team as it grows. Look carefully at the demographics of the members and watch how work is allotted among them. Monitor the social dynamics of your team; unhealthy teams develop cliques.

Turnarounds

The Grand Canyon problem is the team not mixing; there are polarized factions. The fix is simple: Adopt strategies that will mix them up. For example:

- Change the seating plan so that the factions are interspersed. This might consume valuable development time, but a day of desk moving might win weeks of productivity.

- Introduce team meetings to spread information.

- Start pair programming, mixing senior and junior programmers. Get the junior one to drive, while the senior navigates. This is a discipline for the senior and educational for the junior.

- Begin a mentoring scheme to train junior developers. Although this will emphasize the skills divide, it will also force the factions closer.

- Look at all the developers' job titles—do they foster a dangerous and unnecessary pecking order?

Success Strategies

Treat everyone as an equal, as a peer.

- If you're a senior programmer, recognize that the juniors need to learn. You were once a novice too and didn't understand how the world worked. Don't hog all the interesting programming tasks. Be willing to let others take responsibility.

- If you're a junior programmer, ask for more challenging tasks. Seek to learn. Perform your current task as well as you can; this will prove that you are ready for greater responsibility.

Quicksand

It takes just one person, one sour apple, one loose cannon, to bring a team to its knees. You need a group of good programmers to make a good team, but you only need one bad programmer to make a bad one. A team stuck in Quicksand has unwittingly fallen foul of a rogue member. This can be subtle: Maybe no one has spotted where the problem starts, and the culprit has no intention of causing any harm.

You might get stuck in Quicksand for a number of reasons:

- A technically *incompetent programmer* (probably the Cowboy coder we saw on page 302) is on board. This guy isn't easy to spot immediately, and no one will notice while he's writing poor code. The time bomb has been laid, and the project will be stalled later until his mess has been purged and replaced.

- A *morale drain* is sitting under a little black cloud and demoralizes the entire team, sucking out all enthusiasm and cheer. Within a few weeks, no one can bring themselves to write any code, and they're all considering jumping off the nearest bridge.

- A *mis-manager* is performing the exact opposite actions of a good manager, constantly changing decisions, altering priorities, shifting timescales, and promising the impossible to customers. The team members don't know where they stand because the ground is always moving under their feet.

- A *time warp* programmer is bending the laws of relativity so that time slows down around him. Anything coming his way takes a phenomenally long time to process. Decisions stall on his input, his coding work doesn't get done, and meetings always start late because he can't make the start. There's always a good reason—perhaps he is doing other very important jobs—but he amasses a backlog of tasks and never gets around to anything. Eventually other programmers get fed up and bypass him.

In a Quicksand team, one member's weakness can quickly destroy the entire team's productivity. This is especially dangerous when the culprit is high up on the food chain. The more responsibility he has, the more dire the consequences.

Warning Signs

Look for the one guy who doesn't fit in with the team. He's the person that everyone complains about[6] or the programmer who always works alone (because everyone avoids him).

Turnarounds

The most drastic but probably the easiest fix is to get rid of the Quicksand cause. But first you have to identify him, and sometimes that's quite difficult. Calls of unfair dismissal frighten managers, who will be reluctant to fire someone because a few people can't get along with him. It takes some major league incompetence to make this plan happen.

So you've got to find a way to minimize the chaos he can cause, or work out ways to integrate him into the team better.

Success Strategies

Most importantly: Don't be the Quicksand![7]

Presuming you're not, try to insulate yourself as much as possible from the effects of a Quicksand team member. Limit interaction with him, for the sake of your blood pressure. Don't rely on his code too much, and try to avoid his input as much as possible. Don't get sucked into his bad practices, and don't over-react to him—acting the exact opposite and making matters worse.

---

[6] They'll complain behind his back, which is a part of what drags the team into Quicksand. No one addresses the problem head on. No one likes to rock the boat. It will take more effort to confront him than anyone can be bothered to invest.

[7] Luke 6:42

THE MIS-MANAGER AT WORK

The developers were a good team. They enjoyed their work. They were working really hard. Sadly, they had (at best) mediocre management.

Early one morning, the manager (who looked like he was having a particularly bad day) called a meeting to complain that the developers didn't understand the "real world," that they were slacking, and that they never met the (impossible) deadlines he set them (having already sold products that didn't exist). He'd noticed that people were somtimes not at work between the core hours, and that from now on everyone had to be. Or else.

It went down really well.

The programmers did no work at all that afternoon. Nothing. They decided to work strictly to the core hours: no more unpaid overtime. I estimate that manager killed productivity and morale by at least 50 percent in one fell swoop.

Lemmings

Like a group of cute, furry animals with an insane urge to launch themselves off the nearest cliff, this team is far too willing—even eager—to accommodate the brief they've been given. Even when it's bogus.

The team is comprised of very trusting, very loyal members. They are technically competent but don't see beyond their specific instructions. Their enthusiasm and eagerness are commendable, but without a visionary member—someone who asks *why*, who looks beyond the spec to what's really required—the team is in constant danger of delivering what was asked but not what was needed.

Lemming teams are particularly vulnerable to the demands of startup companies. The disease starts when managers say, "Write this code quickly; we'll redo it properly later." Later never comes; instead the Lemmings hear, "The company needs more code, fast, so just bolt this on quickly too." Before long, the team culture is to dance when someone plays music. The work slowly becomes more and more difficult, with ever-more herculean tasks and an ever-decaying codebase.

Eventually, the team finds itself a broken mess at the bottom of a 60-foot cliff. Game over.

Warning Signs

If you're not happy with the specification you're currently working to, you may be in a team of Lemmings. Without faith in your current project, you're a mere code mercenary. When you find yourself listening to vacuous promises and being committed to unreasonable work, and when no one argues or points out flaws in the plan, you're definitely in Lemming country. We hope you enjoy your stay.

Turnarounds

Review what your team is doing right now. Don't stop working, but take a look, from the customer requirements right through to final delivery. Will the code you're working on provide what is ultimately needed? Is it a short-sighted hack that won't stand the strain of many years in your codebase or many years of use?

Success Strategies

Question the work you are given. Understand the motivation for it. Stand up for good programming principles, and never believe that you'll be allowed to fix code later unless you can see it scheduled on a plan that you believe in.

Personal Skills and Characteristics for Good Teamwork

It is amazing what can be accomplished when
nobody cares about who gets the credit.
—Robert Yates

Of course, not every team is doomed. Now, let's see how to make some sense of this mess and how to do things right. In the rest of this chapter, we'll look at techniques that will improve your software development team and hopefully avoid these pitfalls. Although tools and technology do help to improve productivity, the largest gains are related to the human aspects of relationships between people and their work.

Every software team is comprised of individuals. To start improving your team's performance, you can begin close to home—by addressing *your* attitudes toward the team and the joint development effort. We're not all managers, so this is really the main area that we have any influence over.

To be a high-quality programmer, you must be a high-quality team player. There are number of nontechnical skills, characteristics, and attitudes that an effective team member must develop before we can even consider his or her programming language dexterity or design capability.

Communication

Teamwork is dead without communication. Individual parts cannot move as a whole without communication. The goal and vision cannot be shared without communication. Projects really do fail because of a lack of good communication.

Intra-team communication occurs in several ways: conversations between individual engineers, phone calls, meetings, written specifications, email correspondence, reports, and instant messaging. Sometimes we even communicate in pictures! Each medium has a particular usage dynamic and is most appropriate for a specific kind of discussion.

The most effective communication should involve (or at the very least be visible to) all relevant parties. It should be sufficiently detailed but shouldn't consume too much time or effort. It should be performed in a suitable medium—for example, design decisions should be captured in a written specification, not verbally agreed upon and shared by word of mouth.

We've already seen how code itself is a form of communication. A programmer *must* be able to communicate well. This requires both good input and good output—the ability to:

- Write unambiguous specifications, to describe ideas clearly, and keep things succinct.
- Read and comprehend specifications correctly, to listen carefully, and to understand what you are told.

In addition to intra-team communication, we must also consider communication *between* teams. The classic example of bad communication seen in most companies exists between the marketing department and the engineers. If marketing doesn't ask the engineers what is possible, then it will sell products that the company can't make. This problem is cyclical: once it has occurred and people have been burned, the two teams are less likely to talk to each other (due to resentment). It will then happen again and again.

KEY CONCEPT *Clear lines of effective communication are vital to a well-functioning team. They must be established and cultivated. A good programmer is able to communicate well.*

Humility

This is an essential characteristic and one that is often lacking in our profession.

Humble programmers want to make a contribution to serve the team. They don't slack off to let others do all the work. They don't believe that they are the only talented people capable of making a worthwhile contribution.

You can't hoard all the good work for yourself; it's just not possible for one person to do everything. You have to be willing to let another team member contribute—even if it's something you *want* to do.

You should listen to and value the opinions of other people. Yours is not the only point of view, not the only solution. You don't necessarily know the only or the best way to solve every problem. Listen to others, *respect them*, value their work, and learn from them.

Dealing with Conflict

We have to be realistic: Some people can't help winding each other up. In this situation, we must be mature and responsible in our attitudes and learn to avoid (or learn to resolve) conflict situations. Conflict and animosity will severely degrade the performance of a team.

However, harnessed and channeled conflict can be a major success factor in your teamwork. Teammates who stimulate and provoke each other produce the best designs. Disagreement can act as a refining process, ensuring that ideas are valid. Knowing that your work will be cast under a critical eye keeps you focused.

It's important to keep this kind of conflict constructive—on a strictly professional, *not* personal, level.

COMMUNICATION BREAKDOWN

There are many communication methods in our highly connected world, and we must learn to use them effectively to support and facilitate our team interaction. The key to this lies in understanding their particular dynamics, etiquette, and individual merits.

Telephone

Best used for communication that requires an urgent response, a phone call interrupts what you are doing. For this reason, it's inconvenient to be called for non-urgent matters: Use another method instead. With mobile phones, we are far more connected than we used to be; this is a blessing and a curse at the same time.

Being audio only, you can't see the other person's face or their subtle body language cues. It's easy to misinterpret someone on the phone and draw an incorrect conclusion.

Too many techies are scared of using the phone. Don't be: For urgent communication it's invaluable.

Email

An asynchronous, out-of-band communication medium. You can specify a level of urgency, but email is never immediate; it's not a real-time conversation. It's a rich medium, allowing you to quickly send attachments and compose replies when it's convenient for you. It is often used for memo-style broadcasts to many recipients. Your email history provides a reasonably permanent record of communications. Email is an immensely powerful communication mechanism.

You must learn to use email as a tool instead of becoming a slave to it. Don't open every new mail as it arrives; your coding will be interrupted far too often and your productivity will take a hit. Designate email reading times, and stick to them.

Instant messaging

A quick, conversational medium that requires more attention than email, yet one that can be ignored or sidelined more easily than the telephone. It is an interesting and useful middle ground.

Written report

A written report is less conversational than email communication and more permanent. Written reports and specifications are formal documents (see Chapter 19). They take longer to prepare, and are consequently harder to misinterpret. Written reports are generally reviewed and agreed on, so they are more binding.

Meetings

Desipte all this modern techno-wizardry, it's hard to beat good, old fashioned, face-to-face conversations for getting things sorted out quickly and effectively. All too often, programmers try to avoid human interaction (we're not a social species by nature!), but meetings have a valuable place in our teamwork. We'll look at this in more detail in "Meeting Your Fate" on page 340.

Learning and Adaptability

You must continually learn new technical skills, but you must also learn to work as a team. It's not a God-given gift. A new team has to learn how to work together, how each member reacts, each member's strengths and weaknesses, and how to capitalize on individual skills to the group's benefit (see "Team Growth" on page 341 for more on this).

Emerson wrote, "Every man I meet is in some way my superior." Look at what you can gain from your peers. Learn from what they know, learn what they're like, and learn how they react. Learn to communicate with them. Seek criticism from them at all levels, from the formal code review to their passing opinions offered in conversation.

Adaptability is tied closely with learning. If the team has a need that no developer can currently fulfill and it's not possible to bring in an outside resource, then a solution needs to be found. Adaptable programmers learn new skills quickly to fill the gap and serve the team.

Know Your Limitations

If you are committed to work that you know you can't do or work you discover you're unable to complete, then you should make your manager aware of this *as soon as possible*. Otherwise, you will fail to deliver your piece of the project, and the whole team will suffer as a consequence.

Many people feel that admitting inability is a sign of weakness. It's not. It's better to admit your limitations than to be a point of failure in the team. A good manager will provide extra resources to help you do the work, and along the way, you will learn the new skills that you previously lacked.

Teamwork Principles

Here are the key team precepts that, once absorbed into your group's DNA, will change the way you write software. They shift focus away from individuals to the software and its collaborative development. Remember: For these principles to be effective in your team, you must make a purposeful change toward them; don't just agree they're good ideas and carry on coding as you always have.

Collective Code Ownership

Many programmers are territorial about their work. This is natural: Programming is a very personal, creative act. We're proud when we craft an elegant module, and we don't want anyone to trample all over it, destroying the masterpiece. That would be sacrilege.

But effective teamwork demands that we shed egos before entering the software factory. Don't complain that "Fred fiddled with my code." It's a team effort: The code is not owned by you; it's owned by the team. Without this attitude, each programmer builds his or her own empire, not a successful software system.

KEY CONCEPT *No programmer owns any part of the codebase. Everyone in the team has access to the whole code and can modify it as is appropriate.*

With this culture in place, the team immunizes itself from the danger of little Programmer Kings, each ruling their own islands of code. If no one has ever been allowed to see a certain person's code, what happens when that person leaves the project? Losing a local expert will severely disadvantage the team.

It's not wrong to feel a sense of parental responsibility for the code you produce, to be protective of it, and to want to nurture it. But this must be connected to a healthy team focus. Instead of *ownership*, consider code *stewardship*. Stewards don't own their charges, they are appointed to maintain them *on behalf of* the owner. A steward has primary responsibility for a piece of code's upkeep, weeding it, and tending the borders. Usually the steward makes all changes, although trusted team members can also make changes that would ultimately be verified by the steward. This is a constructive approach to your code and one that will serve the team well.

Respect Other People's Code

Even in an enlightened development culture without code ownership, you must still respect other people's code. Don't tinker with it at random. This holds especially true if they're working on it right now. You can't change something under another programmer's feet; it will cause untold confusion.

Respect for others' code means that you should honor the presentation style and design choices currently in place. Don't make gratuitously inappropriate modifications. Honor the method of error handling. Comment your changes appropriately.

Avoid making quick hacks that you'd be embarrassed to see in a code review. They slip in when you need to get your code working quickly and one small tweak elsewhere makes your stuff compile. If you forget to tidy the tweak, then you've just degraded someone else's code. Even temporary modifications must show respect.

Code Guidelines

For collaborative development to produce reasonable code, your team *must* have a set of code guidelines. These are dictates on the standard of code a programmer must write, ensuring that everything in the system reaches a certain minimum quality.

It's important not to stir arguments over code layout (although it is better if all code follows one style). However, there must be consensus on the standard and mechanism for code documentation, for language use and common idioms, for the act of interface creation, and for architectural design.

Teams that get by without such guidelines still do have them: just as unwritten conventions. The problem with such implicit knowledge is that a new team member's code won't match the existing codebase until he or she has been integrated into the code culture.

Define Success

To feel like they're achieving something and that they're working well together, the team members need a clear set of targets and goals. This must be more than milestones on a project plan, although milestones *can* be good motivators: Define lots of small milestones as short-term goals, and celebrate when you hit them.

You must define the criteria for success, so the team knows what it looks like and how to reach it. What does success mean for your current project? Is it work delivered on time, to a certain quality,[8] with a satisfied customer, bringing in a particular revenue, or with a certain bug count? Prioritize these factors, and let the programmers know the main motivator behind their development work. It will change what they do and how they do it.

Define Responsibility

All effective teams have a well-defined structure with clear responsibilities. This doesn't mean that your team has to be hopelessly hierarchical with a strict pecking order and multiple levels of management. The team structure must just be clear and recognizable. It should be clear:

- Who has the final say on important decisions? Who maintains the budget, who makes hire/fire decisions, who prioritizes tasks, who approves designs, signs off code releases, manages the schedules, and so on? These are not all necessarily roles *within* the team, but they are all roles that the team must know about.

- Where does the buck stop, and whose head will roll if the project is an unmitigated disaster?

- What are the members' *responsibilities* and *accountability*? What have they been assigned individual authority for, what is expected of them, and to whom are they accountable?

Avoid Burnout

No team should have impossible goals. Sanity check the project you're embarking on—there's nothing less motivating than knowing failure is inevitable.

Watch how the work is split between programmers. Avoid giving all the difficult work or all the high risk work to a few individuals. This is a common fault, especially when a team cultivates Programmer Kings. If they burn themselves out working many extra hours or worrying about the implications of a mistake, they'll jeopardize the project and demoralize the team.

Congratulate the team when it does well and works hard. Do it publicly. Keep feeding the team members praise and encouragement. It's surprising how refreshing some support and enthusiasm is.

Mix up people's jobs; don't force someone to repeatedly do the same kind of task until they get bored and give up. Give everyone a chance to learn and to develop new skills. "A change is as good as a rest." Even if there's no chance to slacken the development pace, a little variety can prevent programmer burnout.

---

[8] And how will you measure this?

The Team Life Cycle

Coming together is a beginning, staying together
is progress, and working together is success.
—Henry Ford

It's important to see our software teams in the light of their entire lives.
Teams don't spring out of holes in the ground, and they don't last forever.

KEY CONCEPT   *Successful teams are grown and run on purpose; they don't happen by accident.*

There are four distinct stages of a team's life: creation, growth, work, and
closure. At each stage, the focus of activities is different. Sometimes you might
iterate through these a few times in different orders, but every team will go
through each stage. Subteams within the main development project team
will undergo a similar process; this is a recursive model. We'll look at the
details of each stage in the next few sections.

Team Creation

There is a new project looming. It needs a development team. *On your marks.*
Get set. Go. A leader is appointed by the powers that be, and it is his responsibility to pull the team together. Members may be drawn from other teams or
hired specifically for this project. Wherever people come from, they have to
fit together as an effective team—the success of the project (and the leader's
job) depends on it!

So it all starts here. Formation establishes the core team members. At
this early stage, the team has not begun working in earnest yet, nor has it
jelled together properly. There are a number of important considerations as
the team is forged:

- You must establish where the team sits in the organizational food chain.
  Which other teams will it interface with? Set up communications channels with them, so it's clear how work will flow between departments and
  who the contacts are.

  Think about this carefully, and try to minimize communication
  across team boundaries to make work as simple as possible. At this
  stage, you can design your team to have the most chances for success by
  eliminating unnecessary bureaucratic overhead.

- To be effective, the team requires competent, talented members who have
  the potential to become a single high-performance unit. They must cover
  all critical areas of experience and expertise *before* it's needed; otherwise
  development will stall while another person is sought. Plan to grow the
  team as required, and figure out when you'll need to start looking for
  more people.

- Choose and communicate an appropriate teamwork model; otherwise
  the team will adopt an ad hoc structure and chaotic working practices.
  Arrange the team structure to eliminate management overhead and
  internal communication paths, keeping things as nimble as possible.

MEETING YOUR FATE

Programmers trapped in the software factory quickly develop an aversion to meetings for the simple reason that they are forced to go to countless meetings, all of which are awful. Meetings absorb huge amounts of valuable time that could be spent programming to prevent project disaster. The same few points are debated endlessly until the meeting disbands, then everyone forgets what was said and repeats it all at the next meeting.

To run effective software teams, we *must* learn to run effective meetings. It's not that hard; it just requires a little planning and discipline. Here's a seven-point guide to getting the most out of meetings: the rules of combat. Responsibility for this is placed on the person calling the meeting:

1. Meetings are important and inevitable. Don't shy away from calling a meeting when it's needed. However, don't call one when an informal chat in the hallway would resolve the problem more quickly and with less overhead.

2. Give plenty of notice of a meeting—days, not hours. Invite the *right* people: not too few people (no work can get done because the decision makers are absent), and not too many (no work can get done because everyone's struggling to make themselves heard).

3. Convene the meeting at a reasonable time. Not ridiculously early in the morning when only half of the attendees are normally awake, and not so late in the day that everyone's tired, fed up, and itching to get home.

4. Set a strict time limit, and declare it up front. Stick to it. This way, attendees know how much of their day remains to do other work. If you overrun, defer business to another meeting.

5. Make sure that everyone knows what the meeting is about and why they have been asked to attend. Distribute an agenda with the meeting announcement. Ensure that everyone who needs to make prior preparation is aware of their expected input.

6. Make sure that everyone knows where the meeting is being held. Ensure that the location has appropriate facilities: a whiteboard, a computer, and even enough chairs (this sounds silly, but is often overlooked).

7. Define roles *before* the meeting begins. You must have at least:

   A chairman
   This person leads the meeting, keeps discussion on topic, and to the agenda. He or she makes sure the meeting concludes on time, with a suitable resolution (perhaps this is the scheduling of another meeting).

   A secretary
   This person takes minutes of the proceedings, writes them up afterward, and circulates them to the appropriate audience (this is probably a larger group than the meeting attendees).

   Decision maker(s)
   These people have the final say on each issue. Without a defined authority, discussions go around and around with no conclusions.

Understand the purpose of the meeting. Most meetings are either *informational* (to disseminate information; attendees are largely a captive audience), or for *conflict resolution* (to work out a solution to a pressing problem). To run an effective meeting, everyone must understand this and act appropriately. Personal agendas can quickly steer an informational meeting in a random direction; the chairman must spot this and prevent people from hijacking a meeting for their own purposes.

The initial aim when forming a team is to create more than a mere *group*. You don't need another collection of people or a little social club; you need a cohesive, working unit of people who are motivated and aiming for a single common goal.

Don't bring a team together until you *really* know what it exists to do. If people are asked to start working without actually being given anything to do and they are left awaiting further instructions, then the team's long-term ethos will be to hold back; there will forever be untapped potential. If the team can't begin working from the outset, don't bring it together yet.

Team Growth

After creation, once the team is populated with a core staff, the project begins to gain momentum. The team must grow to accommodate the increased workload. There are several facets to this: The team must grow in numbers, but also in experience and in vision. It must grow *inward* and grow *outward*.

Inward Team Growth

As they work together, the members get to know each other on a personal and professional level. The team settles into a work pattern, and a coding culture is established. At first, this must be subtly guided so the culture is healthy and will serve the team structure and goals. This is dubbed *jelling* by Tom DeMarco; the point where individual members jell into a cohesive team. (DeMarco 99)

This stage aligns personal and team objectives and determines the individual roles and relationships. The team's feel at this point sets the tone for the whole project, so watch out for skepticism or bad will.

If it hasn't already been provided, the team infrastructure is laid down as the work builds up. Tools like source control and groupware are deployed. The project specifications are written, objectives are solidified, and the scope of the work is determined.

Outward Team Growth

Outward growth sees the accretion of more members. This is the visible kind of team growth. At its zenith, the team contains each of the following roles. These are not necessarily individual job titles; it depends on the size of the team. In a small team, individual members take on more than one role, either full or part time. Large projects may have whole departments per role.

Analyst
The liaison between the programming team and the customer. The analyst (also called a *problem domain specialist*) studies and understands the Real World problem well enough to write a specification that the developers can implement.

Architect
A high-level design authority who devises a system structure based on the analyst's requirements.

Database administrator
Designs and deploys the database infrastructure for the project.

Designer

Works below the architect to design components of the system. This is often a facet of the programmer's job.

Programmer

Naturally the most important person on the entire team!

Project manager

Takes overall responsibility for the project, making crucial decisions. The manager balances contending project forces (e.g., the budget, deadlines, requirements, feature set, and software quality).

Project administrator

Supports the manager, deals with the day-to-day running of the project team.

Software quality assurance engineer

Produces QA plans and ensures the code produced is of an appropriate standard.

User educator

Writes product manuals, ensures marketing is accurate, draws up training schedules, and so on.

Product delivery specialist

Otherwise known as a *release engineer*, plans how to package, manufacture, distribute, and install the final product.

Operations/support engineer

Supports the product in the field, once it's in the hands of end users.

A successful project must make sure that all these activities are covered. As the need for each role is felt, but before the need is acute, people must be brought in. Appointing members needs management insight, both of a candidate's personality type, his or her technical skills, and the job requirements. Once the team is established, new people must match the working practices and complement existing team members.

Teamwork

This is the point of performance when the team is functioning fully with everyone in place. The cogs turn, and the software construction process grinds relentlessly onward.

The majority of a team's life is spent in this phase, working out the project's objectives. To do this, the single large task is decomposed into a series of smaller tasks. Team members are assigned their own work packages and kept synchronized (perhaps by a project meeting or by close communication). Their work is integrated as it's completed. Slowly, the software takes shape.

Although working to a predetermined development process, the team must adapt to changes as they arise: handling unforeseen problems, changes in the team, or the dreaded Shifting Requirements Syndrome. As work progresses, each member must identify and manage outstanding issues and risks.

The team must get into a development groove—finding the appropriate pace of work, and meeting targets at each step of the way. However, you must prevent the groove from turning into a rut. Don't be frightened to shake up working practices—if required—to ensure that the team doesn't get complacent or lazy or to counter ineffective team members who might jeopardize progress.

Team Closure

Eventually, even the most delayed project will come to an end. That end might be successful software that makes the customer happy; it might be a doomed product and prematurely abandoned development. Either way, the project concludes, and the team is removed from it.

From the very beginning of development, a clear end point must be in sight. No team can continue forever or plan to work indefinitely. The lure of completion actually motivates people, and many programmers won't invest much effort until confronted with a hard deadline.

For this reason, every team must plan to disband, dissolve, or transition to a different kind of team (perhaps a maintenance or support team) upon project completion. This plan must cover both normal and abnormal completion conditions.

Team disbanding doesn't happen suddenly. Projects don't halt without warning; they slowly ramp down. We usually transition people off a project gradually as they become surplus to requirements. No team needs people kicking around doing nothing, absorbing resources. As each person leaves the team, ensure that all his or her important knowledge and work products are captured. It's easy for information to leak between the cracks of a splitting team.

KEY CONCEPT   *Don't lose information when people leave a team. Perform a hand-over, and capture all important knowledge from team members. Include all code documentation, test harnesses, and maintenance instructions.*

What happens once a team gets to the end of a project? You could take one of the following steps:

- Move the team into support mode, maintaining the product.
- Start some new development work (perhaps a new version of the same software).
- Instigate a post mortem if the project was a failure.
- Split the team up to work on separate projects (or release them if their contract expires).

Whether a team is recycled or disbanded is a difficult choice, and one that's often made badly. Just because a team was successful on one project doesn't mean that they will be on the next. A new project may require a different mix of skills or a different development approach. However, it's wise to keep a good team together. Well-integrated teams with competent members and an effective work culture are rare. Don't throw them to the wind needlessly.

When there's a choice, it should be made based on the characteristics of the next project. Sometimes this choice is made for you: In small development organizations the project team *is* the whole development team. It's simply not possible to mix and match programmers, and you are forced to use the same people on the next project.

PEOPLE POWER!

Here are a few simple guidelines for managing and maintaining a team of software developers. Without programmers you don't get programs, so we need techniques that release the potential in people and help them to work together. Even if you're not in a leadership position right now, you can use these as a simple yardstick to judge how your team is run and how people are treated. They distill a lot of the wisdom we've already seen into practical bite-sized chunks.

Use fewer and better people.
   Larger teams require more lines of communication and more management, provide more potential points of failure, and are harder to share vision with.

Fit tasks to capability, and also to motivation.
   Avoid the Peter Principle:[*] Excellent programmers should not be promoted to managerial positions they are not suited for or interested in.

Invest in people.
   You'll get more out of them if you build something into them. Technology moves fast; don't leave their skills out of date. Otherwise they'll move somewhere where they will gain better experience.

Don't cultivate experts.
   It's dangerous when one programmer becomes the only expert in a certain area. That person becomes a single point of failure.[**] Some people actively try to become Programmer Kings, while others are forced into it, not being allowed to work on anything else. When your expert needs a new challenge, he'll leave. How will you maintain the software now?

Select complementary people.
   The team members can't all be world-class experts. Equally, they can't all be inexperienced programmers. You need a healthy skills mix. You also need a healthy interpersonal mix, with personalities that jell and work together well.

Remove failures.
   Someone who doesn't fit should be removed. It's not easy to do, but a rotten part can quickly spoil the whole—and the consequences of procrastination can be dire (see "Quicksand" on page 330). Don't wait to see how things will pan out or just hope they'll improve. Deal with the problem.

   Team members make or break a development team. A successful organization chooses them well and uses each person to his or her full potential.

---

[*] A theory that originated from Dr. Laurence J. Peter: Successful people are promoted to their highest level of competence and, as they can do that job, then promoted one step more—to the level at which they are *not* competent.

[**] Project managers joke about a project's *truck number*: the number of people who could be hit by a truck without the project collapsing.

In a Nutshell

The important thing to recognize is that it takes a team,
and the team ought to get credit for the wins and the losses.
Successes have many fathers, failures have none.
—Philip Caldwell

Programmers only really care about writing good code, so does all this matter? Yes: The health and structure of our software teams has a direct affect on the health and structure of our code. They are inextricably linked. Software is written by humans. Just as the software components have to fit together, communicate well, and form a cohesive structure, so must the programmers building it.

Good teamwork comes from more than a well-defined process or a fixed structure. Good teamwork stems from good individuals. "The whole is greater than the sum of its parts," or so the saying goes. This is, of course, only true if all the parts are working well. If any single part is failing, then the whole will be compromised. Our individual attitudes affect the quality of our teams, and therefore the code produced. We must address these attitudes to create good code. Understanding your natural attitudes and responses will help to improve your programming skills.

A professional programmer *has* to be able to work in a team. Alongside technical skills, you must be able to create a piece that will fit into the larger jigsaw. This means being able to communicate and work with others. It means understanding your role and carrying it out appropriately, working to the best of your ability. It means cooperating with other team members and being team-focused, not self-focused.

Later chapters develop some of these collaborative themes further: We will cover source control, development methodologies, and estimation and planning techniques.

Good programmers . . .

- Are not territorial about the code they write
- Will perform any kind of development task if it advances the software system
- Learn and grow while contributing to the team; they have personal objectives without sacrificing the team
- Are good communicators; they always listen to other team members
- Are humble, serve the team, and respect and value the other members

Bad programmers . . .

- Try to build code empires and make themselves invaluable
- Want to do their own thing and search for the most glamorous assignments
- Work their personal agendas at the expense of the team's effectiveness
- Always want to assert their personal opinions
- Believe the team exists to serve them and that they're the best member of the team—God's gift to the coding community

See Also

Chapter 16: Code Monkeys
The personal skills and characteristics of good programmers.

Chapter 18: Practicing Safe Source
Software teams collaborate on code, and without a source control system this is almost impossible.

Chapter 22: Recipe for a Program
Development methodologies: how teams interact and develop code together.

Action Sheet

Look at the following action sheet. Take some time to fill it in, and figure out how to put what you've learned into practice.

Teamwork — ACTION SHEET

Take some time to fill in this form thoughtfully. Answer honestly.

Team infrastructure

Rate your team's use of the following tools. Check *yes/no* answers, or rate your team on a scale of 1 (*very bad*) to 5 (*very good*).

	We have it (yes/no)	We have an administrator/owner for it (yes/no)	We all know how to use it (yes/no)	It's easy to use (1–5)	We use its features well (1–5)	It contributes to effective teamwork * (1–5)
Source control						
Fault/bug tracking						
Groupware						
Methodology/development process						
A project plan						
Specifications						

* If any items don't contribute to effective teamwork: Why?

Team members

Rate each of the following statements from 1 (*strongly disagree*), through 3 (*neutral*), to 5 (*strongly agree*).

- ☐ We have team members with a good range of skills
- ☐ There is a low turnover of coding staff
- ☐ Adequate training is provided

- ☐ All necessary roles are covered (look at the **Team Growth** section), and
- ☐ These roles are formally defined and recognized
- ☐ All team members are competent
- ☐ We couldn't live without any team members
- ☐ No one is overloaded with work
- ☐ There are problem members
  (1 = big problems, 5 = no problem members)
    – What are the problems?
    – How can you resolve them?

Team structure and work

Code structure vs. team structure
- ☐ Our code design shapes the team structure
- ☐ Our team structure shapes the code design
(reverse scoring: 1 = strongly agree, 5 = disagree)

Documentation
- ☐ We share documentation well, using revision control
- ☐ We record meeting minutes and design decisions

Working practices
- ☐ We have a mentoring scheme in place
- ☐ We perform pair programming
- ☐ We perform code reviews
- ☐ We perform document reviews
- ☐ We don't have a 'code ownership culture'
- ☐ We have a clear set of code guidelines

Management
- ☐ We are managed well
- ☐ My needs are valued, as well as the team's success

About the plan
- ☐ There is a development plan
    - ☐ Everyone knows where it is
    - ☐ It's up to date
    - ☐ Everyone knows when the next deadline is
    - ☐ The deadlines are realistic
- ☐ We know what we're aiming for
- ☐ We know how we're achieving this

Team health
- ☐ The team is motivated
- ☐ The team is growing (should it be?)
- ☐ The team is shrinking (should it be?)

Communication
- ☐ Team communication is effective
- ☐ We have good meetings, run well
- ☐ I know what everyone else is doing
- ☐ I know who is in charge of each technical area

The big picture

For each separate team in the organization, rate the following statements from 1 (*strongly disagree*) to 5 (*strongly agree*).

Add to this list any other teams that you work with.

	We have good communication with them	We have a good relationship with them	We work together effectively	We know who is in the team
Other development teams				
Test				
Marketing				
Management				
The customer				

Review

Finally, review all the answers you have given.

- What do these answers tell you about your team?
- Did you achieve predominantly high or low scores?
- What measures will improve problem areas?

Get Thinking

A detailed discussion of these questions can be found in the "Answers and Discussion" section on page 533.

Mull It Over

1. Why write software in teams? What are the real advantages over writing a system on your own?

2. Describe the telltale signs of good and bad teamwork. What are the prerequisites for good teamwork, and what characterizes bad teamwork?

3. Compare software teamwork with the construction metaphor (see "Do We Really *Build* Software?" on page 177). Does it reveal insights into our teamwork?

4. Will external or internal factors do the most to ruin the effectiveness of a software development team?

5. How does a team's size affect the team dynamics?

6. How can you insulate a team from problems caused by inexperienced members?

Getting Personal

1. What kind of team are you working in right now? Which of the stereotypes on pages 322 through 332 is it most like?

   a. Is it like this by design?

   b. Is it a healthy team?

   c. Does it need to be changed?

   What factors have you encountered that prevent good teamwork?
   If you haven't done so already, fill out the action sheet on the previous page carefully. Make sure you work out how to improve your team and start to make the changes.

2. Are you a good team player? How could you work better with your teammates and build better software?

3. What is the exact responsibility of a software engineer on your current team?

PRACTICING
SAFE SOURCE

Source Control and Self-Control

The superior man, when resting in safety, does not forget that danger may come. When in a state of security he does not forget the possibility of ruin. When all is orderly, he does not forget that disorder may come. Thus his person is not endangered, and his States and all their clans are preserved.

—Confucius

No master jeweler crafts an exquisite diamond necklace and then leaves it in an unlocked workshop where it could be stolen by a passing thief. When a car manufacturer brings a new model to market, it doesn't instantly forget how to support and service the old models. Both would be professional (and financial) suicide, reckless attitudes toward valuable work.

The code we write is similarly precious: With our time and effort invested, it is both financially valuable and also emotionally important. We must safeguard source code like any other precious object and adopt working practices to ensure that we don't break, endanger, or lose it.

KEY CONCEPT *Code is valuable. Treat it with respect and care.*

In this chapter, we'll play minder, bodyguard, and warden, working out essential techniques to keep our code well protected. Who (or what) are we protecting it from? With varying degrees of melodrama, we're fighting against:

- Ourselves and our own silly mistakes
- Our teammates and their silly mistakes
- Inherent problems in the collaborative development process
- Mechanical failure (exploding computers and evaporating hard disks)
- Thieves who want to exploit the software

Your sanity, your happiness, and even your livelihood depend on the contents of this chapter. Those of you nodding off in the back should pay attention!

Our Responsibility

As conscientious software craftsmen, we must take responsibility for our work. Not only must we write high-quality code, we must ensure that our work is:

Safe and secure
It won't be accidentally lost after three months of development, and it can't be leaked out of the company as top secret information.

Accessible
The appropriate people can modify it easily. It is visible to the appropriate people and not to anyone else.

Reproducible
Once released, the source isn't lost or thrown away. It can still be used to build *exactly* the same application image 10 years later, when tool versions have changed and the original language isn't supported anymore.

Maintainable
This doesn't just include using good programming idioms, but also ensuring that the code can be modified by the whole programming team. Can more than one programmer work on it simultaneously without courting disaster? Is it possible to make fixes and updates to older products while developing a new product version?

We achieve these aims by adopting safe development practices. In this chapter, we're not considering the security of our running executables;[1] we're looking at our development techniques. These issues might seem tediously removed from the act of writing code, but we should not discount their importance. A craft involves the process of creation as much as the final product.

---

[1] That's covered in Chapter 12.

Source Control

For team members to collaborate on code development, they must all be able to work on the codebase at the same time. This isn't as easy as it would first appear—you must ensure that concurrent code modifications don't interfere and that no work is lost on the way. There are some low-tech ways to collaborate on code:

- The most basic is to share a single computer and take turns to edit code. Two programmers won't fit in the same chair without a struggle, and so no code edits will conflict. However, you'll suffer a massive productivity loss, since only one person can code at a time.

    You can put two chairs in front the machine and pair program for a potential productivity gain (see "It's All Going Pair Shaped" on page 319). But this doesn't work when three, four, or more programmers all try to work on the same code at the same time.

- Alternatively, you could share the code on a network fileserver. Then other developers can see source files and even edit them alongside each other. But this is far from ideal. The code is shared but not safe, because you can't prevent two people from working on the same file at the same time. This will cause all sorts of confusion—and lost work—when they both hit the Save button. What happens if someone edits a central header file halfway through your build? The answer: An inconsistent executable that will either crash or behave in wildly unpredictable ways.

For this reason, when programming teams evolved from the primordial digital soup, they invented the *source control* tool to act as a central storehouse for, provide access to, and marshal concurrent modification of their source code. But source control is important even if you're working by yourself; as we'll see, a central code repository is an incredibly useful facility.

KEY CONCEPT   *Source control is an* essential *tool for software development. It is vital for teams to work together safely.*

Source control enables one or more people to work on the same *repository* of source code in a controlled manner, avoiding all these problems. It allows each developer to create (or *check out*) his or her own personal copy of a common source repository and work on it in isolation. This copy is known as a *sandbox*, since local code changes cannot escape to pollute others' work. The sandbox can be brought up to date with other users' changes—as and when required—by asking the tool to resynchronize with the repository. When complete, changes are *committed* (or *checked in*) to the main repository for other developers to see.

To achieve this, source control systems will follow one of two access models:

Strict locking
Some systems physically prevent users from editing the same file at the same time, using a file reservation mechanism. At first, all files in the sandbox are read-only; you can't edit them. You must tell the

system that you want to edit foo.c; it becomes writeable, and no one else can edit the file until you commit your changes or release the file unmodified.[2]

Optimistic locking

More sophisticated systems allow users to edit the same files concurrently. There is no reservation step, and the sandbox files are always writeable. Changes are merged together as they are checked in. Merges usually happen automatically. Occasionally, conflicts occur and the developer has to merge manually (this is not generally a difficult task). This is known as *optimistic locking* (although there's really no locking at all).

People hold passionate beliefs about which mode of operation is best and swear by one approach or the other. Concurrent modification works best for a widely distributed set of developers, working over the Internet. When people are harder to shepherd, lower process hurdles are preferable; locking files for modification can become frustrating.

A WAR STORY

Poor source code management can combine with source control to produce painful development headaches. Seemingly sane, simple rules can accidentally stifle software development.

One large project in a well-known company had a policy of strict locking—all code checkouts were exclusive, preventing developers from modifying the same file at the same time. Unfortunately, the coding policy dictated that all enums must be placed in the same source file. This file grew and grew and grew.

The net result was not hard to predict: The file became a checkout bottleneck. The developers were constantly hanging around waiting for this file to become available.

Revision Control

Source control systems don't just hold the latest revision of each file. The repository records the differences made at each check-in. With this important revision information, you can obtain any version of a file over its entire development history. For this reason, we also talk about *version* (or *revision* or *change*) *control systems*. This is a very powerful weapon: Any change can be fully reversed—you have a code time machine! The repository's file versioning means that you can:

- Undo any change that you make, at any point in history
- Track changes made to the source as you are working on it
- See who changed each file and when they did it (and even do complex searches to see how much work a single developer has done on a particular product—useful when development spans many years)
- Check out a copy of the repository as it stood at some particular date

---

[2] It's therefore considered bad practice to lock a file for too long—it might prevent other programmers from carrying on with their work. This is an inherent limitation of this access model.

CONTROL FREAK

What kinds of files should you put into a source control system? To manage and version your software effectively, you must collect your *entire* source tree in one repository. This includes:

- All source code

- The build scaffolding

- Unit test code and any test harnesses

- Any other assets required to create a packaged distribution (graphics, data files, configuration files, and so on)

The ultimate goal is to perform an entire build out of the repository. Starting with just the build toolchain and the source control tool, you should be able to generate a complete product in a few simple steps (i.e., check out the repository and type make)—without needing to supply any more files or modify anything by hand. If you have to add anything else to the source tree, then your software is *not* under change control.

But why stop there? We can extend this list to be really thorough:

- Consider placing the whole development environment under change control. Check in every build tool update, and keep these files synchronized with each release version of your software.

- Revision control all documentation: specifications, release notes, manuals, and so on.

All good source control systems allow you to create named *labels* (or *tags*) and apply them to specific versions of a set of files. This allows you to mark important repository states: You can identify all the files that comprised a specific code release and retrieve them easily with this label at a later date. This is helpful when you're working on product version 3, but an important customer finds a critical bug in the first release, and you need the code ASAP.

With each check-in, you can attach metadata: at the very least, a textual description of the change you have made. Using these messages, you can get an overview of development by viewing a file's revision log. More sophisticated tools allow you to add arbitrary metadata to file revisions, including references to fault reports, supporting documentation, test data, and so on.

Good source control tools version directories as well as files. This enables you to track modifications made to the file structure, including the creation, deletion, moving, and renaming of files. Some source control tools record changes on a file-by-file basis; when you check in many files at once, each one is versioned individually. Other tools implement *changesets*: They record each batch of file changes as an atomic modification. This helps you to visualize how one piece of work affected many files simultaneously.

Access Control

A source code repository can be held locally on your computer or on a remote machine, accessed over a network connection. With the appropriate security measures, it can be accessed by developers worldwide via the Internet, removing the burden of developers in different time zones coordinating their work.

The source control tool also governs which users have access to which parts of the codebase. With this you can enforce visibility rules and modification rights. A project's buildmaster is usually responsible for administering the source control tool, assigning these access rights, and ensuring that the repository is kept tidy. It's important to have a designated source control administrator. If all developers are given admin privileges to the repository, it will encourage them to fiddle with it and make careless administrative changes. Even with the best intentions, things will go wrong.

Working with the Repository

There are two ways to develop code in a revision-controled repository:

- In the *little and often* check-in approach, each file is checked in whenever a small change is made. The repository therefore contains many, many revisions of each file. Doing this makes it easy to track the changes you make during development and helps you to visualize all the modifications made in the file's lifetime. However, you'll see a proliferation of file revisions which are potentially confusing.

- The alternative approach (presumably called *big and seldom*) is to only check in the important changes: to check in a revision for each release of the product or whenever you've successfully added an *entire* feature to a code module. This makes it easier to obtain a particular previous version of the code but much harder to track all the individual changes that it comprised.

Favor the little and often approach. Repository labels allow you to mark each major milestone, so it lacks none of its counterpart's capabilities.

You must be disciplined when checking in code modifications. Your work can be seen immediately by every other developer, so test your code thoroughly first: Don't check in anything that will break the build or make automated unit tests fail. You won't be popular if your fault brings the entire team to a grinding halt. Many teams enforce a penalty for this kind of antisocial check-in to encourage people to work carefully. This is nothing severe—perhaps public ridicule by email or buying the next round of drinks.

KEY CONCEPT   *Treat the repository with respect. Never check in broken code that will stall other developers.*

Leave Branching to the Trees

One of the most powerful source control facilities is *branching*: a mechanism to make multiple parallel streams of development on a file or a set of files. Branches have many applications, including:

- Adding multiple features to the codebase concurrently
- Providing personal workspace for a developer to check in potentially broken work in progress, without breaking the main codebase
- Maintaining an old software version while working on a new one

Suppose you sell an image processing application, and you need to add some new drawing tools. You also want to start a second development effort on the same source files to port the code to a new operating system. The two tasks must begin separately, but eventually they will merge back together. This is a common development scenario. For each task, you create a *branch* in the repository, and commit code revisions onto the branch rather than onto the main line of code development. This keeps the two tasks in separate worlds. One developer works on the drawing tools, another concentrates on the porting effort. Their work does not interfere.

As the name implies, branches create a tree structure of parallel file revisions in the repository. There is always at least one line of code development called the *trunk* (for obvious reasons). Figure 18-1 shows this in practice for a particular file being branched. It was created (at *version 1*) and intially developed on the trunk—the center column. At *version 2*, we create the first feature's branch (for new drawing tools) and perform a number of check-ins down it. None of these affect code in the trunk at all. Work on the trunk continues concurrently, and at *version 3*, a second branch is created to accommodate the porting task.

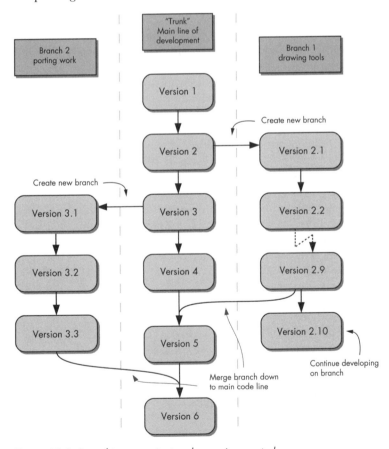

Figure 18-1: Branching a project under version control

Work progressing down a branch can be *merged* with any other branch or back down onto the trunk. This means, for example, that you can try some exploratory bugfix work in a branch and, when proven stable, you can merge it back into the main code. If it was a development dead end, then you can abandon the branch—with no effect on the trunk. Very useful. In our example, the first branch is merged at *version 2.9* into main's *version 4*. This results in main's *version 5*. Later, the second branch is also merged down to main.

Even if you're not simultaneously developing features in your codebase, branching can be usefully applied to single-track development. This scheme leaves the trunk version stable: always a complete, tested product—probably the latest release version of the code. Each feature is developed on its own feature (or release) branch, and the product itself is released from this branch. When complete, we merge it back down to the trunk and create a new branch from there for the next feature. This keeps the mainline code free from potentially broken work in progress and keeps all related work collated together on a development branch rather than scattered down the mainline alongside a host of other feature development work.

A Brief History of Source Control

There are many different source control systems available with both open and proprietary licenses. Often, the choice of source control system is enforced by company practice. ("We've always used . . . , and we know how it works.") Sadly, this does not necessarily mean that it is the right, or best, tool for the job. Many companies run legacy systems; the investment and complication of migrating large chunks of code out of one source control system to another is prohibitive.

The father of all version control systems is *SCCS (Source Code Control System)*, developed at Bell Labs in 1972. It was superseded by *RCS (Revision Control System)*. The most commonly used source control tool in the open source world is currently *CVS (Concurrent Versions System)*, although it is beginning to show its age. CVS was originally built upon RCS and introduced a collaborative environment where several developers could work on the same file at the same time. Whereas RCS implements the file reservation model (described in "Strict locking" on page 351), CVS is concurrent. The modern successor to CVS is called *Subversion*, and it improves on most of CVS's shortcomings.

Although they have subtle functional differences, most source control tools have both command-line and GUI façades. They can all be embedded in popular IDEs. If you're looking for a source control tool to begin to use on private projects, take a look at Subversion and one of the available GUI front ends.

Configuration Management

Software *configuration management* is a subject bound closely with, although often mistaken for, source control. It's actually a world beyond the storage of source code.

TERMS AND DEFINITIONS

Source control is our primary weapon in the battle to safeguard code. It's an essential tool that no software craftsman could live without. We've already seen the various names used to describe it. They are used interchangeably, but each one reveals a specific aspect of its operation:

Source control
Also known as *source code management*, this is a mechanism to manage the files of code that we write. It maintains the files and their directory structure; it also marshals concurrent access to and modification of the code.

Version control
Otherwise known as *revision control* or *change control*, this is a source control system that records the changes you make to a file. It allows you to inspect, retrieve, and compare any version of the file over its entire development history.
  Version control usually works best for text-based file formats—they can be easily scanned for differences—but you can version other kinds of files too: documents, graphic files, and so on. The source files for this book are held in a revision control system so I can track development history.

Configuration management
Builds on version control to provide a reliable environment in which software development is carefully managed and processes are enforced.

Some commonly-used source control acronyms are: SCMS (source code management system), VCS (version control system), and RCS (revision control system).

We've seen that the aims of source control are to:

- Store your source code centrally
- Provide a historical record of what you have done to the files
- Allow developers to work together without interfering with each other's work
- Allow developers to work on separate tasks in parallel, merging their efforts later

Configuration management builds on this foundation to manage software development throughout a project's life. It encompasses source control and adds a development procedure to its use. Software CM is formally defined as "The discipline of identifying the configuration of a system at discrete points in time for purposes of systematically controlling changes to this configuration and maintaining the integrity and traceability of this configuration throughout the system life cycle." (Bersoff et al. 80) It controls the project's *artifacts* (the things you put in source control) and its development *processes.*

Some source control tools provide configuration management capabilities and can integrate with project workflow tools; for example, managing fault reports and change requests, tracking their progress, and linking them to physical changes in the codebase.

Configuration management involves:

- Defining all the individual software components in a system and which artifacts are required to construct them (this is especially useful when one codebase can be configured to generate multiple product variants or can target several platforms).

- Managing the released versions of a product, and which versions of the constituent components each release comprises.

- Tracking and reporting the status of the code and its components. Is it in a *beta* state or is it now a *release candidate*? (See "Alpha, Beta, Gamma . . ." on page 140.)

- Managing formal code change requests, tracking which ones have been prioritized and approved for development; tying change requests to the necessary design work, investigation, code modification, testing, and review work.

- Determining which documentation relates to specific product variants and what sort of compilation environment is required.

- Verifying the completeness and correctness of software components.

How do you currently manage the configuration of your codebase?

Backups

This is good old-fashioned common sense. Backups are your insurance policy, guarding against the accidental deletion of a file, computer system failure and, if held offsite, loss of data when the office burns down. They don't yet cure the common cold, but some enterprising backup company is probably working on it.

Everyone knows that they should make regular backups of their work. But we're human; just because it is both rational and sensible to perform a task doesn't mean we will—there are far more pressing (and fun) things to do. Hindsight isn't helpful: When you're sitting amidst the smouldering ruins of your computer, with hardware beyond hope of repair and all data lost in digital purgatory, you'll curse the day you decided to play solitaire instead of back up your code. Days' worth of work must be rewritten, and while you'll remember most of it, it always seems harder and more tedious (and certainly soul destroying) the second time around. If you're near a deadline, this could be a real disaster.

Think about it: Is all of your source code backed up? I'm frightened when I discover how much work is done on computer systems and workstations that aren't backed up. The level of risk is preposterous.

KEY CONCEPT *Back up your work. Don't wait for disaster to strike before you think about a recovery strategy.*

You must establish a sound backup procedure. Don't rely on a manual backup plan, like performing file copy operations by hand. One day you will forget to kick off that critical backup, leave it too long between backups, or manually copy the wrong thing. Remember Murphy's Law (on page 5): *If it can go wrong, it will.* That goes double for anything *you* do! Instead, ensure that all important files are placed on a filesystem that *is* being backed up. When using a workstation that is not backed up, I will save my code on a network-mounted fileserver that is backed up rather than on the unsafe local disk.[3]

To be useful, backups must be:

- Done regularly
- Checked and audited
- Easily retrievable
- Automatic (both automatically initiated and able to run without intervention)

Critically, all source code repositories must be held on a server that is backed up. Otherwise, you're putting things in a safe but not shutting the door. In fact, "little and often" check-ins reduce reliance on personal computer backups—most of the work you've done is checked into a backed up repository. The loss of files on your workstation will not be critical to the entire project.

The bottom line is: Your work is *not safe* unless it's retrievable in the event of human or mechanical failure. Even if it's "only" code for personal use, protect it with backups. A small investment in some backup software, the extra storage, and a little administration time is immeasurably worthwhile. The cost and hassle of a failure far outweighs this meager outlay.

Releasing Source Code

Source code sometimes needs to leave your tight grip and set off to explore the Big Wide World. Perhaps you sell a library: Your shipping product *is* the source code itself. Perhaps you've been contracted to ship code alongside an executable. Even if you don't intend to release your source code, it might one day be sold to a new owner, or you might need to collaborate with outsiders on a new feature. We must take reasonable measures to ensure code safety and accessibility in these situations too.

The scale of horror that this entails depends on the nature of your code. Proprietary source code—written specifically for internal use in a company's products—is closely guarded *intellectual property*, and it's generally considered commercial suicide to release it openly, where your competitors can find it

---

[3] Of course, there's a trade-off. This simple approach makes file access slower, since network latency and fileserver delays have been introduced. But I can live with this (usually) minor inconvenience.

and exploit it. The polar opposite is *open source* or *free* code, written specifically to be released: freely viewable and modifiable. The choices and nature of a software release differ in each case:

- If you are releasing some closed proprietary code then you need to obtain a signed *non-disclosure agreement (NDA)* before you let the third party see it. This is a standard contractual agreement to ensure that they don't abuse, share, or use the code in a way that violates the agreement. It is legally binding, and its main purpose is to keep the company's lawyers at bay while the technical staff gets on with the important business of creating exciting software.

  If the people you are releasing to will exploit the code for commercial gain, you must also enforce a licensing agreement to ensure that you profit, too. This really concerns the marketing or sales staff, and mere mortal programmers need not worry about this side of corporate wrangling.

- Open source developers must choose an appropriate license to dictate what users can do with the code and whether they must share any derivative works. For more on software licensing, see the sidebar.

In both cases, you must ensure that the source files are presentable. The code *must* be all your own work, or you must own redistribution rights to all the parts that aren't. This is why a lot of old commercial code can't be open sourced: if a company doesn't hold all rights to its source code, then they can't release it freely without costly modification.

To stand on firm legal ground, ensure that every source file contains a copyright notice attributing it to the correct owner (the author or company) and a short description of the license it is released under. Then, if someone finds the code, it's obvious that it is confidential material. See "File Header Comments" on page 83 for more on file header comments.

Beware of an accidental source release: Prevent easy reverse engineering of your executables. It is sometimes possible to reconstruct source code from a distributed binary. This is a particular problem in byte-code compiled languages like Java and C#. Consider obfuscating the byte code; there are tools that can do this for you.

Wherever I Lay My Source

Finally, think about where you put your source code. Top-secret company work shouldn't be left on a laptop in an unlocked car. Likewise, source code should not be left on a publicly accessible network.

Ensure that your login passwords are kept secret. Outsiders (or malicious coworkers) should not be able to sabotage work using inappropriate access rights.

LICENSES

A software license defines the rights that users have over it. This holds for both binary distributed programs and the source code that creates it. Most proprietary licenses withdraw the rights of copying, modification, lending, renting, and use on more than one machine. On the other hand, open source licenses strive to protect your right to copy and distribute the software at will.

Software authors choose their licenses based on specific goals and ideologies. Indeed, an author can chose to release software under multiple licenses, covering different usage patterns and permitting different price and support models. There are many types of source code licenses, although only a few are commonly used. They differ in:

Permitted use
Can the licensed code be exploited commercially, or may it only be used in free software? It's not really making money that's the issue, but whether proprietary closed products can incorporate your work without permission. Some open source licenses require the user to release any code built with their software. A typical commercial license lets you do what you want, as long as you pay.

Terms of modification
If you change the code, must you publish those changes? Or can you ship derived works without any further obligation? Some open source licenses are described as "viral" because any change you make must also be released under the same open source license, and likewise any code you ship using it.

Commercial licenses are drawn up by company lawyers to suit their nefarious purposes (that is, protecting the company's commercial investment). However, there are many common free or open source licenses. *Open source* is a term coined by the *Open Source Initiative (OSI)*, an organization that certifies software licenses. The availability of source is not enough to characterize a product as open source. It must provide certain rights: to allow free modification and redistribution of the code or any modifications, but with the restriction that these rights must be given to all and be non-revocable.

Open source conflicts with the Free Software Foundation's concept of *free* software. The FSF (steward of the GNU Project) is rather more ideological and promotes software licenses that are *free, as in speech*, not just *free, as in beer*—the word *free* is used in the sense of the French *libre*. OSI accept some free-as-in-beer licenses, which does not endear them to the GNU faithful. GNU's famous licenses are the GNU *General Public License (GPL)* and the GNU *Lesser General Public License (LGPL)*. The latter is a more lax "library" version that allows linking with proprietary code.

In a Nutshell

> *We must respect the past, and mistrust the present,*
> *if we wish to provide for the safety of the future.*
> —Joseph Joubert

It's not the size of your code, it's what you do with it that counts.

In this chapter, we've looked at various working methods to ensure that we take responsibility for the source code we create, developing it in a safe and controlled manner. These things really do matter; a mishap at the wrong moment could spell disaster for your development project. You must protect your mission-critical codebase.

Source control is the essential weapon in our battle to develop code safely. It facilitates team interaction, ensures that group development is predictable and safe, helps to manage product revisions and configurations, and acts as a historical archive of all development work. It's a development safety harness, and your life would be considerably worse without it.

Good programmers . . .	Bad programmers . . .
• Take responsibility for their work and know how to safeguard code development	• Wait for disaster to strike before considering their code's security and accessibility
• Use source control carefully, ensuring that the repository is always in a consistent and usable state	• Presume that someone else will think about backups and security for them
• Never check broken code in to source control	• Don't care about updating documentation
• Use all tools thoughtfully, with the intent to produce maintainable, accessible code	• Don't consider the state of their code in the repository—they check in broken code and leave a mess behind them for others to clean up

See Also

Chapter 7: The Programmer's Toolbox
The tools we use to develop software effectively.

Chapter 10: The Code That Jack Built
The accessibility of your code affects how easy it is to perform a build—either of the cutting-edge codebase or a historical version that needs to be reworked.

Chapter 12: An Insecurity Complex
The other safety concern—security issues *within* running programs, rather than in the development process.

Get Thinking

A detailed discussion of these questions can be found in the "Answers and Discussion" section on page 539.

Mull It Over

1. How can you reliably release your source code to other people?
2. Of the two models for repository file editing (locking file checkouts or concurrent modification), which is best?
3. How do the requirements for version control systems differ between a distributed and a single-site development team?
4. What is a sound rationale for selecting a source code management system?
5. How can you separate bleeding-edge code under active development from stable code during team development?

Getting Personal

1. Does your development team make effective use of source control?
2. Is your current work backed up? How important are backups to your development team? When are backups made?
3. On which computers is your source code held?

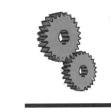

PART V

PART OF THE PROCESS

Writing high-quality software isn't just about churning out good code. Obviously, good code helps. A little. But there's much more to it than that. Good software is created intentionally; it takes planning, foresight, and a robust battle plan. We'll see exactly what this battle plan looks like in the next section. However, before we assemble the troops, we must know what they should do. It helps to point them all in the same direction.

This section looks at some specific parts of the development process, the extra activities we schedule time for that help us to intentionally craft excellent code. We'll see:

Chapter 19: Being Specific
How to write and read software specifications. The correct approach to recording what you will do, and what you have done. This chapter shows how specifications can make your life easier, rather than get on your nerves.

Chapter 20: Review to a Kill
A discussion of *code reviews*—an important practice that ensures you are writing high-quality code.

Chapter 21: How Long Is a Piece of String?

Software timescale estimation—an essential activity in the planning process, yet still one of the mystic black arts of the software development community. This chapter busts some estimation myths and provides practical advice to use on the front line.

The relentless pressures of the software factory continually drive us to work faster and harder. The only way to cope is to learn ways to work smarter. We need to employ each of these pracices to stand a chance in the endgame.

BEING SPECIFIC

Writing Software Specifications

I've never known any trouble that an hour's reading didn't assuage.

—*Charles De Secondat*

Almost everything worth using is documented. Your DVD player has an instruction manual. Your car has a maintenance manual. A contract has small print. Chocolate cake has a recipe. There are books and magazines dedicated to practically every pursuit known to man. If your software is worth using, it also should be well documented.[1]

We all know that the carefully tested software we give to our customers needs to have documentation. Just how much documentation is a moot point. The user of an office suite certainly thinks there should be more than the publisher does. Without a manual to describe the usage mechanics of your software, whatever form it takes, people will falsely assume that it can do more than it was designed to, or use it for purposes no sane programmer would have ever imagined.

---

[1] Of course, that's no excuse to craft a bad interface; it must still be easy and intuitive to use.

Developers can just as easily make the same kinds of mistakes during coding. Just as the final software product needs documentation, so do the intermediate development steps. This is the sort of documentation that the end user will (usually) never see. These are the definitions of how the program will be designed and built. These are the software *specifications*.

Writing and working with specifications is an important skill of the practicing programmer. Communicating in English (or any other natural language) is just as important as communicating in code.[2] Like eating your vegetables and exercising regularly, specifications are "good for you" and good for your software. However, like cabbage and the gym, we avoid them, feel guilty, and then live to regret the consequences: We end up with unhealthy, flabby software development.

The traditional notion of a software specification involves a huge wedge of paper filled with dense text, cryptic tables, and meaningless terminology. It's a highly uninspiring prospect: a document that requires more maintenance effort than the code it describes. Developers live in perpetual fear of being forced to work with the spec.

But it doesn't have to be this way. Used correctly, specifications oil the development process. They reduce development risk, help you to work effectively, and make your life a lot easier. In this chapter, we'll investigate the sorts of specifications we need, what should be in them, and why reality differs so greatly from this ideal.

What Are They, Specifically?

*Apply your heart to instruction and
your ears to words of knowledge.*
—*Proverbs 23:12*

Specifications are formal documents that form part of the development process, providing internal software documentation. There are many different types of specification (we'll see them shortly) containing different information and targeted at different audiences. Each one is appropriate to a particular stage of the software construction process, from the conception of a project to its final deliverable. We use them to capture exactly what the user requires (or exactly what they are going to get, if the two differ—they usually do), to detail the architecture of a software solution, the interface of a particular code module, the design and implementation decisions for a piece of code, and more.

Specifications help you to work smarter and to produce better software. But a bad specification can do quite the opposite. Like your code, the quality of a software specification is vital. Good specifications and documentation are generally taken for granted, whereas poor specifications rapidly become loathed; a millstone around the project's neck.

KEY CONCEPT   *Not just the existence, but also the quality of software specifications is vital to the software development process.*

---

[2] Indeed, Dijkstra once remarked, "Besides a mathematical inclination, an exceptionally good mastery of one's native tongue is the most vital asset of a competent programmer."

Specifications are a form of inter- and intrateam communication. We've seen that projects can die from a lack of communication. We should therefore exploit specifications as a communication medium—where appropriate. (Projects can just as easily fail because too much time is spent writing documents, and not enough time is actually spent writing software!)

Specifications become increasingly important as the size of a project increases. This is not because specifications are unimportant in smaller projects but because larger projects have more to lose—there are more people whose lack of communication and coordination will have a greater negative impact on the outcome of the software development process.

KEY CONCEPT   *Specifications are an important communication mechanism for software developers. Use them to capture information that must not be lost or forgotten.*

Writing specifications helps to make your information:

Safer

Information isn't stored in people's heads where it can be lost, forgotten, or remembered incorrectly. With all important facts written down, there's less risk when people leave the project: The amount of information loss will be minimized, and there will be a solid base to help any replacement programmer get up to speed.

Thorough, complete specifications reduce the risk of two people making different sets of assumptions—the classic reason why two separately created modules do not work together when first integrated. Specifications help to prevent subtle bugs.

Accessible

All information is conveniently recorded in a known place. New people can join your project and understand what each component does and how they fit together, just by reading the documentation. They don't have to search for the information in a hundred different people's heads before they become productive.

More accurate

When all information is gathered and captured, you are more likely to see problems, to indentify missing parts of the design, and to spot any unfortunate consequences or side effects. A few disconnected thoughts floating around your brain are not as easy to validate.

The Types of Specification

Each type of specification forms an intermediate gate of the software process: A method of handover between separate parts of the development process. For example, a specification for the API of a software component is written by the group of people who are scoping its functionality and interface. The programmer works to this specification; it is complete enough to implement all the code. The same specification is a contract detailing how the systems integrator can stitch it into the system and how other programmers can use it. It also describes expected behavior, so the test department can validate that the software is working correctly.

In this way, the output of one specification flows naturally into the contents of the next, leaving a trail of documents in the wake of the rapidly evolving software. An example of this paper trail is shown in Figure 19-1. We see a natural hierarchy of documents generated as a project matures—each subcomponent has a similar set of documents to the overall project; its development can be managed as a mini-project.

Since software design is an iterative process, this is not a one-way flow of information (otherwise you're trapped in a waterfall methodology straight-jacket—see "Waterfall Model" on page 427). As you discover missing information or need to adjust the software design, the specifications must be updated accordingly. If your documents are not malleable and maintainable, your software development will suffer. Bureaucratic development processes try to stifle good software development by ensuring that all work is performed to The Specification, even if it's 10 years old and completely out of date. Good programmers consider their specifications to be just as malleable as their code.

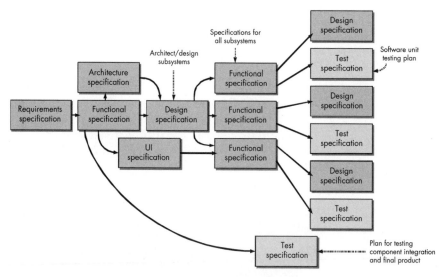

Figure 19-1: The typical specification paper trail

Let's look at the different types of software specifications and see how they enhance your code-writing lifestyle. Unfortunately, in the Real World, these documents are called by many different names. A *requirements specification* is variously called a *user requirements specification* and a *functional constraints specification* by different people.

Requirements Specification

If all other specifications disappeared in a software development process meltdown, this is the one document that you should fight for. It's the head of the merry software development parade and the stumbling block for many failing projects. The information in here is vital. It will keep you sane.

The requirements for a project are never clear at first; customers can't tell you *exactly* what they want their software to do (they're not computer experts, so they don't know). This can cause all kinds of problems, so there must be a single document that pins down what your software is supposed to do and the characteristics of an acceptable implementation: the *requirements specification*. It lists in great detail (or at least appropriate detail, which will usually be great) how the code is expected to behave. It must cover all the important, high-risk, high-value areas of system behavior, comprehensively and unambiguously.

The requirements are usually written as a series of numbered sentences each containing a single factual piece of information. For example:

> *1.3.5 The user interface shall consist of a black rectangle containing the words Don't Panic in a red sans-serif typeface at 13pt.*

Uniquely numbering each requirement enables easy cross-referencing in subsequent documents and helps you to trace a particular design or implementation decision back to a single requirement.

We must consider:

Functional requirements
These requirements detail what the program must do. For example: *Must process BMP images and convert them to either JPEG or GIF format.*

Performance requirements
These requirements show how fast it must work and whether there are operations with deadlines. For example: *The user must receive feedback for every operation within one second, and all operations must complete within five seconds.*

Interoperability requirements
These requirements describe the other software, hardware, and external systems that it must interact with. For example: *Must support HTTP and RS232 communication with an upgrade server.*

Future operation requirements
These requirements determine what functionality must be *accommodated* now, even if it's not implemented right away. For example: *Must provide a skinnable UI so that the user can customize the look and feel.*

These requirements fall into two camps. *Discrete requirements* are binary. You can easily check whether your program meets them by looking at the source: There will be a chunk of code dedicated to each bit of functionality. You can write specific tests to ensure that each discrete requirement is honored.

Nondiscrete requirements are less tangible. You can't check whether your program meets them just by inspecting the source. These include the required fault-tolerance of a system, the required uptime of a server, a program's mean time between failure, its security, or its scalability. These kinds of requirements can be massively important and remarkably hard to verify.

The process for creating a requirements specification will differ from company to company, and often depends on the project characteristics and the customers (how smart and competent they are). The requirements specification is collated by the marketing team, a future product focus group, or a *business analyst* whose job is to understand the problem domain and scope the work required. Usually the customer, or a representative of the customer, is involved.

The customer must agree to and sign off on the requirements specification; it forms an effective contract between the software developer and its client. The supplier agrees to ship a product whose functionality meets these requirements; the customer agrees to pay for it. Without an agreed specification, the customer can refuse the product on a whim, and the developers will have spent a lot of effort to no avail. Sadly, this is a common problem in the software factory that I have seen many times, especially when the customer is not a technical expert and doesn't know what a good software solution looks like. When the requested software is finally built, the customer realizes that what it asked for wasn't what it actually wanted: *Rewrite it in pink.* You're back to square one. This sort of thing happens all the time; the requirements specification is your insurance policy.

Sadly, many software factories skip requirements gathering or do not give it sufficient import. It's *vital* to agree on the requirements early on, before software design has started and certainly before any code has been written. We use the functional requirements specification:

- To keep the project on track and on time—by preventing (or at least reducing) the tardy addition of new features that will postpone delivery.

- To improve customer satisfaction—by setting expectations up front.

- To reduce bugs—by restricting *feature creep*, we avoid last-minute code additions, which helps to avoid scary bugs.

- To maintain your sanity—without requirements specifications, developers rapidly lose their hair.

Depending on the type of development methodology you employ, a single monolithic requirements specification might be written up front before any software development begins, or it might be developed incrementally alongside the code. Understand how your requirements are gathered from the customer and how this impacts the way you develop code.

KEY CONCEPT   *Software requirements must be captured early to set expectations, to prevent feature creep, and to reduce developer angst.*

Also consider your *developmental requirements*: the things that you as a developer must have in order to develop the software. For example, you might require a certain kind of internal architecture to provide adequate future extensibility, and you *need* version control to develop software (it is not optional). Some of these might justifiably belong in a requirements specification.

Functional Specification

Perhaps the document most frequently used by programmers, the *functional specification* describes the observable behavior of a piece of software. It is derived from—and must satisfy—the requirements specification. There are usually a number of functional specifications in one project: one for the overall product and then individual specifications for individual software components.

For a software component, the functional specification includes a complete and unambiguous description of its public interface. This equates to a list of every method or function in the module's API, together with a description of what they do and how to use them. It contains details of all external data structures and formats, and all dependencies on other components, work packages, or specifications.

This is more than a user guide to a piece of software. There is enough detail to build the component from it. Two teams could read the document and work separately on implementions. Although the implementations will differ, both components should behave identically.

This fact is exploited in practice: Some NASA spacecraft employ five computers to do the job of one; four computers implement the specification for a particular computation, running independently developed implementations. The fifth computer is used to average the results of the four calculations (or to decide if one computer wildly disagrees with the others).

If you're writing a software component without a functional specification, begin by writing one yourself. Show it to all interested parties so they can agree that what you'll build is sufficient and so they won't be surprised when it is delivered.

KEY CONCEPT   *If your software task is not adequately specified, don't start coding until you've written a functional specification, and people agree that it's correct.*

System Architecture Specification

The *architecture specification* describes the overall shape and structure of the software solution. It encompasses such things as:

- Physical computer layout. (Is it distributed client/server software or a single user desktop application?)
- Software componentization. (How is it split up? Which parts do we need to write; which can we buy in?)
- Concurrency. (How many threads run at the same time?)
- Data storage (including database design).
- All other aspects of the system's architecture (redundancy, communication channels, and more).

It is important to specify these things in detail before too much development work happens. The architecture affects the later stages of development; a mistake or ambiguity here will filter down to become serious flaws in later phases. Of course, nothing is set in stone: If you discover a flaw in the architecture specification, then it must be fixed, regardless of how much work has already occurred. Don't accept a bad architecture specification as a millstone around your neck. However, it is important to perform adequate architectural design up front. We discuss software architecture in detail in Chapter 14.

User Interface Specification

This document contains information about the user interface: what it will look like and how it will react. This is how we present the system's capabilities to the user. It might describe a GUI application or a web-based interface, an audible phone menu system, a braille accessibility interface, or a simple, single-LED display.

Sometimes the user's view of the system is very different from the implementation behind the shiny façade. Here are two examples:

- A highly networked system can be deployed on a single box and hidden behind a unified UI.
- The available functionality can be simplified for ease of use or to create a cut-down cheaper version.

The UI specification describes the interface conventions and metaphors and shows how the user sees the functions interact. It is comprised of a textual description, with pictures and screenshots. It often contains a *storyboard* representation of the UI in action—a pictorial map of each UI state, its transitions, and what is displayed in each. It includes every screen that the user will see and all detail (that is, all graphics, fields, lists, buttons, and the on-screen layout of each). It will also detail acceptable response times for each operation and the behavior in common error cases (this isn't exhaustive—trying to enumerate *all* possible error conditions is a practically endless task!).

This work may include or lead to a *UI prototype*. Prototypes can be made with varying levels of detail and accuracy; this depends on the application and how much testing and review will be done. Inevitably, the UI design is incomplete at this stage, but this is your first chance to see what the finished product will look like. Although prototypes help to envision how the interface will behave, it's not until the system is integrated that the UI can be properly reviewed and tweaked.

Design Specification

A *design specification* (or *technical specification*) documents the internal design of a component. It describes how a functional specification will be, or has been, implemented. The design specification describes all internal APIs, data structures, and formats. It should detail all key algorithms, execution paths, and thread interactions. It describes the choice of programming language and the tools used to build the code. All of this is critical information for the code implementers and maintainters.

Many heavyweight development processes mandate the production of a design specification prior to implementation; it is reviewed before coding begins to prevent work from progressing down a dead end. However, in most software factories, this document is written alongside, or after, the code.

It sounds like such a good idea, but most design specifications are a big waste of time! They need continual maintenance to stay in sync with the code being described. Without care, they quickly rot and are left inaccurate and incomplete—potential snares for unwary readers. For this reason, I suggest that you *don't write a design specification*!

But wait, before you run off unencumbered, there's more. Replace it with something that contains the same information but is easier to keep accurate. *Literate programming tools* (see "Practical Self-Documentation Methodologies" on page 66) are a great documentation mechanism that can replace heavyweight design specifications by generating documentation from the code itself. You need only supply any extra commentary in specially formatted code blocks.

KEY CONCEPT   *Use literate programming tools to write your technical documentation. Don't write a word-processed document that will quickly go stale.*

You don't need the complete production code to use literate documentation tools in this way. You can document your intended code structure in the same manner: Mock up some code and run the tool over it. This automatically generates design documentation, serves as prototype proof-of-concept code and, with care, can evolve into the production code.

Test Specification

The *test specification* describes the testing strategy for a particular piece of software. It shows how to validate the implementation against its functional specification so you know when the software is acceptable for release. Naturally, the size and scope of this task depends on what is being tested: whether it's a single software component, an entire subsystem, a desktop application, or an embedded consumer product.

The test specification contains a list of every test that must be performed. Each test is detailed in a *test script*: a set of simple steps to run the test, together with its acceptance criteria and the environment in which the test will run. The scripts themselves may be written in separate documents or included in this one.

As we've seen in Chapter 8, many code-level tests can be performed *in code* themselves and run as an automated part of the development process. These tests stand distinct from high-level tests that can only be performed by running the software in its final context with scripted human input.

Wherever you can create programmatic unit tests for your software, prefer to do this rather than create a lengthy test specification. Just as design specifications can rapidly become out of date, test specifications written at the code level will rot as the system evolves around them. Use programatic test code as the documentation of your testing strategy—you can write literate test code as easily as literate normal code. Automated test cycles will also force you to keep the tests up to date with the code; your tests will fail if you don't!

DEVIL'S ADVOCATE

Specifications are expensive: Reading and writing them requires both time and effort. They require extra work. Are all of these documents *really* necessary? Yes, they are—to write high-quality software, you need to consciously generate all this information and then record it somewhere where it can be retrieved when necessary. Specifications encourage us to follow good development practices—to track requirements, perform design, and construct a test plan—and we've seen how they facilitate communication.

Agile processes (see "Agile Methodologies" on page 433) place far less emphasis on writing specifications, but they don't advocate coding by the seat of your pants. Since specifications don't write themselves, can easily get out-of-date, and require extra work to maintain, and programmers have more than enough to do already, it's sensible to only write as many documents as necessary. We should always avoid lengthy procedural hurdles. *But any specification you remove must be replaced by an equivalent store of information.* Don't skip a specification unless you have conciously replaced it with something of equal quality containing the same set of information.

Extreme Programming doesn't produce a lengthy requirements specification, but it captures all requirements in an equivalent set of *user stories*, held on a stack of *story cards*. Design specifications are eschewed: *The code is its own documentation.*

Agile practice also promotes *test-driven design*, where codified tests act as additional documentation of the code and its behavior. This full and clear suite of unit tests can replace the test specification for individual components but is seldom suitable to verify the final product against its validation criteria.

What Should Specifications Contain?

The contents of each type of specification are naturally very different. However, the information in any specification must be:

Correct

This might seem obvious, but it is absolutely vital. An incorrect specification can cause days of wasted effort. It must be kept up to date or it will become dangerously misleading: It will waste readers' time, cause confusion, and may lead to bugs being introduced as a consequence.

If a specification can be interpreted in more than one way, then the "specification" isn't specific—it's not doing its job. Two readers could make different interpretations of the ambiguous information, with inevitable unfortunate consequences. Make sure that your specifications can only be interpreted as you intended.

The text must not contradict itself. When a specification gets reasonably large, it becomes difficult to ensure consistency. This becomes a particular problem when a maintainer (different from the original author) makes modifications—it can be very easy to alter information in one place and not change any subsequent sections that allude to the same information.

A specification should be carefully written to comply with all relevant standards (for example, language definitions and company coding standards). It should follow the document standards/conventions of your company and use any document templates that exist.

Comprehensible

An effective specification is inviting to read and easy to understand. It makes sense to every reader. If it's so technical that only engineers can understand it, then non-techie departments (like marketing and management) will not feel part of the audience and will not look at it carefully. Problems won't be spotted until it's too late.

Like good code, the best specifications are written from the perspective of the reader, not the writer. The information is organized to make it comprehensible to a newcomer, rather than convenient for the author. Blaise Pascal once apologized, "I made this letter longer than usual because I lack the time to make it short." Good writing is concise and doesn't hide the main point behind a wall of words. This does require more work and will take more time, but it's worth it if the result is simpler to understand.

Don't feel compelled to write reams of boring prose in a specification. Consider using devices to compress it and make it easier to read. Bulleted and numbered lists, diagrams, headings and subheadings, tables, and judicious use of whitespace break up the flow and help the reader to create a mental map of the material.

Complete

A specification should be self-contained and complete. That doesn't mean it should contain *all* possible information; it is perfectly acceptable to reference other relevant documents, as long as the reference is precise (consider document revisions in your references) and will allow the reader to easily locate the document.

The level of detail in a specification should be significantly less than the detail in the implementation; otherwise it is either overly prescriptive or too dense to understand. People tend to ignore complicated specifications, so they become abandoned. Left festering in a corner, they only serve to confuse readers who don't realize that they're no longer authoritative.

Verifiable

A specification for a software component interface will lead to the production of two things: the software implementation and a test harness to verify it. The contents of a specification must, therefore, be verifiable. In practice, this largely equates to being correct, unambiguous, and complete.

Modifiable

Nothing is set in stone, neither code nor documents. If a specification needs updating (perhaps to correct a factual error) then this should be easy. A cast-iron specification prevents the world changing underneath your feet. However, it's no use if the specification is wrong. The document must be editable (i.e., you should be able to get to the source, not just a PDF copy), and its release and update procedure must not be too troublesome.

In order to make modifications easily, the document must be carefully structured and no bigger than absolutely necessary.

Self-describing

Each specification must contain at least:

- A *frontsheet*, clearly showing the document title, subtitle, author(s), revision number, date last modified, and document release status (e.g., company confidential, supplied externally under NDA, or a public release).

- An *introduction* to the document, providing a brief summary of its aims, scope, and the target audience.

- All relevant *terms and definitions* that the reader needs in order to understand the contents. (But don't patronize the reader: If your audience is made up of software engineers, don't explain what RAM stands for.)

- A set of *references* to other related or cross-referenced documents.

- A *history* section that lists all important modification and revision information.

Traceable

There should be a document control procedure (akin to a source management system) and a central file store in which all documents reside. Every release version of a specification should be lodged in the repository and must remain be accessible, so you can discover which version of a spec you were working to a year ago; one day you'll need it again. Consider using a revision control system—it's a great tool for versioning any sort of file.

The document frontsheet contains control information (version number, date, author, etc.) so you can check that you have the most up-to-date copy.

KEY CONCEPT *Think about the contents of your specification as you write it. Choose a structure and vocabulary that the audience will understand, and make sure that the document is correct, complete, and self-describing.*

The Specification-Writing Process

*What is written without effort is in
general read without pleasure.*
—Samuel Johnson

Now knowing the types of specification we must produce and what should go in them, we're armed and ready. It's time to write something! The specification-writing process is simple:

1. Select the appropriate document template to start from. This may be provided as part of a defined project development process. If there is no template, base it on an existing specification.
2. Write the document. Okay, this is the hard part. What you write naturally depends on the type of specification.
3. Arrange for the document to be reviewed. Include all the people with an interest in it.
4. Once it's agreed upon (and, if your process demands, formally signed off on), put a versioned copy in the document repository and release it to the appropriate audience.
5. If there are any later problems, raise a change request for the specification and make sure that you understand how the modification affects the scope of your development work. If you don't, then the coding effort will double without anyone noticing.

This is a simple procedure to list, but it isn't simple to do. It's easy to focus only on step 2—we skip the rest for an easy life. But without these other actions, you haven't created a formal identifiable document; this may cause problems later.

Consider these spec-writing guidelines when composing your literary masterpiece. The first few relate to authorship and to your artistic sensibilities:

- Writing usually works best when there is one author per document. It's hard to coordinate multiple authors and accommodate different writing styles. If you are documenting a big system, then split the specification into parts and give one to each person to work on separately. Create an umbrella document that links them all together.

  Contrary to some opinions, it is not at all egotistical to have one person's name on the front of a specification. Someone needs to take credit for it—praise when it's a good job and blame when it's not.

  If you significantly extend someone else's document, don't feel embarrassed to add yourself to the list of authors. But don't remove someone from the author list unless his or her original input has now been removed.

LANGUAGE BARRIERS

I hate definitions.
—*Benjamin Disraeli*

Compose your specification's text very carefully. Compared to code, the English language is full of ambiguity and complexity. These *genuine* newspaper headlines show just how ambiguous seemingly simple English statements can be: "Stolen painting found by tree," "Kids make nutritious snacks," "Red tape holds up new bridge," and "Hospitals are sued by 7 foot doctors."

Specifications are formal documents and they must not be chatty or verbose; this tends to hide the important facts behind a wall of words. Non-native English readers may struggle. However, a terse document is hard to follow. This is a delicate balance, and document review helps to determine the correct style of writing.

Formal documents are written in the third person, in present tense. An accurate selection of words is very important. A useful convention is defined in the Internet RFC document #2119. This defines the following key terms for protocol specifications (which are also very useful in requirements specifications):

Must
The word *must* (or *shall* or *is required to*) means that the following definition is an absolute requirement of the specification.

Must not
The words *must not* (or *shall not*) signify an absolute prohibition of the specification.

Should
Use *should* (or the adjective *recommended*) to indicate an optional requirement—behavior that may be ignored, but only when the full implications are understood and have been carefully considered.

Should not
Use *should not* (or the adjective *not recommended*) to describe a particular behavior that should be avoided unless there are valid reasons to choose it—again, the consequences must be fully understood.

May
Using *may* (or the adjective *optional*) means that an item is truly optional. An implementer can choose to support it or ignore it but, when applied to protocols, it must interoperate with another implementation that made a different choice.

This is the word that should often be used when people write *can*. *Can* is a commonly misused word in specifications and standards; it is ambiguous and, depending on the reader's interpretation, could be taken to mean *must* or *may*.

- The author must be the right person. The marketing department doesn't write your functional specification; it provides requirements. Managers don't design the code; the developer with the right skill and knowledge does it. The author must be capable of writing—it's a skill that's learned, a muscle that requires exercise.

- Each document must have a defined *owner* who takes responsibility for it. The owner may be different from the original author; it might be the technical authority or the document's maintainer now that the primary author has moved on.

Here are some tips for the document writing process:

- It's good to have a *best practice* example of each kind of specification. This will help authors to understand what is expected of them as they write.

- Early drafts of a specification should be marked as such, with a disclaimer stating that it is incomplete. This will prevent people from mistakenly interpreting it as complete—they can't moan at you about the content (yet). Maintain a list of the incomplete sections and open issues within the document itself.

- Document review is important: It checks that the contents are correct and well presented. It is a mechanism to get others' agreement with your decisions and to thereby bestow authority on the document. This is especially important for specifications that are sent outside the project: to the customer or to other departments.

- Once you've finished the specification, don't forget about it. Keep it alive and up to date. A functional specification is not complete when the design phase is over. Requirements inevitably change, and we continue to learn more about the system's operation. Capture all of this in revised specifications.

Why Don't We Write Specifications?

I do not understand what I do. For what
I want to do I do not do, but what I hate I do.
—Romans 7:15

Decent specifications are conspicuous by their absence in the Real World. We know it's not good practice to avoid them, so hasty developers gloss over their absense and pretend that there's no problem. It's not unusual to be given a coding task without an adequate requirements or functional specification. (This is a procedural problem that must be overcome by persistent moaning, education, and abuse of the powers that be.)

But it's equally common for sloppy programmers to sidestep their own document writing. Why is this? There are a few excuses we meet repeatedly. Developers don't write specifications because:

- They don't know that they should
- They forget
- They don't have the time
- They consciously decide not to, thinking they can get by without them ("Who reads specifications, anyway?")

None of these reasons are defensible. An experienced developer certainly shouldn't fall foul of the first two if a specification is an expected deliverable of his or her work.

Programmers like to program, not write long documents. Most programmers don't have good writing skills; they write elegant code but awful English. It's hardly surprising that they try to avoid writing specs: It's hard work, uninteresting, or they just don't like doing it. Often it's seen as a time wasting activity that isn't really necessary. Or they think, *I'll code first, then come back to the documentation later.* Bitter experience shows that this does not happen.

The depressing thought that *no one will ever read my beautiful specification* puts many more programmers off of the idea of committing their brainwaves to prose. And it's probably true: No other soul may ever read your literary masterpiece. But so what? The act of specification writing forces *you* to engage your brain: a very important step. Sure, a few Gurus can code on the run and produce excellent work. But most programmers, whether they admit it or not, simply can't. We need to design. Carefully. First. That design should then be captured: in a document. Potentially, this document will be for your eyes only. But, if one day you hear a higher calling and run off to become a Croatian monk, how can a maintenance programmer pick up your work? The specification will outlive you. Think of it as your legacy.

Not having time is the only scenario that *you* don't have control over: Sometimes a coding task lands in front of you and there genuinely isn't enough time to write a good specification for it. If you have no time to write a specification, then you probably don't have time to write the code properly either. Make sure you're aware of when you're doing things properly and when you're rushing code out without any real discipline—that sort of code really doesn't belong in a production release.

Saving time by avoiding specifications is almost certainly a false economy; specifications help to *save time* communicating. When you write a specification, you only have to describe how the program works once. If you skip this step, at least the same amount of communication happens anyway, but on an ad hoc basis—over a longer space of time and in a less controlled manner. This communication is far less effective and will actually take *longer*, because you will have to explain the same things over and over again with a slightly different spin for each audience.

KEY CONCEPT *It is dangerous and unprofessional to avoid writing specifications. If there isn't enough time to write a specification, there probably isn't enough time to write the code.*

Of course, few people write detailed specifications at home for their own personal pet projects. This is an extreme case of an appropriately detailed specification. Any reasonably large project (which could be determined by the number of source files, modules, developers, or customers) really does require specification support.

In a Nutshell

Words are, of course, the most
powerful drug used by mankind.
—Rudyard Kipling

They're not the most glamorous part of a software developer's life, but specifications are an important part of our code-writing routine. Learn to read and write them effectively—to record the right information in the right place, in a way that will save time and hassle later. But don't become enslaved by a paper-chain bureaucracy.

Good programmers . . .	Bad programmers . . .
• Understand the importance of specifications and use them to make their development lives easier	• Dive headlong into a code task without a thought for design, documentation, or review
• Know the *appropriate* level of documentation required	• Don't think about the text they are writing; they produce unstructured, hard-to-follow specifications
• Want to improve their writing skills and seek reviews and chances to practice	• Avoid writing documents, thinking it's boring and pointless

See Also

Chapter 4: The Write Stuff
Self-documenting code is a solid technique that helps to eliminate some code documentation. Good code is so easy and intuitive to work with that it doesn't need a long manual.

Chapter 18: Practicing Safe Source
Consider change control and a backup strategy for your specifications—they're as vital as your code and need protecting.

Chapter 20: A Review to a Kill
Just like your code, any document you write should be reviewed to ensure that it's correct and of a high quality.

Chapter 22: Recipe for a Program
Specifications are an essential part of the software development process and are often the gates between development phases.

Get Thinking

A detailed discussion of these questions can be found in the "Answers and Discussion" section on page 544.

Mull It Over

1. Is a poor specification better than no specification at all?

2. How detailed does a good specification have to be?

3. Is it important that all the documents in a company/project have a common presentation style?

4. How should you store documents? Should you provide an index of them (by type or by project), for example?

5. How should you conduct a specification review?

6. Does self-documenting code render all specifications useless? Specific ones?

7. How can a document be collaborated on by more than one author?

Getting Personal

1. Who decides on the contents of your documents?

2. Consider your current project. Do you have:

   a. A requirements specification?

   b. An architecture specification?

   c. A design specification?

   d. A functional specification?

   e. Any other specification?

   Are they up to date? Are they complete? Do you know how to get the latest versions? Can you access historical revisions?

3. Do you revision control your documents? If so, how?

A REVIEW
TO A KILL

Performing Code Reviews

Reviewing has one advantage over suicide: in suicide you take it out on yourself; in reviewing you take it out on other people.

—*George Bernard Shaw*

How do you learn to be a good carpenter? You become a carpenter's apprentice. You watch the master work, help him daily, gradually take on more responsibility, and learn from his advice. You don't jump in feet first without any practical ability and expect to churn out quality woodwork right away.

We don't have a version of that in the coding world, even though programming is as much a craft as it is an engineering discipline (possibly more so). A good programmer learns the difference between good and bad code by experiencing it firsthand, discovering what works in Real Life and what doesn't. This is the stuff that books can't teach you, and only a lucky few ever learn these things from a mentor. *Code reviews* are about as close as most of us will ever come to this ideal.

Code reviews (also called *inspections* or *walkthroughs*) are similar to the open source model of software development—providing a structured opportunity for others to eyeball your precious code and for you to inspect others' work. They facilitate knowledge interchange. But their primary goal is to increase software quality. They help you to spot faults before they become raging disasters.

Code reviews also have another subtle advantage: They encourage you to take greater responsibility for your handiwork. When you know that the code isn't just for *you* to look at, but that it will be viewed, used, maintained, and criticized by others, your approach tends to change. You're less likely to make the quick-and-dirty fix that you'll never have time to revise. The accountability brought on by code reviews brings a greater quality to your coding. They help to establish the "collective code ownership" culture described in "Collective Code Ownership" on page 336.

Sound good, don't they? Let's pop the hood and see how they work. . . .

What Is a Code Review?

A review places source code under the microscope—really aiming to criticize and verify it. This is not to ridicule or get at the author, but to improve the quality of software that the team produces. The process normally generates a list of must-fix issues (the size of the list is a reflection of the quality of your programming skills!). Sometimes you will spot improvements that are not worth making now; chalk up those discoveries for future experience.

We look for bugs and any code that could be improved. The code review weeds out problems at several levels:

- The overall design (we check the choice of algorithms and external interfaces).

- The expression of that design in the code (its breakdown into classes and functions).

- The code in each semantic block (we check that each class, function, and loop is correct, follows appropriate language idioms, and is a practical implementation choice).

- Each individual code statement (each must follow project coding standards and best practices).

Code reviews can be:

Personal
   The author carefully and methodically reviews his or her own work to make sure that it's good. Don't get this confused with casually reading your code after typing it; a personal code review is a more detailed and involved task.

One-on-one

You walk another programmer through your code. The other programmer checks the logic and looks out for faults as you lead through it. These reviews tend to be informal, driven by the author. The code is therefore approached from the author's perspective: with his or her set of assumptions, rather than from a more objective, outside view.

Formal

Involving other programmers brings new expertise, more experience, and more eyeballs to the task and shifts the perspective from which the review is run. Large-scale reviews are consequently harder to coordinate and require greater overall effort, but they are more likely to root out problems. It's difficult to delve this deeply in a personal review; often the author is too close to the code, and it's easy to overlook flaws.

This usually takes place in a formal meeting, but it can be run as a virtual review: online, with no physical meeting.

Each type of review can be used at a different time in the development process. One-to-ones might be used daily throughout code development, as an integration review before modifications are committed to the main source tree. Formal reviews are brought in toward the end of code development, as a final software quality audit.

Apart from the obvious benefits of correct code, reviews have other useful side effects. The cross fertilization that comes from looking at each other's code ensures that coding style is more uniform across a whole project. A review also spreads knowledge about the inner workings of core bits of code, so there is less risk of losing information when people leave a project (a very real problem—see "Team Closure" on page 343).

KEY CONCEPT   *Code reviews are excellent tools to detect and eliminate hard-to-find bugs, to increase code quality, to enforce collective code responsibility, and to spread knowledge.*

When Do You Review?

> *If you are not criticized, you may not be doing much.*
> —*Donald H. Rumsfeld*

In an ideal world, every bit of code would be carefully reviewed prior to release. According to the Software Engineering Institute at Carnegie Mellon University, a thorough code review should take at least 50 percent or more of coding time (personal code review is included in this statistic). (Humphrey 98) That would take longer than most Real World projects are prepared to invest.[1]

KEY CONCEPT   *As we write a system, we need to ask* whether *to review the code and, if so, exactly* which *code to review.*

---

[1] The fact that they're rarely prepared to invest *any* time in code review is a more serious problem.

REVIEWING THE ALTERNATIVES

There are a number of development techniques that have been argued to make formal code reviews redundant. These are:

Pair programming
When you pair program (described in "It's All Going Pair Shaped" on page 319), your code is effectively reviewed on the fly. Two pairs of eyes are better than one and will find many, many more faults—*as* they are entered. However, code reviews can catch even more problems by employing reviewers who are physically and emotionally removed from the implementation work.

Open source
Opening and freely releasing the source code allows anyone to see it, to judge the code's quality, and to fix problems. Some call this the ultimate code review. However, it doesn't actually guarantee that anyone *will* inspect the source. Only really popular open projects have actively maintained codebases. Making your code open source will not instantly bring code review–like benefits.

Unit tests
These are an automatic means to show that a modification hasn't degraded the *correctness* of your code's output (see "Look! No Hands!" on page 144), but they don't help to increase the overall quality of the written code statements. Your code could be a jumbled mess of spaghetti, but if it passes the unit tests, no one will notice. If the unit tests aren't rigorous, bugs could still slip through, regardless.

Not reviewing
Alternatively, you can just trust the programmer to get it right—that's his job after all. If this is a winning strategy, then you don't need to test the code either. Good luck!

None of these, on their own, can honestly replace the code review. Perhaps a combination of them and a particularly effective development team culture would render reviews less necessary, but I've yet to meet a team where that has been the case.

Whether to Review

We've seen that bugs are inevitable, and that you can be sure your code contains some classic mistakes. There will be obvious flaws that you'll find quickly and many more subtle problems that would only be spotted by a fresh pair of eyes approaching the code with no preconceptions. It's hard for the original author to see the inherent faults in his own work—he's too close to the codeface, suffering the psychological *cognitive dissonance* described in. (Weinberg 71) If your code is at all important (clue: it is, or you wouldn't have written it) and if you care about its quality (clue: you do, or you're a disgrace), then you *must* review it.

Not reviewing code drastically increases the chance of faults slipping into your production software. That could spell your embarrassment, a lot of expensive rework and in-the-field upgrades and, in extreme cases, your company's financial ruin. The effort of a code review pales in comparison to the consequences. According to Humphrey, "Students and engineers typically inject 1 to 3 defects per hour during design and 5 to 8 defects when writing code. They only remove about 2 to 4 defects per hour in testing but find 6 to 12 per hour during code review." (Humphrey 97)

People often make excuses to justify avoiding reviews. They say, "The code's too large to review fully," or "It's too complex; no one person could ever understand it—there's no point in even *trying* to review it." If a project can muster enough man-hours to write a large program, it can find enough time to review it. If the code is too complex, then it desperately needs to be reviewed! In fact, it probably needs something a little more drastic. Well-written code is decomposed into self-contained sections that can undergo separate reviews.

Which Code to Review

Any project will quickly produce a ton of source code. For all but the most stringent development processes, there simply isn't enough time to review every last scrap of code. So how do you decide which parts to review? That isn't easy.

You must select the code that will benefit most from review. This is the code that is most likely to be bad or that is most important to the correct functioning of your system. You could try these strategies:

- Select core bits of code in the central components.
- Run a profiler to see where most CPU time is spent, and review those parts of code.
- Run compexity analysis tools, and review the worst offending code.
- Target areas that have already exhibited a high bug count.
- Pick on code written by programmers you don't trust (a code review vendetta!).

The most practical approach is probably a hybrid of all of the above. Pick the best code candidates based on a sober assessment of your team, the codebase, and the current system characteristics (performance, bug count, etc.).

KEY CONCEPT *Select the code you review carefully. If you can't review everything, make informed choices about review candidates. Don't guess—you might waste your precious time.*

Performing Code Reviews

> *That which we persist in doing becomes easier,*
> *not that the task itself has become easier, but that*
> *our ability to perform it has improved.*
> —*Ralph Waldo Emerson*

Simply *having* a code review is not enough. It's not going to solve all the problems itself. You also need to make sure that you review *properly*. The next few sections describe how to do this.

Code Review Meetings

The most common review setting (at least in high-ceremony development processes) is the formal *code review meeting*. There is a fixed agenda (to ensure that no action is forgotten) and a defined ending (not necessarily a time limit, but a definition of exactly which code you are reviewing, and which you aren't—it's very easy to be unclear about this).

An example code review meeting procedure is described below.

Where?

The best place to hold a code review meeting is in a quiet room. The reviewers should not be disturbed. There should be coffee (and, for those who must, tea) available.

A suite of networked laptops with code editors may be useful, as may a computer hooked up to a projector. Old-school programmers swear by print-outs and pen-and-paper notetaking—detaching from the computer screen can help to find new faults. This really depends on how much respect you have for trees and electricity consumption.

When?

Obviously, at a mutually convenient time. Common sense tells us that Friday at 5 PM is not a good time. You need to devote serious time to this, so make sure that you won't be disturbed or distracted.

If the code is too large, split the review into a number of separate sessions. You can't sit people in an enclosed space for hours on end and expect the quality of their review to remain high.

Roles and Responsibilities

One of the most important factors contributing to the success of a code review meeting is who attends. Each attendee should be assigned a specific role; in small groups it is likely that people will take on multiple roles. These roles will include:

Author

Obviously the person who wrote the code should attend the review to describe what he or she has done, refute unfair or incorrect criticism, and listen to (and subsequently act on) valid, constructive feedback.

Reviewers

The reviewers should be carefully picked, people with available time and skill to review. It helps if the code is within their area of expertise or if they are involved with it in some way. For instance, the writer of a library should be invited to review a program that uses the library to diagnose incorrect API usage.

There should be an appropriate number of experienced software engineers present. There should possibly be a representative from the QA or testing department (see "Quality Assurance" on page 132) so QA can be assured of the software's quality and of the quality of the development process.

Chairman

Any meeting needs a chairman, or chaos will ensue (see "Meeting Your Fate" on page 340). This person leads the review and guides the discussion. He or she ensures that the conversation keeps to the point and that the meeting doesn't get sidetracked. Any minor issues that don't need to be discussed in the meeting should be quickly taken offline by the chairman. Given half a chance, programmers will discuss a minute technical detail for hours at the expense of the rest of the code review.

Secretary

The secretary takes minutes. This means writing down all points that arise, to make sure that nothing is forgotten after the review. If there is a review checklist (see the example on page 398), the secretary fills it in. The secretary role should not be fulfilled by the same person who acts as chairman.

Before arrival, everyone is expected to have familiarized themselves with the code. Everyone must have read the supporting documentation (any relevant specifications, etc.)[2] and must be aware of any project coding standards. Whoever organizes the meeting should highlight these documents in the meeting announcement to prevent misunderstanding.

Agenda

To organize the code review meeting:

- The author signals that their code is ready for review.
- The chairman arranges the meeting (booking an appropriate location, setting the time, and assembling the correct set of reviewers).
- All required resources (computers, a projector, printouts, etc.) are arranged.
- The meeting must be called sufficiently ahead of time to allow the reviewers to prepare.
- After the meeting announcement, the author cannot change the code gratuitously—this is not fair to the reviewers.

The code review meeting is run as follows:

- The chairman arranges for the room to be prepared beforehand so the review can start on time.
- The author takes a few minutes (no longer!) to explain the purpose of the code and a little bit about its structure. This should be prior knowledge, but it's surprising what misunderstandings can be caught at this first stage.
- Structural design comments are invited. These are comments relating to the structure of the implementation—not the code at statement level. This could include the breakdown of functionality into classes, the split

---

[2] Naturally, all supporting documentation will have been thoroughly reviewed beforehand.

of code into files, and the style of function writing. (Is it sufficiently defensive, and are there good tests?)

- General code comments are invited. These may relate to a consistent incorrect coding style, bad application of design patterns, or incorrect language idioms.

- The code is carefully stepped through in detail, a line or block at a time, to look for flaws. The things to look out for are described later (in "Code Perfection" on page 395).

- A number of example scenarios of code usage are considered, and the flow of control is investigated. If there is a complete suite of unit tests (there should be) then these detail all the scenarios to explore. This helps the reviewers cover all execution paths.

- The secretary notes all changes required (recording the filename and line number).

- Any issue that might percolate out to the wider codebase is recorded for further investigation.

- When the review has finished, a follow-up step should be agreed upon. The possible scenarios are:

Okay
> The code is fine, no further work is necessary.

Rework and verify
> The code needs some rework, but another code review meeting is unnecessary. The chairman nominates someone to act as *verifier*. When the rework is complete, the verifier checks it against the recorded minutes of the code review meeting.
>
> A reasonable deadline should be imposed for any rework, so that the detail of and reasons for actions stay fresh in people's minds.

Rework and re-review
> The code needs a lot of rework, and another code review is deemed necessary.

Remember, the aim here is to identify problems, not to fix them during the meeting. Some problems require considerable thought to fix, and this is a job for the author (or modifier) after the review has finished.

You may find it useful to use the code review checklist at the end of this chapter when conducting your reviews.

Integration Reviews

Code review meetings are a high-ceremony review method. They're hard work, but they undoubtedly find many problems that would otherwise go undetected.

Other, less intense review procedures exist, providing most of the benefits of code review meetings but packaged in an easier-to-swallow pill. Perhaps the most effective is the *integration review*, performed whenever new code is integrated onto a mainline code branch.

This could be when:

- A new piece of code *is about to be* checked into source control
- A new piece of code *has just been* checked into source control
- A code package is merged from a feature development branch onto the main release branch

At such a point, the code in question is marked for review, and a suitable reviewer is picked: either someone responsible for that module (the code integrator or maintainer[3]) or a *shadow* (or *code buddy*) who is assigned to verify that author's work in a one-on-one review session.

These gated code check-ins are often implemented with a software tool that is integrated with the source control system. They're quite hard to arrange manually and are usually left as a check-in discipline: You are not supposed to check any code in until it has been peer reviewed. This approach is quite hard to police; errors can slip past in hurried, last-minute check-ins.

The actual review step here is usually a lot less formal than the meetings described earlier. The reviewer scans the code to check that it isn't obviously broken, tests it (perhaps reviewing the available unit tests to ensure that they're valid), and then authorizes it for inclusion in the mainline. Only then will the code integrator migrate the verified code into the release tree. For more serious projects, or at more sensitive times (just before a major release milestone, for example) this review step may become much more stringent—requiring more eyeballs and more effort.

Since the reviewer and author don't need to actually meet face to face (although it is preferable to do so), this can be considered a form of virtual review process.

Review Your Attitudes

Do to others as you would have them do to you.
—Luke 6:31

Code reviews require a constructive attitude—you need to approach a review with the correct mindset, or it will be unsuccessful. This works two ways: for the author and the reviewer.

The Author's Attitude

Many people shy away from a code review for fear it will expose their inadequacies. Don't do this. Having your code reviewed is a good way to learn new techniques. You must be humble enough to admit that you're not perfect and are willing to accept criticism from others. Your coding style will improve as you learn from the changes made to your work.

---

[3] Compare this with an open source project's maintainer, who collates patches submitted by other hackers and integrates them into the main source tree, performing periodic software update releases.

METHOD IN OUR MADNESS

Code reviews are a universally acknowledged technique and have been around since people punched their programs into stacks of cards. We've looked at two review procedures in detail, but there are many subtle variants. Programming teams pick a review mechanism to suit their members and the nature of their work. (Poor teams perform no code review at all.)

Here are two other common review methods:

Fagan inspections

This is a well-respected process for formal reviews, much as described in this chapter, defined by Michael Fagan in his *Defect Free Process*. (Fagan 76) Fagan emphasizes the importance of an ability to review and shows how to improve review skills. Fagan inspections identify problems both with the work product and with the process that created it.

Shadowing

This is a a halfway house between pair programming and code reviews. Each code module has a *lead developer* who works on the code. A *shadow developer* is also assigned; periodically the shadow reviews the module with the lead. As design solidifies, the shadow developer verifies the decisions that are made. As the code fills out, the shadow reviews progress and offers constructive advice.

In more formal settings, the shadow is given authority to approve the code for release. No module can be integrated until the shadow developer agrees that it's ready for inclusion in the release build.

KEY CONCEPT   *No one's code is above review and peer scrutiny. Actively invite review of your code.*

As an author, do not be defensive about your code. There is a natural tendency to take all criticism personally and assume that it's an assault on your abilities. To cope with a code review, you need to reduce ego and personal pride. Understand that no one writes perfect code: Even the most awesome programmer's code will be criticized for tedious little problems in a code review.

This is *egoless programming*, described by Gerald M. Weinberg in his 1971 book *The Psychology of Computer Programming*: a timeless description of the critical attitude that makes reviews work. (Weinberg 71) Programmers who aren't afraid of bugs in their code or of others finding those bugs will generate better, safer, more correct software. A willingness for others to help find faults in your work is an essential attribute of the master programmer.

When you're in the hotseat, try not to waste other people's time. Before you present your code for review, run a dummy review by yourself first. Imagine you're presenting your work to the others. You'll be surprised by how many little flaws you'll filter out, and it will help you to be more confident in the real review. Don't rush out half-baked code and expect others to review the flaws away for you.

The Reviewer's Attitude

When reviewing code and making criticism, you must be sensitive. Comments must always be constructive and not intended to lay blame. Do not launch personal attacks on the author. Diplomacy and tact are important. Address your comments to the code, rather than the coder; prefer to say *The code does this*... rather than *You always do this.* ...

Code review is a *peer process*: Every reviewer is considered equal. Seniority doesn't matter, and all views are considered. It is interesting that even the least experienced programmer will have something worth mentioning in a code review. And just as the author learns from the review, so may a reviewer.

Over time, you will perform many, many reviews (especially if you perform integration reviews). Be careful that your review process doesn't become a mundane chore; it'll soon be an ineffective waste of everyone's time. Maintain a positive approach to your code reviewing. As a reviewer, always try to have something useful to say at each review. Sometimes this is easy; sometimes it is very difficult to say anything interesting. But by forcing yourself to make comments, you won't fall into the easy review rut, becoming a yes man who adds nothing to the process.

KEY CONCEPT *The success of a code review depends heavily on the author and reviewers adopting a positive attitude. The aim of a review is to collaboratively improve the code, not to apportion blame or to justify implementation decisions.*

Code Perfection

> *When perfection comes, the imperfect disappears.*
> *—1 Corinthians 13:10*

We haven't yet considered what type of code will pass review and what code will fail. It's beyond the scope of this chapter to describe what good code looks like—the first 15 chapters of this book describe important aspects of high-quality code. As we look for bad code design and hunt software bugs, there are a few recurring themes. The reviewed code must be:

Bug free
> Bugs are our enemy, the nemesis of good software development. We must be confident about the quality of our work and need to find faults as early as possible in the development process. The earlier we try to find problems, the more we are likely to find and fix and the less cost and hassle they incur (see "The Economics of Failure" on page 157).

Correct
> The code must meet all relevant standards and its requirements. Ensure that all variables are of the correct type (e.g., there is no chance of numeric overflow). Comments must be completely accurate. The code must meet any memory size or performance requirements (especially important for embedded platforms). Check that there is appropriate use of libraries and that all function parameters are correct.
>
> The code is validated to conform with its requirements and functional specifications. The content of its specification is taken to be correct; if it wasn't, then the task would be herculean! Sometimes code review

comments might feed up to the specification (for example, where clarification is needed), but this is not our goal at code review—don't get sidetracked into discussions on whether the specification is wrong; the secretary should record the issue in the minutes, and the review should continue.

Complete

The code must implement the entire functional specification. It must have been integrated and debugged satisfactorily and pass all test suites. The test suites must be comprehensive.

Well structured

Check that the implementation's design is sound, that the code is easy to understand, and that there is no duplication or redundant code. Look for any obvious *cut-and-paste programming*, for example.

Predictable

There must be no unnecessary complexity and no unexpected surprises. The code should not be self-modifying, must not rely on magic default values, and must not contain the subtle chance of infinite loops or recursion.

Robust

The code is defensive. Wherever possible, it protects against detectable run-time errors (divide by zero, number-out-of-range errors, etc.). All input should be checked (both function parameters and program input). The code handles all error conditions and is exception safe. All appropriate signals are caught.

Data checking

Bounds checking is performed on C-style array access. Other similarly insidious data access errors are avoided. Multithreaded code has correct use of mutexes to prevent race conditions and deadlock. The return values of *all* system/library calls are checked.

Maintainable

The programmer has been wise in his or her use of comments. The code is kept under correct revision control. There is appropriate configuration information. The code formatting meets house standard. It compiles quietly, without spurious warnings.

KEY CONCEPT   *If you don't know what good code looks like, then you can't make a valid judgment of other people's work.*

Beyond the Code Review

A review process is key to the production of any high-quality item, so it is not solely useful for source code development. A similar review process is used for specification documents, lists of requirements, and so on.

In a Nutshell

It is easier to be critical than to be correct.
—Benjamin Disraeli

Code reviews are an essential part of the software development process and help us to maintain a high quality of code. Just as an apprentice learns a trade from knowledge passed on, code reviews spread knowledge and teach coding capability. As more of a peer-to-peer than master-apprentice activity, they provide a learning opportunity for author and reviewer alike.

Write your code to be reviewed. Remember that it's never just for you to read; other people must be able to maintain it as well. The author is always accountable for the quality of his or her work. A good programmer cares more about crafting great code than his or her own pride.

Good programmers . . .

- Desire code reviews and are confident in their code quality
- Accept others' opinions and learn from them
- Can sensitively and accurately comment on other people's code

Bad programmers . . .

- Are scared of code reviews and frightened of others' opinions
- Take criticism badly; they are defensive and easily offended
- Use reviews to demonstrate their superiority over lesser abled coders; their comments are unduly harsh and unconstructive

See Also

Chapters 1 through 15
Each of the opening chapters of this book describes important aspects of good code.

Chapter 9: Finding Fault
A description of the types of bugs that may exist in your code.

Chapter 19: Being Specific
Code is reviewed against its *specification*. The specification also requires careful reviewing.

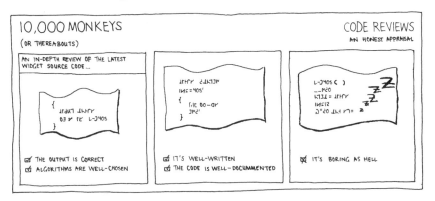

Checklist

Many review processes involve a *checklist*—a set of characteristics of good (passable) code to check off as you go along. If your code doesn't meet these criteria, then it has failed the review. These checklists vary in detail, length, and subject matter.

The following code review checklist is an example. You can use it to help direct your review work. Unlike some checklists, it doesn't systematically list every potential problem in every possible language; it just helps to guide the review process and figure out when to continue to the next review step.

Code review — CHECKLIST

Use this form to help you perform a code review.

About the code

Module name: _____
Version reviewed: _____
Code author: _____

Reviewed by: _____
Date: _____
Language: _____
Number of files: _____

Automated inspection

☐ The code compiles without errors
☐ The code compiles without warnings
☐ There are unit tests
 ☐ They are sufficient (include all boundary cases, etc.)
 ☐ The code passes them

☐ The code is kept under source control
☐ The code has been tested with inspection tools
 Tool name   Results
 _____   _____
 _____   _____
 _____   _____

☐ Continue to next section   ☐ Stop review here

Design

☐ The code is complete (against its specification)
☐ There is a good choice of algorithms
☐ Optimizations are necessary and appropriate
☐ Any missing functionality is marked clearly in the code

General observations about the code's design

☐ The code is well structured
☐ There is design documentation
 ☐ The code matches the documentation

☐ Continue to next section   ☐ Stop review here

General code comments

General comments about the quality of the written code

Style
 ☐ The code layout is clear
 ☐ It follows project style guidelines
 ☐ There is a good (unambiguous) public API
 ☐ There is a good choice of names

Defensive programming
 ☐ Array access is guarded and safe (C/C++)
 ☐ There is a correct choice of types
 ☐ All input is validated
 ☐ There is no use of compiler-specific features

General comments
_____
_____
_____

Error handling
 ☐ Error conditions are routinely handled
 ☐ Assertions are used to validate logic
 ☐ The code is exception safe
 ☐ Errors are propogated, not hidden
 ☐ There are no resource leaks

☐ The code uses multiple threads
 ☐ It is thread safe
 ☐ There isn't potential for deadlock

Structure
 ☐ There is no redundant code
 ☐ There is no cut-and-paste programming

☐ Continue to next section   ☐ Stop review here

Statement-level review

Fill out the table below, and move on to a new sheet as required. Rate issues on a scale from 0 (cosmetic/nice to have) to 5 (must fix).

File	Line	Issue	Rating
____	____	_____	____
____	____	_____	____
____	____	_____	____
____	____	_____	____
____	____	_____	____
____	____	_____	____

Continue on a separate sheet (or mark up a paper copy of the code)

Follow-up

Conclusion:
 ☐ Code OK
 ☐ Rework and verify
 ☐ Rework and re-review

Record the outcome of the review here

Complete work by: _____

Assigned verifier: _____

Get Thinking

A detailed discussion of these questions can be found in the "Answers and Discussion" section on page 547.

Mull It Over

1. Does the required number of reviewers depend on the size of the code being reviewed?
2. Which tools are useful aids for code reviewing?
3. Should you perform a code review before or after running it through source code checking tools?
4. What preparation is required for a code review meeting?
5. How do you differentiate review comments to be acted upon immediately from those to chalk up for experience on the next project?
6. How do you run a virtual review meeting?
7. How useful are informal code reviews?

Getting Personal

1. Does your project perform code reviews? Does it perform *enough* code reviews?
2. Do you work with any programmers whose code is considered to be above review?
3. What percentage of your code has ever been subject to code review?

HOW LONG IS A PIECE OF STRING?

The Black Art of
Software Timescale Estimation

I never guess. It is a shocking habit—destructive to the logical faculty.
      —Sherlock Holmes (Sir Arthur Conan Doyle)

How long *is* a piece of string? Or for our purposes, how long does a piece of string take? It's as simple a question to answer, and it makes about as much sense.

This chapter is about *software timescale estimation*, an important skill of the professional programmer. It's one of the mystical black arts of development, based more on hunches than science, with frequently inaccurate results. It's complicated, but an essential part of the software development process, and is something that every programmer must learn to do.

The rules of the software factory are necessarily governed by economics: the flow of money. Timing estimates are important, since the bulk of the cost of software development is manpower—programmers aren't cheap. Development environments and hardware costs pale into insignificance. To make a software product, we must know how much work is involved, how many people are required to build it, and when it will be completed and ready to make money. This tells us how much construction will cost. The marketing department will predict how much it will make in sales. These two predictions go head-to-head in a dramatic fight to the death; the bean counters draw up budgets to work out whether a project is financially viable.

This is an odd thing called *planning*, something at which most programmers don't excel. Don't worry: That's why we have managers. But you have to understand the rules of the game if you really want to play well. Writing commercially successful software requires a huge amount of foresight and planning. Oh, and nerves of steel.

To construct a development plan, we perform a high-level design of the software system, break it into components, and estimate how long each component will take to write. There's rarely enough time to seriously scope and design each one, so this is a very rough science. Choosing a software development model (see "Development Processes" on page 425), we assemble the estimates on a plan, spread across a number of programmers, and use this to work out the economics. The quality of this plan is clearly founded on the quality of the timescale estimates. Catastrophically bad guesses could spell financial ruin, so it's important stuff!

Without plans, you're creating products by luck, not on purpose. Estimation is an integral part of the project planning process—but that doesn't mean that it's done by the project planners! The only people able to provide timescale information are the programmers who have to do the work. That's you! This is part of the commercial reality of life in the software factory.

A Stab in the Dark

In any company, on any project, at any point in time, software timescale estimates are nothing more than educated guesses—or else they wouldn't be estimates. Guesswork doesn't sound very professional, does it? But it's the best you can do: You'll never know exactly how long a task will take until it's complete, when it's generally too late for the information to be useful.[1]

The quality of an estimate is primarily determined by how well you understand the task being estimated. That is, how well you *really* understand it, not how well you *think* you do. It also depends on how much time you have to create the estimate, and therefore how much effort you can put into a realistic design effort or feasibility review. With a very precise specification, you can make an estimate in a short time; with a vague specification, it could

---

[1] Except, of course, as experience to base future estimates on.

take ages. A reasonable, justified estimate might require several prototypes to investigate implementation choices—different options could have radically different time consequences and levels of inherent risk.

Without enough time to do this, you need to concoct a worst-case figure that development should not exceed. The less effort you put into a timescale estimate, the less the confidence you may have in the figure, and the greater the likely variance of reality from the estimate. Development could take half of the estimate, the full period or—even worse—could require more time. We manage this risk by building *contingency* into the development plan to balance risky areas. How much contingency do you provide? You have to guess! We'll look at this later.

KEY CONCEPT   *Software timescale estimation requires* educated guesswork. *Each estimate should come with a gauge of your confidence in it.*

While good estimates are reasoned and justified, bad estimates are little more than a stab in the dark. This is a standard engineering issue, requiring a perceptive and flexible management. It has been an engineering issue for centuries.[2] Managers and planners deal with estimations for the whole project. That's *exceptionally* hard. We'll just look at estimating single programming jobs. Thankfully, that's not exceptionally hard, just *really* hard.

Why Is Estimation So Hard?

I live in Cambridge, UK; my family lives in Bristol. Software timescale estimation is like estimating how long it will take me to visit them. Given a strong tailwind and no traffic, I can tell you how long the drive takes. But if there is road work or a traffic jam, if my car breaks down, I leave late, or I travel at rush hour, then this estimate becomes a lot less reliable. Foreseeing some of these problems, I will commit to a likely arrival window. I know the best-case journey time; I have an idea of the worst case (I've had some nightmare trips). I can judge an expected arrival time somewhere between the two. However, I can't ever fully account for the unforeseen—if my car breaks down, I'm stuck. Mobile phones are helpful in this situation: If I'm going to be late, I can call and let my folks know to keep dinner heated (and preferably out of the dog's bowl).

The software development process follows a similar pattern. When planning software, there are foreseeable potential problems to account for, third-party dependencies to manage, and a need for contingency to cope with the unforeseen. You can give a best-case development time for a slice of work, and you need to consider a worst-case time. Of course, the impact of a bad guess isn't just your dinner inside the family pet—it's the success or failure of a project, and possibly the solvency of your company.

---

[2] For a Biblical example, see Luke 14:28!

> ## THE WEAKEST LINK
>
> Unforeseen problems can trip you up in unexpected places. Recently, my linker couldn't cope with the size of executable image I was generating, and I needed to go off and fix the linker before I could run my code. The development time more than tripled its original estimate.

This begins to show us why estimating the length of a development task is so hard and so crucial. There are plenty of things conspiring to make this a tricky task:

- There are lots of variables to consider. They come with the inherent complexity of the problem, the implications of your code design, and the existing software ecosystem it must fit into. Some of those variables may change from day to day.

- Requirements will change under your feet, leading to software scope increases. As the feasibility of a project is investigated, new problems and user-level requirements are unearthed at a phenomenal rate. This makes the estimation job tricky—you've got to work hard to keep up with it all (see "Requirements Specification" on page 371 for strategies to manage this).

- You can't give an accurate estimate without knowing *all* the work involved. Perhaps you'll need to rework existing libraries that don't provide enough functionality or refactor to enable safe extension of existing code. If you haven't discovered this, then your estimate will be too low.

- Few projects start on a blank canvas. You must learn the existing system before you can estimate how long work will take. You seldom have time to do this properly before the estimate is delivered.

- If the task is something that has not been attempted before, then it is harder to figure how long it will take. You have no prior experience to base the estimate on.

- Many projects rely on third parties, and these dependencies can prove to be nightmarish. The source of the dependency could be an operating system vendor, a small but significant code library, an external specification, even the customer. You can't control the third-party delivery; your estimates depend on it shipping on time. This increases the risk of delay and must be monitored carefully.

Estimation is hard. But that doesn't absolve us from responsibility. We must account for the things that are genuinely foreseeable: Like road work or bad weather, we can reasonably expect some of these pitfalls. You need to find the right balance of pessimism, optimism, and—somewhere in the middle—realism.

KEY CONCEPT   *Creating timescale estimates is a genuinely hard task. Don't underestimate how much work is involved. Appreciate the repercussions of making a bad estimate.*

The story doesn't end there: It's not just making the estimate that's hard. Living with the consequences can be just as painful.

- Estimates become contractual, used to set delivery schedules with customers. Once set in concrete, these dates are hard to move and costly to get wrong.

- It is hard to work to someone else's estimate—were you not up to the task if you miss a deadline, or was the estimate wrong?

- New tasks are often discovered during development which need accounting for and slotting into the schedule, pushing everything else back. Similarly, you'll only discover specification problems once the development work is actually under way. These specification changes will affect the amount of work required, and therefore the time estimate.

- There are *always* unforeseen problems. You can absorb the impact of small problems by working a little harder to stay on schedule. You didn't need to sleep this month, did you? But large problems introduce buckets of extra work and cause schedule mayhem.

- The estimate is just *another* responsibility: You are not only accountable for creating the code, and for it to be good, well-designed, maintainable code; you also have to deliver it to a timescale that you have promised. Pity the poor programmers!

Under Pressure

The software factory is not a reasonable place, and the temptation to give optimistic estimates is strong. Programmers new to the estimation game are particularly vulnerable. There is pressure from above to promise short schedules so that we can win contracts, announce new releases, maintain internal political stability, and so on. This is an understandable, sad reality; no company exists in a vacuum, and the shareholders want to be kept in caviar and champagne.

But the pressure isn't entirely from above. It also comes from a programmer's personal pride. Techies like to promise an optimistic timescale; we are motivated people who are proud of what we deliver and how fast we can do it. It's tempting to think, "Oh, it shouldn't take too long." But there's a very real difference between a quick code hack or prototype effort and a full, production-ready piece of work. Our timescales must be grounded in reality, not in hopeful ideals.

KEY CONCEPT   *Everyone (including you) wants shorter development timescales. Don't kid yourself about what is technically possible in the given development time. Don't promise a hack timescale when you must deliver production code.*

We must be aware of this pressure and react to it carefully. Beware of the danger of an extreme opposite reaction. It is easy to be a pessimistic doomsayer, to imagine a task lasting indefinitely, and compensating with a stupidly large timescale estimate. The very real danger of an overestimate is that projects inevitably expand to fit the available time! You'll always find bits of code to polish when there are a few days spare.

In an ideal world, project deadlines are established *after* a feasibility review that proves the project is possible in reasonable time. The Real World is rarely that kind. Instead, you are given a deadline ("Get it shipping by Christmas"), and then have to figure out how to deliver. If the work doesn't fit, you must negotiate how you'll get there: Remove features, add programmers, outsource risky parts, or perhaps provide a later upgrade with more functionality. Sometimes this planning becomes more of a marketing exercise and gets quite creative!

No one said that it was supposed to be easy.

A WAR STORY

The company had just taken the biggest and most strategically important order in its five-year history. This one was *make or break*. Sales fought hard to close the deal, agreeing to a hard customer deadline: The software *must* ship by the end of the year. With contracts signed, everyone patted themselves on the back.

But no one had the time (or wit) to confer with the technical staff to ensure that the project was feasible. It wasn't. Managers started panicking, but with an immobile deadline and fixed feature set, there wasn't much they could do. The engineers complained and waved their project plans aloft, but were told to "just make it fit." They worked hard day after day, late into the night, and were soon exhausted. Each week saw them slip further away from the hopelessly optimistic schedule.

In one last herculean effort, they completed the code by their deadline, only to be tripped up by an unforeseen hardware problem that delayed the project by two months. There was no contingency in the plan to account for this disaster.

The project was a failure, the engineers got burned out, nerves were fraught, and the customer was unhappy. Not long into the next project, most of the development team quit.

Practical Ways to Estimate

With the increasing pressure to be prophets as much as programmers, how do we meet expectations? Estimation, like many other skills, is something you get better at it with experience. It's not an old man's game, but if you don't work against a backdrop of schedules and set yourself targets to work toward, then you won't grow in the skill. Practice makes perfect.

In the Real World, we rarely have the luxury of practice projects or a sandbox to experiment with timescale estimation. Somewhere along the road from junior programmer to guru, you have to pick up this skill! Sadly there is no magic formula or easy recipe for coming up with an estimate. But following these simple steps will immeasurably improve your accuracy:

1. Break the task down into the smallest blocks possible, effectively performing a first pass of system design.

2. When you reach a fine resolution with suitably comprehensible parts, provide a timescale estimate for each block in *man-hours* or *man-days*.

3. Once you've estimated all of the individual timescales, place them back-to-back, add up their durations, and voilà: an instant timescale estimate.

This strategy works because you can fully comprehend and accurately estimate a series of smaller activities more easily than one gargantuan task. Estimates should *never* be made in units larger than man-days: Such large tasks show that you don't really understand the problem yet; your estimate cannot be at all reliable. Mercilessly decompose large tasks until you end up with fine-grained—estimatable—work units.

KEY CONCEPT *Time estimates should be made for small tasks whose individual scope is easy to understand. The measurement should be in units of man-hours or man-days.*

Of course, development work can often be parallelized between people; by breaking it into small comprehensible parts, we can juggle tasks around and work out how to run them concurrently, bringing forward the completion date. This becomes a project planning issue.

Set aside a reasonable amount of time to make an estimate. The requisite high-level design is not immediate; don't presume that timescales can be guessed easily. You'll fool yourself by producing a finger-in-the-air estimate with no foundation on prior experience and no basis in a system design.

It is vital to consider *every* activity that will be required to deliver the software. This means including time for:

- Performing adequate thoughtful design
- Any exploratory work or prototyping required
- The actual code implementation work
- Debugging
- Writing unit tests
- Integration testing
- Writing the documentation
- Any research or training you'll be undertaking in the period

This list shows that less time than you might expect is spent writing code, compared to other peripheral activities. Programming isn't just about cutting code; don't forget to include testing and documentation in your timescale estimates. They are essential. Without testing and documentation, you'll deliver code that doesn't work properly and can't be fixed later because no one knows how to use it.

Don't try to calculate *elapsed time* (by incorporating distractions from other projects, reading email, browsing the web, drinking coffee, and answering the call of nature). It will inevitably be very different from the actual time spent on the task. The task may run concurrently with another, or be interrupted to provide space for another project. We deal with this on a project plan (described in "The Planning Game" on page 409).

How conservative should your estimate be? Should you veer toward optimism or pessimism? The correct answer is: The estimate must be realistic. Anticipate likely problems and factor them in, but don't invent 1,000 ways a simple task could fail and use it as an excuse to give an inflated estimate. Don't overestimate just to cover your tracks, or to give yourself more slack to fill with games of solitaire. Our individual task estimates can't mitigate for everything that can go wrong. Risk should be managed at the *project level*; the scheduler takes our estimates and works them into a reasonable plan with suitable contingency.

To make more accurate estimates, consider these important issues:

- The more concrete and specified a project is, the easier it is to estimate. Have you been given a good spec?

    Without a specification, there is no traceability, and a lot of the work involved in each package will be assumed. Two people could assume very different things about the project scope and expect different things at the project deadline. Rigorous specifications avoid this problem.

    Delivering the wrong system on time can be just as damaging as delivering the right one, late. If there is no specification, write one and get it approved by the task stakeholders.[3] At the very least, document all assumptions that you have made about the work.

- The more functionality requested, the harder the estimate is to make. Try to shave off all unnecessary work. An excellent approach is to stage the delivery of the software, giving estimates for each deliverable iteration.

    Feed estimate information back upstream. The project decision-makers can then balance the importance of each requirement against its technical difficulty. It helps to see which small feature requests will double development time.

- If you don't fully comprehend the entire problem, then you'll make a very bad estimate. Spend time getting to know exactly what the software must do. If you need more time to make an estimate, then ask for it, or indicate your confidence in the time values. Never guess an estimate and hope that it's about right—if you can't justify an estimate, then don't give it.

- If the task depends on third-party input, then it is harder to estimate. Who is responsible for chasing the third party for delivery? You may need to factor this into your development estimate. Get the third party's estimated delivery date, and then add time to integrate its work with your codebase (it never "just slots in"). Consider how much you trust the third party, and include a suitable amount of contingency as a buffer to accommodate problems.

- Different people will work on the same task at different rates. This is natural; everyone has a different set of skills, level of experience, confidence level, and relative number of distractions (e.g., older projects vying for attention or home commitments). You need to gauge how fast you work, and have a good understanding of the task you're embarking on. Estimation is personal.

KEY CONCEPT   *Understand whether you're creating an estimate for work that* you *will do (on a system* you *understand well) or that someone else will do (who might have to learn it first).*

---

[3] Of course, that will take time you didn't plan for!

- Don't accept pressure from above to be optimistic. Don't promise unrealistic timescales, thinking you can make it up if you work overtime. Have an appropriate response to managers who say, "It just has to be done faster."

- Perhaps most importantly, *never* plan up front on working overtime.

A simple way to improve your estimates is to ask for help with them. If you don't understand a problem, then find someone who does, and ask for his or her opinion. James Surowiecki's book *The Wisdom of Crowds* describes how large groups of people can be smarter than an elite few. Taking this extreme approach, get all the developers in your team to give rough estimates for all tasks on the plan, and then take the average of their individual estimates. That estimate might not be too far off!

KEY CONCEPT *Don't make estimates in isolation. Solicit other people's opinions to help improve your estimates.*

The Planning Game

A few disconnected timescale estimates are no use to anyone. You have to join them up and convert them into something useful: a project plan with which you can manage the development schedule. Based on their individual timescale estimates, tasks are assembled on a timeline and allotted to developers. Dependencies between tasks are identified and factored in to the plan (obviously, dependent tasks cannot start before their dependencies have completed). The final result is a pictorial chart with time running along the horizontal axis and tasks positioned concurrently on it, looking something like Figure 21-1 (a variant of the classic *Gantt chart*).

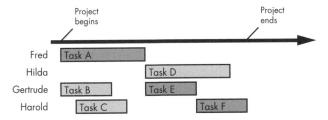

Figure 21-1: A Gantt chart

Project planning is about allocating tasks to developers and working out how to schedule development effort. But that's the easy half of the game. The important part is *risk management*—creating a safe and sensible plan in the face of uncertainty and hidden traps.

The safest project plans:

Reduce the *critical path*
This is the single line of back-to-back tasks that trace from the start to the end of the project, shown by the darker blocks in the diagram above. A slip in any one of these tasks will force back all the tasks depending on it and push out the final deadline.

There is always—by definition—a critical path on the plan. This is what gives project planners grey hair! We aim for the optimum juxtaposition of tasks to provide the smallest (or least risky) critical path.

Are not massively parallel

The standard planning misconception when trying to compress a large project is that throwing more developers at a problem will speed it up. This rarely works. An extra burden is imposed when managing more people—there are more lines of communication, more people to coordinate, and more points of failure. This is the subject of Brooks's seminal essay, "The Mythical Man-Month." (Brooks 95)

You mustn't over-parallelize a project plan, and you shouldn't parallelize individual developers, either. If you put one developer against two tasks concurrently, you can't expect them to finish in the same length of time as those two tasks serialized. This sounds obvious, but it often happens in practice: You might be asked to support an old project and simultaneously start development work on another. Significant time is taken up switching between tasks, which reduces your overall efficiency. If you did the two tasks back to back, then you'd complete faster (but probably fail to meet the business requirements of your organization).

Are not too long

A lengthy project plan is too ambitious. One small problem on the critical path at any point could jeopardize the entire project.

This is where iterative and incremental development (see "Iterative and Incremental Development" on page 432) brings benefits, by breaking large development schedules into smaller, less risky iterations that can be more easily managed. This makes the plan more dynamic; it is effectively re-created at each delivery point. Although this approach is inherently safer and will highlight problems earlier in the development process, it consequently involves more work overall. Many managers don't like this—they like the illusion of an up-front waterfall plan that cannot be deviated from.

Good plans don't just butt timescale estimates back to back. They account for the reality of the software factory and build in important risk-reducing structures. This includes accounting for:

Vacation

The amount of vacation allocated to each developer is known in advance and must be built in to the schedule. We must also include public holidays and any company shutdown over a Christmas break. On average, a developer takes half a day a week as vacation.

Loading

To be realistic, the plan must factor in normal interruptions (meetings, training, sickness, and so on). It's normal to employ an 80 percent loading on the plan for each developer to accommodate this. People who are in more demand are spread more thinly. You must be honest about this, or the "popular" developers will slip against the schedule, despite their hard work, and will quickly become frustrated.

Contingency

This is the biggie. You have to account for the problems seen looming on the horizon and provide space for the unforeseen disasters that might stand between you and your release date. This is where the risk management rubber hits the road.

Risk is best managed at this project level, rather than within individual timescale estimates. On a development plan, we can accommodate potential problems by making informed judgments in full sight of the whole development process. The alternative, a series of pessimistic estimates placed on a plan, will inevitably be wildly out.

The million dollar question is: How much contingency should you add in? You can't simply multiply the plan by three and call it contingency! A good strategy is to give each task a confidence value. Based on this, provide an extra pseudo-task on the plan for the riskiest tasks as "danger time." Make this a fraction of the original task length, based on your confidence value.

Integration

A task is not done once a component is code complete and unit tested. Reserve adequate time to glue all of the components together, and to test that the entire system works as expected. There will be debugging required and issues that only surface when components meet (performance issues or interface mismatches, for example).

Support

The longer people have been within an organization, the more call there will be on them to support old projects, answer bug reports from the field, and so on. Ensure that this is incorporated into their loading, and that they then stick to the plan, highlighting when other projects are demanding more of their time.

Projects slip subtly when key people are stretched in all directions.

Mopping up

Provide time to tidy up at the end of your plan. In the battle to release software, corners are cut to meet the deadline. This is known as amassing *technical debt.* Despite our preaching about good design and coding practices, this isn't necessarily evil; it's quite pragmatic. However, you must set aside time to tidy up and maintain a good, clean codebase. Otherwise, the next development iteration will build upon a broken, crufty codebase. Left unaddressed, this increasing pile of short-term hacks will become a burden to your programmers.

Think of this exercise as part of the *previous* job (despite occurring after the release deadline), and not as the beginning of the next one. Pay off your debt in the project that accrued it.

Never let these tidy-ups been viewed as optional extras; they are an important integral part of the project. In the frantic world of the software factory, optional tasks placed at the end of the schedule simply will not happen. Guard these tasks carefully.

KEY CONCEPT *Create development schedules that will leave your codebase in a clean state. Plan to repay your technical debt.*

An in-depth investigation of project planning is outside the scope of this book; it's a large, complex task. But it is important to understand the basic principles. You must be able to develop software according to a plan, and must understand the rationale behind a plan to truly understand what you're asked to do.

The are many planning models: formal methods of making educated guesses. *Program Evaluation and Review Technique (PERT)* is a classic planning method developed in the 1950s by the US Navy. It's like my arrival window calculation when driving to Bristol. For each task, you estimate three times corresponding to different likelihoods of meeting delivery dates: a best case, worst case, and likely case. This ties into a scheduling procedure that identifies the critical path and calculates the best- and worst-case project completion time. The bigger the gap between each task's estimate, the bigger the risk associated with the task. Perhaps it will need more careful management or to be given to a more experienced member of the staff.

Boehm's *Constructive Cost Model (COCOMO)* dates from 1981 and is an estimation model based on analysis of real software projects. It has evolved into *COCOMO II*, which more accurately reflects the nature of modern software projects. (Boehm 81) *Projects in Controlled Environments* (known by the rather contrived acronym *PRINCE*) is a classic British piece of bureaucracy embodied in project management form; if it could mandate standing in queues, it would![4] Its scope is the entire project life cycle, from start to closure. The PRINCE planning process comprises seven steps, covering designing the plan, through estimation and scheduling, to plan completion. It too has evolved, into a method imaginatively called *PRINCE2*.

Keep Up!

> *How does a project get to be a year late?*
> *... One day at a time.*
> —*Frederick P. Brooks Jr.*

As work slips and the project deadline looms, engineers work very hard and get little credit. The idea of rigorous testing is squeezed out in a mad rush to get something passable out the door on time. Bad estimates are a prime cause of this software circus. They foster managers' incorrect assumptions about the difficulty of the development work, since they have no way to know the schedule was incorrect in the first place. When we make an estimate, it is therefore essential to get it right.[5]

---

[4] Queueing is a popular British pastime, like drinking tea and playing cricket.

[5] Ironically, *good* estimates can also cause this problem. DeMarco and Lister recount a genuine episode where a project lead reported their 100 percent confidence that the project would complete on time and to budget. (DeMarco 99) The managers, taken aback by this unexpected piece of good news, consequently decided to bring the deadline forward! No matter how good the engineer, you can always build a better manager to destroy his or her hard work!

IT'S ALL ABOUT PLANNING

The development team was getting quite large, and our working space had become *really* cramped. After a lot of effort, a new office was found and the team was told on Friday that we'd be working in the new location on Monday. Over the weekend, all the computers, servers, cables, routers, printers—everything—would be manhandled into vans and transported to the new location. We were assured that it would be seamless and that everything would be ready on Monday morning.

On Monday morning, we turned up at the new office and, sure enough, everything had been set up and worked perfectly! All the IT infrastructure had been installed. The servers were back online and fully operational. Everyone's workspace had been set up. A truly herculean effort.

But there was one small problem: There were no chairs. Not one. They had somehow been forgotten in the move plan, had gotten lost, and couldn't be found anywhere! We had no chairs for three days.

Now *that's* what you call planning.

Given a realistic estimate for a software task, there are a few key ways to keep to schedule and prevent this kind of last-minute squeeze:

- When starting a new task, check whether or not the allotted timescale really *is* practical—especially if you didn't have the luxury of making the estimate yourself. Even if you did make the estimate, start by verifying it. Don't rush headlong into a code editor, *hoping* that you can complete on time; be sure that you are genuinely able to deliver. A little sanity checking up front can save you from a world of pain and embarrassment later.

- Refer to the schedule—it matters. Keep a constant eye on how long you're taking against scheduled time. Write down your timescales and keep them close at hand. Add personal estimates for any intermediate tasks that don't figure on the main software plan, and run yourself as a mini-project. If you hit your internal milestones, you'll have more chance of keeping on track with your externally visible timescales. Repeatedly review your list—at least once a day.

  If you discover that you won't hit the deadline, make this known as soon as possible so the plan can be adjusted. Like phoning ahead when I'm traveling to Bristol, it is better to get this fact out in the open as soon as possible. If the possibility of overrun is foreseen, then different scheduling decisions can be made to minimize the impact of the overrun.

  This happens far too rarely in practice. If an important project has five programmers who must all report their progress, then none of them wants to be the first one to admit falling behind the schedule. This is known as playing *schedule chicken*. The result is everything seems to be fine, but then suddenly the project is hugely late. It was getting late one day at a time, but no wanted to admit it. Break this cycle and broadcast a warning as early as possible.

KEY CONCEPT   *Continually monitor your progress against the plan. Then you will never be surprised that your task has slipped.*

- Do as much work as necessary, and no more. It might be fun to add that cute extra feature. But don't. There are more important—planned—things to be done. Ask for important extras to be scheduled in later if they aren't *really* needed now. An ill-chosen detour on my route to Bristol will really set back my arrival time—even if it is a lovely scenic drive—so I take the sensible straight route to arrive on time.

- Careful design exploiting modularity tends to reduce component dependency, and so reduces the ill effects of slippage and the bunching up of tasks on the schedule. Agree on component interfaces early on, and provide stub components so development can continue while others parts of the system are being built.

- Write good code, with a thorough set of unit tests. As keen craftsmen, this should be self-evident! It helps to reduce debug and maintenance time radically.

  Don't forget to finish coding with time to document and test thoroughly. Don't build up to a final coding sprint in the last few days of the schedule. You need time to prove that your code works. Otherwise, you'll slip as debugging inches out beyond your deadline. If you don't have time to complete all this work, say so and get the timescale extended. Don't skip these things—they'll bite you later.

- Watch out for changing requirements and specifications and track how this will affect your timescales. If it's an adverse change, report it immediately. Don't silently absorb functionality changes.

- Be strict with distractions. Don't work on other tasks unless they are accounted for on a plan. Learn to say *no* to old projects, extra work from other departments, and intrusions from the phone and email.

  Guard against these external distractions, even the short ones that seem harmless; they can really lower the quality of your work. It takes time to *get into the zone*, that productive place where your mind is on the task and the code is flowing freely from your fingertips (psychologists call this state *flow*). Even short distractions interrupt this effectiveness, and when you return to work, you must spend more time getting back into the zone. The impact of interruptions can be more than three times their duration. (DeMarco 99)

  Foster a development culture that's conducive to getting work done. Respect each other's brain-space: a person's time to think and work. Make sure that every meeting really is necessary—don't pull developers into random, time-wasting get-togethers.

- Maintain a positive and optimistic approach. Believing a project is doomed is a surefire way to make that happen in reality.

In a Nutshell

Good luck is a lazy man's estimate of a worker's success.
—Anonymous

Timescale estimation and planning help us to develop commercially successful software. However, there is no rigorous method to accurately determine software timescale values. That's why it's *estimation*.

Aim to develop your estimation techniques, and become wary of potential problems that can ruin your neatly scheduled development plan. Learn how to work to a schedule and to identify when your schedules are impractical.

Good programmers . . .

- Create good timescale estimates by considering all parts of the development process, based on a sound component breakdown
- Try to produce tested code with full documentation, properly integrated within the timescales
- Highlight timescale problems early on so that they can be dealt with

Bad programmers . . .

- Produce hopeful estimates, based solely on hunches and gut feelings
- Can hack out some code within their timescale estimates but will not produce production quality, bug-free code
- Think that admitting a timescale problem is a sign of weakness, and work themselves silly trying to catch up—when they fail, they look silly (and tired)

See Also

Chapter 13: Grand Designs
Good timescale estimates can only be based on a sound initial code design.

Chapter 19: Being Specific
Making an estimate requires a well-defined scope of work, which must be captured unambiguously in a *specification*.

Chapter 22: Recipe for a Program
Development methodologies determine how tasks are slotted together and placed on a project plan.

10,000 MONKEYS (OR THEREABOUTS)

IT'S COMIC TIME
BETTER LATE THAN NEVER?

I WAS GOING TO WRITE AN ENTERTAINING COMIC STRIP

I SPENT THREE WEEKS THINKING UP AN IDEA

THE ONLY PROBLEM: I RAN OUT OF TIME TO DRAW IT

Get Thinking

A detailed discussion of these questions can be found in the "Answers and Discussion" section on page 550.

Mull It Over

1. How can you rescue a slipping project and bring it back on track?
2. What's the correct response to having a deadline imposed on you before feasibility or planning work commences?
3. How do you ensure that a development plan is genuinely useful?
4. Why do different programmers work at different rates? How can you reflect this on the plan?

Getting Personal

1. What percentage of the projects that you've worked on have run to schedule?
   a. For those that did: What contributed to the success of the planning effort?
   b. For those that failed: What were the main problems?
2. How accurate are your timescale estimates? How far off target are you normally?

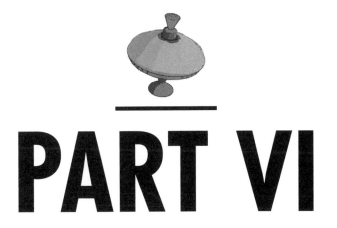

PART VI

VIEW FROM THE TOP

The air's getting thinner, but the view's getting better. Several hundred pages ago we started our journey at the lowest level, grubbing around the seedy underbelly of source code construction. In this last section we complete our journey by climbing to the very top of the software development mountain and surveying the territory below. I hope you're not afraid of heights.

Here we'll look at how the final parts of the jigsaw fit together.

Chapter 22: Recipe for a Program
The code cookbook: how we actually write software in our development teams. This chapter describes both software development methodologies and software development processes. It shows how we manage to produce programs in a predictable, timely manner (or, at least, attempt to).

Chapter 23: The Outer Limits
A look at the different code-writing disciplines out there: applications programming, games programming, distributed programming, and more. Each of these branches of programming has its own special problems and important skills. Understanding these will equip you to write the most suitable code for each occasion.

Chapter 24: Where Next?
The end is in sight. . . . This is the final, tearful farewell. We look at where to go next in your continuing study of code craft. This book is just the beginning.

RECIPE FOR A PROGRAM

Code Development
Methodologies and Processes

They always say time changes things, but you actually have to change them yourself.

—Andy Warhol

Ingredients

1 bunch programmers (preferably fresh)

1–2 tsp language

1 target platform

1 project manager

1 pinch luck

1 sachet dehydrated training

Various industry buzzwords

Instructions

Marinade programmers in training. Add language, target platform, and season with project manager. Stir briskly until well mixed. Add buzzwords to taste. Sprinkle evenly with luck and leave to cook in a hot software oven until deadline. Remove, tip onto wire rack, and allow to cool before handing on to customer.

I know at least four recipes for sponge cake. They vary depending on whether you want a fat-free or an egg-free cake and also on the method you want to prepare with. Writing software is like that. There is no one recipe or magic formula; the same system could be built in many different ways, with no one necessarily better than any other. There are different ingredients that you may choose to feed the development process and different methods to follow. Likely as not, they will each produce a slightly different cake; different in terms of features, structure, stability, extensibility, maintainability, and more. These recipes describe the *software life cycle*: the phases of development ranging from the very beginning (conceptualizing the software) to its very end (decommissioning it).

As software engineers, we should be able to predictably (and to some extent reproducibly) create software by following a defined procedure. As software craftsmen, we should be able to harness a particular development procedure as a tool to help fashion the best software possible. In this chapter, we'll investigate some of the recipes for creating software; we'll compare, contrast, criticize, and see how they affect the way we code.

We programmed a ZX spectrum differently from a modern palmtop PDA, and that differently from a mainframe stock control system with a high-capacity web interface. We program differently alone than we would working in a pair, and differently than we would in a 200-strong worldwide project team. Differences in the target platform and development team (and their levels of experience) will shape the choice of recipe. The art of programming is much more than just edit, compile, link, and run.

KEY CONCEPT   *Good programmers are aware of how they program—the methods and practices that shape their work.*

What are these programming recipes?

Programming Styles

A programming style describes how a software problem is mapped out and how its solution is decomposed and then modeled by the target language. We have to *model* a solution, since useful systems can't be entirely held in the mind of a single developer. The programming style shapes how we split a project up into manageable pieces; it is the design paradigm used to express your code's intent.

Different programming languages support different programming styles. Some are tailored to a specific one; some cater for a number of them. The programming styles fall into two main camps: *imperative* and *declarative*.

- Imperative (or *procedural*) languages allow you to specify the explicit sequence of steps to follow to produce the program's output. It's what most programmers are used to.

- Declarative languages describe relationships between variables in terms of inference rules (or functions), and the language executor applies some fixed algorithm to these rules to produce the result. (This description might turn into understandable English once when we take a look at functional and logic programming.)

The programming language you choose will go some way to determine the style you design with. (However, it would be better to select a language that supports the style you want to use.) The programming language is not the ultimate determinant, though. It is perfectly possible to build structured code in an object-oriented language, in the same way that it is possible to write hateful code in any language. The next few sections describe the popular programming styles.

Structured Programming

This common imperative design method applies *algorithmic decomposition*—a process of breaking a system into parts, each of which represents a small step in the larger process. Design decisions focus on the flow of control and create a hierarchy of functional structure. As Dijkstra observed, "Hierarchical systems seem to have a property that something considered as an undivided entity on one level is considered as a composite object on the next lowest level of greater detail: as a result, the natural grain of space or time that is applicable at each level decreases by an order of magnitude when we shift our attention from one level to the next lower one. We understand walls in terms of bricks, bricks in terms of crystals, crystals in terms of molecules, etc." Indeed, it was Dijkstra's seminal paper "Go To Statement Considered Harmful" that popularized structured programming. (Dijkstra 68)

Structured programming is a control-centered model and follows a top-down design technique. You start with the whole program in mind (e.g., do_shopping). Then you decompose it into sequential sub-blocks (e.g., get_shopping_list, leave_house, walk_to_shop, collect_items, pay_at_checkout, return_to_house, put_shopping_away). In turn, each sub-block is decomposed until it is at a level that can be easily implemented in code. The blocks are assembled into a whole, and the design is complete.

The implications of a structured approach are:

- Each step of the decomposition should be within the programmer's intellectual understanding. (Dijkstra said, "I now suggest that we confine ourselves to the design and implementation of intellectually manageable programs.")
- Control flow should be carefully managed: Avoid the dreaded goto statement (an unstructured jump in the code to some arbitrary place), and instead prefer functions to have a single entry and single exit point (this is known as *SESE code*).
- Looping constructs and conditional statements are used within functional blocks to provide code structure. Short-circuit jumping out of the middle of a loop or from within a nested block of code is held in similar disdain to goto.

Common structured programming languages are C, Pascal, BASIC, and more venerable languages like Fortran and COBOL. Most other imperative languages can be easily used to write structured code, although it's not their design specialism; structured programmers often adopt new fashionable languages without adopting new idioms.[1]

Object-Oriented Programming

Booch describes OO programming as "A method of implementation in which programs are organized as co-operative collections of objects, each of which represents an instance of some class, and whose classes are all members of a hierarchy of classes united via inheritance relationships." (Booch 94) It is another imperative style, but one that allows us to more naturally model the world in our code designs; we focus on the interacting entities being modeled rather than on the notion of a particular flow of execution.

This is very much a data-centred model (as opposed to structured programming's process-centric view). We think about the life of our data and how it moves about, rather than the sequence of steps that need to be taken to get the job done. Objects (the data) have behavior (they do things) and states (which change when they do things). This is implemented at language level by *methods* on *classes* of *objects*. We think of OO programs as sets of collaborating software components, rather than as monolithic lists of CPU instructions. OO design has allowed us to effectively model larger systems.

Object-oriented programming exploits the following computer science concepts:

Abstraction

The art of selective ignorance—abstraction allows us to design code so that the higher levels of control can ignore gory implementation details below. Who cares whether get_next_item does a binary search in a list, indexes an array, or makes a phone call to Frankfurt? It returns the next item (whatever that is), and that's all the calling code has to care about.

Dijkstra's earlier exposition of hierarchy—go back and read it again— revealed a form of abstraction.

Encapsulation

Encapsulation is the placing of cohesive units of execution into one tightly bound package that can only be accessed through a well-defined API: a code capsule. Users of that capsule can only call the defined API and cannot tinker directly with internal state. This provides a clear separation of concerns, helps us to reason about metaphysical questions like *What is an object?* and provides some assurance that no evil programmer can tinker with your innards when you're not looking.

---

[1] This is not necessarily a Bad Thing, unless the programmer believes that he's moved beyond structured coding without changing the way he designs code.

Inheritance

A mechanism to create an object type that is a specialized version of a parent object. Consider a parent type called Shape, with inherited child types Square, Circle, and Triangle. The inherited types provide more detail, specializing behavior (for example, knowing the exact number of sides the shape has). Like any other programming concept, inheritance can be abused to create unfathomable, surprising programs or leveraged to create logically sound, elegant code. Good OO programmers know how to create appropriate inheritance hierarchies.

Polymorphism

This allows the same code to use different underlying data types (what most OO programming languages call *classes*) depending on the context in which it runs. This technique emphasizes programming to explicitly defined interfaces, not to an implicit implementation—polymorphism provides a clear separation of concerns as you write code. There are two types of polymorphism, *dynamic* and *static*.

Dynamic polymorphism, as the name suggests, determines the actual operation to be performed at run time, based on the type of an operand or target object. This often exploits inheritance hierarchies: a client that deals with Shape types might currently be using a Square or a Triangle object—which one is figured out at run time.

Static polymorphism determines the exact code to be run at compile time. Language features that provide static polymorphism include: *function overloading* (functions with the same name accept different parameter lists—the compiler deduces the correct function to invoke from the arguments supplied), *operator overloading* (where you can define certain operations on types—including +, !=, <, and &—these functions are called when the types of operands match), and *generic programming facilities* like C++'s *template specialism* (where you can overload a template based on the template parameter type).

These facilities are all possible to use in non-OO languages, using non-OO practices. However, OO languages express them directly and OO designs exploit them to create a cohesive system.

Object-oriented programming started with Simula around 1970 and has been recently popularized by C++ and Java. One of the few pure OO programming languages is Smalltalk. These days, OO is en vogue, and there are many OO languages; a number are structured languages with fashionable OO bolt-ons.

Functional Programming

This is a declarative programming style based on typed *lambda calculus*, a more mathematical model of programming. You work with values, functions, and functional forms. Functional programs are generally compact and elegant, although seldom compiled. They are therefore reliant on a language executor. The program's performance is governed by these executors—they can be quite slow and memory hungry.[2]

The structured and OO styles are far more popular in mainstream use than any declarative languages, although that doesn't diminish the usefulness of this breed of programming. They have different strong points and uses. Functional programs require a totally different approach to code design from the procedural methods.

Common functional programming languages are Lisp (although it does contain nonfunctional elements), Scheme, ML, and Haskell.

Logic Programming

This is another declarative style, in which you provide the executor with a set of axioms (rules) and a goal statement. A set of built-in inference rules (over which the programmer has no control) are applied to determine whether the axioms are sufficient to ensure the truth of the goal statement. Program execution is essentially the proof of the goal statement.

Interest in artificial intelligence was a huge boost to the development of logic programming languages. They are widely used for automatic theorem proving and in *expert systems* (which model large problem domains and generate specific answers based on the amassed body of knowledge).

The best known logic programming language is Prolog.

Recipes: The How and the What

There are two different aspects we'll investigate. Software "recipes" employ a *development process* and also a *programming style*. The two are separate and connected:

- The process is the larger picture: It describes the steps taken to construct software. This encompasses the *entire* development organization, not just the programmers. Most software construction is not a one-person job; the process explains how to get a number of people to build a coherent whole. Or at least, it should attempt to.

- The programming style is the smaller picture: It is an underlying approach for dissecting, building, and gluing software components together. It will quite likely be influenced by the choice of development process, but doesn't have to be.[3] It's more likely to be influenced by a target language or the designer's prior experience.

---

[2] This is not a problem solely encountered by declarative languages (for example Java has an executor, the JVM). However, comparatively less optimization effort has gone into the declarative breed of language executors—they're more often backed by academic institutions than wealthy corporations.

[3] For example, OO styles are often picked in "iterative and incremental" processes; this is mostly by convention. (If you don't know what this means, *don't panic*! It will all be explained in "Iterative and Incremental Development" on page 432.)

You'll see both of these construction aspects called *methodologies*, so it's easy to get them confused.[4] We'll look in turn at styles and then development processes. It's important to have a grasp of the different development methods out there, to give you a better programming worldview and to help you choose a process, should you ever have the opportunity.

KEY CONCEPT   *Our software development efforts are molded by the* styles *and* processes *we employ. These have an inevitable effect on the shape and quality of our code.*

The following sections do not provide a textbook description of these topics; they provide a suitably hand-wavy overview to help us compare and contrast. If you want or need more detail, you can easily find a hard-core software engineering textbook.

Development Processes

There are as many development processes as there are people who feel like inventing them. Many are slight evolutions of one or two basic development models. We'll look here at those basic variants. Some of them are closely related, as you will see.

Your choice of development processes determines how projects are planned, how work flows between phases, and how the project team interacts. Processes vary along a number of axes:

Thick/thin

A *thick development process* is heavyweight and bureaucratic. It generates a lot of paperwork, regiments developer behavior, and presumes a certain team structure. It's characterized by the ISO 9000 organizational model, where every work procedure is slavishly written down in great detail, without regard for whether the process is flawed or appropriate.

At the other end of the process spectrum, *thin development processes* eschew unnecessary bureaucracy, favoring leaner, people-centric principles. Agile processes, described in "Agile Methodologies" on page 433, are built around thin practices.

Sequencing

Some development processes sensibly recognize that the world is not a predictable place and attempt to model and plan for this by running a number of iterations around a process loop. This provides an opportunity for the developers to incorporate feedback from one iteration into the work of the next. They can adapt to the natural changes that occur as software develops (changing customer requirements, unexpected problems encountered, etc.).

Other processes are more regimented and linear—predicting a formal progression of development from one phase to the next. They involve heavy up-front planning efforts and try to foresee the future in great detail. These predictions make it hard to change direction late in development.

---

[4] If you want to make a distinction, then what I call programming *styles* are often called methodologies (with a lowercase *m*). Development *processes* are often called Methodologies (with an uppercase *M*); a kind of high-church/low-church classification. That's far too subtle. In this chapter I'll stick to styles and processes.

Design direction

A *top-down design* creates the system from an initial undetailed overview. Each top-level package is refined and split into subcomponents. This process iterates until the software is specified sufficiently to begin work. Top-down design emphasizes planning and a good understanding of the final system, and presumes that few requirements change en route.

The opposite, *bottom-up design*, specifies individual parts of the system in detail and then determines how best to connect them to form a cohesive whole. This helps us to leverage existing software components in a new design. Modern processes tend to blend these two polar opposites—some idea of the entire system is required to begin initial planning, then the design progresses by identifying and coding low-level components and objects.

No one style of development process is better than any other. Extreme religious views are held about the correct position on any one of these axes. The correct methodology for any project is determined by a number of factors, including the development culture of the organization, the type of product being developed, and the experience of the development team.

Now please buckle your seat belts for our roller coaster ride through the range of software development processes. Hold on tight.

Ad Hoc

This is a starting point, but it's really an anti-process. Here there is no process, or else it is undocumented. Everybody works to his or her own agenda, no one knows what anyone else is doing, and hopefully something useful will drop out at the end. Perhaps your team works like Figure 22-1?

If an organization doesn't know how it builds software, then it's in an unforgivable state, even if it's a small outfit and it doesn't think it needs a process. In this state, there is no guarantee that the software will be delivered on time, since there's no accountability. Who can guarantee that all the features will be implemented?

A lot of open source software is created using this chaotic method.[5] If you have an infinite number of monkeys and an infinite number of computers, you might eventually get a program out—however it isn't feasible to wait the requisite infinite amount of time. Even back-of-napkin designs are a step toward a more formal, predictable development process.

KEY CONCEPT   *Without a development process, your team is in a state of anarchy. Your software will be produced by luck, not on purpose.*

This case is development anarchy. Individual programmers may work hard, and their heroic efforts might eventually produce something of value. Such an outcome cannot be seriously relied upon, though. The team is likely to be very inefficient and will probably never deliver anything of value.

---

[5] And there, perhaps, it doesn't matter so much, since there's no paying customer and no formal set of requirements—a lot of open source software is developed because the programmer feels like it. However, applying some development process to ad hoc open source work will almost certainly yield better programs.

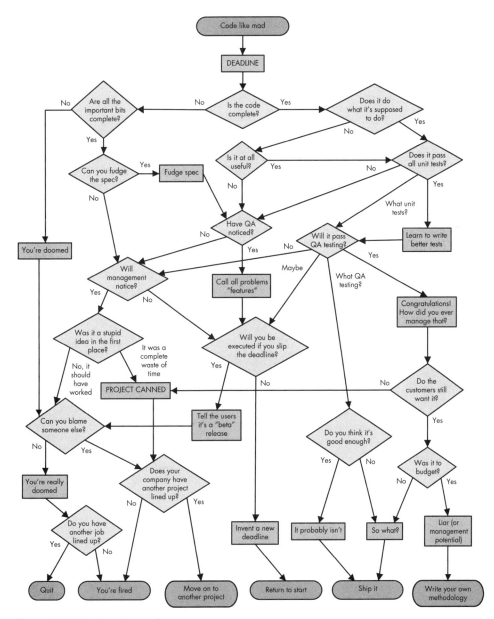

Figure 22-1: Engineering a release

Waterfall Model

The *waterfall model* is the classic software development life cycle model. It has been much criticized for its simplicity (even for being old fashioned). However practically every other development process is in some way based on it. It has numerous flaws, and yet it is still an instructional starting point in process study. It's modeled after a more conventional engineering life cycle and was described by W.W. Royce in 1970. (Royce 70) It's the most predictive of the development processes.

STAGES OF DEVELOPMENT

The waterfall model describes five stages in the life of a software development process. Many other processes identify the same phases but order them differently or change their relative emphasis.

Requirements analysis

First, the requirements for the software project are established. This scopes its goals, the services it will provide, and what constraints it needs to work within. This step is often preceded by a feasibility study to kick the project off, or feasibility is done at the same time. The feasibility study asks questions like: *Will this project work? Should we develop this software? What are the alternatives?*

Design and specification

The established requirements flowing from the first stage are converted into software or hardware requirements. The software requirements are then transformed into a form that can be readily implemented in a computer program, perhaps by splitting into separately developed components.

Implementation

This is where the programs are created. Each program or subcomponent is a *unit*, and is unit tested. The unit test ensures that each unit meets its specification as defined in the previous step.

Integration and testing

All units are combined and the whole system is tested. We test that the code integrates correctly, that the entire system behaves as it should, and that it implements all system requirements. When successfully tested, the software is considered complete.

Maintenance

Finally, the product is delivered. We should never presume software is finished when it ships; it is naïve to do so. The largest phase of the software lifecycle is *maintenance* (see "Maintenance of Existing Code" on page 288). There will be bugs to fix, unnoticed requirements to accommodate, evolution of the original requirements, and other product support work for software deployed in the field.

It is a simple idea; the development process is broken up into a number of stages, which run one after the other. This is likened to a waterfall because of the steady, irreversible flow from one stage to another. Just as water always flows downward toward the river, the development always flows downward through each stage toward release.

The traditional waterfall model is shown in Figure 22-2.[6] You can see the five standard stages; these are described in the "Stages of Development" text box. Once a stage is successfully completed, progression is made via some *gating process* (usually a review meeting) to the next stage. The output of most stages is a document; a requirements specification, a design specification, or something similar. If the review finds an error or problem, it is fed back upstream, setting that stage back again.

---

[6] This is a common simplicfcation of Royce's original paper. Royce *did* allow feedback up the waterfall, but didn't actively encourage it. Zealous managers imagined software development to be a strictly linear process, and soon removed these upstream paths; the waterfall was tarnished.

Following this model, you can't easily backtrack to make changes; it's like a salmon expending massive amounts of time and energy swimming back upstream. While salmon are genetically programmed to do this, programmers aren't. This means that the process is not helpful when changes are made late in the development process. The requirements must be fixed before system design, and it is difficult to accommodate too many alterations after the process is underway. Generally, problems at the design stage are not discovered until system testing.

In its defense, though, it is simple to manage—at least conceptually—and is the basis for most other development models. The waterfall doesn't scale well to very large projects; it works fine for a two-week project. Other development models exploit this by running many, smaller, waterfalls over the life of a large project.

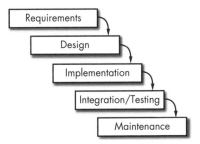

Figure 22-2: The traditional waterfall model

SSADM and PRINCE

Although *SSADM* sounds like development only partaken by consenting adults, it actually stands for *Structured Systems Analysis and Design Methodology.* It is a structured and rigorous method following the waterfall approach, perhaps the most regimented waterfall variant you'll encounter.

It covers analysis and design, not implementation and testing, and is a well-defined open standard, heavily used in UK government organizations. SSADM consists of five main steps (each subdivided into many other procedures), which for our purposes are self-descriptive:

- Feasibility study
- Requirements analysis
- Requirements specification
- Logical system specification
- Physical design

Projects In a Controlled Environment (PRINCE) and its imaginatively named successor, *PRINCE2*, were created in 1989 and 1996 to supercede SSADM. Like SSADM, they define a heavyweight, document-centric model. They list regimented steps (this time in eight separate phases) that can be followed to produce a product, aiming to meet identified requirements and quality standards.

V Model

This process model derives from the classic waterfall and was developed to regulate the software development process within German administration and military. It shares much in common with the waterfall model (including a propensity to attract criticism) but rather than model the processes as a cascade, it is visualized as a *V*, as shown in Figure 22-3.

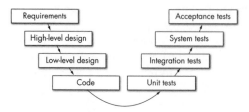

Figure 22-3: The V model

On the left, we see the development phases leading up to software construction: the planning, design, and implementation work. The right-hand stream governs testing and approval.[7] Each level of test work is measured against the specification generated from the corresponding left-hand phase.

The V model's difference from the waterfall is more than the orientation of a diagram. The testing phases (in the right branch) can begin in parallel to the development work (the left branch), and are given an equal importance. This is good because:

- Traditionally, testing is squeezed out during the dying stages of a slipping project. This is dangerous. Emphasizing testing as a keystone of the development process highlights this fact and helps to ensure product quality.

- We should always test more than the final software: reviewing and validating at *all* stages of development work, from the requirements specification through to the completed software. The V model highlights this.

- In the Real World, testing and bug fixing often take up more than half of a project's total time. The waterfall model doesn't accurately reflect this.

- This model can shave time from the entire development process, since the test plans can be drawn up as soon as each development phase is complete. This streamlined, parallelized work will bring forward the project's end date because we don't need to wait for the waterfall's implementation phase to end before beginning test activity.

Prototyping

Despite our many years of research and experience in software development processes, the waterfall is still a standard reference model since it has a clear logic to it—you obviously can't perform useful implementation

---

[7] Note how development flows downward, like the waterfall, but testing is seen as an uphill effort—a reasonably accurate model of software development!

before requirements analysis or any design work. However, the waterfall makes it hard to evaluate a software system until development is complete. It is also hard to demonstrate the software to your customer until the integration phase has completed and the system is ready to alpha test.

The *prototyping approach* attempts to work around this limitation. It helps to explore and evaluate implementation as development progresses and to refine unknown or ambiguous requirements (users never know what they *really* want).

The essence of the prototyping process is to create a number of throwaway prototypes of the software system. Each prototype is evaluated, shown to the customer, and customer feedback is used to shape the next prototype. This continues until enough is known to develop and deploy the real product.

We see an analogy with other industries here. If you were developing a new car, you'd create many prototypes until you hit on exactly the right design. We aim to do the same with our software. However, there is an important difference that must be observed. When building a car, the major cost is in the manufacturing, not the development. It works the other way around with software. You can make multiple copies of the code for free; the development is the costly part. For this reason, the prototyping cycle needs to be controlled; it can't be repeated an unlimited number of times.

PROTOTYPE BLUES

Releasing prototypes can cause severe maintenance problems.

I did some work for a company that had a policy of only using one GUI library for its Java front ends. But in practice, it had some systems that used the library and some that didn't. Whenever a bug cropped up, the maintenance programmers had to jump through hoops to work out what the front end code was doing. They didn't understand the other GUI libraries, and often their fixes introduced yet more problems. The more this happened, the less respected the company's products became.

It didn't take much software archeology to discover the cause of this problem: The front ends that didn't use the correct GUI library had been prototypes that "accidentally" became products. A little time spent releasing correct code would have saved months of work later on and wouldn't have destroyed the company's reputation.

The prototypes are developed quickly in very high-level languages. Sometimes they are simply drawn: The use of automated tool support[8] can speed prototype production immensely. The prototypes are proofs-of-concept, so efficiency, stability, or a complete feature set are not primary concerns. For this reason, prototyping works best for systems with an emphasis on the user interface.

Prototypes help us to manage risk. We can use them to ensure that customers really do want what they *say* they want. We can also use prototypes to explore the use of a new technology or to check that our design decisions will stand up to real use.

---

[8] For example, *Rapid Application Development (RAD)* tools with simple GUI builders.

The danger with prototyping is the temptation to continue developing the inefficient, quickly produced, not fully thought-out prototype code into a real release. This is especially true when a project is running out of time and the real development might not fit the schedule. Without education, customers will confuse the prototype with the finished product and be surprised that it takes a lot longer to receive their completed software. It needs very careful management to work. The best way to avoid this problem is to leave your prototypes deliberately rough around the edges, and to never get them near a releasable state. A prototype that has too much functionality is not a prototype!

Iterative and Incremental Development

All the recent advances on the waterfall approach are basically variations on a theme. The major improvement is performing development in an *iterative and incremental manner.* That is, many trips (iterations) around a small development life cycle run back to back (incrementally), with each cycle adding more and more functionality to the system until it is complete. Each single run of a mini lifecycle tends to follow the waterfall model and may last a number of weeks or months (depending on the scale of the project). Each phase of the waterfall therefore gets executed more than once. At each iteration end is a software release.

Incremental development is neither a top-down nor a bottom-up approach. A complete version of the code is created for each code release, with all requisite high- and low-level components. During each iteration, the system grows, and subsequent design work can be done based on the existing design and implementation. There is a parallel to prototyping here, but we're not so focused on quick demonstrative hacks. With this approach each stage is less complex and easier to manage—and process progress is more easily monitored; you know how much of the system is built and integrated.

This kind of process works well for projects whose requirements are less understood at the start. Let's face it: That encompasses most projects in the Real World. It is more resilient to change, and it saves the lengthy redesign and reimplementation of the entire system that you'd encounter in the waterfall approach. Iterative and incremental development works well because it fits the fundamental nature of software development, it consequently helps us to better control the inherent chaos. Because iterative cycles are much shorter, there is greater opportunity for feedback and correction; you don't have to wait until the end of your project to find out that it's failing.

Spiral Model

The *spiral model,* proposed by Barry Boehm in 1988 (Boehm 88), is a good example of the iterative and incremental approach.[9] The development process is modeled as a spiral, like Figure 22-4. It starts in the center and fans outward toward the later stages of the process. We start working on a very rough notion of the system, becoming more detailed over time, as we enter later stages of the spiral. Each 360-degree turn of the spiral sees us go through a single waterfall, and each iteration typically lasts six months to two years.

---

[9] Boehm's process wasn't the first iterative model, but he was the first to popularize and emphasize the importance of iteration.

Features are defined and implemented in order of decreasing priority; the most important facilities are created as soon as possible. This is a way of managing risk; it's safer because as you inch toward the ship date, you can be sure that the majority of the system is complete. In fact, it is very pragmatic approach; the programmers will not be spending 80 percent of their time on the trifling (but fun) 20 percent of the system.

Figure 22-4: The spiral model

Boehm splits the spiral into four quadrants or four distinct phases:

Objective setting
Specific objectives for this phase are identified.

Risk assessment and reduction
The key risks are identified and analyzed, and information is sought to reduce these risks.

Development and validation
An appropriate model is chosen for next phase of development.

Planning
The project is reviewed, and plans are drawn up for the next round of the spiral.

Agile Methodologies

These were developed as a backlash against the bureaucratic and heavyweight methodologies that tried to straitjacket the software development process. Agile practitioners observed that software development cannot easily be made a predictable process; they claim that it is *very* different from the established engineering procedures, like constructing a bridge.[10] The old-fashioned,

---

[10] This is a religious debate: Many programmers believe that it *is* possible to make the software development process a repeatable, predictable thing, but the industry is currently not mature or disciplined enough to do so.

monumental methodologies only serve to get in the way of people trying to write good software, and so they should be thrown away.

Agile methodology is an umbrella term that describes a number of development processes, including the much-hyped Extreme Programming, as well as Crystal Clear and Scrum. Agile processes focus on nimbleness and risk reduction rather than on long-term planning or forcing (pretending to have) predictability.

Agile processes share these central tenets:

- Minimize risk by performing many small iterative development cycles. The software and all process artifacts are complete, consistent, and of releasable quality at the end of each cycle. Although the software seldom *is* released, it can be passed on to the customer to review and to comment on. This gives the customer reassurance of the team's progress.

  Agile process iterations tend to be much smaller than iterative and incremental process loops (typically lasting a number of weeks, rather than months).

- Minimize risk by placing far more emphasis on a suite of automated regression tests that are run continually, rather than on a lengthy test cycle at the end of development.

- Reduce the documentation that plagues heavyweight processes. Agile processes view the code itself as the design and as the implementation documentation. Good code stands on its own and doesn't need to be lumbered with bureaucratic documentation processes.

- Emphasize people and aim to facilitate communication, preferably face-to-face rather than through documents. This keeps the customer (or a customer representative) as close to the development team as possible, to take part in implementation and prioritization decisions.

- Consider *working software* as the measure of progress and performance, not specification writing or a manager's opinion of the team's position in a fictitious development cycle. The developers meet problems and respond to changes by modifying the code as development progresses.

The agile approach is not always appropriate. It tends to work best on smaller projects, with teams of less than 10 high-quality programmers who are geographically co-located. Agile processes excel in domains with a high degree of requirements change. They are hard to run in companies with a heavy process culture.

Other Development Processes

There are many other development processes: variations on these themes, each with its own distinct features. There are modified waterfall processes that overlap certain phases or contain subprojects, managed as mini-waterfalls. The *evolutionary prototyping* approach starts with an initial concept, designs and implements a prototype, iteratively refines the prototype until it is acceptable, and then releases this, perhaps planning to include some throw away prototypes in the process.

Staged delivery follows a sequential process up to architectural design and then implements the separate components showing them to the customer as each is completed, going back to previous development steps if needed. *Evolutionary delivery* is essentially a cross between evolutionary prototyping and staged delivery.

Rapid Application Development (RAD) emphasizes user involvement and small development teams, and it makes heavy use of prototyping and automated tools. In a slight twist on other processes, the development time frame is established up front and considered immovable. Then as many features as feasible are incorporated into the design to accommodate the deadline—some features may be sacrificed.

The *Rational Unified Process (RUP)* is a notable commercial methodology that stems from Ivar Jacobson's 1987 *Objectory Process*. It's a heavyweight but flexible object-oriented process that leans heavily on UML diagrams, with *use case–driven design* (a use case describes a single user activity or interaction with the software system). It favors iterative development, continuous testing, and careful change management. As a commercial process, it is supported by a suite of commercial tools.

Enough, Already!

If you've read this far and haven't gotten bored yet, then you're doing well. Finally, and perhaps more importantly, what are the key points to draw from all this? A software craftsman has a good working understanding of development processes and programming styles, but anyone can get this from the right books. How do we apply this stuff usefully to our work? How can it improve our skill set?

All of these processes share some common threads. The phases described in "Stages of Development" on page 428 are present in each. The processes really only differ in the length and relative positioning of these stages. Each activity is vital to the production of good-quality software. The better processes ensure that testing is not left as an afterthought, but is carried out continuously—and monitored—throughout the development process.

It's hard to compare or evaluate the different processes and programming styles. Which is best? Which will ensure that a high-quality product is shipped on time and to budget? There is no answer, because those are not the right questions. Which process is suitable depends on the nature of the project and the culture of your company. If you have 20 programmers who know nothing of object-oriented development and only ever use C, then trying to build an OO Java product is clearly a stupid idea.

KEY CONCEPT *You'll pick a software recipe for a number of reasons—make sure they're good ones. The motivation for your choice of process says a lot about the maturity of your organization.*

We can see two procedural extremes: The anarchy of the ad hoc method contrasts with the strict regime of a rigid process. In the latter, any experimentation that could yield a more elegant architecture is discouraged. The user's real requirements may never filter down to a developer since it's lost in a sea of bureaucracy; the programmer just codes to a specification that's passed on to him from the previous process phase.

Following the *Goldilocks prinicple*, the most flexible approach is somewhere in between. You *do* need to know the process you're working to and where it's defined. Effective development requires discipline; you need a coherent strategy to get something out of the door on time (having a realistic schedule is another topic in its own right—see "The Planning Game" on page 409). Experienced programmers know the value of their development processes, as well as the faults. They know how to work with it and when to step outside it. Good programmers don't just program. They understand their recipes and how to adapt them as appropriate. This is why our science is still a craft.

It's important not to be uptight and legalistic about the process you follow, but you must have an agreed framework for producing software. It must be appropriate for your development team—not every organization needs a high-ceremony process with many hoops and hurdles to navigate and lengthy forms to fill in.

KEY CONCEPT   *The process you adopt doesn't have to be high-ceremony and hard to follow. In fact, the exact opposite characteristics are generally hallmarks of a good process. You must have a defined process, though.*

New methodologies spring up (or rather evolve) from time to time. They tend to arrive with a big fanfare and a spurt of fireworks; they're claimed to be the silver bullet, the panacea that will make development better for our children and our children's children. Sadly, it's never the case. When it comes down to it, no matter which life cycle you follow, the programming team is only as good as its programmers. If there is no intuition, no flair, no experience, and no motivation present then, regardless of the development process you use, you won't reliably produce good code. You might be better able to track how far behind schedule you are, though.

Pick a Process

Many factors contribute to a good choice of development process. However, the choice is seldom made on sensible grounds; a development process is used because *It's the way we always do it, It works well enough,* or *It was the first thing we could think of.*

How do you know what development method is appropriate? Ultimately, if the process works for your team—if you collaborate well and produce good software on time—then you have a good development approach.

A good choice of process is based on the type and size of the project. Small modifications to an existing codebase don't need a large iterative development cycle; three-year industrial projects starting from scratch probably do. A good process choice suits the experience of the existing team members, has the developers willing (even eager) to use it, and is something that the project manager really understands.

On the flip side, there are plenty of bad reasons to choose a development process. There's no point in moving to a new process just because you feel like a change; a new process must be introduced to fix a problem with the current development model. There's no point in trying to make a political statement (I know people who've tried to foster an open development culture, just to swing the organization toward open sourcing their internal codebase). The ultimate bad motivation for picking a particular process is fashion. More buzzwords do not necessarily mean a more useful process.

This *is* important: An inappropriate process really can ruin the quality of your code; you'll spend more time pandering to the demands of a procedural straitjacket than delivering software. A good process does not get in your way. Indeed, it enables your team to create more software, better and faster.

KEY CONCEPT   *Process is vital. Most projects fail for nontechnical reasons. And bad process is almost always high on the list of reasons.*

In a Nutshell

Building software is like crime: It's better when it's organized. Every now and again, an undisciplined team will pull off something spectacular and create a software masterpiece. However, that *is* the exception. The development process needs to be defined and understood and carried out by team members with appropriate skills to stand a chance of working well. Otherwise, you'll end up with software that's criminal.

We need to use proven development processes and established design styles to allow us to build software that meets expectations against a backdrop of timescales, budgets, and changing requirements. Building software is hard—and we've just looked at another way to make it easier.

Good programmers . . .	Bad programmers . . .
• Understand the programming style and development process they are expected to work within	• Ignore development process issues, and attempt to do things their own way
• Exploit their development process to shape interactions with other software factory inhabitants; when the process becomes constraining, they'll sidestep it	• Do not know how the process shapes their interaction with other developers
• Appreciate the pros and cons of different development recipes and can pick the appropriate one for any given situation	• Avoid thinking about this kind of stuff—*it's for managers to worry about*

See Also

Chapter 8: Testing Times
Testing is a key phase of the development process. Often the pressures of Real World deadlines try to squeeze out room for it.

Chapter 17: Together We Stand
Teamwork: the cornerstone of large scale software development.

Chapter 19: Being Specific
Specifications are often the gates between phases of the development process.

Get Thinking

A detailed discussion of these questions can be found in the "Answers and Discussion" section on page 553.

Mull It Over

1. How do the choices of programming style and development process influence one another?

2. Which is the best programming style?

3. Which is the best development process?

4. Where does each development process listed in this chapter fall on the classification axes we saw in "Development Processes" on page 425?

5. If development processes and programming styles are recipes, what would a software development cookbook look like?

6. With a suitable process, can software construction become a predictable, repeatable task?

Getting Personal

1. What development process and programming language style are you currently using?

   a. Has it been formally agreed upon by the development team, or do you use it by convention?

   b. How was it chosen? Was it chosen specifically for this project, or is it the recipe you always use?

   c. Is it documented anywhere?

   d. Does the team stick to the process? When problems arise and your back is against the wall, do you maintain the process, or is all ivory tower theory ignored in a rush to produce something—anything?

2. Are your current processes and styles appropriate? Are they the best way for you to develop your software right now?

3. Does your organization appreciate that there are other development models that might be worth investigating?

THE OUTER LIMITS

The Different Programming Disciplines

Everything that irritates us about others can lead us to an understanding of ourselves.

—Carl Jung

I like sweeping generalizations and tenuous metaphors. Sue me. I've also been doing my research. I found that there are over 40 churches in the city I live in. Each one of these is subtly different; different types of people attend, and they do different things. They have different concerns and ways of working. They're located in different areas. However, they're all doing roughly the same thing.

What on earth has this got to do with programming? I hear you ask. If you forgive the tenuous link, software development works in pretty much the same way. Okay, we don't all file into a building every Sunday morning (well, most of us don't). But, to outsiders, we do appear to engage in bizarre rituals and invoke arcane rites to get our own way with things that are out of the control of normal human beings.

The real comparison I draw, though, is that there is no single way to program, no one methodology that solves every problem. There is no one programming language. There are different classes of problems to be solved in many, many different arenas. The work in each differs by more than mere technology (i.e., which tools and code libraries are available); they differ by technique. Each requires a different skill set, a particular mindset, and subtly different ways of working. The differences might seem slight, but there is no replacement for specific experience of programming a particular type of system—if there was, job advertisements for programmers would be a lot more vague. It's important to know your field well and to appreciate its unique concerns. In a particular programming arena, the craftsman knows how to ply his trade, how to work his medium, and how to best use his tools.

KEY CONCEPT *There are various types of programming, in different problem domains. Each presents its own unique problems and requires specific skills and experience.*

In this chapter, we'll explore this. We'll take a guided tour of the vast field that is computer programming, discover some of the common problem domains we program in, see how they differ, and learn the particular problems and challenges of each.

Some of these arenas overlap. That's natural. Nothing is ever quite as clear-cut as you'd imagine. The following descriptions are necessarily general, since each of these is a big field with lots of variations within. Nonetheless, this should give you a taste of what's going on out there.

Applications Programming

This is what most non-techies think of when you mention the word *programming*.[1] It's probably the broadest category we'll consider in this chapter.

It is programming *applications*—self-contained programs—typically for single-user, workstation-like computers. This world focuses on end users and how they use their desktop machines. For commercial reasons, we usually target the mainstream platforms—currently Windows and Mac OS. Although you hear a lot about Linux programming these days, that's still not where the applications work is (at least, at the time of writing). As portable devices become more powerful and their application development environments become richer, mobile applications work has moved from the embedded realm (see "Embedded Programming" on page 447) into this class of more general-purpose applications programming; the specific embedded hurdles have largely been removed.

There are many languages and environments for this kind of work; C and C++ are common. We also see common use of Visual Basic and Delphi, Java, and .NET, plus a number of libraries and frameworks like MFC and Qt. This choice is made according to what is convenient for the developers—something that's well-enough known and provides all required features.

---

[1] Which, of course, you don't. Admitting your job at a party can be an instant conversation killer. Well, unless it's a party full of nerds, in which case you're probably trying to escape, anyway!

Modern applications programming has advanced rapidly since the dawn of personal computing. We now have rich development environments to work in with helpful framework code that automates a lot of tedious boilerplate stuff. We have threading support, libraries of standard user interface components, and facilities for network transparency. There is a lot of operating system support provided to make applications programming easier, but this also means that there's a lot to learn as you get started. You have to know a lot to *really* understand what's going on around you.

All this extra support raises the bar to determine what a good application is. What was acceptable application behavior years ago is not today. People expect high-quality, robust programs, with a standard interface and look-and-feel, good responsiveness, user-friendliness (the ability to cope with the most inept user), and a plethora of features (even if the user will only take advantage of a fraction of them). The huge professional applications marketed today are the results of large development teams with departments specifically focusing on usability issues.

We are seeing a move toward web-based systems, applications that run on browsers, over a network. We'll look at them separately; this also cuts into the enterprise or distributed programming arenas somewhat (see "Distributed Programming" on page 450).

There are two main markets for applications programming: shrink-wrap software and custom applications.

Shrink-Wrap Software

Shrink-wrap software is developed for the mass market. It's used by a large number of people, or at least that's what the marketing departments are praying for. This is key: The market is speculative, so the software has to appeal to the broadest cross-section of consumers possible in order to make money. Since no customer commissions or pays for the development of shrink-wrap software, you must establish a profitable market before you begin work, or else you're throwing away time and effort. The software needs to differentiate itself from competing products in terms of features, performance, or a unique approach to the problem.

Shrink-wrap software might be bought over the counter in a box neatly wrapped in cellophane (hence the name), or it could be downloaded from the Internet. It could even be a subscription-based web service. The key point is the way you sell it and how that forces you to develop it.

Life is hard for shrink-wrap applications programmers. You can't control the environment the code runs in. It must gracefully handle all versions of the operating system, on different machine configurations, with different libraries and other apps installed, and it has to cope reliably with them all. That's a testing nightmare! Web applications programmers win half the battle (as we'll see later)—you have control over the server deployment. But you still have the headache of browser compatibility to contend with: Your web pages must render correctly on a wide range of target platforms.

Custom Applications

Custom applications are made-to-order—developed to a specific brief for a specific customer. Therefore, the focus isn't so much on an inviting UI, a never-ending feature list, or even to get it perfect and bug free. There's no commercial imperative to do this. Get it working. Get it shipped. Get the cash. This is a more certain business model.

Since a customer commissions this work, it will use this software or use nothing. With no real competition, the software only needs to be good *enough*. Given half a chance, programmers will keep tinkering and improving their code until it reaches some mythical state of perfection. But in this situation, it doesn't make commercial sense to do so. It doesn't really matter if the program works fine, but crashes once a week; it costs less to restart it periodically than to engage in a lengthy bug hunt (assuming that it doesn't trash any data as it goes down).

THE RUNDOWN

Application work is fun. Modern PCs are powerful, so you don't have to worry too much about code size or performance, and you can concentrate on writing neat, elegant code. It's a buzz to know your application is used by tens of thousands of people around the world.
—Steve (applications programmer for a major company)

Typical products
Typical shrink-wrap products are desktop applications like web browsers, spreadsheets, and so on. Custom software could be anything—a highly tailored inventory management system for a large retailer, for example.

Target platform
This tends to be the same kind of machine you are doing the development on (more often than not, an x86 Windows PC).

Development environment
You'll normally build code on the same workstation you run the program on. Modern *integrated development environments (IDEs)* provide comfortable working environments, bringing the editor, compiler, debugger, and help systems together in a single unified point-and-click interface. Many third-party components are available to simplify the development of common tasks. The full gamut of languages is employed here: from low-level C/C++, through BASIC and Java, to scripting languages.

Common problems and challenges
Users expect high-quality programs that conform to standard interface principles. More features than any person could remember are the order of the day; this is a serious commercial requirement, and usually what differentiates one product from the next. New product revisions these days tend to introduce more features (and bugs) than any problems they might solve. This is what the market demands.

Games Programming

The exciting and glamorous world of games programming is a specific form of applications work, usually developing shrink-wrap software. A lot of the battle is waged with captivating marketing and a very good initial concept for the game play. This is a fine line that differentiates a great, successful game from the also-rans.

These games often involve first-person, massive, immersive, 3D environments. To provide an absorbing experience, the graphics capability of the hardware is fully exploited, and the CPU is maxed out managing maps, enemies, and puzzles, while performing serious modeling of the physics of moving objects. This must all be coordinated in real time and stresses the hardware to its limits. A significant portion of games programming is optimizing the code to the execution platform. As faster hardware is released, the problem doesn't lessen; to stand out from other games, more optimization is required to squeeze a better experience out of the new platforms. This field is very much about staying on the cutting edge and using the latest state-of-the-art technology to do the coolest thing.

THE RUNDOWN

Professional games development is about fun, but it's a hugely competitive industry where developers are expected to keep up with the latest technologies, furious deadlines, and nonnegotiable, last-minute change requests. Sweat, blood, and tears are required to write the software, only for it to meet the harsh public glare of a highly critical specialist press. But it can be hugely rewarding—once finished, you've made something that people can see, understand, and enjoy.
—Thaddeus (professional games programmer)

Typical products
First-person, immersive, 3D games, strategy games, online puzzles.

Target platform
Desktop PC, games consoles, mobile devices (PDAs and mobile phones), arcade machines.

Development environment
Dedicated games platforms (including high-end graphics cards in standard PCs) have tailored development environments to help exploit their power. It still takes very talented developers to fully capitalize on the platform's functionality.

Common problems and challenges
Getting excellent game play; balancing features, user response, aesthetics, atmosphere, and difficulty. A good game unfolds very much like a story, and draws the player in.
Optimization is required to capitalize on the execution platform.

Modern games development teams often have a cast more akin to Hollywood movie production than to standard bean-counting software. We see teams including graphics artists and level designers and the development of storyboards, concept art, and proof-of-concept designs.

The software might target a (suitably souped-up) PC platform or dedicated games consoles. These machines have specific hardware to accelerate the many graphics operations required per second and special tools to help you harness their power. Console manufacturers provide development kits (special versions of the hardware and tailored software tools) to help you create products, assisting with code loading, testing, and debugging, while helping to avoid security features on production hardware that would impede development.

Multiplayer games provide richer game play. This brings network collaboration into the mix and requires some skill to get acceptable real-time performance out of slow Internet connections.

The quality of the ultimate product is determined by the feel of the game play. Everything is tweaked until the game feels right: the level design, the physics models, the graphics, the color of your underwear. Nothing is sacred. You might write the most beautiful code in the world; the program might never crash; it might do everything it was specified to do; it might be highly efficient. But if it lacks that special spark that makes it a compelling, addictive game, it will not be successful. Tricky stuff.

Systems Programming

Applications sit atop rich system libraries: layers of code for networking, graphical interfaces, multitasking, file access, multimedia, peripheral control, inter-process communication, and more. If applications programmers receive a lot of support from the underlying system, then someone's got to supply that underlying system. This is systems programming.

It is generally for workstation machines too, but it's not aimed at the end users. Systems software is aimed at the application developer; the public façade is a set of APIs to be used by software layers higher up the food chain. Systems software is concerned with the low-level logic that interacts with the computer at a very basic level, and also middle-level support frameworks that don't interface directly to hardware but provide important services to the rest of the system.

Work in this arena typically includes writing device drivers (controlling devices such as printers, storage media, output devices, etc.), writing common shared libraries and utilities for managing scarce resources, implementing the actual operating systems controlling the computer, and providing components such as filing systems and network stacks. Even compilers and installation tool suites can come under this heading, as they are support services for application programmers and are often intimately entwined with the program run-time environment.

THE RUNDOWN

*I wrote the USB stack for a proprietary operating system.
I had to understand the OS, USB hardware, and the USB
protocol, so there was a lot to take in. I had to keep up
performance so the system worked well. Acting as the
middleman, I was abstracting the hardware interfaces
and providing a neat API for applications to use. I had to
make this platform agnostic, which added extra
complexity.*
—Dave (systems component writer)

Typical products
Operating systems, device drivers, a window manager, or a graphics subsystem.

Target platform
Since every execution environment needs some form of run-time support, there is
system-level software in almost every electronic device. Systems software is
required in the smallest embedded device and the largest mainframe computer.

Development environment
Writing device drivers and operating system components tends to screw with the
computer and make your system unstable, so it's common to develop on one
machine and run the code on a second system. C is by far the most common
language in this arena, although some library-level work is done in other languages (C++ is popular, as it aims to be a systems-capable language).

Common problems and challenges
The key here is *stability*, since these are foundational blocks of the entire computing
environment. While an application might crash and have a chance to save work
and gracefully recover, a device driver rarely has such a luxury; it is required to
work correctly the entire time it runs. This could be an awfully long time, so even
small memory leaks can become major problems.
The code must be efficient (enough), both in terms of space and speed, and will
need to be appropriately tailored to the particular operating environment.

Embedded Programming

Computer technology shows up everywhere in our daily lives, whether we're
aware of it or not. We're constantly using devices and gizmos, from micro-
waves to watches, radios to thermostats. These consumer electronics products
require software for control and operation. More often than not, this software
is invisible to the device's user. It's not just consumer electronics appliances
that contain embedded software: Anything with a microcontroller (e.g.,
laboratory instruments or the machines that issue parking tickets) is software
driven. We must write programs that are embedded in the hardware devices:
embedded software.

Embedded developers work under tight constraints:

- There are usually very scarce resources: restricted CPU power and/or strict memory limits. Memory limitations concern both ROM (for the program image) and RAM (space for the code to execute and to store information). On platforms without much capacity, you have to shoe-horn a lot of software into the available device space. Sometimes this requires quite creative (and heroic) solutions, like decompressing program code or data on the fly.

- The opportunities for user interface are quite limited: how do you pack all user interaction into two buttons and an LED? Indeed, there may be no user interface at all; there may be no direct interaction with a user—the software is expected to just work.

These constraints have a profound impact on the nature of the code you write. Sadly, in the embedded environment (more than others), we end up sacrificing the purity of our code to get something working. Fast code that fits into the device's ROM and works is more important than theologically correct but large and slow software.

Embedded systems are designed to do one job and to do it reliably. It should appear as if the software is not there; the embedded device should just work, all the time. Failure is rarely an option; it might physically break the hardware. Contrast this to a desktop computer—it's a general-purpose machine. It has to be able to word process, play movies, browse websites, read email, manage your accounts, and so on. As users, we've been conditioned to accept the odd crash and a bit of instability. We'll sacrifice a little convenience for power and flexibility. Embedded work is a totally different ballpark.

A good example is the modern car industry. We see vehicles manufactured with many embedded systems, controlling all sorts of things: engine management, ABS brakes, safety features like air bags and seat belt pre-tensioners, climate control, the odometer, and so on. However, the users (in this case the driver and/or passengers) don't have to be at all aware that there are any microprocessors whirring away under the hood. They expect the car to just work. When an engine management system fails, the user becomes acutely aware of the software! Think also about mobile phones. They are obviously computer-driven devices, but few consumers think of them as a computer. We pack a lot of power into these small packages, but there are still strict operational limits that the software must work within.

An embedded system is typically the combination of a small computer, some dedicated hardware, and either a real-time operating system or a simple controlling program. It will have direct control over the hardware on the device. Embedded systems are usually made-to-order: developed for specific hardware, for a specific purpose. Simple embedded systems have only one piece of software running on them; no highly complex threaded programming environments are used—not even an operating system.

The code is usually stored in firmware, permanently held in a read-only memory chip. It is seldom updatable, so it has to work correctly the first time. There's no chance to get it wrong and ship a version 1.1. One simple mistake can render your miracle product a failure.

Recently, memory and CPU power have become a lot cheaper as more and more mass market devices are created. Embedded environments have become more powerful and the constraints are widening. However, there will always be the need for very small devices with little horsepower that achieve just what they need to. Just.

You might consider that programming applications for handheld devices like PDAs is embedded-level or applications-level work, depending on where you stand.

THE RUNDOWN

I like working near the metal—it really forces you to think about what's going on. You need tight code and a good understanding of what the hardware's doing. It can be tricky to debug problems, but these challenges are what makes it interesting.
—Graham (embedded software developer)

Typical products
Control software for washing machines, hi-fis, mobile phones.

Target platform
Small, custom-made devices with very limited resources and meager UIs.

Development environment
Since you work with custom-made devices, the toolchain is also often custom made. Frequently, it's not very advanced at all, compared to the relative luxury of the applications programmer. (As the market broadens, we are seeing improvements here.) The code is developed in a *cross-compilation* environment, where the target platform is different from host compilation environment. (Clearly you can't compile C on a washing machine . . . yet.)

We write specialized software for each specific device. Embedded programming almost universally uses C, apart from really low-level work, which resorts to assembly code. C++ is making inroads into this area, and ADA has also been used.

Common problems and challenges
There are all sorts of problems you can encounter, largely depending on whether you are working with a commodity, *off-the-shelf* embedded platform or building your own. There are issues of real-time programming (for example, timely handling of hardware events and interrupts), direct hardware interfacing, and controlling peripheral connections, plus tedious low-level concerns like byte endianness and physical memory layout.

To ensure the system is robust, there must be a great emphasis on product testing.[*]

---

[*] Of course any good software development—not just embedded work—needs a great emphasis on testing. In *all* environments, testing tends to suffer as it is squeezed out by overzealous marketing and management departments who do not really understand the nature of software. However, desktop applications can be more easily updated than the firmware in an embedded device.

Distributed Programming

Distributed systems are comprised of more than one computer. As we'll see later, the World Wide Web is effectively a huge distributed system with information being stored on many computers across many continents and with applications delivered remotely via your web browser. It's not all about web browsers, though. Multimachine architectures are used in many situations. Working with and designing distributed systems ushers in a whole new world of problems.

You might need to distribute a software system for a number of reasons. Perhaps some types of computers are more suited to particular tasks than others. Perhaps the system is in high demand, and you can share the workload among many machines on a network to improve performance. Perhaps there are physical location restrictions for certain machines that mandate distributing the system. Perhaps you need to interoperate a new installation with a legacy system or some old hardware.

The goal is to design a system that is composed of a number of programs on different machines that all work as a cohesive whole. Tied together by a network connection, they might be physically co-located in a corporate server room or scattered across the globe, communicating over the Internet.

The disparate parts need to be glued together somehow; each of the programs needs to communicate, and it is desirable to call functions on remote machines as if they were locally linked to the code. This is known as *remote procedure call (RPC)*, and such facilities are provided by a number of available *middleware technologies*. These act as brokers for data transfer between machines; they describe how you discover and talk to services on other machines and how you publish your services for other programs to call. Middleware manages the policies involved with interoperability: there are security issues (Who's allowed to call whom?), network latency issues (What happens if a remote function call takes too long or a computer goes down?), considerations for balancing synchronous remote function calls with asynchronous calls, and more.

Some middleware systems employ object-oriented technologies; some take more of a procedural approach. The middleware is simply connectivity software and allows some degree of platform neutrality. As long as the middleware runs on a given platform, the client code shouldn't care what platform it's calling into—it could even be a ZX spectrum—the function calls all look the same. Of course, in the design of a distributed system, you will select the appropriate hardware for each task. It's doubtful you'll see any ZX spectrums hanging around!

Commonly used middlewares are CORBA, the Java RMI, Microsoft's DCOM, and .NET remoting. Using these, we split the system between user interface elements, the business logic (real workhorse code), and any storage required (e.g., a database and query engine). The user interface client may be a GUI program or a web-based front end. This is the classic *tiered architecture approach* (described in "Client/Server Architecture" on page 271). We also see the emergence of *web APIs*—communications methods for services that use standard web protocols.

Grid computing and clustered systems are specific distribution mechanisms that help numerical programming work (more on this later), enabling the creation of high performance, distributed computational algorithms. Clusters are tightly coupled systems; usually all the machines are in the same room, using the same hardware and OSes, linked by a specific cluster middleware. Grids are loosely coupled; they could be geographically scattered and run heterogeneous environments. They communicate via standard web protocols (e.g., HTTP/XML).

THE RUNDOWN

The Smallpox project, completed in 2003, was a grid computing project to help find a cure for smallpox by screening a huge number of potential drug molecules. It was a collaboration between scientists, universities, and businesses that identified 44 strong candidates for treatment of the disease.

Typical products
An online purchase system, splitting work between front-end applications (web interface, in-shop kiosk, and/or phone ordering system), business logic (manages stock control, implements ordering system and secure billing) and the shared storage.

Target platform
Many different computer systems connect via a middleware, almost always sitting on top of standard networking protocols.

Development environment
Many and varied. This will depend on languages used, the nature of each computer in the system, and the type of middleware employed. Remotely callable interfaces are often defined in some form of *interface definition language (IDL)* and compiled to an implementation language representation that provides all the calling glue and provides hooks for each function implementation to be slotted in to.

Common problems and challenges
Designing the correct split of services between computers and streamlining the communications involved. This can severely affect the *scalability* of a distributed system. What works for a few transactions per day may not work efficiently for 100 transactions per minute. This calls for a real need to design carefully. You also have to deal with computer availability and cope gracefully if one of the computers in the system becomes unavailable.

Web Application Programming

In 1990, Tim Berners-Lee created the first HTML browser and server, and the World Wide Web was born. Today it is a pervasive technology, and servers can not only deliver static pages of information, but they can dynamically create pages based on programs running on the webserver. This is a very specific form of distributed computing, where the user interface is hosted on a remote client: the web browser.

Examples of this kind of application include:

- Online shopping
- Bulletin boards, messaging services, and web-based email packages
- Ticket availability and booking systems
- Internet search engines

Most people now use web applications without thought; it's as natural as a local word processor. These programs clearly have different characteristics from ordinary (so-called *rich client*) desktop applications. There are different things that each can do well. Without heroic JavaScript coding, interaction in a browser-based application UI is a lot more limited.

THE RUNDOWN

A web app makes you treat the web browser as your OS. All good web developers start by learning client-side browser technologies inside out. Then you learn to write good server-side code (i.e., fast, concurrent, transactional, distributed, and correct). The best thing about the Web is that it is constantly evolving and users' expectations are always rising. The bad thing about the Web is that users' expectations are always rising and your code never stands still.
—Alan (web applications programmer)

Typical products
Interactive services that require up-to-date information and feedback: ticket booking or shopping systems.

Target platform
The back end is a webserver (commonly Apache or IIS). This choice is under your control, since you deploy the web app. The clients are web browsers, and there are many variants. Each has its own quirks, and you have no control over what is used. You have to produce web pages that are compatible with most of these.

Development environment
The environment consists of the specific webserver and the applications programming language you write the system in, running on that server. Common languages are Perl and PHP.

Common problems and challenges
Coping with different browsers; scalability.

The web application operational model is different from vanilla applications programming—session state is held on a remote machine, which must manage numerous simultaneous client connections, storing their state between HTTP interactions and gracefully handling clients that stop connecting. To facilitate this, some information is stored on the server (e.g., the items each customer is ordering are placed in a database) and some on the local client (using web browser *cookies*—nuggets of stored session state—to record the current user/session ID). Frameworks like ASP.NET and

Java Servlets exist to speed web application development. Numerous off-the-shelf systems exist, such as content management systems and shopping cart systems.

Many open standard protocols and encoding systems are used to represent and transfer information. HTTP is the common data transfer mechanism, and XML is often used to encode data packets (e.g., SOAP is a web-based communication protocol based on an XML schema).

The problems faced by web application programmers mainly revolve around interoperability with the many types of browsers that might be used, handling their HTML peculiarities and their odd JavaScript quirks. It's not unusual to develop tortuous HTML output to cope with all manners of flaws in the popular browsers. Web programmers often have to interface with legacy systems (customer databases, existing order management systems, etc.) to generate their information; this can get quite messy. Scalability is a real concern: A system might work fine when tested by five simultaneous users. But when it goes live, it must withstand 500 users accessing it at the same time. *Load testing* is important here (see "Load testing" on page 139).

Enterprise Programming

Enterprise is one of those tedious buzzwords that floats around, more management-speak than any programmer dialect. An enterprise is literally a business organization. So enterprise programming provides systems for entire companies, gluing all their separate systems together to form a unified, cohesive whole. Enterprise programming almost always means the development of large distributed systems.

They'll commonly be deployed on a company intranet (internal network) and link the different departments of the business together to improve workflow. The systems may or may not be customer facing. Once the organization is running an integrated computer system, it's generally not too hard to have automated customer interaction—for example, through a web-based shop interface. Perhaps an enterprise system will need to interface to other companies' systems too, to track the delivery status of goods being shipped, for example.

Enterprise programming shares a lot of characteristics with made-to-order applications software. The product only really needs to be good *enough*, since it's developed under contract for a specific customer, rather than speculatively for a general-market release. Quality here is not the measure of success (at least as determined by general stability and a larger feature set than any competitor); meeting the customer's objectives is.

Enterprise systems are written for installation on specific machines in a company's server room or on locked-down desktop machines. You have reasonable control over the execution environment, so you don't need to worry about making the code work on every release of the operating system and under every conceivable hardware configuration. This deftly sidesteps a lot of the headaches that applications programmers suffer.

THE RUNDOWN

*I work in the IT department of a large city bank. We write soft-
ware to solve specific business needs. It's mission critical; what
we do makes a real difference to the company's profits, so we
have to take it seriously. With many thousands of dollars going
through the system every hour, there's no room for error.*
—*Richard (Enterprise programmer)*

Typical products
Business systems for an entire company, managing its commercial operations.

Target platform
A tailored distributed system.

Development environment
Same as for distributed systems. We'll probably be working with huge data stores,
perhaps various database technologies from previous internal systems (legacy
systems in manager-speak). XML is all the rage here.

Common problems and challenges
Same as for distributed systems.

Numerical Programming

This kind of work involves scientific, highly technical tasks making heavy use
of mathematics. This is a very specialized area that requires writing applications specifically targeted at particular numerical problems. The programs
are often aimed at supercomputers, the fastest type of computers, capable of
massive number-crunching operations. Although we're living in times when
the fastest computer changes from year to year, these are very expensive
platforms, employed for specialized applications that require immense
mathematical calculations.

Weather forecasting, for example, requires a supercomputer (or perhaps
a gift of prophesy!). We also see supercomputers used for animated graphics,
fluid dynamic calculations, and other areas that require highly complex
mathematical investigation and calculation.

A supercomputer is not a mainframe. The latter is a high-performance
computer designed to concurrently execute as many programs as possible,
often used as a centralized computing resource in a business setting. A supercomputer channels all its power into executing a few programs as fast as
possible. There are a number of different supercomputer architectures
exploiting different technological advances, each requiring different algorithmic approaches to fully exploit their power. General-purpose machines
are now becoming powerful enough for serious numerical work—clustered,
they can respectably make a poor man's supercomputer.

Numerical work requires high-performance algorithms that execute
calculations rapidly, to capitalize on the performance of the computing
platform. It is common to make use of carefully designed, heavily optimized
numerical libraries and to make explicit use of parallel processing, designing
this into the computational algorithms and processes. This will involve both

task and data parallelism: either performing many similar tasks on many CPUs at once or pipelining the algorithm, performing different parts of it on different CPUs.

This branch of programming requires heavy optimization to the characteristics of the target platform to achieve acceptable performance.

THE RUNDOWN

I work on software systems for an engineering firm. We model large mechanical installations to figure out where physical problems might lie now or in the future. I have to represent the real world in a mathematical way, figuring out how things (should) work. Once I've done this, it's a case of finding the right mathematical constructs to represent the systems in an acceptable, accurate way.
—Andy (Numerical programming expert)

Typical products
Fields involving highly complex mathematical investigation like nuclear energy research or petroleum exploration.

Target platform
Supercomputers or grid-based computing clusters.

Development environment
Although there is work on advancing numerical programming support in C++, and some of this work is performed in C, a lot of numerical programming is done in Fortran, which has excellent numeric support (that was what it was designed for: formula *translation*).

Common problems and challenges
Crafting efficient algorithms to really exploit the power of the supercomputer.

So What?

Freedom from the desire for an answer is essential to the understanding of a problem.
—Jiddu Krishnamurti

How do these programming niches affect us? What do they make us do differently? To be a good programmer, a true craftsman, you must know:

- What your discipline is—the kind of software you're producing.

- How the discipline affects your architecture. (Is it a tiered enterprise system or tightly woven ball of embedded code? See Chapter 14.)

- What is an appropriate code design in this field and what isn't. (For example, should you sacrifice clarity and elegance for performance, try to squeeze the executable image into the smallest size possible, or perhaps incorporate many hooks for future extensibility?)

- The tools you use—what's available and what isn't.

- Which is the most appropriate choice of programming language and which coding idioms you should employ.

KEY CONCEPT *Know your discipline. Learn its intricacies. Understand how to write excellent software that appropriately meets its requirements.*

In a Nutshell

> *Still round the corner there may wait,*
> *A new road or a secret gate.*
> *—J.R.R. Tolkien*

We've dipped a toe in the water and sampled the different flavors of programming going on out there. Of course, there are other areas than those we've seen: some well defined, others more ephemeral. For example, *safety-critical software* drives high-reliability systems like medical equipment and aircraft control. Here failure is not an option, and the code must be *provably* correct; this has a profound affect on the way you design and write it.

What have we learned? These fields all have one thing in common: their differences. Each requires fundamental design decisions to be made to suit software to them. Application-level code is not generally suited to an embedded environment. A workstation application design may not scale when applied to a distributed system.

This means that software developers tend to specialize in particular fields and learn to think in particular patterns that suit their worlds. Understanding the very real concerns of each environment will make you a more flexible and mature programmer. Ultimately, you must know your programming church and practice its rites and rituals well.

Good programmers . . .	Bad programmers . . .
• Understand the nature of the problems they face • Tailor their code and designs to the problem domain	• Have a naïvely narrow software worldview; they don't understand the forces that drive other types of software development • Write code ill-suited for the problem domain (choosing unsympathetic architectures or inappropriate code idioms)

See Also

Chapter 7: The Programmer's Toolbox
Different niches have different qualities and ranges of development tools.

Chapter 14: Software Architecture
Different problem domains call for very different software solutions.

Get Thinking

A detailed discussion of these questions can be found in the "Answers and Discussion" section on page 557.

Mull It Over

1. Which of the programming niches we've looked at here are particularly similar or share common characteristics? Which are particularly different?
2. Which of these programming disciplines is hardest?
3. Is it important to be an expert in one particular area or to have a good grounding in all of them without a particular specialism?
4. Which programming niche should trainee programmers be introduced to?

Getting Personal

1. What programming arena are you working in right now? How does it affect the code that you're writing? What specific design and implementation decisions has it led you to make?
2. Do you have experience working in more than one programming discipline? How easy was it for you to switch mindsets and apply appropriate techniques in a different world?
3. Are any of the people you work with unaware of the forces that shape the particular kind of code you write? Do you have embedded software being written by programmers who only understand applications work? What can you do about this?

WHERE NEXT?

All's Well That Ends Well

What we call the beginning is often the end. And to make an end is to make a beginning. The end is where we start from.
—*T.S. Eliot*

Congratulations! You've reached the end of this book. Either that, or you're the kind of person who likes to spoil an ending by reading the last page first. (If you are: *The butler did it.*) Presuming that you've read every chapter, by now you should have:

- Learned many practical code-writing techniques that have already improved your source code.
- Gained an understanding of how to write code in the Real World and the tricks that help you to produce useful code in the madness of the software factory.
- Worked out some personal ways to improve your skill set. (You did attempt the questions, didn't you? If not, try them now.)
- Discovered how to write effective code as part of a team, establishing practical steps to improve the way your team currently works together.
- Found out more about cartoon monkeys than you ever really needed to.

But more importantly, you should now appreciate that an exceptional programmer is one with the right attitude: one who always seeks to write the best code in any situation, who works well with others, and who can make pragmatic decisions in the heat of the software factory. The craftsman knows how to manage technical debt and seeks to address problems early, before they become software snares.

KEY CONCEPT *Becoming a good programmer requires you to adopt effective* attitudes—*the angle of approach you take to software construction.*

But What Now?

> *The important thing is not to stop questioning. Curiosity has its own reason for existing. One cannot help but be in awe when he contemplates the mysteries of eternity, of life, of the marvelous structure of reality. It is enough if one tries merely to comprehend a little of this mystery every day. Never lose a holy curiosity.*
> —Albert Einstein

As a code craftsman, you'll never reach perfection; the best you can ever achieve is a continual state of improvement. There's always more to learn. So what should you do now? The very fact that you're asking that question is pivotal—one of the most important charateristics of a code craftsman is a desire to improve.

If I wanted to become a skilled soccer player, I might find some books on soccer, buy a soccer training video, and then sit down with some popcorn and a few beers to learn how to play the game. Great. Ask me how it's going two months later. If I say, "I've read loads about it, and I know all the top moves of the premier players," then you won't be at all impressed: How well can I actually *play*? It is a geniunely good idea to read about the game and to study it, but couch potato soccer skills aren't any real use.

I can only learn soccer by doing it—by getting dirty, out on a field, playing the game. *Practice makes perfect.* I need to play with people who are skilled and who can train me well. I need to expend energy, feel the burn, and perhaps make a fool of myself in front of others. Slowly, gradually, painfully, I'll get better.

I hate to break it to you, but that's the only way to get good at code craft too. Just reading this book won't cut it. You have to get out there and *do it*. Properly. So how can we translate this into practice? Here are a few simple ideas:

- Place this book on your bookshelf. Put what you've learned into practice as best you can right now. You can always refer to a specific chapter when you run into problems later on.

  After a few months of working with this advice, pull out the book once more and give it another read. Pay particular attention to the questions in the "Getting Personal" sections—work out what your next steps must be to improve your code. Each time you go through this process, you'll identify new ways to improve your skills.

- Maneuver your career into the path of great coders, and glean all you can from them. Learn what makes their code good and their attitudes constructive, and how you can apply these characteristics to yourself. Seek their advice, criticism, review, and opinion. Ask them to mentor you. (Bribe them with popcorn and alcohol if you have to!)

- Keep programming, and expand your horizions. Write more code. Try out new techniques. Tackle new problems, different languages, and unfamiliar technologies.

- Don't be afraid of making mistakes; you won't become a perfect programmer overnight. As you learn, you will almost certainly make many embarrassing faux pas. Don't let these stunt your growth or define you as a programmer. Unless you try out new techniques, you'll never learn and won't improve. George Bernard Shaw wrote, "A life spent making mistakes is more useful than a life spent doing nothing."

    Receive advice and code review comments with a constructive attitude. Look back at what you've done, and see how it can be improved.

- Develop outside interests that you can use as a frame of reference for technical knowledge. If all you ever study is programming, then you will become a very two-dimensional person and will not be able to fit code craft into the context of the Real World.

- Find the classic books in your field. (*Code Craft* is obviously one of them!) Get a copy of each, and digest it well. Every disicpline and every language has its renowned gurus—ensure you know who they are and what they've written.

    Read the classic software tomes, like:
    - *The Mythical Man-Month* (Brooks 95)
    - *The Psychology of Computer Programming* (Weinberg 71)
    - *Peopleware: Productive Projects and Teams* (DeMarco 99)
    - *The Pragmatic Programmer* (Hunt Davis 99)
    - *Code Complete* (McConnell 04)
    - *The Practice of Programming* (Kernighan Pike 99)
    - *Design Patterns: Elements of Reusable Object-Oriented Software* (Gamma et al. 94)
    - *Refactoring: Improving the Design of Existing Code* (Fowler 99)

    Ask your peers which books they have found valuable. Seek out relevant magazines, websites, and conferences.

- Teach. Mentor a lesser abled programmer. You'll learn a lot more by passing on your wisdom.

- Broaden your skills base by joining a professional organization like the British Computer Society (BCS), the Association for Computing Machinery (ACM), or the ACCU (www.accu.org). Then join in—contribute. The more you participate, the more you'll invest in yourself. The ACCU, for example, is highly contributory. It runs mentored developer projects and encourages members to write for its periodicals. These organizations run programming contests, provide forums for social networking, and often have local chapters where you can meet like-minded people who care about the craft of programming.

- Have fun! Enjoy cutting code to solve tricky problems. Produce software that makes you proud. Confucius said, "If you enjoy what you do, you'll never work another day in your life."

KEY CONCEPT   *Take responsibility for improving your skills. Never lose your passion for programming or your desire to do it with excellence.*

ANSWERS AND DISCUSSION

Principles for the Development of a Complete Mind:
Study the science of art. Study the art of science. Develop
your senses—especially learn how to see. Realize that
everything connects to everything else.
—*Leonardo DaVinci*

This part contains my musings on the questions at the end of each chapter. It's not a straight answer set—few of the questions have a definite *yes* or *no* response. Compare your answers with these.

The point of these questions is simply to get you thinking, to make you delve deeper into each subject, and to spur you to improve your programming skills.

If you're thinking of reading this just to get the "answers" without having thought about the questions first, I'd really encourage you not to. Spending even a little time mulling things over and getting personal will really pay off. As Confucius said, "I hear and I forget. I see and I remember. I do and I understand."

Chapter 1: On the Defensive

Mull It Over

1. **Can you have *too much* defensive programming?**

Yes—just as too many comments can degrade code readability, so can many defensive checks, if they are bad. Redundant checks can be avoided with careful coding; for example, by making a good choice of types.

2. Should you add an assertion to your code for every bug you find and fix?

Fundamentally, it's not a bad practice. But think about where you'd add the assertions. Many, many faults are due to incorrect honoring of API contracts. If you passed garbage into a function, you would want to put some *precondition* checking inside that function, rather than put a test at the call site. If the function returned garbage, you would either fix the function so that it won't again (and prove it's fixed) or write some *postconditions.*

It would be more beneficial to add a new unit test for every bug you find and fix.

3. Should assertions conditionally compile away to nothing in production builds? If not, which assertions should remain in release builds?

People hold passionate beliefs on this subject. The answer isn't black and white; there are powerful arguments for both sides. There are always some very nit-picky assertions that really don't *need* to be left in production builds. But some assertion occurrences may still interest you in the field.

Now, if you do leave any constraint checks in releases, they *must* change behavior—the program shouldn't abort on failure, just log the problem and move on.

Remember: Genuine run-time error checks should *never* be removed; they should never be coded in assertions anyway.

4. Are exceptions a better form of defensive barrier than C-style assertions?

They can be. Exceptions behave differently; while propagating back up the call stack, an exception can be caught and ignored—suppressing its effect. This makes exceptions more flexible tools. You can't ignore an assert that aborts execution; assertions are lower-level mechanisms.

5. Should the defensive checking of pre- and postconditions be put *inside* each function, or around each important function *call*?

In the function, without a doubt. This way, you only need to write tests once. The only reason you'd want to move them out is to gain flexibility, to choose what happens when a constraint fails. This isn't a compelling gain for such an explosion in complexity and potential for failure.

6. Are constraints a perfect defensive tool? What are their drawbacks?

No, they are nowhere near perfect. Redundant constraints can be pests at best and hindrances at worst. For example, you could assert that a function parameter i >= 0. But it's much better to make i an unsigned type that can't contain invalid values anyway.

Treat constraints that can be compiled out with a certain degree of suspicion: We must carefully check for any side effects (assertions can have subtle indirect consequences) and for timing issues in the debug build that alters its behavior from a release build. Ensure that assertions are logical constraints and not genuine run-time checks that mustn't be compiled out. It *is* possible to put bugs in the bug-defense code!

But carefully used, constraints are still far better than dancing barefoot over the hot coals of chance.

7. **Can you *avoid* defensive programming?**

    a. **If you designed a *better* language, would defensive programming still be necessary? How could you do this?**

    b. **Does this show that C and C++ are flawed because they have so many areas for problems to manifest?**

Some language features certainly could be designed to avoid errors. For example, C doesn't check the index of any array lookup you perform. As a result, you can crash the program by accessing an invalid memory address. The Java run time, on the other hand, checks *every* array index before lookup, so such an catastrophe will never arise. (Bad indexes will still cause an error though, just a better defined class of failure.)

Despite the long list of "improvements" you could make to the liberal C specification (and I urge you to think of as many as you can), you'll never be able to create a language that doesn't need defensive programming. Functions will always need to validate parameters, and classes will always need invariants to check that their data is internally consistent.

Although C and C++ do provide plenty of opportunity for things to go wrong, they also provide a great deal of power and expression. Whether that makes the languages flawed depends on your viewpoint—this is a topic ripe for holy war.

8. **What sort of code do you not need to worry about writing defensively?**

I've worked with people who refused to put any defensive code into an old program because it was *so bad* that their defenses would make no difference. I managed to resist the urge to whack them with a large mallet.

You might argue that a small, stand-alone, single-file program or a test harness doesn't need this sort of careful defensive code or any rigorous constraints. But even in these situations, not being careful is just being sloppy. We should aim to be defensive all the time.

Getting Personal

1. **How carefully do you consider each statement that you type? Do you relentlessly check every function return code, even if you're *sure* a function will not return an error?**

I bet you don't check everything. It's far too easy to overlook certain function return codes, especially since some are deemed more important than others. How many C programmers check the return value of `printf`? How many actually *know* that it returns anything?

2. **When you document a function, do you state the pre- and postconditions?**
   a. **Are they always implicit in the description of what the function does?**
   b. **If there are no pre- or postconditions, do you explicitly document this?**

No matter how obvious you think a contract is (from the function name or its description), explicitly stating the constraints removes any ambiguity—remember, it's always better to remove areas of assumption. Explicitly writing *Preconditions: None* will document a contract explicitly.

Of course, you don't want every function to explicitly restate a global precondition. It would be laborious and tedious. If an entire API expects that pointer values mustn't be null, it's arguably better to document this once, globally.

3. **Many companies pay lip service to defensive programming. Does your team recommend it? Take a look at the codebase—do they really? How widely are constraints codified in assertions? How thorough is the error checking in each function?**

Very few companies have a culture of excellent code with the right level of defense. Code reviews are a good way to bring a team's code up to a reasonable standard; many eyes see many more potential errors.

4. **Are you naturally paranoid enough? Do you look both ways before crossing the road? Do you eat your greens? Do you check for every potential error in your code, no matter how unlikely?**
   a. **How easy is it to do this thoroughly? Do you forget to think about errors?**
   b. **Are there any ways to help yourself write more thorough defensive code?**

No one finds it naturally easy—thinking the worst of your carefully crafted new code is contrary to a programmer's instincts. Instead, expect the worst of any people who will be using your code. They're nowhere near as conscientious a programmer as you are!

A very helpful technique is to write unit tests for each function or class. Some experts strongly advise doing this *before* writing a function, which makes a lot of sense. It helps you to think about all the error cases, rather than happily trusting that your code will work.

Chapter 2: The Best Laid Plans

Mull It Over

1. **Should you alter the layout of legacy code to conform to your latest code style? Is this a valuable use of code reformatting tools?**

It's usually safest to leave legacy code however you find it, even if it's ugly and hard to work with. I'd only entertain reformatting if I was absolutely sure that none of the original authors would ever need to return.

By reformatting, you lose the ability to easily compare a particular revision of the source with a previous one—you'll be thrown by many, many formatting changes which may hide the one important difference you really need to see. You also risk introducing program errors in the reformatting.

As far as code reformatting tools go, they're nice curiosities, but I don't advocate the use of them. Some companies insist on running source files through beautifiers before checking any code into their repository. The advantage is that all code is homogenized, pasteurized, and uniformly formatted. The major disadvantage is that no tool is perfect; you'll lose some helpful nuances of the author's layout. Unless all the programmers on your team are gibbons, don't use a reformatting tool.

2. A common layout convention is to split source lines at a set number of columns. What are the pros and cons of this? Is it useful?

As with many presentation concerns, there is no absolute answer; it is a matter of personal taste.

I like to split my code up so that it fits on an 80-column display. I've always done that, so it's a matter of habit as much as anything else. I don't disagree with people who like long lines, but I find long lines hard to work with. I set my editor up to wrap continuous lines rather than provide a horizontal scrollbar (horizontal scrolling is clumsy). In this environment, long lines tend to ruin the effect of any indentation.

As I see it, the main advantage of fixed column widths is not printability, as some would claim. It's the ability to have several editor windows open side by side on the same display.

In practice, C++ produces very long lines. It's more verbose than C; you end up calling member functions on objects referenced by another object through a templated container. . . . There are strategies to manage the many, many, long lines this may lead to. You can store intermediate references in temporary variables, for example.

3. How detailed should a *reasonable* coding standard be?

    a. How serious are deviations from the style? How many limbs should be amputated for not following it?

    b. Can a standard become too detailed and restrictive? What would happen if it did?

Six limbs should be amputated for deviations from any coding standard.

The correct answer really depends on the exhaustiveness of the coding standard and the coding culture you work in. There are usually much bigger software problems to address than a misplaced bracket, but brackets are easier to moan about. I have seen many coding standards that are so pre-scriptive and paralyzing that the poor programmers have just plain ignored them. To be useful and to be accepted, a coding standard should provide a little room for maneuvering, perhaps with a *best practice* approach given as an example.

4. When defining a new presentation style, how many items or cases need layout rules? What other presentation rules must be provided? List them.

If you write out each layout rule individually, there will be an awfully large number of cases to consider. Coding style is a delicate interplay of many forces: indentation, yes, but also internal spacing, naming, positioning of operators, presentation of parentheses, contents of files, use and ordering of header files, and more, and more.

The following list of presentation items *is* long, but it's far from complete. It's a good starting point for a style checklist. In practice, some items are more important to standardize than others. As you read this list, make sure that you have considered a personal preference for each item. Also make sure that you know the correct convention for your current software project.

Code margins

- The number of spaces per indent shapes the left edge of the code. It's common to see two- or four-space indents, though some programmers diplomatically choose three spaces. Smaller indents mean that you don't run into the right margin as quickly, but they look cluttered and make it harder to differentiate among levels. Larger indents are more distinct, but you run out of space more quickly.

- Whether to indent with tabs or spaces is a long-running debate that has driven many programmers to therapy. Spaces are more portable; they'll display the same width in any editor. When displaying code using a variable width font,[1] tabs can give better alignment.

- Page width determines how you format the right-hand code edge. You can limit lines to a fixed number of columns or let them grow forever, requiring horizontal window navigation. Fixed pages are often 79 or 80 characters wide. This is historic; 80 characters is a common terminal width, but the last column was not always usable for display.

- There are choices for aligning certain constructs. At which level do you put `public:`, `private:`, and `protected:` in a class declaration? Where do `case` labels go in `switch` statements? How do you format labels for the goto statements you never use?[2]

Spacing and separation

- You can line up pieces of code with an internal tabular layout; for example, aligning operators in the same column across subsequent lines. This provides visual emphasis for the function of a block of

---

[1] More common in published code than in a source code editor.

[2] Because, of course, no high-quality programmer will use gotos in these enlightened times—see "Structured Programming" on page 421.

statements. However, it does require extra typing and maintenance effort, and some programmers don't feel it is justified. A tabular horizontal layout would look something like:

```
int    cat   = 1;
int    dog   = 2;
char *mouse = "small and furry";
```

- Whitespace can appear pretty much anywhere, and there are different ways to space out individual code statements. It's a good idea to put spaces around operators, like this: `hamster = "cute"`. It's akin to having spaces between words when you write. The alternative, `hamster="ugly"`, looks cramped and dense.

- Similarly, function calls can be spaced in various ways. You might employ one of the following formats:

```
feedLion(mouse)
feedLion( hamster )
feedLion (motherInLaw)
```

Many view the latter option as bad—a mathematical equation wouldn't have a space after the function name. (The mother-in-law, however, might be a genuinely edible commodity.)

Should you follow a similar convention for keywords? How does `while(lionIsAsleep)` look? Cramped. Keywords aren't functions; they read more like words, so it's most common to see spaces around them.

- If code gets too long for a single line, it must be split, but *where* to split is another choice. Naturally, you'd break in the most logical place, but one man's logic is another man's folly. Lines are generally broken around an operator, but whether before or after it—whether the operator appears on the end of the previous or beginning of the next line—is a matter of taste.

Variables

- A classic C/C++ contention is where to put the asterisk in a pointer declaration (a battle often called Star Wars). You can chose between these three:

```
int *mole;
int* badger;
int * toad;
```

The first two associate the "pointeryness" with the variable and with the type, respectively. The problem with associating with type is it doesn't work as expected for statements like this: `int* weasel, ferret;`. The third version is a reasonable fence-sitting alternative, but isn't as common.

- Some C/C++ standards mandate that all constant names should be in uppercase letters to make them clear. Some argue that only preprocessor macro names should be capitalized.

Lines of code

- Exactly *what* goes on each line is a layout concern; it is often mandated that every individual statement goes on its own line, making each one distinct and clear.

- This leads on to the issue of *side effects* in statements; should you allow code like `index[count++] = 2` or permit assignments in `if`s?

- Some presentation styles will place code on the same line as an opening brace:

```
for (...) { ostrich++;
            buryHead(ostrich);
          }
```

Constructs

- Should you always include braces, even if there's only one statement within them? You might allow braces to be missed when the code follows on the same line, like this:

```
if (weAreAllDoomed) startPanicking();
```

- It's common to see `else` clauses aligned in the same column as their respective `if`, but you'll sometimes see them placed at a subordinate indent level.

- How important is it to make *special cases* clear? Some coding standards mandate that fall-throughs between `switch` statement cases should be flagged with comments. Similarly, *no-ops* in loops should be flagged to avoid confusion; otherwise, this little bodiless loop that finds the end of a C string `str` may confuse the unwary:

```
char *end;
for (end = str; *end; ++end);
```

- Should C++ inline methods be put inside the class declaration, outside it (directly afterward), or in a separate source file?

Files

- The most basic decision is how to split a project into files and what information to put into each one. Is there one file per class or per function? Or can you split files into smaller or larger units than this, perhaps per library or section of code? What if there are a lot of very small related classes? Do you really want lots of very small related files?[3]

---

[3] Java answers this by mandating the physical mapping of classname to filename.

- Conventions for splitting a file into sections differ. Some programmers like to insert a number of blank lines as a separator, some prefer comment blocks, some like reams of ASCII art.

- In C/C++, the exact order of #included files may be fixed by a presentation style. There are different schools of thought here. Some prefer to neatly order system includes first, then project includes, then file-specific includes. Others feel that the exact opposite is safer; it *can* prevent one header file from accidentally relying on headers normally included before itself. Some standards suggest that no *header file* should *ever* #include another, leaving it to be done long-hand in every implementation file.

Misc

There will always be plenty of other issues specific to particular coding situations. How do you format embedded SQL commands in code that performs database access? Do you require consistent formatting in a project across different languages?

5. **Which is more important—good code *presentation* or good code *design*? Why?**

This is really a very artificial question. Both are fundamental for good code, and you should never be asked to sacrifice one for the other. If you ever are, beware. However, which one you just chose may say a lot about you as a programmer.

Bad formatting is certainly easier to fix than bad design, especially if you use clever tools to homogenize your code's formatting.

There is an interesting connection between presentation and design: Bad presentation often shows that the code was produced by a bad programmer, which probably means that it suffers from bad internal design too. Or it may imply that the code has been maintained by a series of different programmers, with a subsequent loss of the initial code design.

Getting Personal

1. **Do you write in a consistent style?**

   a. **When you work with other people's code, which layout style do you adopt—theirs or your own?**

   b. **How much of your coding style is dictated by your editor's auto-formatting? Is this an adequate reason for adopting a particular style?**

If you can't alter the way your editor positions the cursor for you, you shouldn't be using it (either you're too inept, or your editor is).

If you can't write code in a consistent style, you should have your programmer's license revoked. If you can't follow someone else's presentation style, you should be forced to maintain BASIC for the rest of your career.

Guard your attitude: The typical programmer cares more about his code, personal practices, and individual layout fetishes than the overall health of the project. Too often, there is an *individual versus team* dilemma. If a programmer rebels against an imposed house style or can't maintain code using its existing presentation style, it is a bad sign. This suggests that the programmer can't see the big picture.

2. **Tabs: Are they a work of the devil, or the best thing since sliced bread? Explain why.**

   a. **Do you know if your editor inserts tabs automatically? Do you know what your editor's tab stop is?**

   b. **Some *hugely* popular editors indent with a mixture of tabs and spaces. Does this make the code any less maintainable?**

   c. **How many spaces should a tab correspond to?**

Since this is such a religious issue, I'll just say *Tabs suck!* and back away quickly. Well, actually I'll add that the only thing more evil than indenting with tabs is indenting with tabs *and* spaces—a nightmare!

If your editor *is* inserting tabs (and probably spaces) without you noticing, try using another editor for a while to appreciate how frustrating it is. Try setting your tab stop to a different value, and see what a mess it makes of the code. *Everyone uses the same editor, so it doesn't matter* is not a professional attitude. Everyone doesn't use the same editor, so it *does* matter.

You'll hear people recommend their choice of tab-stop length and carefully justify their opinions. That's all very well; in fact a respected study claims that a *three-* or *four-*space tab stop provides optimum readability. (I favor four spaces because I don't like odd numbers!) However, a tab should correspond to *no* fixed number of spaces. A tab is a tab, which is not a space or any multiple thereof. For code laid out using tabs, it shouldn't matter exactly how many spaces the tab is displayed as—the code should read well, regardless. Unfortunately, I have rarely seen tab-indented code that works this way. All too often, tabs and spaces are mixed together to make code line up neatly. This works fine with a tab stop set as the author intended. But it makes an unholy mess with any other setting.

3. **Do you have a preferred layout style?**

   a. **Describe it in a series of simple statements. Be complete. Include, for example, how you format `switch` statements and split up long lines.**

   b. **How many statements did it take? Is that what you expected?**

   c. **Does your company have a coding standard?**

   d. **Do you know where it is? Is it advertised? Have you read it?**

      i. **If yes: Is it any good? Perform an honest critique, and feed your comments back to the document owners.**

ii. **If no: Should it? (Justify your answer.) Is there a common unwritten code style that everyone adopts? Can you drive the adoption of a standard?**

e. **Is there *more* than one standard used, perhaps one per project? If so, how is code shared among projects?**

Make sure you are aware of any style guides (or undocumented conventions) that you should work to.

This question was partly motivated by personal experience: I was working in a large organization with several isolated departments, each following its own set of guidelines. As the separate products slowly converged, it made technological (and sound financial) sense to combine some parts of the codebases. The result was a mess of code with different styles of interface, different presentation, even different language use. It looked unorganized and unprofessional and was very hard to work with. It was painful.

4. **How many different layout styles have you followed?**
   a. **Which did you feel most comfortable with?**
   b. **Which was the most rigorously defined?**
   c. **Is there a link?**

After a few years of programming, it's easy to settle into your own peculiar layout style without really thinking about how or why you arrived at it. Undoubtedly, it was a result of other code you've read and worked with, mixed with your own personal tastes. Take some time to consider this, and ensure that your coding style is sound. Perhaps now is the time to modify and improve it.

Changing your style isn't straightforward. There will still be your old legacy code to deal with—should you convert it to the new style, or leave it in the previous state?

Grab a text editor and type in this bit of code; it calculates the nth prime number. It's written in one particular coding style. Present it as *you'd* like to see it. Don't try to change the implementation at all.

```c
/* Returns whether num is prime.*/
bool
isPrime( int num ) {
    for ( int x = 2; x < num; ++x ) {
        if ( !( num % x ) ) return false;
    }
    return true;
}

/* This function calculates the 'n'th prime number.*/
int
prime( int pos ) {
    if ( pos ) {
        int x = prime( pos-1 ) + 1;
```

```
        while ( !isPrime( x ) ) {
            ++x;
        }
        return x;
    } else {
        return 1;
    }
}
```

That is a representative bit of Real World code, so don't dismiss this as a stupid and tedious exercise.

Note that I haven't given any suggested answer here. My reformatting is just as valid as yours, and indeed as valid as the original format. That's why this is a *Getting Personal* question.

If you're reading these answers without chewing over the questions at all, go on—give this one a try. The book can wait while you type in a few lines. . . .

Now, take a look at what you've written.

- How different is your version? How many specific changes did you make?

- For each change, ask yourself: Is it a personal aesthetic preference, or can you justify the change with some rationale? Question this rationale—is it truly valid? How strongly would you be prepared to defend it?

- How comfortable were you with the original format? Did it bother you to read? Could you work in that coding style if you encountered code like it? *Should* you be able to become comfortable with it?

Give yourself bonus points if you wanted to reimplement the code to be more efficient, and extra bonus points if you resisted the temptation. (Premature optimization is a Bad Thing—see "The Nuts and Bolts" on page 206.)

Chapter 3: What's in a Name?

Mull It Over

1. **Are these good variable names? Answer with either** *yes* **(explain why, and in what context),** *no* **(explain why), or** *can't tell* **(explain why).**

   a. `int apple_count`

   b. `char foo`

   c. `bool apple_count`

   d. `char *string`

   e. `int loop_counter`

The quality of a name depends on its context, and we can't honestly tell whether any of these are good or bad names. That's why the question asks for example contexts. There are some obvious contexts where the names might be bad: `apple_count` wouldn't be a particularly good name for a grapefruit counter.

foo is *never* a good name. I've yet to see anyone counting *foo*s. `loop_counter` is also bad; even if a loop gets too big for a short counter name, you can still pick a more descriptive name, one that reflects the actual *use* of the variable rather than its role as a loop counter.

We can't really tell whether `bool apple_count` is a good name, but it looks like it isn't—a boolean cannot hold a number. Perhaps it's recording whether a separate count of apples is valid, but if this was the case, it ought to be called something like `is_apple_count_valid`.

2. **When would these be appropriate function names? Which return types or parameters might you expect? Which return types would make them nonsensical?**

   a. `doIt(...)`

   b. `value(...)`

   c. `sponge(...)`

   d. `isApple(...)`

What each of these might mean depends on where you find them. A name depends on its context for meaning; that context is provided by the enclosing scope of the function. Context information can also be given by function parameters or return variables.

3. **Should a naming scheme favor the easy reading or easy writing of code? How would you make either easy?**

   a. **How many times do you write a single piece of code? (Think about it.) How many times do you read it? Your answers should give some indication as to the relative importances.**

   b. **What do you do when naming conventions collide? Say you're working on camelCase C++ code and need to do STL (using_underscore) library work. What's the best way to handle this situation?**

I've worked on C++ codebases that used such a collision of naming conventions to their advantage. The internal logic used camelCase, whereas libraries and components that extended the standard library followed STL naming_conventions. It actually worked quite well, neatly marking separate parts of the project.

Unfortunately, it doesn't always work that nicely. I've seen plenty of inconsistent code where there was no rhyme or reason behind the changing styles.

4. **How long should a loop be before you need to give a meaningful loop counter name?**

This depends on how long your piece of string is. It's clear, though, that a 100-line loop with a counter called i is not best practice.[4] Whenever you insert new code into a loop, check the counter name to see if it now needs adjustment.

---

[4] But generally a 100-line loop itself is not best practice.

5. In C, if assert is a macro, why is its name lowercase? Why should we name macros so they stand out?

assert isn't capitalized because assert isn't capitalized. In an ideal world it would be, but standards being what they are, we have to live with this second-rate macro name. Sigh.

Fire is useful, but it can also be very dangerous. Macros are the same. Macros and #defined constant definitions *are* dangerous—adopting the UPPERCASE name convention will prevent nasty collisions with ordinary names. It's as sensible as wearing safety goggles when a lunatic is walking around with a big pointy stick.

Because macros can be so painful, you should choose names that are very unlikely to cause headaches. More importantly, avoid using the preprocessor as much as humanly possible.

Long calculations can be made more readable by putting intermediate results in temporary variables. Suggest good naming heuristics for these types of variables.

Bad temporary names are tmp, tmp1, tmp2, and so on, or a, b, c, and so on. These, unfortunately, are all common intermediate names.

Like any other item, temporary names should be meaningful (like circle_radius in a trigonometric calculation or apple_count in an arboreal analysis routine). In fact, in a complex calculation, good names can really serve to document the internal logic and show what's going on.

If you find a value that really has no nameable purpose, if it truly is an arbitrary intermediate value that's hard to name, then you'll begin to understand why tmp is so popular. Avoid calling anything tmp if possible—try to break the calculation in some other way that makes more sense.

6. What are the pros and cons of following your language's standard library naming conventions?

Standard libraries are often a source of language best practice, so it can be valuable to follow their conventions. Other programmers are used to the naming style, so they will have fewer nasty reading surprises and will feel at home with your code.

On the other hand, the library might not always present best practices, so think first! C's horribly named assert macro is a good example of this.

7. Can you wear out a name? Is it okay to repeat a local variable name in many different functions? Is it okay to use local names that override (and hide) global names? Why?

It is perfectly acceptable to repeat a local variable name in many different contexts. Sometimes it's good practice to: Why use a different loop index counter name all the time? It would only serve to make your code harder to read.

Don't hide global names with local variable names; it's really confusing. This is an indicator of brittle code.

8. **Describe the mechanics of Hungarian Notation. What are the pros and cons of this naming convention? Does it have a place in modern code design?**

Hungarian Notation is a naming convention that adorns variable and function names with cryptic prefixes to denote type. It's seen predominantly in C code. There are several subtly different dialects, but the most common Hungarian prefixes are shown in Table 1.

Table 1: Common Hungarian Notation Prefixes

Prefix	Which means . . .
p	pointer to . . . (lp means *long pointer*, an old architectural issue—if you don't know, don't ask)
r	reference of . . .
k	constant . . .
rg	array of . . .
b	boolean (bool or some C typedef)
c	char
si	short int
i	int
li	long int
d	double
ld	long double
sz	zero-terminated char string (Note: *not* p)
s	struct
C	class (You can define your own class abbreviations, too.)

Hungarian Notation was relatively unbearable in C (not to mention unnecessary once the language became more strongly typed), and is rapidly nauseating in C++, since it doesn't really scale up to the many new type definitions you can introduce.

If you really want to confuse a maintenance programmer, use Hungarian Notation and then, a few months later, change the types of all the variables without correcting every single variable name (since it would take far too long to do *that*). This is a real weakness with the naming scheme.

KEY CONCEPT   *Avoid Hungarian Notation like the plague.*

Some naming conventions have diluted Hungarian leanings. Witness the foo_ptr and m_foo ideas mentioned earlier in the chapter. There are other cute conventions with similar intent: Some programmers call their global variables theFoo and their member variables myFoo. Perhaps this shows that *some* Hungarian Notation is a good idea in principle; but taken to its logical extreme, it's a dictatorial tyrant of a convention. Be on your guard.

9. **We see many classes containing member functions acting as *getters* and *setters*; reading and writing the value of certain properties. What are the common naming conventions for these functions, and which is the best?**

While some argue that the existence of get and set methods shows a weak design, we nonetheless see a lot of classes written like this. Some languages actually have built-in support for these operations.

There are several naming conventions to choose from. If you're writing in C++, using camelCase, and have some property called *foo* of type *Foo*, you might pick:

```
Foo &getFoo();
void setFoo(const Foo &) const;
```

or

```
Foo &foo();
void setFoo(const Foo &) const;
```

or perhaps

```
Foo &foo();
void foo(const Foo &) const;
```

Your choice may be dictated by a coding standard; otherwise, it's down to your sense of aesthetics. This is a case where I'd violate the *Function name should always contain a verb* rule and go for the second option, since it reads the most naturally in code. Try it and see.

If a "getter" method has to perform a long calculation the first time it's run (even if it can cache the answer for future invocations), then I'd be wary. It's no longer a simple retrieval function, and these naming schemes don't imply this. `Tree::numApples` is a good getter name, unless the operation could block for a minute while an image recognition system detects all the apples. In that case, I'd like to see the behavior implied by name. `Tree::countApples()` hints at some greater activity—it's the verb in the name.

Getting Personal

1. **How good are you at naming? How many of these heuristics do you follow already? Do you consciously think about your naming and these sorts of rules, or do you just *do it* all naturally? In which areas can you improve?**

Go back over the section "The Nuts and Bolts" on page 44. Compare those guidelines with the last piece of code you wrote. How does it match up? How much of your naming necessarily follows existing coding conventions (as you're exhorted to do on page 50), and how much have you established from scratch?

2. **Does your coding standard mention naming at all?**
   a. **Does it cover all the cases we've looked at here? Is it *sufficient*? Is it useful, or just superficial?**
   b. **How much naming detail *is* appropriate in a coding standard?**

Sometimes a coding standard with comprehensive naming mandates can make it *harder* to invent names—you have so many rules to try to satisfy that it's hard to remember and reconcile them all. Look with caution at anything more prescriptive than the guidelines laid out in Chapter 3.

Good code craftsmen habitually name well, and don't need coding standards to "help" them. The standards-setters often claim that their standards will help less-experienced programmers to name well. But more often than not, these standards are not that helpful—inexperienced programmers commit more programming sins than just bad naming. Code reviews are required to ensure that their work is appropriate.

3. **What's the worst name you've come across recently? How have names ever misled you? How would you have changed them to avoid future confusion?**

Did you spot this in a formal review of someone else's work, or while trying to maintain some old, long-forgotten code?[5] Finding and correcting bad names just after they've been written (when you still know what the thing should really be called) is best. And it takes the least effort. Working it out months later can sometimes be quite painful.

4. **Do you have to port code between platforms? How has this affected file-names, other names, and the overall code structure?**

Older filesystems limited the number of characters you could use in a filename. This made file naming much messier (and more cryptic). Unless you have to port code to such an archaic system, this kind of limitation can be safely ignored.

File-based polymorphism is a cunning way to exploit filenames to achieve code substitutability at build time. It's often used to select platform-specific implementations in portable code. You can set up header file search paths, allowing one #include to pull in a different file depending on the current build platform.

---

[5] Obviously, it would never be a problem you found in your *own* code!

Chapter 4: The Write Stuff

Mull It Over

1. **Grouping related code will make its relationships clear. How can we perform this grouping? Which methods document the relationships most strongly?**

Obvious grouping devices are common name prefixes and suffixes; file-system location; and putting items in the same class or structure, C++/C# namespace, Java package, source file, or code library. Can you think of more?

Relationships enforced by the language are the strongest—both obvious to read and also automatically checked for you. However, proximity of code layout is a more potent association than you'd think. Ordering also implies a lot—you'll think that the first item is more important than subsequent items. Exploit these facts to document your code.

2. **We should avoid using *magic numbers* in our code. Is zero a magic number? What should you call a constant value representing zero?**

The number zero has magic properties in many different contexts; in C code it is used as a *null* pointer value, and the initial value for most loops. What *could* you replace 0 with?

- A single shared constant called ZERO is no better than writing 0; it's *just as* magic. The name doesn't imply what any zero actually means—is it a null pointer value, or a loop initialization value? This approach would defeat the purpose.

- A different name for each zero constant would get very tedious because you'd have to create many similar variations on the theme of `for (int i = SOME_ZERO_START_VALUE; i < SOME_END_VALUE; ++i)`. None of these zero constant names gives any new meaningful information, anyway.

You'd have to think carefully about names for zero constants. The obvious choice would be something like NO_BANANAS, meaning *no bananas counted*. But this NO_ prefix could be confused as an abbreviation for number (like NUM_).

3. **Self-documenting code makes good use of context to convey information. Show how you do this, and give an example of how a particular name would lead to a different interpretation in different functions?**

There are many ways to exploit context to your documentation's advantage. Consider a Cat class. Inside it, member functions don't need to be called setCatName, setCatColor, and so on; the *cat* part is implicit from the class context.

Many English words have a dual meaning. You'd expect the `count` variable in a search function to hold different information than one in a vampire database schema. More practically, a `name` variable in our `Cat` class clearly holds the cat's name, whereas one in an `Employee` class is more likely to hold a human's—with first name, last name, and title information. Same variable name, different contents. Exploit context information as much as possible, but ensure that the context in which you write is truly obvious.

4. Is it realistic to expect a newcomer to pick up some self-documenting code and understand it totally?

Yes, that's our aim—it *is* realistic. However, the reader will still need overview and design documents describing the entire system, what it does, and how it's structured. If the code comments try to explain this, then they're in the wrong place (or it's a very small system).

With good code documentation, a newcomer should find it perfectly clear what a particular *section of code* is doing. Comprehensive API docs show the meaning of any function call the newcomer may come across.

5. If code is truly self-documenting, how much other documentation is required?

It depends on the size and scope of the project. You'll require functional specifications and design documents. You may still need an implementation overview, and will definitely require thorough test specifications.

To document the design of a single piece of code, good literate comments mean that you shouldn't need any other documentation.

6. Why must more people than the original author understand any piece of code?

It's a reality of the software factory. Being the only person who understands some code is good job security for the unscrupulous programmer. Writing code that's worse than a cryptic crossword puzzle will guarantee you a job for life (or until the company folds, whichever happens first). The downside is that you'll spend your days immersed in your own foul concoctions.

In reality, code is dangerous if it can't be understood by anyone else. If you leave the company, move to another department, get promoted, or no longer have time to perform maintenance, then someone else must be able to take over. And if it doesn't come down to that, sometime down the road, when you've forgotten how your code works, a fatal fault will turn up that must be fixed by last Tuesday.

Code reviews can help to ensure that code is well understood and adequately documented.

7. **This simple C *bubblesort* function could use some improvement. What specific things are wrong with it? Write an improved, self-documenting version.**

```c
void bsrt(int a[], int n)
{
    for (int i = 0; i < n-1; i++)
        for (int j = n-1; j > i; j--)
            if (a[j-1] > a[j])
            {
                int tmp = a[j-1];
                a[j-1] = a[j];
                a[j]   = tmp;
            }
}
```

The first problem is that a bubblesort algorithm should never be used. There are plenty of better sorts. There's also probably a much better, generic language library function available; in C you can call qsort, for example. I've used bubblesort here as a simple code example.

The function's interface isn't clear *at all*. The function name is too cryptic, and the parameter names mean nothing. I'd like to see an API documentation comment provided too, but I'll leave that out in the rewrite below.

Internally, the code is a mess. Its intent would be much clearer if the code that transposes array values is split out as a swap function. Then the reader can see what's going on. A little more massaging leads to this:

```c
void swap(int *first, int *second)
{
    int temp = *first;
    *first = *second;
    *second = temp;
}

void bubblesort(int items[], int size)
{
    for (int pos1 = 0; pos1 < size-1; pos1++)
        for (int pos2 = size-1; pos2 > pos1; pos2--)
            if (items[pos2-1] > items[pos2])
                swap(&items[pos2-1], &items[pos2]);
}
```

This is adequate C, although there are some more changes you might prefer. Depending on your religion, you might want braces around the loops. swap could be made into a macro for efficiency. This isn't a clever optimization though; you should really choose a more efficient sort algorithm.

In C++, I'd consider making swap inline, and take its parameters by reference (documenting the fact that they will be changed). The best choice would be to use the std::swap facility available in the language libraries.

8. Working with code documentation tools brings up some interesting issues. What's your opinion on these?

   a. When you review the documentation, should you perform a *code review*, looking at the comments in the source files, or a *specification review*, looking at the generated documents?

   b. Where do you put documentation of protocols and other non-API issues?

   c. Do you document private/internal functions? In C/C++, where do you place this documentation—in the header file or implementation file?

   d. In a large system, should you create a single, large API document or several smaller documents, one per area? What are the advantages of each approach?

My thoughts on these questions are:

a. Review the generated spec; don't get too hung up about the layout of the comments in the source file. You're reviewing the content, not the code.

b. Don't be fooled into thinking documentation must be put in a *header file* or in an *implementation file*. Even if documentation tools are a Good Thing, it's not evil to have some separate "traditional" documents as well. Write about your protocol there.

c. Document any internal functions that *need* documentation. You don't necessarily have to write exhaustive docs on all private parts. These docs should be hived off into the implementation file if they're reasonably large, to keep the public interface neat and simple.

d. Both! Use different invocations of the tool to generate a single, large document and documents for each subsystem.

9. If you're working on a codebase that isn't literately documented, and you need to alter or add new methods or functions, is it a good idea to give them literate documentation comments, or should you leave them undocumented?

The craftsman *wants to* document and automatically feels the need to write comment blocks. Now, if the code has a separate specification document, then your documentation should go in there alongside everything else. Otherwise, it's not too bad to start adding literate comments. Make sure that the original programmer isn't going to take offense, though!

10. Is it possible to write self-documenting assembly code?

You can give it your best shot, but it's not going to be easy. Assembly code isn't particularly expressive; you're not programming at the level of intent, more at the level of *do this, you dumb microprocessor*. Your code will be mostly comment blocks (probably good practice for assembly, anyway). Except for subroutine labels, there's not much else to self-document with.

Getting Personal

1. **What do you consider to be the best documented code you've come across? What made it so?**

    a. **Did this code have a large number of external specifications? How many of them did you read? How can you be sure you knew enough about the code without reading them all?**

    b. **How much of this do you think was due to the author's programming style, and how much was because of any house style or guidelines he or she worked to?**

Well-documented code does not necessarily have any separate description documents. Internally, it employs good naming, logical modularization, simple techniques, clear layout, documented assumptions, and good commenting. House styles help, but they are no substitute for astute, sensitive programming. An idiot can follow the most stringent guidelines and still produce shabby shreds of code.

2. **If you write in more than one language, how does your documentation strategy differ in each?**

Different languages are more or less expressive, and so what can and can't be documented within the language syntax varies. As much as anything else, this will affect how many comments you'd write.

You're probably better at writing self-documenting code in your most familiar programming language.

3. **In the last code you wrote, how did you make the important stuff stand out? Did you hide private information away appropriately?**

Think carefully about this—the natural tendency is to dismissively say, *Yeah, I wrote it okay.* Look at your code as if it had been written by some other muppet. Criticize it.

4. **If you're working on a team, how often do others come to you to ask you how something works? Could you avoid this with better-documented code?**

A good two-pronged strategy to cope with this is:

a. If the question is genuinely about something unclear in your code, after having explained it to the curious programmer (and learned what he really *needed* to know), capture the information in some appropriate documentation. You can email this to him afterward, too, to ensure he took away the right information.

b. If the question was about something that was already explained in the documentation, point him at it, shout RTFM,[6] and give him a poke in the eye.

---

[6] *Read The* (ahem . . .) *Manual.*

Chapter 5: A Passing Comment

Mull It Over

1. How might the *need for* and the *content of* comments differ in the following types of code:

    a. Low-level assembly language (machine code)

    b. Shell scripts

    c. A single-file test harness

    d. A large C/C++ project

    Assembly language is less expressive, providing fewer opportunities for self-documenting code. Therefore, you'd expect more comments in assembly code, and you'd expect those comments to be at a much lower level than comments in other languages—assembly language comments generally *would* explain how as well as why.

    There isn't an enormous a difference between the remaining three. Shell scripts can be quite hard to read back; they are proto-Perl in this respect. Careful commenting helps. You're more likely to use literate programming techniques on a large C/C++ codebase.

2. You can run tools to calculate what percentage of your source code lines are comments. How useful are these tools? How accurate a measure is this of comment quality?

    This kind of metric will give insight into the code, but you shouldn't get too concerned about it. It isn't an accurate reflection of code quality. Well-documented code might not contain *any* comments. Enormous revision histories or large corporate copyright messages can dominate small files, affecting this metric.

3. If you come across some incomprehensible code, which is the better way to factor in some intelligibility: adding comments to document what you think is going on, or renaming variables/functions/types with more descriptive names? Which approach will most likely be easier? Which approach will be safer?

    You should do both, as appropriate. Renaming is arguably the best approach, but it's dangerous if you don't know exactly what a function does. You might be giving it another equally bad name. When renaming, you must be sure you know the nature of the item you're changing.

    Use the code's unit tests to ensure that your modifications don't break any behavior.

4. **When you document a C/C++ API with a code comment block, should it go in the public header file that declares the function or the source file containing the implementation? What are the pros and cons of each location?**

This question was the cause of a big fight at one place I worked. Some argued for descriptions to go in the .c file. Being close to the function means that it's harder to write an incorrect comment and harder to write code that doesn't match the documentation. The comment is also more likely to be changed in line with any code changes.

However, when placed in a header file, the description is visible alongside the public interface—a logical location. Why should someone have to look into the implementation to read any public API docs?

A literate programming documentation tool should be able to pull comments out of either place, but sometimes it's quicker to just read comments in the source instead of using the tool—a bonus of the literate code approach. I favor placing the comments in header files.

Of course, in Java and C#, there's only one source file anyway; you'd conventionally use the Javadoc or C# XML comment format.

Getting Personal

1. **Look carefully at the source files you've recently worked on. Inspect your commenting. Is it honestly any good? (I bet as you read through the code you'll find yourself making a few changes!)**

When you read and review your own code, it's very easy to skip the comments, presuming they're correct or at least adequate. It is a good idea to spend some time looking at them and assess how well you've written them. Perhaps you could ask a trusted colleague to give you his or her (constructive) opinion on your commenting style.

2. **How do you ensure that your comments are genuinely valuable and not just personal ramblings that only you can understand?**

Some considerations for this are: write whole sentences, avoid abbreviations, and keep comments neatly formatted and in a common language (both the native language and the selection of words used from the problem domain). Avoid inside jokes, throw-away statements, or anything that you're not entirely sure about.

Code reviews will highlight weaknesses in your comment strategy.

3. **Do the people you work with all comment to the same standard, in about the same way?**

   a. **Who's the best at writing comments? Why do you think that? Who's the worst? How much of a correlation does this bear to these individuals' general quality of coding?**

    b. **Do you think any imposed coding standards could raise the quality of the comments written by your team?**

Use code reviews to inspect the comment quality of your peers and to move your team toward a consistent quality of commenting.

4. **Do you include history logging information in each source file? If yes:**
    a. **Do you do maintain it manually? Why, if your revision control system will insert this for you automatically? Is the history kept particularly accurate?**
    b. **Is this *really* a sensible practice? How often is this information needed? Why is it better if placed in the source file than in another, separate mechanism?**

It's human nature not to keep a history accurate, even with the best intentions in the world. It requires a lot of manual work that gets skipped when time is tight. You should use tools to help maintain a history and put the right information in the right place (which I don't believe is the source file at all).

5. **Do you add your initials to or otherwise mark the comments you make in other people's code? Do you ever date comments? When and why do you do this—is it a useful practice? Has it ever been useful to find someone else's initials and timestamping?**

For some comments, this is a useful practice. In other places, it's just inconvenient—extra comment noise that you have to read past to get to the really interesting stuff.

    It's most useful with temporary `FIXME` or `TODO` comments, marking work in progress. Released production code probably shouldn't have these; no finished code should need a reader to understand the author or date of a particular change.

Chapter 6: To Err Is Human

Mull It Over

1. **Are *return values* and *exceptions* equivalent error reporting mechanisms? Prove it.**

Return values are equivalent to global *status variables* because the same reason code information can be sent back by both mechanisms (although it is easier to ignore a status variable). You can write code that works in a similar manner using both of these approaches.[7]

---

[7] They are not quite the same, though. In C++ you can return a *proxy* value type that has behavior in its destructor. This infuses extra magic into the return code mechanism.

Exceptions are a very different beast. They involve a new control flow, something very different from simple reason codes. They are tightly bound into the language and program run time. While you *can* simulate exceptions by hand-crafting code that propagates errors, you'd have to carefully consider:

- How to represent errors as arbitrary objects, not just as integer reason codes
- Supporting exception class hierarchies and providing the ability to catch by base class
- Propagating exceptions through *any* function, even those without try, catch, or throw statements

It's that final point which shows most clearly why the two are *not* equivalent. Implemented at a language level, exceptions are not at all intrusive in your code. A hand-crafted facsimile must manage the possibility of failure at every point. Every function is forced to return an error code—even if it cannot fail itself—just to propagate other error information. This requires serious adaptation of the code.

2. **What different implementations of *tuple* return types can you think of? Don't limit yourself to a single programming language. What are the pros and cons of using tuples as a return value?**

In C you can create a struct for every return type, linking it with an error reason code. This would look something like:

```
/* Declare the return type */
struct return_float
{
    int reason_code;
    float value;
};

/* A function using it ... */
return_float myFunction() { ... }
```

This is messy, tedious to write, cumbersome to use, and hard to read. You can exploit C++ templates or Java/C# generics to automatically build this scaffolding, or you can use C++'s std::pair class. Both approaches are seen in production C++ code. Both are tedious to use, with the extra declarations and the machinery necessary to return these types. Some languages, like Perl, support lists of arbitrary types; this is a much easier implementation mechanism. Functional languages also provide such a facility.

We've just seen some of the disadvantages of this technique: It's very intrusive in the code and not at all sympathetic to the reader. It is also not an idiomatic coding practice. There may be a performance hit when returning more than one argument, but this is not a compelling argument, unless you're working at the machine code level. The notable advantage is that a separate reason code doesn't interfere with any return value.

3. **How do exception implementations differ between languages?**

The four main implementations we'll consider are: C++, Java, .NET, and Win32 structured exceptions. Win32 exceptions are bound to the operating platform, the others to their languages. Languages *may* be implemented in terms of such underlying platform facilities, or they may not be.

They all follow a similar approach; you can throw an exception, which is later handled by a catch statement placed after code wrapped in a try block. They all follow the termination model's behavior.

Java, .NET, and Win32 also have a finally construct. It contains code that is run whether execution leaves the try block normally or abnormally. This can be a good place to put cleanup code to ensure that it always gets called. finally can be simulated in C++, but it isn't pleasant.

The raw Win32 exceptions (minus any language support provided by compilers) don't clean up as they unwind the stack, because the OS has no concept of destructors. They must be used with care—they are intended to handle situations more akin to signals than code logic errors.

Java exceptions (deriving from Throwable) and C# exceptions (deriving from Exception) automatically provide a diagnostic backtrace—very helpful in later debugging. .NET's CLI allows anything to be thrown, but C# does not expose the ability to do so (it does expose the ability to catch them, though). Other .NET languages can throw whatever they like.

4. **Signals are an old-school Unix mechanism. Are they still needed now that we have modern techniques like exceptions?**

Yes, they are still needed. Signals are a part of the ISO C standard, and so they aren't easy to remove, anyway. Signals date from (pre) System-V Unix implementations. They are an asynchronous mechanism to report system-level problems/events. Exceptions solve a different problem, reporting code logic errors that can percolate up to a handler. It makes no sense to throw an exception for signal-type events, especially using the termination model—it doesn't provide asynchronous handling.

5. **What is the best code structure for error handling?**

There is simply no answer to this question. Different code strategies will work best in different situations. What's important is to reliably detect and handle errors with clear, readable, maintainable code.

6. **How should you handle errors that occur in your error-handling code?**

Errors signaled within error handlers should be dealt with as you would any other error. It gets nasty fast, though—you end up with error handlers nested within error handlers nested within error handlers. Be very careful about this, and check for a neater way to structure your code.

A better approach is to only perform operations that are guaranteed to succeed (or that honor the nothrow exception guarantee) in your error handlers. That way, your world is a much nicer place to be.

Getting Personal

1. How thorough is the error handling in your current codebase? How does this contribute to the stability of the program?

There is a direct correlation between good error handling and stable code. Either your program is not required to be robust, or it *must* systematically detect and handle all error conditions. If this isn't deeply rooted in the program's philosophy, then you will not have a reliable system.

2. Do you naturally consider error handling as you write code, or do you find it a distraction, preferring to come back to it later?

It's natural to dislike error handling; no one wants to focus on the negative aspects of program functionality all the time.[8] However, heed this important advice: Don't put it off until later. If you do, some potential errors will inevitably be missed, one day causing unexpected program behavior. Get into the habit of thinking about errors *now*.

3. Go to the last (reasonably sized) function you wrote or worked on, and perform a careful review of the code. Find every abnormal occurence and potential error situation. How many of these were actually handled in your code?

**   Now get someone else to review it. Don't be shy! Did they find any more? Why? What does this tell you about the code you're working on?**

This is a telling insight into how thorough a programmer you really are. Make sure that you perform this exercise carefully—and *do* ask someone else. Even the most accomplished programmer will miss some error cases.[9] If these are unlikely to manifest as bugs, you'll probably never notice and live forever in the shadow of potentially weird behavior.

   When using exceptions, you can't easily ignore an error case—exceptions force their own way up the call stack, regardless of whether you handle them or not. You *can* still write bad code if it isn't exception safe (it may exit in a bad state, or with leaked resources) or if it performs over-eager catches (consuming errors that can't actually be handled at that level—for this reason, don't write catch(...) to catch all exceptions).

4. Do you find it easier to manage and reason about error conditions using *return values* or *exceptions*? Are you sure you know what is involved in writing exception-safe code?

To some extent, this depends on what you're used to. Exceptions complement and extend return values. An exception user can also understand return values, but the opposite doesn't necessarily hold. Return values are more obvious, hence easier to use properly.

---

[8] If you are inclined that way, you'd probably make a very good software tester. But don't change careers just yet—really thorough programmers are few and far between.

[9] How often does anyone check for errors from C's printf, for example?

If you do use exceptions, it's important to know what issues to be aware of. Exception safety affects *all* of your code, not just the parts that raise and catch errors. Exception safety is a large and involved subject that needs much study. Don't underestimate how seriously it affects the way you program.

Chapter 7: The Programmer's Toolbox

Mull It Over

1. **Is it more important for everyone in a development team to use the same IDE, or for each person to pick the one that suits him or her best? What are the implications of different people using different tools?**

All professional programmers should be responsible and informed enough to select the tools that make them most productive. No two programmers are the same, and different people will naturally prefer different tools. As long as the choice is made based on practical considerations, the team's overall effectiveness will be improved. But forcing strong-minded techies to use particular tools rarely enthuses them to work well.

If the people on a team *are* all using different development environments, then they must work together properly. They must build *identical* code, and each editor mustn't fight the others' layout rules every time a source file is edited.

2. **What is the minimum set of tools that any programmer should have at his or her disposal?**

You can't get by without at least:

- Some rudimentary form of editor
- The minimum language support required (either a compiler, an interpreter, or both—it depends on the language)
- A computer to run them on

But that minimum set won't make a very productive programmer. You need a toolbox of other tools to get any serious work done.

- There must be a revision control system, or work is downright dangerous.
- A reasonable set of libraries will prevent reinventing wheels and lower the risk of introducing avoidable bugs.
- You also need a build tool to help construct the software system.

That's a more realistic minimum set. The more fundamental tools you add in, the easier it is to develop, and the better the code that will be produced.

3. Which are more powerful: command-line or GUI-based tools?

I should break your arm if you even began to answer this question. Command-line and GUI tools are different. End of story.

An interesting philosophical question is: *In this context, how do you define "powerful?"* Does it mean having more esoteric features? Does it mean how easy the tool is to use? Does it mean how fast it runs? Or does it determine how well a tool fits into the rest of the toolchain? Decide on a definition, and then try justifying your answer in terms of that. Then I might not break your arm.

4. Are there construction tools that aren't programs?

We already categorized languages and libraries as tools, so the answer is *yes*. Other good examples to consider are:

- Regular expressions
- Graphical components (GUI "widgets")
- Network services
- Common protocols and formats (like XML)
- UML diagrams
- Design methodologies (like CRC cards)

5. What's most important for a tool?
    a. **Interoperability**
    b. **Flexibility**
    c. **Customization**
    d. **Power**
    e. **Ease of use and learning**

Each of these is important. The balance probably changes for different types of tools and the situations in which you'll use them.

Power is important; your tools must be powerful *enough* for the tasks you set them to, or your life will be hell. If this weren't the case, programmers would edit their source code using Notepad or vi.

Getting Personal

1. What are the common tools in your toolbox? Which do you use every day? Which do you use a few times a week? Which do you only call on occasionally?
    a. **How well do you know how to use them?**
    b. **Are you getting the most from every tool?**

c. How did you learn to use them? Did you ever spend any time improving your skill with them?

d. Are these the *best* tools you could be using?

The last question in that list is critical. Honestly appraise whether there are any better tools you could be using. It really is worth spending some time looking around. If there are better tools, get your hands on them and start experimenting.

2. **How up to date are your tools? Does it matter if they're not the latest cutting-edge versions?**

Out-of-date tools can cause nasty problems, but so can the latest tool versions. The nastiest problems occur when one tool version is out of sync with rest of the toolchain. There may be a subtle functional mismatch because of the version skew, causing the toolchain not to work together properly. The symptom is seldom a toolchain failure, but code that behaves in surprising ways.

Out-of-date tools may miss important bug fixes. An update might not seem important until you've been bitten by the bug it addresses. Hindsight is a wonderful thing. If you get out of date, you could end up relying on tools that are no longer supported, written by companies that no longer exist. This can become a serious problem in a critical project.

Of course, you can't always download and install a new tool version on a whim. It may not be practical to upgrade for a number of reasons. It may cost more than you can afford. The upgrade may force you to upgrade your OS or other critical parts of your toolchain, when this isn't practical.

3. **Do you favor an integrated tool set (like a visual development environment) or a discrete toolchain? What are the advantages of the *other* approach? How much experience do you have with *both* ways of working?**

A careless answer here might cost you your arm (see the answer to question 3 in the "Mull It Over" section on page 492). Try to come up with a serious list of the benefits of the other way of working—to ensure you avoid a narrow-minded and opinionated view.

4. **Are you a *Default Dan* or a *Tweaker Tom*? Do you accept the default settings in your editor, or do you customize them to within an inch of their lives? Which is the "better" approach?**

You learn to use and get the most out of your editor by discovering how to configure it. In that case, Tom *might* have the most sensible approach. A pragmatic stance is probably somewhere between the two (a good example of the *Goldilocks principle*; behavior at the extremes is rarely best). There's no point configuring features you'll never touch. Some things really don't matter—I'm not all that worried about the color scheme an editor uses. But others things do matter—I don't want to be forced to accept a default code layout style if it's grotesque.

It's far better to code to your carefully chosen layout style than have it dictated by the editor's default settings. Indeed, your house coding style may *require* it. I'd rather configure my editor to automatically format code as I want, rather than fight its cursor positioning every time I hit ENTER.

This kind of discussion scales beyond editors to any kind of configurable software tool.

5. How do you determine your budget for software tools? How do you know whether a tool is worth its cost?

It depends on what kind of organization you're working for and the kind of work you're doing. If your project has the tools budget of a small country's GDP, then the cost of tools is of no consequence—buy the best tools (which may not necessarily be the most expensive ones) and enjoy them. But a lone hacker working at home can't justify the same kind of expense for a top-notch toolchain. Often the freely available tools are more than adequate for this kind of home use.

Indeed, the freely available tools are often of a very high quality, which makes it hard to draw the line as to when paying for tools is worthwhile. Paying for a toolchain usually means that you can *expect* good product support and demand future bug fixes or development work. However, this doesn't always pan out—companies go out of business and products are discontinued. This is *perhaps* an argument for picking the most popular, widely used tools. There's safety in numbers.

If all reasonable criteria fail, the more expensive a tool is, the larger its box should be. If it costs a fortune but comes in a small box, don't buy it!

Chapter 8: Testing Times

Mull It Over

1. **Write a test harness for the greatest_common_divisor code example earlier in this chapter. Make it as exhaustive as you can. How many individual test cases have you included?**
   a. **How many of these passed?**
   b. **How many failed?**
   c. **Using these tests, identify any faults and repair the code.**

There are a large number of tests you should run, even though there are very few invalid input combinations. Thinking of invalid inputs first: Test for *zero*. It may or may not be an invalid value (we've seen no spec, so we can't tell), but you'd expect the code to cope reasonably with it.

Next, write tests considering combinations of usual inputs (say of 1, 10, and 100 in all orders). Then try numbers with no common multiple, like 733 and 449. Test for some very large numbers and for some negative numbers.

How do you write these test cases? Write a simple unit test function, and then place it into an automated test framework. For each test, don't programatically calculate what the correct output value should be;[10] just check against a known constant value. Keep your test code as simple as possible:

```
assert(greatest_common_divisor(10,  100) == 10);
assert(greatest_common_divisor(100, 10)  == 10);
assert(greatest_common_divisor(733, 449) == 0);
... more tests ...
```

There are a surprisingly large number of tests for this simple function. You could argue that for such a small piece of code, it's easier to inspect, review, and prove correctness rather than laboriously create a set of tests. This seems like a valid argument. But—what if later on, someone makes modifications? Without the tests, you'd have to carefully reinspect and revalidate the code, an easy task to overlook.

Did you find the mistake in greatest_common_divisor? There's a clue coming up. If you don't want the puzzle spoiled, then look away now. . . . *Try feeding it a negative argument.* This is a more robust (and more efficient) version written in C++:

```
int greatest_common_divisor(int a, int b)
{
    a = std::abs(a);
    b = std::abs(b);
    for (int div = std::min(a,b); div > 0; --div)
    {
        if ((a % div == 0) && (b % div == 0))
            return div;
    }
    return 0;
}
```

2. **How should the testing of a spreadsheet application and an automatic aircraft pilot differ?**

In an ideal world, there would be no faults in either. In this utopia, both would be exhaustively tested and not released until perfect. Reality is somewhat different. Whereas you expect spreadsheets to crash from time to time,[11] you expect an autopilot to contain no errors at all. When human lives hang in the balance, software is developed in a very different way—far more formally and with much greater care. It is tested rigorously. There are safety standards at play here.

---

[10] This would open the door to more coding errors—imagine the pain of bugs in the test code!

[11] It's sad we've been conditioned to accept this.

3. Should you test all of the *test code* that you write?

If you think about this for long enough it will give you a headache. You can't keep testing test code—how can you be sure the test code for your test code's test code is correct? The trick is to keep tests *as simple as possible*. This way, the most likely testing errors will be lack of important test cases, not problems with the actual lines of test code.

KEY CONCEPT   *Keep test code as simple as possible to prevent the introduction of errors.*

4. How does a programmer's testing differ from a QA department member's testing?

Testers are more concerned with the black box style of testing and usually only perform product testing. It's rare to have testers working at the code level, because most products are executable software; there are comparatively few code library vendors.

Programmers are more concerned with white box tests, making sure their masterful creations work as they planned them to.

The secret aim of any programmer writing tests is to prove that his code works, not to find cases where it doesn't! I can easily write a load of tests to show how perfect my code is by deliberately avoiding all the bits I know are problematic. This is a good argument for getting someone other than the original programmer to create test harnesses.

5. Is it necessary to write a test harness for every single function?

You don't need to be quite so extreme. Some functions are easy enough to verify by inspection. Be careful not to get sloppy, though—remember to read the code *cynically*. Simple getter and setter functions don't need a slew of individual tests.

At what code size do test harnesses become attractive? Generally when the code becomes sufficiently complex to require it. When a single glance can't prove the code is correct, write some test cases.

6. *Test-driven development* encourages you to write tests first, before any code. What sort of tests should you write?

Without having written any code, these can only be black box tests. Either that, or test-driven developers need a gift of prophecy.

7. Should you write C/C++ tests to check for the handling of NULL (zero) pointer parameters? What's the value of such a test?

If zero is an expected input value, then of course you must test for it.

But you don't always need to test for null pointers. If you don't specify magic behavior for a zero pointer value, then your function is quite within its rights to fall over when you pass it a bad pointer. In this case, zero could be as bad as a pointer to deallocated or invalid memory. It's rarely possible to test that the code will survive all bad pointers.

However, it *can* be valuable to write code that is robust in the face of zero pointers, since they tend to fly around a lot. Many allocation routines return zero pointers for failure, and undefined pointers are often set to zero. If the dog might bite, it's a good idea to put a muzzle on it.

8. **Your early code tests might not be on the final platform—you may not yet have access to it. Is it safest to defer testing until you *do* have a target test platform, or to steam ahead now?**

    If the code is intended to run in a different environment (perhaps on a high-capacity server, or some embedded device), how can you be sure that your tests are representative and adequate?

It depends on the nature of the code you're testing—whether it's a simple function doing housekeeping work or some hardware access logic. You must understand the differences between the development platform and the target environment. Memory constraints or processor speed may affect how the code runs. This probably isn't a big deal for the majority of the code you write, for which it is perfectly possible to create local test harnesses.

If your code exploits particular target platform features (parallel processors or particular hardware facilities), then you can't test fully without them. There may be simulators to check that the code runs; they are helpful, but not the definitive answer.

Putting all testing off until you have a target platform is a dangerous practice. By then you'll have a large body of code that you will have neither the time nor the inclination to test fully. For maximum confidence, test as early as you reasonably can.

9. **How do you know when you've finished and can stop testing? How much is *enough*?**

Since testing can't prove the absence of faults, you can never really tell when you're done. The task is potentially endless, and we're trying to come up with a test plan to make it a realistic exercise.

For simple blocks of code under black box testing, successfully running all the test cases in "Choosing Unit Test Cases" on page 142 is sufficient. The larger your code gets, the more work you have to do.

You can measure the adequacy and exhaustiveness of your tests by the angle of attack you're taking. There are a few key strategies:

Coverage-based testing
    The test plan is specified in terms of *coverage* of the software. For example: You may plan to execute every line of code at least once, execute every conditional branch both ways, or ensure that all system requirements are exercised at least once.

Fault-based testing
    This is based on weeding out a certain percentage of program faults. You start with a hypothetical number of faults, generally picked from prior experience. You then aim to detect and remove, say, 95 percent of them.

Error-based testing

This approach focuses on the common points of error, where the software is likely to be brittle. For example, you'd eliminate off-by-one errors by testing all boundary values.

Based on this, here are some good reasons to stop testing:

- Regression test cases complete with a certain percentage passed (and no major *show-stopping* failures remaining).

- Coverage of code, functionality, or requirements reaches a specified point.

- Exhibited bug rate falls below a certain level.

Beyond these are some physical barriers, seldom movable, which will have a final say in determining an end point:

- Hitting scheduled deadlines (testing deadlines or release deadlines). Development work has a nasty habit of overrunning and eating into the scheduled test time; this requires very careful management.

- The test budget is depleted (a very sad criteria for stopping).

- The beta or alpha testing period ends.

In most organizations, the decision to stop testing and ship the product comes at a deadline. It's a compromise based on the remaining known faults, their severity, and the frequency of their occurrence, pitched against the need to get to market. The tests allow an informed judgment to be made about how acceptable the software is.

Getting Personal

1. **For what percentage of your code do you write tests? Are you happy with this? Are your tests an automated part of the build process? What sort of testing do you give the remaining code? Is this adequate? What will you do about it?**

Don't feel obliged to write a test harness for every scrap of code. But don't forget to use your brain, either. The implementation of a small function is often a no-brainer—so you tend to code it with no brain—and voilà: stupid errors. Since a simple function only needs a simple test, it's probably valuable to write it. In my code shop, we have a simple rule: *Every* piece of code has a unit test, or it's not in the codebase.

Be sure that you *are* performing the adequate and appropriate testing for which you are responsible, not just skipping an unpleasant task. Ask yourself this: How many of the errors that have bitten you recently could have been prevented by a good set of tests? Make sure you do something about it.

If your tests are not a part of the build system, then how do you ensure that the tests are ever run and that all the code passes them?

2. How good is your relationship with the people in your QA department? What personal reputation do you think you have with them?

It is vital to establish good working relationships between the QA department and the software developers. Rivalry often brews; the testing department is seen as a bunch of people who aim to get in the way of developers and hinder the path to release, rather than as a team who is helping to build a stable product. Usually the test and development departments sit far, far away from one another, only taking orders from their individual tribal chieftains.

Forget that.

Make them coffee. Take them out for lunch. Head down to the bar with them. Anything to prevent fostering a *them and us* attitude.

Develop a professional working relationship. Make sure that you provide them with good, well-tested code—not just any old hurried junk. Throwing them your scraps to mop up will give the impression that you see them as servants working *for* you, not colleagues working *with* you.

3. What's your usual response to finding an error in your code?

There are several possible reactions:

- Disgust and disappointment
- An urge to blame someone else
- Happiness, if not downright *excitement*
- Pretending you didn't find it, ignoring it, and hoping it will go away (as if *that's* likely)

Some of those are so plainly wrong that I'll assume you can rise above them. Does it seem a little crazy to suggest that you might be *happy* to find a fault? Surely that's the reasonable reaction for a quality-conscious engineer— it's far better to find faults during development than for a user to find them in the field.

Your level of excitement will depend on where in the development life cycle the fault is found. Discovering a show-stopping bug the day before release won't make anyone smile.

4. Do you file a fault report for every code problem you uncover?

It's not really necessary to do this for every single fault: If no one's seen your code yet and it's not been integrated into the wider system, then you don't need to broadcast your incompetence! If you don't report a fault in the database, then you must make methodical notes so that you don't forget about it. For this reason, you might find it easier to use the fault-tracking system from the outset. You might be forced to raise fault reports if delivery is so late that people *need* visibility of the remaining problems.

As soon as any code is released, you should make all of its faults public; you *have* to file fault reports. This shows that you have identified each issue and have a plan to deal with it.

Whenever you discover a code fault, you should write a test case that excercises it and incorporate it into your suite of automatic tests to be run as a regression check. This acts as a form of documentation for the fault and ensures that it won't be reintroduced accidentally, later on.

5. How much testing are the project engineers expected to do?

It's important to know what's expected of you and to deliver that level of testing. But above this, don't just do what's *expected*—do what *needs* to be done.

Write a unit test for *every* piece of code you create. If you need to modify someone else's work, write a test for it first if there isn't one. That way, you will know how well it currently works, what needs to be fixed, and how to prove that your modifications haven't busted anything.

Chapter 9: Finding Fault

Mull It Over

1. Is it best for faults to be fixed by the original programmer who wrote the code? Or is the programmer who discovered the problem better placed to make a fix?

It's always helpful to approach any problem with a fresh pair of eyes. When debugging, this method avoids the common problem of a programmer reading what he *meant* to write, not what the code actually says—too many bugs stay hidden that way.

On the other hand, the original programmer *is* probably best placed to make the fix. He understands the code inside out (hopefully). He knows what repercussions a particular change will have. He'll be the quickest to pinpoint the location of a fault.

In Real World organizations, the choice of who makes a fix may be determined by individual free time and what other commitments the team has. For bugs that have been in the program since time immemorial, the original programmer is probably no longer available. He may have left the company, moved projects, or (worst of all) been promoted to management.

2. How can you tell when to use a debugger and when to use your brain?

Obviously, even the use of a debugger should be with your brain engaged. (Remember the golden rule of debugging?)

My rule of thumb is: Don't fire up a debugger until you know exactly what information you need to get out of it. The danger lies in using a debugger to putter around in the running code, not really knowing what you are looking for. You can waste hours doing this, with no real reward.

3. **You should learn unfamiliar code before you start trying to find and fix faults in it. But the time pressures of the software factory often dictate that you can't spend any serious time studying and understanding the program you're repairing. What's the best way forward?**

In your dreams, you'd slap the people who wrote the schedule and take as long as necessary to fix the fault properly. Wake up, Alice. . . .

The best you can do is try to learn the code as you go along. Proceed with extra caution when working through it, and don't trust what you *think* is happening—always make sure that the code is doing what you expect it to. When you think that you've found the cause of the bug, see if anyone on your team knows about the offending section of code. Discuss with them what you're going to do. Often when you describe the situation, you'll explain *to yourself* the obvious thing you've just missed.

4. **Describe good techniques to avoid memory-leak bugs.**

These are some good approaches:

a. Use a language where you're less likely to be bitten by them, such as Java or C#. (You can still be bitten by memory leaks in these languages. Do you know how?)

b. Use "safe" data structures that manage memory for you, so you don't have to worry about it.

c. Employ helpful language idioms, such as C++'s `auto_ptr`, to avoid problems.

d. Be rigorous and methodical in your handling of memory. For every allocation point, make sure there is a balancing deallocation point and that it will always be called.

e. Run your code through memory validator tools to ensure no bugs have crept through.

5. **When is it justifiable to have a quick stab at finding and fixing a fault, rather than adopting a more methodical approach?**

You *always* need to think about what you're doing. Even quick fiddling should be done with your brain firmly in gear. Don't blindly pepper the code with breakpoints to start digging around in the internals; try to think about how the code is designed and what it should be doing.

Gut feelings and your instant reactions may find a fault quickly in *very small programs* (say, a few tens of lines). But in a program that's many thousands of lines long, you really need to know what's going on. There is no substitute for insight. There's nothing wrong with tracing the program's execution in a debugger to examine what it's doing, but chose the test points methodically.

Getting Personal

1. **How many debugging techniques/tools do you routinely use? What others have you seen that you might find useful?**

Obviously the answer is *none*. You always write perfect code the first time!

2. **What are the common problems and pitfalls in your language(s) of choice? How do you guard against these kinds of bugs in your own code?**

It's important to know this kind of thing. It's what sets mediocre programmers apart from the experts. If you don't know where the dragons live, then you don't know how to avoid them.

3. **Are most of the bugs that occur in your code sloppy programming errors, or are they more subtle issues?**

If you get bitten over and over again by little language snafus, it shows that you should write code more carefully. Take time with your code. Proofread it, and then reread it—you'll save time overall. A classic mistake is fixing one fault, not testing that it works, and then being bitten by undesirable side effects of your "fix."

There's no shame in having bugs in your code. Everyone gets them. Just make sure they're not stupid mistakes that you could have easily prevented.

4. **Do you know how to use a debugger on your platform? How routinely do you use it? Describe how to:**
    a. **Produce a backtrace**
    b. **Inspect variable values**
    c. **Inspect value of fields within a structure**
    d. **Run an arbitrary function**
    e. **Swap thread contexts**

If you use a debugger all the time, then that's *too much*. If you never use one, then that's *too little*. Don't be afraid of your debugger, but don't use it as a crutch, either. Intelligent use of a debugger will allow you to hone right in to the location of a fault in little to no time.

Chapter 10: The Code That Jack Built

Mull It Over

1. **Why should people with nice integrated development environments worry about using a command-line make utility, when they can just hit a single button to build their project?**

Besides learning what's really going on behind the build button, knowing how to use make is a route to more powerful, flexible software construction. Rarely does a GUI build tool compare to the capabilities and malleability of makefiles. Simplification often *is* a good thing, and GUI tools can help developers to create software quickly, but this simplicity comes at an expense.

GUI build tools simply do not scale well and are of little use on really large projects. Make does have a cryptic syntax, but it lets you do far, far more. For example, makefiles allow nesting of directories, creating a build hierarchy. Simplistic GUI tools only provide one level of depth, the nesting of projects inside a workspace.

People complain about make's complexity and that you can foul things up using it. This is a valid concern, but it is the same as with any power tool—you might injure yourself if you don't use it properly.

This doesn't mean that you should throw away all GUI build tools and start writing a raft of replacement makefiles. On the contrary: Use the right tool for the job. Balance simplicity and integration with power and extensibility; choose the tool that's required each time.

2. Why is it important to treat the extraction of source code as a separate step from building it?

The two *are* logically different steps. In a properly crafted build system, you should be able to check out *any* version of the software, no matter how old, and then issue the same make instruction to build it. Later you should be able to clean the tree and rebuild it using the same instruction, without checking everything back out again.

It's no loss to have these as two separate steps. You can easily wrap a script around them to make a single-step retrieve/build procedure—this will then be useful for an overnight build script. For these overnight scripts, it's vital to start from a fresh source tree each time (to avoid being caught out by problems carried over from the last tree). This is a good test of your source tree; by deleting it and performing a complete rebuild, you'll check that no files are missing or out of date (you might have forgetten to check something in).

Other problems with binding source extraction into the build step include the following:

- You don't want the build system to automatically check files out of the source repository as you do a build. You rarely want the whole world changing under your feet each time you rebuild. It's important to be in control of the code you're working on, not a slave to the build system behavior.

- There is a bootstrapping problem: If extraction is a part of the build process, where do you get a source tree from in order to start the build? You'd have to check it out manually anyway! Or you'd have to recite more magic incantations to partially check out the build portions of the tree in order to perform a real checkout and build. Don't go there.

3. **Where should the intermediate files from construction steps (e.g., object files) be put?**

Some build systems dump object files beside the source file that generated them. Advanced build systems can create a parallel directory tree and build objects into *there*, leaving the source directories intact. This keeps things neat, distinguishing source files from the build-generated files. There are downsides, though: It's harder to search around the hierarchy. You might want to force a source file recompilation by deleting a .o file, but with split trees you have to navigate further from the source to do so.

Another neat approach for object file placement is to put intermediate files within the source tree, but in their own subdirectory; out of way of the source files, but still close to hand. You'd end up with a directory hierarchy looking like Figure 1.

This is a good way to support the building of *multiple targets* from one source tree—each target has its own build subdirectory. Without this mechanism, you could start a debug build, finish it off in release mode, and have a link stage that's a disaster. Adopting this approach leads to a build tree looking Figure 2.

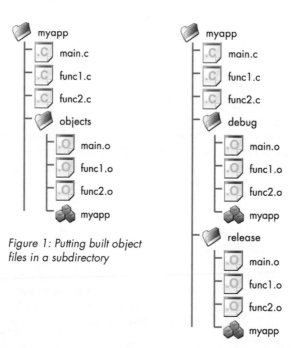

Figure 1: Putting built object files in a subdirectory

Figure 2: Even better: Putting object files in a named subdirectory

4. **If you add an automated test suite to the build system, should it run automatically after the software is built, or must you fire a separate command to invoke the tests?**

You can easily provide a separate command (something like a *tests* makefile target; you'd type make tests after make all). However, this extra step would be less likely to be performed—there's no requirement to do so. The tests may be overlooked. This is quite likely, human nature being what it is. The untested code could cause all sorts of problems, making the effort of writing tests fruitless. Ensure your unit tests are a part of the main build procedure.

Automated stress tests and load tests probably shouldn't be part of this build step, though. They might take too long to execute, only intended to be run on the overnight build. In this case, make an automated scaffold to run them, but don't trigger it during a normal build.

5. Should the overnight build be a *debug* or *release* build?

Both. It's very important to test the release build configuration as early as possible. Debug builds shouldn't be released to the QA department, let alone outside the company.

It's important to test that both release and development build processes work—not just once when the build system is created, but on an ongoing basis. It's remarkably easy to make a minor update that breaks one or other build. If a build isn't tested until the last minute, you're going to be very angry when it fails with a deadline looming.

There may be serious differences between executables generated by debug and release builds. Some compilers exhibit markedly changed behavior in debug and release mode. One popular compiler is happy to pad out data buffers in debug builds, so memory overruns are harmless and go undetected—hardly a good debugging aid. If you only ever tested the debug build, switching to release mode just before the product ships means that you are bound to run into problems.

6. Write a make rule to automatically generate dependency information from your compiler. Show how to use this information in the makefile.

There are several ways to achieve this, depending in part on how you get dependency information from your compiler. Say the hypothetical compiler takes an extra -dep parameter that cajoles it to create a dependency file as well as the object file. Let's say that the format of this generated file is already in make's dependency format.[12] Using GNU Make, you can specify a compilation rule that has the side effect of generating dependencies:

```
%.o: %.c
    compiler -object %.o -dep %.d %.c
```

You can then incorporate all generated dependency files directly into the makefile by putting this at the bottom of Makefile:

```
include *.d
```

---

[12] These are quite reasonable assumptions; many systems work like this.

It's that easy! Of course, this is the simplest mechanism that will work. There are many refinements to clean this up. For example:

- You can direct the dependency files into a separate directory. This prevents them from cluttering up the working directory and covering up the important files.

- You can write an include rule to only pull in the *correct* .d files. There may be other .d files lying around that you shouldn't include, making the wildcard include line dangerous: The inclusion of random information from invalid files will confuse make. This problem can crop up easily: If you remove a source file from the makefile but don't clean the build tree first, the old .o and .d files will hang around in the working directories until you remove them manually.

- If the compiler permits, you can write a separate rule to create .d files, making them first-class citizens of the build system. This has the downside of slowing down the build process—the compiler will now be invoked *twice* for each source file.

7. **Recursive make is a popular method of creating a modular build system spanning several directories. However, it is fundamentally flawed. Describe its problems and suggest alternatives.**

Conventional wisdom suggests that all large codebases built with makefiles should use the recursive make technique. Yet as powerful as recursive make is, it's fundamentally flawed. Don't ignore it, though. It's important to understand how recursive make works (or doesn't work) because it's so prevalent (many codebases employ recursive make), and you need to you know its problems to understand what makes a better solution.

What renders recursive make a liability? It has a number of pitfalls:

Speed

It's so *slooooooow*. If you try to rebuild a source tree that's already up to date, a recursive build still has to trawl faithfully through each directory. For a reasonably sized project this takes ages, which is nonsensical when no action is necessary.

Each directory is built as a *separate* make invocation.[13] This circumvents many potential optimizations; shared include files will be inspected over and over and over again. Although filesystems can cache information, this is still an unnecessary overhead. A sensible build system would only need to inspect each file once.

Dependencies

Recursive make cannot follow dependencies correctly; subdirectory makefiles have no way of determining all dependency information. Your module makefile can observe that its local func1.c source file depends on a shared.h header in another directory. It will happily rebuild func1.c every time shared.h is changed. But what happens if

---

[13] Just think of the overhead of starting up all those child processes!

shared.h is automatically generated by a separate module, based on some template file shared.tmpl? Your module can't know about this extra dependency. Even if it could, it doesn't know how to rebuild shared.h—that isn't its job. So if shared.tmpl is changed, func1.c will not be rebuilt appropriately.

The only way to plaster over this crack is to arrange for shared.h to be built first, *before* func1.c's module. The programmer must carefully define the *order* of recursion to make sure the software rebuilds correctly.[14] The more indirect dependencies that exist, the worse the mess gets.

Faced with this problem, programmers devise nefarious work-arounds, like making several build passes over the tree or manually removing certain files to force a rebuild every time. These hacks only serve to slow the build down more and unnecessarily complicate the procedure.

Puts onus back on the developer

Make was created to manage the complexity of rebuilding code. Recursive make turns this inside out and forces you to get involved in the build process again. We've seen how the programmer has to manage the order of recursion, kludging each makefile to work around limitations.

Subtlety

Recursive make's problems are not at all obvious. That's why many people still think it's a good idea. When things go wrong, they do so in strange ways. The cause of a problem is rarely clear, so it'll be dismissed as "one of those freak events."

This adds up to a build system that is dangerously brittle.

These are all problems people wrongly attribute to make itself, arguing that it is defective. But in this respect, make is an innocent bystander. It's our *use* of make that is at fault. The recursion introduces each of these problems; it inhibits make from doing its proper job.

So what's the solution to this mess? Clearly we don't want to throw away the nesting in our source trees. We need a build process that supports nesting but doesn't split up the build process recursively. This isn't too hard; we'll call the technique *nested make*. It simply involves putting all build information in one master makefile. There is no longer a need for individual subdirectory makefiles. The über-makefile manages all source nesting internally.

KEY CONCEPT *Contrary to popular belief, recursive make is a* bad *build technique. Avoid it in favor of a more robust* nested make *approach.*

You might be thinking that this is a more complex and less flexible approach. How can you manage a large build tree with just a single makefile?

---

[14] This is a one-up for GUI tools—without recursive make, they tend to manage dependencies properly.

A number of practical implementation techniques make it easy:

- Use make's include file mechanism. Put the list of each directory's source files in *that* directory—it's far more maintainable and clear that way. Place this list in a file called something like files.mk, and include that from the master Makefile.

- You can retain recursive make's modularity—entering *any* component subdirectory to type make—by defining more intermediate targets. These targets construct specific parts of the project. Constructing modular builds this way can be more meaningful than recursive make's arbitrary directory-based approach, and it ensures that each intermediate target is always built properly.

Nested make is no more complex than recursive make; in fact it can be *less* complex. It produces more reliable, accurate, speedy builds.

Getting Personal

1. **Do you know how to perform different types of compilation using your build system? How can you build a debug or release version of the application from the same sources, with the same makefiles?**

In an earlier answer, we saw a good solution to this problem: Build objects into different subdirectories, created by the build script, based on the type of build (one directory for debug files and one for release files).

You can achieve this in GNU Make by massaging filenames. Here's an example:

```
# Define the source files
SRC_FILES = main.c func1.c func2.c

# Default build type (if none specified)
BUILD_TYPE ?= release

# Synthesize the object filenames
# (This is a magic GNU Make incantation that swaps
# the .c file suffix for .o)
OBJ_FILES = $(SRC_FILES:.c=.o)

# Now the clever bit: add the build-type directory
# prefix to object filenames (more GNU Make magic)
OBJ_FILES = $(addprefix $(BUILD_TYPE)/, $(OBJ_FILES))
```

You'll obviously be doing more with the selected BUILD_TYPE, altering the compiler flags, for example. Don't forget that you'll need a rule to create the subdirectories, or your compiler will complain when it tries to generate output. Here's how to do this on Unix:

```
$(BUILD_TYPE):
    mkdir -p $(BUILD_TYPE)
```

Now you can type these two commands, one after the other, knowing the build system will cope perfectly:

```
BUILD_TYPE=release make all
BUILD_TYPE=debug make all
```

You *can* create a simpler system without this subdirectory technique, but it will rely on doing a cleanout whenever you change the BUILD_TYPE.

2. **How good is your current project's build process? Does it rate well against the characteristics in this chapter? How could you improve it? How easy is it to:**

   a. **Add a new file to a library?**

   b. **Add a new directory of code?**

   c. **Move or rename a file of code?**

   d. **Add a different build configuration (say, a demo build)?**

   e. **Build two configurations in one copy of the source tree without doing a clean in between?**

This shows both how well you know the build process and how maintainable it is. Comparing your build mechanism to other projects' is a good idea—it will show where your processes are inadequate and need improvement.

Consider moving and renaming source files. Both are common during refactoring and are very easy to overlook. These simple actions *can* cause build systems to calculate dependencies incorrectly and build flawed code. I've been bitten more than once by such a problem; it takes a while to notice when this goes wrong.

Often there is "no time" in the programmers' busy schedules to spend on improving the build system; they are all far too busy trying to get a product out the door. This is a dangerous misconception. The build scripts are a part of the code and require as much maintenance and careful extension as any other source file. A safe and reliable build system is so important that time spent sorting it out is *not* time wasted. It's time invested in the future of the codebase.

3. **Have you ever created a build system from scratch? What drove you to its particular design?**

As with any programming task, the shape of your solution is influenced by a number of factors:

- Your prior experience
- What you know
- Your understanding of the problem *at the moment*
- The limitations of the technology available
- The amount of time you have to set it up

Generally, a little time and a little usage will tell how good your design decisions were. You never appreciate all the requirements at first, and things change that no one can anticipate:

- Requirements change—if the product becomes really successful, you may need to build different internationalized versions or target a new processor architecture. The build system must accommodate extension.

- The code may need to be moved across to a new build toolchain, when no one ever anticipated that this should be a selectable option.

How easily these modifications can be incorporated is a testament to the quality of your design. You'll learn with each change, gaining valuable experience for the next build system you craft.

4. **Everyone suffers from flaws in a build system from time to time. When programming a build script, you're as likely to introduce bugs as you are when programming real code.**
   What kinds of build errors have you been bitten by, and how could you fix, or even prevent, them?

Common build errors include:

- Picking up dependency information incorrectly

- Not coping gracefully with file system failures, like running out of disk space or incorrect file permissions; the build may continue with no indication that one of the steps failed

- Source control problems: merges go wrong, or the wrong version of some source code is checked out

- Library configuration errors, often using incompatible or out of date versions

- Programmers not understanding how to use the build system, and making silly mistakes

When something's not going as expected, step back and consider whether or not the build system is playing a part in the problem.

Chapter 11: The Need for Speed

Mull It Over

1. **Optimization is a process of making trade-offs—sacrificing one quality of code for another desirable quality. Describe the kinds of trade-offs that lead to a performance increase.**

The kinds of decisions that profoundly influence a program's performance are:

- Number of features versus size of code

- Program speed versus memory consumption

- Storage and caching versus computation on demand
- Guarded approach versus unguarded; optimistic versus pessimistic
- Approximate calculations versus exact calculations
- Inline versus function call; monolithic versus modular
- Indexing an array versus searching a list
- Passing a parameter by reference or address versus passing a copy
- Implemented in hardware versus software
- Hard-coded, direct access versus indirect access
- Predetermined, fixed value versus variable and configurable
- Compile-time work versus run-time work
- Local function call versus remote call
- Lazy computation versus eager computation
- "Clever" algorithm versus clear code

2. **Look at each of the optimization alternatives listed in "Why Not Optimize?" on page 202. Describe what trade-offs are being made, if any.**

Some of these alternatives *could* be considered optimizations, depending on how much of the system is under your control. If you specify the hardware platform that your program will run on, using a faster machine *is* an optimization. If not, it's more of a work-around.

Many of the alternatives have hidden complexity costs. For example, relying on a certain host platform configuration (i.e., what services or background programs are running) leads to specific environmental dependencies that are hard to capture and easy to miss during installation or later maintenance.

3. **Explain these terms and their exact relationship:**
   - **Performance**
   - **Efficiency**
   - **Optimized**

The *efficiency* of code determines its *performance*. *Optimizing* is the act of improving the code's efficiency in order to improve performance. Notice that none of these terms directly describe *speed of execution*; the quality required may not be speed, but rather memory footprint or data throughput.

4. **What are the likely bottlenecks in a slow program?**

It's common fallacy to think that everything is contending for the CPU and that bad code will be consuming all the processor time. Sometimes the CPU can be running almost idle, yet performance is dire. A program may stall for a number of reasons:

- Memory is being thrashed to and from swap space on the hard disk.
- It is waiting on disk access.

- It is waiting on slow database transactions.
- There is bad locking behavior.

5. How can you avoid the need to optimize? What methods will prevent you from writing inefficient code?

We've seen how important it is to *design* performance into a software system from the very beginning. You can only do this if you already have a firm idea of what the required performance characteristics are.

Once you have a sound design in place, write your code sensibly. Be aware which constructs are most efficient in your language, and avoid using the inefficient ones. For example, in C++, pass const references rather than expensive temporary copies.[15]

It's useful to have a rough idea of the relative costs of different operations. If we scale time so that a processor executes one instruction a second, then a function call typically takes a few seconds, a virtual function call takes 10 to 30 seconds, a disk seek takes a few months, and the time between keystrokes of an average typist is several years. Try to work out this kind of measure for operations like a memory allocation, claiming a lock, creating a new thread, and a simple data structure lookup.

6. How does the presence of multiple threads affect optimization?

Threading can cause as many problems as it's supposed to solve. Naïvely threaded designs can introduce extra bottlenecks, particularly when locks are used badly, leading to long periods of deadlock.

Multithreaded programs are harder to profile, unless the profiler has good thread support; you need to interpret the profiler's results based on the relative thread priorities. If the threads are supposed to cooperate, you have to work out how the overall execution is progressing as several threads of control weave around one another.

7. Why *don't* we write efficient code? What stops us from using high-performance algorithms in the first place?

There are many perfectly valid reasons for not writing optimized code on the first attempt:

- You don't know the final pattern of usage. With no Real World test data, how can you choose the code design that will work best?
- It's hard enough to get the program *working*, let alone working *fast*. To prove it's feasible, we choose designs that are easy to implement so that prototypes get finished quickly.

---

[15] Conversely, this reference might inhibit other performance gains. Copies are guaranteed not to have aliasing issues; some compiler optimizations cannot be performed if there are potential variable aliases. As always, you must measure and work out what works best.

- "High-performance" algorithms can be more complex and daunting to implement. Programmers naturally shy away from them, since it's an area where faults can be easily introduced.

Programmers often think that the time taken to run some code is proportional to the amount of effort spent writing it.[16] You might have written some file-parsing code in hours, but it will always takes ages to execute, because disks are slow. The complex code you spent half a week getting right may only consume a few hundred processor cycles. In fact, neither the efficiency of a piece of code nor the amount of time you need to spend optimizing it bears any relation to the amount of time you spent writing it.

8. A List data type is implemented using an array. What is the worst case algorithmic complexity of each of the following List methods?

   a. The constructor

   b. append—places a new item on the end of the list

   c. insert—slides a new item in between two existing list items, at a given position

   d. isEmpty—returns true if the list contains no items

   e. contains—returns true if the list contains a specified item

   f. get—returns the item with a given index

The worst cases are:

a. The constructor is O(1) since it only needs to create an array; the list is initially empty. However, it's worth considering that the size of this array will affect the complexity of the constructor—most languages create arrays fully populated with objects, even if you don't plan to use them yet. If the constructors for these objects are nontrivial, then the List constructor will take some time to execute.

   The array size might not be fixed—the constructor could take a parameter to determine this size (effectively setting the maximum possible list size). The method then becomes O(n).

b. The append operation is O(1) on average: It simply has to write an array entry and update the list size. *But,* if the array is full, it will have to reallocate, copy, and deallocate—a worst case complexity of O(n), at least (it depends on the performance of your memory manager).

c. insert is O(n) on average. You might be asked to insert an element at the very beginning of the list. This requires all the elements in the array to be shuffled down one place before writing the first element. The more items in the List, the longer this will take. However, the worst case, again, involves memory reallocation and could be much more than O(n).

---

[16] That looks stupid when you see it written down, but it's a very easy trap to fall into at the codeface.

d. Unless you have a ridiculously bad implementation, isEmpty is O(1). The list size will be known, so the return value is a single calculation based on this number.

e. contains is O(*n*), presuming the list contents are unordered. In the worst case, you will be asked to look for an item that doesn't exist and will have to traverse every single list item.

f. get is O(1), thanks to the array implementation. Indexing an array is a constant time operation. If List had been implemented as a *linked list*, then this would have been an O(*n*) operation.

Getting Personal

1. **How important (honestly) is code performance in your current project? What is the motivator for this performance requirement?**

The performance requirements should not be arbitrarily chosen. They should be justified, not just a time limit pulled out of thin air. Every performance requirement is important; there are no specifications that don't matter. How much concern a particular requirement generates depends on how hard it is to meet. Whether it's hard or not, you still have to come up with a design that satisfies it.

2. **In your last optimization attempt:**
    a. **Did you use a profiler?**
    b. **If yes, how much improvement did you measure?**
    c. **If no, how did you know whether you made any kind of improvement?**
    d. **Did you test that the code still worked after optimizing?**
    e. **If yes, how thoroughly did you test?**
    f. **If no, why not? How could you be sure the code still worked properly for *all* cases?**

Only the most dramatic performance improvements can be detected without a profiler or some other good timing tests. Human perception is easily fooled—when you've just slaved to speed up the program, it will always *appear* faster to you.

Test performance improvements carefully, and discard those that are not worthwhile. It's better to have clear code than a minuscule speed increase and unmaintainable logic.

3. **If you've not yet attempted to optimize the code you're currently working on, take a guess at which parts are the slowest and which bits consume the most memory. Now run it through a profiler—how accurate were you?**

You'll probably be quite surprised at the results. The larger the program you profile, the less likely you are to correctly judge these bottlenecks.

4. **How well specified are your program's performance requirements? Do you have a concrete plan to test that you meet these criteria?**

Without a clear specification, no one can really complain that your program isn't fast enough!

Chapter 12: An Insecurity Complex

Mull It Over

1. **What is a "secure" program?**

A secure program is able to stand up against attempts to abuse it, to break into it, or to use it for a purpose it was not intended for. This is more than a robust program; robust code meets its specification and doesn't crash when you apply a little pressure. However, a robust program might not have been designed with security in mind and could still leak sensitive information under some extreme conditions. Sometimes it's preferable to crash when used wrongly, rather than provide unintended output. So secure code *might* crash!

The definition of a secure program depends on the security requirements for the application. These are defined in part by what you can expect from the supporting services (the OS and other applications). Given these, your application's objectives could be any of the following:

Confidentiality
The system will not disclose information to the wrong people. They will get an access denied message, or will have no idea that the information exists in the first place.

Integrity
The system won't allow unauthorized changing of information.

Availability
The system works continually—even while being attacked. It's hard to guard against *all* possible attacks (what if someone removes the power?), but it's possible to resist many attacks by including a level of redundancy in the design, or by providing a rapid restart after attack.

Authentication
The system ensures that users are who they say they are, usually with a login and password mechanism.

Audit
The system records information about all important operations, to catch or monitor the activities of attackers.

2. **What input must be validated in a secure program? What sort of validation is required?**

All input must be validated. This includes command-line parameters, environment variables, GUI inputs, web form inputs (even those with client-side JavaScript checking), CGI-encoded URLs, cookie contents, file contents, and filenames.

You should check the input's size (if it's not a simple numeric variable), the validity of its format, and the actual contents of the data (that numbers are in range, and there are no embedded query strings).

3.   How can you guard against attacks from the pool of trusted users?

Not very easily. They have been given a specific level of privilege because they are trusted not to abuse it. Most users will not intentionally abuse your software, but a small number will try to subvert programs for their own advantage.

There are a few techniques to manage this:

- Log every operation so you know who made what change and when.
- Require two users to authenticate all really important operations.
- Wrap each operation in an undoable transaction so it can be unrolled.
- Back up all data stores periodically so you can retrieve lost data.

4.   Where can an exploitable buffer overrun occur? What functions are particularly prone to buffer overrun?

Buffer overrun is probably the biggest security vulnerability, and it is a simple problem that is easy for an attacker to exploit. It can occur anywhere that a multi-location structure is addressed—either by copying data into or out of it or by indexing into it to access a specific item. Arrays and strings are the most common culprits.

It is most often seen in user input routines, although this is not the only habitat—it can exist within any data manipulation code. Exploitable buffers can be situated both on the stack (where function-local variables are placed) or on the heap (the pool of dynamically allocated memory).

5.   Can you avoid buffer overruns altogether?

Yes—as long as you are diligent in validating each function's input and can be sure that the stack of software leading up to each input (possibility implemented in the OS input routines or your language's run-time library) is safe.

Here are some key techniques to safeguard your code:

- Use a language with no fixed-size buffers—for example, a language that has automatically extending strings. It's not just strings that are dangerous, though: Look for bounds-checked arrays and safe hash maps.
- If you can't rely on language support, you *must* bounds check all input.
- In C, always use the safer standard library functions `strncpy`, `strncat`, `snprintf`, `fgets`, and so on. Don't use stdio routines like `printf`, and `scanf`—you can't guarantee their safety.

- Never use third-party libraries that aren't provably safe.
- Write your code in a managed execution environment (like Java or C#). Then buffer overrun attacks become almost nonexistent—the executive traps most overruns automatically.

6. How can you secure the memory in use by your application?

There are three times to think about memory security:

a. Before you use it. When you claim some memory, it contains arbitrary values. Don't write code that accidentally relies on the contents of uninitialized memory. A cracker could exploit this to attack your code. To be extra safe, zero all allocated memory before you use it.

b. During use. Lock memory containing sensitive information so it can't be swapped to disk. Obviously you must be using a secure OS—if one application can read any other's memory, then you've already lost!

c. After use. Often forgotten by application programmers is that when you release memory, it should be cleaned before you hand it back for the OS to recycle. If you don't do this, a rogue process could mine memory for the secret data you leave behind.

7. Are C and C++ inherently less secure than alternative languages?

C and C++ produce more than their fair share of insecure applications and *allow* you to write code containing classic security vulnerabilities. You definitely have to keep your brain switched on; even experienced developers must pay attention when writing C/C++ code to avoid buffer overruns. These languages don't exactly encourage secure programming.

However, other languages don't avoid all security problems either, just the ones C and C++ have made famous. A different language will most likely avoid potential buffer overruns, but you shouldn't have a false sense of security; many other problems that can't be avoided in the language itself remain. You must be aware of security issues when using *any* language—you can't pick a "safe" language and forget all about security.

Indeed, buffer overrun is a vulnerability that can be very easily audited and worked around. If you need to program secure applications, then the language you use is a small concern among all the other problems.

8. Has the experience of C led to C++ being a better, more securely designed language?

C++ has gained an abstract string type that manages its own memory internally. This goes a long way toward avoiding buffer overruns, although traditional C-style char arrays remain for those who still want to shoot themselves in the foot. The vector is another handy device: a memory managing array. However, it is possible to overrun both of these structures—do you know how?

C++ could be considered more dangerous than C, because it stores a lot of function pointers on the heap (this is where virtual function tables are stored). If an attacker can overwrite one of those pointers, then he can redirect operation to his own evil code.

In many ways, C++ is more secure, or rather, it is more easy to use securely. However, it was not designed with security solely in mind, and provides its own set of security problems that the developer must be aware of.

9. How do you know when your program has been compromised?

Without detection measures, you'll have no idea—and you will just have to keep an eye out for unusual system behavior or different patterns of activity. This is hardly scientific. A hacked system can remain a secret indefinitely. Even if a victim (or his software vendor) *does* spot an attack, he probably doesn't want to release detailed information about it to invite more intruders. What company would publicize that its product has security flaws? If it is conscientious enough to release a security patch, not everyone will upgrade, leaving a well-documented security flaw in many operational systems.

Getting Personal

1. What are the security requirements for your current project? How were these requirements established? Who knows about them? Where are they documented?

Answer this honestly. It's not too hard to make up something that sounds plausible. But unless the security requirements are formally documented, security has not really been addressed by your project. This should be something that every developer is aware of and knows how to fulfill.

2. What's the worst security bug in one of your shipped applications?

It's important to know about this, even if it's now ancient history. You have to know what you've got wrong in the past to stand any chance of avoiding it in the future. If you don't know of any past security vulnerabilities, then you've probably not been thorough in security testing—you've not been paying attention, or you've been very lucky to have nothing discovered.

3. How many security bulletins have been posted against your application?

Have these been caused by silly developer mistakes like stupid code errors, or do they stem from larger design problems? Most common problems that get documented in bulletins are the former.

4. Have you ever run a *security audit*? What kinds of flaws did it reveal?

Unless you have a professional security specialist running this test, it will surely miss some security vulnerabilities. However, the audit will still uncover many glaring problems and is *very* worthwhile.

5. **What kind of person is most likely to attack your current system? How is this influenced by**
    - **Your company**
    - **The type of user**
    - **The type of product**
    - **The popularity of the product**
    - **The competition**
    - **The platform you run on**
    - **The connectedness and public visibility of the system**

Everyone is a target to someone: a malicious user, unscrupulous competitors, and even terrorist organizations. Who do you trust?

Chapter 13: Grand Designs

Mull It Over

1. **How does project size affect your software design and the work involved in creating it?**

The larger a project gets, the more architectural design it requires in proportion to low-level code design. More time needs to be spent up front ensuring the design is right, because bad choices will have more serious consequences.

2. **Is a well-documented bad design better than an undocumented good one?**

Documentation is part of what makes a design good. A well-documented bad design provides a route in to the code, even if it's a brightly illuminated dirt track to a cesspit. At the very least, it will teach you never to touch the code again.

A sufficiently simple piece of code shouldn't need reams of documentation, but any reasonably complex piece of software becomes hard to work with when there isn't adequate description.

Which is better? The undocumented good design is best: If it is a truly high-quality design, then it *should* be obvious and self-documenting.

3. **How can you measure the design quality of a piece of code? How can you quantify its simplicity, elegance, modularity, and so on?**

Quality is difficult to quantify; it's largely an aesthetic judgment for design. What makes a picture beautiful? The kind of thing you can't hold in your hand and count. Hindsight will show how easy the code was to pick up or to modify. But that doesn't really help when you first come across some code.

If I have two designs *A* and *B*, and I think *A* is more elegant, but in practice *B* turns out to be more usable and copes with the pressures of reuse much better, then it is hard to argue that *A* is the better design.

The only way to judge design quality is to *look* at the code. Reading a little code generally gives a good impression of overall quality; if one small bit appears good, then the rest is likely to be of reasonable quality too. This doesn't always hold, but it's a handy yardstick. A realistic approach is this: If that little bit of code is bad, expect the whole codebase to be terrible. If the little bit is any good, then just suspect the codebase of harboring more subtle problems.

Running code tools that inspect the source, producing diagrams and documentation, can also help to gauge design quality.

4. Is design a team activity? How important are teamworking skills in creating a good design?

Very important. Programming tasks are seldom a lone activity. In the software factory, most large-scale design activities involve more than one designer. Even if the work is split into separate areas, those areas interface at some point—so the designers must interface. If there *is* only one designer, he or she must still be able to document and communicate the design effectively.

5. Are different methodologies more suitable to different projects?

Yes, the scope of some projects will render certain design approaches unnecessary. If you are writing a set of device drivers, you won't find *much* use in a full-blown OO design process.

If you are working on a very formal project, perhaps for a government agency, you'll need to use a very formal process that documents every stage and provides accountability for every design decision made. This may be quite different from an exploratory R&D project in a software lab.

6. In what ways can you determine whether a design is highly cohesive or weakly coupled?

Ultimately you have to look at the code and see how it fits together, but that's boring! You can get a good feel for coupling in a C or C++ project by looking at the #includes at the top of the file. If there are tons of them, the coupling is probably disastrous. Alternatively, you can run inspection tools that produce pretty pictures of your code.

7. If you've solved a similar design problem in the past, how good an indicator is it of how difficult *this* problem will be?

Experience teaches you how to design, so learn and then exploit your knowledge. But employ wisdom with this knowledge; don't run on autopilot. Different situations present different challenges—don't presume that one problem is the same as another just because it looks like it on the surface.

If you know how to use a hammer, don't make every problem into a nail.

8. **Is there a place for experimentation in design?**

Yes, any design *is* experimental until it has been implemented and found acceptable. Consider the "build one to throw away" approach that Frederick Brooks described. (Brooks 95) There's a lot to be said for experimentation.

Design is an iterative process; during each iteration you can try out design alternatives and decide which is most sensible. The more iterations you go through and the smaller in scope you make each one, the less painful any bad design decisions will be.

Getting Personal

1. **Look back and think about how you learned to design code. How could you convey the knowledge you've gained to a total novice?**

How much do you honestly think you *could* teach, and how much would have to come from the novice's inherent abilities and experience? Could you create a set of exercises based on your experience that would help someone else?

You wouldn't give a novice a large system to design at first. You'd start him off on a small self-contained project, and then perhaps get him to make extensions to existing programs, all the time keeping a mentoring eye on what he's doing.

Most programmers didn't get this kind of help themselves when they were learning to design. They learned through a process of trial and error. Do consider teaching and mentoring a novice—it really helps you to grow in your own abilities.

2. **What experience do you have with using particular design methodologies? Were these good or bad experiences? What was the resulting code like? What might have worked better?**

Was the taste left in your mouth by a methodology influenced by your prior experience and preferences? If you don't know how to use a particular methodology, it will be hard work and uncomfortable. A hard-core C programmer may dislike any form of object-oriented design, and his OO designs will be appalling. But that doesn't make OO a flawed approach.

3. **Do you find it important to stick rigidly to the methodology you're using?**

The design approach is a tool, a utility, like a programming language—you should only use it up to the point it remains *useful.* If it stops being useful, it's no longer a utility! A methodology won't work if no one on the team knows how to perform it; use something they do know, or teach them first.

4. **What was the best designed code you've ever seen? What was the worst designed?**

I bet you'll easily remember the worst designed code. Bad code sticks out like a sore thumb, and likewise sticks in your memory. Well-designed code looks simple and obvious, so you probably won't step back and say, "What a great design!" You probably won't even notice there was much design work involved.

5. **A programming language is essentially a tool to implement your design, not a religion to argue about. How important is it _really_ to know language idioms?**

It's very important, or you'll end up with code that doesn't make sense.

Some architectural decisions may be language independent, but low-level code design is _heavily_ influenced by the implementation language. An obvious example: Don't create a flat procedural design when you're coding in Java—it's just plain wrong.

6. **Do you think programming is an _engineering discipline_, a _craft_, or an _art_?**

Quite simply, it depends on how you do it. It has elements of all three.

I prefer to think of programming as a craft—it requires skill, workmanship, discipline, and experience. Its products can be at once functional _and_ beautiful. There is an element of artistry in it; it's a creative process. Allied with this artistry is the mastery of tools and techniques. These are the hallmarks of a craft.

Chapter 14: Software Architecture

Mull It Over

1. **Define where _architecture_ ends and _software design_ begins.**

In truth, both terms can be defined to whatever suits you. In their common usage, the distinctions are as follows:

- **Architecture** is the high-level structural design. It looks at the wide-ranging implications of its choices, seeing how it will impact construction and maintenance costs, overall system complexity, ability to accommodate future extensions, and marketing concerns. The architecture is devised at the start of a project. It has serious consequences, at the very least on the further software design.

- **Software design** is the next level down, a more refined and focused activity. It's concerned with code details—data structures, function signatures, and the exact flow of control through modules. Software design is conducted on a per-module basis. Its consequences are nowhere near as significant to the system as a whole.

Exactly where the two meet depends in part on the size of the project. Software construction is an iterative and incremental process—although architecture is created first, design results can feed back up to the architecture.

2. **In what ways can a bad architecture affect a system? Are there parts that wouldn't be affected by architectural flaws?**

Bad architecture will undermine any effort to write good software. It is fundamental to the quality of your code. If some code isn't affected by the flawed architecture, then it's probably either a stand-alone library or it never really belonged in the system in the first place.

3. **How easy is it to repair architectural deficiencies once they become apparent?**

During the early formative stages of a project, it's relatively easy to massage the architecture. But once development is committed to that architecture, with sufficient investment (design and code) slotted into its scaffold, it's very, *very* hard to change. You might as well try rewriting the entire product from scratch.

This is why it is so important to get the architecture right the first time. You can refactor small bits of code, but not an entire structural foundation.

Of course, it is easier for us to rip up software and start it afresh than it is in the physical construction industry, but economics dictate that we can't do it. We usually only have one chance to get the architecture right, and if we don't, we will have to live with the consequences for the entire lifetime of the software system.

4. **To what extent does architecture affect the following things?**
   a. **System configuration**
   b. **Logging**
   c. **Error handling**
   d. **Security**

The architecture has a profound impact on each of these, or more correctly, each of these has a profound impact on the architecture. You need to establish requirements for these areas before embarking on serious architectural design. It will be hard to graft such features into the code at a later date, let alone into the overriding architecture.

a. The architecture determines *what* should be configurable (a lot or a little) and *how* it should be configured. The kind of configuration mechanism is determined by several factors: the importance of a shared "configuration manager" component, whether or not the system supports remote configuration, and who has rights to perform configuration (is it just the developers; should the software be tweaked by installers, maintainers, or users?). All of these concerns are fundamental architectural issues.

b. The separate components may log information using some shared facility, or they might use their own custom mechanisms. The architecture will define which approach is acceptable, how you access the logs, and also the sort of logging information that's important. This needs to address the requirements of the software developers as well as the software users. Should development logging information be produced by release versions?

c. Architectural error management concerns include whether or not there is a central error-logging service and the error-reporting scheme (how does an error propagate from the seedy back-end components to the user's sanitized GUI interface?). It also defines what kind of error mechanisms are used: perhaps a centralized table of error codes shared across all components or a common exception hierarchy. It will address how errors from third-party code are incorporated into the system.

d. Security issues will depend on the kind of software under development. A distributed Internet-based shop-front system has different security requirements from a small piece of code that will only ever be deployed on a stand-alone computer. Security is an important topic and can't be grafted in at the last minute; it must be addressed in the early architectural designs.

5. What experience or qualifications are required to be called a *software architect*?

You can decide to *call* yourself an architect, but you can't gain insight and experience overnight or magically conjure up the wisdom to make good design decisions.

Good architectural design requires a wealth of prior experience—learning from, devising, and refining real software systems. This can only be learned by actually doing it, not by watching someone else. Be wary of people who call themselves architects after working on just one release of software.

You can work on software architecture and not be called an architect; the use of this moniker often depends on company structure and culture. No formal qualifications are required before you claim the title—however in some countries, it is illegal to call yourself any kind of architect without professional accreditation.

6. Should sales strategy influence architecture? If so, how? If not, why?

Yes, commercial concerns will inevitably affect the technical architecture. Otherwise, you'll build a system that is not a viable product; you'll rapidly find yourself out of a job and your company in receivership.

We *must* address the commercial implications of our designs—for example, considering the consequences of failure modes and the cost associated with return-to-base or on-site system support. The architecture must minimize these events if they are problems (you can provide remote access and rich diagnostics to avoid such intense product support).

Commercial concerns also affect these architectural areas: customer support facilities (including how easy the system is to administer), the installation approach (performed by trained personnel or by an automated CD installer), and maintenance support and fee structures.

7. **How would you architect for *extensibility*? How would you architect for *performance*? How do these design goals affect the system, and how do they complement one another?**

There are a number of architectural decisions that follow from these two requirements.

- **Extensibility** can be supported through architectural devices such as plug-ins, programmatic access to code (reflection), more language bindings, scripting capabilities, and extra levels of indirection.

- **Performance** is achieved by streamlining the architecture, keeping it mean and lean. You must remove all unnecessary components and ensure the connections provided are timely and adequate. Perhaps caching layers must be incorporated to boost data throughput.

As you can see, these two have little in common; every hook for extensibility will consume some, no matter how little, performance. Extra indirection has a cost—the indirection. If your goal is extensibility, this is an appropriate price to pay. A good architecture makes the correct high-level compromises to suit the perceived requirements.

Getting Personal

1. **How diverse is the range of architectural styles to which you are accustomed? What do you have the most experience with—how does it affect the software you write?**

Architecture affects us in many ways. Different architectural styles lead to different design and coding techniques. We are creatures of habit, and these techniques will shape how we think and code, even when working within a different architecture later on.

It is healthy to be exposed to a number of different architectures and to be able to work with them. In practice, you will focus on one particular style. Make sure you understand how your code is shaped by this architecture, and check that you're writing sympathetic code when you do change architectures.

2. **What personal experience do you have of architectures that succeeded or failed? What made them winning solutions or a hindrances?**

First, we must define what architectural *success* means. Is it an architecture with technical merit? Is it a system that achieves commercial profitability? Is it a bit of both? Place your answer here.

Software that buckles under the weight of inappropriate architecture usually suffers because the architecture was not suitably extensible. Important features cannot be accommodated. This inevitably means the product loses market share to the more nimble competitors. History is strewn with software products that have fallen by the wayside like this.

Another danger is legacy; a huge investment in architectural baggage is a great hindrance. It requires real insight and a fair bit of courage to throw away an old system or architecture and start from scratch. A rework must always learn lessons from the previous version.

An over-engineered architecture is just as dangerous as an insufficient one. If the architecture supports too much, it will make the product overly complex, cumbersome, and unacceptably slow. It usually means that even the simplest change requires modifying many components.

3. **Get every developer on your current project to draw a picture of the system architecture—individually (without talking to anyone) and without any reference to system documentation or the code. Compare the pictures. See what strikes you about each developer's efforts—aside from the relative artistic merit!**

Be fearful if the pictures bear no resemblance to one another. Don't worry if there are minor variations; different people will miss different small components, and each may be focused on different parts of the system. But if the diagrams contain wildly different components or the communication paths are not similar, then the team does not have the same mental model of the code. This will almost certainly lead to disaster. Pull the developers together and make sure they know what the system really looks like.

If all the diagrams *do* look similar, then give yourselves a pat on the back. You get bonus points if the components are positioned similarly on each sheet of paper. This is a hint that there is a central architecture specification and, more importantly, that everyone understands it.

4. **Do you have an architectural description that's commonly available for your current project? How up to date is it? Which kinds of view are you using? If you needed to explain the system to a newcomer or a potential customer, what would you really need to have documented?**

Note how far your ideal documentation is from reality. What opportunities do you have to improve this situation? In a busy commercial environment, you'll rarely be able to schedule specific time to document the entire architecture, but you can plan to capture parts during the design and specification of new modules. In this way, you can construct a good architectural overview, piece by piece.

5. **How does your system's architecture compare to the architecture of your competitors in the marketplace? How has your architecture been defined to determine your project's success?**

It's important to understand how your architecture is designed to meet all your requirements and to ensure your success. (If it has not been designed with this in mind, then you're in trouble.) We've seen how architecture has the most fundamental affect on the shape and quality of a software system—it therefore really does have a large influence on your product's success or failure. You'll rarely see software products thriving *despite* their bad architecture. If you do know of a successful one, it probably won't be around for very much longer.

An architecture must be able to support at least the same core functionality as competing systems and provide good support for the unique features that will cause someone to choose your product over anyone else's. The simple features that don't require architectural support are rarely as compelling as core functionality embedded deeply in the system.

Chapter 15: Software Evolution or Software Revolution?

Mull It Over

1.   What is the best metaphor for software growth?

There is none. In the immortal words of Forrest Gump, "Software is as software does." (Groom 94) Code construction has many correlations, yet no metaphor fully conveys its subtleties, just as you could never fully describe the beauty of a sunrise in words.

Analogies can be misleading; software is a very different substance from any physical item, and building it is accordingly different. There are fewer physical constraints, and you can manipulate it in many more ways.

There is a glimpse of truth in each metaphor. Learn what you can from them, but don't be tunneled into an incorrect view of software.

2.   Looking at a program's development through the colorful lifetime metaphor I talked about in the introduction, what Real World events correspond to a program's:
- **Conception**
- **Birth**
- **Growth**
- **Coming of age**
- **Sending out into the Big Wide World**
- **Middle age**
- **Growing tired**
- **Retirement**
- **Death**

Although we've seen that metaphors are imperfect, investigating this one does teach us a lot about the lifetime of a software system. It's certainly not practical to try to place one developmental stage before the preceding steps—you can't release software until it has come of age. Well, you can, but the consequences are dire.

Conception

The company observes an opening for a new product. The market requirements are established. The decision is made to build it.

Birth

A project is initiated to build the software. Designers and programmers are drafted in. An architecture is established. The code is started.

Growth

The code develops, and the program matures. It becomes more and more functionally complete. Deadlines loom.

Coming of age

Finally, the code is complete. It passes all tests to QA's satisfaction. It's considered a job well done, and hopefully it wasn't too far behind schedule.

Sending out

The program is released as version 1.0. It successfully meets the market's needs.

Middle age

The program is heavily used by clients and has been deployed for some time. Now, several revisions later, it has accumulated extra functionality and a degree of bloating.

Growing tired

Eventually, more nimble competition overtakes the program, with a greater feature set and better performance. No new customers choose our program, but existing customers clamor for upgrades. The software has become hard (even uneconomical) to extend.

Retirement

Finally, the company decides to give up on development and cease support. It announces support is ending in *x* months: a formal *end-of-life* statement. Development stops, although some maintenance work continues.

Death

We reach the inevitable: All development and maintenance stops. There is no longer anything offered by way of support. The world has moved on; soon, no one will remember what the program was called, let alone how to use it.

3. Is there a limit to software life—how long can you keep developing and working on a program before you have to start afresh?

This depends more on the market for the program than the quality of the software itself. Code can last indefinitely if it's well maintained and extended carefully. However, technologies go out of date rapidly, and trends change. Operating systems evolve quickly, hardware platforms become obsolete, and something that began as state-of-the-art, market-leading functionality will be given away for free a few years later. You must work hard to maintain the program's competitive advantage. Perhaps you'll have to continually add new functions, or port the software to new platforms.

Open source software is not immune to these competitive and market-related issues; in some cases the problem is worse. There may be little or no money involved, but there is a still a real market with advancing technology, lower barriers to entry, and greater chances to switch products.

4. Does the size of a codebase correspond to the maturity of the project?

No. On many occasions, I have vastly improved a system by *removing* code from it. Duplication can lead to massive code growth with little functional gain. The use of external libraries provides a lot of functionality without any discernible increase in project code size.

Many people quote *lines of code* as a good measurement of development progress. Such metrics are useless unless interpreted correctly. This is merely a view of the *amount of code written*, not of its quality or the purity of its design. It is certainly not a measure of its functionality.

5. How important is *backward compatibility* when maintaining code?

This depends on the individual project and how it has been deployed. More often than not, it is very important to retain backward compatibility when you change code—especially with regard to file formats, data structures, and communication protocols. Few applications can justifiably break this rule—only systems with small deployments and no need to store, retrieve, or communicate legacy data.

You should also consider *forward compatibility*. That is, designing code for extension and ensuring that future events will not render it inoperable. The Y2K bug is a good example of this rule being ignored, with expensive and potentially disastrous consequences.

6. Is code likely to rot more quickly if you alter it or if you leave it alone?

Code rots quickest when you attempt to alter it. It's true that leaving a program to slowly stagnate will ensure your competitors gain an advantage, eventually rendering your code worthless. Your *product* will hear its death knell, but the *code* itself is as beautiful as it ever was.

Careless maintenance and sloppy extension will really cripple code. New faults are introduced all too easily as other problems are cleaned up. The pressure for rapid turnaround leads to modifications that degrade code clarity and structure. Maintaining code often renders it unmaintainable.

It takes good programmers and informed project management to avoid this.

Getting Personal

1. Is the majority of the code you write brand new or a modification of existing source?

   a. If it's brand-new code, do you create entirely new systems or new extensions to existing systems?

   b. Does this affect *how* you write? In what ways?

Different forces come into play in these different scenarios. When extending existing code or fitting new software into an old framework, you have to do a *lot* of investigation up front to understand how all the existing stuff works. If you don't, you'll end up writing bad code that doesn't fit in properly, causing headaches in the future.

Brand-new code must be created with a view to future modification. It must be clear, extensible, and malleable to prevent such problems from cropping up later.

2. Do you have experience of working with preexisting codebases? If so:

   a. How has it shaped your current skill set? What lessons did you learn?

   b. Was it predominantly good or bad code? What did you have to judge it against?

A few years experience helps you to judge what's good software and what's bad. The telltale signs become clear, and you're able to quickly detect code that must be handled with care.

Although vaguely masochistic, it can be good experience to work with someone else's trashy code—it teaches you what *not* to do, how one programmer's shortsightedness can make other programmer's lives painful later on. It helps you to appreciate the importance of taking responsibility for the code you write.

3. Have you ever made changes that degraded the quality of code? Why?

Common reasons (or excuses) are:

- I didn't know any better at the time.
- I was pressed for time and had to ship the code quickly.
- It was too much work to do any other way.
- I could only modify code that was under *our* control—the problem was in another team's code or in third-party library code that we only had binaries for.

None of these reasons are satisfactory.

For bonus points, come up with counter arguments against each of those excuses and find ways to avoid each situation. For example, if you're pressured to ship a code release quickly, you can make a simple hacky change now, and revise the work once the software is released to create a more engineered solution.

4. **How many revisions has your current project gone through?**

   a. **How much changed functionally between revisions? How did the code change?**

   b. **Has it grown by *luck*, by *design*, or something between the two? How is this evident now?**

Here are some important things to consider.

a. The two are not necessarily connected. Even some very simple functional changes may require fundamental code rewrites. I've seen many projects where this was the case, where the system architecture didn't support future requirements and had to be radically altered.

   And I've also seen the opposite: releases that were functionally identical to their predecessor, but where almost everything had changed under the covers. There is no point in performing a complete project rewrite if the system is spiraling toward its death, but when it has a viable commercial future and the current code cannot accommodate future requirements, such action may be justified.

   It might be commercial suicide to release a new version with no new features—customers will refuse to upgrade unless it's worth their while. Therefore, a few minor features tend to be thrown in as bait, or the revision is released with a certain amount of spin (i.e., *This revision includes significant bug fixes*).

b. You must know the history of your codebase to understand how it grew to this current shape and to be able to make informed modifications and appropriate tidy-ups.

5. **How does your team safeguard code so that it can't be changed by more than one programmer at once?**

Employ a *revision control system* to manage code changes. Blocking file checkouts prevent more than one person from modifying a file at once. However, this is not enough. One change can be checked in with a contradictory change immediately following. You need to *manage* the development carefully, so that each developer with access to the source code understands what his or her peers are doing and who is responsible for making which changes. Code reviews help to detect and correct when this kind of problem has occurred.

   A good suite of regression tests will ensure that any modification you make does not break functionality.

Chapter 16: Code Monkeys

Mull It Over

1. How many programmers *does* it take to change a light bulb?

The question's wrong. It's a hardware problem, not a software one. Get the hardware engineers to fix it. Of course, the hardware engineers will want to work around the problem in software. . . .

2. Is it better to be enthusiastic and less skilled (not incompetent) or to be incredibly talented and unmotivated?

a. Who will write the better code?

b. Who is the better programmer? (Not the same thing.)

Which does more to shape the code you write: your technical competence or your attitude?

There are various types of software systems, and the creation of each requires a different set of skills. That's how programmers can carve out niches in embedded programming, web services, financial systems, and so on. The coding task also differs with the heritage of the code. You might write:

- Simple "toy" programs
- New systems from scratch
- Extensions of existing systems
- Maintenance work on old codebases

Each task requires a different level of skill and discipline, and a very different development approach. We'll see this in the next question. Not every programmer who can write a personal "toy" can create a brand-new, industrial-strength system.

For all of these, the quality of the resulting code is determined as much by your technical competence as your *attitude* regarding the task—indeed, the two must complement one another. If you lack some technical skills, then you must have an attitude that acknowledges this and compensates for it.

Your attitude can do more to shape the code you write than your current skill set can. If you're less skilled but desire to do a good job, then you're more likely to work well. You're also more likely to learn and to improve your skills.

3. There are various different types of programs we write, differentiated by code "heritage." How does writing the following types of code differ?

a. A "toy" program

b. A brand-new system

c. Extensions to an existing system

d. Maintenance work on an old codebase

It might not look like there's a great difference between these code scenarios, but they require surprisingly different approaches.

A toy program

This might be a small fun hack for your own use or a little utility to help develop a larger system. This program doesn't need to be bulletproof, have in-depth design, or have exhaustive features. It just needs to do enough to solve the immediate problem. Then it's thrown away.

Speed and ease of development is probably more important than design elegance or the theological purity of the construction process.

A new system

Creating a brand-new professional system from scratch requires serious design and careful planning. You must take into account future use and extensions, and ensure that the whole system is adequately documented.

Extensions

Few projects create a new system from the ground up. More often, we extend existing code, adding new features to an old codebase. The new work must knit correctly into the existing system. This can't be done properly without a thorough understanding of the original code and the ability to make changes that sit well alongside existing work.

Maintenance

The most common software activity is the maintenance of existing code, fixing any remaining faults, and ensuring that it remains operational as the world around it changes. This needs a careful methodical approach. It probably requires a lot of exploratory work; it will stretch your deductive powers since few systems are ever documented well enough to easily maintain, especially as they grow old and near obsolescence.

4. **If programming is an art, what is the correct balance of consideration and planning versus intuition and gut instinct? Do you program by gut or by plan?**

As we've seen, effective programmers use both approaches. Intuition and the artist's aesthetic sensibilities will help craft elegant code. Thoughtful planning works alongside to ensure the code is sound, pragmatic, and delivered on time.

We can't formulate an exact ratio or formula for the optimum balance. Effective programmers have both and know how to moderate the use of each.

Chapter 17: Together We Stand

Mull It Over

1. **Why write software in teams? What are the real advantages over writing a system on your own?**

Software development might be easier on your own; you don't have to work with other weird programmers, you don't need to coordinate work or suffer ineffective management. However, it isn't hard to see the many benefits of software development in teams.

In a team you can solve larger problems by decomposing them between individual members. And you can create code faster too. Groups of developers combine talents to make something greater than the sum of their parts. In cases where there is no well-established design or prior art, the wider skill set and knowledge of the group has a distinct advantage; a collaborative approach will filter ideas and generate better solutions. Peer reviews ensure that work is sound.

There is also a personal motivation: Techies like working on cool projects. You can work on systems well beyond your own ability when developing in a team. This might be software that is much larger than an individual could tackle, which requires specialized skills, or that provides the chance to work alongside more experienced programmers.

In a Real World organization, even a lone developer is part of a larger team. If you're not working with other software developers, you are still part of a corporate team, working to create a final polished product. Without those other people, your software would never be released.

2. **Describe the telltale signs of good and bad teamwork. What are the prerequisites for good teamwork, and what characterizes bad teamwork?**

For effective teamwork, all of these factors must be in place:

- The correct spread of people, with a range of appropriate technical skills.

- Team members with a range of experience, who are each able to learn from others. A whole team of trainees will clearly be very unlikely to succeed. (However, they'd be much easier to mold and manage than a bunch of Demigurus who are far more set in their ways.)

- Team member personality types must be complementary. To succeed, the team needs encouragers and motivators, not people who will drag morale down.

- A clear and realistic goal (even better if it's an exciting project that the team members really want to see completed).

- Motivation (whether financial or emotional).

- Suitable specifications provided as soon as possible, so all members understand what they are building and to ensure that the individual pieces of work fit together.

- Good management.

- As small a team as realistically possible, but no smaller. Adding more people makes teamwork harder: There are more lines of communication, more people to coordinate, and more points of failure. We should try not to make things unnecessarily difficult.

- A clear and universally understood software engineering process for the team to follow.
- Backing from the company, not hindrances and unnecessary bureaucracy.

In contrast, these are sure indicators of a team that is not able to work effectively. Note that this list includes a mix of internal and external factors:

- Unrealistic schedules with deadlines established before the team has scoped their work.
- Unclear project objectives and a lack of project requirements.
- Communication failures.
- Bad or unqualified team leaders.
- Badly defined individual roles and responsibilities—who's responsible for doing what?
- Individual bad attitudes and personal agendas.
- Incompetent team members.
- Management not valuing individual engineers, and treating them like minions instead.
- Individual appraisals based on criteria that don't match the team objectives.
- Rapid turnover of team members.
- No change in management procedure.
- A lack of training or mentoring.

3. **Compare software teamwork with the construction metaphor (see "Do We Really *Build* Software?" on page 177). Does it reveal insights into our teamwork?**

There are a number of different metaphors that can be used to describe our work (for example, DeMarco's *sports team* or *choral society* and the *factory* we joke about here). (DeMarco 99) The problem with any metaphor is that it can only tell a partial truth. Software engineering has its own problems and challenges. Chemical engineering is different from civil engineering, which is different from making a movie, which is different from writing software.

While not perfect, *building construction* is a useful metaphor. After all, we construct software according to a plan, from different components (some of which we build ourselves, others which we buy or bring in). These are the useful parallels:

- You need a team: You can't single-handedly build a skyscraper or an enterprise-level highly complex software superstructure.
- The team has a goal: It works to finish the construction on time and on budget.
- Someone commissions the work, for a purpose: There is an end-purpose for the work.

- Each team member does something different: Different roles help to get the job done. There are architects, builders, carpenters, plumbers, electricians, foremen, office staff, security guards, and more. Each makes a valuable contribution.

- There are team members with responsibility: The foreman is the people manager.

But of course, buildings are very different from programs. Buildings can't be developed in an iterative and incremental manner. Any change to a building's specification will result in costly demolition prior to rebuilding. In our world of pure thought stuff, we can tear down and rebuild with very little material cost (but with the costs of time and labor). In software, we are better able to build abstract interfaces between blocks. The engineering discipline is different, but that doesn't mean we can't learn from the parallels with other professions.

4. Will external or internal factors do the most to ruin the effectiveness of a software development team?

They'll both conspire to destroy your development work. Internal factors like:

- Ineffective team members
- Conflict
- Confusion
- Show-stopping bugs late in development
- Inaccurate plans

Mix with external factors like:

- Unclear or shifting requirements
- Unrealistic deadlines
- Bad management
- Corporate bureaucracy

This makes the life of a software developer incredibly difficult. Internal and external pressures are equally likely to destroy your teamwork, although it's widely recognized that most projects fail for nontechnical reasons.

One thing is certain: There are far more detrimental influences on team performance than there are success factors. For this reason, you must guard your team's work closely, attempting to insulate yourself from both internal and external attacks.

5. How does a team's size affect the team dynamics?

With more people, the team members suffer increased

- Coordination effort
- Communication effort (more people introduce more separate paths of communication; this grows exponentially)

- Cooperation effort
- Dependency on others (direct and indirect)

Each of these *can* make your work harder. However, it's clear that a team of programmers can produce greater software than a single coder. This means that there must be an appropriate balance of team size versus size of task; this will change depending on the kind of system being developed.

As a team gets bigger, there is more likelihood that individual programmers will slacken the effort they put in, since they can be carried by the rest of the team. Brooks's *The Mythical Man-Month* shows that adding people to a project does not necessarily make it complete sooner. (Brooks 95)

With a larger project, there is more chance that management talent will differentiate success from failure and more scope for management to provoke catastrophic failure.

In general, smaller development teams are better; but they must still be large enough to accomplish the task.

6. How can you insulate a team from problems caused by inexperienced members?

There will always be inexperienced programmers. This is the same in any field of endeavor. In many professions, new recruits undergo some form of apprenticeship period and must complete a stage of academic study. This ensures that their skills are already honed to a reasonable level. Although ripe with academic programming courses (of varying quality), our software profession doesn't recognize any formal form of apprenticeship. Mentoring new programmers is a fantastic way to quickly bring fresh recruits to a reasonable standard.

A few techniques contribute to making inexperienced coders' work less risky:

- Have realistic expectations; don't expect miracles from them. Allot trainees appropriate tasks.
- Monitor their progress, and ensure they aren't afraid to raise questions and problems.
- Don't require too much prior experience: Use popular languages and tools that will require less time to get up-to-speed.
- Don't use bleeding edge technologies and techniques.
- Standardize tools across teams so trainees only need to learn a toolset once.
- Train them.
- Review their code.
- Mentor them.
- Pair program with them.

Getting Personal

1. What kind of team are you working in right now? Which of the stereotypes on pages 322 through 332 is it most like?

   a. Is it like this by design?

   b. Is it a healthy team?

   c. Does it need to be changed?

      What factors have you encountered that prevent good teamwork?

      If you haven't done so already, fill out the earlier action sheet carefully (see "Action Sheet" on page 347). Make sure you work out how to improve your team and start to make the changes.

Work out how you will carry out any required changes. Set goals and review the team's health in a few months' time.

Common team problems include:

- Unbalanced team composition
- Ineffective team members
- Bad management
- Unrealistic deadlines
- Shifting requirements
- Communication failure

2. Are you a good team player? How could you work better with your teammates and build better software?

Look again at the personal characteristics in "Personal Skills and Characteristics for Good Teamwork" on page 333. Determine how closely you model each of these and how you can improve.

3. What is the exact responsibility of a software engineer on your current team?

How much responsibility and authority does a software developer have? Are there several ranks of programmer job titles—if so, how do these roles differ? Does a development role involve any of the following activities?

- Forming the project scope and objectives
- Analysis
- Estimating timescales
- Architecture
- Design
- Review
- Project management
- Being a mentor

- Investigating and implementing performance
- Documentation
- Integrating systems
- Testing (to what level?)
- Interaction with the customer
- Planning enhancements or the next software revision

This detail will differ from company to company and from project to project. Are there clear lines of accountability in your team? Are there technical and pastoral managers to whom developers are assigned?

Do you have a job description? Do you have a set of personal objectives? If so, are you fulfilling them right now, or are they actually incorrect?

Chapter 18: Practicing Safe Source

Mull It Over

1. How can you reliably release your source code to other people?

The easiest option for proprietary source code is *not* to release it—then you'll avoid all sorts of problems. If you must ship code, don't forget to sort out licensing and get NDAs in place first. Know the size and extent of your audience and, if it's important to you, take measures to ensure that the code doesn't leak further afield.

For open source projects, this is not such a big concern; by their nature, they ship as source.

Before release, make sure that there are clear copyright and license notices in every source code file.

There are several mechanisms for a source code release, with differing abilities to guard against your code getting into the wrong hands:

- Allow the external viewer to have access to your source control system. You can lock this down through an account that is granted read-only access, possibly using a shared *anonymous* account if your code is publicly available.

  Obviously, to see your VCS server, users must have some level of privilege and network access to your development environment, so this must be closely managed—both so that they don't do anything untoward and so that crackers can't get in to look at your code.

- *Tarball* the source tree (create a compressed archive of files—this term is named after Unix's tar command). This tarball can be emailed, FTPed, or sent on a CD. Ensure that your method of dispatch is appropriately secure.

Include a set of release notes with your code, and clearly display the source tree revision information (usually a source control version or build number) for later reference. Mark the released code in your source control repository with a label so that you can retrieve it at a later date.

2. Of the two models for repository file editing (locking file checkouts or concurrent modification), which is best?

Neither model of operation is better or worse than its counterpart. Each hides different file editing problems and forces users to work differently when modifications might collide.

- The locking model requires you to check out a file to reserve it before making any modifications. You can be sure that no other developer's change will interfere with your work and that you have sole access to that file until you check it back in or release the file unchanged. The downside is that a reserved file is blocked until the owner has relinquished control. You have no immediate way of knowing how long this will take.

  If the owner sits at the desk next to you, then it's annoying but not hard to work out. However, if the owner is on another continent, works different hours, or accidentally leaves the file checked out while on vacation, then you're stuck. The best you can do is subvert the checkout by fiddling with the owner's computer to release the file. This will undoubtedly cause hassle and confusion later.

- The concurrent model avoids this problem and ensures that you can continue coding unhindered at all times. The hidden danger is the possibility of conflicting file modifications. If Fred alters lines 10 through 20 of foo.c, while George alters lines 15 through 25, a race is on! The first developer to check in the file won't have any problems, so if Fred wins, his work on lines 10 through 20 will be put into the repository. But when George tries to check in, the SCMS will tell him that his source tree is out of date—he has to merge Fred's change into his copy of foo.c first. The five conflicting lines will need to be merged manually; George must do extra work to understand Fred's change and integrate it with his own. Only then can he check his work in.

  This isn't ideal, but it happens very rarely in reality, and most conflicts are not at all contentious. The more common case is when Fred modifies lines 10 through 20 and George modifies lines 40 through 50; the two modifications don't conflict and the SCMS can merge the changes automatically. If you do encounter conflicting concurrent modifications, it's often a sign that the code needs some refactoring.

Neither mode of operation is perfect; but each works fine. Which you choose depends on the operation of your source control tool and the development process and culture you work in.

3. How do the requirements for version control systems differ between a distributed and a single-site development team?

If a SCMS can accommodate remote sites, it will definitely be able to cope with a single-site development team, so we're mostly considering a set of *extra* requirements for multisite operation. These extra requirements include:

- There must be a scaleable client/server architecture.
- The tool must work effectively over low-bandwidth network links (which are common for satellite sites), *or* your deployment must include a really

high-quality intersite connection. Low-bandwidth links require intelligent data compression and sensible communications protocols (for example, the tools should send small file differences, rather than entire files).

- There must be a centralized method to administer user accounts so that collaboration is seamless across sites.

There are two main designs: wide area network communication and remote repository replication. The first performs all client communication with a central server hosted at the parent location. This requires a sufficiently fast and reliable communication channel between sites. The latter method reduces communication overhead by replicating the repository onto a remote server at low-load times. However, this adds a lot complication to the development process; you need to understand that the two repositories are not costantly synchronized, and you must work out sensible branching strategies to avoid conflicting lines of development work.

When evaluating source control systems, don't ignore these requirements, even if you only have one development site. In the future, you may need to add a secondary site or support for telecommuters. Bear this in mind as you scope your system.

4. What is a sound rationale for selecting a source code management system?

Good criteria for selecting a SCMS include:

Reliability
Check that it is proven technology and won't suddenly lose your source files. The server must be robust and not prone to crashing every few days.

Capacity
The tool must scale up well, handling large teams and large projects as well as small ones. In more demanding situations, does it consume a lot of disk space, soak up all network bandwidth, or take an excruciating time to run? Perhaps you require multisite repository synchronization, or does it work well enough on a low-bandwidth link?

Flexibility
Does it provide all the operations and reports that you need? Does it handle all the filetypes that you want to control? Can it manage binary files? Does it support Unicode? Does it version directories, allowing the renaming and moving of files? Does it manage atomic change sets, or is each file individually versioned?

Branching
To support more than one release, product variants, concurrent feature work, or to help with logical development, the tool *must* support branching. Does it support sub-branches? Is merging easy, or is it prohibitively difficult?

Platforms
Make sure that it works on all the platforms, hardware configurations, and operating systems that you work with.

Costs and licensing

The SCMS must meet your budget constraints (remember, there are some *very* free source systems). Consider whether there are extra license costs per client. Sometimes these are hidden extra costs; as your team grows, you must pay an SCMS tax.

Audit

The repository must record who makes each change: Don't force everyone into one SCMS user account. The system must support your access policies, allowing you to restrict modification rights as required. Do you want it to provide automatic notification of changes?

Simplicity

The tool must be easy to use, configure, and deploy. This is especially important if you don't have a full-time designated SCMS administrator.

5. **How can you separate bleeding-edge code under active development from stable code during team development?**

You need a strategy to separate the two in the source control repository. Your choices are:

- Don't separate them. Everyone has bleeding-edge code and must learn to cope with it. Don't check in anything that is obviously broken or nonfunctional.

- Employ branches. Perform each line of development work on a separate branch, and merge the branches down at appropriate stable points. With this scheme, integration problems are only discovered on a merge; this places the burden of maintenance on the branch merger (which might be the developer working on the branch or a separate system integrator).

- Use a *stable* label, applied to the entire source tree as a *baseline*. Developers check out this labeled baseline and then move the components they are developing to the latest version. They can then work and commit changes without affecting anyone else's stable source tree. When new development work is deemed stable (fit for public consumption) the label is moved. This change is picked up by other developers when they next synchronize to the baseline.

Which you chose depends on the facilities of your SCMS and your development culture.

Getting Personal

1. **Does your development team make effective use of source control?**

Ultimately, does your SCMS help you to develop software easily, and does it facilitate collaboration better than any alternative? Consider tool setup issues like:

- Are you using the right tool with the right feature set?
- Do you have an SCMS administrator, or is it managed on an ad hoc basis?

- Does everyone know how to use it? Is there an appropriate training scheme?
- Is the repository integrated with your defect management or fault-tracking tool?

Consider asset management issues like:

- Is there agreement over the contents of check-in messages and the use of other revision metadata?
- Do you have a consistent labeling scheme to mark important source tree revisions?
- Do you have a defined (and documented) branching strategy, with provably correct merging?
- Can you automatically create release notes from the source repository?
- Are you able to re-create old builds? Have you addressed when the build toolchain altered, affecting code compatibility?
- Can you build a product entirely from the contents of the repository, or do you need to supply any extra files?

How important are each of these issues to your development team?

2. Is your current work backed up? How important are backups to your development team? When are backups made?

If you can be bothered to write some code, it must be important, and so it must be backed up. There are several levels at which backups can be employed:

- Personal workstation backups. These will ensure that no work is lost from your local hard drive or from your source tree sandbox.
- The server holding the source control repository. This ensures that you won't lose the central source tree files and their revision histories.

The latter is the most important: It's criminally insane not to back up a source repository. If your workstation only contains sandbox development areas, then it's not as critical to back it up; there should be little work at any time that isn't checked in (remember to perform *little and often* check-ins), so a loss of a local disk is not critical.

Consider also how you back up documents and any other non–source tree items you produce. Either check them in to the repository somewhere or make sure that they are stored in logical places on a shared fileserver, somewhere that is backed up. Without revision control, you will have to perform manual document versioning—it's as important to keep historical versions of specifications as it is to version the source code.

In a multiuser environment, the systems administrator will determine when backups are made. This is usually during the night when there is less computer activity and less information changing on the filesystems being backed up. (But what about multi-continent projects with massive time zone delays?)

3. On which computers is your source code held?

Obviously, it is held on the development servers and workstations within the company network. These sit safely in the office behind a corporate firewall. But also consider whether your code is held on laptops or on the home machines of telecommuters. How sensitive is the work? How should these machines be digitally and physically protected?

Chatper 19: Being Specific

Mull It Over

1. Is a poor specification better than no specification at all?

A factually incorrect or painfully out-of-date specification is definitely worse. It will send readers down a blind alley and waste a lot of their time. The false information it contains could easily lead to broken code that will cost a lot of time, energy, and money to fix later on.

If a specification is ambiguous or misses important information, then you're hoping that the readers are experienced enough to recognize the problem and interpret the information carefully. Hopefully they'll all make the same set of assumptions about the missing information. A specification should really stand on its own and not require the intuition of its readership.

If a specification is too verbose and hides information, then it is probably better (in the long run) to rewrite it.

The number of factual inaccuracies in your company's specifications will probably frighten you! In my experience, very few companies have a set of consistently good specifications.

2. How detailed does a good specification have to be?

The answer is: *appropriately detailed*, where the value of "appropriate" depends on the project, the team, the contents, the quality of related documents, and the lunar phase. Too much detail can definitely be counter-productive: Clearly, if a design specification was too detailed it would *be* the code itself. However, ambiguity in key areas is a road to disaster.

3. Is it important that all the documents in a company/project have a common presentation style?

This is about as important as a uniform code style. That is, there are plenty of more important things to worry about, even if this is the most immediately visible problem with a specification. The importance of visual consistency depends (in part) on whether the documents are released outside the company or not. It looks more professional to ship consistent documents, all written in a similar style with the same template.

Ultimately, the content of your documents is far more important than their appearance.

4. **How should you store documents? Should you provide an index of them (by type or by project), for example?**

You must be able to quickly locate and retrieve a document that has been written. The actual storage scheme is unimportant, provided that it's well known and universally followed.

It usually makes sense to store all documents on a single central filestore, and group them by work package (this could be by project, by customer, by component, or by feature). It's helpful to maintain a central list of all stored documents to aid retrieval. However, this adds management overhead, and if not maintained, it will quickly fall out of use.

Large companies employ people to deal with the storage and retrieval of documents. Though experts at this task, their presence adds more steps to the working procedure and more links in the development process chain.

It's essential to keep documents under some form of revision control and to monitor which versions of the documents apply to which versions of the code. This is part of a *configuration management* strategy (see "Configuration Management" on page 356).

5. **How should you conduct a specification review?**

Document reviews work similarly to code reviews. They generally take place in a meeting, in which case there are some important prerequisites: the correct set of reviewers must be selected, and the material for review should be distributed with enough time for reviewers to adequately prepare.

Alternatively, the review can be run virtually by soliciting email feedback or by giving a printed copy to each reviewer and receiving his or her marked-up copies for inspection.

The review will address a number of things; the importance of each should be agreed upon up front:

- The quality of the contents. (Is it complete, correct, and so on? This is paramount.)
- The quality of the presentation style. (Does the document conform to project guidelines?)
- The quality of the writing style. (Does the author write like Shakespeare or a five year old? For software specifications, both are bad!)

In a meeting context, it's best to discuss general comments about the material and the overall approach first. (But be careful here: It's very easy to get waylaid by more specific technical issues at this stage.) Then the specifics of the material can be discussed. Since all the reviewers have looked at the material beforehand and have already amassed their comments, stepping through, section by section, is usually appropriate. Long sections might be traversed paragraph by paragraph if necessary.

6. **Does self-documenting code render all specifications useless? Specific ones?**

Not entirely. Self-documenting code can avoid the need for design specifications or other maintenance documents. Literate API documentation placed in code comments can even replace functional specifications in *some* cases, if the docs are really thorough. Be careful, though: If you try to write a lot of documentation in literate comments, you'd probably find it easier to type the same information into a word processor. Literate code documentation can never replace a requirements specification or a test specification.

A comprehensive set of automated test cases *could* replace a software component's test specification, if the test were sufficiently clear and maintainable. However, they are seldom sufficient to replace final product validation tests.

7.   How can a document be collaborated on by more than one author?

With difficulty—few documentation systems provide the same collaborative facilities as a source code control tool. Look at wiki-webs for shared text editing, if you can cope with your documents being in an HTML-derivative form.

Otherwise, you have to split the document into sections and give one section to each person. Each section will have an inevitable difference in writing style, quality of content, and will be based on a different set of assumptions; check for this as the work is stitched back together. You might find it easier to split the sections into their own documents and put an umbrella document over the top of them. A leader must be appointed to coordinate the work of several people—to guide the writing process, collate the parts, and encourage people to complete their sections on time.

An alternative approach is to give one person overall writing responsibility, but with a strong element of peer review. The document's content and structure is agreed upon in meetings beforehand, then the writer retires to craft the document alone, before offering it for group review.

Be careful with any of these approaches, as writing by committee can produce laborious documents and can take a very long time.

Getting Personal

1.   Who decides on the contents of your documents?

This is defined by a company's development process, by a document template, or by convention. But just because there is a convention doesn't mean that it's actually good practice. Check that the types of documents you write, as well as their contents, are genuinely valuable to your software development process.

2.   Consider your current project. Do you have:
   a.   A requirements specification?
   b.   An architecture specification?
   c.   A design specification?
   d.   A functional specification?
   e.   Any other specification?

   Are they up to date? Are they complete? Do you know how to get the latest versions? Can you access historical revisions?

If you don't have some of these or they're substandard, why? How can you remedy the problem?

Whose job is it to keep the documents up to date? Document versioning is an important aspect of specification generation—make sure that you have a clear plan for doing this.

3. Do you revision control your documents? If so, how?

Several techniques for managing document revisions are seen in the field:

- Store them in an SCMS alongside the code.
- Use a document (or even a workflow) management system.
- Use the filesystem: Encode the document revision in its filename (possibly archiving old versions in a separate old directory).
- Store old revisions in an email attachment sent to a "magic" user (grotesque, but—yes—I *have* seen a company do this).

Whichever scheme you use, it must address these issues:

- Ease of use and document accessibility
- How to prevent two people from editing the same document at the same time
- Differentiating the latest release version from the copy currently under development
- How to avoid accidental deletion or overwriting the wrong document version
- How to maintain the document history with each change
- The ease of referencing a specific document revision

Chapter 20: A Review to a Kill

Mull It Over

1. Does the required number of reviewers depend on the size of the code being reviewed?

Not really. If your code is particularly important, then you might consider inviting a few more reviewers, or you might make a particular effort to select reviewers with the most experience.

However, if the code is too large, you don't need more reviewers—you need a rewrite!

2. Which tools are useful aids for code reviewing?

Common sense, a keen pair of eyes, and an alert brain!

A number of software tools are also useful. Many different tools can inspect your code and help you to gauge its quality and relative risk to the entire codebase. They can trace the flow of execution, work out which code is executed most often, and calculate a value for each function's code complexity. This last metric is very useful when identifying which pieces of code need to be reviewed as soon as possible. A visual design program may help you to understand the code structure and its dependencies (particularly useful for reviewing class hierarchies in object-oriented languages).

3. Should you perform a code review before or after running it through source code checking tools?

After. Reviewers should probably use these tools themselves during review preparation, but authors must perform all possible checking on their own code before releasing it for review. They'd be foolish not to. It makes no sense to waste reviewers' time on code that could have been easily improved. Reserve review time to find more interesting problems.

If an issue is detected during a review, thought should be given to whether the same issue can be automatically detected in the future using a tool.

4. What preparation is required for a code review meeting?

The author has completed the code satisfactorily (otherwise he or she is wasting the reviewers' precious time). The chairman has arranged the meeting properly so that it will run smoothly. More interestingly, before the meeting, each reviewer must have already:

- Read (and understood) the specification
- Become familiar with the code
- Drawn up a list of issues and questions (this step enforces discipline; if you don't force yourself to do this, it's easy to superficially skim the code and not really know it well enough to review thoroughly)

There will always be things you'll find during methodical inspection in a review meeting that you missed beforehand. Even so, this prior preparation is essential to prevent the meeting from wasting a lot of people's time.

5. How do you differentiate review comments to be acted upon immediately from those to chalk up for experience on the next project?

You must make a decision based on:

- How important the identified problem is
- Whether it's a matter of personal aesthetics or it breaks an agreed best practice
- How much work is involved in the fix
- How serious the effect of the change is on the rest of the code
- How wrong (or misleading) the code is without the fix
- How fragile or dangerous the change work is
- Where the project is in the development cycle—you only want to make *essential* changes near a release deadline

There is no easy rule. If there is any ambiguity in a review meeting, then the chairman makes the ultimate choice. Sometimes problems are rated between *must fix* and *nice to have*—the author implements as many high priority fixes as feasible in the available time. Other issues may be deferred to the next iteration of the component's development.

6. How do you run a virtual review meeting?

Virtual reviews are commonly run by email. The review is organized by a chairman, who is usually the hub of communications. Certainly, the author must *not* be the hub of communications; it would be too easy for him to select which comments are important and to ignore all the things he doesn't like. This is obviously a bad idea.

There is an important question with this approach: Do the reviewers get to see each other's comments? In a virtual review, debate is much harder to facilitate, especially if emails are directed only to the chairman. However, a 1,000-email conversation broadcast to all reviewers quickly becomes irritating and diverting. As an alternative, you could meet in a virtual chat room, use an instant messenger, a dedicated newsgroup, or a mailing list.

An alternative virtual review mechanism is to distribute printouts of the code in question. The reviewers scribble comments on their copies and return them to the author. You can run a similar scheme using a wiki: Post your code on the wiki and let reviewers add comments to the page. The format of how you conduct a review is less important than simply doing it somehow.

7. How useful are informal code reviews?

Informal reviews are much better than no review at all, but since they are less thorough, they'll inevitably find fewer faults (for the same quality of code reviewer).

Although terms are not officially defined, McConnell describes two types of informal review: (McConnell 96)

Walkthroughs
These are very informal gatherings where programmers look over the code together. This could be in front of an editor, with changes made on the fly.

Code reading
The author distributes copies of the code to a set of reviewers, who make comments on it and send them back to the author.

Getting Personal

1. Does your project perform code reviews? Does it perform *enough* code reviews?

Even if it makes a vaguely regular event of code reviews, there probably still isn't enough reviewing going on. Too little value is put on this practice; if the code seems to work, then people think that there's no point wasting valuable time reviewing it.

This attitude is careless. The time taken to track lingering code faults is often far greater than the effort of review. Code reviews are a sensible and pragmatic way to take control of your development process and ensure that your software is of high quality.

What can you do to improve on this in your current project?

2. Do you work with any programmers whose code is considered to be above review?

A respected Guru programmer (see "The Guru" on page 299) is often held in awe, and no one ever suggests that his work should be reviewed. No one probably dares. This reverence is misguided and dangerous.

In my experience, Gurus write some of the most review-worthy code you'll ever see: full of deep, incomprehensible, unmaintainable magic. The fact that they never put their code forward for review illustrates their incorrect attitude toward the task and the team. No one's code is above review; all code should be carefully scrutinized.

3. What percentage of your code has ever been subject to code review?

Unless you're a very unusual beast, this amount is undoubtedly small. How formal have the reviews been? How useful was each review, and how much did it contribute to the final quality of the code?

How much of your unreviewed code was pair programmed? How much *should* have been reviewed? How much unreviewed code was critically important commercial code? How many bugs slipped through into production software, and how many of those bugs caused later problems?

Even if it's not a part of your project culture to run code reviews, make a point of inviting formal review for your work. Don't worry if no one else does it—your code will be exceptional by comparison!

Chapter 21: How Long Is a Piece of String?

Mull It Over

1. How can you rescue a slipping project and bring it back on track?

One technique to protect yourself from a failing project is to run, fast, like a rat from a sinking ship. It's not very professional, though!

Once a project is behind schedule, there's rarely anything you can do to bring it back on track—that is, unless there was a monster amount of contingency allocated. You might instead consider these strategies:

- Reschedule the project; see if you can agree a later delivery date with the customer.

- De-scope the first release, possibly agreeing to a later release with the missing functionality. It's better to commit to doing less stuff, but doing it better and within the allotted time, than to implement loads of unnecessary functionality and slip badly.

Don't blindly throw more developers at the project to speed things up. Brooks lucidly described how bad this idea is, especially when a project is failing. (Brooks 95) It would take the existing developers time to get the new guys up to speed, and there would then be extra overhead in managing the larger team. Any benefit would almost certainly be outweighed by the costs of new personnel.

2. **What's the correct response to having a deadline imposed on you before feasibility or planning work commences?**

Tact! The fixed delivery deadline might be a valid business requirement: You'll make money if you ship software on time; you'll make nothing if you don't. You can't always do the theologically correct thing and move a deadline or adjust the scope of the work.

Sometimes it helps your design effort to have early visibility of the anticipated project deadline. This information shows you how pure and well-thought-out your design can be, and it will help you to scope out the amount of code required and whether future flexibility can be considered. Ultimately, it will show you whether or not you need to hack out a quick-fix solution or the elegantly engineered code you always want to write. It might help you to make buy versus build decisions and to set the final quality expectations for the delivered software.

Make it clear that this is not an ideal way to develop software. *Hopefully* someone will listen, and the managers will learn to stop promising such risky deadlines—it's a careless form of gambling with the success of a project and the future of an organization.

3. **How do you ensure that a development plan is genuinely useful?**

High-quality development plans are:

Accurate
They include all the tasks required to build the software and are based on sound timescale estimates.

Fine-grained
There aren't a few large tasks with rough estimates, but many small tasks carefully sequenced. Our confidence in the accuracy of a small task's timescale is higher, so the quality of the overall plan will be higher.

If you think that a task comprises several parts (e.g., it is dependent on a third party and splits into the third-party release milestone, followed by a period of integration and bug fixing) then make this explicit on the plan.

Agreed

Everyone buys into the plan: Management is happy with the level of inherent risk, while programmers agree that the timescales are accurate, no tasks are missing, and all the dependencies are correctly mapped out.

Visible

They are used to make important decisions by individual developers and by managers. Timescale changes are communicated through the plan. The plan is versioned, and progress against the plan is recorded clearly.

Monitored

If the schedule is poorly monitored, the timescale estimates become a worthless statistic. Progress must be checked against the plan. The course of the development effort is steered by this measurement.

4. **Why do different programmers work at different rates? How can you reflect this on the plan?**

Programmers differ in many ways:

- They have different technical abilities and reason about problems in different ways. This affects the quality of work produced.

- Different levels of experience lead to different design choices.

- People have different levels of commitment: responsibility for old projects, levels of enthusiasm for the company or project, respect for the craft of software construction, and external commitments (family pressures, socializing, etc.).

- Some people are highly motivated and prepared to put in hours of over-time to get a project finished. Others want to work their minimum hours and then go party.

It's not just the duration of a work package that differs between programmers. The quality of their code, the soundness of their design, and the bug count of their programs will differ too. It will even differ when the same programmer attempts the same task multiple times—with more experience, a programmer will work better the second time.

To reflect this on a project plan, check which developer each task is allocated to. If the task is not within his or her core competency, then increase the timescale estimate, or add in a block of contingency to the end. Consider putting in an extra up-front task to get the developer up to speed with the work, and make sure that you include any training that might be required.

Getting Personal

1. **What percentage of the projects that you've worked on have run to schedule?**

   a. **For those that did: What contributed to the success of the planning effort?**

   b. **For those that failed: What were the main problems?**

It's easier to characterize failure than success; you'll identify the single reason that something went wrong far more easily than a delicate balance of things working together well. When everything on a project is healthy, the whole thing appears to just work.

Iterative and incremental development helps to accommodate problems and de-risk the plan. Well-understood work packages, a fine-grained plan, and a good initial design are also key. High-quality testing performed early and often makes development much safer. Talented developers are also very useful!

2. How accurate are your timescale estimates? How far off target are you normally?

This is a skill that you can continually improve. Experience is a great teacher. Hopefully, your later estimates have been more accurate than your earlier ones. Is this the case?

If you haven't yet been asked to make timescale estimates, start practicing now! Make a mini-plan for your current development task. Estimate timescales for the small parts of this mini-plan and see how accurate you are. This has the added benefit of making you think carefully about what you're doing, putting a good initial design into place. It will also force you to leave enough time for testing, debugging, and documentation—all good things.

Chapter 22: Recipe for a Program

Mull It Over

1. How do the choices of programming style and development process influence one another?

They don't need to have any bearing on one another, but hopefully they're the kinds of things you think about together as you begin a project.

Iterative processes are easier to implement with programming methodologies that support componentization—the object-oriented paradigm. Linear processes are suitable for all types of programming styles, but are not necessarily the best match.

The developers' prior experiences and their personal preferences for programming style will have the greatest affect on these choices.

2. Which is the best programming style?

Trick question! If you actually gave an answer, put down this book and give yourself 30 lashes with a wet noodle.

3. Which is the best development process?

You can't possibly have fallen for this too? Electric shock therapy with a 9-volt battery is your only option.

4. **Where does each development process listed in this chapter fall on the classification axes we saw in "Development Processes" on page 425?**

First, a quick recap: The thick/thin classification relates to the bureaucracy and paperwork involved in a process, *sequencing* describes how linear and predictive the process is, and the *design direction* determines whether design starts from the minuscule implementation details or from the grand overview:

Ad hoc

Who knows how to classify this mess? An ad hoc process could be anywhere on any axis, even constantly moving. Ad hoc developers are typically low on bureaucracy, but with no discipline at all, things fall through the cracks or are repeated time and time again. There's no sequencing whatsoever, so this anti-process rates off the scale, and if there *is* any design, then it probably has nothing to do with what is actually being built, anyway!

Waterfall model

This is a reasonably thick, very linear process. It generally leads to a top-down design, although it doesn't enforce this.

SSADM

This scores full marks on the thick scale—there's paperwork and heavily documented steps aplenty here. The sequencing axis is full throttle toward linear.

V model

Another thick, linear process (although some parts of this process are explicitly parallelized for efficiency). As with other waterfall variants, it leans toward top-down design.

Prototyping

An explicitly cyclical process (although by fixing the number of prototypes anticipated, we can enforce some level of linearity on the development process). This tends to edge toward the thin camp, sometimes too much so: Prototypes by themselves are not sufficient to capture user requirements or design decisions, so when prototyping, it's dangerously easy to avoid capturing decisions in specifications.

Iterative and incremental

Again nonlinear by design, this process can be as bureaucratic as you like, but some variants (especially as seen in the agile movement) can be quite thin. Iterative and incremental processes tend to stick in the middle of the design direction axis—at each iteration, we perform high-level design right through to low-level design. These design decisions are revised in the next cycle, and additional work repeat the top-level and bottom-level design.

Spiral model

A thick version of an iterative and incremental process.

Agile methodologies

Agile processes are thin and nonlinear. They do not fix a design direction; you are constantly redirecting the design. Compare design to driving to Paris: In a traditional process, you would point your car at Paris and drive; in an agile process, you'd start driving and make constant streering tweaks. You *might* even map out sections of the middle of the journey before determining the best route out of your hometown.

Remember that an organization's implementation of a specific process model will be inevitably tailored to its particular ways of working. (This is perfectly healthy.) These tweaks can make a significant difference. For example, you might base your development around the V model but aim to make the interphase handoff procedure as lightweight as possible, to reduce unnecessary bureaucracy.

5. **If development processes and programming styles are recipes, what would a software development cookbook look like?**

It would probably look dangerously like a software engineering textbook. There probably wouldn't be that many mouth-watering pictures! Just as the Naked Chef's[17] recipes differ from Rachael Ray's, you could imagine a number of different approaches to a mythical software development cookbook.

You don't really see that many software development cookbooks because people don't shop around for new recipes that often. These things only tend to spring up when a marketing machine can gather sufficient momentum behind the next big thing.

6. **With a suitable process, can software construction become a predictable, repeatable task?**

We're still not in a position where the software industry is able to make this claim. No matter how hard we try to homogenize the development process, the quality of code produced is ultimately determined by the quality (e.g., experience, ability, intuition, and flair) and the particular mood (e.g., ability to concentrate, being in the zone or constantly interrupted, see page 414) of the programmers doing the work. A master craftsman will produce more elegant, robust, and well-fashioned designs than a fresh apprentice.

With such variance, it's hard to reproducibly create software, even with the most prescriptive process. Using the same programmers, the same process, and trying to produce the same piece of software, you'll never get the exact same result. On different days, the team will make different choices, which will lead to radically different software with different inherent faults and strengths. (This point is hypothetical anyway; the same team would learn from its mistakes the first time around and create a different—probably better—piece of software on its second attempt.)

---

[17] If you think that sounds rude, see www.jamieoliver.com.

Agile methods exploit this, and celebrate the unpredictability of software construction. They attempt to address uncertainty by choosing pragmatic approaches that minimize the inherent risk of an unpredictable task.

Getting Personal

1. **What development process and programming language style are you currently using?**

    a. **Has it been formally agreed upon by the development team, or do you use it by convention?**

    b. **How was it chosen? Was it chosen specifically for this project, or is it the recipe you always use?**

    c. **Is it documented anywhere?**

    d. **Does the team stick to the process? When problems arise and your back is against the wall, do you maintain the process, or is all ivory tower theory ignored in a rush to produce something—anything?**

This question is probing how organized your development team is—and whether you develop software on purpose or by accident. Do you really *know* how you produce software, or do you still rely on the heroic efforts of a few key team members to get your work done?

Can you point to a specific reference for your way of working? Is it documented? Is it understood? Is it understood by *all* the developers, by *all* the process managers, and by *all* those who play some part in the construction process?

2. **Are your current processes and styles appropriate? Are they the best way for you to develop your software right now?**

If you don't know how you're producing software, or if you're not using the best approach, what would be better, and why?

Watch for the danger of ad hoc methods. I've seen numerous organizations where there is no agreed method; one person produces wholly OO designs while another avoids OO and performs structural design. The code produced is ugly and inconsistent.

3. **Does your organization appreciate that there are other development models that might be worth investigating?**

Understand who makes decisions about this kind of thing—is it the developers, the software team leader, or the managers? Are these people sufficiently informed about software development processes? Understand why they've chosen to work in the current way: what problems have they already solved? Often the reason for an odd development procedure is historical—organizations evolve a set of working practices, they don't fashion them consciously.

What would it take to persuade your organization to adopt another process model?

Chapter 23: The Outer Limits

Mull It Over

1. **Which of the programming niches we've looked at here are particularly similar or share common characteristics? Which are particularly different?**

There is more in common than you might think. Crossovers include:

- Games and web applications could both be considered specific forms of applications programming.
- Web programming is a form of distributed programming.
- Some enterprise work can take the form of web applications.
- Some systems implementation is for embedded platforms.
- Numerical work is sometimes optimized by parallelizing and distributing the computation.

2. **Which of these programming disciplines is hardest?**

Each type of programming presents a different set problems, and every individual program is complex in its own way. Otherwise, programming would take very little skill and any idiot could do it. (The fact that many idiots *do* program doesn't bear discussion here!)

The "harder" programming worlds could be considered to be the ones that demand more formal processes to ensure adequate quality is met. For example, the world of safety-critical software (mentioned in "In a Nutshell" on page 456) is particularly fraught. Watertight specifications, very formal development and testing models, and certification to regulated standards are essential in this world, along with the inclusion of reliable failsafes.

Numerical work, in particular, would be hard for someone who doesn't have a head for math and designing complex algorithms. It requires extra statistical or scientific skills.

3. **Is it important to be an expert in one particular area or to have a good grounding in all of them without a particular specialism?**

An understanding of each area is helpful. However, to truly excel in a given area requires specific skills and expertise that can only be gained from experience in the trenches. To get this good experience, you'll probably have to focus on one particular work area. Vincent van Gogh remarked, "If one is the master of one thing and understands one thing well, one has at the same time insight into and understanding of many things." Learn the particular intricacies that set your discipline apart from the others.

4. **Which programming niche should trainee programmers be introduced to?**

This is seldom thought about by the writers of programming courses. It's a sad oversight; many courses are not tailored to programming in the Real

World—more to some theoretical, androgynous branch of programming. Of course, this makes teaching programming much easier, and there are fewer issues to confuse the trainee with. But it is important to understand how to make appropriate coding choices when you're in the thick of the software factory, and someone has to teach this.

Compared to the other programming areas, applications programming is relatively unencumbered by specific rituals and practices, so this is presumably the easiest area to introduce programmers to. Because trainees rarely appreciate the wider world of software development, this is probably what they'd expect to learn anyway.

Getting Personal

1. **What programming arena are you working in right now? How does it affect the code that you're writing? What specific design and implementation decisions has it led you to make?**

It's important to understand the type of code you write so you can make the correct programming decisions. If you can't explain how your code has been shaped by the demands of the problem domain, then you may not have been thinking hard enough about what you're doing. Software has to survive in— and must therefore be shaped by—its environment.

2. **Do you have experience working in more than one programming discipline? How easy was it for you to switch mindsets and apply appropriate techniques in a different world?**

Be careful of the temptation to dismiss these differences and hop thoughtlessly from one domain to another. It can lead you to write bad code. You probably won't realize that your code isn't appropriate until the end of the game, when you're working on tedious bugs or trying to optimize your system to get it to meet the original requirements (e.g., code size or scalability). If that's when you realize your work isn't molded to its environment, then you're in a sticky position.

3. **Are any of the people you work with unaware of the forces that shape the particular kind of code you write? Do you have embedded software being written by programmers who only understand applications work? What can you do about this?**

Programmers who don't tailor their work to the requirements of the problem domain endanger your project. If they don't understand the inherent constraints (scalability, performance, code size, interoperability, and so on), their code will not match the specifications, and they will be weak links in the development chain.

Code and design review will help to catch this, as would pair programming.

BIBLIOGRAPHY

(Alexander 79)
Alexander, Christopher. *The Timeless Way of Building.* Oxford University Press, 1979. 0195024028.

(Aristotle)
Aristotle (384–322 BC). *Rhetoric.* Book 1, Chapter 11, Section 20. 350 BC.

(Beck 99)
Beck, Kent. *Extreme Programming Explained.* Addison-Wesley, 1999. 0201616416.

(Belbin 81)
Belbin, Meredith. *Management Teams: Why They Succeed or Fail.* Butterworth Heinemann, 1981. 0750659106.

(Bentley 82)
Bentley, Jon Louis. *Writing Efficient Programs.* Prentice Hall Professional, 1982. 013970244X.

(Bersoff et al. 80)
Bersoff, Edward, Vilas Henderson, and Stanley Siegel. *Software Configuration Management: An Investment in Product Integrity.* Longman Higher Education, 1980. 0138217696.

(Boehm 76)
Boehm, Barry. "Software Engineering." *IEE Transactions on Computers.* Vol. C-25, No. 12, pp. 1,226–1,241. 1976. http://www.computer.org/tc.

(Boehm 81)
Boehm, Barry. *Software Engineering Economics*. Prentice Hall, 1981. 0138221227.

(Boehm 87)
Boehm, Barry. "Improving Software Productivity." *IEEE computer*, Vol. 20, No. 9. 1987.

(Boehm 88)
Boehm, Barry. "A Spiral Model of Software Development and Enhancement." *IEEE computer*, Vol. 21. May 5, 1988.

(Booch 97)
Booch, Grady. *Object Oriented Analysis and Design With Applications*. Benjamin/ Cummings, 1994. Second Edition. 0805353402.

(Briggs 80)
Briggs Myers, Isabel. *Gifts Differing: Understanding Personality Type*. Consulting Psychologist's Press, 1980. 0891060111.

(Brooks 95)
Brooks, Frederick P., Jr. *The Mythical Man Month*. Addison-Wesley, 1995. Anniversary Edition. 0201835959.

(DeMarco 99)
DeMarco, Tom, and Timothy Lister. *Peopleware: Productive Projects and Teams*. Dorset House, 1999. Second Edition. 0932633439.

(Dijkstra 68)
Dijkstra, Edsger W. "Go To Statement Considered Harmful." *Communications of the ACM*, Vol. 11, No. 3, pp. 147–148. 1968.

(Doxygen)
van Heesch, Dimitri. *Doxygen*. http://www.doxygen.org.

(Economist 01)
"Agility counts." *The Economist*. September 20, 2001.

(Fagan 76)
Fagan, Michael. "Design and code inspections to reduce errors in program development." *IBM Systems Journal*, Vol. 15, No. 3. 1976.

(Feldman 78)
Feldman, Stuart. "Make—A Program for Maintaining Computer Programs." *Bell Laboratories Computering Science Technical Report 57*. 1978.

(Fowler 99)
Fowler, Martin. *Refactoring: Improving the Design of Existing Code*. Addison-Wesley, 1999. 0201485672.

(Gamma et al. 94)
Gamma, Erich, Richard Helm, Ralph Johnson, and John Vlissides. *Design Patterns: Elements of Reusable Object-Oriented Software*. Addison-Wesley, 1994. 0201633612.

(Gosling et al. 94)

Gosling, James, Bill Joy, Guy Steele, and Gilad Bracha. *The Java Language Specification*. Addison-Wesley, 2000. Second Edition. 0201310082. http://java.sun.com.

(Gould 75)

Gould, John. "Some Psychological Evidence on How People Debug Computer Programs." *International Journal of Man-Machine Studies*. 1975.

(Groom 94)

Groom, Winston. *Forrest Gump*. Black Swan, 1994. 0552996092.

(Hoare 81)

Hoare, Charles. "The Emperor's Old Clothes." *Communications of the ACM*, Vol. 24, No 2. ACM, 1981.

(Humphrey 97)

Humphrey, Watts S. *Introduction to the Personal Software Process*. Addison-Wesley, 1997. 0201548097.

(Humphrey 98)

Humphrey, Watts S. "The Software Quality Profile." *Software Quality Professional*. December 1998. http://www.sei.cmu.edu/publications/articles/quality-profile/.

(Hunt Davis 99)

Hunt, Andrew, and David Thomas. *The Pragmatic Programmer*. Addison-Wesley, 1999. 020161622X.

(IEEE 84)

IEEE Standard Glossary of Software Engineering Terminology. ANSI/IEEE, 1984. ANSI/IEEE Standard 729.

(ISO 84)

ISO7498:1984(E) Information Processing Systems—Open Systems Interconnection—Basic Reference Model. International Standard for Information Systems, 1984. ISO Standard ISO 7498:1984(E).

(ISO 98)

ISO/IEC 14882:1998, Programming Languages—C++. International Standard for Information Systems, 1998. ISO Standard ISO/IEC 14882:1998.

(ISO 99)

ISO/IEC 9899:1999, Programming Languages—C. International Standard for Information Systems, 1999. ISO Standard ISO/IEC 9899:1999.

(ISO 05)

ISO/IEC 23270:2003, Information technology—C# Language Specification. International Standard for Information Systems, 2005. ISO Standard ISO/IEC 23270:2003.

(Jackson 75)

Jackson, M.A. *Principles of Program Design*. Academic Press, 1975. 0123790506.

(Javadoc)
Javadoc. Sun Microsystems, Inc. http://java.sun.com/products/jdk/javadoc.

(Kernighan Pike 99)
Kernighan, Brian W., and Rob Pike. *The Practice of Programming*. Addison-Wesley, 1999. 020161586X.

(Kernighan Plaugher 76)
Kernighan, Brian W., and P.J. Plaugher. *Software Tools*. Addison-Wesley, 1976. 020103669X.

(Kernighan Plaugher 78)
Kernighan, Brian W., and P.J. Plaugher. *The Elements of Programming Style*. McGraw-Hill, 1978. 0070341990.

(Kernighan Ritchie 88)
Kernighan, Brian W., and Dennis M. Ritchie. *The C Programming Language*. Prentice Hall, 1988. Second Edition. 0131103628.

(Knuth 92)
Knuth, Donald. *Literate Programming*. CSLI Publications, 1992. 0937073806.

(Kurlansky 99)
Kurlansky, Mark. *The Basque History of the World*. Jonathan Cope, 1999. 0224060554.

(McConnell 96)
McConnell, Steve. *Rapid Development*. Microsoft Press, 1996. 1556159005.

(McConnell 04)
McConnell, Steve. *Code Complete: A Practical Handbook of Software Construction*. Microsoft Press, 2004. Second Edition. 0735619670.

(Meyers 97)
Meyers, Scott. *Effective C++*. Addison-Wesley, 1997. Item 34: Minimize complication dependencies between files. 0201924889.

(Miller 56)
Miller, George A. "The Magical Number Seven, Plus or Minus Two: Some Limits on our Capacity for Processing Information." First published in *Psychological Review*, 63, pp. 81–97. 1956.

(Myers 86)
Myers, Ware. "Can software for the Strategic Defense Initiative ever be error-free?" *IEEE computer*. Vol. 19, No. 10, pp. 61–67. 1986.

(Page Jones 96)
Page-Jones, Meilir. *What Every Programmer Should Know About Object-oriented Design*. Dorset House Publishing Co., 1996. 0932633315.

(Royce 70)
Royce, W.W. "Managing the Development of Large Software Systems." Proceedings of IEEE WESCON, August 1970.

(Simpsons 91)
Simpsons, The. "Do the Bart Man." Geffen, 1991. GEF87CD.

(Stroustrup 97)
Stroustrup, Bjarne. *The C++ Programming Language.* Addison-Wesley, 1997. Third Edition. 0-201-88954-4.

(UML)
Unified Modeling Language. Object Management Group. http://www.uml.org.

(Vitruvius)
Vitruvius Pollio, Marcus (c. 70–25 BC). *De Architectura.* Book 1, Chapter 3, Section 2.

(Weinberg 71)
Weinberg, Gerald. *The Psychology Of Computer Programming.* Van Nostrand Reinhold, 1971. 0932633420.

(Wulf 72)
Wulf, William A. "A Case Against the GOTO." Proceedings of the twenty-fifth National ACM Conference, 1972.

INDEX

flowcharts, 256
foo, 44
formatting, 24. *See also* code,
      formatting
Fortran, 24, 422, 455
forwards compatibility, 529
frameworks, 274
free software, 361, 388. *See also* open
      source
Free Software Foundation (FSF), 361
functional
    decomposition, 254, 421
    programming, 423
    specification, 373
    testing, 140
functions, 62, 244
    naming, 45
    return values, 13
    Single Entry, Single Exit (SESE),
        17, 24, 62, 102, 421
functors, 47

G

games programming, 205, 445
Gantt chart, 409
garbage collection, 14, 159
Garbage In, Garbage Out (GIGO)
      principle, 105
General Public License (GPL), 361
getters and setters, 54, 478
GIGO (Garbage In, Garbage Out)
      principle, 105
glass box testing, 141
GNU, 361
    code standard, 30
    indentation, 29. *See also* code,
        layout styles
goals, 337
Goldilocks principle, 436, 493
goto, 24, 468
    in error handling, 102
    and structured programming, 421
GPL (General Public License), 361
Grand Canyon team, 329
grep, 119
grid computing, 451
grouping, 64

groupware, 321
growth, 279, 280, 290
    and teams, 341
guesswork, 402
GUI, 44
    response, 204
    specification, 374
    tools, 113, 181, 492, 503
Guru, 299, 550

H

hackers, 228, 302. *See also* crackers
hardware, 137, 532
    optimization, 204, 511
header file, 48, 49, 50, 83, 88, 193,
        471, 486
    dependency, 180, 506
heap, 230, 516, 518
hierarchy, 250, 421. *See also* class,
        hierarchy
    of abstractions, 249
    file, 193
    layers, 270
    structure, 421
    team, 324
high-level design, 262
hit-and-run programming, 9
holiday, accounting for, 410
Holy Wars, 35, 465
honeypot, 234
horizontal organization, 319
house interface, 250
house style, 31
HTML, 384, 451, 546
humility, 300, 334
Hungarian Notation, 44, 45, 51, 477

I

IBM OS/360, 316
IDE (integrated development
        environment), 28, 60,
        113, 176, 444
Ideal Programmer, 308
identity, 40
idioms, 43, 252, 255, 392
IDL (interface definition language),
        272, 273, 451

if-then-else, 15, 61
imperative language, 420
implementation
  file, 50
  view, 264
important stuff, 64
improvement, 308
incremental development, 432, 554.
    See also iterative and incre-
    mental development
Incompetent Programmer, 330
indentation, 29, 81, 468. *See also*
    code, layout styles
Indian Hill Recommended C Style
    and Coding Standards, 30
indirection, 202, 211, 525
  extra levels of, 251
infinite loops, 160, 396
  monkeys and, 298, 426
infinite recursion. *See* recursion,
    infinite
inheritance, 250, 423. *See also* class,
    hierarchy
inline, 214
input, 230, 234
inspections, 386. *See also* code,
    reviews
instant messaging, 335
integer overflow, 231
integrated development environ-
    ment (IDE), 28, 60, 113,
    176, 444
integration, 408, 411, 428
  testing, 139
intellectual property, 359
interaction, 40
interface definition language (IDL),
    272, 273, 451
interfaces, 47, 248, 251, 272
interoperability, 371
interpreters, 125, 177
intranet, 453
invariants, 17, 19, 105, 216
ISO 9000 organizational model, 425
iterative and incremental develop-
    ment, 410, 432, 554

J

Java, 19, 50, 92, 160, 177, 179, 189,
    274, 360, 423, 486, 501
  comments, 75
  documentation, 68
  exceptions, 93, 96, 104, 107, 489
  garbage collection, 14
  standard, 121
JavaBeans, 274
javac, 189
Javadoc, 68, 486
JavaScript, 177
just-in-time (JIT) compilation, 178

K

K&R indentation, 27. *See also* code,
    layout styles
Keep It Simple, Stupid (KISS), 288.
    See also complexity; simplicity
Knuth, Donald, 66

L

labels, 353
language, 124
  byte-compiled, 179
  compiled, 178
  interpreted, 177
  methodology, 420, 424
  object-oriented (OO), 177
  scripting, 178
  structured, 178
  types, 176
lawyers, 360
layers, 241, 270
layout, 23. *See also* code, layout styles
lead developer, 394
learning, 335
legacy code, 4, 288, 450, 467, 526
lemming team, 332
Lesser General Public License
    (LGPL), 361
libraries, 122, 125, 182, 191, 193
licenses, 361
life cycle, software, 420
limitations, identifying, 336
linear time, 212

naming, *continued*
 foo bar (baz) 44
 functions, 45, 63
 Hungarian Notation and, 45, 47.
  See also Hungarian Notation
 macros, 48
 namespaces, 47
 packages, 47
 types, 45, 46
 variables, 44
NDA (non-disclosure agreement),
  360, 363, 539
NDEBUG, 18
nested make, 507
nesting, 62, 64
.NET
 building with, 181
 exceptions, 93, 104, 107, 489
 garbage collection, 13
non-disclosure agreement (NDA),
  360, 363, 539
non-discrete requirements, 371
notation, 255
 complexity of, 212
 flowcharts as, 256
 Hungarian, 45, 477
 UML, 255
numerical programming, 205,
  454, 557

O

object, 47, 254, 422
 code, 182
 file, 182, 183, 187, 189, 508
object-oriented programming
  (OOP), 11, 202, 215, 254,
  273, 422
 naming conventions, 44
 optimization and, 215
Objectory Process, 435
offensive programming, 19
Old Timer, 303
OOP (object-oriented programming), 11, 202, 215, 254,
  273, 422

open source, 361, 386, 388, 529. *See
  also* free software; Open
  Source Initiative (OSI)
 development, 325, 426
 security, 233
Open Source Initiative (OSI), 361
 network model, 270
optimistic locking, 352
optimization, 62, 194, 199, 219,
  288, 455
 alternatives to, 204
 avoiding, 217
 code changes and, 213
 design changes and, 210
 laws of, 200
 procedure for, 206
 profiling code and, 207. *See also*
  profilers
organization, 316, 318. *See also*
  teams, organization
OSI (Open Source Initiative), 361
 network model, 270
overflow, 231
overruns
 buffer, 229
 memory, 159
 schedule, 413
overtime, 409
ownership, 336

P

packages, 64, 243, 480
 naming, 47
pair programming, 167, 319, 388, 394
paperwork, 425
parallelization, 407
paranoia, 5
parent types, 423
parsers, 120
partitioning, 249
Pascal, 28, 422
 Blaise, 246, 377
 Case, 46
passwords, 226, 235, 236, 360, 515
patterns
 architectural, 255, 275
 design, 275. *See also* design patterns

prototype
  evolutionary, 434
  process, 430, 554
  UI, 374
pseudocode, 256
Python, 177

Q

QA (quality assurance), 131, 132,
    133, 342, 390
quadratic time, 212
quality
  assurance, 131, 132, 390. *See
    also* QA
  code, 289, 395
  comments, 73
  programmer, 408, 552
  specifications, 368
  tools, 113
Quicksand team, 330
quicksort, 212

R

race conditions, 160, 231, 236
RAD (Rapid Application Develop-
    ment), 431, 435
RAII (Resource Acquisition Is Ini-
    tialization), 103, 252
Rational Unified Process (RUP) 435
RCS (Revision Control System), 356
real time, 139, 205
reason code, 92
recipe, 419, 437
recognition, 40
recursion, 105, 192, 214
  infinite, 396. *See also* infinite
    recursion
recursive make, 192, 506
  is bad, 506
refactoring, 209, 285
regression testing, 139, 145, 190,
    289, 434, 498
relationship, 40
release, 190, 342, 375
  candidate, 140, 358
  note, 148, 194, 539
  source code, 359

religion, 35. *See also* Holy Wars
remote procedure call (RPC), 450
repetition, 202
reports
  communication, 335
  error, 91
  fault, 147, 164
repository, 351
requirements, 404, 414, 428, 431
  architecture and, 267
  discrete, 371
  non-discrete, 371
  security, 233, 515
  specification, 371
Resource Acquisition Is Initializa-
    tion (RAII), 103, 252
respect, 334, 337
responsibility, 318, 338, 350, 386
return values, 92, 95
reverse engineering, 360
reviews, 288, 385. *See also* code
    reviews
revision control, 120, 183, 185, 192,
    351, 352, 356, 547. *See also*
    source control
Revision Control System (RCS), 356
rewriting, 66, 284, 288. *See also*
    refactoring
RFC document #2119, 380
rich client, 452
risk, 408, 409, 434
RMI, Java, 450
roles and responsibilities, 106,
    249, 263
rot, 281. *See also* code, rot;
    comment, rot
RPC (remote procedure call), 450
RTFM, 484
RTTI, 211
run-time errors, 164. *See also* bugs,
    run-time errors
RUP (Rational Unified Process), 435

S

safety, 8, 93, 246, 349, 362. *See also*
    defensive programming;
    threads, safety
safety critical systems, 30, 456, 557

sales team, 360. *See also* marketing, department
salmon, 429
sandbox, 351
Satellite Station team, 327
scalability, 451, 452, 453
scanf, 159, 229, 516
scarce resource, 13, 159
   ye olde days, 223
SCCS (Source Code Control System), 356
schedules, 409, 412
scientific method, 164
SCMS (source code management system), 357
scope, 11
scripting language, 126, 178
Scrum, 434
secretary, 340, 391
security, 223, 349
   audits, 235
   code implementation, 235
   compromises, 225
   designing for, 229, 234
   exploits, 227
   flaws, 227
   vs. functionality, 233
   through obscurity, 235
   privilege escalation and, 225
   procedures and, 236
   requirements, 233, 515
   specifications, 381, 384, 545
   system installation and, 233
   tapping into data, 225
   vulnerabilities, 227, 229
sed, 119
segmentation faults, 158
self-documenting code, 59, 70, 376, 545
   comments in, 75
   errors in, 98
   example of, 60
   techniques for writing, 61
self-improvement, 65, 308
semantic errors, 158
server, 272
SESE (Single Entry, Single Exit) functions, 17, 24, 62, 102, 421

seven, 41
seven-layer trifle reference model, 270
shadowing, 393, 394
shell scripts, 126, 178
short circuit evaluation, 216
shrink-wrap software, 443
side effects, 17, 63, 470
signals, 95, 96
Simonyi, Charles, 45
simplicity, 10, 61, 203, 226, 242, 246, 268, 288. *See also* complexity
Single Entry Single Exit (SESE), 24. *See also* SESE functions
singleton, 144, 255
slacker, 306
Smallpox, 451
smalltalk, 46, 423
smart pointers, 103, 218
soak testing, 139
SOAP, 453
social engineering, 226
software
   architect, 265
   architecture, 261. *See also* architecture
   licenses, 361
   life cycle, 420
solution domain, 263
source code, 182
source control, 31, 320, 351, 356, 357
   access control and, 353
   backups and, 359
   baseline, 542
   branching, 354
   change control and, 352
   check in/out, 351
   check-in schemes, 354
   history, 356
   labels, 353
   repository, 351
   revision control and, 352
   stable labels and, 363, 542
   tags, 353
   version control and, 352
   what you control and, 353
Source Code Control System (SCCS), 356

Electronic Frontier Foundation
Defending Freedom in the Digital World

Free Speech. Privacy. Innovation. Fair Use. Reverse Engineering. If you care about these rights in the digital world, then you should join the Electronic Frontier Foundation (EFF). EFF was founded in 1990 to protect the rights of users and developers of technology. EFF is the first to identify threats to basic rights online and to advocate on behalf of free expression in the digital age.

The Electronic Frontier Foundation Defends Your Rights!
Become a Member Today!
http://www.eff.org/support/

Current EFF projects include:

Protecting your fundamental right to vote. Widely publicized security flaws in computerized voting machines show that, though filled with potential, this technology is far from perfect. EFF is defending the open discussion of e-voting problems and is coordinating a national litigation strategy addressing issues arising from use of poorly developed and tested computerized voting machines.

Ensuring that you are not traceable through your things. Libraries, schools, the government and private sector businesses are adopting radio frequency identification tags, or RFIDs – a technology capable of pinpointing the physical location of whatever item the tags are embedded in. While this may seem like a convenient way to track items, it's also a convenient way to do something less benign: track people and their activities through their belongings. EFF is working to ensure that embrace of this technology does not erode your right to privacy.

Stopping the FBI from creating surveillance backdoors on the Internet. EFF is part of a coalition opposing the FBI's expansion of the Communications Assistance for Law Enforcement Act (CALEA), which would require that the wiretap capabilities built into the phone system be extended to the Internet, forcing ISPs to build backdoors for law enforcement.

Providing you with a means by which you can contact key decision-makers on cyber-liberties issues. EFF maintains an action center that provides alerts on technology, civil liberties issues and pending legislation to more than 50,000 subscribers. EFF also generates a weekly online newsletter, EFFector, and a blog that provides up-to-the minute information and commentary.

Defending your right to listen to and copy digital music and movies. The entertainment industry has been overzealous in trying to protect its copyrights, often decimating fair use rights in the process. EFF is standing up to the movie and music industries on several fronts.

Check out all of the things we're working on at http://www.eff.org and join today or make a donation to support the fight to defend freedom online.

ELECTRONIC FRONTIER FOUNDATION · 454 SHOTWELL STREET · SAN FRANCISCO, CA 94110 · 415.436.9333

More No-Nonsense Books from  **NO STARCH PRESS**

WRITE GREAT CODE, VOLUME 1
Understanding the Machine

by RANDALL HYDE

Write Great Code, Volume 1 teaches machine organization, including numeric representation; binary arithmetic and bit operations; floating point representation; system and memory organization; character representation; constants and types; digital design; CPU, instruction set, and memory architecture; input and output; and how compilers work.

NOVEMBER 2004, 464 PP., $39.95 ($55.95 CDN)
ISBN 1-59327-003-8

WRITE GREAT CODE, VOLUME 2
Thinking Low-Level, Writing High-Level

by RANDALL HYDE

Today's computer science students aren't always taught how to choose high-level language statements carefully to produce efficient code. *Write Great Code, Volume 2: Thinking Low-Level, Writing High-Level* shows software engineers what too many college and university courses don't: how compilers translate high-level language statements and data structures into machine code. Armed with this knowledge, readers will be better informed about choosing the high-level structures that will help the compiler produce superior machine code, all without having to give up the productivity and portability benefits of using a high-level language.

MARCH 2006, 640 PP., $44.95 ($58.95 CDN)
ISBN 1-59327-065-8

WRITE PORTABLE CODE
An Introduction to Developing Software for Multiple Platforms

by BRIAN HOOK

Write Portable Code contains the lessons, patterns, and knowledge for developing cross-platform software that programmers usually must acquire through trial and error. This book is targeted at intermediate- to advanced-level programmers and will be a valuable resource for designers of cross-platform software, programmers looking to extend their skills to additional platforms, and programmers faced with the tricky task of moving code from one platform to another.

JULY 2005, 272 PP., $34.95 ($47.95 CDN)
ISBN 1-59327-056-9

THE TCP/IP GUIDE
A Comprehensive, Illustrated Internet Protocols Reference

by CHARLES M. KOZIEROK

Finally, an encyclopedic, comprehensible, well-illustrated, and completely current guide to the TCP/IP protocol suite for both newcomers and seasoned professionals. This complete reference details the core protocols that make TCP/IP internetworks function, as well as the most important TCP/IP applications. It includes full coverage of PPP, ARP, IP, IPv6, IP NAT, IPSec, Mobile IP, ICMP, and much more. It offers a detailed view of the TCP/IP protocol suite, and describes networking fundamentals and the important OSI Reference Model.

OCTOBER 2005, 1616 PP., HARDCOVER, $79.95 ($107.95 CDN)
ISBN 1-59327-047-X

THE ART OF ASSEMBLY LANGUAGE

by RANDALL HYDE

Presents assembly language from the high-level programmer's point of view, so programmers can start writing meaningful programs within days. The CD includes the author's High Level Assembler (HLA), the first assembler that allows programmers to write portable assembly language programs that run under either Linux or Windows with nothing more than a recompile.

SEPTEMBER 2003, 928 PP., W/CD, $59.95 ($89.95 CDN)
ISBN 1-886411-97-2

PHONE:
800.420.7240 OR
415.863.9900
MONDAY THROUGH FRIDAY,
9 A.M. TO 5 P.M. (PST)

FAX:
415.863.9950
24 HOURS A DAY,
7 DAYS A WEEK

EMAIL:
SALES@NOSTARCH.COM

WEB:
WWW.NOSTARCH.COM

MAIL:
NO STARCH PRESS
555 DE HARO ST, SUITE 250
SAN FRANCISCO, CA 94107
USA

COLOPHON

Code Craft was laid out in Adobe FrameMaker. The font families used are New Baskerville for body text, Futura for headings and tables, and Dogma for titles.

The book was printed and bound at Malloy Incorporated in Ann Arbor, Michigan. The paper is Glatfelter Thor 60# Smooth, which is made from 50 percent recycled materials, including 30 percent postconsumer content. The book uses a RepKover binding, which allows it to lay flat when open.

UPDATES

Visit **http://www.nostarch.com/codecraft.htm** for updates, errata, and other information.